HOUGHTON MIFFLIN SOCIAL STUDIES

To See a World

World Cultures and Geography

*T*o see a **World** in a Grain of Sand
And a Heaven in a Wild Flower,
Hold Infinity in the palm of your hand
And Eternity in an hour.

William Blake

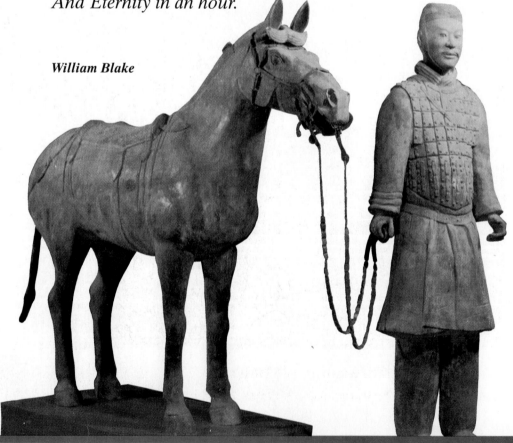

Beverly J. Armento
J. Jorge Klor de Alva
Gary B. Nash
Christopher L. Salter
Louis E. Wilson
Karen K. Wixson

To See a World

World Cultures and Geography

Houghton Mifflin Company • Boston

Atlanta • Dallas • Geneva, Illinois • Princeton, New Jersey • Palo Alto • Toronto

Consultants

Khalid Yahya Blankinship
Assistant Professor of Religion
Temple University
Philadelphia, Pennsylvania

Kees W. Bolle
Professor Emeritus of History
University of California
Guest Professor, Religion, Reed College
Portland, Oregon

Mark Cummings
Editor in Chief
Encyclopedia Americana
Grolier, Incorporated
Danbury, Connecticut

Charles C. Haynes, Ph.D.
Executive Director
First Liberty Institute at George Mason
  University
Fairfax, Virginia

Mary N. MacDonald
Assistant Professor of Religious Studies
LeMoyne College
Syracuse, New York

Shabbir Mansuri
Director, Council on Islamic Education
Tustin, California

The Most Reverend Desmond M.
  Tutu, D.D. F.K.C.
Bishopscourt, Claremont
Cape Town, Republic of South Africa

Taitetsu Unno
Jill Ker Conway Professor of Religion
  and East Asian Studies
Smith College
Northampton, Massachusetts

Rabbi Alfred Wolf, Ph.D.
Director, Skirball Institute on American
  Values
American Jewish Committee
Los Angeles, California

Teacher Reviewers

Linda Crain
Broward County Schools
Ft. Lauderdale, Florida

B. J. Dancer
Ector County Independent
  School District
Odessa, Texas

Susan M. Denhardt
Glenwood Middle School
Glenwood, Maryland

Glenn Diedrich
Walker Middle School
Milwaukee, Wisconsin

William F. Frew
Whitney Young
  Intermediate School
Cleveland, Ohio

Joyce Hecht-Hulslander
Largo Middle School
Pinellas County School
  Board
Clearwater, Florida

Jeanie Heginbotham
Baxter Elementary School
Anchorage, Alaska

Beverly Leonard
Blue Springs R-IV School
  District
Blue Springs, Missouri

Nancy Meyer, R.S.M.
Archdiocese of Cincinnati
Cincinnati, Ohio

Kathy J. Nye
Baltimore County Public
  Schools
Baltimore, Maryland

Virginia Tang
Woodland School
Weston, Massachusetts

Bonnie S. C. Wood
Tumwater Middle School
Tumwater, Washington

ISBN: 0-395-54893-4
   56789-VH-97 96 95

Development by Ligature, Inc.

Acknowledgments

   Grateful acknowledgment is made
for the use of the material listed below.
   The material in the Minipedia is
reprinted from *The World Book*
Encyclopedia with the expressed permission of the publisher. © 1993 by World
Book, Inc.

–Continued on page 723.

From Your Authors

They were probably some of the world's first exchange students. They came from China, Tibet, and as far away as Japan. During the fourth century, students from all over Asia filled the classrooms of the University at Nalanda. It was a long trip to northern India, but worth it.

So begins the story of a real event in the culture of ancient India. Could college students from 1,600 years ago and halfway around the world have anything to do with you? Well, as Chapter 14 explains, you can thank such ancient scholars for your math homework tonight. That's right. Indian mathematicians invented the number system that you use today.

In this book you'll find many surprising connections to cultures from distant times and remote places. Your world has been shaped by the customs and decisions of many people— ordinary people as well as great leaders. Ideas you believe in may have been passed to you through many generations and many countries. Things we take for granted— from marriage to makeup to marathons— have roots in the past.

Many present-day people affect your life as well, even though you've never met them. That's why in this book you'll read about modern as well as ancient cultures. While there isn't time to visit every culture, you'll touch down in many fascinating places.

We hope that as you proceed, you'll ask questions like these: "Why did people settle here?" "What makes this culture unique?" "What would it be like to grow up in this society?"

Most of all, we hope you catch the excitement of thinking about your world—its past, present, and future.

Beverly J. Armento
Professor of Social Studies
Director, Center for Business and
Economic Education
Georgia State University

Gary B. Nash
Professor of History
University of California—Los Angeles

Louis E. Wilson
Associate Professor
Department of Afro-American Studies
Smith College

J. Jorge Klor de Alva
Professor of Anthropology
Princeton University

Christopher L. Salter
Professor and Chair
Department of Geography
University of Missouri

Karen K. Wixson
Associate Professor of Education
University of Michigan

Contents

About Your Book xiv

Map and Globe Handbook xx

UNIT 1 Looking at the World	1	Chapter 1 *Exploring Culture*	2
		Lesson 1 *A World of People*	4
		Lesson 2 *What Shapes and Changes Cultures?*	12
		Lesson 3 *How Do We Learn about Culture?*	20
		Chapter 2 *Exploring Geography*	26
		Lesson 1 *Location and Place*	28
		Lesson 2 *Interaction*	32
		Lesson 3 *Movement*	38
		Lesson 4 *Regions*	42

UNIT 2 Origins of Today's World — 50

Chapter 3 *The Fertile Crescent* — 56
- Lesson 1 *Life in Prehistoric Times* — 58
- Lesson 2 *Ancient Mesopotamia* — 66
- Lesson 3 *The Origins of Judaism* — 73

Chapter 4 *Ancient Egypt and Nubia* — 80
- Lesson 1 *Kingdoms on the Nile* — 82
- Lesson 2 *Ancient Cultures Linked Together* — 87
- Lesson 3 *Great Achievements* — 93

Chapter 5 *Two Early Asian Civilizations* — 100
- Lesson 1 *Ancient India* — 102
- Lesson 2 *Hinduism and Buddhism* — 108
- Lesson 3 *Ancient China* — 114
- Lesson 4 *China's Cultural Heritage* — 117

Chapter 6 *Early Civilizations in the Americas* — 126
- Lesson 1 *Early Americans* — 128
- Lesson 2 *Aztec Civilization* — 132
- Lesson 3 *Andean Civilizations* — 138

UNIT 3 The Mediterranean and Southwest Asia — 146

Chapter 7 *The Mediterranean World* — 152
- Lesson 1 *Ancient Greece* — 154
- Lesson 2 *Ancient Rome* — 168
- Lesson 3 *Early Christianity* — 175

Chapter 8 *The Arabian Peninsula* — 182
- Lesson 1 *Islam Develops* — 184
- Lesson 2 *The Spread of Islam* — 189
- Lesson 3 *Saudi Arabia Today* — 193

Chapter 9 *Iran* — 202
- Lesson 1 *Iran's Land and Traditions* — 204
- Lesson 2 *Iran's Proud Legacy* — 208
- Lesson 3 *Modern Iran* — 213

UNIT 4 **Africa**	220	**Chapter 10** *Egypt*	226	Lesson 1 *Rulers from the North* — 228 Lesson 2 *Islamic Egypt* — 232 Lesson 3 *A Trip Down the Nile* — 239
		Chapter 11 *Mali*	246	Lesson 1 *From Empire to Colony* — 248 Lesson 2 *Mali and Its People* — 255 Lesson 3 *Republic of Mali* — 259
		Chapter 12 *Ghana*	266	Lesson 1 *The Asante: A People of Tradition* — 268 Lesson 2 *Growth and Change* — 273 Lesson 3 *A New Nation* — 280
		Chapter 13 *South Africa*	290	Lesson 1 *A Divided Land* — 292 Lesson 2 *The Fight for Land* — 296 Lesson 3 *A New South Africa* — 304
UNIT 5 **Asia**	310	**Chapter 14** *India*	316	Lesson 1 *A Hindu Empire* — 318 Lesson 2 *Foreign Rulers* — 322 Lesson 3 *Modern India* — 329
		Chapter 15 *China*	338	Lesson 1 *Mandate of Heaven* — 340 Lesson 2 *China after Mao* — 347 Lesson 3 *China Today* — 351
		Chapter 16 *Japan*	358	Lesson 1 *Island Culture* — 360 Lesson 2 *History of Japan* — 366 Lesson 3 *Japan Today* — 374
		Chapter 17 *Southeast Asia*	384	Lesson 1 *The Geography of Southeast Asia* — 386 Lesson 2 *The Philippines* — 390 Lesson 3 *Singapore, Indonesia, and Vietnam* — 395
UNIT 6 **Europe**	402	**Chapter 18** *The Making of Europe*	408	Lesson 1 *The Power of the Church* — 410 Lesson 2 *Feudal Europe* — 414 Lesson 3 *The Renaissance* — 424 Lesson 4 *The Reformation* — 430
		Chapter 19 *The Rise of Spain, Great Britain, and Russia*	436	Lesson 1 *Spain: The First Modern Empire* — 438 Lesson 2 *Great Britain's Sea Empire* — 444 Lesson 3 *Russia's Land Empire* — 452
		Chapter 20 *Europe: 1900 to the End of the Cold War*	458	Lesson 1 *World War I* — 460 Lesson 2 *Russia Becomes the Soviet Union* — 464 Lesson 3 *World War II and the Cold War* — 468
		Chapter 21 *Europe and Russia Today*	478	Lesson 1 *Europe Today* — 480 Lesson 2 *Western Europe Today* — 484 Lesson 3 *Eastern Europe Today* — 490 Lesson 4 *Russia and the Former Soviet Republics* — 493

UNIT 7 500
The Caribbean,
Central and South
America

Chapter 22 506
The Caribbean

Lesson 1 *Geography of the Caribbean* 508
Lesson 2 *The Caribbean: Cradle of the Americas* 512
Lesson 3 *The Caribbean Today* 518

Chapter 23 526
*Central and South
America*

Lesson 1 *The Land and Its History* 528
Lesson 2 *South America* 536
Lesson 3 *Central America* 542

Chapter 24 548
Brazil

Lesson 1 *The History of Brazil* 550
Lesson 2 *The Geography and Economy of Brazil* 555
Lesson 3 *Brazil Today* 562

UNIT 8 570
North America

Chapter 25 576
Mexico

Lesson 1 *The Forming of Mexico* 578
Lesson 2 *Regions and Resources* 584
Lesson 3 *A Blending of Cultures* 588

Chapter 26 596
Canada

Lesson 1 *Geography and Native Peoples* 598
Lesson 2 *History of Canada* 601
Lesson 3 *Canada Today* 607

Chapter 27 616
*From Many, One
Nation*

Lesson 1 *Land of Diversity* 618
Lesson 2 *People from Many Lands* 622
Lesson 3 *For the Good of All* 632

Chapter 28 642
*The United Nations,
Israel, and South
Korea*

Lesson 1 *The United Nations* 644
Lesson 2 *Israel and the United Nations* 648
Lesson 3 *South Korea and the United Nations* 653

Time/Space 659
Databank

Minipedia 660
Countries of
  the World 674
Atlas 678
Glossary of
  Geographic Terms 690
Gazetteer 692
Biographical
  Dictionary 696
Glossary 701

Index 708
Acknowledgments 723

Understanding Skills

Each Understanding Skills feature gives you the opportunity to learn and practice a skill related to the topic you are studying.

Fact, Judgment, and Opinion: Evaluating Information   18
Thematic Maps: Comparing Two U.S. Maps   46
Graphic Organizers: Using a Flow Chart   61
Visual Evidence: Interpreting Egyptian Art   96
Organization: Identifying Patterns   107
Evidence: Identifying Main Ideas   143
Conclusions: Comparing Greece and Rome   174
Historical Sequence: Making Parallel Timelines   199
Current Events: Making Predictions   217
Historical Evidence: Evaluating Sources   238
Arguments: Identifying Supporting Evidence   263
Critical Thinking: Interpreting Proverbs   272
Note-Taking: Recording Information   303
Reference Sources: Using the *Readers' Guide*   328
Written Reports: Presenting Information   355
Cartograms: Interpreting Symbols   372
Topography: Analyzing Elevation Maps   399
Critical Thinking: Making a Hypothesis   419
Graphic Information: Comparing Graphs   451
Visual Learning: Interpreting Political Cartoons   475
Conflict: Resolving Conflicts Peacefully   483
Others: Using Constructive Criticism   517
Oral Reports: Presenting Information   541
Critical Thinking: Recognizing Assumptions   554
Historical Evidence: Interpreting Artifacts   583
Diagrams: Reading a Process Diagram   606
Relationships: Identifying Stereotypes   637

Exploring

The story of the past is hidden all around you in the world of the present. Exploring pages tell you the secrets of how to find it.

Greek Architecture in Your Community   162
African Jewelry   278
Japanese and U.S. Schools   380

Making Decisions

Much of history is made of people's decisions. These pages take you step-by-step through fascinating problems from history and today. What will you decide?

Where Should We Put Our Trash?   36
The Great Wall   122
Voting For or Against a United Europe   488
Rain Forests: Preserve Them? Use Them?   566
Should Puerto Rico Be the 51st State?   638

Understanding Concepts

Each Understanding Concepts feature gives you more information about a concept that is important to the lesson you are reading.

Cultural Diffusion   15
Natural Resources   34
Dynasty   84
Empire   136
Democracy   157
Kinship   270
Social Justice   306
Communism   345
Feudalism   367
Colonialism   440
Genocide   471
Inflation   560
Borders   586
Naturalization   626

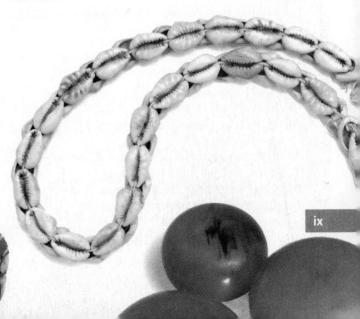

Literature

Throughout history people have expressed their deepest feelings and beliefs through literature. Reading these stories, legends, poems, and shorter passages that appear in the lesson will help you experience what life was like for people of other places and times.

A World of Poems	10
"The Luring of Enkidu" from *Gilgamesh,* retold by Bernarda Bryson	62
"Demeter and Persephone" from *Book of Greek Myths,* retold by Ingri and Edgar Parin D'Aulaire	164
"The Cow-Tail Switch" retold by Harold Courlander and George Herzog	284
Japanese Poetry, written by Sanpū, Bashō, and Gokason	364
Chapter Six from *Valentine & Orson,* re-created and illlustrated by Nancy Ekholm Burkert	420
From *The Captive,* by Scott O'Dell	534
"Ginger for the Heart" from *Tales from Gold Mountain,* by Paul Yee	628

Primary Sources

Reading the exact words of the people who made and lived history is the best way to get a sense of how they saw themselves and the times in which they lived. You will find more than 50 primary sources throughout this book including the following:

Guglielmo Marconi	12
Elihu Burritt, from *The Irish Potato Famine: Victims of the Great Hunger*	38
The Ten Commandments	76
Homer, from the *Odyssey*	93
Ashoka, Rock Edict I	113
John Lloyd Stephens, *Incidents of Travel in Central America, Chiapas, and Yucatán*	131
"Pericles' Funeral Speech," from Thucydides, *The Peloponnesian War*	158
Ar-Razi's diagnosis of smallpox from *al-Judari wa Hasbah,* A.D. 910	189
Barry Rosen, *444 Days: The Hostages Remember*	216
Arab historian Ibn Khaldun, description of 14th-century Cairo	232
Leo Africanus, diary account of life in ancient Mali	253
Kwame Nkrumah, *I Speak of Freedom*	280
Nelson Mandela	294
Turkish Sultan Mahmud of Ghazna	322
Xiao Wenxin, Chinese teacher	351
Tokugawa Ieyasu, a decree on proper behavior	368
Pope Pius XII	394
Martin Luther, *Ninety-Five Theses*	430
Columbus, from *History of the Indies,* by Bartolomé de las Casas	442
Anne Frank: The Diary of a Young Girl	470
Nickolai Karanko, a Ukrainian teenager, on democracy	495
Unnamed survivor of Haitian revolution	515
Rigoberta Menchú	542
From the letter of Pero Vaz de Caminha to King Manuel, written at Porto Seguro, Brazil, May 1, 1500	551
Miguel Hidalgo y Costilla, *Grito de Delores*	580
Captain James Cook	600
Von, Vietnamese immigrant	632
From the Preamble to the United Nations Charter	644

A Closer Look

Take a closer look at the objects and pictures spread out on these special pages. With the clues you see, you'll become a cultural detective.

The Great Migration	40
Cuneiform Writing	70
The Emperor's Tomb	119
Inca Highways	141
Arabian Hospitality	195
Persian Miniatures	211
The Rescue of Abu Simbel	241
Kente Cloth	275
Mining in South Africa	300
Monsoons	330
The Voyages of Zheng He	343
Volcanoes	388
Britain, Transplanted	449
The Last Czar	466
European Currency	486
Steel Drums	521
The Amazon River	558
Día de los Muertos	592
Canadian Animation	611

A Moment in Time

A person is frozen at an exciting moment. You'll get to know these people by reading about where they are and the objects around them.

An Anthropologist	22
A Nubian Princess	91
A Roman Engineer	172
A Mali Metalsmith	252
A Tea Master	369
A Crusader	417
A Gaucho	538
A Gulf War Soldier	634

Charts, Diagrams, and Timelines

The visual presentations of information help give you a clearer picture of the people, places, and events you are studying.

What Is Culture?	6
Institutions and Culture	9
Technology and Culture	17
Endangered Species	35
What's in Our Garbage?	37
Major Rivers of the Ancient World	54
The Earliest Humans, 2,400,000–15,000 B.C.	60
Steps Toward Civilization	61
The Ten Commandments	76
Ancient Egypt and Nubia, 3000 B.C.–c. A.D. 350	85
Building the Great Pyramid, 2500s B.C.	88
The Meroitic Alphabet	95
The Four Noble Truths	111
The Eightfold Path	112
Ancient and Modern Writing	117
Dynasties and Inventions of China, 1766 B.C.–A.D. 1279	120
Aztec Exchange Rates, c. 1525	134
Regional Rainfall	150
How an Aqueduct Works	171
Performing the Pilgrimage	184
Five Pillars of Islam	187
Largest Muslim Populations	190
Wheat Production, 1975–1990	198
Making Parallel Timelines	199
Society under the Pahlavis	214
Oil Production in Iran	215
African Population	225
Religious Groups in Egypt	242
Populations Compared by Age, 1990	261
Cocoa Prices, 1955–1965	281
Population and Land	294
Creation of Modern South Africa	298
Famous Mountains	314
Pacific Rim Trading Partners	315
City Population Density	315
Major Religions of India	333
Literacy Rate	334
China's Population	348
Camera Production	374
East vs. West: Church and Culture	413
Medieval Life: Serfs and Lords	415
Spain's Empire, 1492–1898	441
Foods in the Columbian Exchange	442
Great Britain's Empire, 1600–1931	445
World Trade, 1780–1820	451
World Trade, 1820	451
Russia's Empire, 1462–1917	453
Modern Europe and Russia	470
Per Capita Income in Europe and the United States	485
Comparing Canals	505
The Largest Caribbean Islands	520
Vertical Zones	528
Central America	530
South America	531
Population, 1818	552
War and Revolution	581
Mexican Exports, 1981–1989	587
How a Lock Works	606
Acid Rain	612
Patterns of U.S. Immigration, 1820–2000	625
Projected U.S. Population, 1990–2090	633
The Founding of Israel	649
Population of Israel	650
Population	652
The History of Korea	654
Countries Receiving Korean Exports	655

Maps

Each culture has been shaped by the places in which it developed. Each map in this book tells its own story about these cultures and regions.

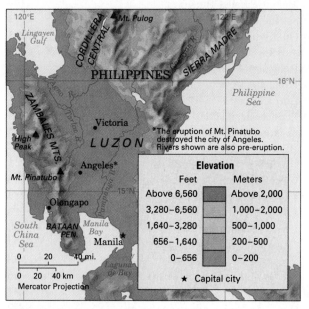

Korea and Japan: Political	G1
Australia: Political	G2
Mexico City: A Downtown Section	G3
The World: Hemispheres	G4
Southeast Asia: Political	G5
Mercator Projection	G6
Peters Projection	G6
Goode Projection	G7
Robinson Projection	G7
Africa: Physical and Profile Map	G9
Time Zones of the Western Hemisphere	G10
Roman Expansion, 338 B.C.–133 B.C.	G11
The Conquests of Alexander the Great	G12
Argentina: Land Regions	G13
Argentina: Population Density	G13
African Migration and Language	G14
United States: Regions	43
World: Regions	44
United States: Physical Regions	46
United States: Land Use and Resources	47
Africa: Annual Precipitation	49
Early Civilizations	53
Early Farming Areas	59

Fertile Crescent, 6000–2000 B.C.	67
Assyrian and Babylonian Empires	71
Ancient Egypt and Nubia	83
Ancient Cities of the Nile	86
Ancient Trade Routes and Resources, c. 2500 B.C.	104
China: Physical	115
Early Migration to the Americas	129
Mesoamerican Civilizations, 1200 B.C.–A.D. 1521	130
Andean Civilizations, 2500 B.C.–A.D. 1532	139
Western Eurasia: Political	149
Greek Civilization, c. 550 B.C.	149
Persian Empire, c. 500 B.C.	149
Roman Empire, c. A.D. 117	149
Western Eurasia: Climate	150
Greek City-States and Trade Routes, c. 550 B.C.	155
Rise of the Roman Empire, 338 B.C.–A.D. 117	169
Spread of Early Christianity by A.D. 395	178
Performing the Pilgrimage	184
The Expansion of Islam, A.D. 622–750	190
Modern Iran	205
Empires of Persia	209
Persian Gulf Oil Production, 1991	215
Africa: Political	223
The Expanding Deserts of Africa	224
Major Grain–Producing Areas of the Roman Empire	230
Expansion of the Ottoman Empire	234
Egypt: Population, 1990	240
Mali Empire, c. 1337	250
Songhai Empire, c. 1500	250
French Occupation, 1924	251
Modern Mali	251
Western Africa: Vegetation Regions	256
Ashanti Empire, 1820	269
Modern Ghana	282
South Africa, 1990	294
Groups Living in Southern Africa, c. 1400	297
Southern Africa, 1854	298
Asia: Political	313
Asia: Rainfall and Monsoon Winds	314
The Gupta Empire, c. A.D. 400	318
Muslim Rule and Indian Resistance, c. 1700	324
The Indian Subcontinent: Physical	331
Indian States and Languages, 1993	333
The Mongol Empire in China, c. 1294	341
Modern China: Population and Arable/Non-arable Land	348
Dialects in China, 1950	355
Japan: Physical	361

World: Political	372	Central America: Major Products	543
World: Petroleum Resources	373	Brazil: Geographic Regions	551
World: Gross National Product	375	Brazil: Resources and States	557
Southeast Asia: Political	387	North America: Political	573
Manila Galleon Trade Routes, 1565–1815	391	The Last Ice Age, c. 16,000 B.C.	574
Western Indonesia: Physical and Profile Map	399	Volcanoes and Earthquakes since 1900	574
Northern Philippines: Physical	401	Mexico: Changing Borders, 1835–1853	580
Europe: Political	404	Mexico: Physical Regions and Resources	585
Europe: Areas Affected by Acid Rain	406	Mexico: Population, 1990	590
Division of the Christian World, c. A.D. 950	413	Canada: Vegetation Regions	599
Feudal Europe, c. 1100	416	Mackenzie's Explorations	602
Spread of the Plague, c. 1347–1353	419	Four Peaks of U.S. Immigration	624
The Spread of Protestantism, c. 1560	433	Peace Missions of the United Nations	647
Spanish Empire, c. 1600	441	Changing Boundaries of Palestine and Israel	649
British Empire, c. 1860	445	Israel and the Occupied Territories, 1993	652
Russian Empire, c. 1600	453	North and South Korea, 1993	653
People of Europe, 1914	462	World: Political	678
Berlin and Germany, 1989	473	World: Physical	680
Eastern and Western Europe, 1993	481	Eurasia: Political/Physical	682
The European Economic Community, 1993	485	Pacific Rim: Political/Physical	684
Russia Today	494	Africa: Political/Physical	685
Central and South America: Political	503	North America: Political/Physical	686
Central and South America: Vegetation Regions	504	South America: Political/Physical	687
Caribbean: Natural Resources	509	World: Religions	688
European Presence in the Caribbean	514	World: Climate	688
Indentured Servants to the Caribbean	516	World: Land Use, Land and Ocean Resources	689
Central and South America: Climate Regions	529	World: Population	689

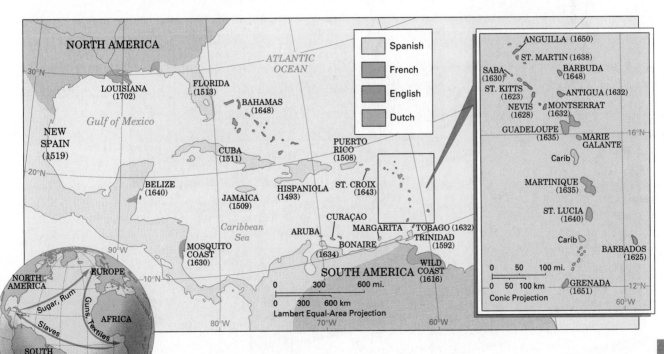

ABOUT YOUR BOOK

Starting Out

What makes this textbook so special? This book is about a whole world of people and landscapes. It is about your world—the one that exists today, and the one you will live in during the 21st century.

Unit Opener Striking images introduce each unit. Your journey to the various countries and cultures of the world begins here.

Unit Overview These four pages of maps and charts help you get the big picture— of a continent or other large region.

Unit 5 Overview
Asia

Asia can boast some of the greatest contrasts of geography and climate of any continent—volcanoes and plains, deserts and rain forests. The tallest mountain range in the world, the Himalayas, forms a huge arc north of India. One Asian city is one of the wettest places on earth. An average of more than 100 inches— almost 9 feet—of rain falls each June on Cherrapunji, India.

China and India rank first and second as the most populous countries in the world. Although Asia is home to some of the world's oldest cultures, much of it is also quite modern. Today many Asian nations are among the world's fastest-growing industrial nations.

◄ *Many of Asia's waterways are busy with activity, like this floating market in Thailand.*

Chapter 22
The Caribbean

From Cuba to Guadeloupe to Trinidad and Tobago, the tropical world of the Caribbean is a region of diversity. Different cultures have met and influenced one another, and they all have been shaped by the history of colonialism. Although different ethnic traditions have been kept, a unique Caribbean culture has been produced.

1492

Chapter Opener Pictures and a timeline let you see at a glance what is covered and when. The timeline for each lesson narrows it down, so you always know where you are in time.

xiv

B.C. A.D.

500

639

500

TODAY

L E S S O N 2

Islamic Egypt

THINKING FOCUS

How did Egypt become an Islamic nation?

Key Terms

- sultan
- isthmus

How Do We Know?

CULTURE The writings of Ibn Khaldun (1332–1406) give a picture of how people lived in old Cairo. An Arabian born in Tunis, Ibn Khaldun used aspects of culture, such as geography and family ties, to understand societies of the past. Before settling in Cairo, he advised rulers in North Africa and Spain.

It is the metropolis of the universe, the garden of the world, the nest of the human species. . . . [It is] the glory of Islam and the orchard of the world.

These words are from the Arab historian Ibn Khaldun (IHB uhn kal DOON). The place he described was a city in the Egyptian desert, al-Qahirah (ahl KUH hee ruh). We know it as Cairo (KY roh).

According to one legend, the birth of Cairo happened this way: In A.D. 969 a group of Shiite Muslims prepared to break ground for a new city. They hired astrologers

to tell them when the digging should begin. Workers raised their shovels. The astrologers watched the sky. When the moment arrived, they would give the signal to begin by pulling on a bell rope.

The planet Mars rose in the sky, but before the astrologers could give the signal, a raven landed on the rope and jingled the bells. The new city was named al-Qahirah, Arabic for Mars the victorious. Whatever the true story of Cairo's founding, the city quickly grew. By the 1300s, Cairo was the greatest city in all of Africa, Europe, and Southwest Asia.

Arab Rule

The Arab Muslims came to Egypt in A.D. 639, when the Byzantines ruled. Like Alexander the Great, the Arabs entered Egypt with little trouble. The Byzantine Empire was too weak to fight. In addition, Egyptian Christians still disliked the Byzantines because of the split with the church at Constantinople.

Arab rule was fairly mild. The Arab ruler, Caliph Umar, did not allow Muslims to take Egyptian land. Instead, Egypt had to pay tribute. "Tribute is better than booty [stolen goods]," Umar said. "It lasts longer."

The Arabs also demanded tribute from Egypt's ancient neighbor, Nubia (see Chapter 4). A treaty made during the mid-600s required Nubia, which

was then largely Christian, to do business with Muslim traders, build a mosque, and send 360 slaves to Cairo each year. Yet the treaty also required Cairo to send yearly gifts of food, horses, and cloth to Nubia.

An Islamic Nation

Like Egypt's Greek and Roman rulers, the Arabs allowed the Egyptians to worship as they chose. Although many Egyptians remained Christians, Egypt slowly became an Islamic nation.

The message of Islam, its five basic duties, and the caring community that it provided appealed to the people of the Nile. The practices of Islam were, in some respects, familiar. Like the beliefs of the ancient Egyptian religion and of Christianity, Islam gave Egyptians hope even when the Nile failed. It was the hope of a paradise that worshipers would enter after death.

The Rise of Cairo

Besides a new religion, the Arabs brought Egypt a new culture. Shortly after arriving in Egypt, they built a new capital called al-Fustat (ahl FUH staht) on the banks of the Nile. Later a newer capital was built at a site not far from al-Fustat. This new capital was Cairo.

The map on page 685 of the Atlas shows why the Arabs moved the capital from Alexandria. This capital of the Ptolemies bordered the Mediterranean Sea. The Greeks and Romans who had ruled Egypt from Alexandria looked across the sea, toward their homelands in Greece and Italy. The Arabs had little use for a capital that had to be defended from attack by sea. From Cairo the Arabs' ties lay southeast, toward the Muslim holy city of Mecca.

Across Time & Space

An earthquake that hit Cairo on October 12, 1992, did a great deal of damage to the city's modern buildings. The pyramids and Sphinx outside the city fared better. The 40-second quake wiped out many older homes and killed hundreds of people.

The Muslim ruler Saladin built this fortress, the Citadel of Cairo, to protect Egypt from Christian invaders.

Chapter 10

Thinking Focus This question is a guide suggesting what to keep in mind as you read a lesson.

Key Terms As you read a lesson, watch for these words and phrases listed on the lesson's opening page. Each term is highlighted in heavy black type and is defined, both in the lesson and the Glossary.

Important Connections *Across Time & Space* connects what you're reading to events that happened centuries ago or continents away. *How Do We Know?* explains where information about a particular culture comes from.

A Closer Look From the lavish life of a Russian czar to exploding volcanoes, special subjects get extra attention on these pages.

A Moment in Time In these features, time stops for a moment in the daily lives of people from many cultures.

XV

Continuing On

As you read about different peoples and their cultures, you'll need a variety of tools to help you understand and remember them. The many features shown here are useful guides for learning and remembering.

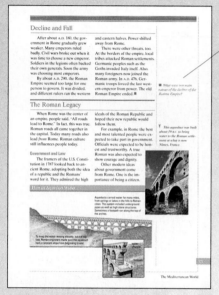

Charts and Graphs Information is presented in different ways to make it easier to understand. This is a diagram of an aqueduct.

Lesson Titles and Subtitles Red titles in the text tell you the main topics discussed. Blue titles are subtopics.

Margin Checks Find the red square at the end of the text. Match it to the square in the margin. If you can answer the question there, you probably understood what you have just read.

Letters, Diaries, Books Passages from these primary sources help you understand the cultural traditions of peoples all over the world.

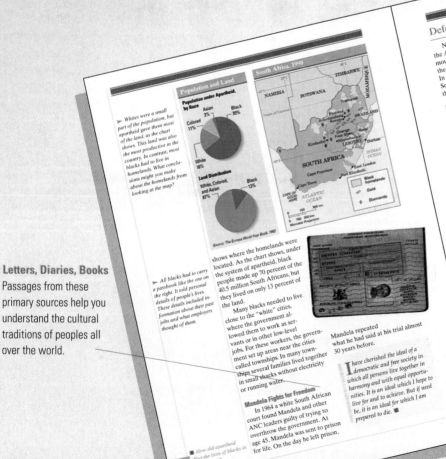

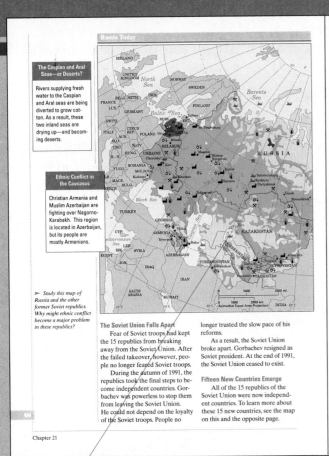

The Caspian and Aral Seas—or Deserts?

Rivers supplying fresh water to the Caspian and Aral seas are being diverted to grow cotton. As a result, these two inland seas are drying up—and becoming deserts.

Ethnic Conflict in the Caucasus

Christian Armenia and Muslim Azerbaijan are fighting over Nagorno-Karabakh. This region is located in Azerbaijan, but its people are mostly Armenians.

➤ Study this map of Russia and the other former Soviet republics. Why might ethnic conflict become a major problem in these republics?

The Soviet Union Falls Apart

Fear of Soviet troops had kept the 15 republics from breaking away from the Soviet Union. After the failed takeover, however, people no longer feared Soviet troops.

During the autumn of 1991, the republics took the final steps to become independent countries. Gorbachev was powerless to stop them from leaving the Soviet Union. He could not depend on the loyalty of the Soviet troops. People no longer trusted the slow pace of his reforms.

As a result, the Soviet Union broke apart. Gorbachev resigned as Soviet president. At the end of 1991, the Soviet Union ceased to exist.

Fifteen New Countries Emerge

All of the 15 republics of the Soviet Union were now independent countries. To learn more about these 15 new countries, see the map on this and the opposite page.

Chapter 21

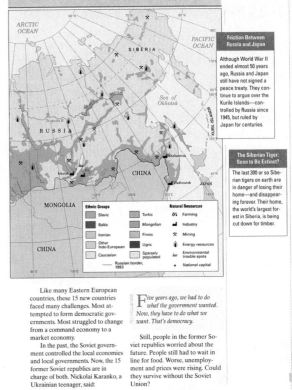

Friction Between Russia and Japan

Although World War II ended almost 50 years ago, Russia and Japan still have not signed a peace treaty. They continue to argue over the Kurile Islands—controlled by Russia since 1945, but ruled by Japan for centuries.

The Siberian Tiger: Soon to Be Extinct?

The last 300 or so Siberian tigers on earth are in danger of losing their home—and disappearing forever. Their home, the world's largest forest in Siberia, is being cut down for timber.

Ethnic Groups
Slavic
Baltic
Iranian
Other Indo-European
Caucasian
Turkic
Mongolian
Finnic
Ugric
Sparsely populated
Russian border, 1993

Natural Resources
Farming
Industry
Mining
Energy resources
Environmental trouble spots
National capital

Like many Eastern European countries, these 15 new countries faced many challenges. Most attempted to form democratic governments. Most struggled to change from a command economy to a market economy.

In the past, the Soviet government controlled the local economies and local governments. Now, the 15 former Soviet republics are in charge of both. Nickolai Karanko, a Ukrainian teenager, said:

Five years ago, we had to do what the government wanted. Now, they have to do what we want. That's democracy.

Still, people in the former Soviet republics worried about the future. People still had to wait in line for food. Worse, unemployment and prices were rising. Could they survive without the Soviet Union?

Europe and Russia Today

Maps You'll find maps showing landforms, oceans, waterways, ancient empires, trade routes, migrations, and brand new countries only weeks or months old.

Understanding . . . Two kinds of Understanding features give you tools for learning. One covers skills you'll need throughout your life, such as Understanding Topography, which explains how to read elevation maps.

More Understanding A second type of Understanding feature looks at concepts—the big ideas that help you put all the pieces together. This feature defines dynasties.

Reviews At the end of the lesson, take time to review what you've read. These questions and activities help you focus on the lesson and connect it to what you've already learned. A Chapter Review then ties all the lessons together.

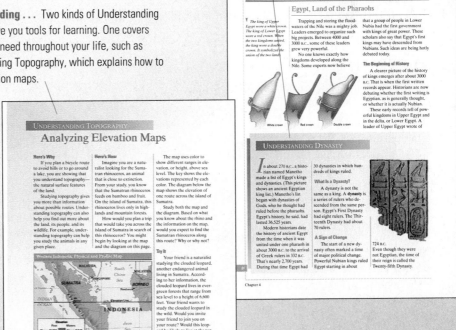

UNDERSTANDING TOPOGRAPHY
Analyzing Elevation Maps

Here's Why

If you plan a bicycle route to avoid hills or to go around a lake, you are showing that you understand topography—the natural surface features of the land.

Studying topography gives you more than information about possible routes. Understanding topography can also help you find out more about the land, its people, and its wildlife. For example, understanding topography can help you study the animals in any given place.

Here's How

Imagine you are a naturalist looking for the Sumatran rhinoceros, an animal that is close to extinction. From your study, you know that the Sumatran rhinoceros feeds on bamboo and fruit. On the island of Sumatra, this rhinoceros lives only in highlands and mountain forests.

How would you plan a trip that would take you across the island of Sumatra in search of this rhinoceros? You might begin by looking at the map and the diagram on this page.

The map uses color to show different ranges in elevation, or height, above sea level. The key shows the elevations represented by each color. The diagram below the map shows the elevation of one route across the island of Sumatra.

Study both the map and the diagram. Based on what you know about the rhino and the information on the map, would you expect to find the Sumatran rhinoceros along this route? Why or why not?

Try It

Your friend is a naturalist studying the clouded leopard, another endangered animal living in Sumatra. According to her information, the clouded leopard lives in evergreen forests that range from sea level to a height of 6,600 feet. Your friend wants to study the clouded leopard in the wild. Would you invite your friend to join you on your route? Would this leopard be likely to live at the top of Mount Kerinci?

Apply It

Research an animal found in your state. At what altitudes does it live? Find a topographic map of your state in an atlas. Use the map to pinpoint areas in your state where the animal would most likely be found.

Southeast Asia

Egypt, Land of the Pharaohs

Trapping and storing the floodwaters of the Nile was a mighty job. Leaders emerged to organize such big projects. Between 4000 and 3000 B.C., some of these leaders grew very powerful.

No one knows exactly how kingdoms developed along the Nile. Some experts now believe that a group of people in Lower Nubia had the first government with kings of great power. These scholars also say that Egypt's first kings may have descended from Nubians. Such ideas are being hotly debated today.

The Beginning of History

A clearer picture of the history of kings emerges after about 3000 B.C. That is when the first written records appear. Historians are now debating whether the first writing is Egyptian, as is generally thought, or whether it is actually Nubian. These early records tell of powerful kingdoms in Upper Egypt and in the delta, or Lower Egypt. A leader of Upper Egypt wrote of

The king of Upper Egypt wore a white crown. The king of Lower Egypt wore a red crown. When the two kingdoms united, the king wore a double crown. It symbolized the union of the two lands.

UNDERSTANDING DYNASTY

In about 270 B.C., a historian named Manetho made a list of Egypt's kings and dynasties. (This picture shows an ancient Egyptian king list.) Manetho's list began with dynasties of Gods, who he thought had ruled before the pharaohs. Egypt's history, he said, lasted 36,525 years.

Modern historians date the history of ancient Egypt from the time when it was united under one pharaoh in about 3000 B.C. to the arrival of Greek rulers in 332 B.C. That's nearly 2,700 years. During that time Egypt had 30 dynasties in which hundreds of kings ruled.

What Is a Dynasty?

A dynasty is not the same as a king. A **dynasty** is a series of rulers who descended from the same person. Egypt's First Dynasty had eight rulers. The Thirteenth Dynasty had about 70 rulers.

A Sign of Change

The start of a new dynasty often marked a time of major political change. Powerful Nubian kings ruled Egypt starting in about 724 B.C. Even though they were not Egyptian, the time of their reign is called the Twenty-fifth Dynasty.

Chapter 4

xvii

Map and Globe Handbook

At the very front of the book, you'll find a resource section on maps, globes, and geographic skills. Reviewing this section will help you make sure that you can use all the maps in your textbook.

Also Featuring

Each unit includes special features and learning activities to increase your understanding. At the back of this book, you'll find more information in the Time/Space Databank, including an atlas of world maps.

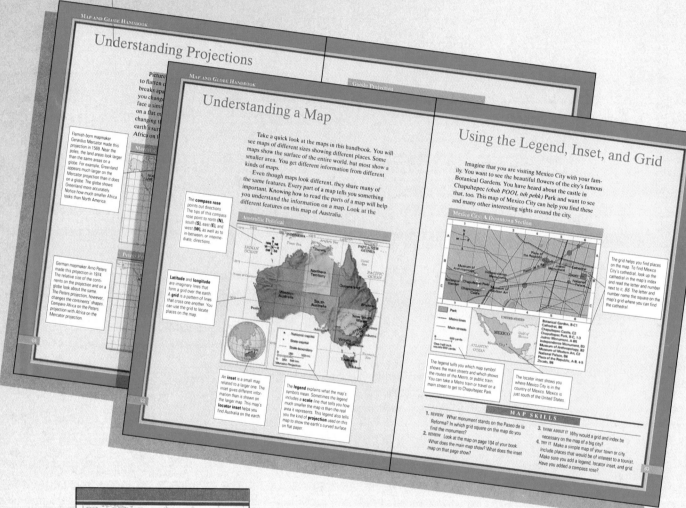

Literature Stories and writing are an important part of every culture. Each unit includes a work of literature that relates to the topic you are studying. These haiku were written by Japanese poets.

Atlas The Atlas adds to the wealth of maps in this book. Special maps also show languages, religions, climates, and resources.

The Minipedia A small version of an encyclopedia is bound into the back of this book. You'll find facts, charts, graphs, and articles to help you as you study.

Making Decisions What would you do? In each unit, this feature describes an important choice that others have faced. You have the chance to choose for yourself — and get good practice making decisions.

Exploring An Exploring feature appears in each unit. These activities take you outside the classroom, for exploring ideas at home or in your community.

This scale model of Buckingham Palace is entirely made up of interlocking plastic bricks. What elements of Greek architecture can you identify?

Map and Globe Handbook

*Y*ou are about to begin a journey through space and time. First you'll visit Korea and Japan, and then Australia. You'll go to Africa to scale the heights of Mt. Kilimanjaro. Later, you will follow the ancient route of Alexander the Great's army. By using maps and globes, you can explore lands nearby or on the other side of the world.

Your adventure begins in the pages of this handbook, which will help you unlock the secrets of maps and globes. Turn to page G1, and get ready to start your journey.

Contents

Mapping Our Planet	**G1**
Understanding a Map	**G2**
Using the Legend, Inset, and Grid	**G3**
Understanding Globes and Hemispheres	**G4**
Using Latitude and Longitude on Maps	**G5**
Understanding Projections	**G6**
Observing the Seasons	**G8**
Reading Different Kinds of Maps	
A Physical Map with a Profile	**G9**
A Time Zone Map	**G10**
A Historical Map	**G11**
A Route Map	**G12**
Comparing Maps	**G13**
A Cultural Map	**G14**
Using Geographic References	**G15**

Mapping Our Planet

A map is a representation of all or part of the earth's surface. Look at the pictures and map on this page. The picture on the right shows our planet in space. You can hardly see any details of the land. The picture below shows a smaller area of the earth. You can see the islands of Japan. You can also see North and South Korea and other parts of the East Asia coast. Now look at the map of the same area. Notice how carefully the mapmaker has drawn the shapes and sizes of the coastal lands and islands. The map is like a diagram of the area in the picture.

◄ You can see that Japan is really many islands and that North and South Korea are on a peninsula. In both pictures, computers have added color to make the images clearer.

Korea and Japan: Political

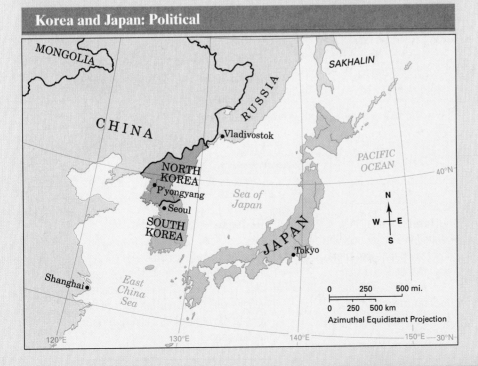

MONGOLIA

SAKHALIN

RUSSIA

CHINA

•Vladivostok

PACIFIC
OCEAN

40°N

NORTH
KOREA
•P'yongyang

Sea of
Japan

N
W—E
S

•Seoul

SOUTH
KOREA

JAPAN

•Tokyo

Shanghai•

East
China
Sea

0   250   500 mi.
0   250   500 km
Azimuthal Equidistant Projection

120°E   130°E   140°E   150°E — 30°N

◄ Look at the coastline of Japan on the map and in the photo above it. Check to see how accurately the mapmaker drew this coastline.

Understanding a Map

Take a quick look at the maps in this handbook. You will see maps of different sizes showing different places. Some maps show the surface of the entire world, but most show a smaller area. You get different information from different kinds of maps.

Even though maps look different, they share many of the same features. Every part of a map tells you something important. Knowing how to read the parts of a map will help you understand the information on a map. Look at the different features on this map of Australia.

The **compass rose** points out directions. The tips of this compass rose point to north **(N)**, south **(S)**, east **(E)**, and west **(W)**, as well as to in-between, or intermediate, directions.

Latitude and **longitude** are imaginary lines that form a grid over the earth. A **grid** is a pattern of lines that cross one another. You can use the grid to locate places on the map.

Australia: Political

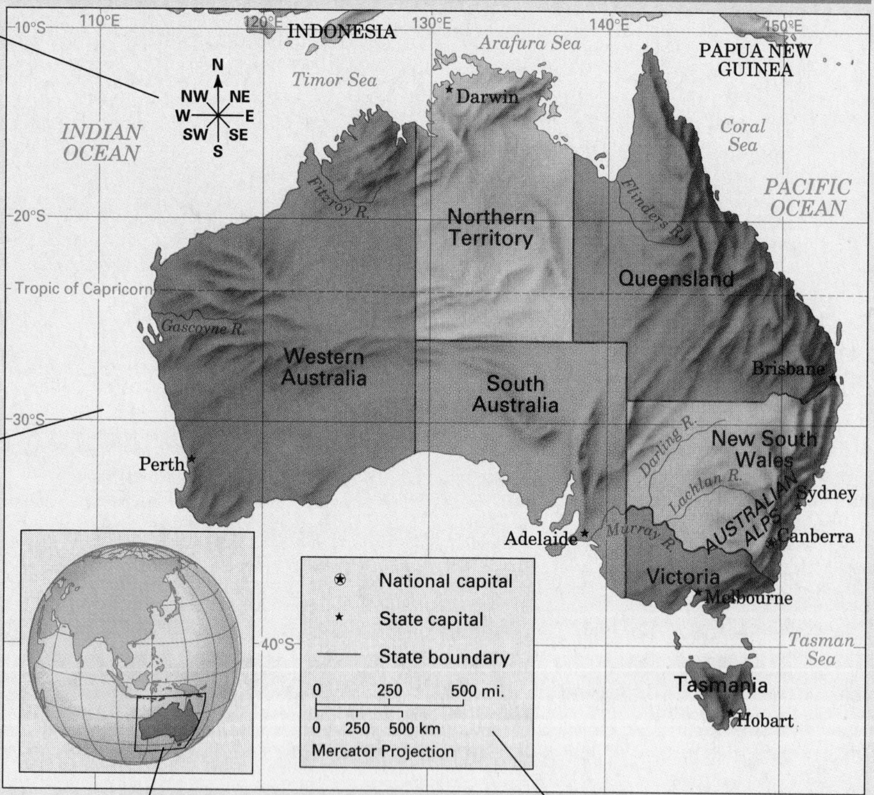

10°S   110°E   120°E   INDONESIA   130°E   Arafura Sea   140°E   150°E

PAPUA NEW GUINEA

Timor Sea

* Darwin

INDIAN OCEAN

Coral Sea

PACIFIC OCEAN

20°S

Fitzroy R.

Northern Territory

Flinders R.

Queensland

Tropic of Capricorn

Gascoyne R.

Western Australia

South Australia

Brisbane

30°S

Perth *

Darling R.

New South Wales

Lachlan R.

AUSTRALIAN ALPS

Sydney

Adelaide *

Murray R.

Canberra

Victoria

Melbourne

⊛   National capital

★   State capital

State boundary

40°S

Tasman Sea

0   250   500 mi.

0   250   500 km
Mercator Projection

Tasmania

Hobart

An **inset** is a small map related to a larger one. The inset gives different information than is shown on the larger map. This map's **locator inset** helps you find Australia on the earth.

The **legend** explains what the map's symbols mean. Sometimes the legend includes a **scale** line that tells you how much smaller the map is than the real area it represents. This legend also tells you the kind of **projection** used on this map to show the earth's curved surface on flat paper.

Using the Legend, Inset, and Grid

Imagine that you are visiting Mexico City with your family. You want to see the beautiful flowers of the city's famous Botanical Gardens. You have heard about the castle in Chapultepec (*chuh POOL tuh pehk*) Park and want to see that, too. This map of Mexico City can help you find these and many other interesting sights around the city.

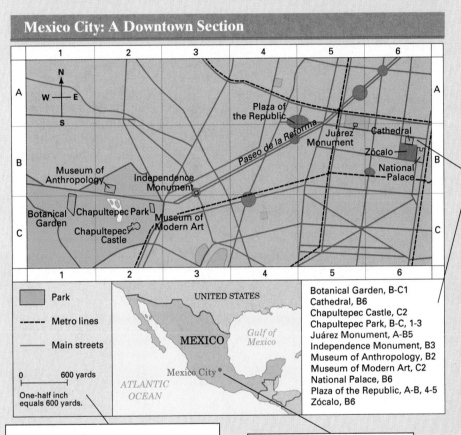

Mexico City: A Downtown Section

The grid helps you find places on the map. To find Mexico City's cathedral, look up the cathedral in the map's index and read the letter and number next to it, *B6*. The letter and number name the square on the map's grid where you can find the cathedral.

Park

----- Metro lines

——— Main streets

0   600 yards

One-half inch
equals 600 yards.

Botanical Garden, B-C1
Cathedral, B6
Chapultepec Castle, C2
Chapultepec Park, B-C, 1-3
Juárez Monument, A-B5
Independence Monument, B3
Museum of Anthropology, B2
Museum of Modern Art, C2
National Palace, B6
Plaza of the Republic, A-B, 4-5
Zócalo, B6

The legend tells you which map symbol shows the main streets and which shows the routes of the Metro, or public train. You can take a Metro train or travel on a main street to get to Chapultepec Park.

The locator inset shows you where Mexico City is in the country of Mexico. Mexico is just south of the United States.

MAP SKILLS

1. **REVIEW** What monument stands on the Paseo de la Reforma? In which grid square on the map do you find the monument?

2. **REVIEW** Look at the map on page 104 of your book. What does the main map show? What does the inset map on that page show?

3. **THINK ABOUT IT** Why would a grid and index be necessary on the map of a big city?

4. **TRY IT** Make a simple map of your town or city. Include places that would be of interest to a tourist. Make sure you add a legend, locator inset, and grid. Have you added a compass rose?

Understanding Globes and Hemispheres

Both maps and globes show the location of land and water on the earth. However, a globe does something a flat map can't do. A globe shows that the earth is shaped like a ball, or sphere. Geographers use certain imaginary lines of latitude and longitude on the globe to divide the earth into halves, or hemispheres. When you want to locate a place on a globe, it helps to know in which hemisphere the place can be found.

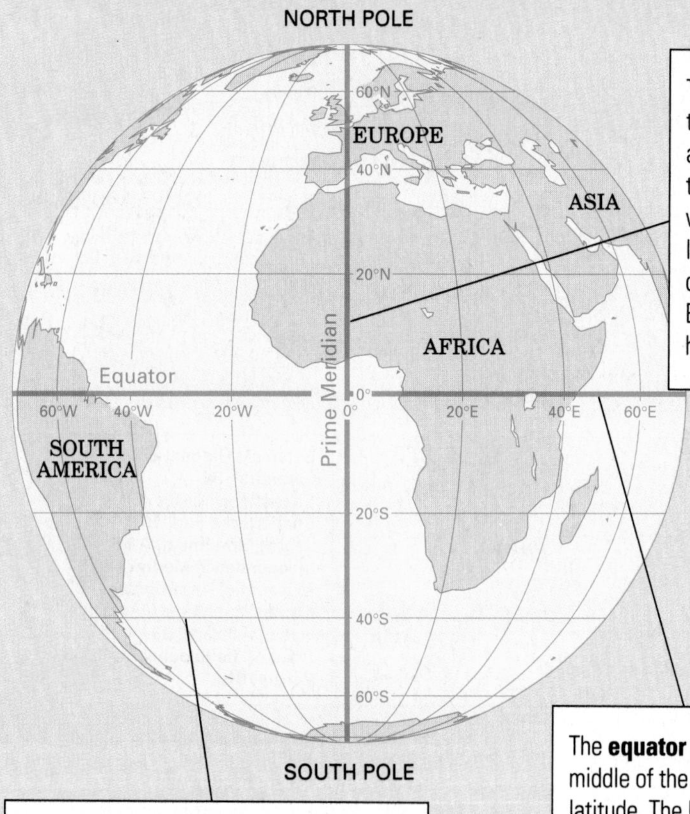

Northern Hemisphere
Detroit

Southern Hemisphere
Melbourne

Western Hemisphere
Rio de Janeiro

Eastern Hemisphere
Dar es Salaam

▲ *Above, you can see the four hemispheres and a major city in each.*

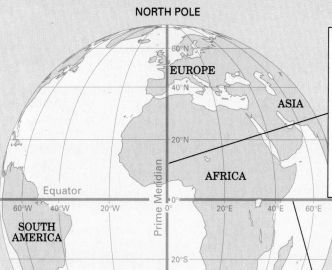

NORTH POLE

60°N

EUROPE

40°N

ASIA

20°N

AFRICA

Equator

Prime Meridian

0°
0°

60°W 40°W 20°W   20°E 40°E 60°E

SOUTH
AMERICA

20°S

40°S

60°S

SOUTH POLE

The **prime meridian** runs through western Europe and West Africa at 0° longitude. Halfway around the world is the 180° line of longitude. These two lines divide the earth into the Eastern and Western hemispheres.

The **equator** circles the middle of the earth at 0° latitude. The Northern Hemisphere is north of the equator. The Southern Hemisphere is south of the equator.

Lines of **latitude** cross the globe from east to west between the equator and the poles. Lines of **longitude** run from the North Pole to the South Pole. Both kinds of lines are measured in degrees (°).

GLOBE SKILLS

1. **REVIEW** Why is it helpful to know the four hemispheres of the earth?

2. **THINK ABOUT IT** One continent lies in four hemispheres. What continent is it and how is this possible?

3. **TRY IT** Find three countries on a globe. Give the name of each country to a classmate. Have each classmate find the country on the globe and tell you the two hemispheres in which it lies.

Using Latitude and Longitude on Maps

Suppose someone asks you the location of the small country of Singapore. You might say it is in Southeast Asia. If you need to tell exactly where Singapore is, you can give its latitude and longitude. Singapore is located at about 1° north latitude and 103° east longitude. That means Singapore lies one degree north of the equator and 103 degrees east of the prime meridian.

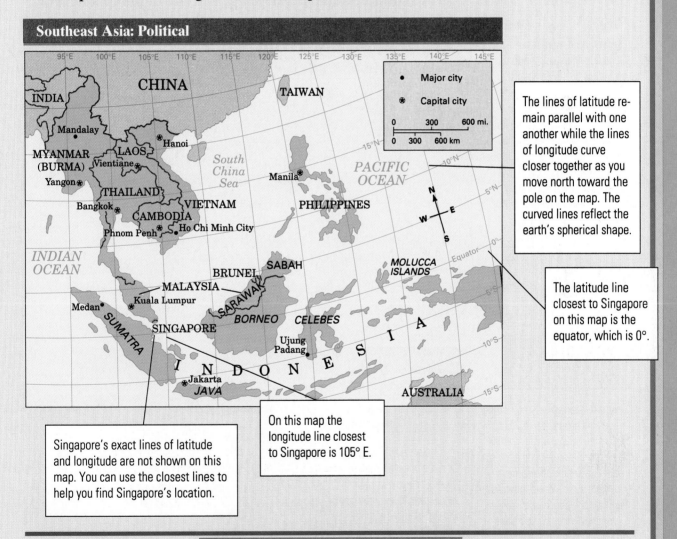

Southeast Asia: Political

The lines of latitude remain parallel with one another while the lines of longitude curve closer together as you move north toward the pole on the map. The curved lines reflect the earth's spherical shape.

The latitude line closest to Singapore on this map is the equator, which is 0°.

On this map the longitude line closest to Singapore is 105° E.

Singapore's exact lines of latitude and longitude are not shown on this map. You can use the closest lines to help you find Singapore's location.

MAP SKILLS

1. **REVIEW** Use latitude and longitude to tell the location of Ujung Padang on the island of Celebes in Indonesia.
2. **THINK ABOUT IT** How could you use latitude and longitude to tell the location of an entire nation, such as Vietnam in Southeast Asia?
3. **TRY IT** Use a globe or atlas to find the lines of latitude and longitude closest to your city or town.
4. **TRY IT** Look at the map of Eurasia on pages 682–683. List European and Asian cities located near 45° N latitude and cities near 45° E longitude.

Understanding Projections

Picture yourself peeling an orange. Once you finish, try to flatten out the peel. What happens? Most likely, the peel breaks apart. Because the peel is shaped like a sphere, or ball, you change its shape when you try to flatten it. Mapmakers face a similar problem when they show the sphere-shaped earth on a flat map. Each map uses a certain projection, or way of changing the size or shape of oceans and continents on the earth's surface. Compare the shape and size of the continent of Africa on four projections.

Flemish-born mapmaker Gerardus Mercator made this projection in 1569. Near the poles, the land areas look larger than the same areas on a globe. For example, Greenland appears much larger on the Mercator projection than it does on a globe. The globe shows Greenland more accurately. Notice how much smaller Africa looks than North America.

Mercator Projection

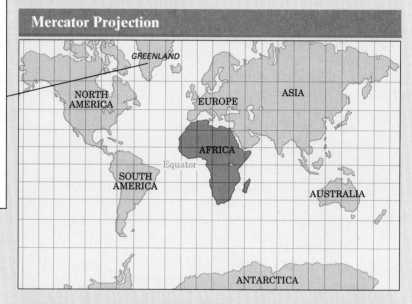

German mapmaker Arno Peters made this projection in 1974. The relative size of the continents on the projection and on a globe look about the same. The Peters projection, however, changes the continents' shapes. Compare Africa on the Peters projection with Africa on the Mercator projection.

Peters Projection

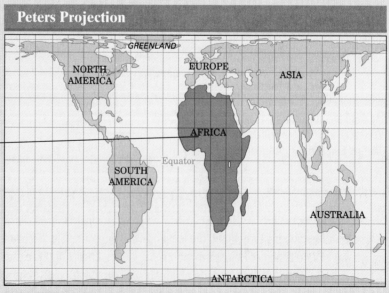

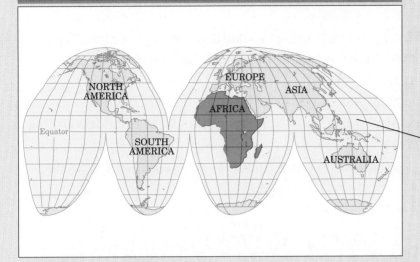

In 1923 American map-maker Paul Goode created a projection showing the continent sizes and shapes as they appear on a globe. Because this projection divides the earth into segments, or pieces, near the poles, the distances between places cannot be easily measured.

Robinson Projection

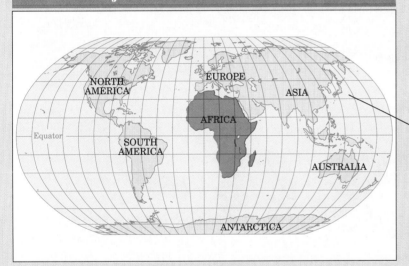

Another American map-maker, Arthur Robinson, made this projection in 1963. The sizes, shapes, and distances of land and water areas on this projection are closest to the ones on a globe. Most of the world maps in this book use the Robinson projection.

MAP SKILLS

1. REVIEW Which projections show Africa closest to the way it looks on a globe?

2. THINK ABOUT IT Look at Africa on the Mercator projection and the Goode projection. Why do you think Africa looks alike on the two projections when Greenland and other areas at the top of the projections are so different? Use a globe to help you answer the question.

3. TRY IT Find the land areas of Greenland, Antarctica, and Africa on a globe and trace them. Compare each tracing to the same area on a flat world map. They will not be exactly the same because your globe and map are different sizes. Notice differences in the shapes of the land areas. Which shapes show the most change? Why did the changes occur?

Observing the Seasons

Why do the seasons have to change? Why can't you enjoy your favorite weather all year long? The diagram below gives the answer.

Seasons change because the earth tilts or slants as it revolves around the sun. The parts of the earth tilted toward the sun have warm weather. At the same time, those parts of the earth that are tilted away from the sun have cooler weather.

The Northern and Southern hemispheres each tilt toward the sun for about six months and away from the sun for six months. In June when the North Pole tilts toward the sun, the Northern Hemisphere has summer while the Southern Hemisphere has winter.

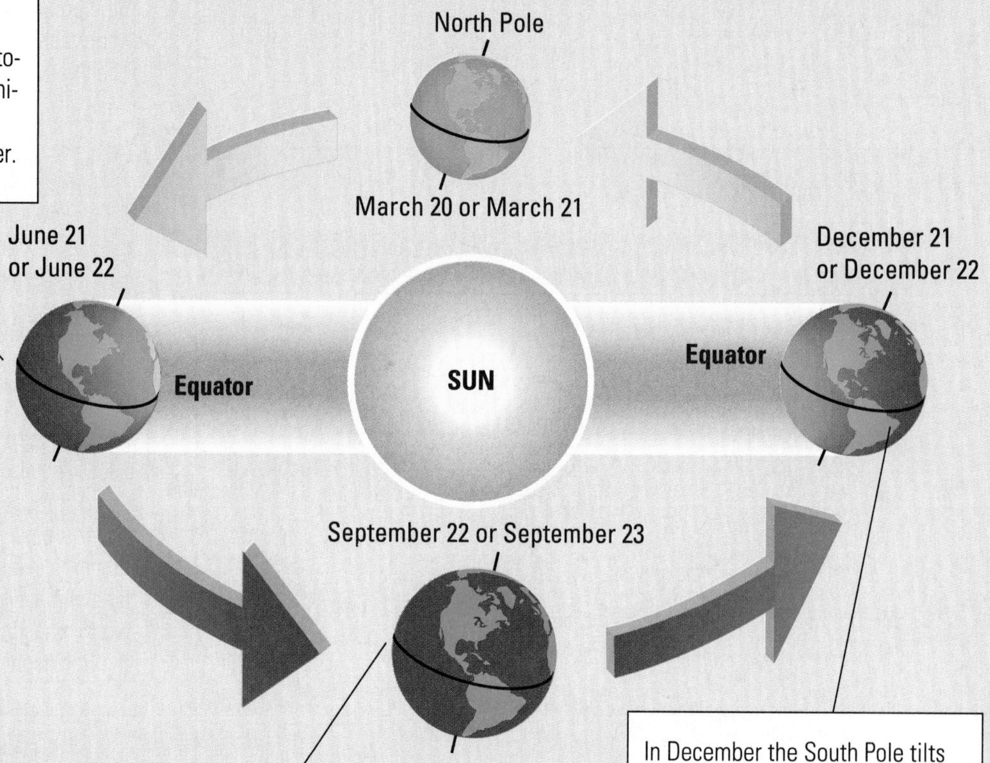

North Pole

March 20 or March 21

June 21 or June 22

December 21 or December 22

Equator

SUN

Equator

September 22 or September 23

▲ *This Indonesian mother uses an umbrella to protect herself and her baby from the hot sun. Indonesia lies on the equator where the weather is hot all year round.*

On two days each year, both hemispheres are about the same distance from the sun. In the United States those days are the first day of spring (March 20 or 21) and the first day of autumn (September 22 or 23).

In December the South Pole tilts toward the sun bringing summer to the Southern Hemisphere. At the same time, the Northern Hemisphere tilts away from the sun and has winter.

GLOBE SKILLS

1. **REVIEW** When does summer begin in Australia? Why?
2. **THINK ABOUT IT** What season is it right now in the nation of Chile in South America? How do you know?
3. **TRY IT** Place a ball on a table. Hold a smaller ball and move it around the larger ball. Draw two dots on the smaller ball, one for the North Pole and the other for the South Pole. Watch how its position changes in relation to your "sun." Use the balls to explain to a classmate why winter in the Northern Hemisphere begins in December.

Reading Different Kinds of Maps

Maps do more than show the shape of the land. Study the maps on the following pages and think about what you learn.

A Physical Map with a Profile

A physical map shows the elevation of land, or its height compared to sea level. Sometimes a physical map includes a diagram called a profile. The profile below shows a side view of the mountains, hills, and flat lands you would see in the area marked by the red line on the map.

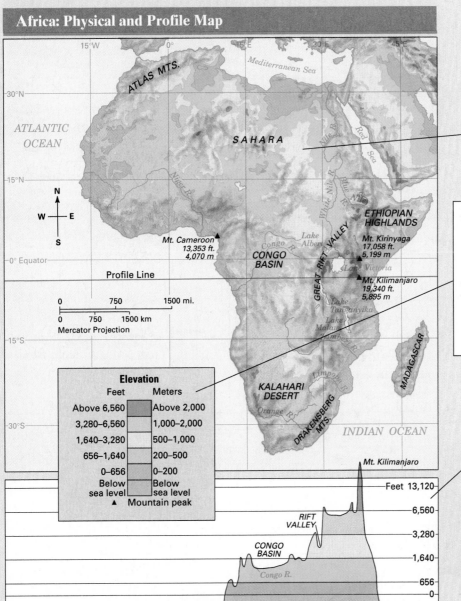

Africa: Physical and Profile Map

On the map, the color of an area shows the land's elevation.

The legend tells you what elevation each color represents. An elevation of "0" means that the land is at sea level. The number "6,560" means that the land rises 6,560 feet higher than sea level.

This map's profile shows how the land falls and rises across the Congo Basin, the Great Rift Valley, and Mt. Kilimanjaro. The Profile Line on the map shows where this profile, or side view, cuts across Africa. Notice that Mt. Kilimanjaro is the highest point on the profile and the map.

Elevation	
Feet	Meters
Above 6,560	Above 2,000
3,280–6,560	1,000–2,000
1,640–3,280	500–1,000
656–1,640	200–500
0–656	0–200
Below sea level	Below sea level
▲ Mountain peak	

A Time Zone Map

When you want to call a friend in another part of the country, think about the time zone where your friend lives. When it is 12:00 noon in Los Angeles, California, the time is 10:00 A.M. in Honolulu, Hawaii, and 3:00 P.M. in Miami, Florida.

Before official time zones existed, people had difficulty planning travel and doing business far from their homes. Each area set its own time. In order to end the confusion, government leaders agreed in 1884 to divide the earth into 24 time zones.

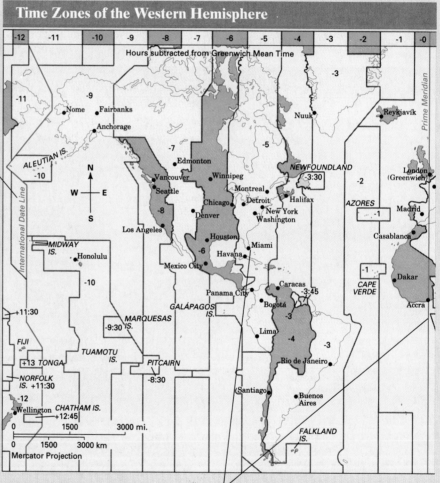

Time Zones of the Western Hemisphere

When you go west across the International Date Line at 180° longitude, the date immediately changes to one day later. It is Monday noon west of the International Date Line at the same time that it is Sunday noon east of the Line.

▼ *This diagram shows why the earth has 24 time zones. The earth rotates, or spins like a top. It takes 24 hours for the earth to make a complete rotation. At all times, half of the earth is getting daytime sunlight while the other half has nighttime darkness.*

The zone that contains the prime meridian is the starting point of the time zone map. West of the prime meridian, the time gets earlier. Miami is in the "-5" time zone that is five hours earlier than the prime meridian time zone.

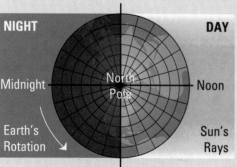

6 P.M.

NIGHT

DAY

Midnight

North Pole

Noon

Earth's Rotation

Sun's Rays

6 A.M.

Comparing Maps

These two maps show different facts about the country of Argentina. The land regions map shows the main physical areas in Argentina. The population density map shows the number of people in different areas of Argentina. You can compare the maps to figure out why people in Argentina live where they do.

Argentina: Land Regions

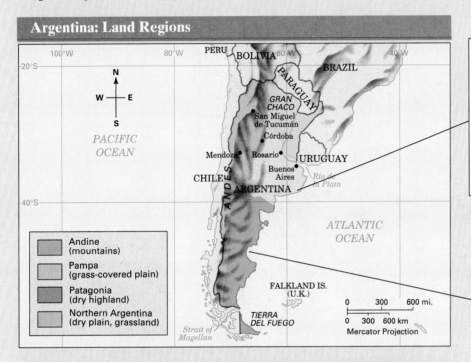

Legend:
- Andine (mountains)
- Pampa (grass-covered plain)
- Patagonia (dry highland)
- Northern Argentina (dry plain, grassland)

The pampas, a large plain, extends from the Atlantic coast inland to central Argentina. The land here is fertile and good for farming. Buenos Aires, Argentina's capital, is in this region on the coast.

Patagonia, Argentina's dry and windy plateau, extends from the coast to the Andes Mountains, south of the pampas. Patagonia has poor soil for farming. Sheep ranchers, who need a lot of land for grazing, can make a living here.

Argentina: Population Density

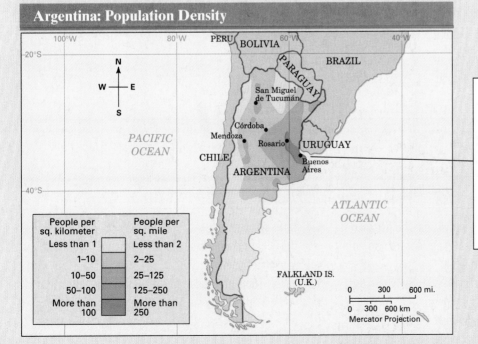

People per sq. kilometer	People per sq. mile
Less than 1	Less than 2
1–10	2–25
10–50	25–125
50–100	125–250
More than 100	More than 250

The population map shows that Buenos Aires has more than 250 people per square mile. In most parts of the world, the greatest number of people live in fertile, low-lying lands, where enough rain falls to grow the crops needed to feed them.

A Cultural Map

A people's culture includes everything that is part of their way of life. Cultural maps can show how all or part of one group's culture spread and influenced other people. This map shows what happened as a result of the Bantu migration in Africa.

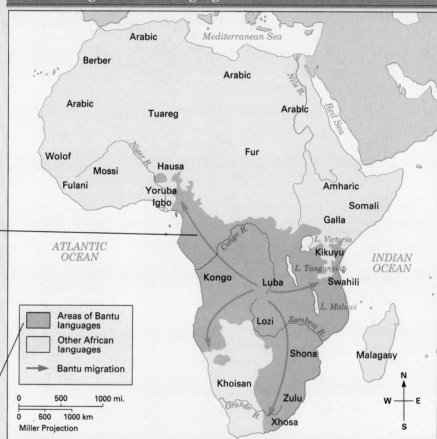

African Migration and Language

Arrows show the directions of the Bantu migrations from the interior of Africa, starting more than 2,500 years ago. As they traveled, they split off into many smaller groups with similar languages. To which part of Africa did the Bantu bring their language and culture?

The map uses color to show the area where the Bantu language spread and the areas where other major languages not related to Bantu are spoken in Africa.

MAP SKILLS

1. **REVIEW** Which has a higher elevation, the Congo Basin or the Rift Valley? What map feature can help you answer this question quickly?

2. **REVIEW** Look at the map on page 234. By what year did the Ottomans gain land in Egypt?

3. **REVIEW** Compare the map of climate regions on page 529 with the Atlas map on page 689 showing land use. What kind of climate do most of the large farming regions of South America have?

4. **THINK ABOUT IT** How would the route map of Alexander the Great's conquests help you write a report about Alexander?

5. **TRY IT** Think of three to five places in the United States you would like to visit. Then imagine your family going on a two-week vacation to see these places. You might travel by car, plane, train, or even boat. Trace a map of the United States. On it, draw a route map of your imaginary vacation.

Using Geographic References

What countries border El Salvador? What does a volcano look like? Where is Haiti? The different parts of the Time/Space Databank on pages 659–708 of this book will help you answer many geography questions.

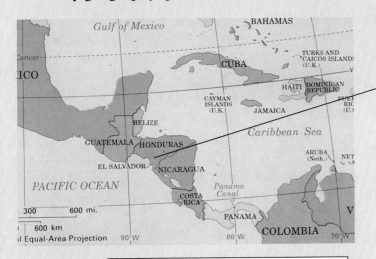

The Atlas on pages 678–689 has maps of the world and continents. This segment from the Atlas shows the northwest corner of South America, Central America, and major islands in the Caribbean Sea. You can see that El Salvador is bordered by two countries, Guatemala and Honduras.

The Glossary of Geographic Terms on pages 690–691 shows some of the earth's natural features. This entry for volcano tells you what a volcano is and shows a picture of what one looks like.

This entry from page 692 of the Gazetteer tells you where the city of Alexandria, Egypt, is. It tells the city's latitude and longitude and on what page you can find Alexandria on a map.

A

Accra (capital of Ghana)	6°N	0°	282
Aegean Sea (part of the Mediterranean Sea)	39°N	25°E	155
Alexandria (city in Egypt founded by Alexander the Great)	31°N	30°E	178
altiplano (high plateau, as in the Andes region)	19°S	68°W	687
Amazon R. (in South America; largest in the world)	1°S	52°W	557

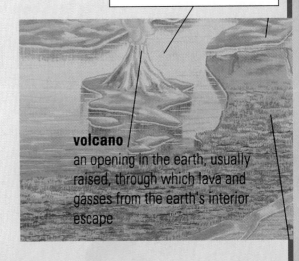

volcano an opening in the earth, usually raised, through which lava and gasses from the earth's interior escape

MAP SKILLS

1. **REVIEW** Which part of the Time/Space Databank will have a map of the world's vegetation regions? Look at the vegetation map there and find out which continent is mostly desert.

2. **REVIEW** What is the exact location of Cairo, Egypt? On what page of your book will you find a map of Cairo?

3. **THINK ABOUT IT** What is the difference between a canyon and a cliff? Which part of the Time/Space Databank helped you answer this question?

4. **TRY IT** Suppose you are the new editor of the Time/Space Databank. You decide to add more information to the Glossary of Geographic Terms. Pick two geographic features, write their definitions, and draw pictures of them.

Unit 1

Looking at the World

A mountain climber raises his arms in triumph as he reaches the peak of Mont Blanc, France. This moment of celebration is a solitary one, for the man is alone in this barren and cold place. Soon, however, he will come down from the mountain. He will return to the lowlands where people make their homes on farms and in villages. There he will be able to tell others of his experience and to share his achievement.

Mountain climber atop Mont Blanc, France

Chapter 1

Exploring Culture

The people in the pictures on these pages are from different places in the world. Yet they are doing many of the same things that you might do. Some are talking together. Some are celebrating a holiday, as you might celebrate your birthday or the Fourth of July. Some are working with their hands to make something beautiful. No matter where people live, they all work, play, and learn, and they observe important events. The different ways in which they do these things is the subject of this chapter.

These sixth-grade students represent many different cultures, yet share the responsibility of being citizens of the world.

This Mexican woman sells her weavings to tourists.

Wole Soyinka of Nigeria, the first black African to win the Nobel Prize in literature, is interviewed in Stockholm in 1986. Soyinka won the prize that year for his plays, poems, and novels.

Korean girls take part in a harvest festival.

Painter Ewelina Peksowa of Poland displays her paintings done on glass.

A World of People

Key Terms

- culture
- custom
- institution
- belief
- value

Dear Kenji,

My name is Lilla. I live in Chicago, which is a big city here in the United States.

I am in middle school. My favorite subject in school is English. I also like science. After school on Mondays, I go to soccer practice. Most days I have homework to do. My mom says I have to finish my homework before I can watch TV.

I like Saturdays best because I can go to a friend's house to listen to music and talk. Sometimes, my friends and I go shopping. This week I bought a new pair of sneakers for school. My old ones were a mess!

I hope you will write and tell me all about yourself.

Your pen pal,
Lilla

Dear Lilla,

Thank you for your letter. I am happy to have a pen pal from the United States.

I am twelve years old. My favorite subject is Japanese. I study Japanese and other subjects every day in school and at home after school. Some days I also go to classes in kendo, an old martial art.

On Sundays, I like to meet my friends for ice cream and shopping. Last week I bought a new T-shirt. I do not wear it to school, however. I wear a uniform to school.

Please write again soon.

Your pen pal,
Kenji

Lilla and Kenji have just become pen pals. They are discovering that they have a lot in common. They both enjoy shopping and being with their friends. They both go to school, where they study a language. They are learning that there are differences between them, too. The languages they study are different. So are the clothes they wear to school and the sports they play.

Through their letters Lilla and Kenji tell each other about the things friends talk about—school, sports, clothes, hobbies, and so on. As they write to each other, they also learn about how someone in another country lives. In other words, they learn about a different culture.

What Is Culture?

What do you notice about the girl in the picture on this page? Perhaps you notice her clothing or the things she is carrying. Almost everything you notice tells you something about her culture. **Culture** is everything a person must learn to live as a member of a group. It includes ways of making things, behaving, and thinking. It includes the types of food, clothing, and shelter that a group uses. It may include a shared religion, language, and forms of art. It even includes ways of having fun and being sad, and of making a living.

The diagram on page 6 can help you understand culture. It shows all the ways of looking at or thinking about culture that are common to most groups the world over.

Cultures Are Alike and Different

As you read this book, you will learn about the cultures of the world. You will see how they are alike and how they are different. You will see that people all over the world have many of the same needs. For example, all people need food, clothing, and shelter. Culture shapes the way people meet their needs. Culture determines what foods people eat and what a group's clothing and shelters look like.

People of all nations also share the same experiences of change, such as birth, childhood, adulthood, old age, and death. They celebrate many of the same events, such as marriage or the birth of a baby. These celebrations differ from culture to culture, however. People everywhere are sad about many of the same losses and failures, too. Culture shapes what people do as they face these losses. For example, people of different cultures act differently when a loved one dies.

▲ *This girl is from the United States. What do you notice about her that tells you about her culture?*

Cultures Include Customs

Ways of doing things that have become accepted by a group are called **customs.** Customs vary from culture to culture. For example, in all countries people get married. They differ, however, in the way they marry. In the United States, at many weddings the bride and the groom feed wedding cake to each other. Jewish couples smash a glass at their ceremonies. In Ethiopia friends of the groom pretend to kidnap the new bride.

The rules about marriage also differ from place to place. In some parts of the world, people marry at an early age. In other places people marry when they have grown up. In some cultures people can have more than one husband or wife at the same time. In the United States, people usually choose their own husbands and wives. In some countries, parents choose the person their son or daughter will marry.

All over the world, people are sorrowful about the deaths of loved ones. However, ceremonies to honor the dead can be very different. After a Hindu funeral procession, the body is burned. Some groups of Australian aborigines place the dead in trees.

Manners are also a matter of custom. In the United States, it is acceptable for people to rest their hands in their laps while at the table. In Germany children are taught that polite Germans rest their wrists on the edge of the table. In the United States, it is the custom to hold a fork in the right hand. In Germany the fork is usually held in the left hand.

The feasts and the festivals celebrated by a group are also customs.

A baby learns about its culture from the moment it is born.

This diagram shows that culture is made up of many different parts of the life of a people.

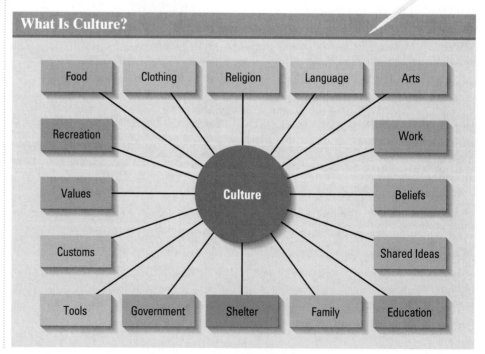

What Is Culture?

Food · Clothing · Religion · Language · Arts

Recreation · Work

Values · **Culture** · Beliefs

Customs · Shared Ideas

Tools · Government · Shelter · Family · Education

HAPPY NEW YEAR

These objects are used in New Year's Eve celebrations in the United States.

Many cultures celebrate the coming of spring. In Italy residents of Florence celebrate the Festa Del Gallo, or cricket festival, on the 40th day after Easter. They say that the cricket's song heralds the coming of spring. For hundreds of years in Great Britain, the first of May has meant a celebration. A May queen is crowned, and people dance around a ribbon-wrapped maypole.

People in almost every country celebrate the new year with a holiday. On New Year's Eve, many people in the United States celebrate with parties and dancing. They hang banners and blow noisemakers like the ones shown above.

Many people the world over celebrate the new year on dates established by their religion. For example, the Jewish New Year, called Rosh Hashanah, is observed during September or early October. The Chinese New Year is celebrated for a month beginning in late January or early February. The objects you see below are used in celebrations of the Chinese New Year.

Shared ceremonies, manners, celebrations, foods, clothing, and so on are an important part of a culture. They draw the people of a culture together as a group.

Cultures Include Institutions

In order to live together as a group, a people must organize orderly ways of doing certain jobs. An **institution** is an organization created by a people to do what one of its members alone cannot do.

Many items used in celebrations of the Chinese New Year are red or orange. These colors are thought to bring good luck. The banner at the right shows characters of the Chinese language that mean "Happy New Year." The red paper square at the left says "good luck"; the one to the right of it says "spring."

Exploring Culture

➤ *At the right a farm family is shown loading hay into a horse-drawn cart in the Slovak Republic. The photograph below shows shelters of Inuit families living in the Arctic.*

The family is perhaps the oldest institution. It came into being because human infants need protection and education for a long time. Therefore, the family has been one of the most important institutions in the world. The pictures on this page show families in different parts of the world.

Families teach many important things—how to speak, how to dress and eat, and how to behave. People rely on another institution—the school—to teach other things they need or want to know. In schools experienced people teach knowledge and skills that students will need to survive in their culture. Many adults go back to school again and again to gain new knowledge and skills.

Government is another important institution. Through government, people can make decisions, enforce rules, settle disagreements, and live together in an orderly way.

The economic system of a culture is also an institution. An economic system allows people to sell or trade what they have and get what they need.

In most cultures people share another of the oldest institutions— religion. Religion helps people in their search to understand how the world came to be, why people are born, and what happens to them after death.

Institutions usually have special buildings in which to carry out their purposes. The building pictured on page 9 has a special purpose too. What is this building used for? The table on page 9 describes other buildings and their uses.

Cultures Include Beliefs

People of all cultures have certain ideas in which they believe. An idea a person holds to be true is a **belief.** Many beliefs are ideas you accept as true that can't be proven correct or incorrect by scientific experiment or measurement. Beliefs often have to do with things that are difficult to measure, such as good or evil, or whether something is beautiful or ugly.

Beliefs are an important part of culture. This doesn't mean that all

Building	School	Skyscraper	Houses of Worship	Stores and Restaurants
Social group	Students and teachers	Office workers	Religious groups	Merchants and customers
Purpose of building	Schools are used for education of students. Teachers and groups of students work together in classrooms.	Skyscrapers provide office space for workers and for storing records.	Houses of worship inspire and educate people about their faith. They provide a place for worship services.	Stores display goods for sale. They have signs to identify them and their products.

members of a cultural group have exactly the same beliefs. It does mean, however, that many members of the group share a large number of beliefs. For example, most persons in the United States believe that people should be free to speak their minds. In some cultures, however, it is considered rude or ugly to say publicly that you disagree with someone, even if you do.

In every culture people are expected to behave in ways that are considered "right" or "good." If they act in ways that are considered "wrong" or "bad," they will be shamed or punished. Often beliefs about right and wrong are part of religion.

Beliefs that people hold about the right way to live and about how a person ought to behave are called **values.** Cultural values are the ideas, qualities, and institutions people prize most. They are used to define individuals and members of a group. Shared beliefs and values draw people closer together, just as a group's customs and institutions do. ■

◄ *A restaurant in Tacoma, Washington, is built in the shape of a teapot.*

■ *How does your culture help you live in the world?*

R E V I E W

1. **FOCUS** Why is culture important to people everywhere?
2. **CULTURE** Describe some customs or celebrations that are important in your culture.
3. **BELIEF SYSTEMS** Why are some beliefs hard to measure or prove?
4. **CRITICAL THINKING** Which of the institutions described in the lesson do you think is most important to you? Why?
5. **WRITING ACTIVITY** Ask your parents to talk about how the culture in which your grandparents grew up is different from your culture today. Then write a paragraph or two describing these differences.

A World of Poems

People around the world share many of the same feelings. Some of these poems were written by children from different nations. As you read, think about the special feelings the poets have about the world and their place in it.

In Lesson 1 you read that the world is home to many different cultures. In the next lesson you will read that cultures are shaped by nature and by the coming together of different peoples. Here young poets share their thoughts about nature and about the world as they see it.

pier a structure extending into water for use as a landing place for boats

I Love the World

I love you, Big World.
I wish I could call you
And tell you a secret:
That I love you, World.
   —Paul Wollner, age 7, United States

The Pier

One very nice day I went to the pier,
There were lots of noises that I could hear,
There I saw so many ships.
They were buzzing; buzzing, buzzing
I couldn't stand it, there was so much noise—
As if the place was full of naughty schoolboys.
However, I didn't want to leave. I had to be brave
Because I was enjoying myself, looking at the waves.
Soon I had to go; night had come, lights went on,
The day had brought me so much fun.
That night I could not sleep; I wanted to sing,
Of ships and waves and bells that ring.
   —Enrique Lozada, age 10, Philippines

A Wish

I want to climb the santol tree
That grows beside my bedroom window
And get a santol fruit.
I want to climb the tree at night
And get the moon the branches hide.
Then I shall go to bed, my pockets full,
One with the fruit, the other with the moon.
   —Tonas Santos, age 7, Philippines

Winter

Animals are restless
Birds are in flight,
Butterflies are not out.
Leaves; a gray blanket,
Winter lurks near.

Icy fingers grasp the world.
Snow falls; graceful, beautiful,
  undisturbed.
Silence creeps about.
     —*John Constant, age 10, Canada*

lurks   lies in wait

Sailing Homeward

Cliffs that rise a thousand feet
Without a break,
Lake that stretches a hundred miles
Without a wave,
Sands that are white through all the year
Without a stain,
Pine-tree woods, winter and summer
Evergreen,
Streams that forever flow and flow
Without a pause,
Trees that for twenty thousand years
Your vows have kept,
You have suddenly healed the pain of a traveler's heart,
And moved his brush to write a new song.
     —*Chan Fang-Sheng, China*
     —*Arthur Waley, Translator*

vows   promises

Further Reading

The Cay. Theodore Taylor. Phillip, shipwrecked in the West Indies, learns to respect the dark-skinned people he finds there.

The Desert Is Theirs. Byrd Baylor. The author describes the characteristics of the desert and its plant, animal, and human life.

Talking to the Sun: An Illustrated Anthology of Poems for Young People. Kenneth Koch and Kate Farrell. This collection of poems combines beautiful works of art from the Metropolitan Museum of Art in New York with poems for young people. The poems include African chants, Japanese haiku, American Indian verse, and much more.

What Shapes and Changes Cultures?

THINKING
F O C U S

What factors influence the way cultures develop and change?

I n 1901 in a hut in Newfoundland, Canada, Guglielmo Marconi *(gool YEHL moh mahr COH nee)* listened on an earphone. Suddenly, he heard a tapping sound. The world's first wireless transatlantic radio message had just been sent through the airwaves from Great Britain. Later, he would say:

I *now felt for the first time absolutely certain that the day would come when mankind would be able to send messages without wires not only across the Atlantic but between the farthermost ends of the earth.*

Physical Environment and Culture

Key Terms

- environment
- social interaction
- cultural diffusion
- technology

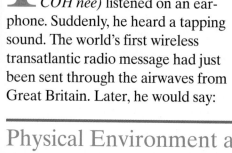

▼ *A woman makes good use of a waterway in her area. She lives on a houseboat in Pakistan.*

Marconi's invention soon enabled people to send messages around the world in a matter of minutes. With advances in communication, cultures came into contact with one another more than ever before. This contact has helped to shape the world's cultures.

Before rapid communication, cultures changed more slowly, and natural surroundings did

much to shape them. Physical, or natural, environment has always been an important factor in shaping culture. **Environment** includes things by which people are surrounded. Physical environment includes all natural features such as air, land, living things,

◄ *As a temporary shelter, this igloo in the Canadian Arctic provides warmth and protection from the wind.*

and climate found in a particular area. An example of physical environment can be seen in the picture on page 12 of a waterway in Pakistan.

Natural features help shape culture in many ways. For example, for thousands of years people have lived near the Arctic Circle. To adapt to this climate of continuous cold, they dressed in animal furs. When hunting, they built temporary shelters, like the one shown above, from snow and ice. Today people still live in the Arctic, and their culture is still shaped by the cold. It has changed, however. For example, many people now use snowmobiles to travel over the snow-covered ground.

A culture adapted to the Arctic probably could not survive in the world's deserts. Some people who live in deserts must travel from place to place looking for water and new pastureland for the animals they herd. They use tents for shelters because they are easy to move and small enough to carry. Like the man in the picture to the right, people take advantage of the desert sun.

Physical Environments Change

A change in physical environment can change culture. The people of Africa's Sahel, an area south of the Sahara, were nomads. When there were rains, they moved through the Sahel in search of pasture for their herds of cattle, camels, goats, and sheep. During periods of little rain, they moved south to more fertile areas.

In 1968, however, the Sahel entered a continuing period of little rain. At the same time, people there came to rely more and more on farming. They settled down to plant crops and graze cows and sheep, no longer herding their animals to new pastures. Because of the lack of rain and because the people used the same lands continuously for farming and grazing, the grass that covered the soil was destroyed. This made it possible for the desert to creep southward, taking over hundreds of thousands of square miles of grassland. Thus, the people of the Sahel lost the land they had once moved to. As a result, those who had survived by following the rains lost their way of life. ■

A man in the desert of Saudi Arabia talks on a solar-powered telephone.

■ *In what ways does physical environment help shape cultures?*

13

➤ *Like these trapeze artists, people of all cultures depend on and cooperate with one another.*

Social Interaction

Within a culture, people constantly come in contact with one another. This contact, in which people communicate and do things with one another, is called **social interaction.** Social interaction is essential to the trapeze artists shown on these pages. They must communicate with one another as they plan, practice, and perform amazing acts of skill.

Special ceremonies and celebrations are an important part of social interaction within a culture. For instance, the young Apache woman in the photograph below is taking part in a ceremony that marks her coming of age as an adult. She is dressed in buckskin and jewelry and is guided through the ceremony by her godmother.

During the ceremony, which continues for four days, Apache elders join in singing chants. In turn, the young woman acts out for everyone the story of the origins of her people. Then she is instructed by her godmother in her responsibilities as an adult, that is, in how she is supposed to interact with others. At the close of the ceremony, she dances from sunrise to sunset for the well-being of her people. Like generations of Apache women before her, the young woman completes an essential ritual that communicates to everyone her willingness to be part of her culture.

Social interaction also occurs when whole cultures come into contact with each other. Social interaction between cultures often

➤ *In Whiteriver, Arizona, an Apache woman takes part in a ceremony celebrating the beginning of her life as an adult.*

brings changes to each of them. Sometimes, elements of one culture spread to the other. This is called **cultural diffusion.**

Examples of cultural diffusion occurred after the Spaniards had come to Mexico in the 1500s. The Spaniards had brought many things with them, including horses, cattle, and sheep. The use of horses spread rapidly, and soon many American Indian groups rode horses. The wild cattle became the longhorns that helped shape culture in the southwestern United States. The Navajo borrowed sheep raising from the Spaniards and turned the making of wool blankets into an art form. Understanding Cultural Diffusion below will tell you more. ■

■ How does cultural diffusion change cultures?

UNDERSTANDING CULTURAL DIFFUSION

Can you imagine pizza or spaghetti without the tangy flavor of tomatoes, or a hamburger without French-fried potatoes? Yet 500 years ago, tomatoes and potatoes grew only in the Americas. People in Italy and France had never tasted them. European explorers who came to the Americas in the 1500s took these foods back home. They quickly became part of European culture. This process has gone on all over the world.

Ideas as well as foods have spread from one culture to another. For example, new farming methods, such as irrigation and the use of plows, were developed in Southwest Asia and spread to many cultures in Europe and elsewhere.

What Is Cultural Diffusion?

The process you have been reading about is called cultural diffusion. The term *diffusion* is used in science. For example, a drop of ink in a glass of water will gradually diffuse, or spread out, until it colors all the water in the glass. In the process of cultural diffusion, an idea or method spreads from one culture to another.

The Spread of Culture

Long ago, mountains, deserts, and oceans kept different groups of people apart. Still, whenever groups of people met—by accident, for trade, or even in war—cultural diffusion might occur. Someone might sample a new food or admire the way a spear point or pottery bowl was made. He or she took the new idea home, making it part of another culture.

Many languages and ways of writing them spread by cultural diffusion. So did religions, farming methods, and skills such as working with metals.

Today, modern travel and communication have shrunk distances. People encounter different cultures often, sometimes every day. As a result, cultural diffusion can occur more often than in the past. You may play a Japanese computer game or watch a program on a television set manufactured in Japan. Japanese students enjoy U.S. rock music, fast foods, fashions, and sports.

15

▶ Cars play a very important role in the culture of the United States. What kind of person might own this car?

Technology and Culture

Through cultural diffusion, ideas and technology move from one culture to another. **Technology** means tools and machines and the knowledge and skills needed to make and use them. New technologies change the cultures that adopt them. Changes in farming, transportation, and communication have all shaped and altered cultures around the world.

Advances in Transportation

An early advance in transportation was the steam engine, developed in Great Britain in the early 1800s and used both for water and land travel. The steam engine quickly changed cultures. In the United States, the steam-run locomotive helped create and then end the cowhand culture. In the 1860s, trains made it possible to ship large numbers of cattle to the eastern cities. Therefore, many cowhands were needed to tend huge herds of cattle on unfenced land called the open range. The cowhands took the cattle on long trail drives to railway stations in the "cow towns."

About 30 years later, changes in technology put most of the

▼ The scene below shows Los Angeles, California, in 1884. At that time, people rode along dirt streets in horse-drawn carriages and trolleys. The picture at the right shows Los Angeles today. The vast majority of people in the Los Angeles area drive to work in cars, vans, or trucks.

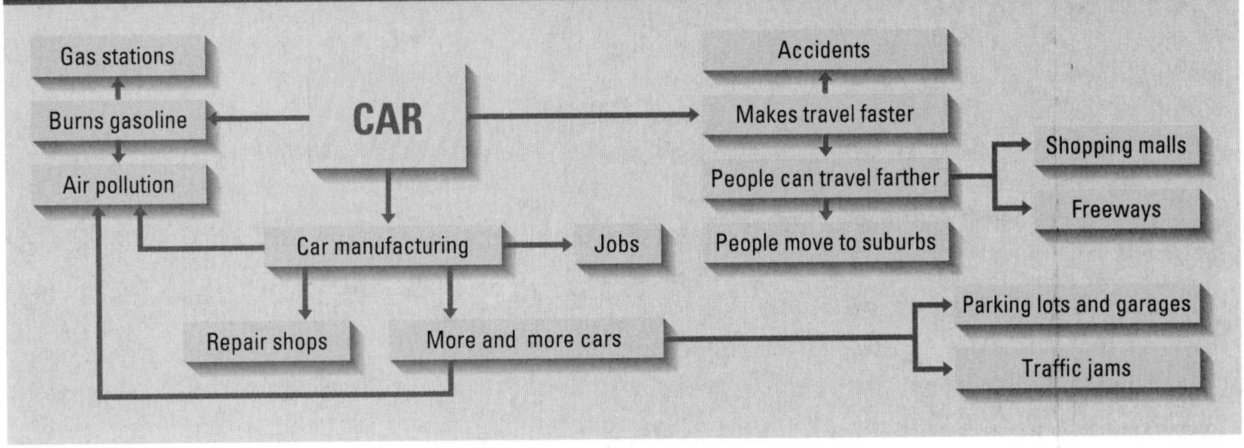

This chart shows the many changes brought about by the invention of the car.

cowhands out of work. The use of barbed wire fences and the spread of farms brought an end to the open range. Railroads expanded to reach the cattle ranches and did away with the need for trail drives. As a result, far fewer cowhands were needed.

Cars brought dramatic changes to culture in the United States. Compare the scenes pictured on page 16. One photo was taken before the invention of the car. The other shows modern downtown Los Angeles.

With the invention of the car, people no longer had to live close to their jobs. Instead, they spread out to live in suburbs. Businesses with drive-in services sprang up near roads across the United States, changing the way people shopped and spent their leisure time. People drove their cars to supermarkets, shopping centers, drive-in banks, and, later, to shopping malls. They traveled to tourist cabins, campgrounds, motels, and resorts. They enjoyed food at drive-in restaurants and films at drive-in theaters. The chart on this page shows not only the benefits but also some problems brought by the car.

Advances in Communication

Advances in communication also have changed our culture. For example, television permits almost everyone, wherever they may be, to share in political, cultural, and other experiences. With television, citizens in the United States witness presidential debates and speeches. Television advertising influences what we eat and wear, the cars we drive, what we do for fun, and how we clean our homes. Through television news, people see and hear about what the government is doing every day and what is taking place throughout the world. Television, therefore, has helped build a common culture from one end of the United States to the other. ■

■ *What are some advances in technology that are important in your life?*

R E V I E W

1. **FOCUS** What factors influence the way cultures develop and change?
2. **GEOGRAPHY** How does physical environment affect the way people in different cultures meet their basic needs?
3. **CULTURE** Give an example of how each of the following has shaped culture in the United States: physical environment, cultural diffusion, technology.
4. **CRITICAL THINKING** Study the information on pages 665–668 in the Minipedia—Highlights in the History of Communication. What developments in communication are important in your life? Why?
5. **ACTIVITY** Look around your house and list five items that come from other countries. Compare your list with other students' lists.

17

Exploring Culture

Evaluating Information

Here's Why

People learn about the past in many different ways. Written records, fossils, artifacts, and oral traditions are all keys to the past. By gathering and evaluating these sources, historians form their ideas about past events.

As you study the past, you also need to evaluate historical evidence. To do this, you must be able to tell the difference between facts, reasoned judgments, and opinions.

Look at the picture below of the gigantic stone statues found on Easter Island. This island is located in the Pacific Ocean about 2,300 miles west of Chile.

The Polynesian name for Easter Island is Rapa Nui *(rah puh NOO ee)*. Its Chilean name is Isla de Pascua *(EEZ lah day PAHS kwah)*.

The statues, called *moai (MOH eye)*, were made hundreds of years ago. Suppose you read an account of how these statues were made. How would you know whether or not to believe the account?

Here's How

To decide whether information is accurate, look for facts, reasoned judgments, and opinions. An interpretation that depends on facts and reasoned judgments is likely to be correct. An explanation that offers only opinions has little value.

Read "The Easter Island Story" on page 19. It contains facts, reasoned judgments, and opinions.

EASTER ISLAND

A fact is a statement that can be proven. There are many forms of proof. The archaeologists' findings can be proof, or they can come from written sources or direct observation.

Find the statement highlighted in blue in "The Easter Island Story." This statement is a fact because there is proof that it is true. Photographs and other records show the statues and the stone picks that archaeologists found at the volcano.

A reasoned judgment is a statement that is based on fact but has not been proven. Key words such as *probably, perhaps,* and *possibly* can help you identify reasoned judgments.

The statement highlighted in pink is a reasoned judgment. It explains how the statues may have been lifted onto their platforms. Can you find the facts that support this idea? They directly follow the reasoned judgment. People on Easter Island tested this idea in the 1950s.

Using three logs as levers and piled stones, they lifted a 25-ton statue. Yet it has not been proven that the statues' makers used logs as levers. It only has been shown that this is possible.

An opinion is a statement of personal preference, feelings, or ideas. Words such as *think* and *feel* often indicate that a statement is an opinion. The statement highlighted in green is an opinion. It tells you how the writer feels about the statues.

Try It
Look again at "The Easter Island Story." Find a fact, a reasoned judgment, and an opinion. Be sure to choose examples that have not been discussed already.

Apply It
Listen to a newscast or read a newspaper or a magazine article. Record one fact, one reasoned judgment, and one opinion. Point out any key words that helped you identify the types of statements.

The Easter Island Story

I think the *moai* of Easter Island are exciting artifacts. They are certain to interest people in the future.

Islanders used stone picks to carve the *moai* from the rock of the extinct volcano Rano Raruku. Both inside and outside of the crater, archaeologists have found many unfinished statues and thousands of stone picks. All of the *moai* are made of a yellow-gray stone called tuff. The tuff comes from the crater walls of Rano Raruku.

The islanders probably dragged the statues from the volcano to the places where they stand now. In the 1950s people from Easter Island tested this idea. They found that it took 180 people to pull a medium-sized statue!

The people who built the statues probably used log levers to lift the statues onto their platforms. Trees grow on the island today. By studying pollen deposits, scientists have learned that there were trees on the island in the past. Also, people in other times and places have used logs for the same purpose.

19

How Do We Learn about Culture?

THINKING
FOCUS

How do people learn about their own and other cultures?

On your paper, write the answers to the "culture test" below.
1. Look both ways before you
   ___ ___ ___.
2. ___ your hands before you eat.
3. The Pilgrims and Native Americans celebrated the first ___.

Check your answers with the ones below.
The answers are:
1. cross the street
2. Wash
3. Thanksgiving

How did you do?

Key Terms

- media
- ethnic group
- anthropologist
- prejudice
- racism

➤ *A young African American girl studies a mural depicting U. S. history.*

Our Own Culture

In schools all over the United States, students know the answers to these questions. How did so many people learn the same answers to the same questions?

From the time people are born, they begin to learn about their culture. Knowledge about one's culture usually begins with the family. When a mother puts a spoon into the hand of her two-year-old child, she learns that, in her culture, people eat with spoons. Her family doesn't use chopsticks or eat with the fingers.

Perhaps the child plays with other children in her neighborhood

or goes to daycare. Through these experiences, she learns what behavior is acceptable. For example, she learns to wait her turn. At about five years of age, she starts school. There she learns to read and write her language.

Meanwhile, the community around her also teaches her about her culture. The crossing guard teaches her to use the crosswalk.

The food that is offered in local restaurants reveals the foods of her culture. She sees the ways nearby stores decorate for special days such as Halloween and Thanksgiving. Everywhere she goes, she learns about the customs, institutions, beliefs, and values of her community.

Culture is also learned through the media and the arts. Every time you decide you want your hair cut like the model's in a magazine ad or you want to see a movie advertised on television, you are being influenced by the media. Through the **media,** including newspapers, magazines, radio, and television, ideas are communicated to many people at once. The arts also teach culture. The girl in the picture on page 20 is looking at a mural showing scenes of U.S. history. ■

◄ *Children everywhere learn much about their culture from family members. Here a six-year-old girl talks with her great-grandmother.*

■ *How do the media teach you about your culture?*

▼ *African Americans celebrate Kwanza, a holiday based on the African festival of the harvest of the first crops. The celebration combines discussions of African American goals and ideals with African practices. People enjoy African foods, dancing, music, and ceremonies honoring ancestors.*

Other Cultures

You have read that people learn about their own culture through social interaction that begins at birth. People can learn about other cultures through social interaction with different ethnic groups. An **ethnic group** is a group of people who share a common cultural heritage. There are many ethnic groups in the United States: for example, Chinese Americans and Swedish Americans. In Chapter 11 you will read about ethnic groups in Mali, including the Bambara and the Fulani. By interacting with members of other ethnic groups, it is possible to learn firsthand about their customs and beliefs.

Culture and the Social Sciences

People in school learn about cultures by studying the social sciences, the basis of social studies.

The social sciences, including geography, history, economics, sociology, and political science, all teach about culture. Geography, for example, provides a look at how physical environment helps shape culture. The study of history also provides valuable clues to solving

Exploring Culture

An Anthropologist

9:25 A.M., November 7, 1993
Coal mine, Boone County, West Virginia

Notebook
Today she notes the tasks of coal loaders. Several are teenagers. Loaders are exposed to coal dust, which causes black lung disease.

Shoulder Bag
She packs a tape recorder. As part of her study, she checks noise levels in the deep mine. She also wants to know how miners adjust to the dangers of their everyday work.

Camera
She photographs the miners both at work and after their shifts. Her articles will include pictures of union meetings and miners' ball games.

Lantern
Like the miners, she checks her lantern. A blue flame means deadly gas fumes are present. Her steel-toed boots protect her from heavy machinery and falling rocks.

Lunch Pail
She eats underground with men and women of the day crew and totes a durable pail like theirs. They arrive before daylight and leave after dark.

How Do Anthropologists Learn About People?

An anthropologist studying this scene might ask:

• What are these people doing? Why?

• How is the woman in the white dress related to the man with her?

• How does the woman feel? How do the people watching her feel?

cultural puzzles. History tells what a culture used to be like. It also tells how a culture has changed over time.

The study of economics—how a group uses its resources—adds details to the picture of its culture. So does learning about political science, the study of how political power is distributed in a group.

Perhaps the social science that adds the most to people's knowledge of other cultures is anthropology. One of the aims of this science is to study how people live as a cultural group. A person who is an expert in this science is called an **anthropologist.** In the box above, you can read some questions an anthropologist might ask when studying a group of people. To learn more about the work of an anthropologist, see A Moment in Time on page 22.

The Value of Each Culture

As people learn more about other cultures, they learn to recognize the value of each one. Without this knowledge and understanding, negative prejudices can develop. This kind of **prejudice** is a dislike or a distrust of certain people simply because they are different.

Sometimes, this prejudice grows beyond dislike or distrust. It turns into something far worse, called racism. **Racism** means disliking or distrusting people because they belong to a different group than you do.

As you will read in this book, the earth is home to different peoples with long and amazing histories. Learning to understand and value other cultures is a way of learning to live on the planet all people share. ■

■ *How do the social sciences help people learn about cultures?*

R E V I E W

1. **FOCUS** How do people learn about their own and other cultures?
2. **CULTURE** How do geography, history, economics, and political science teach people about culture?
3. **CULTURE** Explain how an anthropologist can learn about a culture by living among its members.
4. **CRITICAL THINKING** Why is it important to learn about other cultures?

5. **WRITING ACTIVITY** Imagine you are an anthropologist studying the classroom behavior of students in your school. Spend your next class observing other students. Jot down your observations. For example, do students raise their hands to answer questions? Do students sit in chairs? Then write a short paragraph describing the cultural details you observed.

Chapter Review

Reviewing Key Terms

anthropologist (p. 23)
belief (p. 8)
cultural diffusion (p. 15)
culture (p. 5)
custom (p. 6)
environment (p. 12)
ethnic group (p. 21)

institution (p. 7)
media (p. 21)
prejudice (p. 23)
racism (p. 23)
social interaction (p. 14)
technology (p. 16)
value (p. 9)

A. Write a definition for each of the following key terms. Then give an example of each one, based on your own knowledge and experience.
1. custom
2. ethnic group
3. belief
4. institution
5. value
6. media

B. Write the key term that is suggested by each of the following groups of words. Then explain how each group of words relates to the key term.
1. climate, neighborhood
2. conversations, meetings
3. farm machinery, computers
4. language, religion, recreation, arts

C. Explain the relationship between the key terms in each of the following pairs.
1. prejudice, racism
2. social interaction, cultural diffusion
3. belief, value
4. anthropologist, culture
5. environment, technology

Exploring Concepts

A. On your own paper, copy and complete the outline below. Then use it to write a summary of the chapter. For each main idea, write a short paragraph.

  I. Culture is the way of life of a people.
    A. Customs
    B. Institutions
    C.
  II. Cultures develop and change.
    A.
    B. Social interaction
      1.
      2.
    C.
  III. We learn about culture.
    A. Our own culture
    B. Other cultures
      1.
      2.
    C.

B. Answer each question with information from the chapter or a dictionary.
1. In what ways are people of all cultures alike?
2. List at least eight parts of culture that are common to most cultures.
3. Give two examples of ways in which cultures differ.
4. The English language, as it is spoken in the United States, has become enriched with words from many cultures. Explain how this growth of language is an example of cultural diffusion. Then look up each of the following words in an English dictionary: *gumbo, pinto, skunk, kayak.* Identify the word's origin. Then write a brief definition.
5. Technology and invention have also introduced new words and phrases into the English language. Look up the following examples: *motel, turbo, database, sandwich, braille, dahlia.* Tell how the words were created and what they mean.

Reviewing Skills

1. Guglielmo Marconi received the world's first transatlantic radio message in 1901. How do you know that this statement is a fact?

2. We believe that the cricket's song heralds the coming of spring. What key words tell you that this statement is an opinion?

3. Social scientists think that the family is perhaps the oldest institution. Is this statement a fact, a reasoned judgment, or an opinion? Explain your answer.

4. Customs vary from culture to culture. How do you know that this statement is a fact? Use examples to support your answer.

5. Imagine that you are observing the scene in the picture on page 23. First, you write an exact description of what you see in the picture. Then, you write a statement about what is probably happening in the picture. Finally, you write your feelings and thoughts about the picture. What three types of information are you writing down?

Using Critical Thinking

1. The word *prejudice* contains two Latin word parts: *pre-,* which means "before" and *iudicium,* which means "judgment." Therefore, the literal meaning of prejudice is "a judgment made before." Before what do you think the judgment is made in cases of prejudice?

2. The United States is a multicultural nation. (The word part *multi-* means "many.") What benefits and problems might a multicultural nation have? How, in your opinion, can social interaction and institutions such as schools and government work to solve some of the problems? Explain your answers.

3. Movies made in the United States are seen by people all over the world. Think of a movie you have seen that takes place in the United States. What view of our culture do you think this movie gives? In your opinion, does this movie present a true picture of our culture? Why or why not?

Preparing for Citizenship

1. **GROUP ACTIVITY** The English language, as it is spoken in the United States, contains many idioms. An idiom is a saying that has a meaning different from the meanings of the words that make it up. Such sayings include *by the way, in the meantime, on the other hand,* and *It's up to you.* Idioms are often difficult for people from other cultures to understand. In a small group, make a list of as many of these expressions as possible. Then work together to write definitions for them.

2. **INTERVIEWING** List inventions that have changed your culture in recent years. Then interview older relatives about changes that have occurred during their lifetimes. Report your findings to the class.

3. **WRITING ACTIVITY** On page 15 you read about a change that took place in some American Indian cultures after the Spaniards came to Mexico in the 1500s. Select an American Indian culture to research. Where did the people live, and how did the physical environment shape their culture? What customs, institutions, beliefs, and values were part of the culture? How did the culture change after the arrival of new settlers? Prepare a report to share with the class.

4. **COLLABORATIVE LEARNING** Like many other institutions, a government has special buildings for its activities. With three of your classmates, give a presentation that describes a government building. Choose a building located in your state capital or in the nation's capital. Two can gather information about the building. The other two can prepare a description of the building's purpose, the groups that use it, and the activities that go on there.

Chapter 2
Exploring Geography

A photograph of the earth, taken from outer space, shows a world wrapped in clouds. Close-up photographs show features of the land and evidence of the human, animal, and plant life found on earth. In this chapter you will read about how people study the earth.

A Hawaiian volcano erupts, sending glowing rivers of lava down its sides.

Signposts in the Falkland Islands point the long way home for British troops stationed there. Great Britain rules the Falklands, which are located in the South Atlantic Ocean, about 8,000 miles from Britain.

On the left you see orpiment, or arsenic trisulfide. On the right is malachite, or carbonate of copper. These are just two of the many different kinds of minerals found in the earth.

People enjoy a day at the beach in Atlantic City, New Jersey.

This photograph of the earth was taken in April 1972 by the space-craft *Apollo 16*.

Fossils are the remains or imprints of ancient animals and plants. At the right is a fossil trilobite, an ancient marine animal. At the left are fern fossils.

Location and Place

*What is geography, and
what are its five themes?*

Key Terms

- geography
- landform
- latitude
- longitude

J enny was dreaming. In her
dream she was walking along
a strange street. Yet much of
what she saw was familiar to
her. She could tell she was in a city
because she saw tall buildings
crowded along the sidewalk and
dozens of people hurrying past her.
She saw a school and a church. She
crossed a bridge over a wide river.

Yet some things in this city were
not familiar to Jenny. Many of the
buildings seemed to be hundreds
of years old—much older than the
buildings in most U.S. cities. The
flags flying from storefronts
showed thick stripes of blue,
white, and red—not the thin red
and white stripes and white stars
on blue that make up the U.S. flag.

Do you recognize the city in
Jenny's dream? Perhaps the pictures here can help you name it.

All the things Jenny saw in her
dream help describe a place: Paris,

France. This place has a location.
Location and place are two important ways people who study the
earth organize information about
it. Other important ways are
human interaction with the earth;
movement of people, goods, and
ideas across the earth; and regions
of the earth. Location, place, interaction, movement, and regions are
known as the five themes of
geography.

➤ *Look closely at these
objects. Do you recognize
the language that appears
on the magazines and the
menus? Do you recognize
the small souvenir tower
at the far right? These objects bring to mind a particular place. Do you
know what the place is?*

Locating the Place

Geography is the study of the earth and the relationship of people with the earth. Geography describes physical features of the earth such as the plants, animals, and landforms of an area. A **landform** is a feature on the earth's surface such as a hill, plain, or valley. Geography also looks at how the earth supplies basic human needs for food, clothing, and shelter. In addition, geography explores how people use the earth and how they affect the environment.

Locating places is an important part of geography. Geographers describe location in two ways—absolute location and relative location. Absolute location is identified by a specific address or a point on a map. Relative location is found by looking at where places are in relation to one another.

A Point on a Map

Using a map is one way to find the location of a place. However, a map usually shows a large area with many places. How can you find one particular place on a map? Mapmakers crisscross maps with two sets of imaginary lines that divide up the map. One set of

◀ *The Eiffel Tower is named after Alexandre Eiffel, the engineer who designed it. The tower is an iron framework, 984 feet high. It was completed in 1889.*

lines circles the earth east and west, like the equator. These are lines of **latitude.** All lines of latitude are parallel with one another—they never meet. Lines of latitude are measured in degrees (°). The latitude of a place is its distance north or south of the equator.

The other set of lines circles the earth to meet at the North and South poles. These lines, or meridians, of **longitude** are also measured in degrees (°). The longitude of a place is its distance east or west of the prime meridian, a line of longitude that runs through Greenwich, England.

Together, the lines of latitude and longitude create a grid that breaks up a map into smaller parts. The picture of the globe on page 30 shows lines of latitude and longitude. Every place on the earth can be described through the use of latitude and longitude. The absolute location of a place is the point where a specific degree of latitude crosses

Exploring Geography

one of longitude. You can read more about using latitude and longitude on page G5 in the Map and Globe Handbook.

What Are You Near?

Relative location tells where one place is in relation to another. Giving directions is one way to explain relative location. For example, you might tell a friend how to get to your house from the school that she attends.

A map can also show relative location. The map of a Paris neighborhood on page 31 shows the location of places in relation to one another. ■

■ Describe two ways to identify the location of a place.

A Sense of Place

Location tells you where you are. Paris, for example, is located 49 degrees north of the equator and 2 degrees east of the prime meridian. This doesn't tell you very much about Paris, however. You are probably more interested in its sights—the special buildings, the river, and the stores. All these features give you a sense of place.

When they are describing a certain place—a valley, a desert, a house, a school, a village, a city, or any other place on earth—geographers talk about both the human features and the natural features of this place.

A Human Place

In her dream Jenny recognized a school and a church. She walked along crowded streets and over a bridge. All of these things were built by people. All are human features of Paris. These features illustrate how people affect a place.

➤ This photograph, taken from the air, shows the city of Paris, France.

You may find some of the human features of Paris in a city near you, too. Other human features such as the religions practiced, the flags flown, and the languages spoken help make a city—or any area—unique.

A Place in Nature

The place in Jenny's dream also included a river. This river, the Seine, is a natural, or physical, feature of Paris. You can see the Seine flowing through the heart of Paris in the photograph on page 30. Altitude—or the height of a place, usually above sea level—is a physical feature. The land on which Paris is built is about 250 feet above sea level. The climate of an area is also a physical feature. Parisians enjoy a climate with comfortable temperatures and moderate rainfall most of the year.

Both the human features and the physical features found around the world vary dramatically. Housing—a human feature—varies from igloos used as temporary hunting shelters in northern Canada to towering concrete, glass, and steel skyscrapers in Houston, Texas. Climate—a physical feature—ranges from always hot in the tropics to always cold at the poles.

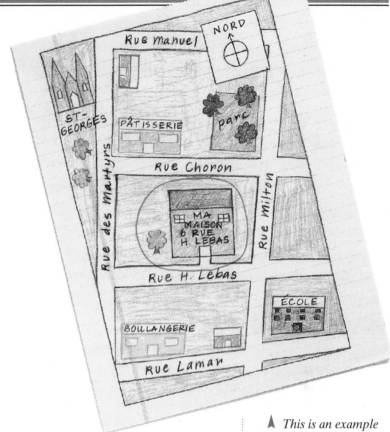

Physical features and human features also change. In 200 years transportation systems in the United States have changed from horses, wagons, and canoes to cars, trains, and planes. The Sahel is a physical feature you read about in Chapter 1. Because of recent periods of little rain, the Sahel is changing as it slowly becomes absorbed by the expanding Sahara. ■

▲ *This is an example of a map that shows relative location. The building in the center of the map is labeled* ma maison, *which means "my house." The map shows where this house is located in relation to other places, including a church, and a school (école).*

■ *What two kinds of features are used to describe a place?*

R E V I E W

1. **FOCUS** What is geography, and what are its five themes?
2. **GEOGRAPHY** How do lines of latitude and longitude divide the world into a grid?
3. **GEOGRAPHY** Describe two human features and two physical features found where you live.
4. **CULTURE** List three ways climate in your area affects the way you live.
5. **CRITICAL THINKING** Draw a map of your neighborhood. Then compare it with the map of the Paris

neighborhood on this page. How are the two places and maps alike? How are they different?

6. **ACTIVITY** Choose four countries from the world map on pages 678 and 679 of your text. Write down the degrees of latitude and longitude that intersect, or cross, in these countries. Then exchange papers with a classmate and take a location quiz. Use the degrees of latitude and longitude on the world map to identify the four countries.

Interaction

Key Terms

- adapt
- deforestation
- pollute
- endangered
- extinct

➤ *La Paz, Bolivia's largest city, lies on a broad stretch of high, level land in the Andes of South America. Most people who work in La Paz live on the slopes of the valley that surrounds the city.*

Matt stumbled to the side of the soccer field and leaned over, his hands on his knees, trying to catch his breath.

"I don't know what's so hard about playing here in Bolivia," he said to his coach. "I seem to be out of breath after just a few minutes of practice."

"Well, La Paz is one of the highest cities in the world," his coach explained. "At 12,000 feet above sea level, the air is thin. Most visitors have more trouble breathing than the people who have lived here a long time. Look out there." The coach motioned toward the mountain peaks in the distance. "Those are the tops of the Andes—and they don't even look very high from here."

Matt stood and gazed at the mountain tops. "You know, Coach, this place is really beautiful. If I had grown up here, I don't think I'd want to leave."

Adapting to Places

Certainly people can enjoy the natural beauty of their surroundings. Yet beauty is not the main factor people consider when they decide where to live. The vast deserts of Africa, for example, may appear beautiful, but few live there.

Where People Live

Most of the world's people live in places that have a comfortable climate, a source of water, fertile soil, and level areas of land. These resources help make it easy to produce food, to build homes, and to meet the needs of business and industry. In other words, people live where they can find work and meet their basic needs. Understanding Natural Resources on page 34 will tell you more.

We Adapt to Places

Some places in the world meet most human needs. For example, British settlers in the area of Sydney, Australia, found land that could support crops and sheep. The mild climate offered a sufficient growing period and enough rain to provide water for people, farms, and ranches. The nearby harbor provided a way to get goods to market. It's no wonder, then, that Sydney continues to grow and is today Australia's largest city.

Not all areas of the world answer every human need so well.

Often people must **adapt**—or adjust—to an area. When pioneers decided to settle the Great Plains of the United States, they found few trees to provide lumber for housing. Yet the climate and soil of the Great Plains did meet many of their needs. So the pioneers adapted. They learned to build houses of sod—chunks of root-tangled earth cut from the land itself.

Sometimes, people's bodies can adapt to their environment. Over the years, the people of the Andes have physically adapted to the lower level of oxygen in the air. They have developed barrel-shaped chests as their hearts and lungs have increased in size. They also breathe more rapidly than people who live at lower altitudes. These physical changes allow them to take in enough oxygen. ■

■ *What factors influence where people live?*

Changing the Environment

Much of what is now the Netherlands was once underwater. The Netherlands grew because the people found a way to claim land that was below sea level. First,

they built dikes. Then they drained away the seawater, uncovering soil that could be turned into rich farmland. They added thousands of square miles to their nation. This is

▼ *This photograph of Sydney was taken with a special camera lens that permits a broad view in the shape of an arc, or curve. Sydney is located in the most heavily populated area of Australia.*

only one of the ways in which humans shape their environment.

Using the Land

People have found ways to use many kinds of places for farmland. Starting thousands of years ago, they have brought water from rivers and wells to dry and desert areas. People have cut into mountains and hills to create flat areas called terraces and planted crops there. From China to Peru, terracing is still practiced.

➤ *The photograph at the right shows an area of rain forest that has been destroyed.*

Human Impact

You have been reading about ways people interact with the environment. In this interaction, or give-and-take, between people and the environment, humans can also do harm. For example, when

people first began to plant crops, they developed the slash-and-burn method. They cut down trees and plants, let them dry out, and then set fire to what remained. They farmed the cleared land until its nutrients were used up. Then the people moved on to slash and burn another area.

This farming method has been a way of life for thousands of years in parts of Africa, Central America,

UNDERSTANDING NATURAL RESOURCES

Since the beginning of time, natural forces have shaped and changed our earth. During the ice ages, massive glaciers inched across the land, carving out lakes and ponds in their paths. The powerful force of earthquakes has pushed precious metals like gold and silver up from deep inside of the earth, while reshaping the face of the earth. Wet, cold climates of northern regions have produced forests of towering trees spreading far across the land.

Nature and Human Needs

Humans have come to depend on these products of nature for their survival. Fresh water from lakes and ponds can meet the water needs of entire communities. Lumber from the trees of the north is used to make strong and sturdy houses. Oil and natural gas found deep within the earth provide energy to run factories and businesses and to heat homes. Metals such as gold, silver, and copper are used to make tools and valuable jewelry.

Resources You Use

These materials that humans find in nature and use for their needs are called natural resources. Without natural resources, life as you know it would not exist. Look around you, and you will see many examples of natural resources. A short list might include the electricity that powers your television set, the plastic (produced from oil) wrapper on your sandwich, the steel used to build your family's car, and the water that runs through your home.

34

Endangered Species

Endangered Species	Species Habitat	Threat	Progress Toward Saving Species
Gray bat	caves, mines, and crevices in rocks in southeastern U.S.	cave exploration, pesticides, deforestation	Population has increased greatly since 1985.
Northern Right whale	shallow ocean waters in Northern Hemisphere	hunted almost to point of extinction	Population has increased little if any since 1935.
Puerto Rican parrot	lowland forest of Puerto Rico	deforestation, logging, hunting, pet industry	A fragile population of 20–25 birds is slowly increasing.
California condor	caves and crevices in the costal moutain range of central California	pesticides and other poisons	Today there are about 60 birds in captivity.

South America, Southeast Asia, and some Pacific islands. Its limited use does not do permanent damage to the land. However, when millions of people do it, aided by giant bulldozers and cutting machines, slash-and-burn becomes a problem. Today **deforestation**—the process of clearing forests—is having a tremendous impact on the environment. For example, widespread logging and cattle ranching are destroying the rain forests of the Amazon. In the picture that appears on page 34, you can see an area of rain forest that has been cleared and burned.

Increased manufacturing the world over has also damaged the environment. Toxic, or poisonous, smoke from industry and cars fills our air. Oil spills and industrial sewage **pollute**—make dirty or unusable—our oceans. Waste dumps contain toxic materials. Even our own homes help pollute the earth, as you will see when you read Where Should We Put Our Trash? on pages 36–37.

Damage to the environment through deforestation and pollution has endangered the earth's plant and animal life. **Endangered** plant and animal species are in danger of becoming **extinct,** or dying off. Once a species has become extinct, it is gone forever. The chart on this page lists some endangered species found in the United States and Puerto Rico. ■

▲ *In 1982 scientists began a program to capture all wild California condors. The last of these wild birds was captured in 1987. Since then, several condors have been born and raised in captivity. Some condors born in captivity have been returned to the wild. Nevertheless, the future of the bird remains in doubt.*

■ *In what ways do humans shape the earth?*

R E V I E W

1. FOCUS How do people interact with the natural world?
2. GEOGRAPHY What are some ways people are harming the environment?
3. GEOGRAPHY The radioactive waste that people create can't be thrown away because it doesn't decompose, or become part of the soil, like most other trash. So the United States is considering putting it all in one place and creating some sort of symbol that would alert everyone for thousands of years to KEEP OUT. What kind of symbol do you think would be most effective?

4. CRITICAL THINKING President Franklin D. Roosevelt once wrote, "The nation that destroys its soil destroys itself." What do you think he meant by this statement?
5. ACTIVITY Choose one of the animals listed on the Endangered Species chart on this page. Research your choice. Then write two or three paragraphs explaining what effect the extinction of this animal might have on the rest of the world. Illustrate your paragraph with a picture of the animal.

Where Should We Put Our Trash?

*W*e are *running out of land-fill space. More important, is the issue really "available space" or is it a question of our right to dig a hole whenever we feel the need to bury our garbage because it seems easier than the role of re-sponsible stewardship [caretak-ing]?*

Peter L. Grogan, president of the National Recycling Coalition

*W*hat *most people don't know about landfills could fill a landfill. At the current rate, if all the nation's solid waste for the next 500 years were piled or buried in a single landfill to a depth of 100 yards, . . . this "national land-fill" would require a square site less than 20 miles on a side.*

Clark Wiseman, professor of economics, Gonzaga University

Background

The first record of a city's plan for trash disposal comes from the Greek city-state of Athens, more than 2,500 years ago. The law simply stated that waste was to be taken at least one mile from the city.

Since the time of the ancient Greeks, the disposal of trash has gone through many changes. Not all of these changes have been for the better. City dwellers in me-dieval Europe simply tossed trash out their windows into the street. When the garbage seeped into the drinking water, people became sick. In 1885 the United States opened its first garbage incinerator on Governor's Island in New York City. Since then, the need for new methods of trash disposal has grown as the amount of trash has grown.

Since World War II the number of products we use once or twice and then throw away has grown consid-erably. The list includes disposable diapers, razors, fast-food containers, and much, much more.

In 1960 approximately 2.7 pounds of trash were discarded each day for every man, woman, and child in the United States. Today, each person in the United States discards about 4 pounds of trash per day, or one-half ton per year. This is roughly twice the amount as in Japan and Western Europe.

Considering Alternatives

The diagram at the right shows what makes up our trash. What should we do with these waste materials? One alternative is to bury solid waste in landfills. Another is to recycle it. Products that can be recycled include glass, aluminum, paper, plastics, and vegetable waste (made into compost). A third alternative is incineration, that is, burning waste to greatly reduce its size. By 1990, U.S. residents were throwing away about 73 percent of their trash in landfills, incinerating about 14 percent, and recycling about 13 percent.

Landfills have given rise to the slogan NIMBY (Not In My Backyard). No one wants a landfill next door. Landfills are unsightly, smelly, and unsafe.

Recycling sounds like a good idea, but most communities can't afford to collect and recycle their citizens' waste. They have barely enough resources to provide police and fire protection, schools, and town dumps. In addition, industries that make new things from recycled materials are still trying to keep up with even the small amount being recycled.

Burning trash has advantages and disadvantages. Some incinerators burn waste to produce steam and electricity. In the process, however, foul odors, toxic gases, and gritty smoke are produced. In 1992 the United States had 140 waste-to-energy plants in operation. The building of more waste-to-energy plants was blocked, however, when citizens became concerned about the plants' impact on their local environments.

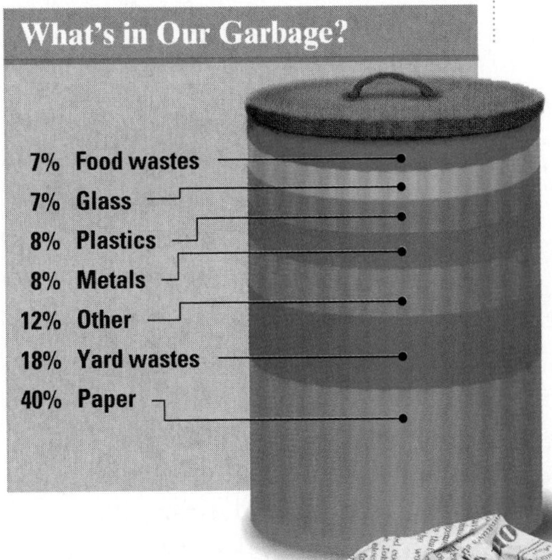

What the chart doesn't show is reduction, that is, reducing the amount of waste each person produces. What if we were to reuse instead of dump, recycle, or burn our trash? What if food producers were to package their products in fewer wrappers, boxes, and bags?

What's in Our Garbage?

- 7% Food wastes
- 7% Glass
- 8% Plastics
- 8% Metals
- 12% Other
- 18% Yard wastes
- 40% Paper

Decision Point

1. What are the advantages of each kind of waste management discussed above? What are the disadvantages of each one?

2. How does your community handle its waste? Do you think this is the most effective way?

3. List at least 10 ways that you yourself can reduce the amount of waste you generate.

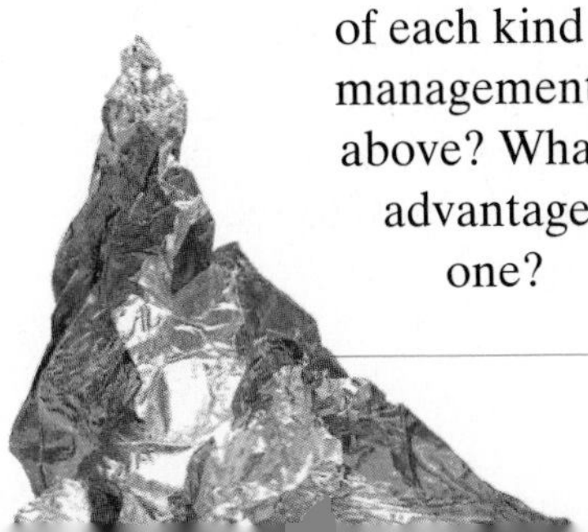

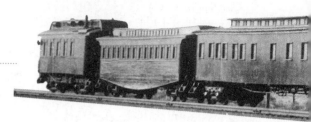

Movement

THINKING
FOCUS

What are the causes and the effects of human movement around the world?

Key Terms

- immigration
- migration
- emigrant
- rural

➤ *Samuel B. Waugh painted this scene, entitled* The Bay and Harbor of New York, *in 1855. It shows people arriving by ship to make their home in the United States.*

> e entered [a cabin] and found a single child about three years old lying on a kind of shelf, with its little face resting upon the edge of the board and looking steadfastly out at the door as if for its mother. It never moved its eyes as we entered, but kept them fixed toward the entrance. It is doubtful whether the poor thing had a mother or father left to her. . . . Never have I seen such bright, blue, clear eyes looking so steadfastly at nothing.

Elihu Burritt, from *The Irish Potato Famine: Victims of the Great Hunger*

This description of a starving child was written after the author had visited Ireland during the potato famine in the 1840s. The potato did not originally grow in Ireland. Instead, explorers returning from South America brought the potato back with them. It grew so well in Irish soil that it became Ireland's main food. When a disease wiped out the potato crop, a million people died, and more than a million left their homeland. All this movement and change was caused by the little, round root crop called the potato.

People, Goods, and Ideas

Movement of goods, services, and ideas around the world is one way in which people interact with the environment. Bringing the potato from South America, for example, eventually offered a new, very healthful food source to many nations, including China, India, and the United States. This movement of the potato—in spite of the Irish tragedy—proved helpful to the people of the world.

Goods and Services

In fact, the movement of goods and services usually benefits humans. This movement is one of the things that allows humans to adapt to their environment. For example, wheat is the world's most important food crop. Western European countries do not produce enough wheat to meet their own needs. So vast amounts of wheat are sold to these countries by countries that produce a surplus of the crop.

Ideas

Ideas, like goods and services, also move throughout the world. In the early days, people could not write. They passed on information by speaking. The Egyptians were among the first to develop a form of picture writing. When the Semites learned of it, they used it to create an alphabet. The Semites passed this new idea to the Phoenicians, who made changes to it and passed it along to the Greeks.

The Greeks introduced it to the Etruscans, who moved the idea along to the Romans. Eventually, the alphabet became our ABCs.

U.S. Immigration

How do goods, services, and ideas get from one place to another? Often they travel with people who are themselves moving. In this way the idea of an alphabet was spread throughout the ancient world.

Today people still bring goods, services, and ideas with them when they move. For example, people from many nations have moved to the United States. In fact, our nation was built on **immigration,** or the movement of people to a new homeland. Immigrants—people who come to a country to live permanently—bring with them the clothing, foods, celebrations, ideas, and skills that are part of their way of life. ■

▲ *This photograph shows a restored Union Pacific passenger train, one of the first trains used to carry travelers across the United States.*

■ *Give an example of how the movement of goods, services, or ideas has benefited people.*

People in Motion

People move for a variety of reasons. The people of the Sahel, about whom you read in Chapter 1, move from the Sahel to the south, then back again, according to the rains. This is called **migration,** or movement from one place to another. Mexico's Tarahumara Indians migrate with the seasons, living high in the Sierra Madre most of the year but moving down the mountainsides during the winter.

In the United States many farm workers migrate as various crops ripen and are ready for harvesting. For example, in California migrant workers harvest lettuce in the Salinas Valley along the southern coast.

The Great Migration

Over several decades beginning in the late 1800s, millions of African Americans left the South. Black recruiters and newspapers from northern cities told of a better life there. Families and individuals moved to Chicago, Detroit, New York City, and other factory centers. From 1916 to 1930, the blacks who headed north created the largest single internal migration in United States history.

Why leave? Southerners had passed laws unfair to African Americans. Also, the amount of farm work declined. Jobs at mills, mines, and docks paid too little or went to white workers.

Black men and women packed and traveled to the North, where they hoped to find better-paying jobs. Also, fewer laws restricted their freedom.

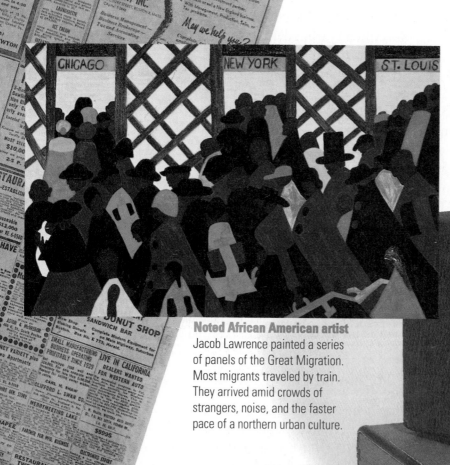

Noted African American artist Jacob Lawrence painted a series of panels of the Great Migration. Most migrants traveled by train. They arrived amid crowds of strangers, noise, and the faster pace of a northern urban culture.

Then they move on. Such workers travel throughout the state, harvesting whatever crops are in season.

For other people, the move is permanent. For example, many Irish immigrants who fled the potato famine in the 1840s settled permanently in the United States. You can read about another example of migration—the African American movement from the South to the North within the United States—in A Closer Look on page 40.

Problems at Home

In the examples of migration you have read about so far, something was pushing people away from where they were. Sometimes the push comes from the climate. People in the Sahel move with the rainfall; the Tarahumara migrate with the temperature. Sometimes the push comes from changes in job opportunities in an area, for example, when a factory closes.

Many who migrate permanently also are pushed to move. As you read, in the 1840s Irish **emigrants**—people who have left their native land to make their home in another country—did so because of the push of starvation. Many of these emigrants came from **rural,** or farming, areas. When they reached the United States, they settled in cities, where they had to become accustomed to city life.

Opportunity and Community

Yet even as they say their good-byes, immigrants often look forward with hope to their new home. Usually, new opportunities wait for them there. Perhaps the climate is better, the food is more plentiful, or more jobs are available. Perhaps the new land promises trade opportunities or religious freedom. All of these factors are called pull factors—attractions pulling people away from their homes and toward their new destinations. ■

▼ *The movement of human beings and their technology has extended into outer space. This photograph, taken on May 13, 1992, shows U.S. astronauts outside the spacecraft* Endeavour, *rescuing a satellite from its orbit around the earth.*

■ *Why do people move from place to place?*

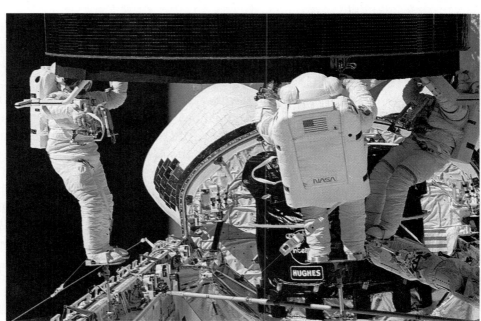

R E V I E W

1. FOCUS What are the causes and the effects of human movement around the world?
2. CULTURE When do people choose to move away rather than adapt to their environment?
3. GEOGRAPHY Give examples of push and pull factors.
4. CRITICAL THINKING Why do you think geographers study the movement of people, goods, services, and ideas?
5. ACTIVITY Imagine you have been put in charge of creating an advertisement that will entice people to settle on the moon. Choose a pull factor you think will work and use it to draw a poster that will attract moon pioneers.

Regions

Key Terms

- region
- urban

▼ *This cafeteria has tables,
chairs, trays, and other
equipment for serving and
eating meals. Other areas
of a school also have special purposes. What areas
are used for special pur-
poses in your school?*

James jumped off the bus and
waved to Harry.

"Hey, Harry!" he shouted
over the din of the student
crowd. "I'll meet you in the social
region."

James ran down the hall to his
locker, where Harry was waiting
for him.

"Listen, I have something to tell
you," James said. "Can you meet
me in the food region at 12 sharp?"

"That's gonna be tough," Harry
explained. "I have to come all the
way from the exercise region and
stop at the administration region to
pick up a note from my dad. I'll be
there as soon as I can."

Regions in the United States

In real life nobody talks the
way James and Harry just did. Yet
you knew exactly what areas of the
school they were talking about. The
social region includes the locker
area and the halls. The food region
is the cafeteria and the kitchen.
The exercise region is the gym and
the playing fields. The administration region is the office and the
nurse's room. Each area can be
called a region because the places
in this area have certain characteristics, or features, in common. A
region is an area that has shared
features that set it apart from surrounding areas.

Like a school, the world can
be divided into regions. Geographers do this so they can study the
features of particular regions and
how they differ. Even the world's
countries, including the United
States, can be divided into regions.

Geographers can define a region by almost any feature. They name the region by the characteristic the area shares. For example, the word **urban** means "city." So an urban region is a city and the area around it. A climatic region is an area that shares a particular climate. Other types of regions include vegetation regions and landform regions. Often, regions are illustrated on thematic maps. You'll read more about this kind of map on pages 46–47.

Your school district is another example of a region—an educational region. The school district also is a political region, with a ruling group voted on by residents.

States as Political Regions

The United States has many levels of political regions. A school district is one; your city is another; your county (in Louisiana, parish) is another. There are also 50 larger regions, each with its own government, each with its own unchanging boundaries. You have probably already guessed that these are the states.

Regions by Location

Look at the map of the United States on this page. Locate the region called the Northeast. You probably knew to look in the upper right-hand corner of the map, because the region's name gives directions to the place. You know it is both in the north and in the east.

The map divides the United States into six regions. The area included in each region shares certain features. For example, much of the Midwest is flat, with fertile land used for farming. On the other hand, the Rocky Mountain region is named after a high mountain range. The mountains have many rich metal deposits. Because of these natural resources there is much mining in this region. Much of the Southeast is characterized by a long coastal plain and a climate that is warm and wet. ■

▼ *The map below shows the United States divided into six regions. Find your state on the map. In what region is it located? How do you think your state is like others in the same region?*

■ *List three examples of political regions found in the United States.*

United States: Regions

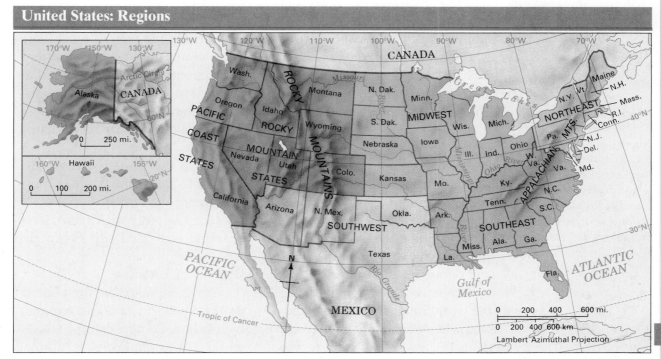

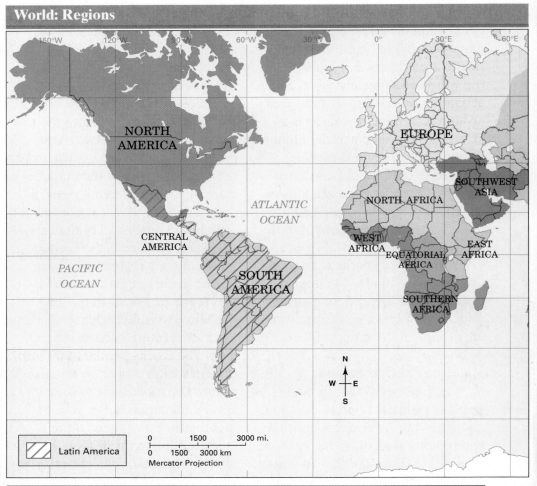

World: Regions

NORTH AMERICA

EUROPE

SOUTHWEST ASIA

NORTH AFRICA

ATLANTIC OCEAN

CENTRAL AMERICA

WEST AFRICA

EAST AFRICA

EQUATORIAL AFRICA

PACIFIC OCEAN

SOUTH AMERICA

SOUTHERN AFRICA

N
W E
S

Latin America

0   1500   3000 mi.
0   1500   3000 km
Mercator Projection

The map on these pages shows different regions of the world. Some regions are identified by their location, for example, North, Central, and South America. The continent of Africa is also divided into regions by location. Latin America, a cultural region, is marked with diagonal lines.

▲ *Guatemala has more people than any other country in Central America. More than half the people of Guatemala are descendants of the Maya. Here, Indian women and children take part in a Holy Week procession.*

Regions of the World

One area can be part of several regions. You have read that your school district makes up one region. It is also part of larger political regions—your state and the United States. In the same way, the world's regions overlap.

Some regions of the world are huge. For example, the regions we refer to as the Northern Hemisphere and the Southern Hemisphere each occupy half the earth. For help in understanding the concept of hemispheres, see page G4 in the Map and Globe Handbook.

Another way geographers divide the world into regions is by landform. The picture of the Alps on page 45 shows a landform region.

Countries as Political Regions

Perhaps the regions most familiar to us are the world's countries. Each country can be considered a political region. Each has its own government and court system. Each provides certain services to its people.

Just as the United States is divided into states, many other countries are broken up into smaller political regions. Switzerland, for example, is divided into 23 cantons.

Regions by Location

You have read that the United States can be divided into regions by location. So, too, can the whole world. For example, one locational

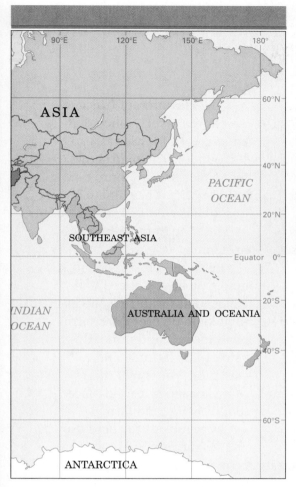

A *The Alps are the largest mountain system in Europe. The entire system is about 750 miles long. At their widest point, the Alps are about 125 miles wide. At their narrowest point, they cover about 75 miles.*

region, the people share cultural features, such as language and clothing. A cultural region can be very small. One example is the region around Lancaster, Pennsylvania, known as Amish country. Here the Amish culture has changed little in 200 years. The Amish share a common religion. Their beliefs require farming as a way of life, but they often refuse to use modern farm machinery. The Amish shun the use of telephones, electricity, and automobiles.

Other cultural regions of the world are vast. Latin America is a cultural region that includes Mexico and most of the countries of the Caribbean, Central America, and South America. Latin Americans share common languages. The majority of the people speak Spanish or Portuguese. ■

region is South America. This region includes all the countries on this continent. Locate South America on the world map above. Then look at the continent of Africa on the map. Into what locational regions has Africa been divided?

Cultural Regions

The world can also be divided into cultural regions. In this type of

■ *Give three examples of shared features that might be found in a cultural region.*

R E V I E W

1. **FOCUS** Why do geographers divide the world into regions?
2. **GEOGRAPHY** Name five kinds of regions mentioned in this lesson.
3. **GEOGRAPHY** Locate your community on a map. List three regions of which it is a part.
4. **CRITICAL THINKING** Why is the United States

considered one of the world's political regions?
5. **WRITING ACTIVITY** Remember that geographers can create a region by using just about any feature. Choose a crop you know is grown in the United States. Research it in an encyclopedia. Then write a paragraph describing the region in which this crop is found. What states are included in the region?

Exploring Geography

Comparing Two U.S. Maps

Here's Why

No single map can show you everything about a region. In fact, there are different kinds of maps, each showing a particular kind of information. For example, one kind of map may show rainfall in a region. Another kind may show elevation, and another kind of map may show land use.

You often can learn more by comparing two maps of the same region than you can by looking at one map alone. For example, you can compare physical regions maps with land use maps of the United States. Using the maps together will help you see how the physical features of our country affect our land use.

Here's How

Look at the map of physical regions on this page. It shows physical features such as mountains, lakes, and rivers. A map key explains which colors on the map stand for which elevations.

Now study the land use and resources map of the United States on the facing page. This map shows you what types of economic activities are found in different areas of the United States.

Compare the two maps. How have geographic factors influenced land use in Chicago, Illinois? First, find Chicago on the physical regions map. You can see that it is located at the southwestern tip of Lake Michigan.

The elevation of Chicago is near sea level. Notice that large areas of lowlands also surround it. The map shows that Chicago is at approximately 42°N. The climate in this area is cold and windy in winter and hot and humid in summer.

From the physical regions map, you have noticed that Chicago has water resources that could be useful for farming, industry, and trade. Because of its latitude and elevation, you might infer that Chicago is a good place to live, work, and farm.

Now look at the land use and resources map to see what economic activities are important to Chicago. The map's key tells you that Chicago is

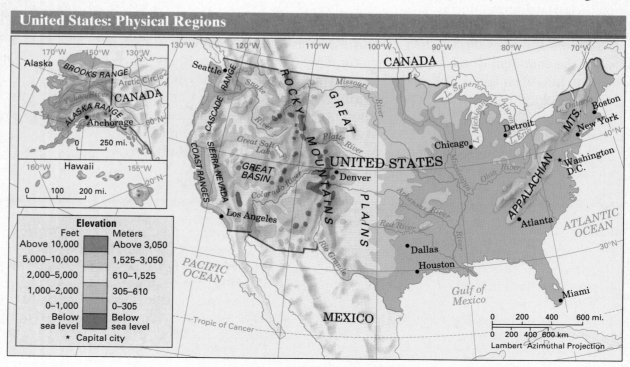

United States: Physical Regions

Elevation

Feet		Meters
Above 10,000		Above 3,050
5,000–10,000		1,525–3,050
2,000–5,000		610–1,525
1,000–2,000		305–610
0–1,000		0–305
Below sea level		Below sea level

★ Capital city

0   200   400   600 mi.
0   200 400 600 km
Lambert Azimuthal Projection

in an urban and industrial area. Most of the surrounding land is used for farming.

Now find Anchorage, Alaska, on the physical regions map. You can see that it is located near the Arctic Circle, at approximately 60°N. This area has long, cold winters. Notice that the elevation of Anchorage is near sea level, with higher elevations nearby.

From the physical regions map, you can tell that because of the latitude and elevation, farming would be difficult if not impossible near Anchorage. You might also infer that few people would live and work in the area.

Now look at the land use and resources map to see what economic activities are found in Anchorage. The map's key tells you that mining and drilling for oil and natural gas are important activities in this area. The key also shows that some of the area around Anchorage is forests. Notice, too, that large areas of this region have little land use.

Try It

Find the Rocky Mountains on the physical regions map. These mountains are the most rugged area of the United States. Now study the land use map. What is the main land use in the Rocky Mountain region? Then look at the eastern coast of the United States. What is the main land use in this region? What geographic features might explain the differences in land use between the two regions?

Finally, locate some urban and industrial areas on the land use map. What information from the physical regions map might explain why these urban and industrial areas are located where they are?

Apply It

Find physical regions and land use maps of your state in an encyclopedia or an atlas. Compare the maps. Then write a short report about how information from the physical regions map helps explain the locations of cities and land use.

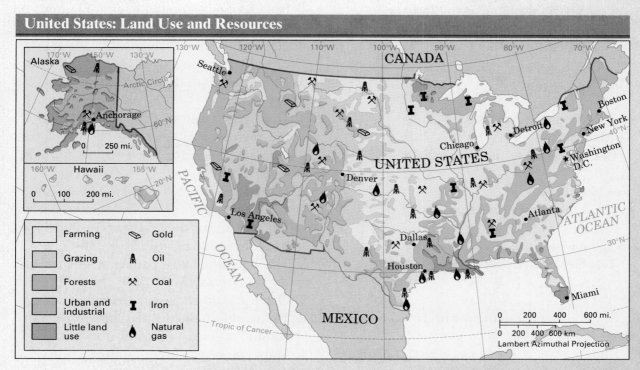

United States: Land Use and Resources

Farming
Grazing
Forests
Urban and industrial
Little land use

Gold
Oil
Coal
Iron
Natural gas

47

Exploring Geography

Chapter Review

Reviewing Key Terms

adapt (p. 33)
deforestation (p. 35)
emigrant (p. 41)
endangered (p. 35)
extinct (p. 35)
geography (p. 29)
immigration (p. 39)
landform (p. 29)

latitude (p. 29)
longitude (p. 29)
migration (p. 39)
pollute (p. 35)
region (p. 42)
rural (p. 41)
urban (p. 43)

A. Read each pair of words. Write a sentence telling how the words in each pair are related.
1. landform, geography
2. rural, urban
3. latitude, longitude
4. endangered, extinct
5. emigrant, immigration
6. adapt, extinct
7. region, landform

B. Write the key term that means about the same as each of the following words or phrases.
1. to make something dirty
2. movement from one place to another
3. adjust
4. the clearing away of trees
5. an area with shared features

C. Give an example of each of the following descriptions.
1. An urban area in the United States
2. An endangered animal
3. A substance that may pollute the environment
4. A place that might be spoiled by deforestation
5. A landform that might contain trees

Exploring Concepts

A. Copy and complete this outline.
  I. Location
    A. Absolute
    B.
  II. Place
    A.
    B. Physical features
  III. Interaction
    A. Adapting to the environment
    B.
  IV. Movement
    A. Goods, services, ideas
    B.
  V. Regions
    A. United States Regions
    B.

B. Support each statement with facts and details from the chapter.
  1. The location of every place on the earth can be described through the use of latitude and longitude.
  2. Geographers use human and natural features to describe a place.
  3. People adapt to their environment in different ways.
  4. Throughout history, people have changed the environment.
  5. Humans depend on the world's natural resources.
  6. Damage to the environment has endangered the earth's plant and animal species.
  7. The movement of goods, services, and ideas has benefited human beings.
  8. Throughout history, people have migrated for many reasons.
  9. One area can be part of several regions.
  10. The world can be divided into political or cultural regions.
  11. Maps can show different information.

Reviewing Skills

1. Study this map. Different colors show the average annual, or yearly, amount of rainfall in various regions of Africa. Which regions get the most rain per year? Which regions get the least?
2. Study the map on page 224. It shows how Africa's deserts are spreading. Use both maps of Africa to describe features that are shared by the northern and southwestern regions of Africa. Make a reasoned judgment about how these features are related.
3. Some plant and animal species are in danger of becoming extinct. Is this statement a fact, a reasoned judgment, or an opinion? How do you know?
4. Study the map on page 44. It shows different regions of the world. Make a reasoned judgment about how rainfall helps define regions on the continent of Africa.

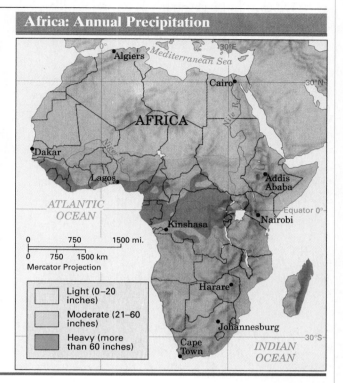

Africa: Annual Precipitation

0 750 1500 mi.
0 750 1500 km
Mercator Projection

Light (0–20 inches)
Moderate (21–60 inches)
Heavy (more than 60 inches)

Using Critical Thinking

1. Make a chart to compare the physical and human features of an urban region and a rural region. Then tell which type of region you would prefer to live in, and why.
2. Think about the physical environment, including the climate and other natural features, of the area in which you live. Make a list of ways people have adapted to the environment of your area, for example, building bridges over rivers, heating homes, or bringing water from far away. Then make a list of ways that you personally adapt to your environment.
3. Describe some pull factors that you think might encourage people to move to your area. What might be some push factors causing people to move away from your area?

Preparing for Citizenship

1. **INTERVIEWING** Interview family members about where they have moved during their lifetime and why. Share your findings with the class.
2. **ART ACTIVITY** Make a poster to persuade people to protect the environment from deforestation or a specific form of pollution or to save a specific animal or plant species from extinction. Combine pictures and written facts to make your message clear.
3. **COLLABORATIVE LEARNING** With three classmates, choose a country in Africa or South America.

Report on:
a. the absolute location of its capital city
b. its relative location (What countries are its neighbors?)
c. its physical features, major products, and natural resources
d. its major cultural groups and some of their customs
e. pull factors that might attract immigrants and push factors that might lead to emigration
f. adaptations to the local environment

49

Unit 2

Origins of Today's World

The exchange of goods and ideas has taken place from the beginning of human experience. Two thousand years ago, the Silk Road passed through these mountains, allowing the great civilizations of China and Rome to trade silk, gold, and silver. The ancient world was crisscrossed with long trading routes, some of which, like the caravan track below, are still in use.

Prehistory

A caravan travels through the Pamirs, a mountain range in central Asia with rocky peaks and deep, narrow valleys.

A.D. 1532

Unit 2 Overview

Origins of Today's World

Imagine that you are an archaeologist looking through the bits and pieces left behind by people who lived thousands of years ago. With slow, careful work, you find a few objects that help tell the story of these ancient people: a piece of pottery, a farming tool, a necklace. Who were these people? How did their culture begin?

From China to the Americas, cultures all shared similar beginnings. People spent much of their time hunting and looking for food. They did not live in any single place but traveled together in small groups. As they learned to plant seeds and tame animals, they began to live together near their fields and herds.

In some places people were able to grow more food than they needed. This allowed some people time for tasks like making pottery or weaving cloth. Communities traded these goods. Villages grew into cities, and cities began to trade ideas as well as goods. In time people developed writing, government, religion, art, and architecture.

▼ *Thousands of years ago, Chinese lived on the shores of the Chang Jiang. Today the Chang Jiang and its branches form one of China's most important trade routes.*

▲ *This ancient Mayan clay figure shows a woman weaving. Weaving—often with brightly colored threads and complicated patterns—is still popular in Latin America today.*

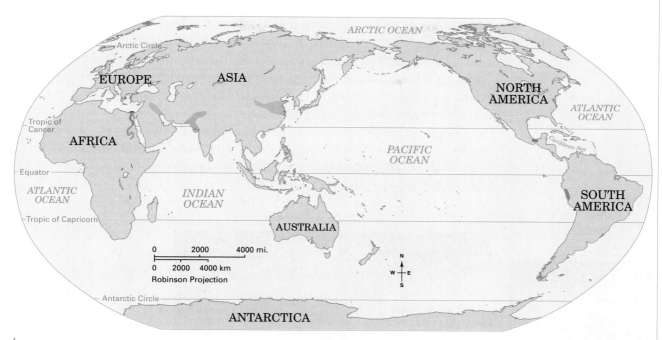

▲ *Early civilizations existed between 3500 B.C. and A.D. 900. On the world map above, identify the location of each civilization depicted on the smaller maps below.*

▼ *The maps below show seven early civilizations in detail.*

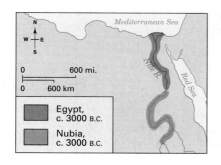

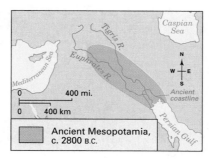

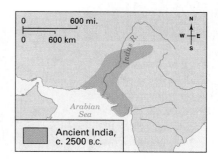

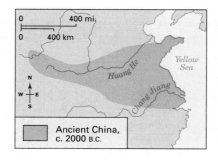

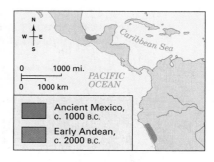

The Ancient World

The Land and People

The world's first cultures developed along the Tigris and Euphrates, the Nile, and the Indus rivers, and between the Huang He and Chang Jiang. These rivers provided water for thirsty fields. When they flooded, they also helped fertilize the soil. All of these rivers flooded, but none could be counted on as much as the Nile. Every summer for hundreds of years, the Nile overflowed onto the surrounding land. Afterward, the water left behind fertile soil called silt.

People living in Peru met different challenges. The flat plains of Peru's coast are a desert. High in the Andes, however, the climate is very cold at night. The Andean peoples grew different crops, depending on how high in the mountains they lived.

▲ *Ancient peoples depended on rivers and lakes for trade, transportation, and water for their fields. In reed boats like these, people traded along the Tigris and Euphrates.*

▶ *The Nile is the world's longest river. Long or short, all the rivers of the ancient world were necessary to support life.*

◀ *Today, as in ancient times, people settle near water. This infrared photo of the Nile delta is red where people live. The desert appears as a vast wasteland.*

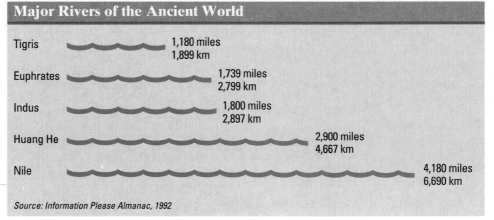

Major Rivers of the Ancient World

Tigris	1,180 miles / 1,899 km
Euphrates	1,739 miles / 2,799 km
Indus	1,800 miles / 2,897 km
Huang He	2,900 miles / 4,667 km
Nile	4,180 miles / 6,690 km

Source: Information Please Almanac, 1992

Throughout the ancient world, people worked together to complete large tasks, including feeding the hungry people of a growing city or building a temple. To get the job done, people divided the work. Someone became a carpenter or a stonecutter. Some people worked to keep everything organized.

Ancient peoples invented mathematics and systems of writing to help them with measurements and keeping records. With the invention of writing, people no longer had to depend on memory to keep track of information and ideas. They could easily pass down more complex ideas and longer histories from one generation to the next.

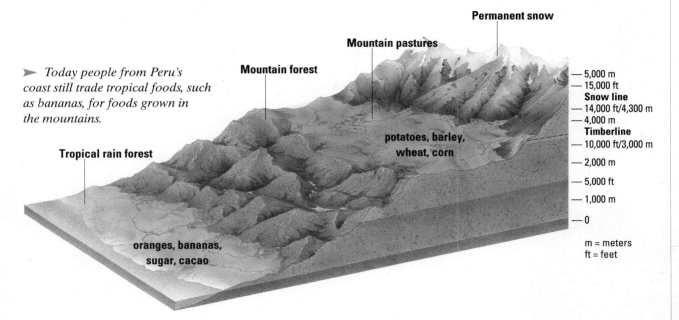

➤ *Today people from Peru's coast still trade tropical foods, such as bananas, for foods grown in the mountains.*

Permanent snow

Mountain pastures

Mountain forest

Tropical rain forest

potatoes, barley, wheat, corn

oranges, bananas, sugar, cacao

— 5,000 m
— 15,000 ft
Snow line
— 14,000 ft/4,300 m
— 4,000 m
Timberline
— 10,000 ft/3,000 m
— 2,000 m
— 5,000 ft
— 1,000 m
— 0

m = meters
ft = feet

▼ *Constructing these ancient buildings required a high level of organization as well as enormous skill.*

Egypt's kings and queens were buried in huge pyramids. The largest measured more than 481 feet (146 meters) high.

Ancient Mesopotamians built temples on top of pyramid-shaped towers called ziggurats. The largest was about 160 feet (48 meters) high.

A wide stairway leads to what was once a temple at the top of this Mayan pyramid, El Castillo. It is 75 feet (23 meters) high and has 364 stairs.

Chapter 3

The Fertile Crescent

The Fertile Crescent, a band of land that crosses Southwest Asia, was one of the world's first farming areas. Early peoples tended crops and herded animals in the rich soil of its river valleys. In time they settled in cities and built complex civilizations. The Israelites established one of these civilizations in a part of the Fertile Crescent called Canaan.

Early peoples developed the first stone tools. They used bowl-shaped querns like this one to grind wild grains into flour.

Prehistory The earliest human development takes place over millions of years. Much later, in ancient Sumer, people begin to produce written records.

Prehistory	8500	6800	5100

about 9000 B.C. Sheep begin to be raised for their meat and, later, for their wool. Today shepherds like the Syrian man above continue to tend flocks of sheep.

Prehistory

The Assyrians knew periods of great power. Archaeologists have found stone sculptures like this battle scene in ancient Assyrian temples and palaces.

Elaborate cases like this one protect some scrolls of the Torah, a group of religious writings central to Judaism. They are handwritten by trained scribes today, just as they were in ancient days.

about 2000 B.C. Abraham moves with his family from the town of Haran to Canaan, an area of Mesopotamia that later will be called Israel.

| 3400 | 1700 | B.C. | A.D. | 1700 |

about 3500 B.C. The civilization of Sumer begins. By 3100 B.C. Sumerians invent writing.

A.D. 70

L E S S O N   1

Life in Prehistoric Times

THINKING FOCUS

How did prehistoric peoples' ways of getting food change with the passing of time?

Key Terms

- archaeologist
- hunter-gatherer
- prehistoric
- agriculture

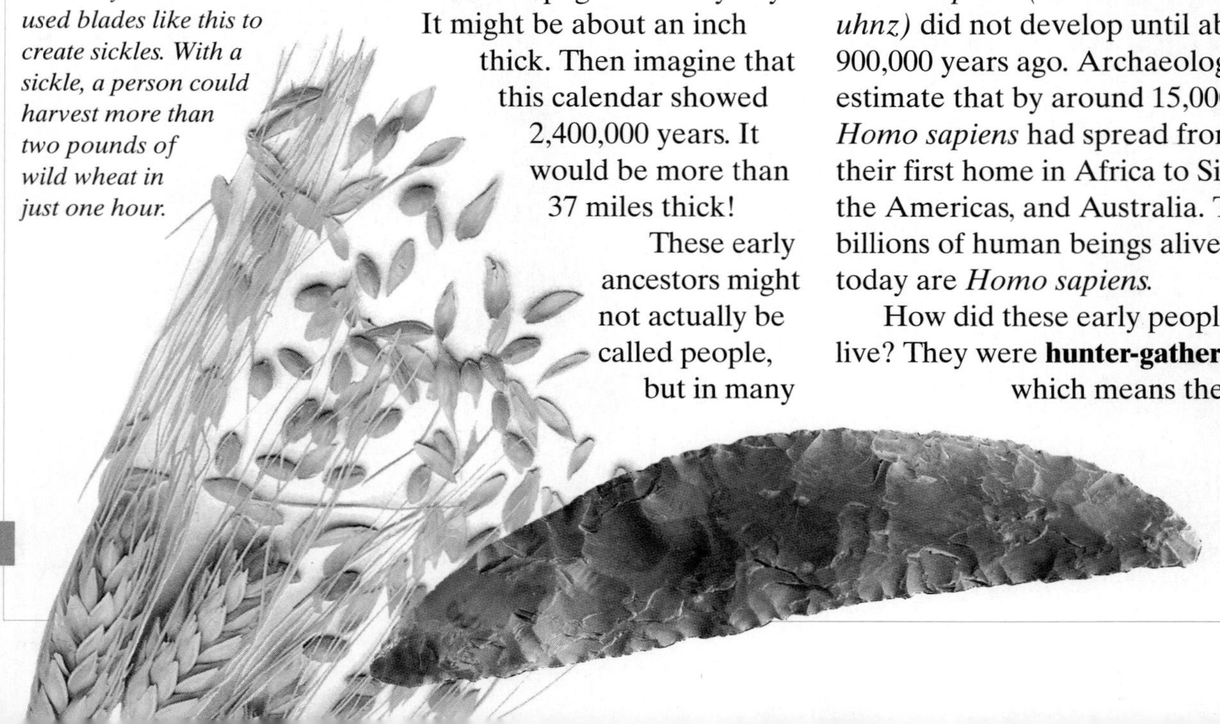

➤ *Early tool makers used blades like this to create sickles. With a sickle, a person could harvest more than two pounds of wild wheat in just one hour.*

You are watching a woman make tools. She puts her foot on a rock to keep it steady. She holds a chisel-like tool called a punch and a hammer, each made from an antler. Working quickly but with care, she splits long, thin pieces from the rock. In a matter of minutes, she has made several blades. They are as sharp as modern knives. The edges are so thin that light shows through them.

Who is this tool maker? She is an **archaeologist** *(AHR kee AHL uh jihst)*. She studies the things people leave behind. Now she is testing how early peoples made stone tools.

If you could ask her why she's interested in archaeology, she might look up with a surprised smile. "Without those first tool makers," she'd say, "we would never have the tools we use today. Our modern ways have deep roots in the world of the earliest peoples."

Lives of the Earliest Peoples

Archaeologists estimate that the earliest human ancestors walked the earth about 2,400,000 years ago. Imagine a one-year calendar with one page for every day. It might be about an inch thick. Then imagine that this calendar showed 2,400,000 years. It would be more than 37 miles thick!

These early ancestors might not actually be called people, but in many ways they looked and acted like humans. They walked on two feet and made tools from rocks and bones.

The kind of humans called *Homo sapiens (HOH moh SAY pih uhnz)* did not develop until about 900,000 years ago. Archaeologists estimate that by around 15,000 B.C., *Homo sapiens* had spread from their first home in Africa to Siberia, the Americas, and Australia. The billions of human beings alive today are *Homo sapiens*.

How did these early peoples live? They were **hunter-gatherers,** which means they hunted animals and gathered wild plants to eat. On page 58 you can see a blade from a tool that might have been used to cut wild wheat, as well as a kind of wheat that was gathered. Some archaeologists believe that very early peoples were also scavengers. That is, they ate prey already killed by animals like saber-toothed tigers.

Most hunter-gatherers lived in **prehistoric** times—that is, before people developed record-keeping. As a result, we must get our knowledge about hunter-gatherers from nonwritten evidence. ■

■ *How did hunter-gatherers obtain food?*

Farming Changes the World

A big change in the way people lived began about 17,000 years ago. No one knows exactly how this change occurred. It took thousands of years to develop and happened in different places and at different times around the world.

People Begin to Farm

The big change was that many people stopped depending only on hunting and gathering for their food supply. They found they could capture some animals and keep them for the milk, wool, and meat they provided. Also, instead of eating all the grains and seeds they gathered, people began to save some to plant later. In this way they could be sure they would have food to eat in the following year. Growing plants for food in this way is called **agriculture.**

Of course, not all the places where people lived were good for farming. You can see where the earliest agriculture developed by studying the map below.

Results of Farming

Agriculture brought tremendous changes to human societies.

▼ *About 8000 B.C. people learned to raise animals for the food they provided. This sculpture from about 2600 B.C. shows the pouring of fresh milk.*

Early Farming Areas

Map: Early Farming Areas (Mercator Projection)

- NORTH AMERICA
- MESOAMERICA c. 7000 B.C.
- SOUTH AMERICA
- ATLANTIC OCEAN
- PACIFIC OCEAN
- EUROPE
- ANATOLIA c. 8000 B.C.
- FERTILE CRESCENT 8000–5000 B.C.
- NILE RIVER VALLEY c. 6000 B.C.
- AFRICA
- ASIA
- HUANG HE VALLEY c. 5000 B.C.
- INDUS RIVER VALLEY c. 2500 B.C.
- PACIFIC OCEAN
- INDIAN OCEAN
- AUSTRALIA
- Equator 0°
- 45°N
- 45°S

Scale: 0 2000 4000 mi. / 0 2000 4000 km

◄ *By 8000 B.C. people were farming successfully in some regions around the world. For help in using latitude and longitude to locate these regions, see page G5 in the Map and Globe Handbook. What similarities among farming regions can you identify from their location on this map?*

59

The Fertile Crescent

The Earliest Humans, 2,400,000–15,000 B.C.

2,400,000 B.C.
Date of oldest human fossil and oldest stone tools

1,600,000 B.C.
Date of oldest *Homo erectus* fossils

900,000 B.C.
Homo sapiens first appears.

2,500,000	2,000,000	1,500,000	1,000,000

2,000,000 B.C.
Upright *Homo erectus* first appears.

50,000 B.C. Hunter-gatherer societies emerge.

15,000 B.C. Hunter-gatherer societies begin to farm.

▲ *Archaeologists have estimated the dates of important developments in early human history. The timeline shows some of these dates.* Homo erectus *is the direct ancestor of* Homo sapiens, *or modern human beings.*

➤ *These sheep are pictured in one of two mosaics that were discovered in 1927 in a royal grave at the ancient city of Ur. You can locate Ur on the map on page 67.*

■ *What changes did agriculture bring to the way early peoples lived?*

As you know, farmers must pull weeds, chase away birds, and care for their plants. As prehistoric peoples took up farming, they tended to stay near their crops. They began to breed and raise the animals they had captured. Since people were now in the same place all the time, they began to build permanent shelters.

Because people had more food, they were healthier. Healthier parents meant that fewer babies died and adults lived longer. Populations grew, and groups of shelters developed into villages and towns.

As farming methods improved, fewer people had to farm. Some people could spend more time making pots or weaving cloth, while others could be full-time religious leaders.

As the population grew, people needed new ways to get along. They needed rules to help divide the land and the crops. They also needed rules to govern how people behaved in the growing communities.

The coming of agriculture began a chain of events that changed the world completely. As you will read in the next lesson, this single change eventually led to very complex human societies. ■

REVIEW

1. **FOCUS** How did prehistoric peoples' ways of getting food change with the passing of time?
2. **HISTORY** How have we learned about the ways early peoples developed and lived?
3. **HISTORY** What kind of evidence must be used to learn about prehistoric peoples? Why?
4. **CULTURE** How did agriculture begin to develop?
5. **CRITICAL THINKING** Early peoples had many uses for

blades like the one described at the beginning of this lesson. Name some possible uses for such blades, and think of similar tools we have today that might serve the same uses.

6. **ACTIVITY** Imagine that you are shipwrecked on a large, deserted island. In a small group with your classmates, discuss how you can find ways to grow plants and raise animals.

Using a Flow Chart

Here's Why

Graphic organizers are pictures and words that show one idea or the relationship among many ideas. A flow chart is one type of graphic organizer. A flow chart shows how one event causes another or how several steps make up a process.

Suppose you wanted to get a better understanding of how farming helped the development of early civilizations. By clearly listing the ideas in order, a flow chart can help you study.

Here's How

Look at the flow chart below. First, read the title of the flow chart, Steps Toward Civilization. The title tells you what information the flow chart contains.

Now look at the flow chart itself. You can see that the arrows between the boxes point to the right. These arrows tell you in what direction to read the flow chart.

Begin by reading the first box on the left, called Farming.

The arrows in the flow chart mean "leads to." If you read the first box, the arrow, and the second box, you can say, "Farming led to surplus food."

Next, the second box and the three arrows tell you that surplus food in early societies led to the three results listed: settlements expanded, the population increased, and people began working at specialized jobs, such as constructing buildings. Finally, read the flow chart from beginning to end: Farming led to surplus food, which led to settlements expanding, to an increase in population, and to people working at specialized jobs, such as constructing buildings.

Compare this flow chart with the material about early farming in Lesson 1. Does the flow chart make the text you read easier to understand? Why or why not?

Try It

Try creating your own flow chart to summarize the following information. Be sure to give your flow chart a title.
- A growing population in Mesopotamia led to a need for more farmland.
- The need for more farmland led to a need for more irrigation.
- More irrigation led to the rise of administrators to manage these irrigation projects.
- More irrigation led to larger crews of workers to take care of the irrigation canals.

Use your chart to help you understand Lesson 2.

Apply It

Make a flow chart that shows a series of events in your life, such as what happens when you get up late for school, or what happens when school is canceled because of the weather. Model your flow chart after the chart on this page.

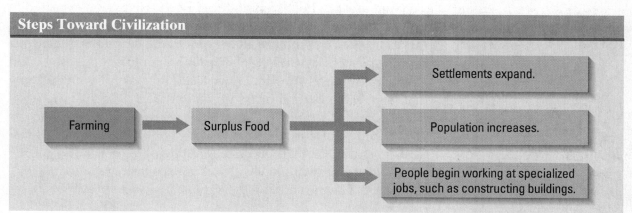

Steps Toward Civilization

Farming → Surplus Food → Settlements expand.

Population increases.

People begin working at specialized jobs, such as constructing buildings.

The Luring of Enkidu

Retold by Bernarda Bryson

Myths about the Mesopotamian king Gilgamesh are some of the oldest stories in the world. They have been retold many times. This selection from Bernarda Bryson's book Gilgamesh *describes Enkidu, a wild man who lives with animals. In this passage, Enkidu begins to learn the ways of humans.*

The hair springs out of his head like a field of grain, and he has the horns of a wild beast!"

"If he stole your catch of game, my son, why didn't you stop him?"

"He is taller and more powerful than Gilgamesh the King. I was numbed with fear!"

"If what you say is true, son, then we must report the matter to the King. But if you have lied, we will be in disgrace forever!"

The shepherd and his son went into the city of Uruk to make their complaint. But there the populace were already spreading rumors about the wild man. Some said, "He is covered with hair from head to foot," and others, "He is taller than a giant and eats grass with the gazelles!"

It was the eldest of the elders who led the hunter and his father before the King. "O Gilgamesh," said the elder, "there is a wild man that terrorizes the countryside. He robs the hunter of his game and disperses the herds of the shepherd. He turns all who see him numb with fear—indeed I've heard that he is taller and more powerful than Gilgamesh the King!"

Gilgamesh, who feared nothing, might have been expected to say, "Then it's I who will go out and subdue him and bring him captive to the city!" Not at all; he sent to the temple of Ishtar for a certain priestess, one called Harim, servant of the goddess.

He said to her, "Harim, I have a certain task for you; it is one that turns the boldest hunters numb with fear!"

"Then I am afraid," said Harim.

The eldest of the elders spoke angrily, "This is not a girl's task, O King; it is a task for a brave man—a hero!"

"Tut tut," said Gilgamesh. "It is a girl's task of smiles and charm. Go, Harim; soften the heart of the wild man and bring him back to the city!"

The poems and stories about Gilgamesh are based on an actual hero-king of ancient Mesopotamia, the region that you will read about in Lesson 2.

populace people

disperses scatters, sends away

subdue quiet, conquer

Harim was led by the hunter to the edge of the forest, and she noted that he began to tremble with fear. "Go back to the hut of your father," she commanded. "If I can tame the wild man, I will lead him into the city alone."

The hunter was shamed by the girl's bravery. "Do not enter the forest, O Harim; I myself will go." But the priestess laughed at him and sent him home.

She went among the dark cedars; she listened to the sounds of birds and of monkeys chattering. She noted the bits of sunlight that filtered through the branches and lit up the flowers, moss, and bracken on the forest floor. "How peaceful a place this is! How could any evil thing lurk here?" Harim found a fresh spring bubbling with cool water. She sat beside it on a stone, untied her sandals, and dipped her feet in the water.

bracken ferns

Enkidu came to the place with the small wild horse and the gazelle. As they drew near, the two beasts became nervous, sniffed the air, and fled. But Enkidu stood still; he wondered what new danger was near, what unknown beast might have come to the water.

When he saw the girl sitting there his breath failed and he was overcome. He had not yet seen a human being, and this creature seemed to him the most admirable, the most enchanting being that he had ever seen. He stood quietly in order not to frighten her.

Harim gazed at this giant figure, his soaring horns, and his unkempt looks and would have run away, but she could not move. She opened her mouth to scream and could not make a sound. She was numb with terror. And Enkidu noting this remained quiet; he had made friends with many timid creatures and he knew their ways.

unkempt rough, uncombed

When the priestess saw the gentleness of his manner, her courage returned to her somewhat. She called out shyly, "Hello!"

Enkidu knew no words. He could babble somewhat as the monkeys did. He could bark quite like a fox, or trill like many birds. He had various calls of greeting for his wild friends, but this new animal made sounds that he could not understand.

He neither barked nor roared, but stood perplexed looking at the girl. Again she spoke, and now held out her hands to him in greeting.

perplexed puzzled, confused

Enkidu approached slowly and sat on the earth beside the white feet of Harim. She said all sorts of things to him and he understood nothing. She asked him many questions and he could not reply. But he felt ecstasy in his heart, and great contentment in merely sitting beside her.

ecstasy great joy

How easy was her conquest of Enkidu! Harim smiled, but she now began to feel a new sort of fear. How could she lead this great fellow, so gentle and so innocent, back to the city of Uruk? Would

jeer   make fun of

the people set on him and kill him? Would they jeer at him? Would the King have him put into a cage and carried through the streets on the backs of soldiers? She shuddered.

No, first she must teach him the ways of people, the conformity of life.

"Al-ka ti-ba i-na ga-ag-ga-ri!" said Harim. "Come, rise from the ground!" But the wild man did not understand. Thus, she taught him the word for standing, and then after that, the word for sitting. She taught him the words for walking, running, talking, laughing, eating, and he repeated each one, learning it. She taught him the words for trees and for stones and for water, for earth and for the trailing vines that grew beside the spring, and for the spring itself. She taught him the words for feet and hands and the names of all the fingers and all the myriad words of love.

myriad   many, countless

Thus patiently, Harim taught Enkidu to be like ordinary men. She cut his hair and combed it in the way of people of the city. She made him bathe; she tore her long tunic into two parts, making of one-half a garment for Enkidu, keeping the other half for herself.

Again she spoke to him, and now he understood, "A-na-tal-ka En-ki-du ki-ma ili ta-ba-as-si!"—"I gaze upon you, Enkidu; you are like a god!"

He brought her gifts—all the things that he had come to know and love in the forest and from the open steppes; wild cucumbers and cassia melon, grapes and figs and caper buds from the dry rocks. He brought her blossoms of golden mimosa and fragrant branches of jasmine.

After some time had passed Harim said, "Now I will lead Enkidu out among the people and everyone will admire him!" But still she feared for his life so she took him first to the hut of the shepherd.

At the edge of the forest Enkidu stopped and turned back. He was overcome with regret; how could he leave forever his friends of the woods and wild places? Who would protect them? Who would release them from the traps? How could he leave behind his friend the little wild horse, or the gazelle, the rabbits, the monkeys that had taught him to play games?

But as he approached they leaped away startled. The rabbit hid trembling in the grass and the birds took off with a wild flutter of wings.

Enkidu threw himself to the ground weeping. "O Harim, what have I done? How have I made all my friends into strangers? Why do they run from me?"

"Enkidu is no longer a wild creature. He is no longer a beast of the forest and the open plain. Enkidu is now a man. He will live among men and be eminent among men!"

eminent   outstanding

Enkidu followed regretfully as the priestess led him toward the hut of the shepherd. This man greeted him with awe and admiration, but his son fled from the place and hid in the sheep-fold. After some time he returned, running. "Father, a lion has entered the fold! It is devouring the lambs!"

Enkidu went to the sheepfold where again he wrestled with the lion, his friend who no longer knew him. Again he overcame the beast, but he let it go free. He lifted the lambs gently, washing and tending the ones that bled. To his great joy they did not shun him or run away. Neither did the young calves nor the barnyard fowl. A dog followed him wagging its tail. A cat smoothed its fur against his legs, and again he was content.

In the hut of the shepherd Enkidu learned to sit on a chair and to wash his hands before eating. He learned how to care for animals, to make plants grow, and to build with mud and brick and reeds. He learned to play on a flute. He ate bread. There he drank the juice of the wild grape. His face shone, he rejoiced; he sang.

Harim smiled. "Now Enkidu has become like a man, we shall go into the city!"

Further Reading

He Who Saw Everything: The Epic of Gilgamesh. Anita Feagles. This book and *Gilgamesh and Other Babylonian Tales* are other versions of the Gilgamesh epic.

In the Land of Ur: The Discovery of Ancient Mesopotamia. Hans Bauman. The author describes archaeological finds in Mesopotamia and tells what they reveal about the ancient civilizations of that area.

A Song for Gilgamesh. Elizabeth Jamison Hodges. The story of a Sumerian potter is woven in with a myth about the hero-king Gilgamesh and his journey to the Land of the Living.

The Three Brothers of Ur. Jennifer G. Fyson. Here is an adventure story about three boys in the ancient city of Ur. The story also teaches about the boys' religion and customs.

L E S S O N   2

Ancient Mesopotamia

**THINKING
FOCUS**

*What were the major
achievements of the
civilizations of ancient
Mesopotamia?*

Key Terms

- irrigation
- civilization
- surplus
- specialization of labor
- class

➤ *One factor that en-
abled Mesopotamia to be-
come a powerful culture
was the richness of the soil
along its rivers. Here a
section of the Tigris River
flows between the modern
cities of Baghdad and
Mosul.*

With an enormous
heave, you lift one
last shovelful of earth
onto the growing pile
a few feet away. Then, taking a rest,
you stand up straight and look
around. The time is about 4,000
years ago. You are knee deep in a
canal that brings water from the
Euphrates *(yoo FRAY teez)* River
to your field.

Behind you are the walls and
towers of the city of Ur. The king's
palace, the temples of the Gods,
and the homes of many traders and
craftsworkers are located within
these walls.

You are a canal digger. Sometimes, you feel important. Without
your work, the farms that feed the
people of Ur would dry up. At
other times, like now, you just feel
tired. You wipe away the sweat on
your forehead with the back of
your hand and again lean over your
shovel. Time to get back to work!

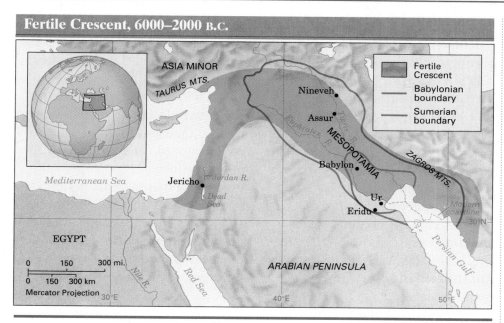

Fertile Crescent, 6000–2000 B.C.

ASIA MINOR
TAURUS MTS.
Nineveh
Assur
MESOPOTAMIA
ZAGROS MTS.
Babylon
Ur
Eridu
Jericho
Jordan R.
Dead Sea
Mediterranean Sea
EGYPT
Nile R.
Red Sea
ARABIAN PENINSULA
Persian Gulf
Modern coastline
30°N
30°E
40°E
50°E

Fertile Crescent
Babylonian boundary
Sumerian boundary

0   150   300 mi.
0   150   300 km
Mercator Projection

◄ *The Fertile Crescent extends over parts of what are now Turkey, Iran, Iraq, Syria, Lebanon, Jordan and Israel. Mesopotamia made up much of the Fertile Crescent. Sumer was centered between the Tigris and Euphrates rivers.*

Sumer: An Early Civilization

The city of Ur was in Sumer *(SOO muhr),* a land in southern Mesopotamia *(mehs uh puh TAY mee uh).* Sumer was one of the early cultures that arose after people began a farming life. It developed about 5,500 years ago.

The Fertile Crescent

The map on this page shows that Mesopotamia is the area between the Tigris *(TY grihs)* and Euphrates rivers. In fact, in Greek the word Mesopotamia means "land between the rivers." This area covers most of present-day Iraq.

Mesopotamia was part of the Fertile Crescent—an area of land that crosses Southwest Asia. The Fertile Crescent stretches from the Taurus Mountains in the north (now part of Turkey) to modern Israel in the south and the Persian Gulf in the east. Plants grow well in the Fertile Crescent because it has water. Much of this water, however, comes from rivers rather than rain. For this reason **irrigation,** or a system for watering crops, was

necessary for the farms around Mesopotamian cities like Ur.

What Is a Civilization?

Civilizations have been defined in different ways. Most scholars agree that when a society develops enough for cities to form, it becomes a **civilization.**

The civilizations of the Fertile Crescent shared at least five specific features. The first was an agricultural **surplus,** or a supply of extra food. A surplus made the other features possible.

Specialization of labor, the second feature, meant that people had specific jobs. These jobs were divided into social levels, or **classes.** This was the third feature. Civilizations also had a form of government, including a system of laws. A government was the fourth feature.

Further evidence of a complex culture was the fifth feature. As you have read, culture includes art, architecture, religion, and music. The first complex cultures also kept written records.

Across Time & Space

Archaeologists try to find out specific dates for important events, such as when Sumer began. However, when early written records cannot be found, archaeologists can only estimate these dates. To show that a date is an estimate, they often use the Latin word circa, *meaning "approximately." Circa is often abbreviated* c. *or* ca.

67

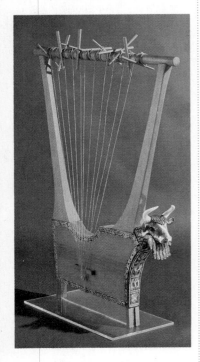

This lyre decorated with a bull's head was made to look like one used at Ur around 2500 B.C.

In the center of Ur, the ziggurat, other temples, and nearby buildings were set off as a religious place within the city.

Life in the City of Ur

Imagine you could take a walk through ancient Ur. All around, you see evidence of the five features of civilization.

As you walk toward the center of the city, you notice carpenters, bricklayers, and other builders. The activities of these workers are a sign of the specialization of labor.

As you look around, you see various kinds of buildings. One building towers above all the others. It is a ziggurat, a huge temple constructed of several levels, like steps.

A ziggurat dominated many Mesopotamian cities. Each ziggurat was dedicated to a specific God, who was believed to rule over the city. You can see a diagram of a ziggurat on this page. Near the ziggurat is a large palace where the king lives.

What do the size and richness of the ziggurat and the palace tell you? The ziggurat indicates that the worship of Ur's God is of the greatest importance to the people of Ur. The location of the palace next to the ziggurat signifies the key role played by the king who lives in the palace.

Around the ziggurat you notice a great deal of activity. From all directions people are bringing the produce of their farms to the city. These riches of the region include vegetables, dates, sesame seeds, and wool. Some of these goods will be used by people of the upper classes, some will be used in the ziggurat, and some will be stored for trading with other countries.

You also notice that people wear different kinds of clothing and jewelry. Some people are obviously wealthier, better fed, and better dressed than others—a sign of different social classes.

Social Classes

In Sumer the upper class included priests, soldiers, and government officials. Some of these officials ran the irrigation system. Others collected taxes and fees, while some served priests in the ziggurat.

Merchants, shopkeepers, teachers, farmers, and laborers belonged to the middle class. The lowest class was made up of slaves. Some slaves were people taken prisoner during wars.

On a walk through the king's palace, you notice someone playing a harp decorated with the carved head of a bull. This tells you that Sumerians enjoy music and make beautiful objects, both signs of a people's culture.

When you go to the ziggurat itself, you are at the heart of Ur's culture. There priests are worshiping some of Sumer's hundreds of Gods. There, too, the goods of the entire civilization are gathered. Scribes or priests are keeping track of the wool, grain, and other products brought to the ziggurat. To record these products, the scribes or priests write on clay tablets.

Some Sumerian Achievements

The Sumerians were important thinkers and inventors. They excelled in the fields of science and mathematics. In fact, Sumerian mathematics was so advanced that we still use some of it today.

For example, it was the Sumerians who created a system for subdividing a day and a year. Their year was made up of 12 months. Their system of mathematics divided a circle into 360 equal parts.

The Sumerians also discovered the importance of wheels. They made wheels out of wood. These wheels were used to build vehicles for farming, trade, and war. Even though we don't know who built the very first wheel, we do know that the Sumerians had wheels about 5,500 years ago. If you don't think that the wheel is an important invention, just try to imagine what your life would be like today without it. ■

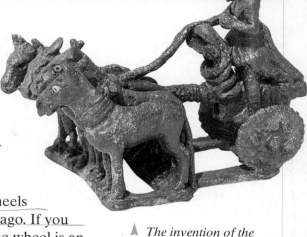

▲ *The invention of the wheel allowed the Sumerians to build vehicles, such as chariots. This copper figurine of an animal-drawn chariot was found in a Sumerian temple.*

■ *Give an example of each of the five features of civilization found at Ur.*

The Babylonians

About 1800 B.C. another Mesopotamian civilization arose. We call it Babylonia. Look for it on the map on page 67. The city of Babylon, in southern Mesopotamia, was the center of Babylonia. The king who first brought together various cities of Mesopotamia to form Babylonia was Hammurabi *(hah mu RAH bee)*. He ruled for more than 42 years, from 1792 to 1750 B.C.

Hammurabi is also known for recording a system of laws called the Code of Hammurabi. This code is considered one of the most important law codes in history. It is a description of what to do in specific cases. There are 282 laws contained in the code.

Many of these laws help us understand the treatment of women in Babylonian society. For example, the code says that if a woman was divorced, she could take back the money her parents had given her husband when she was married. If a woman's husband died, she would have the use of his property.

Other laws give us an idea of what life was like in cities such as Babylon. One law tells us what happened if an ox stabbed someone with its horn and caused that person's death. The code says that in such an event, the owner of the ox had to pad its horns, tie it up, or take responsibility for any further harm the ox might cause.

◀ *Archaeologists found the Code of Hammurabi engraved on a large stone structure called a stele (STEE lee). This engraving at the top of the stele shows one of the Babylonian Gods giving the rod and ring to King Hammurabi, which signified his right to rule.*

The Fertile Crescent

Cuneiform Writing

The ancient Sumerian people, who lived in what is now southern Iraq, were the first to invent writing. At first, scribes drew simple pictures on wet clay tablets, probably to keep track of cows or sacks of grain. Over many centuries, beginning about 3100 B.C., their marks became more complex. This newer script, called cuneiform, could capture ideas such as "life" or "light" in symbols.

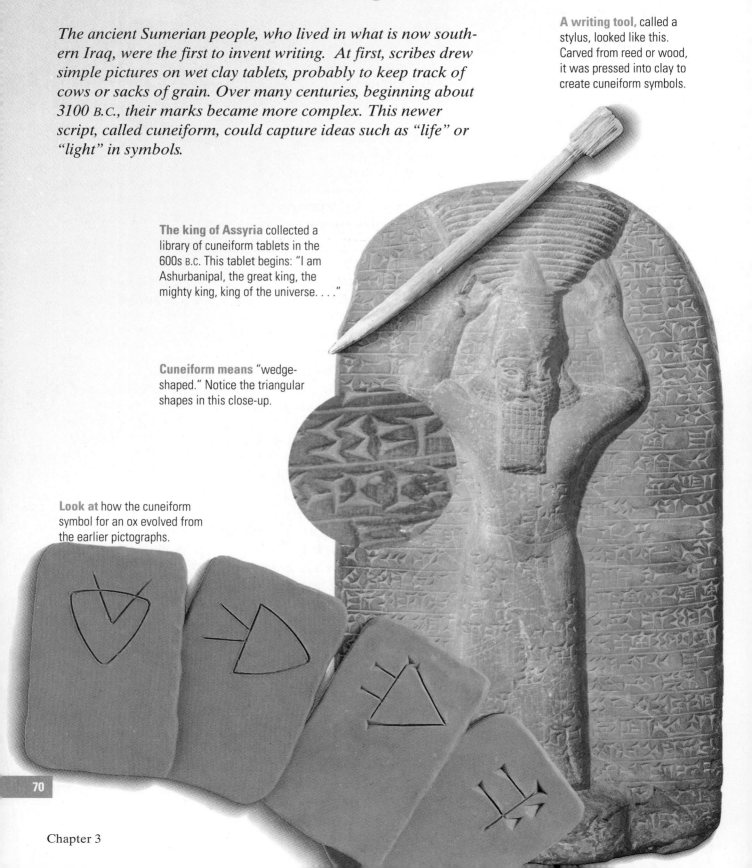

A writing tool, called a stylus, looked like this. Carved from reed or wood, it was pressed into clay to create cuneiform symbols.

The king of Assyria collected a library of cuneiform tablets in the 600s B.C. This tablet begins: "I am Ashurbanipal, the great king, the mighty king, king of the universe. . . ."

Cuneiform means "wedge-shaped." Notice the triangular shapes in this close-up.

Look at how the cuneiform symbol for an ox evolved from the earlier pictographs.

Another law gives the punishment for a builder who "has built a house for a man and has not made his work sound, so that the house he has made falls down and causes the death of the owner of the house." According to the Code of Hammurabi, such a builder should be put to death.

As important and interesting as the Code of Hammurabi is, it was not a law code like those we have today. Instead it was a description of the way Hammurabi felt the laws *should* be. When we examine actual law cases from Babylonian times, we see that the code itself never became the law of the land. ■

■ *How do Hammurabi's laws show what life was like in ancient Babylonia?*

The Assyrians

North of Babylonia another Mesopotamian civilization arose and became powerful about 1350 B.C. This civilization was Assyria *(uh SIHR ee uh)*. Find Assyria on the map on this page.

The Struggle for Empire

The Assyrians developed powerful armies equipped with iron weapons. With these armies they conquered the lands up to the Mediterranean Sea. At times the Assyrians controlled Babylonia as well. They even overran far-off Egypt. The Assyrians formed a large empire, or a state in which one ruler controls several kingdoms or territories.

The conquered peoples often rebelled. Some of them drove the Assyrians away. At other times rebellions failed, and conquered peoples were killed or exiled. Historians have wondered why the Assyrians had such a hard time holding onto their empire. Some think they have found an explanation in Assyrian art. Much of Assyrian art portrays battle

scenes. In these scenes the Assyrians are often shown killing their enemies. Some historians have suggested that conquered peoples may have rebelled against Assyrian rule because there was no other way to escape Assyrian cruelty.

Other historians point out, however, that the Assyrians were no worse than other rulers of the time. We don't know yet why the Assyrians ruled some areas for such a short time. Maybe we never will.

After many periods of strength and weakness, the Assyrians fell from power. In 612 B.C. the last Assyrian capital, Nineveh, was captured by the Medes, people from what is now Iran.

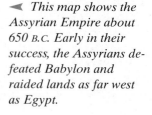

How Do We Know?

HISTORY *We have learned most of what we know about ancient times and peoples from the science of archaeology. All over the world archaeologists carefully dig up ancient artifacts, or tools and other objects made by early humans. By studying these artifacts, archaeologists can determine their age, what they were used for, and something about the culture of the people who made them.*

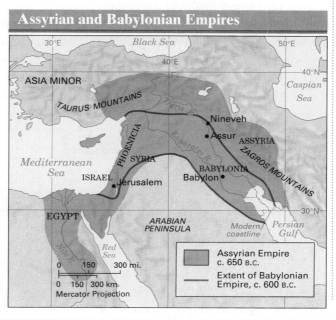

Assyrian and Babylonian Empires

30°E · Black Sea · 50°E · 40°E · 40°N · ASIA MINOR · Caspian Sea · TAURUS MOUNTAINS · Tigris R. · Nineveh · Assur · ASSYRIA · ZAGROS MOUNTAINS · PHOENICIA · SYRIA · Euphrates R. · Mediterranean Sea · ISRAEL · Jerusalem · BABYLONIA · Babylon · EGYPT · ARABIAN PENINSULA · Modern coastline · Persian Gulf · 30°N · Red Sea · Nile R. · 0 150 300 mi. · 0 150 300 km · Mercator Projection

Assyrian Empire c. 650 B.C.

Extent of Babylonian Empire, c. 600 B.C.

◄ *This map shows the Assyrian Empire about 650 B.C. Early in their success, the Assyrians defeated Babylon and raided lands as far west as Egypt.*

71

The Fertile Crescent

➤ In the ruins of Assyrian temples and palaces, archaeologists have found many reliefs. These are stone sculptures that project out from the walls, giving a three-dimensional effect. This relief shows an official giving information to two scribes.

Across Time & Space

Many of the letters of your alphabet were developed 4,000 years ago by the Phoenicians, a trading people who lived along the coast of the eastern Mediterranean Sea. Their names for the first two letters were alef *and* bet. *The Greeks later changed the names of the first two letters to* alpha *and* beta. *From these letters we get our word* alphabet.

■ *What reason do some historians give to explain why the Assyrians often failed to keep control of their conquered peoples?*

Ashurbanipal's Library

Besides its importance as the Assyrian capital, Nineveh is famous for another reason. One of the world's first great libraries was at Nineveh. The last great king of the Assyrians, Ashurbanipal *(ah shur BAH nuh pahl),* created the library. Ashurbanipal's library included books on fables, proverbs, religion, magic, law, science, folktales, and ancient stories. Some of the books were written in the Sumerian language and some in the Babylonian language.

Archaeologists have uncovered more than 20,000 of these "books." All of them are clay tablets. These tablets may have made up only a small part of the collection Ashurbanipal once had.

When archaeologists found Ashurbanipal's library, they did not know that the Sumerian language existed. By studying Ashurbanipal's Sumerian books and comparing them with others that had been found elsewhere, scholars learned to read Sumerian.

It is fortunate for us that Ashurbanipal collected books. Such a large library can tell us a great deal about the Sumerians and other peoples of the time. If Ashurbanipal had not loved knowledge and books so much, we would know far less about Mesopotamia than we do. ■

R E V I E W

1. **FOCUS** What were the major achievements of the civilizations of ancient Mesopotamia?
2. **CULTURE** List and explain three features that make up a civilization.
3. **CULTURE** Give one example of a Sumerian idea that influences our culture today.
4. **CRITICAL THINKING** How might specialization of labor have encouraged social classes to develop in Sumer?
5. **CRITICAL THINKING** Can you think of examples of modern laws that resemble laws from the Code of Hammurabi? List as many as you can think of, and tell how they are similar to those in the Code of Hammurabi.
6. **WRITING ACTIVITY** Write a short story describing how a day in your life would be different if the wheel had never been invented.

LESSON 3

The Origins of Judaism

About 2000 B.C. a man named Abraham lived with his family in a Mesopotamian town called Haran. People in Haran, as in the rest of Mesopotamia, worshiped many Gods.

Abraham, however, worshiped only one God. Today, **monotheism,** or the belief in only one God, is shared by Christians, Muslims, Jews, and millions of other people all over the world. Most scholars agree that 4,000 years ago, however, monotheism was rarely practiced. Abraham started a tradition that lasted and spread over most of the world.

THINKING FOCUS

What are the main teachings of Judaism?

The Promise of Land

Abraham's story is told in a collection of religious writings called the Bible. The Jewish Bible is made up of 24 books that tell the story and the teachings of early Judaism. The Christian Bible includes the entire Jewish Bible under the name Hebrew Scriptures or Old Testament. It is bound together with the New Testament, a collection of 27 books that tell the story and the teachings of early Christianity. Stories about Abraham are also found in the Muslim Qur'an.

Archaeologists continue to discover artifacts and writings that help us understand Abraham's time. Even so, for his story and for information about early Judaism, the Bible is our best source.

From the book of Genesis, the first book of the Bible, we learn that when Abraham was 75 years old, God spoke to him in Haran. God said to him:

Go from your country and your kindred [family] and your father's house to the land that I will show you. I will make of you a great nation, and I will bless you, and make your name great, so that you will be a blessing. . . ."

Genesis 12:1–2

According to Genesis, Abraham obeyed God's command. He left Haran and journeyed to Canaan, an area just to the east of the Mediterranean Sea. There God promised to give this land to Abraham and his descendants. Abraham, his family, and his descendants

Key Terms

- monotheism
- Torah
- prophet
- rabbi
- Talmud

▼ *The ancient Hebrew alphabet was made up only of consonants. Beginning about A.D. 800, scribes added small symbols to the consonants to represent vowels. Here are the first two words—read from right to left—of chapter 17 in Genesis.*

The Fertile Crescent

▲ *One belief central to Judaism is that God gave a set of laws to Moses after the Israelites had left Egypt in the Exodus. This painting illustrates a manuscript page of the Torah in the Bible of St. Paulo di Muri de Roma in Italy. It shows Moses receiving the laws of the Torah from God and presenting them to the Israelites.*

remained faithful to God even though other people in Canaan worshiped many Gods.

Abraham's grandson Jacob, who was also called Israel, had 12 sons. When a serious food shortage threatened the region, Jacob and his family left Canaan. They moved to the nearby country of Egypt.

In Egypt, Jacob prospered, and his family grew rapidly. Each of his sons became the ancestor of an entire tribe. The members of the 12 tribes came to be known as the Israelites.

The Exodus

For hundreds of years, the Israelites were treated well by the Egyptians. Then one of the Egyptian kings began to treat the Israelites as slaves. He made the Israelites work on various building projects.

In time a leader named Moses arose among the Israelites. The Bible tells us that God instructed Moses to lead the Israelites out of Egypt. Their passage from slavery to freedom, called the Exodus, is still celebrated by Jews in their annual Passover festival.

According to the Bible, Moses led the Israelites through the wilderness for 40 years. Early in their journey, they stopped at Mount Sinai. There God gave them a set of laws called the Ten Commandments.

Through Moses, God gave the Israelites other laws and instructions as well. These laws are included in the first five books of the Bible, which together are called the **Torah.** The word Torah means "instruction." The Torah also includes stories about the beginning of the world and early times up to the death of Moses.

Some of the laws in the Torah are like the laws in the Code of Hammurabi and many modern laws. They tell what should be done in specific legal cases. Other laws in the Torah give instructions for worship. They describe behavior on holy days that Jews still celebrate, such as Rosh Ha-Shanah *(rawsh huh SHAW nuh),* the New Year; Yom Kippur *(yawm KIHP uhr),* the Day of Atonement; and Pesach *(PAY sahkh),* the Passover.

The Torah also gives basic rules for living a good life. The best known rules are the Ten Commandments. Also important is the instruction "Love your neighbor as yourself," found in the book of Leviticus.

◄ *In ancient Jerusalem the temple was the center of worship. This model shows what the temple that Solomon built might have looked like.*

Across Time & Space

In A.D. 525, a Christian monk named Dionysius Exiguus introduced the system used today to number the years. He began with the year when many believed Jesus was born. The initials A.D. mean "anno Domini," or "in the year of the Lord." The initials B.C. mean "before Christ." Some non-Christians and Christians alike prefer to use the initials C.E., meaning "common era," and B.C.E., meaning "before common era."

Jerusalem and the Temple

The people who lived in Canaan when the Israelites arrived were called Canaanites. Scholars disagree about whether the Israelites fought with the Canaanites or settled among them peacefully. Nevertheless, by about 1200 B.C. the Israelites controlled Canaan. They regarded it as the land God had promised to Abraham.

For about 200 years after the Israelites had settled in Canaan, there was little unity among the tribes. People called judges brought the tribes together at times of emergency. Kings ruled a united Israel for the following 100 years. One of these kings, David, made Jerusalem the capital of Israel in about 1000 B.C. Another king, David's son Solomon, built a great temple at Jerusalem. You can see what the temple might have looked like in the picture on this page.

The temple became the center of the Israelites' religious life. People came to the temple to worship, pray, and offer sacrifices to God. They also sang and recited songs called psalms. The book of Psalms in the Bible is a collection of these temple songs and similar poems that were composed later. ■

■ *What were the different types of laws given in the Torah?*

Independent Kingdoms

Israel's unity did not last long. By about 900 B.C., after the reign of Solomon, the kingdom had split into two parts, each with its own king. The new northern kingdom was home to 10 of the 12 Israelite tribes. It kept the name Israel. The new southern kingdom was called Judah after the tribe of that name. Residents of Judah were known as Judeans. In later years they were called Jews and their religion was called Judaism.

The Prophets

The Bible tells that during the time of the divided kingdoms, many kings did not worship only the one God. They also allowed the people to worship other Gods. In addition, they allowed the rich to take advantage of the poor.

The Ten Commandments

1. I am the LORD your God. . . . You shall have no other gods before me.

2. You shall not make for yourself an idol [image of a God]. . . . You shall not bow down to them or worship them. . . .

3. You shall not make wrongful use of the name of the LORD your God

4. Remember the sabbath day, and keep it holy. . . .

5. Honor your father and your mother, so that your days may be long in the land that the LORD your God is giving you.

6. You shall not murder.

7. You shall not commit adultery.

8. You shall not steal.

9. You shall not bear false witness against your neighbor.

10. You shall not covet . . . anything that belongs to your neighbor.

Source: The Holy Bible, New Revised Standard Version, 1989

➤ *Although the Ten Commandments were recorded thousands of years ago, many Jews and Christians today still regard them as all-important rules.*

Across Time & Space

Today during worship services in some synagogues, the Torah is carried in a procession to a reading desk. There passages are read aloud or chanted in an ancient melody. Before and after the reading of the Torah, the congregation recites prayers and blessings. The service varies depending on the day of the week and the time of day.

The Bible includes a number of books named for prophets who lived during this time. The **prophets** were religious leaders who were disturbed by the people's actions. The prophets reminded the people of their relationship with God. They preached that the Israelites and the Judeans should worship only the one God of Abraham. They urged the people to treat one another fairly as God had commanded them. If the people failed to obey God, the prophets warned, their land would be destroyed.

The prophets also gave the people hope. They assured the Israelites and the Judeans that God would bring them back even if enemies forced them out of their homeland.

A Period of Exile

In about 722 B.C., the Assyrians destroyed the northern kingdom of Israel. They resettled the Israelites in other parts of the Assyrian Empire. However, the kingdom of Judah remained.

By about 610 B.C., the Babylonians and the Medes had defeated the Assyrians. Under King Nebuchadnezzar, the Babylonians took over Judah in 586 B.C., destroyed the temple, and burned Jerusalem. Nebuchadnezzar forced thousands of Judeans to move to Babylon.

In Babylon the exiled Jews were allowed to live in settlements, farm, and trade. Still, living far from their beloved homeland among people who worshiped many Gods was a test of their faith. One of the psalms records the Jews' struggle: "By the rivers of Babylon—there we sat down and there we wept when we remembered Zion [Jerusalem]. . . . How could we sing the Lord's song in a foreign land?"

The Jews met this test with renewed faith. Now they stressed the importance of their laws and religious traditions even more than they had before the exile.

In 539 B.C. an empire called Persia conquered Babylon. In the following year, the Persian king allowed the Jews to return to their land. They built a new temple in Jerusalem and began to worship in it. Much later, in A.D. 70, the Romans destroyed this second temple in a war against the Jews. They never rebuilt their temple.

From Past to Present

How was it possible for the Jews to maintain their faith without a common land or temple? The answer: A group of teachers, a set of books, and a new place to meet for prayer created a portable homeland for the Jews.

The teachers are called **rabbis.** The word *rabbi (RAB eye)* means "master" or "teacher." Beginning in the first century A.D., rabbis taught the Jews how to live by the instructions of the Torah and the prophets, even if they could no longer worship at the temple.

Early rabbis created the **Talmud,** a collection of books containing the laws and customs that developed in the Jewish tradition. The Talmud was completed in Babylonia in the sixth century.

The place for prayer is called the synagogue *(SIHN uh gahg).*

The word *synagogue* means "meeting" or "gathering" in Greek. Ever since the exile in Babylon, Jews have been meeting for prayer in synagogues. Synagogues can be built anywhere, but they always face in the direction of Jerusalem.

Today there are more than 17 million Jews in the world. About seven million live in the United States, and about four million in the modern State of Israel. Guided by rabbis who interpret the Talmud, Jews worship in synagogues around the world. Wherever they live, they honor the tradition they believe began almost 4,000 years ago with their ancestor Abraham. ■

◄ *The six-pointed Star of David was used in ancient times by several civilizations as a magical sign or decoration. In the 1600s it was used for the first time as a general symbol of Judaism.*

◄ *Today Jewish families around the world celebrate holy days. Here a family celebrates a Seder meal at Passover.*

■ *What helps modern Jews hold onto their traditions?*

R E V I E W

1. FOCUS What are the main teachings of Judaism?

2. GEOGRAPHY Why did Jacob leave the land that he believed God had promised to his grandfather?

3. ETHICS What was the role of the prophets in ancient Israel and Judah?

4. BELIEF SYSTEMS What are the Torah and the Talmud?

5. CRITICAL THINKING Give an example of an event in Jewish history that cannot be proven or disproven by archaeologists.

6. ACTIVITY Find out about Jewish holy days such as Rosh Ha-Shanah or Yom Kippur. Write one or two paragraphs describing one of these holy days and its ceremonies.

Chapter Review

Reviewing Key Terms

agriculture (p. 59)
archaeologist (p. 58)
civilization (p. 67)
class (p. 67)
hunter-gatherer (p. 58)
irrigation (p. 67)
monotheism (p. 73)

prehistoric (p. 59)
prophet (p. 76)
rabbi (p. 77)
specialization of labor (p. 67)
surplus (p. 67)
Talmud (p. 77)
Torah (p. 74)

A. Read each pair of words. Write a sentence telling how the words in each pair are related.
1. agriculture, irrigation
2. civilization, surplus
3. specialization of labor, class
4. hunter-gatherer, prehistoric
5. archaeologist, civilization

B. Each statement below contains one or more key terms from the chapter. Decide whether each statement is correct or incorrect. Give reasons to support your decision using information in the chapter.
1. A <u>surplus</u> of food led to the <u>specialization of labor</u>.
2. <u>Archaeologists</u> study the written records of people who lived in <u>prehistoric</u> times.
3. <u>Hunter-gatherers</u> in the Fertile Crescent developed an important <u>civilization</u> 50,000 years ago.

C. Use a dictionary to find the origin of the following words. Then explain how the meaning of each word applies to Judaism.
1. Talmud
2. monotheism
3. Torah
4. prophet
5. rabbi

Exploring Concepts

A. The timeline below gives important dates and events in the history of ancient Mesopotamia. Copy the timeline on your own paper and complete it by filling in the missing events.

B. Answer each question with information from the chapter.
1. What big change in the way people lived occurred about 17,000 years ago?
2. What helped the people of Mesopotamia to be successful in farming?
3. Why is the area of land that crosses Southwest Asia called the Fertile Crescent?
4. Name the civilizations that developed in Mesopotamia. What kinds of evidence still exist to tell us about these civilizations?
5. What event do Jews celebrate in their annual Passover festival?
6. Compare the laws in the Code of Hammurabi with the laws in the Torah.

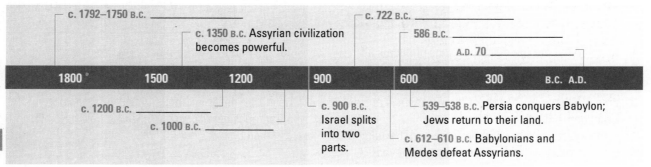

c. 1792–1750 B.C. _____

c. 1350 B.C. Assyrian civilization becomes powerful.

c. 722 B.C. _____

586 B.C. _____

A.D. 70 _____

| 1800 | 1500 | 1200 | 900 | 600 | 300 | B.C. A.D. |

c. 1200 B.C. _____

c. 1000 B.C. _____

c. 900 B.C. Israel splits into two parts.

539–538 B.C. Persia conquers Babylon; Jews return to their land.

c. 612–610 B.C. Babylonians and Medes defeat Assyrians.

Reviewing Skills

1. Create a flow chart to summarize information in Lesson 3. Make a flow chart from the following facts. Be sure to give your flow chart a title.
   - A food shortage in Canaan caused Abraham's grandson Jacob and his family to move to Egypt.
   - The move to Egypt led to the enslavement of the Jews by an Egyptian king.
2. Look at the map of the Fertile Crescent on page 67. Then find a precipitation map of the region in an encyclopedia or atlas. Study the two maps. What is the annual precipitation in this area? How does this fact help explain why Mesopotamian farmers needed to irrigate the land?
3. Which map in the Atlas of this book tells you the names of the countries that lie within the Fertile Crescent region today? List these countries and their capital cities.

Using Critical Thinking

1. Archaeologists often try to make tools from stone and other materials the way early peoples made them. Why do you think they do this?
2. A surplus of food was probably the most important feature of civilizations in the Fertile Crescent because it made all the other features of civilization possible. Why do you think this is so? Explain your answer.
3. One of the main principles of the Code of Hammurabi is that "the strong shall not injure the weak." Do you think the laws we have today are based on this principle? Explain your answer.
4. The prophets in ancient Israel told the Jews that they had strayed from a proper life and warned them that destruction would result if they did not correct their ways. What do modern environmental prophets tell us about the way our society operates today?
5. During their exile in Babylon from 586 to 539 B.C., the Jews' faith was greatly tested. Why might this exile have been so difficult for the Jews?

Preparing for Citizenship

1. **WRITING ACTIVITY** As you read in this chapter, the Jews have a rich tradition that began long ago with their ancestor Abraham. Interview a Jewish family member or other person who lives in your community. Find out about Jewish customs, beliefs, religious services, holidays, and traditions. Write a short report about one holiday or tradition.
2. **COLLECTING INFORMATION** Ashurbanipal's library included books on fables, proverbs, religion, magic, law, science, folktales, and ancient stories. Visit your school or local library. What system does the library use to classify books? What are the main groups into which the books are classified? Share your information with the class.
3. **GROUP ACTIVITY** In ancient times, irrigation for watering crops was necessary to feed growing populations in cities like Ur. In small groups, discover how farmers today try to increase food production. What methods do they use? How successful have these methods been? Are any of these methods dangerous? Then decide how to present your findings to the class.
4. **COLLABORATIVE LEARNING** Many of the crops that Mesopotamian farmers grew are still grown in the Middle East today. Find out what these foods are and how they are prepared. Then plan a Middle Eastern meal. In small groups, prepare some Middle Eastern dishes to serve to your classmates. You may wish to invite friends and parents to your dinner.

Chapter 4

Ancient Egypt and Nubia

An ancient historian called Egypt "the gift of the Nile." The Nile River created a valley of bountiful land in the harsh African desert, giving everything Egyptians needed to live. Yet Egypt was not the Nile's only gift. Farther south, where the river runs through a rocky land, was another great civilization called Nubia. Located at a crossroads of trade, Nubia was home to mighty kingdoms.

Egyptians prepared for what they believed would be life after death. This couple is shown enjoying a bountiful harvest in paradise.

6000	5000	4000	3000

6000 B.C.

c. 6000 B.C. The first culture of the Nile Valley begins in Nubia. Cultures in Egypt develop soon after.

c. 3000 B.C. Powerful kingdoms develop in Egypt and Nubia.

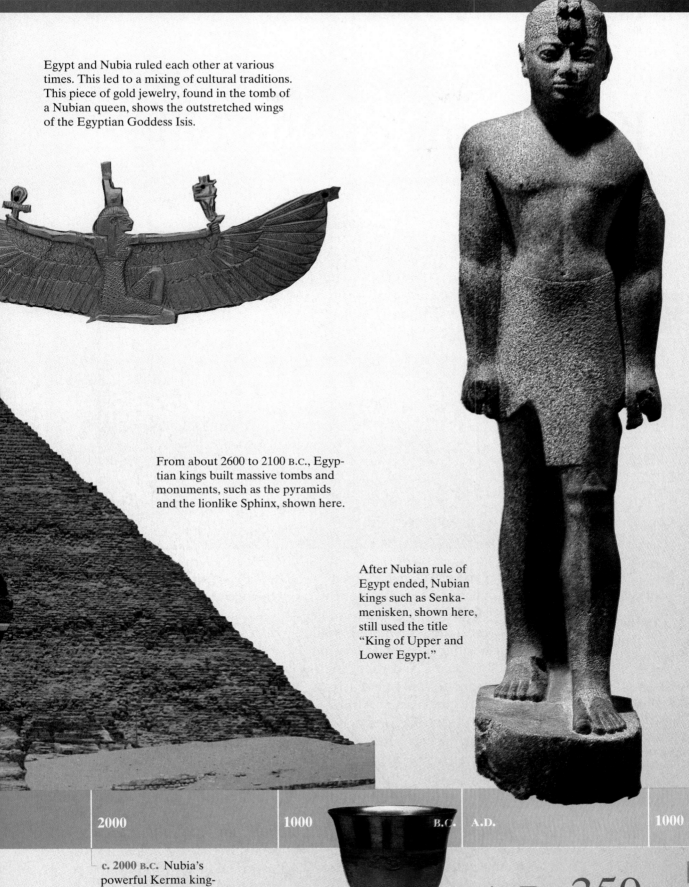

Egypt and Nubia ruled each other at various times. This led to a mixing of cultural traditions. This piece of gold jewelry, found in the tomb of a Nubian queen, shows the outstretched wings of the Egyptian Goddess Isis.

From about 2600 to 2100 B.C., Egyptian kings built massive tombs and monuments, such as the pyramids and the lionlike Sphinx, shown here.

After Nubian rule of Egypt ended, Nubian kings such as Senkamenisken, shown here, still used the title "King of Upper and Lower Egypt."

| 2000 | 1000 | B.C. | A.D. | 1000 |

c. 2000 B.C. Nubia's powerful Kerma kingdom produces some of Africa's finest pottery.

81

A.D. 350

LESSON 1

Kingdoms on the Nile

THINKING
FOCUS

Describe differences in the way kingdoms developed in ancient Egypt and ancient Nubia.

Key Terms

- delta
- cataract
- dynasty
- pharaoh

➤ *This photograph shows how suddenly the green banks of the Nile turn into desert. The rock painting above shows Stone Age people herding cattle in what is now desert. Rock art has been found throughout the Sahara, including a 25-foot-long painting of a rhinoceros.*

I f you stood on the green banks of Egypt's Nile River and began walking west, the green under your feet would vanish within a few miles. Facing you would be a landscape of blistering sand that stretches across the entire continent of Africa.

This desert, the Sahara, is the largest on the earth. Its treeless land and soaring temperatures make life there nearly impossible. Yet the Sahara was not always so empty. At one time the desert was a green grassland. People roamed the land. They fished, herded cattle, and hunted animals such as giraffes, elephants, and birds.

Prehistoric rock paintings like the one above show that the Sahara once supported human and animal life. Such colorful paintings have been found throughout the desert.

The last time the Sahara was green was about 8,000 years ago. As it dried out, animals and people spread in all directions, seeking better land. Many were attracted to the fresh water and fertile land of the Nile Valley.

These refugees from the desert joined peoples who had been living along the Nile for thousands of years. In time the blending of these desert and river peoples created two great civilizations.

The Gift of the Nile

Each year in late spring, monsoons from the Indian Ocean dump tons of rain on the highlands of east-central Africa. The water rushes downward, swelling a river called the Blue Nile. At the city of Khartoum *(kahr TOOM),* the Blue Nile joins the White Nile to form the Nile River. Locate the Nile and its branches on the map on this page and in the Atlas on page 685.

Geography of the Nile

The powerful Nile River digs a long, deep ditch in the Sahara. A thin strip of fertile land lines the riverbanks. The Nile flows from south to north. That is why the southern, higher part is called the Upper Nile. The northern, lower end is the Lower Nile.

Near the mouth of the river, the Lower Nile fans out into a marshy, triangle-shaped area called a **delta**. There the fresh waters of the Nile empty into the salty Mediterranean Sea. From its source at the start of the White Nile to the delta, the river flows 4,132 miles, making it the world's longest river.

While the Nile flows north, the winds in the valley blow south. This makes boat travel easy, since you can drift downstream and sail upstream. From the delta southward, there is clear sailing for 750 miles. Then suddenly a pile of giant boulders looms ahead. The river bends and crashes around this area of rocky rapids called a **cataract**. Find the Nile's six cataracts on the map.

A Fruitful Valley

The land of the cataracts was home to an ancient civilization called Nubia. It was located in what is today southern Egypt and the northern part of the country of Sudan.

Until this century historians knew little about the people of Nubia. They knew much more about Nubia's northern neighbor, ancient Egypt. Yet Nubia and Egypt were closely tied throughout their ancient history.

The first culture along the Nile began in Nubia, near the modern-day city of Khartoum, south of the Sixth Cataract. This part of Nubia had a climate like that of central Africa—hot and rainy. Pieces of pottery from this fertile region show that the Khartoum culture may date back to 6000 B.C.

Other Nile cultures developed over thousands of years, as the drying of the Sahara pushed more people into the valley. These people brought a knowledge of how to grow grains, such as barley. As in Mesopotamia, people in small communities began working together to capture the floodwaters for farming. They used mud from the river's banks to make bricks for houses. The Nile provided everything they needed to live. ■

Ancient Egypt and Nubia

Study the map. Write down two words or phrases that describe the geography of the Nile Valley. Next, look at the inset map. It shows the location of the Nile Valley in the world. For help in using an inset map, see page G3 in the Map and Globe Handbook.

■ *Why was the Nile Valley a likely place for civilizations to develop?*

Egypt, Land of the Pharaohs

▼ *The king of Upper Egypt wore a white crown. The king of Lower Egypt wore a red crown. When the two kingdoms united, the king wore a double crown. It symbolized the union of the two lands.*

Trapping and storing the flood-waters of the Nile was a mighty job. Leaders emerged to organize such big projects. Between 4000 and 3000 B.C., some of these leaders grew very powerful.

No one knows exactly how kingdoms developed along the Nile. Some experts now believe that a group of people in Lower Nubia had the first government with kings of great power. These scholars also say that Egypt's first kings may have descended from Nubians. Such ideas are being hotly debated today.

The Beginning of History

A clearer picture of the history of kings emerges after about 3000 B.C. That is when the first written records appear. Historians are now debating whether the first writing is Egyptian, as is generally thought, or whether it is actually Nubian.

These early records tell of powerful kingdoms in Upper Egypt and in the delta, or Lower Egypt. A leader of Upper Egypt wrote of

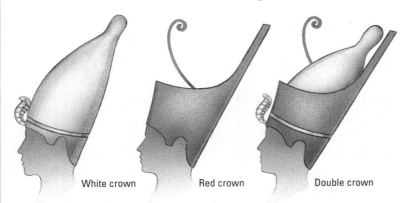

White crown   Red crown   Double crown

UNDERSTANDING DYNASTY

*I*n about 270 B.C., a historian named Manetho made a list of Egypt's kings and dynasties. (This picture shows an ancient Egyptian king list.) Manetho's list began with dynasties of Gods, who he thought had ruled before the pharaohs. Egypt's history, he said, had lasted 36,525 years.

Modern historians date the history of ancient Egypt from the time when it was united under one pharaoh in about 3000 B.C. to the arrival of Greek rulers in 332 B.C. That's nearly 2,700 years. During that time Egypt had 30 dynasties in which hundreds of kings ruled.

What Is a Dynasty?

A dynasty is not the same as a king. A **dynasty** is a series of rulers who descended from the same person. Egypt's First Dynasty had eight rulers. The Thirteenth Dynasty had about 70 rulers.

A Sign of Change

The start of a new dynasty often marked a time of major political change. Powerful Nubian kings ruled Egypt starting in about

724 B.C.
Even though they were not Egyptian, the time of their reign is called the Twenty-fifth Dynasty.

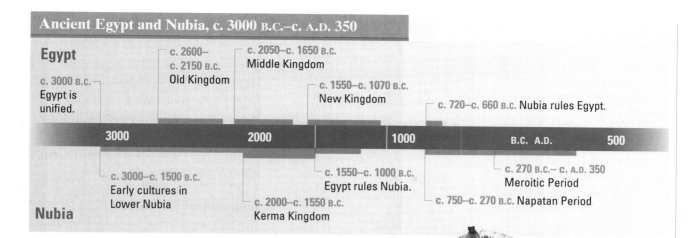

Egypt

c. 3000 B.C.
Egypt is unified.

c. 2600– c. 2150 B.C.
Old Kingdom

c. 2050–c. 1650 B.C.
Middle Kingdom

c. 1550–c. 1070 B.C.
New Kingdom

c. 720–c. 660 B.C. Nubia rules Egypt.

3000   2000   1000   B.C. A.D.   500

c. 3000–c. 1500 B.C.
Early cultures in Lower Nubia

c. 2000–c. 1550 B.C.
Kerma Kingdom

c. 1550–c. 1000 B.C.
Egypt rules Nubia.

c. 270 B.C.–c. A.D. 350
Meroitic Period

c. 750–c. 270 B.C. Napatan Period

Nubia

how he had conquered Lower Egypt to form one country. This union marks the start of Egypt's First Dynasty. See Understanding Dynasty on page 84.

Kings and Kingdoms

Thirty dynasties ruled Egypt for nearly 3,000 years. Historians divide Egypt's ancient past into three periods, called kingdoms. On the timeline above, trace Egypt's Old, Middle, and New kingdoms.

At the start of each kingdom, Egypt prospered. Often the king, called the **pharaoh** *(FAIR oh),* was strong and wise. Near the end of each period, Egypt declined because of weak pharaohs, civil wars, or famine.

In normal times the pharaoh, usually a man, had absolute power. Much of Egypt's land and wealth belonged to him. He controlled taxes, trade, irrigation, and mining.

Many colorful leaders ruled Egypt. Although few rulers were women, one queen, Hatshepsut *(haht SHEHP soot),* rose to great power. She led her country into a time of peace and wealth. King Ramesses II *(RAM ih seez)* built great monuments. Another king, Akhenaton *(ah kuh NAHT uhn),* is famous for his failed attempt to make Egypt a monotheistic country.

The pharaohs had a large appetite for wealth, especially gold. Foreigners believed that, in Egypt, gold was as common as dust. What they did not know was that Egypt got much of its wealth from its southern neighbor—Nubia. ■

▲ *The timeline shows the main historical periods of Egypt and Nubia. The large mask (at left) is of one of Egypt's most famous rulers. He was the boy king Tutankhamon (toot ahng KAH muhn), who died at age 18.*

■ *Who were the pharaohs, and what powers did they have?*

Nubia, a Crossroads of Trade

Nubia became united more slowly than did Egypt, largely because of its rocky land. To this day, a region south of the Second Cataract is called "belly of rock." The rough terrain made travel, communication, and cooperative farming difficult.

Yet Nubia had other resources. These resources led to the growth of trade, which in turn spurred the development of wealthy kingdoms.

Growth of Trade

Hidden in the rocky sands of eastern and western Nubia was a treasure chest of gold and other minerals. Locate Nubia's gold deposits on the map on page 83. The Nubian Nile was home to valuable

How Do We Know?

CULTURE *No one knows what the early Nubians called their land. The Egyptians called Lower Nubia Ta-Sety, or "Land of the Bow"—a reference to the Nubians' famed archery skills.*

> *Where were most of Nubia's capitals—in Lower Nubia or Upper Nubia?*

Ancient Cities of the Nile

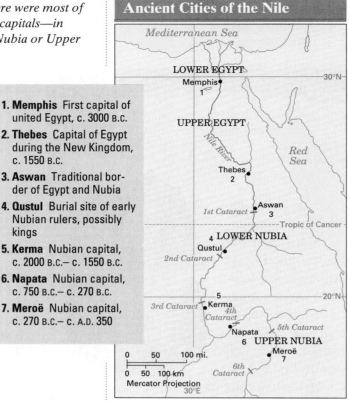

1. **Memphis** First capital of united Egypt, c. 3000 B.C.
2. **Thebes** Capital of Egypt during the New Kingdom, c. 1550 B.C.
3. **Aswan** Traditional border of Egypt and Nubia
4. **Qustul** Burial site of early Nubian rulers, possibly kings
5. **Kerma** Nubian capital, c. 2000 B.C.– c. 1550 B.C.
6. **Napata** Nubian capital, c. 750 B.C.– c. 270 B.C.
7. **Meroë** Nubian capital, c. 270 B.C.– c. A.D. 350

goods from the south and sold them to Egypt and Southwest Asia. One Egyptian trader returned from Nubia with "three hundred donkeys laden with incense, ebony, panther skins, elephants' tusks, throw sticks, and all sorts of good products."

Competition for Power

In time Nubia's trading kingdoms grew to rival the power of Egypt. During its ancient history, Egypt often sought to control Nubia's mines and trade. In times when Egypt's government was strong, powerful pharaohs pushed south, seizing parts of Nubia. In times of weakness, Egyptian forces withdrew.

The Egypt-Nubia border shifted many times. During Egypt's Old Kingdom, the pharaohs often controlled Lower Nubia. After 2000 B.C., however, powerful kingdoms arose in Upper Nubia, a region the Egyptians called Kush.

During the next 1,500 years, Egypt and Nubia often competed for power. In the time of Egypt's New Kingdom, Egypt ruled all of Nubia. Kings from Kush later ruled all of Nubia and Egypt. The map above shows capitals and key cities along the Nile.

When armies crossed the Egypt-Nubia border, parts of their culture crossed over, too. In Lesson 2 you'll read about the cultures of Egypt and Nubia and see how each affected the culture of the other. ■

> *Late in its history, Kush was ruled by queens, like the one shown in this silver mask.*

■ *How did resources bring both benefits and problems to Nubia?*

living resources as well. Hippopotamuses, giraffes, ostriches, and other animals roamed the wilderness. A growing human population had driven many of these animals out of Egypt, so the Egyptians eagerly sought them from Nubia.

Besides its own goods, Nubia also had access to products from the rain forests of central Africa to the south. Nubian traders got luxury

R E V I E W

1. **FOCUS** Describe differences in the way kingdoms developed in ancient Egypt and ancient Nubia.
2. **GEOGRAPHY** How did changes in the climate and land of the Sahara affect the Nile Valley?
3. **HISTORY** What is a dynasty?

4. **CRITICAL THINKING** Why might the Nile's cataracts have affected the history of Egypt and Nubia?
5. **WRITING ACTIVITY** Pretend you are the boy king, Tutankhamon. Write an order for products that you would like to get from Nubia.

LESSON 2

Ancient Cultures Linked Together

For hundreds of years, ancient Egyptian was a lost language. It had begun to fade from use after about A.D. 500, as new languages spread down the Nile. People forgot how to speak the language or read the writing.

Yet all over Egypt, the beautiful symbols of the dead language lived on—in temples, pyramids, and books. The Egyptians wrote in **hieroglyphics** (hy uhr uh GLIHF ihks), a script that uses pictures to stand for ideas, words, or letters. The hieroglyphics, and what they told of Egyptian life, remained a mystery until the early 1800s.

In 1799 French soldiers were building a fort near Rosetta, a village in the Nile delta. There they dug up a black stone covered with writing. This object became one of the world's most famous artifacts. It is called the Rosetta stone.

Inscribed on the stone was the same message in three scripts—two forms of ancient Egyptian as well as ancient Greek. The Greek, a known language, gave clues to the meaning of the Egyptian symbols. In time, scholars decoded the more than 700 Egyptian hieroglyphs.

THINKING FOCUS

Summarize key facts about Egyptian and Nubian culture.

Key Terms

- hieroglyphics
- scribe
- afterlife
- mummy

◄ *The Rosetta stone is nearly four feet high and two and one-half feet wide. Its message praising the Greek king Ptolemy V (TAHL uh mee) was written in 196 B.C.*

Egyptian Society

The Egyptians left volumes of written material—tax records, poetry, religious books, textbooks, and military reports. Once hieroglyphics could be read, they shed new light on this ancient culture.

Egyptian families lived much like people today. Marriage was important, and husbands were urged to respect their wives. Parents taught their children to work hard and to obey. Although children often did chores at an early age, they also enjoyed dolls, games, and sports.

Egyptians loved to look good, too. People who could afford them used makeup, hairpins, wigs, and perfumes. Although few people were rich, life for many was good.

Nearly every Egyptian was in the service of someone at a higher level of society. The society was

87

organized into several levels. From the Middle Kingdom on, slaves made up the lowest level. Next came farmers. Most labored on the farms of wealthy landowners or of the pharaoh. During flood seasons, they built monuments for the pharaoh and served in the army.

On the level above the farmers were the skilled laborers—carpenters, bakers, and jewelers. Above them were the scribes. A **scribe** had the important job of writing. Scribes kept records and wrote letters. Above the scribes were the priests, who worked in the temples.

At the top of society was the all-powerful pharaoh. Thought to be Gods or godlike, the pharaohs were surrounded with wealth and beauty. In fact, the word *pharaoh* means "great house," a reference to the king's grand palace.

Pharaohs were honored in death as well as in life. You can witness this fact at the ancient site of Giza. ■

■ *Describe the layers of Egyptian society.*

Across Time & Space

Khufu's pyramid may have been built in about 23 years. Was this really possible? In 1991 U.S. archaeologists did an experiment at Giza to find out. Using ropes, ramps, and ancient-style tools, 12 stonecutters built a small pyramid in only 21 days. At this rate a king's crew of about 400 stonecutters could have completed the task.

The Great Monument Builders

On the plain of Giza near present-day Cairo, stone structures rise out of the sand. The tallest is 40 stories high and covers an area the size of seven city blocks. If it were hollow, four of the world's largest cathedrals could fit inside it. It is the Great Pyramid.

The Pyramids at Giza

The Great Pyramid was the burial tomb of Khufu *(KOO foo)*, a king in the 2500s B.C. The structure consists of 2.3 million blocks of limestone, most weighing more than two tons. During Khufu's reign thousands of men labored to build the pyramid. One group of workers proudly painted its name—"The Craftsmen Gang"—on a wall deep inside the pyramid. Once in place, the outer blocks were so snug that a knife blade could not fit between them.

Two other pyramids at Giza belonged to Khufu's descendants. The fourth structure is the Sphinx, a stone creature nearly as long as a football field. The Sphinx has the body of a lion and the face of a man, thought to be King Khafre *(KHAH frah)*.

Most of the pyramids were built during Egypt's Old Kingdom. More than 80 pyramids survive to this day. Egyptians hoped that the

➤ *This is an archaeologist's drawing of what the construction site at Giza might have looked like. Shown here are: (1) Great Pyramid of Khufu; (2) ramps; (3) villages for workers; (4) harbor canals; (5) quarries; (6) Khufu's palace complex; (7) tombs of royal relatives and officials; (8) future sites of pyramids of Menkaure, Khafre, and the Sphinx.*

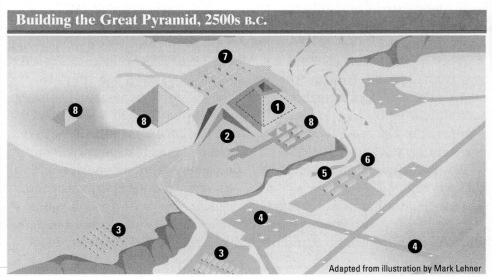

Building the Great Pyramid, 2500s B.C.

Adapted from illustration by Mark Lehner

monuments would cause the pharaohs' names to be remembered. This would fulfill their belief that "to speak the name of the dead is to make him live again." Indeed, the names of Khufu and his successors are still spoken after more than 4,000 years.

Preparing for the Afterlife

Egyptians were once thought to be a gloomy people because they were so concerned about death. Actually, they hoped that the good things they had in this life would continue in the next.

Egyptian religion taught that achieving a happy **afterlife,** or life after death, was not easy. Egyptians believed that the soul is judged and faces either miserable punishment or a happy afterlife.

This journey is described in the Book of the Dead, a collection of chants, spells, and religious texts found in Egyptian tombs. One spell is from the tomb of a scribe named Ani *(ah NEE)*. (See the painting above.) In the text Ani appears before a jury of 42 Gods to prove that he has lived an honest life.

I have not made [anyone] hungry, I have not made [people] to weep, I have not killed, . . . I have not taken the milk from the mouths of children, I have not deprived the herds of their pastures,. . . . I have not built a dam on flowing water. . . . I am pure, pure, pure, pure!

Book of the Dead, Spell 125

A Royal Burial

No burial was more important than the pharaoh's. When Khufu's pyramid was completed, workers filled it with treasures he would need in the afterlife—furnishings, gold, jewels, and even games.

Egyptians believed that without a body, a person's spirit could not enjoy the afterlife. They invented a process called embalming to slow the normal decay of the body after death. Embalming changed the body into a **mummy.**

The jackal God Anubis (uh NOO bihs) weighs Ani's heart against the feather of truth. Egyptians believed that if their hearts were heavy with sin, they would die a permanent death. If their hearts passed the test, they would go on to a happy afterlife.

◄ *To make a mummy, embalmers removed some of the organs from the body and put them into canopic (kuh NOH pic) jars, like the jar on the left. They filled the body with sawdust or linen and dried it for 40 days in salt. The body was then coated in hot tree sap and wrapped in linen. The mummy was often placed in a beautiful coffin.*

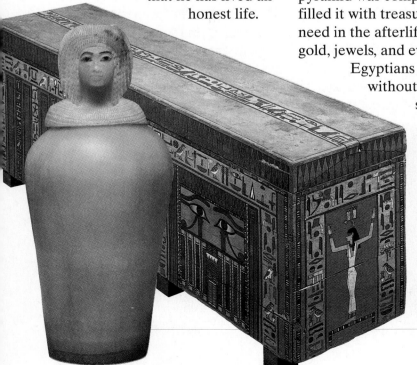

When Khufu died, his mummy was placed in the tomb. After a final prayer, workers slid stone blocks into the doorway to seal the tomb—forever, they hoped. Despite these efforts, thieves found their way through secret vaults and false rooms and stole Khufu's mummy and all of his treasures.

Egyptian beliefs had deep roots that developed over thousands of years. These beliefs governed the daily life of every Egyptian from farmers to pharaohs. So powerful were Egypt's customs that they also influenced other cultures—particularly the neighboring peoples of Nubia. ■

■ *What do the pyramids reveal about the beliefs of the ancient Egyptians?*

Nubia's Unique Culture

Egyptians and Nubians had close contact from very early times, so it's not surprising that each group passed on ideas to the other. Nevertheless, Nubian culture had a flavor quite different from that of Egypt.

While Egyptian pharaohs were building the pyramids, the peoples of Lower Nubia carried on their own traditions. Nubian kings gained great wealth from trade. Nubian soldiers became famous for their archery skills. Because farming took hold slowly in the rocky region, many Nubians raised cattle and hunted and traded for food.

The Rise of Kush

After 2000 B.C. much of Nubia's cultural change took place in the Upper Nubian kingdom of Kush. At Kerma, the Kushite capital from about 2000 to 1550 B.C., workers made knives and tools. Other workers made attractive jewelry. Skilled carpenters carved elegant furniture. Potters in Kerma made some of Africa's finest pottery.

Kerma's kings grew strong enough to capture much of Upper Egypt. In 1550 B.C., however, Egypt struck back. The pharaoh's army marched into Kush, smashed Kerma's walls, and burned the city.

Under Egyptian Rule

For the next 550 years, Egypt ruled all of Nubia. Nubians had to bring payments of gold and other wealth to the pharaoh each year. A Moment in Time on page 91 shows a Nubian princess preparing to take an offering to the pharaoh.

The pharaohs put the Nubians to work. Many were forced to mine gold. To keep the Nubians from rebelling, an official of the pharaoh,

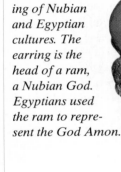

➤ *This earring shows the blending of Nubian and Egyptian cultures. The earring is the head of a ram, a Nubian God. Egyptians used the ram to represent the God Amon.*

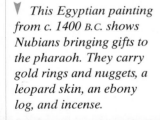

▼ *This Egyptian painting from c. 1400 B.C. shows Nubians bringing gifts to the pharaoh. They carry gold rings and nuggets, a leopard skin, an ebony log, and incense.*

A Nubian Princess

9:11 A.M., May 10, 1341 B.C.
In the home of a Nubian royal family

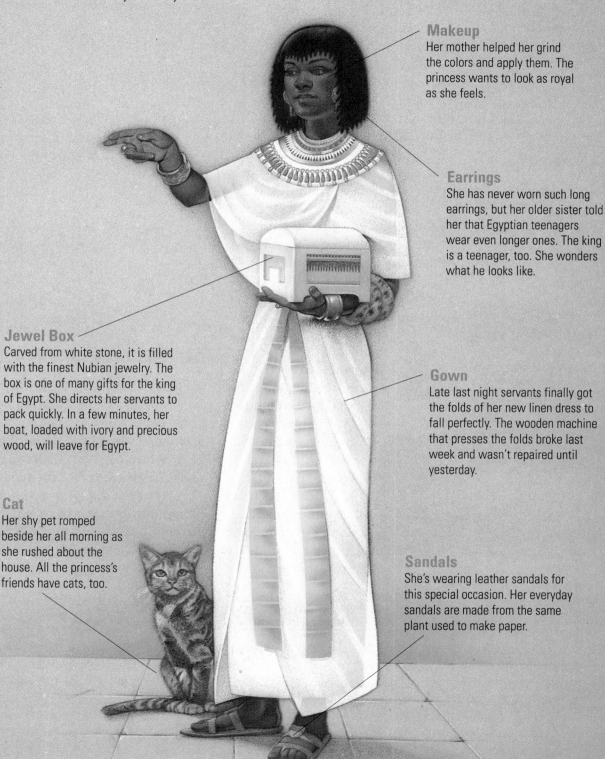

Makeup
Her mother helped her grind the colors and apply them. The princess wants to look as royal as she feels.

Earrings
She has never worn such long earrings, but her older sister told her that Egyptian teenagers wear even longer ones. The king is a teenager, too. She wonders what he looks like.

Jewel Box
Carved from white stone, it is filled with the finest Nubian jewelry. The box is one of many gifts for the king of Egypt. She directs her servants to pack quickly. In a few minutes, her boat, loaded with ivory and precious wood, will leave for Egypt.

Gown
Late last night servants finally got the folds of her new linen dress to fall perfectly. The wooden machine that presses the folds broke last week and wasn't repaired until yesterday.

Cat
Her shy pet romped beside her all morning as she rushed about the house. All the princess's friends have cats, too.

Sandals
She's wearing leather sandals for this special occasion. Her everyday sandals are made from the same plant used to make paper.

called the King's Son of Kush, kept watch over local rulers. He had their sons sent to Egypt as hostages. In time these sons, raised in Egypt, returned home to rule, bringing Egyptian culture with them. ■

Nubia Influences Egypt

➤ *These Kushite pyramids are smaller and steeper than those of Egypt. Like the Egyptians, Nubians also buried small tablets under the pyramid. They thought the tablets, shown below, had power to protect the tomb.*

Eventually, facing problems at home, Egypt retreated from Nubia. Left alone, the Kushites built a new capital at a city called Napata *(NAP uh tuh)*. From this city, in the 700s B.C., Kush invaded and conquered Egypt. A Nubian king took the throne in Lower Egypt. A Nubian princess ruled Upper Egypt.

Restoring Egyptian Culture

Nubian rulers did not force the Egyptians to follow Nubian customs. Instead, Kushite kings helped to bring back forgotten parts of Egypt's own culture. They added to old temples and built new ones in the Egyptian fashion. Their art mixed styles from Egypt's past.

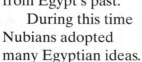

During this time Nubians adopted many Egyptian ideas. They built their own pyramids and began to mummify their dead.

■ *Contrast Egyptian rule of Nubia with Nubian rule of Egypt.*

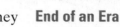

End of an Era

Nubian rule in Egypt lasted only about 60 years. The Assyrians, spreading their huge empire into Egypt (see Chapter 3), drove the Kushites back to their homeland.

After the Assyrian invasion, Egypt never regained its full strength. However, as you will read in the next lesson, the height of Nubian culture was yet to come. ■

R E V I E W

1. **FOCUS** Summarize key facts about Egyptian and Nubian culture.

2. **HISTORY** How did writing help civilization to develop in Egypt?

3. **BELIEF SYSTEMS** Reread the quotation from the Book of the Dead on page 89. How does the Egyptian sense of right and wrong compare with your own?

4. **BELIEF SYSTEMS** Many people today think of tombs as sad places. How was the Egyptian belief different?

5. **CRITICAL THINKING** Why might Egypt have wanted to "Egyptianize" Nubia?

6. **WRITING ACTIVITY** List the things you would want to take with you into the afterlife if you were a pharaoh.

L E S S O N 3

Great Achievements

He was counselor to the king, high priest of the sun, astrologer, and wise man. He was both a scribe and a sculptor. In a sense, Imhotep *(ihm HOH tehp)* represents the genius of Egypt.

About 2650 B.C., Egypt's King Djoser *(DZOH suhr)* asked Imhotep to design the grandest tomb ever. The result was Egypt's first pyramid and the first large monument of cut stone in the world. The Step Pyramid, at Saqqara *(suh KAHR uh),* rose in six levels to a height of more than 200 feet.

Imhotep was most likely a doctor, too, and a brilliant one. He was one of the first people to study how the body worked. He may have known, for example, that blood runs through the body. This fact had to be discovered again by modern medicine 4,000 years later.

Egyptian medicine was famous in the ancient world. Egyptian doctors treated patients in Assyria and beyond. In the *Odyssey,* the Greek poet Homer summed up the world's admiration of Egyptian medicine. He wrote of Egypt,

> Where the rich plantations grow herbs of all kinds, maleficent [harmful] and healthful; and no one else knows medicine as they do, Egyptian heirs of Paian, the healing god.

Imhotep was so admired that cultures in Egypt and beyond made him a God of medicine. For thousands of years, people prayed to him in the hope of being healed.

THINKING
F O C U S

What lasting effects did the Egyptians and the Nubians have on the world?

Key Term

• papyrus

◄ *In Greece, Imhotep was worshiped as a God and was identified with the Greek God of medicine, Asclepius.*

Egypt's Place in History

The works of Imhotep, like those of Egypt itself, lived on. Egyptian ideas spread throughout the ancient world. Some still affect our lives today.

Spread of Egyptian Culture

Trade was one way the ideas of Egypt traveled. Egypt exported paper, pottery, grain, and other goods. An Egyptian statue found on the island of Crete may have been brought there about 1700 B.C.

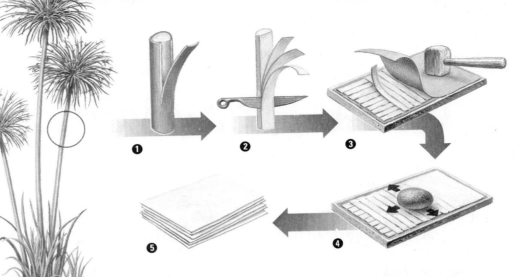

➤ (1) Egyptians cut the stem of the papyrus and removed the core. (2) They cut the core into strips, (3) put one layer across another, and beat them into a single sheet. (4) Then they polished the sheet with a stone and (5) trimmed the edges. The papyrus below is from the largest Egyptian math textbook ever found. It asks questions about the geometry of triangles.

■ *How did Egyptian achievements and ideas spread beyond Egypt?*

A crystal bowl and an Egyptian box from the 1500s B.C. have been discovered in tombs in Greece. Many scholars now believe that Egypt influenced Greek culture.

One Greek visitor was amazed by Egyptian culture. Herodotus *(hih RAHD uh tuhs)*, a historian who sailed the Nile in the 400s B.C., wrote lively accounts of Egyptian customs, such as the building of the pyramids.

Contributions to the World

The page you are reading now is one of the gifts that ancient Egypt passed on to the world. It had its origins in **papyrus** *(puh PY ruhs)*, the plant from which the paper was made (see the diagram above). Papyrus was an Egyptian product that was exported throughout the Mediterranean region.

Egyptians also invented a 12-month, 365-day calendar. Their system was later used by the Romans and is the basis for today's calendar.

To build their pyramids, the Egyptians needed to be able to measure exactly. The base of the Great Pyramid is within about 1½ inches of being perfectly square.

The Greeks said that they had learned how to measure areas and angles from the Egyptians. They in turn improved and passed on this knowledge to us as geometry.

The age of Egypt's pharaohs died out in 332 B.C., when the Greeks took control. You will read about Egypt under foreign rule in Chapter 10. ■

Nubia's Place in History

Long after Egypt had fallen to the Greeks, Nubian culture lived on. The city of Meroë *(MEHR oh ee),* beyond the Fifth Cataract, became the capital of Kush in 270 B.C. The kingdom of Meroë, which lasted until A.D. 350, was Nubia's last major kingdom—and its finest.

Meroë covered a square mile, a huge size for an ancient city. It was in a fertile region of Kush. This part of the Nile had broad banks and rich soil. Good rainfall during the summer and fall made farming and cattle grazing possible.

The Mystery of Meroë

Find Meroë on the map on page 86, and notice its distance from Egypt. Far from Egypt's influence, Nubian culture took its own course during the Meroitic period.

For example, the Nubians at Meroë created their own language and hieroglyphics. Unfortunately, no one has yet figured out how to read the mysterious language.

Meroitic religion shows a break with Egyptian traditions. Egypt's God Amon was still the most important, but a Nubian Lion-God was next. Kings were still buried in pyramids, but the Kushites returned to older Nubian customs, such as placing the body on a bed instead of in a coffin.

As always, Nubia was a crossroads for African trade. Now, however, the Nubians had a new product of their own: iron. Archaeologists have found huge piles of slag, a product of iron making, at Meroë.

Trade brought Nubians into contact with other cultures. Meroitic art shows Egyptian, Greek, Roman, and central African influences. Nubian graves contained numerous items of bronze, glass, and silver from all over the Mediterranean region.

The Meroitic Alphabet

Hieroglyph				
Cursive				
Sound	i	b	k	d

◄ These are a few of the 23 Meroitic hieroglyphs, as well as the cursive characters that evolved from them.

After about A.D. 200, the world began to bypass Nubia, as traders found new routes through the Sahara. Meroë became weak, and in the middle A.D. 300s, it fell to conquerors from the nearby desert.

Survival of Customs

Great kingdoms never rose again in Nubia. However, Nubia makes up part of the modern nation of Sudan. There, Nubian customs survive today. Beautiful pottery, baskets, and furniture are still made in the ancient style. In some parts of Sudan, people use wooden pillows much like ancient Nubian headrests.

Today's Nubians, like the young girl in this picture, are a living part of the ancient culture. After more than 35 centuries, Nubia endures. ■

▼ This Sudanese girl braids her hair just as the ancient Nubians did.

■ Why can it be said that Nubian culture became more independent during the Meroitic period?

R E V I E W

1. **FOCUS** What lasting effects did the Egyptians and the Nubians have on the world?
2. **GEOGRAPHY** Find Meroë on the map on page 86. How did location and geography help to make Meroitic culture independent?
3. **CULTURE** State in your own words the quotation from the Greek poet about medicine in Egypt.
4. **CULTURE** What was papyrus, and how was it made?

5. **HISTORY** What brought about the fall of the kingdom of Meroë?
6. **CRITICAL THINKING** In your opinion, did the ancient world know less about Nubia than about Egypt?
7. **ACTIVITY** Invent your own writing, using symbols to represent letters, words, or ideas. Write a short paragraph in your hieroglyphics, and have a classmate try to read it.

Ancient Egypt and Nubia

Interpreting Egyptian Art

Here's Why

One way to learn about the daily lives and the beliefs of people of the past is to study their art. Suppose you want to learn more about what life was like in Thebes, the capital of Egypt at the time of the New Kingdom. Art from this time period is rich in information about daily life. Yet first you must know how to interpret art from the past.

Here's How

When you look at art from the past, ask yourself these questions:

1. What was its purpose?
2. What is its main subject?
3. What does it tell you about the past?

The illustration on these pages is from a wall painting found in a tomb in Thebes. The tomb, which dates from about 1380 B.C., belonged to Nebamun (*NEHB uh muhn*) and Ipuky (*ee POO kee*). Both were important artists who worked for the king.

Now ask: What was the artist's purpose? Why was the painting created? A tomb artist's purpose was to help ensure a happy afterlife for the person buried in the tomb.

Next, what is the main subject of the painting? To answer this question, you need to figure out who is shown in the painting and what each person is doing.

Notice that the painting is divided into horizontal sections, called registers. Look at the large, seated figure to the left of the registers. In Egyptian paintings, people of high rank are often shown as being larger than the others. In this case the large figure is a supervisor.

Look at the man on the far left of the upper register. He is weighing gold rings against a counterweight shaped like a bull's head. The four seated men in the upper register are all carving symbols. To the right, two craftsmen are fitting the symbols into a framework. They are building a catafalque (*KAT uh fawlk*), an ornamental structure used in funerals.

Now look at the lower register. Here you see six artisans at work. To their left, two men show finished objects to their supervisor.

Now do you know what the painting is about? If you guessed that it shows a royal workshop of artisans, you are right. Both Nebamun and Ipuky were supervisors in the

royal workshop. The items being made were for the king's tomb.

Next, consider the third question. What does the painting tell you about the past? Most important, it shows how deeply the Egyptians believed in the afterlife. As you can see, much effort went into the crafting of items for the next life.

The painting also tells you about Egyptian customs. For example, think about how the people in the painting are dressed. Notice that the supervisor wears a large ornamental collar and a thin, full-length garment. The workers, however, dress in simple cloths wrapped at the waist.

Try It

Look closely at the lower register. Try interpreting the rest of the painting by answering the following questions. What are the six seated men in the lower register making? What kinds of tools are they using? What does this tell you about ancient Egyptian technology? What are the workers wearing? What does this say about Egypt's climate?

Apply It

Now that you have studied some skills for interpreting wall paintings, try your hand at making a painting of your own. Working alone or in a small group, create a mural that shows a scene from your daily life. For example, you might paint a scene from the lunchroom. Or you could paint a scene of your classroom or a special area such as the library. Be sure to show a number of different activities in detail. Display your murals. Then study and interpret one another's paintings.

Chapter Review

Reviewing Key Terms

afterlife (p. 89)
cataract (p. 83)
delta (p. 83)
dynasty (p. 85)
hieroglyphics (p. 87)

mummy (p. 89)
papyrus (p. 94)
pharaoh (p. 85)
scribe (p. 88)

A. Use a dictionary to find the origins of the following words. Then explain how the meaning of each word applies to Egypt and/or Nubia.

1. papyrus
2. cataract
3. scribe
4. hieroglyphics
5. delta
6. dynasty

B. Read each pair of words. Write a sentence telling how the words in each pair are related.

1. pharaoh, dynasty
2. scribe, hieroglyphics
3. delta, cataract
4. afterlife, mummy

C. Each statement below contains one or more key terms from the chapter. Decide whether the statement is correct or incorrect. Give reasons to support your decision using information in the chapter.

1. Because nearly all Egyptians considered the <u>dynasty</u> to be godlike, they buried it with great care.
2. Colorful <u>hieroglyphics</u> written on the temple walls explained how the <u>pharaoh</u> defeated his enemies.
3. The Egyptians' belief in an <u>afterlife</u> resulted in the construction of the pyramids and the practice of making <u>mummies</u>.
4. For more than 1,000 years, <u>scribes</u> tried but failed to decipher the writing system of ancient Egypt.

Exploring Concepts

A. Compare and contrast Egypt and Nubia by copying and completing the following chart.

	Egypt	Nubia
Major resources		
Customs and beliefs		
Contributions		

B. Answer each question with information from the chapter.

1. Why do historians know more about Egyptian civilization after 3000 B.C. than before that time?
2. Why did powerful leaders emerge in the Nile Valley?
3. Why did the Greek historian Herodotus call Egypt "the gift of the Nile"?
4. What effect did trade have on the history of Nubia?
5. Why did the Egypt-Nubia border shift so many times over the years?
6. The Assyrians and, later, the Greeks invaded Egypt. What geographic features protected Egypt from invaders, and what features made it open to invaders?
7. Why were historians able to learn more about ancient Egypt after the early 1800s than they had before?
8. Why did the Egyptians mummify the dead before burial?
9. How did religion influence the Egyptians?
10. Why does Imhotep "represent the genius of Egypt"?

Reviewing Skills

Using what you learned about Egyptian art on pages 96 and 97, evaluate the Egyptian painting on page 90. What do you think was the painting's purpose? What are the people in the painting doing? What are they carrying? What does the painting tell you about the history of Egypt and Nubia?

Using Critical Thinking

1. Historians have a wealth of information about the Egyptians who lived in ancient times. Yet they know much less about the culture of the ancient Nubians. How might this lack of information be explained? Explain your reasoning.

2. On the plain of Giza, various Egyptian pharaohs ordered and supervised the building of four enormous stone structures. The largest, the Great Pyramid, is 40 stories high and covers an area the size of seven city blocks. What were some of the factors that enabled the pharaohs to erect such impressive monuments?

3. Egypt's customs were so powerful that they influenced other cultures. What U.S. customs do you think have influenced other cultures around the world? Do you think that U.S. customs have had a good or bad effect on other cultures? Give examples to support your answer.

4. Although Egypt tried to "Egyptianize" Nubia, Nubian rulers did not force the Egyptians to follow Nubian customs. Instead, the Nubians adopted many Egyptian ideas and helped to bring back forgotten parts of Egypt's own culture. What do you think this reveals about the Nubians?

Preparing for Citizenship

1. **WRITING ACTIVITY** Ancient Egypt and Nubia each influenced the culture of the other. Other cultures have influenced the culture of the United States. Describe a custom of your family or a family you know and explain its origin.

2. **COLLECTING INFORMATION** The Egyptians believed that "to speak the name of the dead is to make him alive again." Thus, they built great temples and pyramids, hoping that the monuments would cause the pharaohs' names to be remembered. Over the years, the people in your community may have erected monuments, statues, or plaques to honor people and to keep their memory alive. Find such a monument, describe it, and explain why it was erected. Does it reveal anything interesting about the culture of the people who built it or of those whom it honors? If possible, include a photograph or drawing of the monument with your description.

3. **GROUP ACTIVITY** In ancient times Egypt got many natural resources from Nubia. Today the United States imports from other countries many of the natural resources on which its industries depend. In a small group, make a list of resources the United States imports and the countries from which the resources come. Then draw a map of the world, and label the countries and the resources that they export to the United States.

4. **COLLABORATIVE LEARNING** Migration is an important part of the history of the United States, just as it was in the early development of the Nile Valley. In small groups prepare a presentation on a migrant culture in the United States. Have one person research and take notes on the reasons that the migration took place. Have another find photographs, artifacts, or articles from that time period. The group can choose a representative, or the entire group can present your findings to the class.

99

Chapter 5

Two Early Asian Civilizations

Like the brightly colored cloth woven in India for thousands of years, the culture of India has been fashioned from many strands. India accepted peoples and ideas from many places. China, surrounded by towering mountains and vast deserts, has a culture that grew with little outside influence. Both civilizations developed traditions that live on into the present.

More than 4,000 years ago, people in the Indus Valley were weaving cotton cloth. Hand looms like this are used today in some parts of India.

Great Hindu poems include a tale about a hero named Rama, one form of a Hindu deity. Indian children today still act out this tale.

2500	2000		1000

2500 B.C.

c. 2500–1750 B.C. The Indus Valley civilization flourishes along the Indus River.

c. 1766–1122 B.C. The Shang dynasty, one of the earliest known dynasties of China, rules the land. The shells of cowries, a kind of snail that lives in warm seas, serve as a form of money during this time.

Buddhism spread from India to China during the Han dynasty. This Chinese bronze sculpture shows the Buddha in a posture of meditation.

B.C.	A.D.	500	1000	1500

c. 124 B.C. A university is established to train Chinese government officials. Civil service examinations, stamped with seals like the one above, later come into use.

A.D. 960–1279 Sung dynasty rules in China. The compass is invented.

A.D. 1500

L E S S O N 1

Ancient India

THINKING FOCUS

What are the ancient origins of Indian civilization?

Key Terms

- tributary
- caste
- untouchable

▼ *Mohenjo-Daro was once a busy city filled with as many as 40,000 people. In addition to carefully planned streets and a well-designed sewer system, this ancient city had many large houses.*

The sun beats down on this dusty place. Temperatures climb to 120°F. Very little grows here, even though the Indus River flows just a few miles away. Yet in this near-desert in 1922, Indian archaeologist R. D. Banerji found small stone seals, or stamps used to make marks in soft clay or wax. He guessed that the seals, carved with writing and images of animals, had been made by people of an ancient civilization. How could the animals on the seals—a tiger, buffalo, and rhinoceros—have lived here? Indeed, how could a civilization have existed here at all?

To find out, scientists began in 1924 to dig at this site, a ruined city called Mohenjo-Daro (*moh hehn joh DAHR oh*). Using hand scoops and brushes, the scientists removed the dust and dirt that covered the ruins. Ancient tools, pots, and even toys were brought to light. What they found confirmed Banerji's hunch, but on a greater scale than he imagined. The city was thousands of years older than any discovered before in India. Mohenjo-Daro was thriving as long ago as 2500 B.C.

Archaeologists do not know what finally ended life in Mohenjo-Daro. Was it an earthquake? A flood? An invasion? Or was it deforestation? There is some evidence for each of these. Perhaps a combination of them brought the city down.

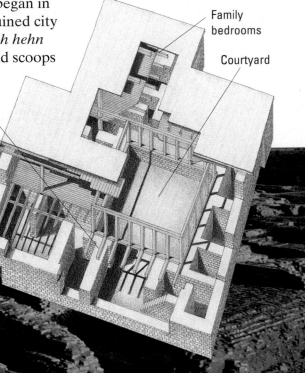

Family bedrooms

Courtyard

Wells

A Great River Civilization

Historians believe Mohenjo-Daro was the southern center of a widespread civilization. The northern center was Harappa, about 400 miles away on a tributary of the Indus River. A **tributary** is a stream or river that feeds into a larger stream or river. About 70 other sites have been discovered in the Indus Valley. They are scattered across a vast plain about three times the size of California.

These sites are part of the same civilization. The buildings, streets, and sewers were made in the same way. Even the baked bricks used in construction are the same size.

The cities were laid out in a grid pattern, with streets crossing at right angles to one another. The two major cities had a large fortresslike building, which may have been as high as five stories. The building contained a place to store grain, an assembly hall, and a public bath. These public baths were similar to those found in Indian cities today.

In ancient times the Indus River often flooded. The flood waters left behind a rich soil in which crops such as wheat, barley, rice, and cotton grew well.

The Indus Valley also had enough rainfall for farming. The strong monsoon winds of Asia created a regular wet season. See A Closer Look in Chapter 14 to find out more about monsoons. ■

Across Time & Space

The Indus Valley is no longer a well-watered plain. The Indus River passes through a dry, desertlike landscape. This area might have been altered by a change in climate, along with deforestation and overgrazing.

■ *What geographic features made possible the growth of a civilization in the Indus Valley?*

An Ancient Trade Network

At sites both in the Indus Valley and far from it, archaeologists have uncovered evidence of an ancient trade network. Once more, clues have come from the seals.

Evidence of Trade

Historians think that merchants used seals, like the one shown on page 104, to mark their property. The seals were made of a soft stone called steatite *(STEE uh tyt)*, on which pictures of animals were carved. Above the animals is writing that has never been decoded and that is unlike any other ancient writing.

Some of these seals turned up in ancient Southwest Asian cities. Archaeologists date a seal found in the Sumerian city of Ur to about 2200 B.C. What goods might have been traded by the people of the Indus Valley with Southwest Asia? Once again, a seal gives a clue. On the back of one of the seals is the imprint of coarse cloth. At this time the Indus Valley people were spinning and weaving cotton. Perhaps they exported cloth to Mesopotamia. The

▲ *These flat-bottomed boats are used today for fishing in the Indus River. Boats similar to these may have been used by the people of the ancient Indus Valley civilization.*

103

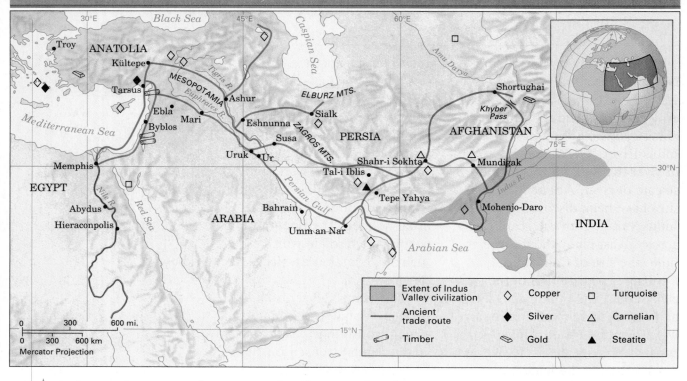

▲ *As the map shows, many of the trade routes used by people of the Indus Valley civilization followed waterways.*

▼ *Beads and seals from the Indus Valley were found as far away as Mesopotamia.*

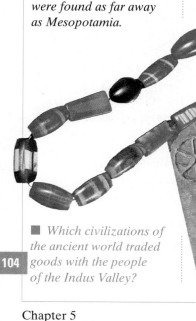

■ *Which civilizations of the ancient world traded goods with the people of the Indus Valley?*

large granaries discovered at the Indus Valley sites suggest that the people grew more grain than they needed to feed themselves. Perhaps they shipped wheat and barley to Southwest Asia also.

Other Trading Goods

Jewelry and beads are other clues archaeologists use to work out puzzles about the past. Shown below is a necklace made of glazed pottery beads from the Indus Valley. Similar beads have been found in Syria. Other beads from the Indus Valley have been found in Sumerian sites.

Neither the ocean to the south nor the mountains to the north were barriers to Indus Valley traders. At Lothal, an Indus Valley site near the Arabian Sea, archaeologists have found the ruins of a dockyard. From there, ships could have sailed up the Persian Gulf to Mesopotamia. By means of overland caravans, the Indus Valley people obtained gemstones and metals from Iraq, Iran, Afghanistan, and central Asia.

At Harappa archaeologists have found metal pins, ax heads, and vases from Southwest Asia. At Lothal they have dug up a seal that most likely came from the area of the Persian Gulf.

The Indus Valley civilization came to an end around 1750 B.C. One of its contributions is still important to us. The next time you put on a T-shirt, remember that cotton cloth was one of this civilization's gifts to the world. ■

Arrival of the Aryans

No one knows what happened to the people of the Indus Valley civilization. Many factors may have brought an end to the civilization. Soon another group of people, who called themselves Aryans *(AIR ee uhnz),* or "nobles," moved into the Indus Valley region from the north. They brought with them a new language, Sanskrit; new Gods; and a new social structure. Their arrival changed the course of Indian history.

Indo-European Migrations

Long before they reached India, the Aryans had lived in the grasslands near the Black and Caspian seas. They were part of a group we call the Indo-Europeans.

The Indo-Europeans were people who herded cattle, goats, and sheep. They had tamed the horse and developed a chariot that had sturdy wheels with spokes. These speedy chariots allowed them to move freely over large areas and to wage war more effectively than warriors on foot.

About 2000 B.C. conditions in their homeland caused the Indo-Europeans to go on the move. Perhaps their pasture lands had dried out. Or perhaps their population had grown so large that they needed more land. Whatever the reason, huge numbers of Indo-Europeans began migrating to new regions. Some groups went west and south. Others, like the Aryans, moved southeast toward India.

By around 1500 B.C., the first Aryans had found their way through the high passes in the Hindu Kush. The Hindu Kush is a mountain range along the northwestern edge

of India. The passes there would serve as highways for other migrating and invading peoples over the next 3,000 years.

The Aryan Religion

The early Aryans lived in houses built of bamboo or wood, which decayed and left no evidence for later archaeologists. The Aryans, however, did leave a poetic record. Their beliefs and daily life are recorded in the Vedas *(VAY duhs),* a collection of sacred hymns and poems. The oldest collection, the Rig-Veda, existed by 1500 B.C. The Vedas were not written down, but were passed on through an oral tradition.

The Vedas are the main source of information about the Aryan people and their way of life. For this reason, historians call the time in India from about 1500 to 600 B.C. the Vedic period.

The Aryans brought with them to India a religion based on many Gods. Priests worshiped by sacrificing food and drink to these Gods in

Aryans made their way through passes like this one in the Hindu Kush.

Across Time & Space

As groups of Indo-Europeans moved into new homelands, they took their language with them. Language experts have discovered that many of the languages spoken in Europe and India today have the same root: the language spoken by Indo-Europeans. These include German, Greek, Indo-Iranian, and the Romance languages such as French, Spanish, and Italian.

Two Early Asian Civilizations

A Vedic fire is still used at upper-caste Hindu weddings. During the ceremony, the Brahmin chants verses from the Vedas.

a sacred fire. To keep the earth's natural forces in balance, Aryan priests fed the ritual fires with melted butter and sang Vedic hymns to the Gods. Because rituals played an important role in their religion, priests became very powerful in Aryan society.

A New Social System

The Aryans introduced into India a new social system made up of four *varnas,* or classes, of people. At the top were the priests, or Brahmins. Next were the ruler and his warriors. The third class were merchants and farmers, while the fourth class consisted of servants.

Only the males of the top three classes were allowed to study the Vedas. They were called the "twice

■ *What do the Vedas reveal about Aryan society and religion?*

born" because they had a second, ritual birth, after which they began their studies.

Each of the classes contributed something important to the society. Priests performed religious rituals. Kings and warriors ruled and protected the society. The third class of merchants and farmers supplied food, clothing, and other goods. The fourth class served the others.

Within each class were subgroups, called *jatis.* A person was born into a *jati* and stayed there his whole lifetime. He married within his subgroup and did the same kind of work as all the others in that *jati.* The Portuguese later gave the name caste system to this social structure. Today, **caste** means a unit into which a person is born and cannot change.

The Aryans were very concerned with ritual cleanliness and ranked jobs according to their purity. The people who performed the dirtiest tasks, such as dealing with dead bodies, fell completely outside the social system. They were known as **untouchables,** because people believed that their impurity could be transferred through touch.

The caste system has continued in India up to modern times. However, as you will read in Chapter 14, Indian reformers have worked to correct some of the injustices of the caste system. ■

R E V I E W

1. **FOCUS** What are the ancient origins of Indian civilization?
2. **GEOGRAPHY** Why is the Indus Valley civilization considered a great river civilization?
3. **CULTURE** What was the caste system of Aryan society? How did it influence the Aryan way of life?
4. **CRITICAL THINKING** Since the Vedas were composed by Aryans, the information in them is presented from an

Aryan point of view. Why is it important to consider point of view?

5. **ACTIVITY** On a map of Europe and Asia, locate the original home of the Aryan people. Trace their route through the Khyber Pass, one of the passes in the Hindu Kush. Show how Aryan settlements spread from the Indus River down to the Ganges River Valley.

Identifying Patterns

Here's Why

Writers use different patterns to organize what they write. The chart below explains some of the most common patterns of organization: chronological, spatial, cause and effect, and compare and contrast.

The chart also gives you clue words to help you identify each pattern. Recognizing these patterns when you read can help you improve your understanding of the material.

Here's How

Find the section on Indo-European Migrations on page 105. It is an example of a chronological, or time-related, pattern. This section describes events in the order in which they happened. Notice that dates are used: "about 2000 B.C." and "by around 1500 B.C." Words that describe time relationships such as "the first" are clues, too.

A cause-and-effect pattern shows which events made other events happen. The story on page 102 is an example of a cause-and-effect pattern. We learn that stone seals found in the near-desert of the Indus Valley led archaeologists to discover the ruins of Mohenjo-Daro and the ancient civilization that once thrived there.

Spatial patterns describe people, places, things, and events. A spatial pattern gives you a visual "snapshot" of what is being described. The description of the Indus Valley in the first paragraph of page 103 is an example of spatial organization.

Compare-and-contrast patterns can show similarities or differences between two subjects. They may show both similarities and differences. In A Great River Civilization, on page 103, the writer shows similarities between the ancient cities of Mohenjo-Daro and Harappa.

Writers use many patterns to organize their work. Often, especially in long passages, you will find a combination of several patterns.

Try It

Turn to the first paragraph of the section A New Social System on page 106. Tell what organizational pattern is used in this paragraph. How did you identify the pattern?

Apply It

Find an article in a magazine or a newspaper that uses one of the organizational patterns explained on this page. Name the pattern and explain how you identified it.

How to Identify Patterns of Organization in Your Reading

Pattern	Definition	Some Clue Words
Chronological	Explains the order in which events happened	as soon as, at last, first, second, third, next, then, before, after, finally, while, by, until
Spatial	Describes people, places, things, or events	above, across, beside, behind, below, beyond, east, farther, in front of, inside, lower, near, next to, north, outside, south, under, within, west; names of places
Cause and effect	Tells what events caused others	as a result, because, consequently, if, nevertheless, since, so, therefore, then
Compare and contrast	Describes similarities or differences between two or more events, ideas, people, and places	although, by contrast, by comparison, compared to, relatively, similarly, unlike

107

LESSON 2

Hinduism and Buddhism

What are the origins and main teachings of Hinduism and Buddhism?

Key Terms

- Hinduism
- reincarnation
- Buddhism

➤ *Lamps burn brightly when Hindus mark their new year. The celebration falls in October or November, according to a lunar calendar.*

All over India on this night when there is no moon, women light hundreds of small oil lamps. They place them in windows and in rows along the rooftops of their houses.

Members of merchant castes say that the lamps are meant to light the way into their homes for Lakshmi, the Goddess of wealth and good fortune. In Bengal, a state in eastern India, the lamps are lit for the Goddess the people call Kali. Still other Hindus say that the lamps honor Rama, who on this night returned to his palace after 14 years in exile.

In some parts of India, this is the first day of the Hindu New Year. It is also the fourth day of Divali, one of the most important Hindu festivals of the year. It is a time for visiting, exchanging gifts, and wearing new clothes.

The Hindu Way of Life

The celebration of Divali begins in late October. Throughout India, Hindus observe this festival of lights in ways that are both similar and different. The deities they worship appear in many different forms and are known by many different names. Yet Hindus all share certain beliefs, values, and traditions. Some of these go back to Vedic times or even earlier. Other beliefs and practices are more recent in origin.

It is this mix of old and new that is **Hinduism,** the major religion in India today. Hinduism is also a distinctive way of life for over 700 million followers.

The Search for Truth

As the Vedic period drew to a close in about 600 B.C., some people in India began to ask difficult questions. Why are some people born into a life of ease and others into poverty? What happens after death? How should we live our lives before death? The answers to these questions helped shape Hinduism as it is known today.

Common to all Hindus is the search for truth, for a true understanding of what the world is really like. Hindus believe that the world they live in now is not real but only *maya,* illusion. *Maya* keeps the individual soul, *atman,* from knowing the world soul, Brahman. The goal of life, then, is to become free of *maya,* and to be united with the world soul, Brahman.

Hinduism teaches three ways to achieve this goal. One way is through devotion, such as worship of a personal deity; another way is through wisdom; and a third way is through right actions. However, to reach the goal by any of these three ways requires a very long time—more than any one lifetime provides. From this idea developed the belief in **reincarnation,** the rebirth of the soul in a new body after death.

In Hinduism, how quickly the soul advances toward freedom depends on the karma that a person has built up. Karma is the sum of all the good and bad actions of the soul's previous lives. Hindus believe that everything a person does influences the status of that person's current or future life.

Gods and Goddesses

You could be a Hindu and work toward the goal of spiritual freedom, and not believe in any personal God at all. However, most Hindus are helped toward their goal by worshiping a personal God. Hindu Gods are usually a form of Vishnu, Shiva, or of the mother Goddess, Shakti.

Usually a person worships the same deity as other members of his or her family, caste, or community. All Hindus, however, are free to choose their own personal deity.

The stories and art of India are rich with tales of Gods and Goddesses and of the various forms they have taken to appear on earth. Vishnu is said to have appeared already in nine of his ten different forms. Some of these include a fish; a man-lion; Rama, the ideal human; and Krishna, the divine cowherder.

Temple and Family Worship

Brahmin priests perform temple worship services called *pujas.* Priests also conduct major religious ceremonies, such as weddings.

Most Hindus, however, keep images of their personal deities in their homes and perform the daily *pujas* themselves. In a *puja,* the deity is treated much like an honored guest. The God or Goddess is first woken up from sleep. Then it is offered water, perfume, flowers, and food.

Life's Four Stages

Hindus who choose the path of right action are encouraged to

▲ *The Hindu God Shiva dances on the body of a demon to free the world of illusion. The surrounding circle of fire represents the cycle of creation, destruction, and rebirth.*

How Do We Know?

RELIGION *We know about Hindu Gods, myths, and religious duties from two long poems called epics. The Mahabharata is the story of a war between two families. The Ramayana is the account of Rama's exile in the forest and of the capture of his wife, Sita, by a demon king.*

carry out the duties of their caste. They are also guided by an ideal of life that is divided into four stages. In the first stage, a young boy studies the Vedas with a teacher. In the second stage of life, a young man marries and becomes a householder.

In the third stage, the householder puts aside everything that he owns and retires to the forest to meditate, or reflect. During the fourth stage, a man gives up everything, including caste identity, to move about the country. ■

■ *In what ways is Hinduism a complete way of life?*

Teachings of Buddhism

The story of another great world religion, Buddhism, begins in a small kingdom in northern India about 2,500 years ago. The king had a son named Siddhartha Gautama *(sihd DAHR tah GAW tah mah).* At the time of his birth, wise men predicted that the child would grow up to be either a great king or a great spiritual leader.

The king did not want his son to lead the life of a wandering holy man, so he tried to protect the prince from any signs of suffering. No sick, old, or poor people were allowed in the palace or in the streets near the palace.

In the end his father's efforts failed. While away from the palace,

➤ *The young Siddhartha (center) is pictured in the royal palace in this modern copy of an Ajanta cave painting. Near Ajanta, India, cave walls are covered with paintings, some dating back to about 200 B.C., around 300 years after Siddhartha lived.*

the young prince saw an old man. Later, he saw a sick man, and on another day a dead man. Siddhartha realized that he, too, would grow old and die. Was there no way to escape life's sorrows?

Then the prince saw a wandering holy man who owned only a single food bowl. In spite of his great age and poverty, the holy man seemed content. Siddhartha decided to give up his riches, to leave the palace, and to search for a way to end suffering in the world.

The story of Siddhartha's birth and childhood may be legend. However, a prince by that name did live in what is now India, from about 563 to 483 B.C. Siddhartha wandered throughout the land, seeking truth by which to live. In time, these ideas became known as **Buddhism,** a major religion of the world today.

Siddhartha's Search

Siddhartha's search for truth took place at a time of great religious activity on the Indian subcontinent. Many others were asking similar questions: Why do people suffer? How can suffering be avoided?

On his journey, Siddhartha met great religious teachers of the day, but he found no answers. He then decided to look within himself for wisdom. Sitting in the shade of a fig tree, he vowed not to leave until he found his answers.

After 49 days of deep thought, Siddhartha discovered the truth he sought. He believed he had found a way to escape suffering. Understanding flooded his mind like a great light. From that time on, he was called the Buddha, meaning "the enlightened one." He had reached the height of understanding that Buddhists call enlightenment.

The Buddha sent his first followers in all directions to spread the Buddhist *dharma,* or law. The Buddha traveled and taught, stopping wherever people would listen. He lived his days in peace, teaching and preaching until his death at the age of 80.

The Way of the Buddha

Following his days of deep thought beneath the fig tree, the Buddha spoke of his Four Noble Truths. These teachings give the Buddhist view on why people suffer and how suffering can be avoided. The chart on this page explains these beliefs.

The Buddha rejected many ideas of his day. He did not believe in *atman,* the individual soul of Hinduism. He had no use for Brahmin or Vedic sacrifices, which required killing animals. He also rejected the caste system, which gave people little choice about how to live their lives.

The Buddha taught that nothing in this world lasts forever. Everyone gets old, most get sick, and all die. He said that people suffer because they want what they cannot have. If they can rid themselves of their wants, he taught, then they would be free. They would be enlightened.

The Chain of Rebirth

Although they have different ideas about the soul, both Buddhists and Hindus believe in reincarnation. Good karma, collected by following Buddhism's Eightfold Path, takes a person closer to enlightenment.

The chain of birth, suffering, death, and rebirth continues until enlightenment is gained. Once enlightened, a person is finally free from further rebirth with all of its earthly suffering. Buddhists call this state nirvana. Nirvana means "blowing out," like blowing out a candle. At that moment a person wants nothing, not even to live or to die or to be reborn.

(top) The Buddha received his enlightenment beneath a sacred tree. This sculpture stands about two feet high. (below) In the Four Noble Truths, the Buddha explained his beliefs about suffering.

The Four Noble Truths
1. Human life is full of suffering and sorrow.
2. Suffering and sorrow are caused by people's greedy desires for power, pleasure, and possessions.
3. Suffering and sorrow will end when people overcome their greed.
4. People can overcome their greed and uncontrolled desires by adopting the Eightfold Path. This path gives eight ways of living a correct, or right, life.

Two Early Asian Civilizations

➤ *The Four Noble Truths and the Eightfold Path together are the heart of the Buddha's teachings.*

The Eightfold Path

Way	Description
Right view	Believing in the Four Noble Truths and the Eightfold Path
Right resolve	Making a firm decision to live according to the Eightfold Path
Right speech	Speaking in a manner that doesn't harm others: not gossiping, lying, or using angry words
Right conduct	Acting in a way that doesn't harm others: not killing, not stealing, and also not acting selfishly
Right livelihood	Earning a living in a way that doesn't harm others
Right effort	Striving to get rid of any evil within oneself
Right mindfulness	Paying attention to every state of the body, mind, and feeling
Right concentration	Thinking deeply for answers to problems

The Three Jewels

Buddhists say that their tradition is made up of three parts, called the Three Jewels. These are the Buddha; his *dharma,* or teachings; and the *sangha (SAHN guh),* or religious community. The *sangha* is made up of monks, nuns, and everyday followers.

Gradually Buddhist missionaries spread their beliefs beyond India. They first traveled to the island of Ceylon, now called Sri Lanka. By about A.D. 650, Buddhism had reached China, Korea, Japan, Tibet, Burma, and other areas of Southeast Asia.

Although Buddhism became less popular in India over the years, it gained followers in other countries. Today more than 300 million people throughout the world are Buddhists. ■

➤ *The image of the Buddha is identified by several symbolic marks on his body.*

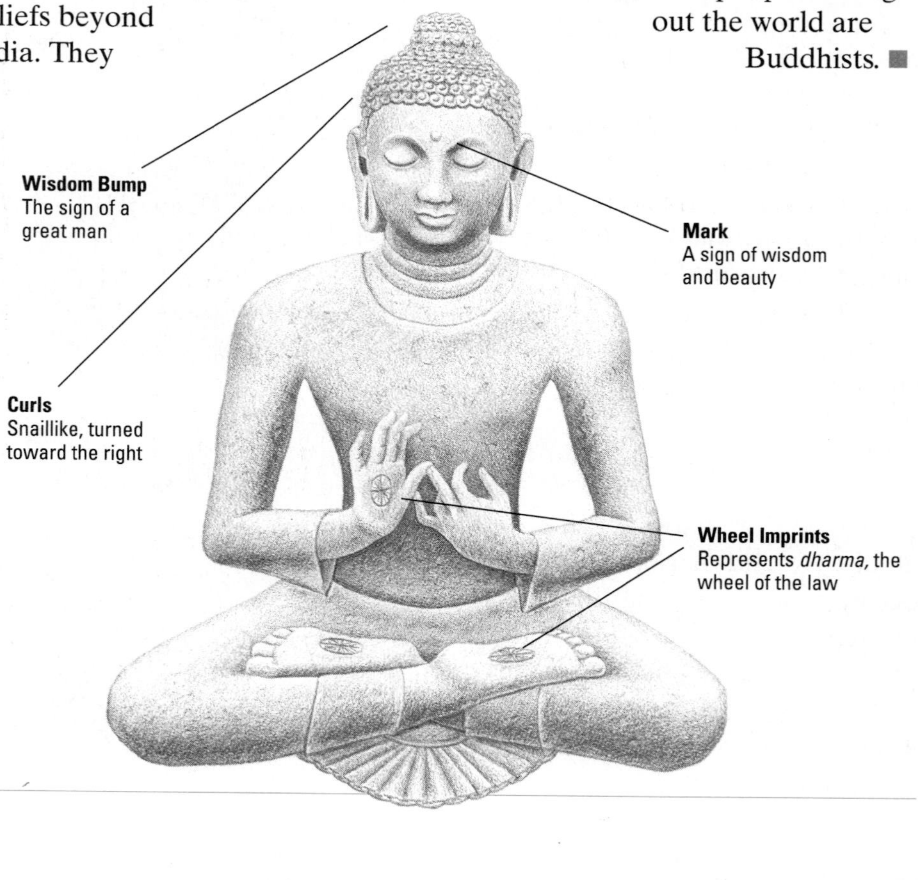

Wisdom Bump
The sign of a great man
Mark
A sign of wisdom and beauty
Curls
Snaillike, turned toward the right
Wheel Imprints
Represents *dharma,* the wheel of the law

■ *What is the Eightfold Path, and what is its importance?*

A Great Buddhist Ruler

The worldwide spread of Buddhism began with the emperor Ashoka *(ah SHOH kah)*. A faithful follower of Buddhism, he was the first ruler to send missionaries beyond India's borders.

Ashoka's Conversion

Ashoka belonged to a line of conquering kings known as the Mauryas *(MOW ree uhz)*, who ruled India from about 324 to 187 B.C. They built the first great Indian empire. It was probably the largest Indian empire in the country's history.

Soon after Ashoka came to power in 273 B.C., he went to war. He conquered Kalinga, an independent area in eastern India, in a series of bloody battles. The violence may have turned Ashoka toward Buddhism.

Ashoka's Edicts

During the rest of his rule, Ashoka sent out Buddhist missionaries. He also spelled out his beliefs in edicts, or public announcements. Ashoka had these edicts carved into rocks and pillars around the empire. Beautiful carvings like the one shown on this page often decorated the tops, or capitals, of pillars.

Rock Edict I explains Ashoka's support of *ahimsa (uh HIHM sah)*, the Buddhist belief in nonviolence. It forbids harming any humans or animals.

No living creature shall be slaughtered here. . . . Many hundreds of thousand living creatures were formerly slaughtered every day for curries in the kitchens of His Majesty. At present, when this edict on Dharma is inscribed, only three living creatures are killed daily, two peacocks and a deer. . . . In the future, not even these three animals shall be slaughtered.

The Kalinga Edict II in eastern India shows how Ashoka felt toward his people:

All men are my children. Just as I seek the welfare and happiness of my own children in this world and the next, I seek the same things for all men.

Ashoka's nonviolent style of ruling did not last. After his death, the empire broke up into little warring kingdoms. In spite of this bloodshed, the peaceful message of Buddhism continued to spread. ■

▼ *This lion capital sits atop an Ashokan pillar. India's national emblem is patterned after it.*

■ *How did Ashoka's Buddhist beliefs influence his rule?*

R E V I E W

1. **FOCUS** What are the origins and main teachings of Hinduism and Buddhism?
2. **HISTORY** What does Hinduism owe to the Vedic religion?
3. **GEOGRAPHY** Trace a map of Asia. Color areas where Buddhism had spread by A.D. 650.
4. **CRITICAL THINKING** Which groups of people in ancient India were most likely to become Buddhists?
5. **WRITING ACTIVITY** In 50 words or less, write a pillar edict as Ashoka might have done. In your edict, instruct people how to act toward other human beings and toward animals. Draw your pillar. Design a carving for its capital.

L E S S O N   3

Ancient China

Key Term

- Mandate of Heaven

➤ *High peaks, fertile plains, desert wastes—these are some of the varied landforms of China.*

*The towering heights of the Southern Mountains
Soar dizzily like a stack
    of cooking pots,
Their sides are furrowed with
    ravines and valleys. . . .
While from their folds the
    mountain streams leap and
    tumble,
Spilling out upon the level
    plains,
There they flow a thousand
    miles along smooth beds,
Their banks lined with dikes
Blanketed with green orchids.*

From "The Shang-lin Park"

Imagine traveling through a landscape like this. Your trip would be a long one, and the sights would be incredible. Over this vast distance, you'd see huge mountains, powerful rivers, and sweeping,

green plains. These are some of the features of China, as the poet Sima Xiangru *(suh mah shahng roo)* described them more than 2,000 years ago.

Surrounding China are mountains, deserts, and the Pacific Ocean. These natural barriers set the ancient Chinese apart from other cultures. Thinking they were at the center of the world, they called their land the Middle Kingdom. Dating back over 4,000 years, China is the world's oldest continuous civilization.

China's Geography

Look carefully at the physical map of China on this page. You can see that China is a vast and varied land. Different landforms and climates cause ways of life to differ from one region to another.

The Himalayas in southwestern China are the world's highest mountains. Grasslands as well as barren deserts stretch across north and northwest China. In the southwest is Tibet, a land of high-altitude plateaus and mountain ranges where little grows. The climate here is dry and very cold.

The Plateau of Tibet is the source of the Huang He *(hwahng hoh),* one of China's major rivers. On the map, trace the Huang He, which means "Yellow River," across northeastern China. Notice how low and flat the land becomes as the river nears the ocean. This plain contains rich soil, thanks to the river floods.

Across central and southern China flows the Chang Jiang *(chahng jyahng).* The basin of this river, called the Yangtze *(YANG see)* in English, is another area of rich farmland. Farmers use the river to send their crops to Pacific ports.

Eastern China is much better suited to farming than western China. In addition to fertile soil, eastern China benefits from rains brought by the monsoons of southern Asia. ■

▼ *As the map shows, nature built a wall around China with mountains, plateaus, seas, and deserts.*

■ *Why is eastern China better suited to farming than western China?*

China: Physical

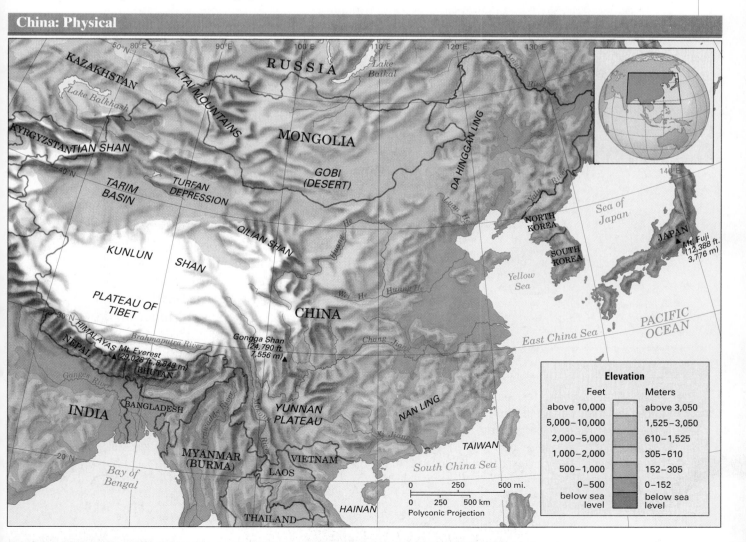

Patterns in Chinese History

As in Mesopotamia and India, civilization in China started beside a river. The Shang, the first dynasty to leave historical records, ruled a large area of eastern China between the Yellow and Yangzte rivers. At this time, Shang China was farmland, but there were also towns and walled cities. Shang rule lasted from about 1766 to 1122 B.C.

The Rise and Fall of Dynasties

How did Shang power come to an end? The answer to this question shows a pattern that repeated itself many times in Chinese history. Shang rulers feared raids from people outside their territory. For protection the Shang rulers sought the help of the Zhou *(joh)* people, who lived west of Shang territory, in patrolling the borders. The Zhou people soon came to believe that Shang rulers were corrupt and immoral, and conflict erupted between the two forces. Eventually, the Zhou leader overthrew the Shang king and started his own dynasty.

Chinese history has gone through many changes of dynasty. A new dynasty usually rose after a period of civil war and unrest. When a new ruling family came to power, it often built up the economy and strengthened Chinese power along the northern and western frontiers.

As the dynasty aged, the central government weakened. Groups along the frontiers took advantage of this weakness. Sometimes they joined with local lords to overthrow a dynasty.

The Mandate of Heaven

Starting with the Zhou dynasty, the Chinese have believed that their emperor ruled through the **Mandate of Heaven.** Heaven to them was a power that demanded right behavior and good government. Heaven gave its support, or mandate, to a good ruler. If the emperor did not rule well, he lost the Mandate of Heaven. Then he could be overthrown.

The end of a dynasty did not signal the downfall of Chinese civilization. Even though the empire went through periods of unrest, Chinese civilization was preserved as a distinct whole. ■

▼ *Shang craftworkers created this 14-inch-high bronze vessel in the shape of a man within a tiger's open jaws. No one knows whether the tiger is protecting the man or eating him. What do you think?*

■ *What was the importance of the Mandate of Heaven?*

R E V I E W

1. **FOCUS** What are some major patterns that appear throughout early Chinese history?
2. **GEOGRAPHY** Of what importance are the Huang He and Chang Jiang?
3. **HISTORY** How and why did dynasties change in China?
4. **CRITICAL THINKING** Where would you guess that most people in China live? Why?
5. **WRITING ACTIVITY** Imagine that you are an ancient Chinese ruler. Write a journal entry describing what problems you are facing as your country's leader. How would you propose to solve them?

2700   1766   1279   1800

L E S S O N 4

China's Cultural Heritage

What strange bones! In their fields, some Chinese farmers found oddly polished bones with strange markings. One man thought they came from dragons. Many Chinese believed that ground-up dragon bones could cure the sick. Knowing their value as medicine, the farmer sold all the bones he found.

Some of the bones turned up in medicine shops in Beijing. In 1899, Chinese scholars guessed that the markings were a form of ancient writing.

The designs on the bones proved to be the oldest known writing in East Asia. Yet the ancient writing was enough like modern Chinese for scholars to read nearly 1,500 words.

The bones were used as oracles, or predictors of things to come. Though meant for looking into the future, these bones make it possible for us to look back into China's ancient past.

Tracing the source of the bones led scholars all the way back to Anyang, the capital of one of China's first dynasties. The scholars were delighted. By decoding the writing on the oracle bones, they had unlocked China's past.

For about 4,000 years, the written language has helped to hold the people of China together. Though the spoken language differed from region to region, the written language was the same. Educated people throughout China used it to communicate with one another for generations.

THINKING

FOCUS

What factors have helped make China the oldest continuous civilization in the world?

Key Term

- Confucianism

◄ *The chart compares an example of oracle bone writing with its modern Chinese counterpart. Both have the same meaning: "On this day . . . it is divined whether on this . . . day it will rain—or not rain."*

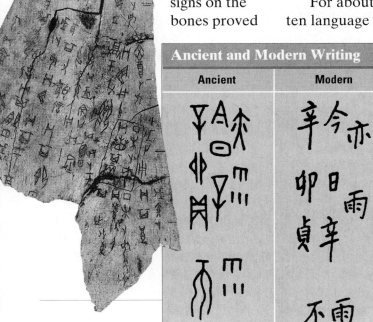

Ancient and Modern Writing

Ancient	Modern

117

Two Early Asian Civilizations

Confucianism and the Social Heritage

➤ *The brush strokes at the top represent the Chinese word for* man. *The two middle strokes represent the number* two. *When written together, these characters change to form* jen—*one person existing in harmony with another. The relationship between two people is central to Confucianism.*

Since ancient times, respect for elders, ancestors, and the past have been key parts of Chinese culture. These values have helped hold Chinese civilization together for many thousands of years. They have been passed on by rituals and by the writings of China's great thinkers. Perhaps the best known is K'ung Ch'iu *(kung chee oo),* or Confucius, as he is known in the West.

Confucius the Teacher

Confucius was born in 551 B.C. and was one of the best-educated men in China. He taught many new ideas on how to improve government and society. These ideas, known as **Confucianism,** still influence Chinese thought after almost 2,500 years.

Confucianism isn't a religion, but it gives people a code of right and wrong behavior. A central idea of Confucianism is *jen. Jen* means "human-heartedness," or loving others. In order to practice *jen,* Confucius said, "Do not do to others what you do not wish yourself."

Five Basic Relationships

Confucius taught that there are five basic relationships. They are those between ruler and subject, father and son, older and younger brother, husband and wife, and friend and friend. In each relationship, people should be sincere, loyal, and respectful.

Three of Confucius's basic relationships are among family members. The family has always been the most important unit in Chinese society. Confucius believed that children should respect their parents at all times.

Over the centuries, Chinese homes have reflected Confucius's ideas about the importance of the family. Children would live with their parents and grandparents and perhaps even aunts and uncles. At the age of 15 or 16, a son might bring his new wife into the family home. A married daughter would move to her husband's home. Family members were buried near the home, and their descendants made offerings to their spirits.

Rulers and Their Subjects

Confucius used the family as a model for how the rest of society should work. A ruler, he believed, should act like a good father. Ruled by a wise and good leader, people

▼ *The family has been central to Chinese life throughout its history. This painting shows a family giving thanks before its family shrine.*

The Emperor's Tomb

Workers digging at Lintong, China, in 1974 discovered a huge buried army. For more than 2,000 years, it stood in an underground chamber, ready for battle. Over 6,000 life-size warriors and horses, made of sculpted clay, guarded the nearby tomb of Qin Shi huangdi, China's first emperor. The entire tomb site has not yet been dug up. It may hide many other treasures of his empire.

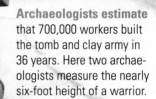

Who needs a clay army? The emperor united China through warfare. Guards protected him from attack. They may have been the models for his clay warriors, meant to protect him after he died.

Archaeologists estimate that 700,000 workers built the tomb and clay army in 36 years. Here two archaeologists measure the nearly six-foot height of a warrior.

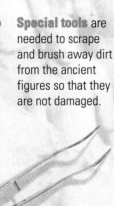

Special tools are needed to scrape and brush away dirt from the ancient figures so that they are not damaged.

221–206 B.C. Qin Dynasty; connection of Great Wall

| 1600 | 1200 | | 400 |

c.1766 – 1122 B.C. Shang Dynasty; development of writing

206 B.C.–A.D.220 Han Dynasty; invention of paper

would be wise and good, too.

Confucius believed in traditional Chinese values such as obedience and order, but his ideas about government were new. Instead of laws and punishment, Confucius thought that government should be based on goodness. He said, "If the ruler himself is upright, all will go well, even though he does not give orders."

The Civil Service

Laws, however, were an accepted part of Chinese civilization. To carry them out, the emperor had a huge body of government workers called the civil service. Confucius taught that government officials should earn their jobs through education and talent. They should not use family connections to get their jobs, as so many did. He gave this advice: "Don't worry about not being in office; worry about qualifying yourself for office."

Many years after Confucius, China set up a system of examinations by which civil servants, or government workers, were chosen. To pass the exams, students had to read and write well. They also had to know the writings of the Confucian classics.

The civil service was an important unifying force in Chinese history. In spite of rebellions, invasions, and changing dynasties, the civil service helped preserve Chinese civilization. This class of well-educated people helped China produce some of the most dazzling achievements of the ancient world. ■

What contributions did the teachings of Confucius make to Chinese civilization?

Chinese Achievements

Take a good look at this book. In every way, it seems to belong to modern Western civilization. Yet it is in your hands today because of several key Chinese inventions. The Chinese are responsible for many achievements that have changed the course of world history.

Silk, Paper, and Printing

Did you ever stop to think what people wrote on before there was paper? In ancient China, scribes used soft brushes to copy words, character by character, onto pieces of silk. Silk was made from the cocoons of silkworms. How to make silk was one of China's best-guarded secrets.

According to legend, Emperor Ho-ti was tired of writing on silk. To please him, a courtier figured out how to make paper from the inner bark of the mulberry tree in about A.D. 105.

Paper replaced silk for many written documents, but painting characters still took a lot of time.

120

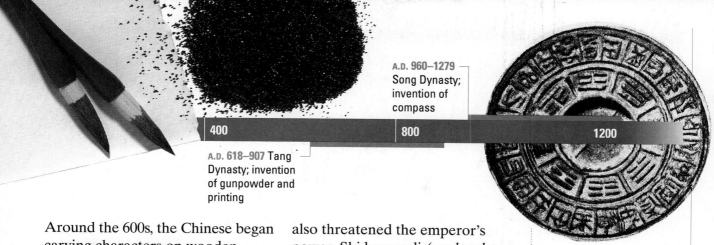

A.D. 960–1279
Song Dynasty;
invention of
compass

| 400 | 800 | 1200 |

A.D. 618–907 Tang
Dynasty; invention
of gunpowder and
printing

▲ *Trace some of the great
achievements and dynas-
ties of ancient China.*

Around the 600s, the Chinese began carving characters on wooden blocks. By applying ink to these blocks, and then pressing the blocks onto paper, the Chinese were able to print many copies quickly. Printing with wood blocks would not start in Europe until the 1400s.

Protection Against Foreigners

Some products from China began reaching Europe about 2,000 years ago. Silk was in great demand. Traders carried it over the Silk Road, from China across Asia and the Middle East to the Mediterranean. These traders, however, were not Chinese. The emperors of China did not want certain secrets to leak out. They even threatened death to anyone who told an outsider the secret of silk or gave away a silkworm.

Preserving and protecting the Middle Kingdom and its culture were of the highest importance to the rulers. They feared invasions by warlike peoples to the north and west. Invaders threatened farming, on which China depended. They

also threatened the emperor's power. Shi huang-di *(see hwahng dee)* was the first ruler to unite large parts of China. To keep out invaders and strengthen his control, he ordered a huge wall to be built in 221 B.C. (see A Closer Look on page 119).

Gunpowder

In spite of its size, the Great Wall was not very successful in keeping out invaders. Warfare was a common ingredient in Chinese history. In addition to fighting off invaders, the Chinese went through periods of fighting among themselves. The need for new weapons seemed constant.

Perhaps the most famous Chinese invention is gunpowder. By the 900s, the Chinese had figured out how to make gunpowder fuses for flamethrowers. They also invented the fire-lance, an early kind of gun. By the 1000s, the Chinese were developing gunpowder rockets, flares, fireworks, grenades, and bombs. Not for several hundred years would Europe do the same. ■

■ *How have Chinese
inventions influenced the
world beyond China's
borders?*

R E V I E W

1. **FOCUS** What factors have helped make China the oldest continuous civilization in the world?

2. **HISTORY** How did the oracle bones provide a window into China's past?

3. **ETHICS** Explain the principle of *jen* in your own words.

4. **CRITICAL THINKING** Which of the achievements of

Chinese civilization described here do you think is the most important? Why?

5. **ACTIVITY** For each of Confucius's five relationships, make up a rule that could be applied in today's world. Do you think Confucius would agree with your rules? Why or why not? Share your ideas with your class.

121

Two Early Asian Civilizations

The Great Wall

The Great Wall still snakes for thousands of miles across modern China. However, the wall that is still standing is not Shi huangdi's wall, but a later version, built during the Ming dynasty.

Had the Great Wall not already existed, Yangdi [the second Sui emperor] would certainly have conceived it. As it was, he had to be content with rebuilding it.

Robert Silverberg,
20th-century historian

Background

Records show that Yangdi's rebuilding of the Great Wall in A.D. 607 required more than one million workers. More than half of them died of overwork or fled the harsh conditions.

The original building of the Great Wall, begun in 221 B.C., also involved a huge work force. Shi huangdi, the Qin emperor who thought of this project, connected shorter walls that had been built along China's northern border centuries before. He also extended the wall for hundreds of miles. The resulting wall was and still is the longest structure on the earth.

Before beginning any massive work, such as the building of the Great Wall of China, a wise decision maker will try to weigh the benefits and the costs of the project. We can look at historical events to try to compare the benefits and the costs of building the Great Wall of China.

These coins, which were issued by Shi huangdi, were the standard currency throughout the empire at the time when the Great Wall was being built.

Benefits and Costs of the Great Wall

The most obvious benefit of building the Great Wall was protection. The wall helped prevent wandering horsemen from invading China's farms along the northern border. Also, it kept farmers living along the border from joining the nomads.

Building the Great Wall helped Shi huangdi to get rid of his enemies. He ordered them to work on distant parts of the wall. He also sent soldiers to work on the wall. As a result, the soldiers could not band together and rise up against the emperor.

However, it is estimated that building Shi huangdi's wall required more than 300,000 workers. Most of them were drafted against their will. Thousands of farmers and merchants were required to supply the workers with food, clothing, tools, and shelter. Most of these supplies never made it

to the work sites; bandits roaming the countryside robbed the supply caravans.

The work of constructing the wall was so difficult and living conditions were so harsh that thousands of workers died. Often they were buried in the wall itself. Thus, the Great Wall of China gained the gruesome title of "the world's longest cemetery."

Sturdy horses, like the one at the left, carried nomads who raided China's northern border. In response, the Great Wall was built, using labor-intensive construction methods as shown. Study the chart for a comparison of the Great Wall's long-range benefits and short-term costs.

Decision
Build Great Wall

↓

Outcomes	
• People are safer.	• Many laborers die.
• More farmers stay on farms.	• People become poorer.
• Fewer threats to emperor arise.	• Supply caravans are often attacked.

Decision Point

1. What were the benefits of constructing the Great Wall of China? What were the costs?
2. Do you think these were the only benefits and costs of the Great Wall? Where would you look to find more information about the role of the Great Wall in Chinese history?
3. Based on the information on these pages and any other information you have found, do

you think the benefits and costs of building the Great Wall balanced out? Explain.
4. Collect information from newspapers and magazines about upcoming plans for large government projects in the United States. Discuss the projected benefits and costs of each project. Decide which projects you would support and which you would oppose.

Two Early Asian Civilizations

Chapter Review

Reviewing Key Terms

Buddhism (p.110)
caste (p.106)
Confucianism (p.118)
Hinduism (p.108)

Mandate of Heaven (p.116)
reincarnation (p.109)
tributary (p.103)
untouchable (p.106)

A. Each statement below uses a key term from this chapter. Tell whether each key term is used correctly. Then explain the reason for your answer.

1. People who fell outside the caste system were called <u>untouchables</u>.
2. <u>Buddhism</u> teaches that in order to reach enlightenment, a person must do the duties of his or her caste.
3. The Chinese believed that the <u>Mandate of Heaven</u> gave the emperor unlimited power to rule; no one could ever question anything he did.
4. According to <u>Confucianism</u>, all people are equal; therefore, no one owes obedience to anyone else.

B. Use a dictionary to find the origins and the definitions of the following words. Then explain how the meaning of each word applies to India.

1. tributary
2. caste
3. reincarnation
4. untouchable
5. Hinduism

Exploring Concepts

A. In this chapter you have read about three important systems of belief in Asia. The chart below will help you compare them. Copy and complete this chart.

Belief system	Goal of life	How to achieve goal
Hinduism		
Buddhism		
Confucianism	right behavior	

B. Answer each question with information from the chapter.

1. Why were archaeologists excited about the discovery of the Mohenjo-Daro and Harappa sites in India?
2. What evidence do we have that the Indus Valley civilization was centrally planned?
3. How did its geographic location affect how people made a living in the ancient Indus Valley?
4. What do we know about the Aryans from the Vedas?
5. According to legend, why did Siddhartha Gautama give up his riches to search for a way to end suffering in the world?
6. How did geography influence the development of a distinctive Chinese culture?
7. How did China's system of writing contribute to stability in the empire?
8. What evidence can you give that the emperors of ancient China shunned the outside world?

Reviewing Skills

Use the clue words in the chart on page 107 to help you answer each of the following questions in a brief paragraph.

1. What were some of the most important events that helped to establish Chinese civilization? Use chronological organization in your answer.
2. Describe the area of China where civilization developed. Use spatial organization in developing your answer.
3. Explain why the population of China was concentrated in the area you just described. Use cause-and-effect organization in your answer.
4. How was ancient China like ancient India? How was it different? Be sure to include both comparisons and contrasts in the answer that you give.

Using Critical Thinking

1. The caste system still exists in India today, although it is not so rigid as in ancient times. Compare this kind of social organization with U.S. society today.
2. The success of crops and trade depended on the regular monsoons. What might have happened if the monsoon was early or late?
3. In the Buddha's time, priests, rulers, and warriors were in the upper classes. How might they have felt about Buddhism? Why?
4. Confucius said, "Riches and honor are what everyone desires, but if they can be gained only by doing evil, they must not be held." What do you think it would take to get government leaders to follow this advice today?
5. The emperors of ancient China did not want the rest of the world to know the secrets of making silk and paper. Do we have similar laws protecting our technology today? Do you think such laws are a good idea? Why or why not?

Preparing for Citizenship

1. **WRITING ACTIVITY** Just as archaeologists did at Mohenjo-Daro, scientists one thousand years from now may start digging up your community for evidence of a past civilization. Write a brief description of what you think they will find. Then tell how they might think these artifacts were used in the late 20th century.
2. **COLLECTING INFORMATION** Archaeologists learn about ancient life and culture by unearthing old cities and artifacts. Based on what they find, archaeologists try to piece together a picture of what life must have been like in the past. Your community has a past. Discover any traces left from its past inhabitants. You could interview older residents; research photographs, maps, and books; or study the buildings and land. Share your research with the class. Explain what you think life was once like in your community.
3. **COLLABORATIVE LEARNING** In this chapter you have read about three of the world's most important systems of belief: Hinduism, Buddhism, and Confucianism. What would each system have to say about proper conduct and attitudes in the classroom? Working with a small group of classmates, choose a different belief system. Your group should develop a list of classroom rules that reflect the values of one of the three belief systems. Here are some questions to get your group discussion started:
   (1) What is the purpose of education?
   (2) What are the teacher's duties?
   (3) What are the students' duties?
   Have a member of your group present the rules to the class. In class discussion, compare the three sets of rules. Which sets are more alike? Which rules do you think would create the best climate for learning?

Chapter 6

Early Civilizations in the Americas

The Atlantic and Pacific oceans form a vast barrier that separates the Americas from other continents. In time people settled in the Americas and developed unique ways of life that became great civilizations. Among these people were the Olmec, the Maya, the Aztecs, and the Inca.

The Mayan Temple of the Warriors at Chichén Itzá is a pyramid with a temple at the top. The statue holds a bowl, perhaps for offerings.

The Olmec sculptured enormous, stone heads that weigh up to twenty tons and stand nine feet tall.

Machu Picchu, the "lost city of the Inca," was unknown to the outside world until 1911. The llama, a relative of the camel, is the main pack animal used in the Andes.

15.000	14,500	1000	500

1000 B.C. Chavín civilization emerges in the Andes.

14,000 B.C.

This huge stone carving represented Aztec ideas of the creation of the world, the universe, and the Aztecs' role in the universe. Called the Calendar Stone, the carving was set near the Great Temple in Tenochtitlan.

1325 Aztecs build Tenochtitlan.

B.C.	A.D.		500		1000		1550

A.D. 250 Mayan civilization thrives in Mesoamerica.

A.D. 500 Teotihuacan is at its height.

A.D. 1532

L E S S O N   1

Early Americans

THINKING FOCUS

How did people first come to the Americas?

Key Terms

- glacier
- diversity
- rain forest

➤ *Clovis points, usually made of flint, a kind of quartz, were fitted onto spear shafts.*

Across Time & Space

In 1990 U.S. President George Bush and Soviet President Mikhail Gorbachev planned the Beringian Heritage International Park. The park will protect the culture of the people in the region along with wildlife and other resources.

W ho were the first Americans? Where did they come from? When did they arrive? How did they get here? Archaeologists have spent years trying to answer these questions. They look for signs of human life, such as the remains of humans, fireplaces, and tools. This search is still going on.

The earliest Americans came from Asia. They arrived by way of a land bridge that once existed between Asia and North America. In the distant past, great masses of ice, or **glaciers,** covered much of northern Europe, Asia, and North America. The glaciers held so much water that ocean depths were as much as 300 feet less than what they are today. This exposed a wide landmass between Asia and North America. Today, scientists call this area Beringia. The map on page 129 shows the location of Beringia.

The First Americans

Archaeologists disagree about the time when people first came to the Americas. Was it within the past 10,000 to 15,000 years? Was it twice that long ago? The actual time is a mystery. Scientists know that stone spearheads found near Folsom and Clovis, New Mexico, date to 11,500 years ago.

In the past 10 years, however, scientists have found signs that people may have arrived much earlier. Bones of a mammoth that may have been killed by humans have been found in a Canadian cave. These bones date to 15,500 years ago. Remains of animal bones and objects that may have been tools have been found in Brazil. The bones are 17,000 years old. In 1992 the archaeologist Richard MacNeish, in Orogrande, New Mexico, found what he thinks are signs of human life dating to 55,000 years ago. The debate about the time—and the evidence itself—continues today.

Some scientists now think that Asians came to the Americas in at least three waves. These scientists, who study language, believe that early Americans can be divided into three groups. Scientists still disagree

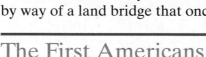

about the route people took. Some scientists think that hunters crossed the Beringian plain by an inland route, following herds of caribou and woolly mammoths. This route is shown on the map opposite. Other scientists think that people traveled by foot or in skin boats along the warmer coast of Beringia. There they could live on fish, sea mammals, and birds.

Hunting-Gathering Societies

Bands of people kept moving southward in search of food. They found mammoths, herds of bison, and other large, grazing animals on the plains of North America.

Over time, small bands of hunter-gatherers occupied an area from the Great Plains to the Andean mountains. They lived apart from one another in widely scattered areas.

The **diversity,** or variety, of plant and animal life in the various geographic regions meant that people in the regions needed different skills in order to survive. They developed belief systems and ways of living that also showed diversity.

Origins of Farming

Sometime between 7000 and 6000 B.C., people began to turn from hunting-gathering to farming. This change took place first in

Early Migration to the Americas

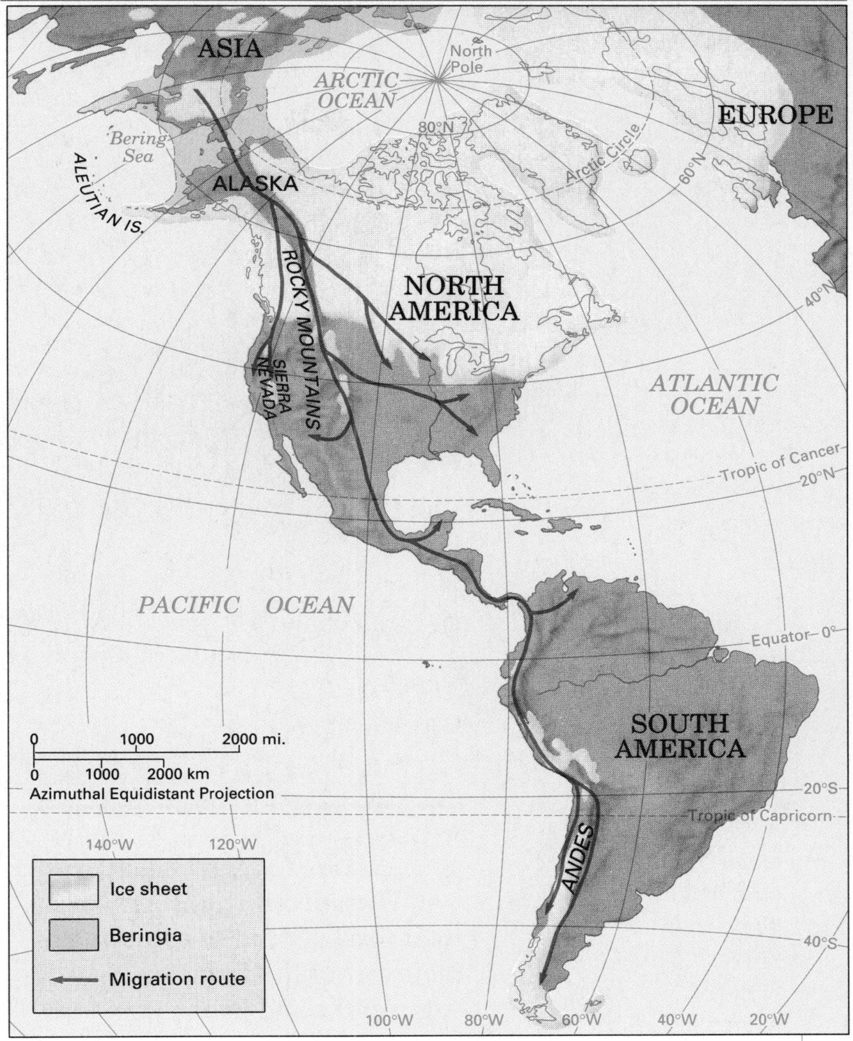

Mesoamerica, the region shown on the map on page 130. Most of Mesoamerica lies in the tropics, where the climate is hot and wet.

Along the swampy coasts of the Gulf of Mexico, farmers began to clear the land and plant crops. The first people to grow corn, however, lived in the highlands of central Mesoamerica. Corn soon became the basic food of early Mesoamericans. Just as wheat supported civilizations in the Fertile Crescent, corn supported the rise of civilizations in early Mesoamerica. ■

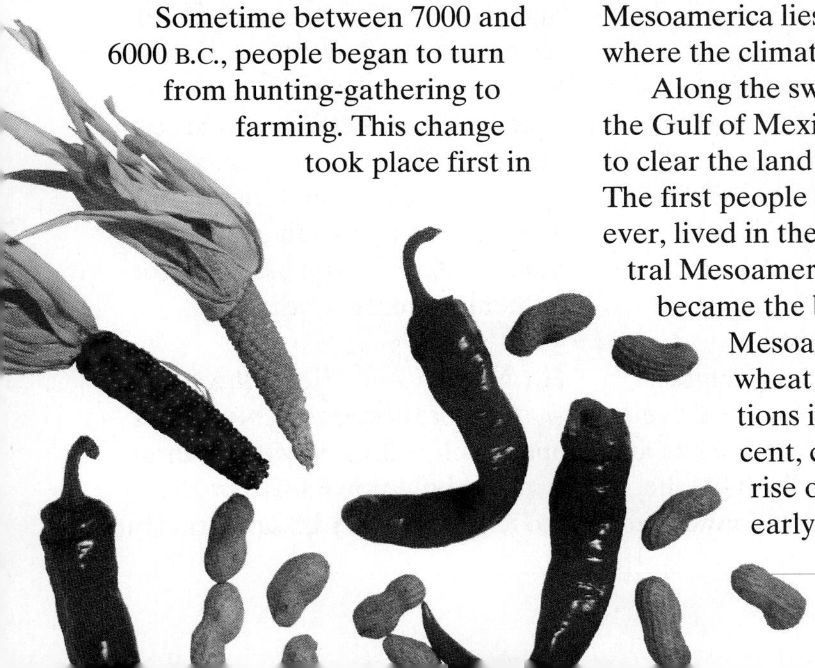

▲ *Beringia was located in the region of today's Bering Sea, as this route map shows. What became of Beringia? For help in using a route map, see page G12 of the Map and Globe Handbook.*

◄ *Early farmers in Mesoamerica learned to grow such plants as corn, chilies, and peanuts.*

■ *How did people's ways of living change in the Americas?*

Early Civilizations in the Americas

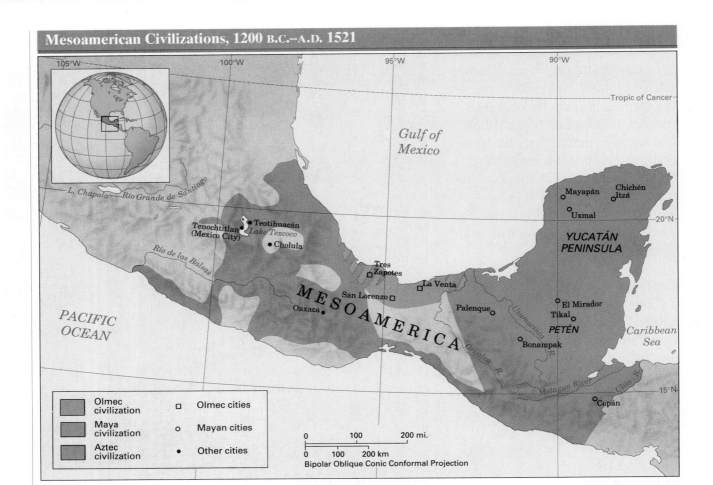

▲ *This map shows the major Mesoamerican cultures and their cities. Judging from the geography of this region, why might it be a favorable place for civilizations to develop?*

Mesoamerican Civilizations

When people begin growing their food instead of gathering it, their way of life changes. They develop crafts and live in larger settlements. Cities grew slowly in Mesoamerica, but in time they became centers of new civilizations.

➤ *The Olmec frequently used jade in their carvings. This one, which is part human and part animal, may have been a religious carving.*

The Olmec

The earliest of these civilizations was the Olmec. Its people lived in the **rain forest,** or damp jungle, along the coast of the Gulf of Mexico.

Religion was the driving force of the Olmec and the civilizations that followed. Knowing that their way of life depended on a good harvest, farmers prayed to their Gods. When rain or sunshine failed, people turned to their priests.

The Olmec built large temples where priests held religious ceremonies. Priests also developed the first calendar in the Americas. To record time and events, they used systems of counting and writing in which pictures stood for numbers and ideas.

In time the Olmec civilization declined, though archaeologists are not sure why. It remained a major influence on later civilizations.

The Maya

One of the most highly developed civilizations of Mesoamerica remained unknown for centuries. In 1839, John Lloyd Stephens came across an amazing sight as he hacked his way through the rain forests of Central America. Stephens was led by local Maya to the ruins of an ancient city. It would prove to be Copán *(koh PAHN)*, a great Mayan city. Stephens later described his feelings about the discovery.

The beauty of the sculpture, the solemn stillness of the woods, disturbed only by the scrambling of monkeys and the chattering of parrots, the desolation [loneliness] of the city, and the mystery that hung over it, all created an interest higher, if possible, than I had ever felt among the ruins of the Old World.

quoted from *Incidents of Travel in Central America, Chiapas, and Yucatán*

The Mayan civilization flourished from about A.D. 250 to 900. The map on page 130 shows its location. For the present-day countries of this region, see the Atlas map on page 686.

Mayan Achievements

Like the Olmec, the Maya built huge religious centers with pyramid temples, palaces, and plazas. Colorful murals adorned the rooms, and sculptures decorated the outside walls. At the height of Mayan civilization, at least 100 cities dotted the region.

By observing the sun and the moon, Mayan priests perfected two calendars. One was a 365-day calendar that kept track of the seasons for planting and harvesting. The other, a 260-day calendar, recorded the times for religious ceremonies.

The Maya also developed a system of numbers that was similar to the Arabic system that we use. In their writing the Maya used hieroglyphics, with symbols standing for ideas. The Maya were great artists, too. Paintings on the walls of their palaces and temples show vivid scenes of their lives.

For many years the meaning of these glyphs remained a mystery. In recent years, however, scholars have translated them. The translations have finally given scholars a written history of the Maya. John Lloyd Stephens had sensed correctly the brilliant and complex civilization that lay within the ruins he saw. ■

▲ *Chichén Itzá, one of the last great Mayan cities, is known for its beautiful temples, such as this Temple of Kukulcán. The detail shows a painting from the Mayan book known as the* Dresden Codex.

■ *What were some of the achievements of the Olmec and the Maya?*

R E V I E W

1. FOCUS How did people first come to the Americas?

2. HISTORY What different ideas do scientists have about the time when people came to the Americas?

3. GEOGRAPHY Why was the Gulf coast a favorable place for a civilization to develop?

4. CRITICAL THINKING Raising corn was an important step for Mesoamerica. Why is a surplus of food necessary in order for a civilization to develop?

5. ACTIVITY Write a paragraph describing the ruins of Copán as Stephens might have seen them.

Early Civilizations in the Americas

LESSON 2

Aztec Civilization

THINKING FOCUS

How did the Aztecs view their place in the world as a whole?

Key Terms

- barter
- currency
- tribute

▲ *This jade mask is from Teotihuacan, a great religious center before the rise of Tenochtitlan. The Aztecs borrowed many ideas from Teotihuacan.*

Against the waters of Lake Texcoco, the island city gleamed white in the sun. Around it stretched lush green gardens built up on the lake. Wide causeways, or raised earthen roads, linked the city to the mainland. From the hills beyond, a raised channel carried fresh water to the city. A wide dike crossing the lake protected the gardens from the salt waters of the lake. This was Tenochtitlan (*teh nawch TEE tlahn*), capital of the Aztec Empire and center of Aztec life. The Aztecs believed they were the People of the Sun, chosen to carry out the Sun God's work.

The Aztecs loved their city so much that they wrote praises to it in their poetry.

*Proud of itself
   is the city of Mexico-
   Tenochtitlán.
Here no one fears to die in war.
Have this in mind, oh princes,
   do not forget it.
Who could conquer Tenochtitlán?
Who could shake the foundations
   of heaven?*

Cantares Mexicanos

Nearby was the great market center that shared the island with Tenochtitlan. This was Tlatelolco (*tlah teh LOHL koh*). Here, goods from all over the empire were traded. People throughout Mesoamerica came to Tlatelolco. Its huge open-air plaza was the center of everyday life for the people of Tenochtitlan.

The Aztecs

The Aztec people, or Mexica (*mehk SHEE kuh*), were the last to appear in Mesoamerica before the Spanish conquest. When the Aztecs first appeared in the Valley of Mexico in the 1200s, they were a wandering, desperate group. They said of themselves, ". . . they had no houses, they had no lands, they had no woven capes as clothing . . ." What they did have, however, was a belief in their own special destiny. In time, these people were to build their great city and carve out a mighty empire.

Origin of the Aztecs

The Aztecs came to the Valley of Mexico from the northwest. Changes in climate may have forced them to seek better land. When they arrived in the valley, they found the best lands already taken. For a while the Aztecs lived on other people's land, but they were soon forced to move on.

In the course of wandering, the Aztecs worked and became soldiers for another group of people. Again, conflicts forced them to flee. They found a home on a small island surrounded by marshes at the western edge of Lake Texcoco.

Tenochtitlan: The Capital

According to their history, when the Aztecs arrived on their island in 1325, they saw an eagle sitting on a prickly pear cactus and holding a snake in its beak. To the Aztec priests, this was a sign that they should build their capital here. They called the site Tenochtitlan, Place of the Prickly Pear Cactus on a Rock.

First, the Aztecs set out to enlarge their small island. In shallow areas along the shore of the island, they cut canals through the marshes. Between the canals they heaped up a mass of weeds to form solid islands. On top of the weeds, they layered mud brought up from the bottom of the lake. On these islands, called *chinampas (chih NAM pahs),* farmers could grow at least two crops each year. With a stable food supply, the population grew. The time had now come for the Aztecs to enlarge and improve their city.

The Aztecs became highly skilled in engineering. They built causeways for roads; raised channels to carry fresh water; and dikes, or earthen banks, to keep the salt water of the lake out of their gardens. They also enlarged the city itself.

Building a city is difficult at best. For the Aztecs, it posed special problems. To keep buildings from

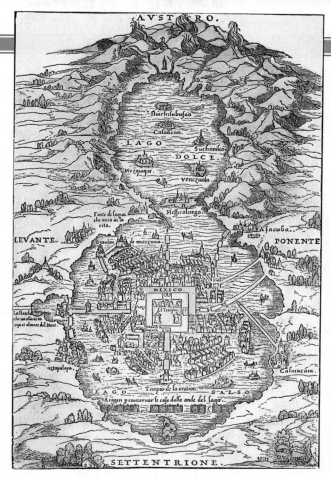

This map of Tenochtitlan, drawn after the Spanish conquest, shows many details of the city. What features of the city can you identify? What can you tell from the map about the artist's idea of the city?

sinking into the soft, marshy land, workers had to drive huge wooden poles into the ground for support. Because no building materials existed on the island, everything had to be brought there. The Aztecs, however, had neither wheeled vehicles nor large animals to pull them. Instead, they depended on human power, along with boats, for transporting goods. They also lacked metal tools.

In the central part of the city, the Aztecs built a great plaza, the main ceremonial center of the city. Facing the plaza was the Great Temple, which was built on top of a pyramid that rose to a height of about 97 feet. A number of other temples also faced the plaza. Beyond the temples were the palace of the ruler, the homes of the nobles, and many of the government buildings. Farther out were the houses of the common people.

Early Civilizations in the Americas

This Aztec stone sculpture shows a porter carrying corn. Porters were of a low class, but they did important work.

Rates of exchange were important to the Aztecs. Because cacao beans were rare and precious, they could be used as money.

■ *Why was trade important to the Aztecs?*

Tlatelolco: The Market

In the northern part of the capital lay the great market of Tlatelolco. It was the main crossroads for trade in the Aztec Empire. Here all kinds of goods were at hand—fruits and vegetables, cooking pots, brooms, herbs, jewels, and colored feathers.

The market was also a crossroads for people. High-ranking nobles, priests, merchants, traders leading slaves harnessed in collars, feather workers, farmers, jewelry makers, potters, and porters—all visited the market.

Among those selling goods in the market were women who brought produce from their own gardens. People came by canoe, carrying their tomatoes, peppers, squash, and fruit, all fresh from the *chinampas*. They displayed these wares in baskets in one section of the market.

Many products in the market differed according to the region that produced them. From the steaming coastal plains came cotton, vanilla, and cacao beans, used to make chocolate. Milder lowland areas grew fruits of all kinds, as well as tomatoes, avocados, and peppers. The Gulf coast and inland salt lakes produced salt, a major item of trade. From highland forests came wood for fire and for building.

The goods that traders brought to the market also differed from region to region and even from village to village. Workers in the old city of Teotihuacan *(teh uh tee WAH kahn)* fashioned knives and spearheads from obsidian, a black volcanic glass. In Xochimilco *(soh chee MEEL koh)* highly skilled workers made jewelry and small figures from jade. Feather workers created gleaming and colorful shields, headdresses, and fans.

The Aztecs did much of their buying and selling by **barter,** the exchange of one item for another without the use of money. At times they did use some forms of money. Cacao beans were the most common form of **currency,** or money. The Aztecs also used gold dust and cotton cloaks as currency.

Markets and Trade

The market at Tlatelolco was held every day of the week. The fifth day, the last day of the Aztec week, was by far the busiest. On this day, 40,000 to 50,000 people met to barter, visit, and share news.

Though Tenochtitlan had the largest market in the empire, every community held a market on a regular basis. These smaller markets were held just once every five days. They offered mostly food and household items, though at times they also had luxury goods.

Luxury items came from many different sources. To get these goods, merchants traveled along ancient trade routes. One route led to the Pacific coast. There merchants traded for shells, turquoise, and jade. Another route led south to Guatemala. There merchants traded for precious stones, cacao, and feathers of parrots, macaws, and quetzal *(KEHT zuhl)* birds. ■

Aztec Exchange Rates, c. 1525	
1 Cotton cloak = 100 Cacao beans	
Item	Price
Dugout canoe	1 Cotton cloak
Gold lip-plug	25 Cotton cloaks
Feather cloak	100 Cotton cloaks
String of jade beads	600 Cotton cloaks

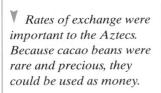

The Aztec Way of Life

In Aztec society each person had a particular role. Nobles served as judges, rulers of cities, and generals in the army. Priests carried out religious duties. Merchants brought goods from distant markets. Skilled artisans made luxury items, and the common people farmed, fished, hunted, and made items for everyday use. Together, the different classes formed an orderly, highly organized society united by its beliefs.

Religion

Like the other peoples of Mesoamerica, the Aztecs were very religious. Many of their daily activities included religious rituals, or ceremonies. Their beliefs influenced their economy, their way of governing, and their ways of waging war.

The Aztecs believed that the God of the sun and war, Huitzilopochtli *(hweets y loh PAWCH tlee),* was in a constant fight with the forces of darkness. For the God

to remain strong and continue his struggle, the Aztecs believed that he and the other Gods needed regular sacrifices that included human blood. At the dedication of Tenochtitlan's Great Temple in 1487, Aztec priests may have sacrificed thousands of captives.

The Aztecs also believed that fate influenced each person's life. The date of one's birth, for example, influenced the course of one's whole life—and even one's death. It was important to choose the best possible day for naming an infant, planting crops, or crowning a ruler. This focus on time explains in part the importance of calendars for the Aztecs. The Aztecs also believed in omens, or signs that told the future. Such omens might be found in the call of birds or the way that certain animals acted.

Because they believed in fate, the Aztecs did not always fear or

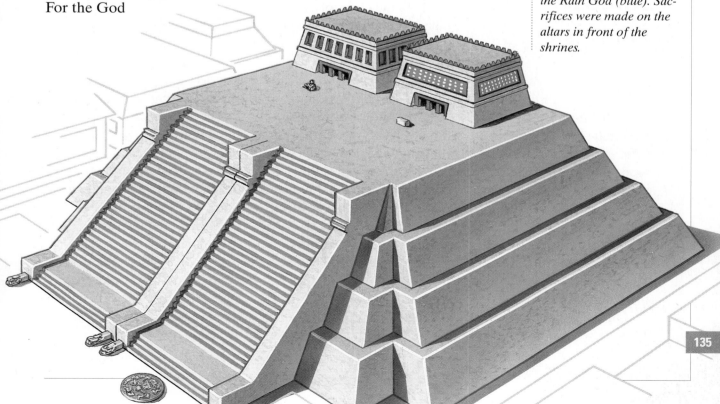

▼ *The Great Temple of Tenochtitlan was sacred to Huitzilopochtli, the Aztec God of the sun and war. This is an artist's idea of how the temple may have looked. Priests climbed the double staircase leading to the shrines for Huitzilopochtli (red) and Tlaloc, the Rain God (blue). Sacrifices were made on the altars in front of the shrines.*

135

➤ *This scene from the Aztec Codex Mendoza shows stages in the life of a warrior. The stages begin with taking the first captive and end with becoming a general.*

resist death. To be sacrificed to the Gods was in fact an honor. At times rulers even sacrificed members of their own families. All Aztecs viewed such actions as a sacred part of their religion.

Aztec Society

The Aztec way of life was an orderly one. Each level of society was divided into several groups. The highest-ranking nobles ruled large city-states. Lesser nobles ruled smaller cities and towns or served as judges or generals in the army. Between the nobles and the commoners were the traveling merchants and the most highly skilled artisans.

Each class lived by strict rules of conduct. For example, the rules

UNDERSTANDING EMPIRE

During the two centuries from about 1300 to 1520, the Aztecs built the last great empire in Mesoamerica. At the same time, the Inca in South America built a huge Andean empire, also the last of its kind. In the space of a few years, both empires fell under the threat of another entirely alien empire—the Spanish Empire.

What is an empire? An empire is a political unit in which one powerful state rules over others. Large in area, empires usually include peoples with both similar and different cultures. Differences may include language, customs, religion, and ways of life.

Once a people such as the Aztecs build an empire, they must decide how to govern it. This control can take different forms. Sometimes the ruling state keeps direct control over the lives of the conquered peoples, as the Inca did. The Inca demanded that conquered peoples adopt their language, customs, religion, and way of life. You will read about the Inca in the next lesson.

The Aztecs, however, did not try to interfere with the language and local customs of the peoples they conquered. They did not set out to control local governments. Instead, they appointed Aztec governors and tax collectors. They also placed soldiers in key locations to ensure control over the area. The Aztecs allowed local rulers to remain in office as long as regular payments of taxes were made to the Aztecs.

The collecting of tribute —a tax paid by conquered peoples, to the conquerors— is another feature of an empire. The new rulers may demand that tribute payments be made on a regular basis, as the Aztecs did, or only as the empire needs it.

The Aztecs and the Inca built empires every bit as real as the empires of the Persians, Romans, and other ancient peoples you will read about in this book. They all conquered other states, extended their control over a large area, and demanded tribute from the peoples they ruled. However, they also risked causing hatred among the conquered peoples.

136

told what kind of clothing people could wear. Only nobles of the highest rank could wear expensive cotton cloaks. Everyone in Aztec society was expected to lead a proper life. Parents taught their children to be honest, to respect authority, and to work hard.

Literature and the Arts

The Aztecs adopted some of their customs and ideas from other peoples in Mesoamerica. They took many of their religious beliefs and art from different groups. Even the calendar was borrowed from other peoples. However, the Aztecs changed these crafts and ideas to make them their own. You have seen the great city they planned and built. They were also skilled sculptors who made fine stone carvings and figures of turquoise and jade. As poets, they wrote beautiful verses that often expressed a sense of sadness. ∎

■ *How did religion influence Aztec life?*

A Powerful Empire

The Aztecs began their conquests in the name of their Sun and War God Huitzilopochtli. They expanded their rule, first over nearby cities and then over regions beyond the Valley of Mexico. In time, their city-state became an empire. Their goal was in part religious—to gain captives to sacrifice. They also sought wealth.

At its height the Aztec Empire included about 400 to 500 small states and perhaps as many as 15 million people. It reached from the Pacific Ocean to the Gulf of Mexico and just into present-day Guatemala.

From conquered peoples, the Aztecs collected **tribute,** payment in the form of goods, services, or currency. Tribute had to be paid regularly and when demanded. The Aztecs sent officials to each conquered province to collect the payments. If a province rebelled, the Aztecs doubled the amount to be paid. Thus, the Aztecs held their empire together by force. They sent troops to any city that failed to send its tribute or that tried to escape from the empire.

In spite of their achievements, the Aztecs failed to win the loyalty of all of the people they conquered. The demand for tribute and the quest for captives to sacrifice caused resentment and anger among many of the conquered groups. When the time came, these conquered peoples would be eager to join the Spaniards in defeating the Aztec Empire. ∎

◄ *Aztec rulers and nobles sometimes wore gold lip plugs as jewelry to show their high status.*

■ *Why did the Aztecs seek to create an empire?*

REVIEW

1. **FOCUS** How did the Aztecs view their place in the world as a whole?
2. **SOCIAL SYSTEMS** What problems did the Aztecs face in building the city of Tenochtitlan?
3. **BELIEF SYSTEMS** How did the Aztecs look upon fate?
4. **CRITICAL THINKING** The Aztecs had worked very hard to establish their own nation. Why then did they set out to conquer neighboring cities?
5. **ACTIVITY** Draw a picture showing some of the people in the market at Tlatelolco.

Early Civilizations in the Americas

L E S S O N   3

Andean Civilizations

Why was water such an important resource to Andean peoples?

Key Terms

- elevation
- distribution

▼ *Six to ten peaks of the Peruvian Andes rise to more than 20,000 feet. Even the passes are high. The pass for crossing the mountains east of Cuzco is above 16,000 feet.*

A second center of early American civilization arose on the west coast of South America. Until recent years, the best-known people of this region were the Inca. They lived in the high Andes of Peru at about the same time as the Aztecs in Mesoamerica. Archaeologists wondered if earlier peoples might have existed in the region. Might earlier peoples—like the Olmec and the Maya in Mesoamerica—have built civilizations in this region before the Inca?

Archaeologists have learned in the past 20 years that such civilizations did indeed exist. In fact the earliest of these cultures arose a thousand years before the Olmec. In their harsh desert and mountain environments, Andean peoples built unique civilizations.

How could people live in such a harsh land? What were special features of their cultures? Archaeologists are still finding answers to these questions. Each year brings new discoveries about these earliest South American civilizations.

Environments and Cultures

Peru is a land of extremes. Its coastal desert—one of the driest on the earth—stretches for 1,500 miles along the Pacific Ocean. Few rivers cross this great expanse. Inland, the Andes reach skyward, their peaks covered with snow.

The climate of Peru is also one of extremes. The coastal desert is cooled by winds off the cold ocean waters. The climate in the mountains varies with **elevation,** or height above sea level.

The earliest Andean cultures arose on the coast. Archaeologists have found that the peoples here, unlike the farmers of Egypt and Mesopotamia, lived mainly on fish. In time these Andean peoples learned to grow plants along the rivers.

For the early Andean peoples, the lack of fresh water was a problem. With almost no rain in their desert home, they had to seek other sources. Because of their

elevations, the peaks of the Andes are covered with snow and deep-frozen glaciers. As these melt in spring and summer, rivers of runoff fall down the slopes and cross the desert. These rivers dry up for months each year, however. To keep a good supply of water, the early Andean peoples built storage ponds and irrigation canals to hold the runoff.

In the coastal settlements, the first signs of civilization appeared.

Here people built huge buildings and pyramids made of stone. Some of these structures may date back to the time of the pyramids in ancient Egypt. Other peoples settled on the altiplano, the high plateau. There they built canals, terraces, temples, and storehouses.

The Chavín

In time a new culture, the Chavín (chah VEEN), appeared and spread across northern Peru. Chavín civilization reached its height between 1000 B.C. and 200 B.C. Chavín de Huantar, with its great temple, was the main center.

The Chavín culture is known for its stone carvings and its pottery and weaving. It borrowed some of its ideas and designs from earlier cultures, and it remained the base for later Andean civilizations.

The Moche

Another civilization that arose in Peru was the Moche (MOH cheh). It flourished from A.D. 100 to 800. The Moche culture was known for its pottery, wall paintings, and beautiful cotton and wool cloth.

Moche culture gained new fame in 1987. In that year, archaeologists discovered tombs of Moche rulers. The tombs were filled with gold and copper ornaments set with jewels. The finds showed that the Moche were among the greatest artists of the ancient world.

The Moche traded far and wide. Jewels came from present-day Chile, jaguar skins and feathers from the Amazon rain forests, and shells and gems from present-day Ecuador and Colombia. These riches were used in the temples and in tombs. ■

▲ *The Moche were highly skilled at working in gold. Here a gold spider, shown above and opposite, rests in its golden web. Notice that the artist has shown the spider with a human face.*

◄ *Deserts and mountains separated the early Andean peoples into many small settlements. Later, regional cultures appeared. What centers of these cultures appear on the map?*

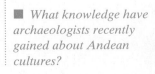

■ *What knowledge have archaeologists recently gained about Andean cultures?*

Andean Civilizations, 2500 B.C.–A.D. 1532

Inca Empire
Road
Present-day boundaries
★ Andean Culture Center

Equator
Quito
ANDES
Marañón R.
Amazon R.
SECHURA DESERT
Ucayali R.
PACIFIC OCEAN
Moche
Huánuco
Chavin
La Florida
Apurimac R.
Machu Picchu
Cuzco
SOUTH AMERICA
Paracas
Nazca
L. Titicaca
Tiahuanaco
80°W
Peru Current
0   300   600 mi.
0   300   600 km
Azimuthal Equal-Area Projection
ATACAMA DESERT
Tropic of Capricorn
ANDES MTS.
Salado R.
70°W   60°W
10°S
20°S
30°S

139

Early Civilizations in the Americas

The Inca

A number of outstanding cultures arose after the Moche. The last and greatest of these was the Inca. Like the Aztecs, the Inca began as a small, struggling group and were latecomers to their region. In about A.D. 1200, they moved into the valley near Cuzco. Also like the Aztecs, the Inca saw themselves as a chosen people. They borrowed many ideas from earlier cultures. Often, however, they destroyed the remains of those cultures or took credit for the cultures' achievements.

Inca Rule

Today, the term *Inca,* which means "sun," is applied to all the people of this culture. To the Inca themselves, however, the term referred only to the emperor and to the nobles who were members of his family. People believed that the Inca was descended directly from the sun. They called him the Son of the Sun. They worshiped not only the sun itself but also the Inca.

The Inca had total power. He made all the main decisions that affected his people. He also directed the use of land and wealth. Gold— "the sweat of the sun"—was his special property.

Inca society was divided into separate classes, but everyone worked for the Inca. The men of the villages worked in the fields. They also worked on roads, terraces, canals, and temples. Some served in the army, mined gold and silver, or served as runners who carried messages over the royal roads. Women, too, worked for both family and state. They spun and wove wool for clothing for the Inca, the members of his court, and the soldiers. Women also prepared food for the soldiers and the men working on state projects.

A Rural Way of Life

The Incan way of life was centered on the land. Farming was the main occupation. Inca farmers built canals, terraces, and storage ponds, and raised a variety of crops. People raised llamas and alpacas at higher elevations. Inca artists used the wool to weave beautiful cloth.

Inca farmers developed special ways of raising and using potatoes. They preserved potatoes by allowing them to freeze, letting them thaw, and then trampling them to force out the water. This method of freeze-drying preserved the potatoes for use during the winter. Inca farmers grew more than 60 varieties of potatoes, which were a staple food.

In addition to farming, the Inca mined gold, silver, copper, and tin. They became highly skilled metalworkers. Some metalworkers created delicate little figures of gold. The Inca also excelled at working in stone. The temple and fortress at Cuzco and the buildings and terraces at Machu Picchu (*MAH choo PEE choo*) are fine examples of Inca stone work. ■

▲ *Andean artists excelled at weaving cloth. This weaving, part of a sleeve, is from the north coast before the Inca conquest. It is made of wool from a llama or an alpaca and cotton. Andean peoples valued decorative fabrics.*

What was the emperor's role in Inca society?

Inca Highways

Rivers, mountains, jungles, and deserts once separated the peoples of western South America. When the Inca built a great network of stone roads, they connected many groups and created an empire. The roads covered more than 10,000 miles. Inca runners sprinted along them to relay messages. In five days a message could travel the length of present-day Peru.

Foods of the Inca included potatoes, maize, beans, chili peppers, and sun-dried meats.

A *quipu* was like an adding machine made of strings. The Inca tied knots in the strings to count llamas, gold, or the foods they sent to villages in need.

Roadside shelters were spaced about a day's journey apart. Here, weary travelers could find food or safely rest.

Steep steps climbed into mountainous regions. Suspension bridges crossed deep gorges and streams.

141

A Widespread Empire

In 1438 Pachacuti *(pah chah KOO tee)*, the ninth Inca emperor, set out to unite the peoples of the Andean region into one powerful empire. In less than 90 years, he and the rulers after him spread their control over about 12 million people. The empire stretched for nearly 2,500 miles.

The Inca imposed their government, law, religion, and language on each group they conquered. They allowed local officials to keep their positions as long as they remained loyal to the emperor. If local groups resisted, the Inca sometimes moved whole villages to the Inca homeland. The empty rebel villages were filled with loyal Inca subjects, who would teach Inca ways.

Soon after a conquest, officials took a census, or count of the people, of the region. They divided the fields into three parts: one for the Gods, one for the Inca, and one for the members of the community.

Unlike the Aztec method of exchanging goods through markets, the Inca state set the **distribution,** or handing out, of goods. It divided the resources and distributed them according to need.

The Inca way of life was highly organized with the Inca himself as the center of power. However, if some misfortune happened to the Inca, who would be in command? Later, even before the Spaniards arrived, the empire had been weakened by disease and war. ■

➤ *The people of Peru still celebrate the Inca pageant called Inti Raymi. Held annually on June 24, it honors the sun.*

■ *How were goods distributed in Inca society?*

REVIEW

1. **FOCUS** Why was water such an important resource to Andean peoples?
2. **HISTORY** How did a recent discovery gain fame for the Moche?
3. **CULTURE** How did the Inca impose their culture on conquered peoples?
4. **CRITICAL THINKING** Empires always risk the danger of revolt. Why do you think Andean peoples were less likely than Mesoamericans to resist their rulers?
5. **ACTIVITY** A number of cultures besides the Chavín, Moche, and Inca developed in Peru. Look back at the centers of these cultures on the map on page 139. Then prepare a report on one of these early Andean cultures.

Identifying Main Ideas

Here's Why

When you read, you need to determine what the writer wants you to understand. Identifying the main idea is the key to getting the most out of anything you read. For example, if you were asked to tell someone what you read in Lesson 3 about the Inca Empire, you would need to use this skill.

Here's How

The main idea of a paragraph is often stated in the topic sentence. This sentence, which is usually the first or last sentence, tells what the paragraph is about. The other sentences of the paragraph provide facts and details that support the main idea.

The main idea of a large section of a lesson may be found in a topic paragraph. Like a topic sentence, a topic paragraph tells you the main idea of the section. The other paragraphs in the section build on and support the topic paragraph.

Look at the summary of the Lesson 3 section, The Inca (box). In this example, a topic paragraph begins the passage. As you can tell from the green highlighting, the paragraph asks why the Inca were successful. Supporting details, highlighted in blue, explain what led to the Inca's success in creating a great civilization.

The main idea of a passage is not always stated in a topic paragraph. For example, if the passage did not include the first paragraph, you would need to look at the rest of the passage for a common idea or ideas. You would study the supporting details to determine the unstated main idea.

Look at the passage. Blue highlights the part of each sentence that tells about some major accomplishment of the Inca. When you determine what these sentences have in common, you can come up with the main idea of the section.

Try It

Turn to page 142 and reread the section called A Widespread Empire. Write the main idea of that section on your paper. Now list several supporting facts or details that reinforce the main idea.

Apply It

Find a magazine article about a topic that interests you. Read the article to get an idea of its content. Then identify the topic sentence or the topic paragraph of the article. Describe how the other sentences or paragraphs in the article support the main idea.

The Inca

The last and greatest of the Andean civilizations was that of the Inca. They began as a small, struggling group but built a vast empire. What factors led to their success?

The Inca people believed their ruler, the Inca, was descended from the sun. Thus, he was not only an emperor but also a God to be worshiped. As ruler, he oversaw the distribution of land, resources, and food. The state also carried on public projects such as building irrigation works and highways. Everyone owed service to the state. Though the Inca demanded much from the people, he also took care of them in time of need.

The Inca way of life was based mainly on farming. Men of the villages worked on the land and on public projects. At high elevations they raised llamas and alpacas. The Inca people also mined valuable minerals such as gold, silver, and copper. Besides caring for their families, Inca women wove cloth and prepared food for the state.

The Inca culture supported many craftworkers, such as metal workers and weavers of beautiful fabrics. Their work shows the accomplishments of the Inca culture.

143

Chapter Review

Reviewing Key Terms

barter (p.134)
currency (p.134)
distribution (p.142)
diversity (p.129)

elevation (p.138)
glacier (p.128)
rain forest (p.130)
tribute (p.137)

A. Read each pair of words. Write a sentence telling how the words in each pair are related.
1. rain forest, diversity
2. barter, currency
3. glacier, elevation

B. Each statement below contains a key term from the chapter. Decide whether each statement is correct or incorrect. Give reasons to support your decision using information in the chapter.
1. When <u>glaciers</u> covered much of Asia and North America, people could not travel from one continent to the other.
2. The <u>tribute</u> that conquered peoples paid to the Aztecs helped to unify the empire.
3. People in the Inca Empire were well cared for in times of need because the ruler controlled the <u>distribution</u> of goods.
4. The <u>diversity</u> of plant and animal life in Mesoamerica led to the growth of markets.

Exploring Concepts

A. Most empires have certain traits in common. These are listed on the chart below. Copy and complete the chart. Write one or more sentences telling how the Aztec Empire illustrated each trait.

Common Traits of Empires	Examples from Aztec Empire
Rule by a powerful state over lesser, conquered states	
A system for ruling the conquered states	
The taking of tribute or payments from conquered peoples	goods, services, or currency often taken by force

B. Answer each question with information from the chapter.
1. Why are recent discoveries in Canada, Brazil, and New Mexico important to archaeologists?
2. Why did priests have a high rank in Mesoamerican societies?
3. In what ways did the earliest Andean civilization differ from Olmec civilization in Mesoamerica?
4. What basic technologies did Mesoamerican and Andean peoples lack when they built their huge projects?
5. On what kinds of resources and materials did the people of Mesoamerica and the Andes rely most? Why might they have valued these things?
6. How were the Aztec and Inca civilizations alike? How were they different?
7. What special methods of farming did the Aztecs and the Inca use?
8. How were Andean peoples able to live and thrive in their difficult environment?

Reviewing Skills

1. Turn to pages 130–131 and reread the section called Mesoamerican Civilizations. Write the main idea of that section on your paper. Then list as many supporting facts or details as you can find that reinforce the main idea.
2. Look at the picture from the *Codex Mendoza* on page 136 and read the caption. What does the picture show? What does it tell you about Aztec civilization?
3. Imagine you are an archaeologist who has just discovered an ancient city in the Peruvian desert. What questions will you try to answer about your find? In what ways might it change people's thinking about early Andean cultures?

Using Critical Thinking

1. Sir Isaac Newton once wrote, "If I have seen further [than other men] it is by standing on the shoulders of Giants." What do you think he meant by that statement? Do you think the same could be said of the Aztec and the Inca civilizations? Explain your answer.
2. Although the Aztecs and the Inca borrowed many ideas from earlier cultures, they often destroyed elements of those cultures. What do you think accounts for this action?
3. Although at times they used currency, the Aztecs did much of their buying and selling by barter. In your opinion, why is barter rarely used today?
4. The cultures that flourished in Mesoamerica and in the Andes are known for their art work, literature, buildings, monuments, and feats of engineering. What do you think people a thousand years from now will consider outstanding about U.S. culture today? Explain your answer.

Preparing for Citizenship

1. **WRITING ACTIVITY** The Aztecs and the Inca conquered and ruled other peoples. If you were a member of a conquered group, in which empire would you have preferred to live? Write an essay to answer this question, including the reasons for your choice.
2. **COLLECTING INFORMATION** Archaeologists find, record, and interpret various forms of evidence about life long ago. Your community also has a past. What evidence exists about earlier inhabitants? You could interview older residents; research photographs, maps, and books; or study the buildings and land to obtain information about earlier times in your community. Share your information with the class.
3. **GROUP ACTIVITY** The Inca built highways to aid the movement of people and goods to distant parts of their empire. The same needs for transportation exist today. Working in small groups, study the various forms of transportation in your state or community. What different types are there? What special purposes does each serve? What routes or places does it connect? Share your findings with the class.
4. **COLLABORATIVE LEARNING** The products that Aztec farmers and artisans brought to market differed from region to region. Working in small groups, prepare a display of food products, from different parts of the United States and from other countries, that are available in your area. Have several students collect products from different regions and countries. Have others locate, on a map of the United States or the world, the regions and countries from which each item comes. Other students might write a brief description of each product and the way it is used. Group members should then decide together how to present the findings to the class.

The Mediterranean and Southwest Asia

The lands around the Mediterranean Sea have been the birthplace of powerful ideas about government, learning, and the arts that still influence people today. From the eastern Mediterranean and nearby Southwest Asia came three great world religions—Judaism, Christianity, and Islam. Some ideas were spread by force, perhaps by mighty armies like this Roman cavalry. Other ideas spread through trade, or simply through their appeal to the human spirit.

1500 B.C.

Carving on base of column honoring Antoninus Pius, Roman emperor, A.D. 138–161

147

Unit 3 Overview

The Mediterranean and Southwest Asia

The Mediterranean and Southwest Asia lie at the meeting point of three great continents—Africa, Asia, and Europe. Many ancient traditions began in this region and then spread throughout these continents and beyond.

Greece and Italy reach far into the Mediterranean Sea. The ancient Greeks used the sea for trade and expansion of power. In their turn, the Romans conquered the Greeks. Then they went on to build a mighty empire. Much of Roman culture, however, copied Greek arts, religion, literature, and science.

The effects of these ancient cultures are still in evidence today. Greek-style buildings are found in many modern cities. Some of today's governments are built on Roman ideas of law and citizenship. Three world religions—Judaism, Christianity, and Islam—spread quickly outward from Southwest Asia. These religions remain major forces in the lives of peoples around the world.

The Olympic Games were first held in Olympia, Greece, in 776 B.C. Early events included chariot racing. This statue of a charioteer is from the Greek city of Delphi.

▼ *Much of Southwest Asia has a desert climate. These olive trees and other plants grow near the few areas that have water.*

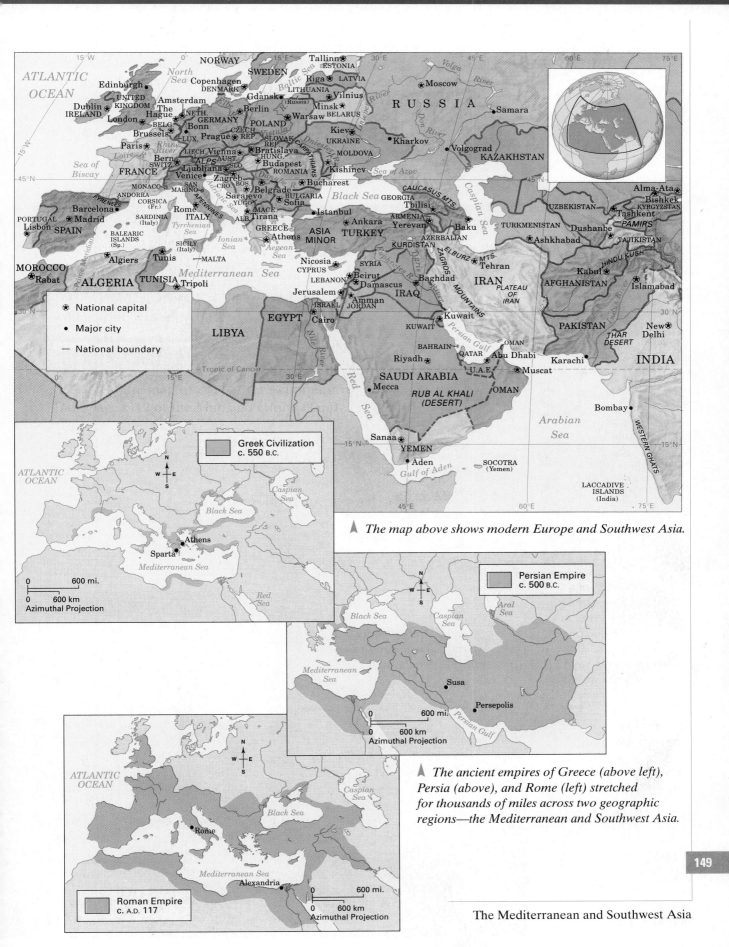

The map above shows modern Europe and Southwest Asia.

Greek Civilization c. 550 B.C.

Athens
Sparta

600 mi.
600 km
Azimuthal Projection

Persian Empire c. 500 B.C.

Susa
Persepolis

600 mi.
600 km
Azimuthal Projection

The ancient empires of Greece (above left), Persia (above), and Rome (left) stretched for thousands of miles across two geographic regions—the Mediterranean and Southwest Asia.

Roman Empire c. A.D. 117

Rome
Alexandria

600 mi.
600 km
Azimuthal Projection

149

The Mediterranean and Southwest Asia

The Land and People

The Mediterranean and Southwest Asia have very different climates. When clouds from the Mediterranean Sea hit the mountains of Southwest Asia, they drop their rain. As a result, the land east of the mountains gets very little rain. For this reason, much of Southwest Asia is hot and dry. Areas near the Mediterranean Sea have warm, dry summers and mild, rainy winters.

➤ *Regions circling the Mediterranean receive plenty of rainfall during winter. To the west, however, the land becomes desert.*

▲ *Frankincense comes from trees grown in Africa and Southwest Asia. In ancient times it was burned during religious celebrations and was a major trading item. Today it is used in perfumes.*

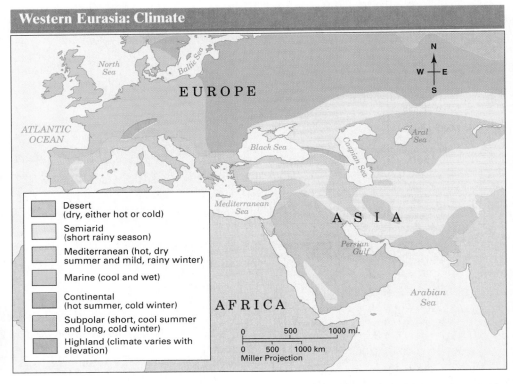

Western Eurasia: Climate

Legend:
- Desert (dry, either hot or cold)
- Semiarid (short rainy season)
- Mediterranean (hot, dry summer and mild, rainy winter)
- Marine (cool and wet)
- Continental (hot summer, cold winter)
- Subpolar (short, cool summer and long, cold winter)
- Highland (climate varies with elevation)

0 500 1000 mi.
0 500 1000 km
Miller Projection

➤ *Saudi Arabia receives less rainfall than almost any other place in the world.*

▼ *Pistachios grow in the dry climate of the eastern Mediterranean and Southwest Asia.*

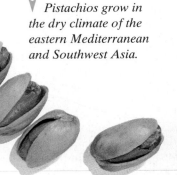

Regional Rainfall

Average Annual Precipitation (in inches) / (in centimeters)

City	inches	centimeters
Athens, Greece	16	38
Rome, Italy	26	63
Tehran, Iran	10	25
Riyadh, Saudi Arabia	4	13

Source: Statesman's Yearbook, 1992–1993

Three world religions began in Southwest Asia. The development of Judaism began when a shepherd named Abraham left Mesopotamia to settle in what is now Israel. His descendants were called Israelites, the ancestors of the Jews. Christianity began almost 2,000 years later and was based on the teachings of Jesus, who had been raised in the traditions of Judaism. In the early seventh century, Muhammad, the founder of Islam, began preaching in Mecca, Saudi Arabia. Today these religions are practiced throughout the world.

◄ *Followers of Islam face toward the holy city of Mecca when they pray.*

▼ *This boy is celebrating his Bar Mitzvah, a ceremony in which he will become a full member of the Jewish community.*

▼ *Followers of the Russian Orthodox church built churches like this one in Alaska. Eastern Orthodox churches are often richly decorated with religious art.*

Chapter 7
The Mediterranean World

On a globe, the Mediterranean is a small sea. Yet it touches the shores of three continents. Many peoples who lived here developed remarkable new ideas. Rich cultures developed in Greece and Rome. The Christian religion began and grew in the eastern Mediterranean. From the Mediterranean world come many of our ideas about what is beautiful, what is just, and what is right and wrong.

438 B.C. The Parthenon, a temple to the Goddess Athena (shown left), is completed as part of Pericles' ambitious building program for Athens. The temple still stands on the Acropolis in modern Athens.

800	600	400	200

800 B.C.

343 B.C. The Greek philosopher Aristotle becomes the tutor of young Alexander of Macedonia, who will grow up to be known as Alexander the Great.

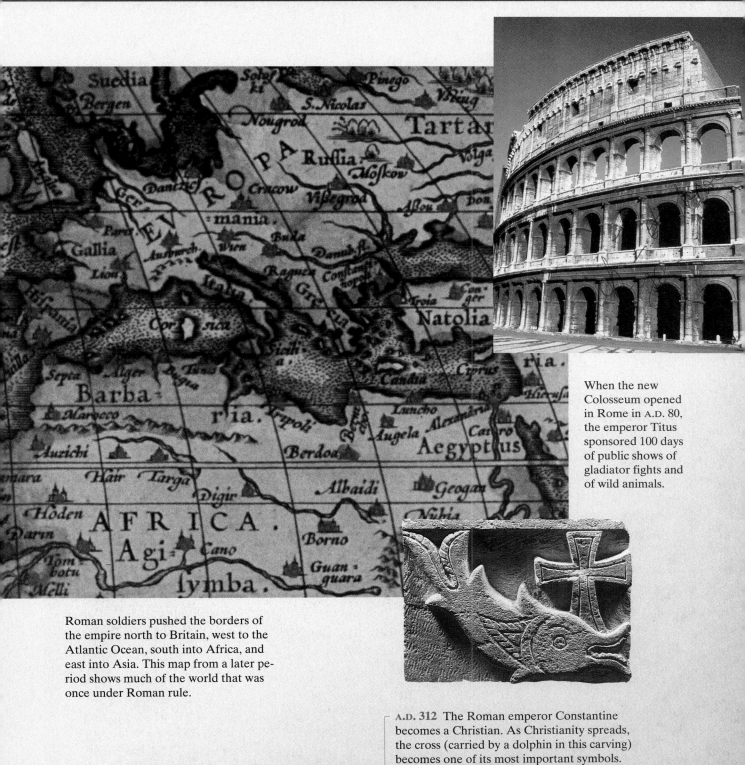

When the new Colosseum opened in Rome in A.D. 80, the emperor Titus sponsored 100 days of public shows of gladiator fights and of wild animals.

Roman soldiers pushed the borders of the empire north to Britain, west to the Atlantic Ocean, south into Africa, and east into Asia. This map from a later period shows much of the world that was once under Roman rule.

A.D. 312 The Roman emperor Constantine becomes a Christian. As Christianity spreads, the cross (carried by a dolphin in this carving) becomes one of its most important symbols.

B.C.	A.D.	200	400	600

58–46 B.C. Julius Caesar conquers Gaul for Rome and invades Britain. He defeats his opponents, returns to Rome a hero, and soon is a powerful ruler.

A.D. 476

153

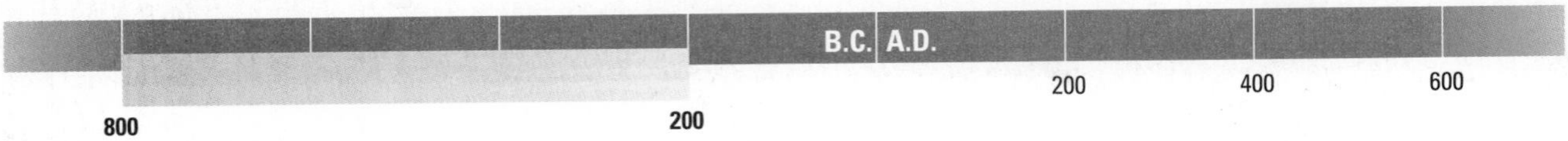

LESSON 1

Ancient Greece

**THINKING
FOCUS**

*How do the achievements
of ancient Greece still
influence people today?*

Key Terms

- peninsula
- city-state
- citizen
- democracy
- philosophy

I am Odysseus, son of Laertes, known before all men for [being clever]. . . . I am at home in sunny Ithaka. There is a mountain there that stands tall . . . and there are islands settled around it, lying one very close to another. . . . But my island lies low and away, last of all on the water toward the dark [the west] . . . a rugged place, but a good nurse of men; for my part I cannot think of any place sweeter on earth to look at.

Homer, *Odyssey*

With these words, the Greek hero Odysseus *(oh DIHS ee uhs)* described his island home. Odysseus—who may or may not have been a real person—had been away from home for many years. With other

Greek heroes, he had been fighting in the Trojan War. His journey home, filled with adventures, took almost 10 years. As he spoke, he was nearing home. Soon he would stand again on Ithaka, the island he loved so well.

Odysseus' speech is part of a long poem, the *Odyssey*, which is about his travels. It was composed in ancient Greece by the poet Homer, perhaps as early as the 700s or 800s B.C. The poem was probably recited at first and not written down until later.

Notice that when Odysseus remembered his home, he spoke of the sea and islands and mountains. He might have been describing the world of all the Greeks.

➤ *Odysseus' journey
took him through the blue
waters of the Aegean and
Ionian seas, which sepa-
rate the Greek islands.
This is the island of
Samos, in the Aegean.*

Map labels:
20°E 25°E 30°E
MACEDONIA
Mt. Olympus ▲
Thasos
THASOS
Byzantium
Sea of Marmara
40°N
Potidaea
Abydos
LEMNOS
PERSIAN EMPIRE
THESSALY
Aegean Sea
LESBOS
AETOLIA
CHIOS
Phocaea
Ithaca
Chalcis
EUBOEA
Chios
Thebes
ATTICA
ANDROS
Ephesus
Corinth
Athens
SAMOS
Mantinea
Argos
Miletus
PELOPONNESUS
DELOS
Sparta
Naxos
Cnidus
RHODES
Sea of Crete
Lindus
Cydonia
CRETE
35°N

Legend:
- Major city-state
▲ Mountain peak
— Trade route

0 50 100 mi.
0 50 100 km
Mercator Projection

The Setting

To understand Odysseus' feelings about his home, look at the map above. Much of what is now Greece is a triangular piece of land that extends into the sea. That is, the Greek mainland is a **peninsula,** a word that means "almost island." Greece also includes many islands clustered in the sea nearby.

The map also shows clearly that rugged mountains cross the Greek landscape. Land and sea, mountains and valleys—these are the geographic contrasts in which ancient Greek culture developed.

Land and Sea

Like most other peoples in ancient times, the Greeks raised crops and herded animals for food. However, Greece is so hilly that fields with good soil are small and scarce. The Greeks could not grow all the food they needed.

As a result, the Greeks turned to the sea. They were fishers and sea traders as well as farmers. The Greeks sailed from island to island but tried not to lose sight of land.

Traders brought home products that the Greeks needed. Still, the lack of good farmland often meant food shortages at home. One solution was to send settlers to start new cities elsewhere.

As a result, ancient Greece included cities in what are now France, Spain, Italy, Russia, and Turkey. Modern Marseilles *(mahr SAY),* France, for instance, began as a Greek settlement. The new cities traded and sometimes fought with each other. Their people were thoroughly Greek in lifestyle.

Mountains and Valleys

In Greece, settlements were cut off from one another by mountains and the sea. Each city developed its own laws and its own government. An independent town, with the land around it, was called a **city-state**.

▲ *The main crops grown in the rugged land of Greece were olives, grapes, and grain. Notice how mountains and sea separate the city-states. Which ones were in the Peloponnesus?*

155

The Mediterranean World

Spartans encouraged sports for both women and men. This bronze statue, from about 520 B.C., shows a girl running.

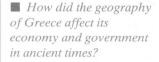

■ *How did the geography of Greece affect its economy and government in ancient times?*

The map on page 155 shows major city-states. There was no single nation called "Greece"—only these separate city-states.

Sparta and Athens

People in separate city-states developed their own customs. Two cities with very different views of life were Sparta and Athens. Eventually they became rivals for leadership of the Greek world.

Sparta is near the southern tip of the Greek peninsula, in a hilly region called the Peloponnesus *(pehl uh puh NEE suhs)*. It was ruled by two kings and a council. Spartans valued physical courage, strength, and bravery in war.

The Spartans expected people to give their first loyalty to the city-state. Boys as young as seven left home for military camps where they were trained to be soldiers. Young Spartan women also were educated and were trained in gymnastics.

Athens is farther north, in a forested region called Attica. Sheep and goats grazed on the hillsides. Some land was good for growing olives and grapes. Athenians had to depend on trade for grain and other food, however. Looking toward the sea, they built a strong navy.

Athenians valued reading, writing, and music, which the Spartans scorned. They also admired bravery in battle. They ran, wrestled, and did other gymnastics to keep both body and mind fit. At its height, Athens did not have a king. It was sometimes ruled by its people, sometimes by one strong ruler.

Both Athenians and Spartans were scornful of the others' way of life. It was partly these differences that made the two cities rivals. ■

The Golden Age

A time of prosperity, creative art, and rich culture is often called a golden age. In Greece, the Golden Age lasted from about 500 B.C. to 338 B.C. Much of the Greek art, literature, and ideas that people admire today come from this period. However, Greece's Golden Age was also an age of war.

From Kings to Democracy

Before about 600 B.C., the city-states of Greece were ruled by kings. By the start of the Golden Age, the government of most Greek city-states included some kind of an assembly, a gathering of the people.

The Assembly in Athens, in fact, governed the city. People met there to vote on questions of defense, trade, and other issues. Only Athenian citizens could vote in the Assembly. A **citizen** is a person who has full rights and duties in a state. For example, a citizen may have both the right to vote and the duty to serve in the army.

Only a small number of Athenians—about 15 to 20 percent—were citizens. All were men. Athenian women had certain privileges, and they could pass citizenship on to their sons. They were not voting citizens, though, and they could not own anything except their clothes, jewelry, and slaves. Upper-class women lived restricted lives inside their homes.

Children and most foreigners were not citizens. Neither were slaves. Slavery was common in many ancient cultures. Most slaves in Athens had been captured in war or were so deep in debt that they had to sell themselves into slavery.

The limits on citizenship meant that all Athenians were governed by a small group of men. From 80 to 85 percent of the people had no say in important decisions. Still,

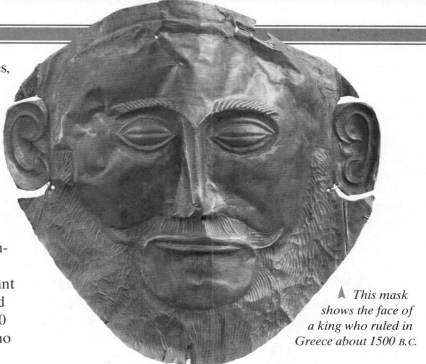

▲ *This mask shows the face of a king who ruled in Greece about 1500 B.C.*

UNDERSTANDING DEMOCRACY

*T*hroughout ancient history, kingdoms and nations were ruled by one powerful ruler or a small group of people. Then, in the sixth century B.C., people of the Greek city-states made a change. Several city-states organized the first lasting democracies—governments in which people ruled themselves. Because historians wrote the most about the city-state of Athens, people still study it today as the birthplace of democracy.

Rule of the People

A democracy is a form of government in which all citizens may take part in governing. The word comes from two Greek words: *demos,* meaning "people," and *kratos,* meaning "power." In any democracy, it is the people who hold the power. Athenian democracy, however, was not like democracy in the United States and other nations today.

Forms of Democracy

There are two types of democracies—direct and representative. In a *direct democracy,* such as Athens, each citizen decides and votes on important issues. Athenian citizens cast their votes with tokens like those at the left. In a *representative democracy,* citizens elect a group of people to make decisions about government.

Direct democracies work best in small communities, such as the early Greek city-states or small towns today. In countries or even big cities, it would be impractical for everyone to meet together to discuss and vote on issues. That is why modern democratic countries have representative democracy. In the United States, citizens vote to elect men and women who will represent them in Congress.

In the future, television and electronics might change how democracy works. With an "electronic town meeting," citizens might be able to sit at home, listen to debates, and vote directly, just as citizens did long ago in the Assembly at Athens.

The Mediterranean World

Pericles' rule in Athens was the height of the Golden Age. He was not only a political and military leader but also a person who loved the arts. This statue shows him wearing a military helmet.

a government in which groups of people—not one ruler—make the laws was something new in the ancient world. It is called a **democracy**.

You can learn more about how it works by reading Understanding Democracy on page 157.

Athens Becomes a Leader

The Greek city-states were not the only powers in the eastern Mediterranean region. Greece's neighbor to the east was the huge Persian Empire. (Part of the Persian Empire is shown on the map on page 155.)

In about 499 B.C., the Greek city-states went to war with Persia. Persian forces were much larger, but the city-states banded together. With great courage and clever strategy, the Greeks won. Two of their greatest victories were at Marathon and Salamis.

After the war with Persia, Athens became the leader of a group of city-states. Its navy protected them from attack. These cities formed a small empire, which made Athens rich and powerful. Sparta headed another group of city-states. They were its neighbors in the southern part of the peninsula.

The years from about 460 to 430 B.C. were the height of Athens's Golden Age. Poets, playwrights, and sculptors worked to create beautiful works of art that still inspire people today. The Athenian leader Pericles *(PEHR ih kleez)* made the city beautiful, too.

Pericles hired architects and sculptors to build new buildings in the heart of Athens. On the top of the central hill was the Parthenon. This temple honored Athena, the city's chief Goddess. A great gold and ivory statue of Athena stood inside its columns. Although the Parthenon has been damaged since Pericles' time, the white marble temple still stands in Athens today.

Cultures in Conflict

Athens's growing power made the Spartans nervous. In 431 B.C. the two rivals began a destructive war. Fighting continued off and on for about 25 years. Historians refer to this time period as the Peloponnesian War. In many ways it was a war between two different cultures. Early in the war, Pericles said:

> It is worth remembering some of the great differences between our way of life and that of our enemies. . . . Our city is open to all the world and everyone is free to look at what he likes in it. This is because we rely not on secret weapons, but on our own real courage and loyalty. There is a difference too in our educational systems. The Spartans, from their earliest boyhood, are submitted to the most strict and laborious training in courage. We pass our lives without all these restrictions, and yet we are just as ready to face danger as they are when the moment comes.

"Pericles' Funeral Speech,"
about 430 B.C., from Thucydides,
The Peloponnesian War

A few months later, many Athenians, including Pericles, died in a dreadful epidemic. As the war went on, people on both sides suffered greatly. Sparta won a final victory in 405 B.C. It captured the Athenian navy and surrounded the city. With their supplies of food cut off, the starving Athenians eventually had to surrender. ■

■ *How did Athens become a leader among the city-states?*

158

Battles at sea were an important part of warfare in ancient Greece. The painting on this vase shows the soldiers' shields above the oars of the warship. The lower picture shows hand-to-hand combat.

The Greek Heritage

After the Peloponnesian War, Greek city-states continued to fight among themselves. The wars drained their money and energy. In 338 B.C. King Philip of Macedonia, a large region north of Greece, took over the entire peninsula.

Philip's son Alexander was brought up to admire the culture of Greece. As Alexander the Great, he later went on to conquer most of the world the Greeks knew about. You will read about Alexander in Chapter 10. His conquests helped spread Greek culture to a wide area.

Greek Religion

The Greeks worshiped many Gods that they believed looked like—and often acted like—human beings. Myths, or stories, were told about the Gods and their adventures. Myths were not just good stories but looked into human nature and the relationships between Gods and humans. Writers and artists still use stories and symbols from the Greek myths. People still enjoy reading them.

There were 12 main Greek Gods. They were seen as members of a large family who fought, got jealous, and otherwise behaved in very human ways. Their home was Mount Olympus.

Zeus, as head of the family, was called "the father of Gods and men." He ruled the sky, while his brothers Poseidon and Hades ruled the sea and the underworld. His wife Hera protected the home.

Greek cities often chose one God or Goddess as their special protector. People also came under their protection. Each God also looked after certain crafts and ideas. For example, Zeus's daughter Athena was the Goddess of wisdom and war as well as crafts such as spinning thread and weaving cloth. Her special city was Athens.

Before making important decisions, the Greeks wanted to make

This fragment of a Roman mosaic shows the young conqueror Alexander the Great on his favorite war horse, Bucephalus. Because of Alexander's conquests, Greek culture spread to many areas.

159

sure the Gods approved. One way to find out was to visit the oracle at one of more than 200 special temples. There, people's questions about the future were answered. Many people asked advice from Apollo, a son of Zeus. He was a popular God, considered the God of truth. His best-known temple was at Delphi.

Greeks honored their Gods at festivals, with dances, songs, and athletic games. The most famous games were the ancient Olympic Games, which honored Zeus. Athletes competed mainly for fame and for honors from their home cities. The prize was a wreath of leaves. There are records of Olympic Games every four years from 776 B.C. to A.D. 217.

Greek Philosophers

The Greek word **philosophy** means the love of knowledge of all kinds. For Greek philosophers, studying philosophy was a way to discover what the universe was like and how to live correctly.

One Athenian philosopher, Socrates *(SOK ruh teez),* used an unusual way of teaching. Instead of telling his students what they should know, he asked careful questions. As students tried to answer, they learned how to think.

This statue is thought to show Zeus, ruler of the sky, getting ready to throw a thunderbolt. Notice how real—but how perfect— the figure appears.

Rich young Athenian men flocked to study with Socrates. One of them, Plato, listened carefully and wrote down the conversations of Socrates and his students.

Plato's works and Socrates' ideas are still studied today.

One of Plato's students, Aristotle *(AIR ihs taht uhl),* became as famous as his teacher. He explored many fields—science, drama, government. His ideas were studied and followed for centuries. Students today still learn Aristotle's theories about drama and poetry. As the teacher of Alexander the Great, Aristotle taught him to love Greek culture.

Ancient Greek Science

For the ancient Greeks, science and philosophy went together in understanding the world. Greek scientists asked "why" about things they saw. For example, in about 400 B.C., Hippocrates *(hih PAHK ruh teez)* taught medicine. He trained doctors to look for physical causes of illness, not to blame it on the anger of the Gods. Doctors today still take an oath named after Hippocrates. This is part of it:

I will follow that method of treatment which, according to my ability and judgment, I consider for the benefit of my patients, and [not do] whatever is [harmful].

After Philip conquered the city-states, Greek scientists worked in other parts of the Mediterranean world. For example, about 200 B.C., Eratosthenes *(ehr ah TAHS thuh neez)* used geometry to estimate the distance around the earth. His result was amazingly close to the measurements made by modern scientists.

A Lasting Artistic Vision

You have read how the ancient Greeks left their mark on government, history, philosophy, and science. They also produced striking works of literature, art, and architecture. You can find out more about the influence of Greek architecture in the feature on the next two pages.

The most famous Greek authors of the Golden Age wrote plays. In comedies, or humorous plays, they poked fun at politicians and current events. In tragedies, writers showed how fate and people's own unwise actions led them into disaster.

Today, if you watch a "situation comedy" or a Shakespearean tragedy, you are seeing a kind of play that was first created by the ancient Greeks. Audiences came to huge outdoor theaters where these plays were given. Playwrights competed to write the best new comedy or tragedy for a festival.

Greek artists of the Golden Age created magnificent sculptures. They tried to show both humans and Gods as perfect. Look at the statue of the God Zeus on page 160. What impression does it give you?

Over the course of 2,500 years, many of the great Greek plays and other writings have been lost. Vases, statues, and buildings have been broken or damaged. Still, the Greek heritage is an amazing one. Anyone today who wants to be a writer, artist, or architect needs to know what was done long ago in Greece. ■

◄ *Greek vases (left) were often decorated with paintings, usually in black or red. They show scenes from the myths and from everyday life—how the Greeks dressed, fought, lived, and worked. Greek theaters were outdoors, like this one (below) at Epidaurus.*

■ *Identify three things in modern U.S. culture that you can trace back to ancient Greece.*

R E V I E W

1. **FOCUS** How do the achievements of ancient Greece still influence people today?
2. **GEOGRAPHY** In Chapter 2, you read about different kinds of regions. What different regions can you identify for ancient Greece?
3. **CULTURE** Describe how Athens and Sparta differed in the way young people were educated.
4. **SOCIAL AND POLITICAL SYSTEMS** How was Athens governed during the Golden Age?

5. **CRITICAL THINKING** How did Greek scientists like Hippocrates set the stage for the way modern scientists work?
6. **ACTIVITY** Many familiar words refer to the Greek myths. Look up the following words in a dictionary to find the meaning and the name of the Greek God or hero to which it refers: *narcissus* (flower), *arachnid, echo, atlas, Herculean.* Then look in a book of Greek myths to read the story behind one of the words.

161

Greek Architecture in Your Community

*Y*ou don't have to travel to Greece to see what the ancient Greeks left to the modern world. Their influence reached far beyond their own borders. For instance, you can explore the Greek contribution to architecture right here at home.

Get Ready

Pack up a sketch book and a pencil. Take along a camera if you have one. You are searching for examples of ancient Greek building styles in your own city or neighborhood.

Find Out

Look for columns—tall pillars that support a roof or ceiling. When you find some, sketch or photograph the capitals—the decorations at the top. Compare

your sketch with those at the left. Are the capitals simple Doric, graceful Ionic, or elegant Corinthian?

Record the location of the building and its name, if it has one. Write down what it is used for: Is it a house? A store? A government building? A bank?

Move Ahead

Back in your classroom, compare your sketches or photographs with the drawings of the capitals on

The three classical types of Greek capitals are Doric (top), Ionic (middle), and Corinthian (bottom).

162

Chapter 7

This scale model of Buckingham Palace is entirely made up of interlocking plastic bricks. What elements of Greek architecture can you identify?

these pages and in the Architecture entry of the Minipedia, on pages 662 and 663. Correct your sketches or labels, if necessary.

Make a list of all the buildings you and your classmates saw. How many are there? What are the buildings used for?

Your class can draw a large mural showing the classical Greek architecture you found in your exploration. You can also combine many of the drawings and the photographs in a collage.

Explore Some More

Use the architectural terms on pages 662 and 663 to identify features of other buildings you find in your city or neighborhood. For example, some of the buildings you see may have a round dome.

The ancient Romans were the first people to borrow the Greek style. Since then, it has been copied often and in many places. In the late 1700s, architects in the United States imitated Greek architecture. Historians call this time the Federalist period of American arts.

Since Greece was the world's first democracy, Greek building styles symbolized the ideals of the new nation. The buildings were statements in stone, reminders of the people's right to govern themselves.

Early Greek temples were painted in many bright colors. As you explore your neighborhood, do you find colors used together with elements of Greek architecture?

Demeter and Persephone

Retold by Ingri and Edgar Parin D'Aulaire

Although Demeter was not one of the major Goddesses of Mount Olympus, the Greek people loved her dearly. She was the Goddess who helped them plant and harvest crops, especially the grain used to make bread and flour. (Even Demeter's hair was the golden color of ripe grain.) As you read this myth, think about the events in nature that it explains.

As you read in Lesson 1, Greek myths are not just stories about Gods and humans. They also tell us a great deal about how the Greeks saw their world.

Persephone
(per SEF uh nee)

Demeter (dih MEET ur)

Hades God of the underworld, brother of Zeus

nymphs young Goddesses of nature

dismal gloomy

Persephone grew up on Olympus and her gay laughter rang through the brilliant halls. She was the daughter of Demeter, goddess of the harvest, and her mother loved her so dearly she could not bear to have her out of her sight. When Demeter sat on her golden throne, her daughter was always on her lap; when she went down to earth to look after her trees and fields, she took Persephone. Wherever Persephone danced on her light feet, flowers sprang up. She was so lovely and full of grace that even Hades, who saw so little, noticed her and fell in love with her. He wanted her for his queen, but he knew that her mother would never consent to part with her, so he decided to carry her off.

One day as Persephone ran about in the meadow gathering flowers, she strayed away from her mother and the attending nymphs. Suddenly, the ground split open and up from the yawning crevice came a dark chariot drawn by black horses. At the reins stood grim Hades. He seized the terrified girl, turned his horses, and plunged back into the ground. A herd of pigs rooting in the meadow tumbled into the cleft, and Persephone's cries for help died out as the ground closed again as suddenly as it had opened. Up in the field, a little swineherd stood and wept over the pigs he had lost, while Demeter rushed wildly about in the meadow, looking in vain for her daughter, who had vanished without leaving a trace.

With the frightened girl in his arms, Hades raced his snorting horses down away from the sunlit world. Down and down they sped on the dark path to his dismal underground palace. He led weeping Persephone in, seated her beside him on a throne of black marble, and decked her with gold and precious stones.

But the jewels brought her no joy. She wanted no cold stones. She longed for warm sunshine and flowers and her golden-tressed mother.

Dead souls crowded out from cracks and crevices to look at their new queen, while ever more souls came across the Styx and Persephone watched them drink from a spring under dark poplars. It was the spring of Lethe, and those who drank from its waters forgot who they were and what they had done on earth. Rhadamanthus *(rad ah MAN thus)*, a judge of the dead, dealt out punishment to the souls of great sinners. They were sentenced to suffer forever under the whips of the avenging Erinyes. Heroes were led to the Elysian fields, where they lived happily forever in never-failing light.

Around the palace of Hades there was a garden where whispering poplars and weeping willows grew. They had no flowers and bore no fruit and no birds sang in their branches. There was only one tree in the whole realm of Hades that bore fruit. That was a little pomegranate tree. The gardener of the underworld offered the tempting pomegranates to the queen, but Persephone refused to touch the food of the dead.

Wordlessly she walked through the garden at silent Hades' side and slowly her heart turned to ice.

Above, on earth, Demeter ran about searching for her lost daughter, and all nature grieved with her. Flowers wilted, trees lost their leaves, and the fields grew barren and cold. In vain did the plow cut through the icy ground; nothing could sprout and nothing could grow while the goddess of the harvest wept. People and animals starved and the gods begged Demeter again to bless

Styx (stihks) river across which souls of dead are carried

Erinyes (ih RIN eez) the furies, mythological creatures who pursued and punished sinners

barren without fruit

the earth. But she refused to let anything grow until she had found her daughter.

Bent with grief, Demeter turned into a gray old woman. She returned to the meadow where Persephone had vanished and asked the sun if he had seen what had happened, but he said no, dark clouds had hidden his face that day. She wandered around the meadow and after a while she met a youth whose name was Triptolemus *(trihp toh LAY muhz)*. He told her that his brother, a swineherd, had seen his pigs disappear into the ground and had heard the frightened screams of a girl.

Demeter now understood that Hades had kidnapped her daughter, and her grief turned to anger. She called to Zeus and said that she would never again make the earth green if he did not command Hades to return Persephone. Zeus could not let the world perish and he sent Hermes down to Hades, bidding him to let Persephone go. Even Hades had to obey the orders of Zeus, and sadly he said farewell to his queen.

Joyfully, Persephone leaped to her feet, but as she was leaving with Hermes, a hooting laugh came from the garden. There stood the gardener of Hades, grinning. He pointed to a pomegranate from which a few of the kernels were missing. Persephone, lost in thought, had eaten the seeds, he said.

Then dark Hades smiled. He watched Hermes lead Persephone up to the bright world above. He knew that she must return to him, for she had tasted the food of the dead.

When Persephone again appeared on earth, Demeter sprang to her feet with a cry of joy and rushed to greet her daughter. No longer was she a sad old woman, but a radiant goddess. Again she blessed her fields and the flowers bloomed anew and the grain ripened.

"Dear child," she said, "never again shall we be parted. Together we shall make all nature bloom." But joy soon was changed to sadness, for Persephone had to admit that she had tasted the food of the dead and must return to Hades. However, Zeus decided that mother and daughter should not be parted forever. He ruled that Persephone had to return to Hades and spend one month in the underworld for each seed she had eaten.

Every year, when Persephone had left her, Demeter grieved, nothing grew, and there was winter on earth. But as soon as her daughter's light footsteps were heard, the whole earth burst into bloom. Spring had come. As long as mother and daughter were together, the earth was warm and bore fruit.

Demeter was a kind goddess. She did not want mankind to starve during the cold months of winter when Persephone was away. She lent her chariot, laden with grain, to Triptolemus,

Hermes (HER meez) Son of Zeus and messenger of the Gods.

the youth who had helped her to find her lost daughter. She told him to scatter her golden grain over the world and teach men how to sow it in spring and reap it in fall and store it away for the long months when again the earth was barren and cold.

reap to harvest, gather

Further Reading

The Avenger. Margaret Hodges. This exciting historical novel is set at the time of the Battle of Marathon (490 B.C.) between the Greeks and the Persians.

Book of Greek Myths. Ingri and Edgar Parin d'Aulaire. The book includes the myth above as well as other familiar stories.

Greek Gods and Heroes. Robert Graves. The author colorfully retells some classic myths and tales.

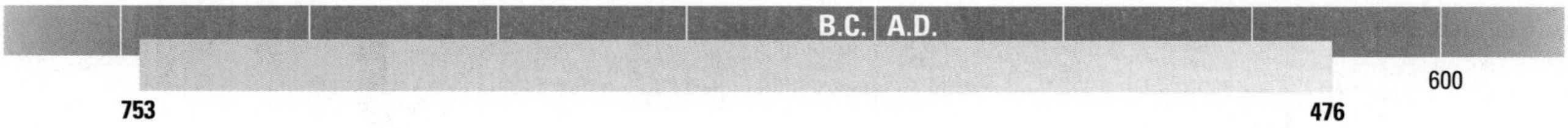

L E S S O N 2

Ancient Rome

THINKING FOCUS

How did Rome rule a huge empire for so long?

Key Terms

- republic
- province
- legion
- aqueduct

This place [Italy] . . . the olive owns, and the joyful herds. From here the war-horse comes, striding in his pride over the plain . . . Remember, too, all the fine cities . . . and the rivers gliding by beneath ancient walls. . . . This land has raised a fierce kind of men . . . Hail, great parent of harvests, land of the God Saturn, hail, great parent of men!

Virgil, *Georgics*, written about 37 B.C.

More than 2,000 years ago, the Roman poet Virgil praised the fertile farmlands and heroic people of Italy. His long poem *Georgics* was written when Rome was powerful but facing great political changes. The poem talked about lasting values. It reflected the pride that Romans had always felt in their home.

In this feeling of pride for their homeland, ancient Romans and Greeks were very similar. In other ways, the people of these two cultures were very different.

The Beginnings

Like Greece, Italy is a long peninsula that juts into the Mediterranean Sea. A chain of mountains runs down the center. Notice on the map that the city of Rome is near the center of Italy, on the Tiber River. Its location helped Rome grow powerful.

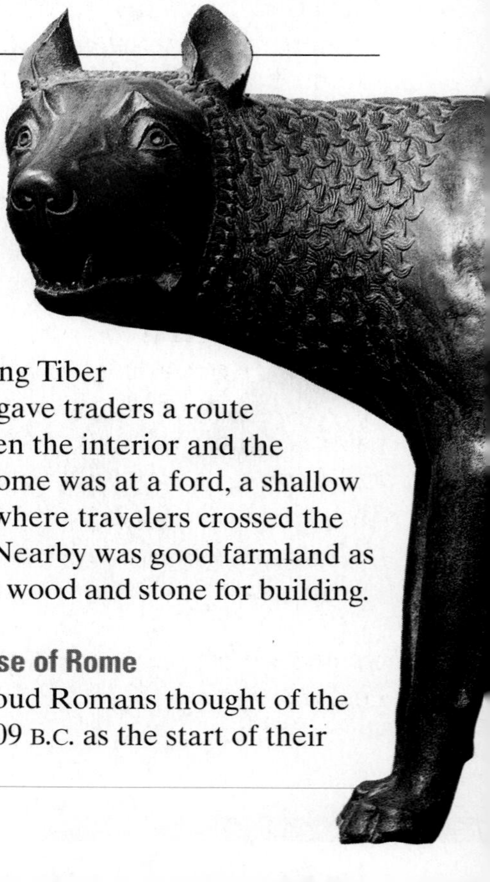

➤ This statue of a mother wolf is a symbol of the city of Rome. Legend says that a wolf rescued and raised twin babies, Romulus and Remus. They supposedly founded the city in 753 B.C. but later fought. Romulus won, giving the city his name.

A City on Seven Hills

When Rome began, several tribes of people lived on the Italian peninsula. In the center were the Latins. Etruscans lived to the north and south. Farther south were other tribes as well as Greek city-states.

The early Romans picked a good place for a town. It was built on seven hills that were easy to defend. The long Tiber River gave traders a route between the interior and the sea. Rome was at a ford, a shallow place where travelers crossed the river. Nearby was good farmland as well as wood and stone for building.

The Rise of Rome

Proud Romans thought of the year 509 B.C. as the start of their

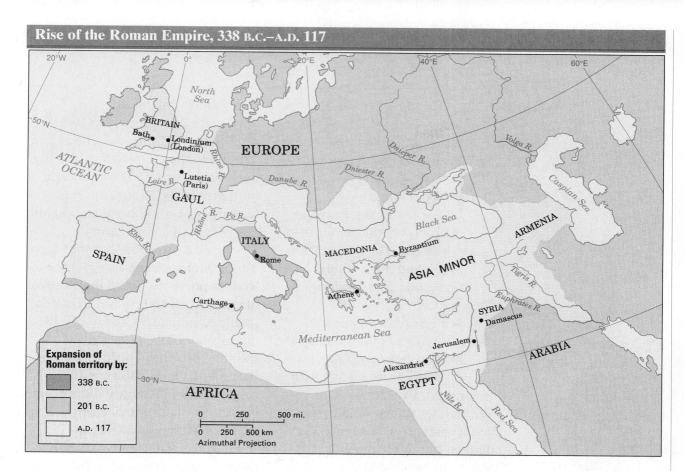

Expansion of
Roman territory by:

338 B.C.

201 B.C.

A.D. 117

0   250   500 mi.

0   250   500 km
Azimuthal Projection

greatness. In that year they overthrew their king, an Etruscan, and set up a new government. It was a **republic**, a state without a king, in which the people have a voice.

Rome was not a democracy like Athens, however. Roman noblemen made up a Senate that advised Rome's leaders. Gradually, the city took over the rest of the Italian peninsula, then began to conquer nearby lands (see page G11 in the Map and Globe Handbook).

Rome's chief rival to the west was the city of Carthage in North Africa, the center of a huge trading empire. For over 100 years, Rome and Carthage fought three wars, called the Punic Wars. Rome won each war. In 146 B.C., Roman soldiers burned Carthage to the ground.

Rome continued to grow by conquering new territory. At home, however, Romans faced problems such as poverty, lack of jobs, and

riots in the cities. Civil wars broke out. After more than 400 years, the Republic was in trouble.

By 44 B.C., Julius Caesar, a military hero, was the most powerful and popular man in Rome. Afraid that Caesar would become king, a group of nobles killed him. This did not save the Republic, however.

Rome now became an empire. In 31 B.C., Caesar's adopted son Octavian became sole ruler. As Augustus Caesar, he ruled until A.D. 14. His rule began a 200-year period known as the Pax Romana—the "Roman Peace." Although wars still went on at the empire's borders, Rome itself was at peace.

Roman emperors after Augustus had supreme power. They were sometimes worshiped as Gods. Yet many tried to rule wisely. The early empire was more peaceful and prosperous than the stormy last years of the Republic. ■

▲ *Through wars and military expeditions, the Roman Republic steadily increased its territory over several centuries. How did Rome acquire the territory around Carthage in North Africa?*

■ *How did Rome become an empire?*

Daily Life

The center of the growing Roman Empire was Rome itself. What was life like for Romans in and out of the city?

The City of Rome

For many, the Roman Forum was the center of daily life. The Senate, temples, and other public buildings stood around this open square.

Men were the leaders in Rome. As head of the family, a Roman father could be as stern as he wished with his children. Roman women, however, did not stay at home as upper-class women in Athens did. They could go out to see a play at the theater, to watch gladiators, or to visit friends. Women owned property and had other legal rights.

Rich and poor lived very differently in Rome. Most people lived in crowded apartment houses, three or four stories high. These rickety buildings often collapsed or caught fire. Wealthy Roman families had their own private houses, built around pleasant courtyards. They owned slaves who did all their everyday work.

Romans enjoyed many kinds of entertainment. Both rich and poor people exercised, bathed, and relaxed at the public baths. Romans also liked to go to the city's huge sports arenas. At the Circus Maximus, as many as 250,000 people could see fast horses and skillful drivers in exciting chariot races. The main sport at the Colosseum was watching gladiators fight hand-to-hand—often to the death—with each other or with wild animals.

The lives of upper-class Romans like this woman were made more comfortable by slaves, who worked as cooks, personal maids, tutors, and in other jobs. This slave tag promises a reward for the return of a valuable runaway slave.

■ *Why did men want to become soldiers in the Roman army?*

The Roman Provinces

By the second century A.D., the Roman Empire stretched from Britain to the Caspian Sea (see the map on page 169). It was divided into **provinces**. Ruling this huge empire took good organization and a strong, often cruel, army.

In each province, the emperor or the Senate appointed a governor to represent Rome. Often the Romans used local officials as well. They made sure that taxes were collected and Roman laws carried out. In farming provinces, people paid their taxes with grain. The grain helped feed people in Rome and the army.

People in provincial towns tried to live like people in Rome. They built public baths and arenas in the Roman style. Being able to say, "I am a Roman citizen" was important in the provinces. Roman laws protected citizens anywhere in the empire. If accused of a serious crime, they could demand a trial in Rome. Only citizens could become officials or army officers.

The Roman army had been important in building the empire. Now it had to guard the empire's frontiers. When people in the provinces resisted Roman rule, soldiers brutally crushed the rebels. Sometimes, thousands died.

The Roman army was divided into about 30 **legions**, or fighting units. A legion typically had about 5,400 soldiers. Army life was hard, but it had rewards. After serving for 20 years, a soldier was given land or a sum of money as well as full citizenship, if he was not already a citizen. Late in the empire, a soldier could rise to become a general or even emperor. ■

Decline and Fall

After about A.D. 180, the government in Rome gradually grew weaker. Many emperors ruled badly. Civil wars broke out when it was time to choose a new emperor. Soldiers in the legions often backed their own generals. Soon the army was choosing most emperors.

By about A.D. 290, the Roman Empire seemed too large for one person to govern. It was divided, and different rulers ran the western and eastern halves. Power shifted away from Rome.

There were other threats, too. At the borders of the empire, local tribes attacked Roman settlements. Germanic peoples such as the Goths invaded Italy itself. Also, many foreigners now joined the Roman army. In A.D. 476, Germanic troops forced the last western emperor from power. The old Roman Empire ended. ■

■ *What were two main causes of the decline of the Roman Empire?*

The Roman Legacy

When Rome was the center of an empire, people said, "All roads lead to Rome." In fact, this was true. Roman roads all came together in the capital. Today many roads also lead *from* Rome. Roman culture still influences people today.

Government and Law

The framers of the U.S. Constitution in 1787 looked back to ancient Rome, adopting both the idea of a republic and the Romans' word for it. They admired the high ideals of the Roman Republic and hoped their new republic would follow them.

For example, in Rome the best and most talented people were expected to take part in government. Officials were expected to be honest and trustworthy. A true Roman was also expected to show courage and dignity.

Other modern ideas about government come from Rome. One is the importance of being a citizen.

▼ *This aqueduct was built about 19 B.C. to bring water to the Roman settlement at what is now Nîmes, France.*

How an Aqueduct Works

Aqueducts carried water for many miles, from springs or lakes in the hills to Roman cities. The system included underground pipes as well as high stone structures. Sometimes a footpath ran along the top of the arches.

To keep the water moving steadily, but not too fast, Roman engineers made sure the aqueduct had a constant slope from beginning to end.

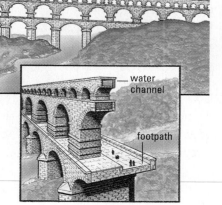

water channel

footpath

A Roman Engineer

10:42 A.M., July 26, 109 B.C.
On what will be the Via Aemilia Scauri, outside Pisa

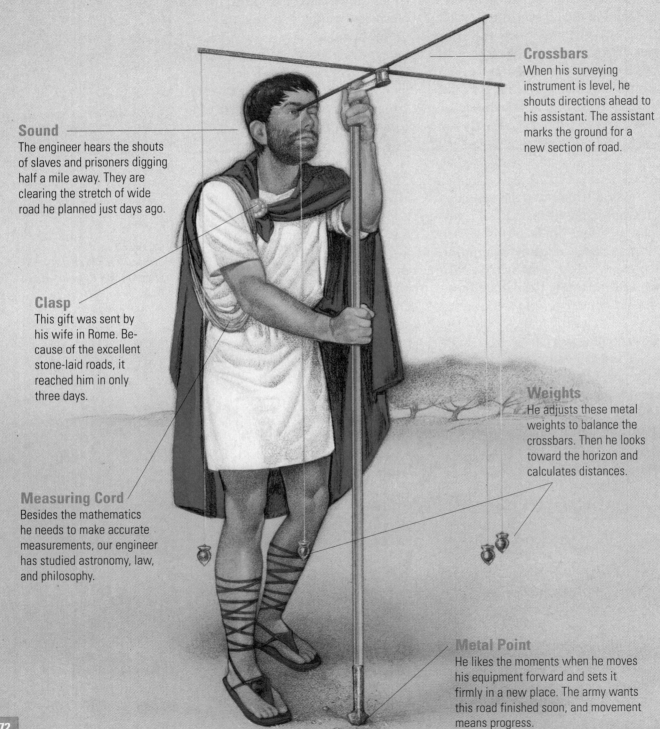

Crossbars
When his surveying instrument is level, he shouts directions ahead to his assistant. The assistant marks the ground for a new section of road.

Sound
The engineer hears the shouts of slaves and prisoners digging half a mile away. They are clearing the stretch of wide road he planned just days ago.

Clasp
This gift was sent by his wife in Rome. Because of the excellent stone-laid roads, it reached him in only three days.

Weights
He adjusts these metal weights to balance the crossbars. Then he looks toward the horizon and calculates distances.

Measuring Cord
Besides the mathematics he needs to make accurate measurements, our engineer has studied astronomy, law, and philosophy.

Metal Point
He likes the moments when he moves his equipment forward and sets it firmly in a new place. The army wants this road finished soon, and movement means progress.

172

As in Rome, citizens of the United States have both rights and responsibilities. Another is the importance of having written laws so that people can read them for themselves.

Architecture

The Romans were practical people who were good engineers and builders. Roman architects used many rounded arches in their buildings. The Colosseum pictured on page 153 is a good example.

Roman aqueducts were also constructed of stone arches. As you can see in the pictures on page 171, an **aqueduct** carried fresh water into a city. Roman aqueducts still stand in Spain, France, and other places where Rome ruled.

The Romans were also famous for their road system. These roads were well built, with layers of stone and gravel. By A.D. 300 there were 50,000 miles of roads throughout the empire. Roads were built mainly for the army but also helped unite the empire. You can see a Roman road engineer at work in A Moment in Time on the facing page.

Language

Anywhere you traveled in the Roman Empire, you were likely to hear someone speaking Latin. Outside Italy, of course, local people spoke their own languages. Latin was the language of Rome, however. Anyone who wanted to succeed had to learn it.

In many places in the empire, people began to speak an everyday Latin that was different from written Latin. In time, most people stopped speaking their old languages. The local forms of Latin developed into new languages. Because these languages came from the language of Rome, they are called Romance languages. More than 400 million people speak these languages today. The largest number speak Spanish, French, Portuguese, Italian, and Romanian. ■

Across Time & Space

What if you did not know what your country's laws were until you broke one? What if an official could change a law without telling you? That is how things were in most early cultures.

In about 451 B.C., the Roman people insisted that their laws be written down. The laws, called the Twelve Tables, were posted in the Forum. Today people still believe that having written laws helps ensure justice.

◄ *A Roman pupil unrolls his scroll to read, while another stands to face the stern-looking teacher.*

■ *Name at least three things modern culture has adopted from Roman culture.*

R E V I E W

1. **FOCUS** How did Rome rule a huge empire for so long?
2. **GOVERNMENT** How was the government of the Roman Empire different from the government of Athens?
3. **CULTURE** Compare the entertainments that Romans enjoyed with those that people enjoy today. Can you see any similarities?
4. **CRITICAL THINKING** Roman generals often fought among themselves for control of the empire. What kind of rules or laws could have helped prevent this type of fighting?
5. **ACTIVITY** Look at the arches in Roman structures such as the Colosseum or an aqueduct (pages 153 and 171). Then look for similar examples of arches in buildings in your community. Are Roman arches common in any particular type of building? Report your findings to the class.

Comparing Greece and Rome

Here's Why

A conclusion is a reasoned judgment based on evidence. To draw your own conclusions, you must first study the facts available and see where they lead.

For example, as you read Lessons 1 and 2, you may have seen both similarities and differences between the cultures of ancient Greece and Rome. What conclusions can you draw about those two cultures?

Here's How

The paragraph on the left below is a summary of facts about Greek and Roman military organization. Use it to draw a conclusion about the strength of Roman legions compared with the armies of the Greek city-states. Follow these steps:

1. **Study the evidence.** As you read, look for facts. The paragraph on military organization includes these important points:
   a. Roman legions had thousands of trained soldiers.
   b. Small Greek armies were made up of citizen-soldiers.
2. **Draw a conclusion.** Use the facts from step 1 along with anything else you know about the subject. Here it is reasonable to conclude that the Roman legions were stronger than the Greek armies. Trained, experienced soldiers are likely to be a stronger force than citizen-soldiers.
3. **Think about the evidence again.** Does it support the conclusion? Be ready to change your conclusion if necessary. During the empire, Roman troops in the legions spent 20 years as soldiers. The legions were well supplied and organized. Certain troops were specially trained. These facts support the conclusion.

Try It

The paragraph on the right below compares Greek and Roman engineering skills. What facts are given? What conclusion can you draw about their relative abilities?

Apply It

Find an article in a local newspaper or magazine. Use the three-step strategy in Here's How to draw a conclusion from it.

Military Organization

The Roman army was a powerful military force. It did not depend only on huge numbers of soldiers but used planning and discipline to defeat its enemies. The small armies of most Greek city-states were made up of citizen-soldiers. In contrast, the Roman army had thousands of trained soldiers who served for 20 years. Roman legions traveled with workers who could make weapons or give medical help, so they seldom needed to return to Rome. In addition, they could adapt to changing battle conditions with troops specially trained as archers, spear throwers, and so forth.

Engineering Skill

The Romans owed much to Greek culture but made many important practical achievements of their own. Engineering skill enabled the Romans to build long-lasting roads throughout the empire. The mountains of Greece, however, made road building difficult, so the Greeks more often traveled by sea. Greek builders skillfully cut and carved stone for their buildings. The Romans, on the other hand, invented a form of concrete, which was strong but lighter than stone. Concrete was used not only for roads but also in huge public works such as bridges, aqueducts, and stadiums.

LESSON 3

Early Christianity

It was the middle of the night, but Paul and Silas, two prisoners in the jail at Philippi, were praying and singing. Paul was an **apostle**—a person who spreads the message of a new religion. Suddenly, an earthquake shook the prison. Doors flew open, but the two prisoners did not run away. The jailer was amazed and relieved, for he would have been punished for their escape. He fell to his knees before the prisoners.

Then he brought them outside and said, "Sirs, what must I do to be saved?" They answered, "Believe on the Lord Jesus, and you will be saved, you and your household."

Bible, Acts 16:30–31

The New Testament of the Bible tells how apostles like Paul spread this message to many people during the first century A.D. They spoke about the new beliefs taught by Jesus.

THINKING FOCUS

How did the Christian religion begin and grow?

Key Terms

- apostle
- Gospel

The Life and Message of Jesus

Scholars are not sure of the historical facts of Jesus' life. Many now agree that he was born a Jew about 6 B.C. in the Roman province of Judea. In Rome, Augustus Caesar was still ruling as emperor. Jesus was put to death in Jerusalem in about A.D. 30. His followers later called Jesus "the Christ." This name refers to the holy oil used when kings were chosen. Jesus' followers are called Christians.

The people who first followed Jesus were Jews. Most of his teachings agreed with Jewish beliefs. As a result, the Christian and Jewish faiths share many common ideas. Most of what they teach about right and wrong is the same.

The part of the Christian Bible called the Old Testament includes the same books as the Jewish scriptures. They are a part of belief and worship services for both Christians and Jews. The rest of the Christian Bible is called the New Testament. It is the source of many basic Christian beliefs.

The Gospels

Four books of the New Testament tell how Christians understand the life of Jesus. Matthew, Mark, Luke, and John describe the

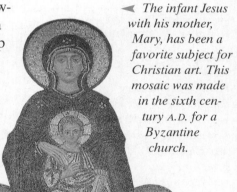

◄ *The infant Jesus with his mother, Mary, has been a favorite subject for Christian art. This mosaic was made in the sixth century A.D. for a Byzantine church.*

175

▲ *Both Christian and Jewish scriptures were originally written down in several different languages and versions. This ancient manuscript in Greek is part of Psalms, a book of the Old Testament.*

message of God's forgiveness that Jesus taught. These books are called the **Gospels**, meaning "good news."

According to Luke, at about age 30, Jesus began to travel and teach. He preached to large crowds about the kingdom of God. He told them he had come as a sign of God's offer of salvation. For Jesus, salvation meant being forgiven by God for your sins so that you could have eternal life. Jesus said that those who truly repented for their sins could enter God's kingdom. He chose 12 apostles to help him spread his message.

The Gospels say that Jesus performed miracles, which were seen as signs of the coming kingdom of God. They tell how he healed the sick, walked on water, and brought the dead back to life.

The Teachings of Jesus

Jesus followed Jewish tradition in teaching that it was important to forgive people. He said, "For if you forgive others their [wrongdoings], your heavenly Father will also forgive you" (Matthew 6:14). Even though humans did not deserve to be forgiven, Jesus said, God offered forgiveness to those who believed in God and were sorry for their sins.

Jesus knew the Jewish scriptures well. One Gospel tells about a lawyer who asked Jesus what part of the Law was the greatest. Jesus answered with verses from the Jewish scriptures:

> Y*ou shall love the Lord your God with all your heart, and with all your soul, and with all your mind." This is the greatest and first commandment. And a second is like it: "You shall love your neighbor as yourself." On these two commandments hang [depend] all the Law and the prophets.*
>
> Bible, Matthew 22:37–40

Jesus' Death and Afterward

According to the Gospels, many people listened to Jesus. They came to believe he was the son of God.

Both Roman officials and local Jewish leaders believed Jesus was dangerous. In about A.D. 30, Jesus was arrested. Under Roman law, he was put to death by crucifixion— fastened to a wooden cross until he died. This was a Roman method for carrying out death sentences.

Jesus' friends were stunned by his death. Christians believe, however, that he was resurrected, or raised from the dead, a few days later. According to the Gospels, Jesus talked to his followers several times after the crucifixion.

For Jesus' followers, the resurrection was a sign of hope. To them, it meant that all who believed in Jesus would gain God's forgiveness and have a life after death. The Christian festival of Easter celebrates the resurrection.

Christians believe that Jesus suffered to save all humanity. In a ritual called Holy Communion or the Lord's Supper, they remember Jesus' last meal with his apostles. He gave them bread and wine as symbols of his suffering. The cross on which Jesus died also became an important Christian symbol. ∎

■ *What did Jesus teach about the Jewish Law?*

The Christian Religion

According to the Gospels, Jesus himself told his close friends to spread his message of God's forgiveness for humanity. In one of his last meetings with the apostles, he had said, "Go into all the world and proclaim the good news to the whole creation" (Mark 16:15).

At Jesus' death, some of his followers returned to Jerusalem. The small group was made up of the apostles and several women, including Jesus' mother, Mary.

The Religion Grows

At first, the new religion was guided by such apostles as Peter, James, and John. Later, other people joined in their efforts. They traveled to nearby cities and countries as missionaries, telling people about Jesus' death and resurrection. The map on the next page shows how groups, or congregations, of Christians formed throughout the Roman Empire.

Some features of the Roman Empire helped Christianity spread. Missionaries used the fine Roman roads. They sailed on Roman trading ships. Some could teach in Greek or Latin, which people throughout the empire understood.

On the other hand, the missionaries spreading the new religion often were in danger. Their preaching angered people who still followed the old Gods of Greece and Rome. It also bothered local officials. Some rulers had missionaries arrested and sometimes put to death. In Jerusalem, an angry crowd chased and killed a young preacher named Stephen.

Probably the most famous apostle is Paul, a Jew born in a Greek city in Asia Minor. For years, Paul was one of the officials who arrested and threatened Christians. According to the Bible, as he traveled to Damascus one day, he saw a blinding light and heard Jesus speaking to him. Paul suddenly became a believer.

For the rest of his life, Paul journeyed from one end of the Mediterranean to another. He began new churches and wrote letters to groups in other cities. A Roman citizen, Paul used his citizenship for protection when he was arrested for preaching. The books of the New Testament include Paul's letters to early churches in Rome, Greece, and Asia Minor.

▼ *Early Christians in Rome were buried in the catacombs—long underground tunnels on the edge of the city. By the dim light of small oil lamps, Christians made their way through the catacombs to hold services at tombs that had become shrines.*

Christianity Gains a Protector

Being a Christian in the Roman Empire was often risky. Some Romans thought the new group was dangerous. Christians did not honor the Roman Gods or accept the Roman emperor as a God. They did not come to public ceremonies or festivals, which honored the Gods. Romans thought this behavior was disloyal to the empire itself. They blamed Christians for fires and other disasters. Christians in both Rome and the provinces were killed, put in prison, or sent to face wild animals in the arena.

Yet, Christians tried to obey Roman law. They also took care of the sick and the needy. Still, their beliefs and actions set them apart from the Roman community.

Gradually, however, the Roman Empire began to accept Christianity along with other religions. Then in A.D. 312, Constantine, who would become Roman emperor, had a vision. It led him to become a strong protector of the Church.

What changed Constantine's mind? According to one source, he was at war with a rival who also wanted to be Roman emperor. The night before the battle, Constantine dreamed that he should paint a Christian symbol on his soldiers' shields. After winning the battle, he became a supporter of Christianity.

Constantine later believed that his support of Christianity made him a successful ruler. He worked hard to make the Roman Empire a Christian empire. His support helped the Church become rich and powerful. Gradually, statues of the old Gods were taken down. In time, Christianity became the official religion of the Roman Empire.

Constantine built himself a city called "New Rome" at the town of Byzantium, near the eastern end of the Mediterranean Sea. In A.D. 330, Constantine made his new city the capital of the Roman Empire. He renamed it Constantinople *(kon stan tih NOH puhl)*. Today it is the city of Istanbul in modern Turkey.

► *By A.D. 200, missionaries had started Christian congregations from one end of the Mediterranean to the other. What were the easternmost and westernmost Christian settlements?*

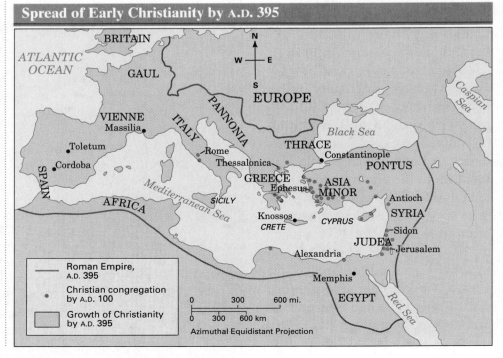

Spread of Early Christianity by A.D. 395

Christians Discuss Beliefs

By the time of Constantine, the Christian Church was well organized. The first apostles had been mainly teachers. They inspired people by preaching, as Jesus had done. Now local churches needed people to lead them and look after day-to-day business. Those chosen as leaders were called bishops.

Bishops became very important in the Church. They decided what would be taught and made rules for people in their congregations. They looked after the Church's money and property. Power was passed on from bishop to bishop.

A declaration of beliefs became a central part of early Christian services. Because this statement was so important to them, Christians argued about several questions of belief. It was the bishops who decided such questions for the Church as a whole. They wrote letters back and forth about their different points of view. They also held meetings, or councils, to discuss them.

One question was this: Was Jesus a human being, or was he divine, like God? Jesus had suffered and died as a human being. How then, some asked, could he be the son of God, as he had said he was? Perhaps he had been only a great prophet or teacher. Finally, a council of bishops agreed that Jesus was both human and divine.

Still another question was about the Trinity, the idea of "threeness." Christians, like Jews, believe in only one God. Those who believed in the Trinity said that this one God included three "persons:" God the Father, God the Son (Jesus), and the Holy Spirit. Others disagreed. Church scholars argued about the idea for centuries. By the end of the fourth century A.D., however, the Trinity became an official teaching of the Church.

Over later centuries, Christianity spread to many parts of the world. The Atlas map on page 688 shows where followers of Christianity and other religions live today. ■

▲ *This painting depicts Jesus' Last Supper with his small group of 12 apostles. This event is still remembered in Christian religious services. The painting is on a wall of the Roman catacombs.*

■ *Why were bishops important in the early Christian Church?*

R E V I E W

1. **FOCUS** How did the Christian religion begin and grow?
2. **HISTORY** How did the organization of the Roman Empire help the apostles in their work of spreading Jesus' message?
3. **BELIEF SYSTEMS** Why did Christianity seem threatening to some Romans?
4. **CRITICAL THINKING** You have read about the troubled times during the decline of the Roman Empire. How might this have helped the spread of Christianity?
5. **ACTIVITY** In your library, do research to find out more about catacombs like the one shown in the illustration on page 177. Write a three-paragraph report describing what you discovered.

Chapter Review

Reviewing Key Terms

apostle (p. 175)
aqueduct (p. 173)
citizen (p. 156)
city-state (p. 155)
democracy (p. 158)
Gospel (p. 176)

legion (p. 170)
peninsula (p. 155)
philosophy (p. 160)
province (p. 170)
republic (p. 169)

A. Each statement below uses a key term from this chapter. Tell whether each key term is used correctly. Then explain the reason for your answer.

1. The rugged geography of Greece contributed to the development of self-governing <u>city-states</u>.
2. Each <u>province</u> of the Roman Empire was like a separate country, with its own laws and rulers.

3. In the Roman army, a <u>legion</u> was a group of generals from which the next emperor would be chosen.
4. As an <u>apostle</u>, Paul arrested and threatened Christians.
5. The four <u>Gospels</u> describe what Christians understand about the life of Jesus.

B. Use a dictionary to find the origin of the following words. Then explain their importance in the ancient Mediterranean world.

1. aqueduct
2. citizen
3. democracy
4. peninsula
5. philosophy
6. republic

Exploring Concepts

A. The cultures of ancient Greece and Rome made many contributions to present-day culture. Copy and complete this chart with information from the chapter. Include at least four items for each culture.

Culture	Contributions
Greeks	tragedy, comedy
Romans	

B. Answer each question with information from the chapter.

1. How did geography affect the way people lived and worked in ancient Greece?

2. How did Greek culture spread to other parts of the ancient Mediterranean world?
3. In what ways was Pericles important in Greek history?
4. How was Roman government different under the Republic and the empire?
5. What were some of the ways in which Roman culture influenced people throughout the Roman Empire?
6. Why was the army so important in Roman history?
7. What different materials do the Old Testament and the New Testament of the Christian Bible include?
8. According to the Gospel of Luke, how and where did Jesus begin to spread his message?
9. How did the Christian religion spread? What obstacles did early Christians face?
10. What was the role of bishops in the early Christian Church?

Reviewing Skills

1. Comparing two maps of the same area can tell you how geography, history, and people's ways of life are related. For example, the maps on pages 169 and 178 show the Mediterranean world in Roman times. Compare the maps to see what they show about the relationship of the Roman world and the spread of Christianity. For instance, what major cities of the empire became the sites of new Christian congregations?

2. From your comparison of the two maps, what conclusions can you draw about the relationship between Rome and the spread of Christianity? Write a statement of your conclusions.

3. Suppose you were a historian doing research on what it was like to be a young student in ancient Rome. What kinds of written sources would you look in to find this kind of information?

Using Critical Thinking

1. In Athens, only free-born males could be citizens or members of the Assembly. Although the Athenian government would not be considered a true democracy today, it is still admired as a model. Write a paragraph telling whether or not you think this is justified.

2. "In Rome, the best and most talented people were expected to take part in government." To what extent is this true in the United States? How would you go about convincing the "best and most talented" people to work in politics and government?

3. Look at the map of Roman expansion on page G11 in the Map and Globe Handbook. Imagine that you are a member of the Roman Senate in 133 B.C., listening to a plan to extend Roman territory. What would be some advantages of doing so? What would be some problems?

4. After Constantine, Christianity became the official religion of the Roman Empire. Do you think it is a good idea for a government to give its support to one religion over all other religions? Why?

Preparing for Citizenship

1. **WRITING ACTIVITY** Although the ancient Greek myths describe the actions of Greek Gods and Goddesses, they actually show much about human nature. Read several Greek myths. Then invent a God or Goddess your own age and write your own myth. How does your main character face one of the problems of growing up?

2. **GROUP ACTIVITY** Citizens in ancient Greece or Rome had both rights and responsibilities. As a class, list rights that United States citizens have. Then develop a list of responsibilities of citizenship. Some are written laws. What are some that are unwritten but still important?

3. **ARTS ACTIVITY** Both Greeks and Romans made mosaics with small stones, tiles, or glass. (The pictures on pages 159 and 175 are mosaics.) Design and make a small mosaic. Your design might show a Greek or Roman God or Goddess, a plant or animal, or a portrait. You can use materials such as colored paper, cellophane, stones, or clay.

4. **COLLABORATIVE LEARNING** The Romans were good engineers and city planners. You have read about their roads, aqueducts, and buildings. Now work as a class to plan a new community of your own. Discuss these questions: What buildings will the community need? What kinds of services? You may want to divide into groups to work on different areas. When your plan has been finished, draw a diagram or an aerial view of your model community, and label all the important parts.

181

Chapter 8
The Arabian Peninsula

In the dry climate of the Arabian Peninsula, towns have clustered near water since ancient times. About 1,400 years ago in the town of Mecca, a religious leader named Muhammad began to spread the message of Islam. Since that time Islam has gained followers around the world. Each year hundreds of thousands of worshipers visit Saudi Arabia to affirm their faith at the holy places of Islam.

Verses from the Qur'an, the holy book of Islam, are embroidered with gold thread in intricate Arabic script on this covering for the Ka'bah.

A.D. 622 Muhammad leads Muslims from Mecca to Medina.

	500		800		1100

A.D. 500

c. 1154 Al-Idrisi, the greatest Muslim geographer, draws this map. He puts northern Europe at the bottom of the map, so that the reader looks upward toward Arabia.

Riyadh, the capital of Saudi Arabia, has some strikingly modern buildings. This shopping mall is protected from the glaring desert sun by a modern air conditioning system.

Hills surround Mecca, where Muhammad delivered the message of Islam. In the center of the picture is the Great Mosque, within which is the Ka'bah.

1932 Abdul Aziz proclaims the formation of Saudi Arabia.

	1400		1700		2000

Today

LESSON 1

Islam Develops

How did Islam develop?

Key Terms

- pilgrimage
- oasis
- caravan
- mosque

▼ *What places do pilgrims visit during the hajj?*

"ere I am, O God, at thy Command. Here I am!" The prayer echoes in the dry air of Saudi *(sah OO dee)* Arabia. Hundreds of thousands of people join in. All are Muslims, followers of the religion of Islam. They are making a religious journey, a **pilgrimage,** to the city of Mecca (see map below).

Among them is Mrs. Sara Sahali from the United States. Two days ago, when she left her family in Michigan, it was snowing. Now she is far from home. Yet, in a way, this hot, sunny place also feels like home. Here are the holy places of her religion.

Mrs. Sahali thinks of the millions of pilgrims who have gone before her. A long time ago, many

pilgrims traveled great distances by foot to get to Mecca.

When she reaches Mecca, Mrs. Sahali will join the pilgrims massed around a large, stone building. This place, the Ka'bah *(KAH buh),* is the focus of Muslim worship (see picture on page 186). All Muslims, wherever they are, turn toward Mecca and the Ka'bah when they pray. It symbolizes the unity of their belief in one God.

The most important part of the hajj, or pilgrimage, is a visit to the Plain of Arafat (see map). There the pilgrims spend the day in prayer and worship. Many climb the small hill called the Mount of Mercy. At its foot the prophet Muhammad gave his last sermon while he was on a pilgrimage to Mecca.

Performing the Pilgrimage

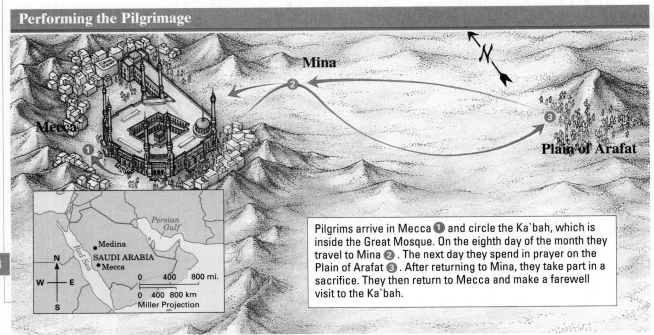

Mina

Mecca

Plain of Arafat

Persian Gulf

• Medina

SAUDI ARABIA

• Mecca

0   400   800 mi.

0   400   800 km

Miller Projection

N
W   E
S

Pilgrims arrive in Mecca ❶ and circle the Ka`bah, which is inside the Great Mosque. On the eighth day of the month they travel to Mina ❷. The next day they spend in prayer on the Plain of Arafat ❸. After returning to Mina, they take part in a sacrifice. They then return to Mecca and make a farewell visit to the Ka`bah.

The Setting

Mecca is in the western part of the Arabian Peninsula. This peninsula is the largest in the world, and lies between the Red Sea and the Persian Gulf. To the south of the peninsula is the Arabian Sea, which is part of the Indian Ocean.

Deserts and Towns

Much of the Arabian Peninsula is a high plain of rocks and sand. There are no rivers. Here and there is an **oasis** *(oh AY sihs)*, a fertile area around a spring or a waterhole. Because water is so precious in this hot, dry land, the oases attracted wandering herders and settlers. Towns grew up around many oases.

The southeastern part of Arabia is called the Empty Quarter. An area the size of Texas, it is covered with dunes of fine, soft sand. People rarely visit this barren region. No rain falls for years at a time, and fierce sandstorms are common.

The mountains along the coasts of the Red Sea and the Arabian Sea are much more inviting. There, enough rain falls for farming. The Yemeni civilization had developed in the southwestern mountains by about 1000 B.C.

Destination Mecca

Traders from southwestern Arabia sailed the seas to India and to eastern Africa, bringing back gems, silk, ivory, and precious spices. On the homeward route, many merchants sailed north on the Red Sea. Some went overland in a caravan. Each **caravan** was a long line of people and camels traveling from one oasis to another. Caravans were like cities on the move. As many as 300 traders,

camel drivers, and guards made up each caravan. Up to 2,500 camels were loaded with goods bound for Mecca. From there, other caravans carried the goods farther north.

Mecca was also the goal of Bedouin *(BEHD oo ihn)* families. For hundreds of years, the Bedouin Arabs had been herders. Each group of Bedouins had its own land. When one area was grazed over, the Bedouins moved on, looking for food and water for their herds of camels and sheep. Each group moved in a regular pattern over the lands it had claimed.

The Bedouins went to Mecca to sell the meat and milk from their camels and the wool from their sheep. From the merchants there, they bought grain, swords, and carpets. Then they visited the Ka'bah.

Like most other people in Arabia in the 500s, the Bedouins worshiped many spirits. They thought that spirits lived in the wind and rain and in bushes and stones. At the Ka'bah they prayed to stone and wooden statues that stood for these spirits. ■

▲ *Mecca may have had houses like the ones in this modern Arabian town. Thick walls keep the buildings cool inside.*

▼ *Frankincense comes from trees in southern Arabia. Incense and spices were valuable items of trade before the time of Muhammad.*

■ *Why was Mecca important to both merchants and Bedouins?*

185

Muhammad and Islam

Each year the Ka'bah is covered with a new cloth woven by hand. Verses from the Qur'an are embroidered on it in gold.

Only a small number of people in the Arabian Peninsula were Bedouins. Most Arabs lived in towns like Mecca.

Trade made Mecca a busy, noisy town. Here the prophet Muhammad was born about the year A.D. 570. Orphaned at an early age, Muhammad was brought up by relatives. He became a successful merchant and married Khadijah *(kah DEE juh),* the woman for whom he worked.

Muhammad's Vision

Muhammad often felt he needed to get away from Mecca's noise and bustle. He went out to the quiet, empty mountains near the town. According to Islamic tradition, around the year 610, when Muhammad was about 40 years old, he had a vision. This experience changed his life—and the lives of millions of other people around the world.

In the silence of the mountains, Muhammad was amazed to hear a voice. The voice seemed to come from everywhere at once. "Recite!" the voice thundered. "Recite in the name of thy Lord!" Twice more the message was repeated. Then Muhammad saw a figure looming against the sky. The figure told Muhammad that he had been chosen to be the prophet of God.

Muhammad rushed back to Mecca to tell Khadijah. She was filled with joy that her husband had been chosen as a prophet of God.

Spreading the Word

Urged on by Khadijah, Muhammad began to preach to other people in Mecca. "There is only one God," he said, using the Arabic word *Allah* for God. He urged the people of Mecca to follow God's word and lead good lives. Several of his friends and members of his family became Muslims, followers of Islam. The word *Islam* means "submission to God." A person who accepts Islam is willing to follow God's teachings in all parts of life.

At first most Meccans did not accept Muhammad's message. They did not want to give up their old religion. They also may have feared that Islam would end the profitable trade with the Bedouins. Some of the people of Mecca threatened the Muslims.

In 622 Muhammad and his followers moved to Yathrib *(YATH ruhb),* about 200 miles north of Mecca. Islam already had supporters there. Soon, Yathrib (now called Medina) became known as Medinat an-Nabi, City of the Prophet. There Muhammad and his followers put up a simple house. It became Islam's first **mosque,** a place to worship.

The migration to Medina is known as the Hijra *(HEEJ ruh).* Muslims begin their calendar on the date the Hijra occurred. The year A.D. 622 is the year 1 A.H.— the first year of the Hijra. (A.H. is Latin for *anno hegirae,* "year of the Hijra," just as the Christian date A.D., *anno domini,* is Latin for "year of the Lord.")

Return to Mecca

Within eight years of the Hijra, thousands of Arabs had become Muslims. With his followers Muhammad returned to Mecca. He destroyed the idols in the Ka'bah and restored it as the center of worship of one God. Later, the Great Mosque was built around it (see page 183).

Muhammad told the Muslims that they should honor the Ka'bah as the house of God. Muslims believe that Abraham rebuilt the original Ka'bah. They honor him as the founding father of the religions based on the belief in one God.

Until his death in 632, Muhammad continued to preach. His followers wrote down what he said on "bits of parchment, thin white stones, and leafless palm branches." These messages were gathered into the Qur'an, Islam's holy book. ■

■ *Why is the Hijra important to Muslims?*

The Teachings of Islam

Because Islam developed in Arabia, some people think of it as a desert religion. Yet Islam developed in the towns of the Arabian Peninsula. As Islam spread, it flourished in the cities.

The Qur'an

The rules guiding the lives of all Muslims are set forth in the Qur'an (sometimes spelled Koran). The table on this page shows the duties of all Muslims. The same duties apply to both men and women.

Under the laws of the Qur'an, the rights of women were broadened. Women can own and inherit property. Although a man may have as many as four wives, he must support all of them equally. A man can divorce his wife easily, but she may keep any money or property she had when she married.

The Qur'an is organized in chapters called suras. It is written in Arabic, the language spoken by the first Muslims (see the Minipedia, pages 660–673, for the Arabic alphabet). Passages such as the one on the next page have inspired faithful Muslims for centuries.

◄ *During the hajj, rich and poor pilgrims dress alike. Men wear two pieces of seamless white clothing called an* ihram. *Women cover their heads and wear simple dresses.*

Five Pillars of Islam	
Duty	**What Muslims Do**
Shahada	They express their faith by saying, "There is no god but God, and Muhammad is the messenger of God."
Salat	They pray five times a day—dawn, midday, late afternoon, sunset, and night—while facing toward Mecca.
Zakat	They give a portion of their income to the poor and to public charities.
Sawm	They fast during Ramadan, the ninth month of the Muslim year. They do not eat or drink between sunrise and sunset.
Hajj	If they are in good health and can afford it, all Muslims must make the pilgrimage to Mecca once in their lifetime.

*I*t is He who fashioned for you hearing, eyes and hearts
 (but little do you give thanks),
and it is He who scattered you through the earth
 (and to Him shall you be mustered [returned]),
and it is He who causes you to die, and to live,
and to Him belongs the alternation of night and day:
 will you not understand?

From Sura 23, the Qur'an

▼ *Flowing Arabic script makes this handwritten page of the Qur'an a work of art. This passage is in the oldest style of written Arabic.*

Ties with Other Religions

Muslims called the Jews and Christians People of the Book, meaning the Bible. The Qur'an has many ideas that parallel ideas from the Jewish Scriptures and the Christian Bible. All three religions look on Abraham as a founder and regard the Jewish prophets as messengers of God. Muhammad believed that he belonged to the same line of prophets as the prophets of the Jews and the Christians.

As a trader, Muhammad doubtless had contact with Jews and Christians. Many Jews lived in Medina, and there were Christian Arabs living in southern Arabia and East Africa.

There are important differences among the three religions. While all three believe in one God, most Christians speak of God as a Trinity and believe that Jesus was the son of God. Neither Muslims nor Jews believe that Jesus was divine. Muslims look on Jesus as a prophet, although Jews do not. Although Muslims regard Muhammad as the last and greatest of the prophets, they do not think he was divine.

Muhammad taught his followers that God's message in the Bible had been misunderstood. Muhammad said that the message of God in its pure form appears in the Qur'an.

Both the Qur'an and the Hebrew Scriptures are very much concerned with daily living. Both deal with the regulation of some parts of daily life—food, dress, customs of the home, and so forth—more than do the Christian Scriptures.

After Muhammad's death, Islam spread to lands outside Arabia. Many people there became Muslims, but many Christians and Jews kept their faith. The Muslim rulers generally allowed these People of the Book to practice their own beliefs. ■

■ *What basic beliefs do all Muslims share?*

R E V I E W

1. **FOCUS** How did Islam develop?
2. **ECONOMICS** Why did Mecca attract both merchants and Bedouins?
3. **BELIEFS** What are the five duties of all Muslims?
4. **CULTURE** Compare the teachings of Islam with the teachings of Judaism and Christianity. In what ways are the three religions alike? In what ways are these religions different?
5. **CRITICAL THINKING** Most religions have holy places that worshipers visit on pilgrimages. Christians may make a pilgrimage to Rome, and Jews go to the State of Israel. What makes the hajj of Islam different from the pilgrimages made by people of other faiths?
6. **MAP ACTIVITY** Use the modern political map in the Atlas (pages 682–683) to list the countries that are now located within the Arabian Peninsula.

LESSON 2

The Spread of Islam

After 632 Islam spread to many new lands. A golden age of learning developed. One feature of this age was an interest in science, especially medicine. Many medical advances came from Persia to the northeast of the Arabian Peninsula (see Chapter 9). A doctor there named ar-Razi was the first to make a careful study of smallpox.

Ar-Razi's work made it possible to make an accurate **diagnosis,** or identification, of disease. For centuries doctors in Europe used his diagnosis of smallpox, quoted at the right, as a model. Ar-Razi's diagnosis describes how a patient with smallpox looked and felt.

The eruption of the Small-Pox is preceded by a continued fever, pain in the back, itching in the nose, and terrors in sleep. . . . then also a pricking which the patient feels all over his body; a fullness of the face, which at times goes and comes; an inflamed color, and vehement redness in both the cheeks; . . . a heaviness of the whole body; . . . a pain in the throat and chest, with a slight difficulty in breathing, and cough; a dryness of the mouth, thick spittle, and hoarseness of the voice; pain and heaviness of the head. . . .

From *al-Judari wa Hasbah,*
A.D. 910

THINKING
FOCUS

Why is the period from 700 to 1100 called a golden age of Muslim culture?

Key Terms

- diagnosis
- caliph

The Caliphs Spread Islam

When Muhammad died, his followers worried because he had not named a successor. Who would lead the Muslims? One of Muhammad's closest followers, Abu-Bakr *(AH boo BAH kuhr),* tried to ease their fears. "O men, if you worship Muhammad, Muhammad is dead; if you worship God, God is alive."

The Early Caliphs

A group of leading Muslims met to choose a **caliph** *(KAY lihf),* a successor to Muhammad. The caliph was not expected to act as a prophet. His job was to serve as head of the Muslim state and be the defender of the faith. Abu-Bakr was chosen as the first caliph.

▼ *This painting from a Persian book shows a pharmacist mixing cough syrup. The written text gives the formula for the medicine.*

189

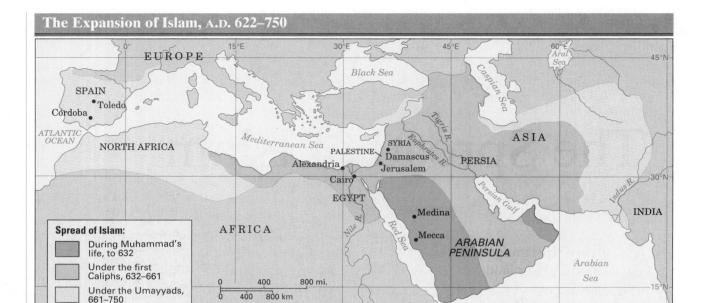

Spread of Islam:
- During Muhammad's life, to 632
- Under the first Caliphs, 632–661
- Under the Umayyads, 661–750

Miller Cylindrical Projection

▲ *This map shows the spread of Islam. What areas did the first four caliphs add? What areas did the Umayyads add? For help in reading a historical map, see page G11 in the Map and Globe Handbook.*

▼ *The chart does not include large countries with a small percentage of Muslims. For example, in 1990 about 2 percent of the U.S. population of about 250 million were Muslims.*

Largest Muslim Populations

Country	Muslim Populations	Percent
Indonesia	160,330,500	87
Pakistan	118,170,700	97
Bangladesh	96,472,400	87
India	95,298,691	11
Iran	59,103,000	99
Turkey	58,608,000	99
Egypt	50,130,000	90
Nigeria	43,248,000	48
Morocco	25,938,000	99
Ethiopia	24,435,000	45

Sources: 1992 World Population Data Sheet, Population Reference Bureau, 1992; The Europa World Year Book, 1991

He and the next three caliphs helped spread Islam beyond the Arabian Peninsula.

A Split among Muslims

The next group of caliphs came from the Umayyad *(oo MY ad)* family. The Umayyads gained power after the murder of the fourth caliph, Ali *(ah LEE)*, in A.D. 661. Ali was married to Muhammad's daughter Fatima *(FAHT uh muh)*. Muslims who supported Ali refused to recognize the Umayyad caliphs. Fighting between the two groups of Muslims led to the murder of Ali's son Husayn in 680.

Today there are still two main groups of Muslims. The larger group is known as Sunni *(SUN ee)*. Sunni Muslims believe that the only sources of Islam are the Qur'an—that is, the word of God—and the traditions of Muhammad. Their name comes from the *sunna*, the deeds and sayings of Muhammad and the actions he permitted. More than 85 percent of the world's Muslims are Sunnis.

The smaller group of Muslims is known as Shi'a *(SHEE uh)* or Shiites. Most Shi'as live in Iran and Iraq. Their name means "party" and refers to Ali's supporters. The Shi'as believe there are three sources of Islam: the Qur'an, Muhammad, and Ali's descendants.

The Appeal of Islam

The Umayyads ruled the Muslim state between 661 and 750, adding vast areas to its territory. By 750 all of North Africa was Muslim. Muslim armies also reached central France before Christian forces pushed them back into Spain. To the east, Islam reached India. The map above shows how far Islam spread in about 125 years.

By 750 the Muslim world included people from many countries and walks of life. Islam had followers among city dwellers, people in villages, and farmers in tropical lowlands. Today many countries have large Muslim populations (see chart).

Why did so many people accept Islam? Some welcomed the idea that all Muslims are equal. "Know that every Muslim is a Muslim's brother," Muhammad had said. Some were attracted by the idea that all Muslims are joined in a community, or *umma,* that requires the same five duties of all followers (see Lesson 1). Islam provides a guide to daily life that all believers can follow. ■

■ *What caused a split among the followers of Islam?*

Muslim Achievements

As the religion of Islam spread, Muslim culture flowered. From 700 to 1100, Muslim culture experienced a golden age. Many cities in the Muslim world had lighted streets. In some homes fountains cooled the air and pleased the ear with the sound of falling water.

Science and Medicine

The caliphs of the golden age built schools and libraries. Cairo, Egypt, was said to have a library with 100,000 books on history, astronomy, Islamic law, and other subjects. At this time learning in Europe was in decline. Yet the ideas of ancient Greek and Roman writers survived. They were preserved in part because Muslim scholars translated the works into Arabic. As learning revived in Europe, these volumes were translated back into Western languages.

The caliphs also promoted science. Physicists studied light and how the eye sees it. Astronomers kept records of the ways the planets move, and biologists described plants and animals. These scientists learned to look with care at the world around them. They made careful notes of what they saw and did experiments to test their ideas. Today's scientists still use methods like those of Muslim scientists.

Muslims also made advances in mathematics. They brought the use of zero and the Indian numeral system to Southwest Asia. From there these numerals spread to Europe.

You know them as our Arabic numerals and use them every day. Muslims also improved on the geometry used by the Greeks and did original work in algebra. In fact, the words *algebra* and *algorithm*—a method for solving problems—both come from the Arabic language.

In Muslim hospitals chemists made oils and ointments to use in medicine. Doctors vowed to care for the sick by repeating the Hippocratic Oath (page 160). They diagnosed diseases and performed surgery. Some devoted their lives to caring for children.

Trade and Geography

Muslim traders regularly moved back and forth from Spain to India and China, using Arabic as a common language. They had maps drawn of trade routes and encouraged travelers to write about their journeys. These accounts added greatly to knowledge of the world.

One of the greatest travelers of all time was Ibn Battuta. In 1325 he set out from Tangier, Morocco, to make the hajj. He returned home 29 years later. During these years Ibn Battuta crossed two continents and traveled 75,000 miles by land and sea.

Across Time & Space

Paintings showing scientists studying the skies reflect Muslim interest in astronomy. The star maps they made show star names that are still used—Altair, Deneb, Rigel, and Aldebaran. All of these names are from the Arabic language.

▼ *Muslim scientists used an astrolabe like this one to figure the time for prayers and to find stars and planets. The Arabic numerals on the dial mark off 360 degrees.*

▲ *The Pearl Mosque in India (above) has domes that borrow from Indian styles of architecture. Muslim designs of brightly colored tiles decorate a wall in Fez, Morocco (right).*

■ *What achievements did Muslims make during their golden age?*

He described the markets and mosques of Southwest Asia, the frozen plains of Russia, bustling cities in India and China, and the many peoples he met.

Muslim merchants traded in an enormous variety of products. They introduced dozens of plant products to Western Europe, including oranges, lemons, apricots, dates, rice, and sugar. The master swordmakers of Damascus, Syria, invented damascene, a way to inlay gold and silver in steel. Damask, a cloth with a finely woven pattern, was another product from Damascus. From Mosul, Iraq, came the sheer cotton cloth called muslin. Books were bound in cordovan leather from Córdoba, Spain.

Muslim Art

Muslim artists created more than swords, cloth, and books. The Qur'an did not forbid pictures of people and animals. Muhammad and many Muslims, however, felt it was disrespectful. They believed that only God has the power to create life. Muslim artists made writing a form of art. They copied verses from the Qur'an in flowing Arabic script. Beautifully handwritten copies of the Qur'an are among the treasures of Muslim art.

Some Muslim artists, particularly in Iran and India, showed figures of people and animals. Many others made designs out of stone and tiles. They formed patterns of stars, circles, and triangles and copied the shapes of flowers and trees. Complex patterns of intertwined lines are called arabesques. Muslim artists today still use designs like these. ■

REVIEW

1. **FOCUS** Why is the period from 700 to 1100 called a golden age of Muslim culture?
2. **BELIEFS** What are the two main groups of Muslims? Explain what still unites these groups.
3. **CULTURE** What contributions did Muslims make to science and mathematics during the golden age of Muslim culture?
4. **CRITICAL THINKING** Explain what Abu-Bakr meant when he said, "If you worship Muhammad, Muhammad is dead; if you worship God, God is alive."
5. **WRITING ACTIVITY** Using ar-Razi's diagnosis as an example, write a description of the symptoms you noticed when you were feeling ill with a cold, the flu, or some other disease.

Chapter 8

L E S S O N   3

Saudi Arabia Today

For centuries, whenever travelers arrived at a Bedouin's tent, they knew they would be given water, food, and shelter. Today, at the start of a business meeting, the Saudis continue this ancient custom of welcoming guests by offering visitors tea to drink.

Every place in the world has its own customs. In Saudi Arabia many customs are tied to the rules of Islam. For example, Muslims may not drink alcohol or eat pork, which is viewed as unclean.

Cleanliness is an important part of worship for Muslims. Before they pray, they wash their hands, faces, and feet. When they enter a mosque, they take off their shoes to avoid tracking dirt inside.

Islam also influences working hours in Saudi Arabia. At noontime, midafternoon, and sunset, stores and businesses close to allow workers to meet their duty to pray (see table, page 187). On Friday businesses are closed for most of the day. Friday is Islam's holy day, when many people go to a mosque for midday prayers.

Some Saudi social customs combine Bedouin and Muslim practices. Since ancient times, for example, the Arabs have believed that women should dress very modestly. In the Qur'an the wives of Muhammad are advised to wear veils. Muslim women are expected to keep their hair covered, and in Saudi Arabia they usually wear face veils in public. These customs show the mixture of Muslim and Bedouin beliefs and ways of life in modern Saudi Arabia.

THINKING FOCUS

How has oil changed life in Saudi Arabia?

Key Terms

- censor
- desalination

▲ *Muslims remove their shoes when entering a mosque. While praying, they touch the floor with their head and hands.*

◀ *The tiny cups in which tea is served are often decorated with floral designs.*

193

The Arabian Peninsula

The Saudi Kingdom

Saudi Arabia is the only country in all the world that is named for its ruling family—the Sauds. If history had been different, it might have been called Rashidi Arabia.

Forming a Kingdom

For many years, the Saud and Rashid families had been enemies. In 1891 the Rashids attacked the Saudi town of Riyadh *(ree YAHD)*. They poured poison into the wells and cut down the date palms. The Sauds fled to the desert on the edge of the Empty Quarter (see page 185). Their leader's 15-year-old son was hidden in a basket strapped to the back of a camel.

The young prince, Abdul Aziz *(AHB dul ah ZEEZ),* vowed to regain Riyadh. One cold winter's night 11 years later, he and a small raiding party climbed the town wall. At dawn, with a loud war cry, Abdul Aziz attacked. When the battle ended, the Saudi forces had won back Riyadh.

By the early 1920s, Abdul Aziz controlled most of the Arabian Peninsula except Yemen. In 1932 he declared himself king of Saudi Arabia. Today Saudi Arabia welcomes representatives from many nations, as shown in A Closer Look on page 195.

Introducing Modern Ways

King Abdul Aziz often said, "The chief of a tribe is its servant." He liked to talk about his plans with the leading men of different families. He encouraged his subjects to come to him with their problems.

Although Abdul Aziz listened to the advice of others, he was the one who made all the decisions. Saudi Arabia is one of the few nations in the world today that is ruled by one person with nearly absolute power. The Saudi ruler has almost complete control, and his word is law. Yet because Saudi Arabia is a Muslim country, its laws must agree with the rules of Islam.

➤ *During the hajj the tent city on the Plain of Arafat stretches to the horizon. Here the Saudi government provides sanitary areas and tents where pilgrims can rest and eat, get first aid, and find friends and relatives who are lost.*

Arabian Hospitality

In their proud tradition of hospitality, the Saudi Arabians built the Tuwaiq Palace to welcome foreign diplomats to the capital city of Riyadh. Like an ancient oasis, the palace offers protection against the desert sun and winds.

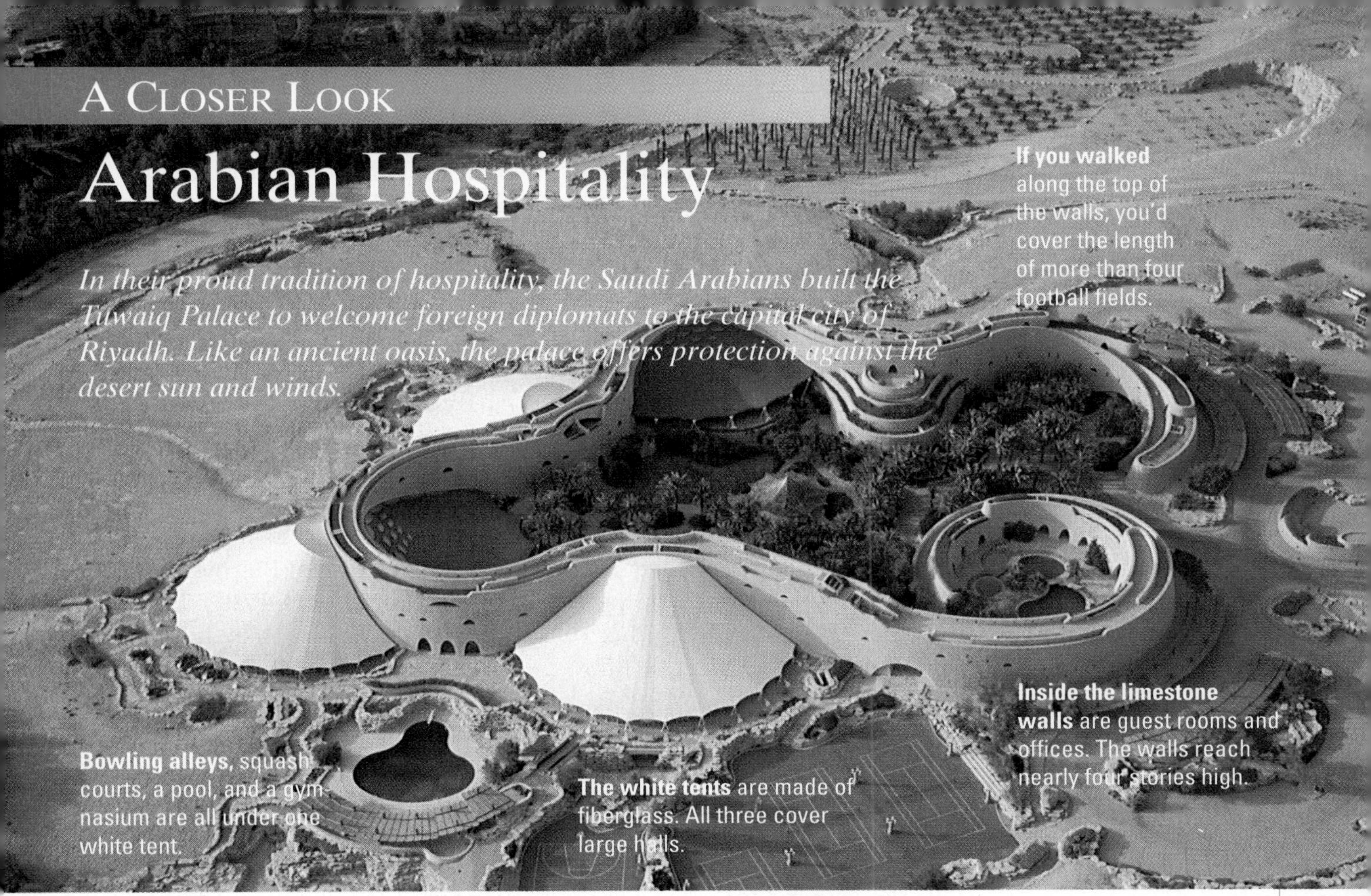

If you walked along the top of the walls, you'd cover the length of more than four football fields.

Inside the limestone walls are guest rooms and offices. The walls reach nearly four stories high.

Bowling alleys, squash courts, a pool, and a gymnasium are all under one white tent.

The white tents are made of fiberglass. All three cover large halls.

When Abdul Aziz first allowed automobiles and cameras into Saudi Arabia, many people opposed him. They said the changes were against the teachings of Islam. One sheik, a religious leader, thought the radio was a tool of the devil. After all, he said, it made words come out of the air!

Abdul Aziz asked, "Would Satan carry God's word?"

The sheik replied, "You know and I know that Satan would never carry the word of God one inch."

The king then led the sheik to the radio. Through the crackle of static, they could hear a voice reading verses from the Qur'an. This convinced the sheik that the radio was not some evil invention.

Changes by Later Kings

Abdul Aziz used similar methods to get roads and railroads built.

By the time he died in 1953, Saudi Arabia had modern cities as well as desert villages. Abdul Aziz's son Faisal *(FY suhl),* who came to the throne in 1964, continued his father's policies. He also supported the schools his wife, Iffat *(IHF iht),* set up to teach boys mathematics and science. She also planned schools for girls, courses in typing, and women's health clinics.

When Faisal's half-brother, Fahd, became king in 1982, he used the title Custodian of the Two Holy Mosques. It emphasized the Saud family's duties toward pilgrims. Each year the government provides transportation and shelter for pilgrims. Caravans of tanker trucks carry water to the pilgrims each day, and kitchens supply them with food.

A printing plant supplies Muslims around the world with about 10 million free copies of the Qur'an

195

The Arabian Peninsula

yearly. King Fahd also decided that the Saudi government should pay for the cost of educating the people of the kingdom and providing them with health care.

Programs such as these cost a great deal of money. How do the Saudis pay for them? The answer lies in the oil that is buried under the desert sands. ■

The Impact of Oil

The kingdom Abdul Aziz had created in 1932 was very poor. It is said that the head of the treasury kept all the nation's money in a box in his home! Abdul Aziz knew that oil had been found in desert areas in other countries. In 1933 he agreed to let a U.S. oil company drill in Saudi Arabia. In March 1938 the drills finally made a major strike. The discovery changed Saudi Arabia forever.

Oil Becomes a Weapon

At the end of World War II in 1945, the demand for oil soared. The largest demand came from industrial countries like the United States. When U.S. oil companies could not meet the demand, companies in Saudi Arabia and other countries filled the gap. Saudi oil was cheap, and the supply seemed endless. Saudi Arabia had over one-fourth of the world's known oil reserves. Soon the Saudi princes were collecting millions of dollars in oil profits each year.

By 1960 the Saudis wanted more control of their oil. They met with four other oil-producing nations—Iran, Iraq, Kuwait *(koo WAYT),* and Venezuela—to form the Organization of Petroleum Exporting Countries (OPEC). Eight other nations later joined them. OPEC raised the price of oil and controlled the amount produced.

Then, in 1973, war broke out between the Arab nations and Israel. Like other Arab leaders, Faisal was opposed to Israel. He stopped shipping oil to nations supporting Israel. Oil and gasoline became scarce in the industrial nations, and prices soared. Worried about how much they depended on foreign oil, people in the United States began to look for ways to use less oil.

Five months later the United States agreed to provide support and help for the development of Saudi Arabia. Faisal reluctantly began to ship oil again.

Worries about Change

Although the Saudis have set up modern industries, they have held onto many traditional values. Many Saudi women teach, run computers, act as doctors, and work in banks. Yet women are usually separated from male co-workers. Male teachers instruct female students over closed-circuit TV. No woman can stay in a hotel, ride in an airplane, or study abroad without

This oil refinery at Ras Tanura is one of the four largest in the world. Oil produces nearly all the kingdom's income. Less than 2 percent of the workers in Saudi Arabia, however, are employed in the oil industry.

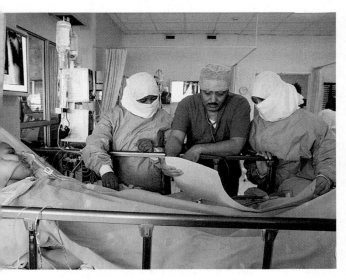

Kuwait. In 1990 Iraq renewed its claims. During a costly war with Iran (page 216), Iraq had borrowed large sums of money from Kuwait and Saudi Arabia, which also had opposed Iran. The Iraqis thought Kuwait should cancel the debt, but Kuwait refused. On August 2, 1990, Iraqi troops invaded Kuwait.

When the Iraqis moved south, King Fahd felt Saudi Arabia was threatened. Industrial nations such as the United States, Germany, and Japan did not want Iraq controlling another major source of oil. The United Nations voted to drive the Iraqis out of Kuwait. Almost all the Arab nations agreed, although Libya, Jordan, and Yemen did not. This was the first time Arab nations had joined forces with the United States for the purpose of attacking another Arab country.

In January 1991 multinational troops sponsored by the United Nations launched an attack called Operation Desert Storm. The troops soon drove the Iraqis out of Kuwait.

New Sources of Income

Oil income has helped the Saud family do many things for the nation. Yet scientists know that the world's supply of oil is limited. Once the present supply of oil has been pumped out of the ground, there will be no more.

▲ In modern wars soldiers wear clothing that blends in with the land around them. The "pyramids" in this picture from the Persian Gulf War are really tents designed to blend in with the desert. Saudi troops played an important role in the war.

written permission from a male relative or an official sponsor.

The Saudi government censors printed materials, music, and films. To **censor** something is to cut out anything that seems objectionable, or stop it from being sold. Censored books may be removed from libraries and bookstores. In the United States, freedom of speech and the press are basic rights. These rights do not exist in Saudi Arabia, but many Saudis are beginning to demand them.

The Saudis also worry about unrest in Southwest Asia. In the past, civil war in Lebanon, war between Iran and Iraq, and clashes between Israel and the Muslim nations have threatened to tear the region apart. (Find these nations on the Atlas map on pages 682–683.) Also, many Muslim nations have large populations but low incomes. They feel Saudi Arabia should share its wealth with less fortunate Muslims.

War in the Gulf

One of these nations, Iraq, had a special interest in Kuwait, Saudi Arabia's oil-rich neighbor on the Persian Gulf. When Iraq became independent in 1932, it claimed

Desalination provides water for irrigation so Saudi farmers can grow larger crops. The graph shows how greatly wheat production increased after irrigation became widely used. Today Saudi Arabia produces all the wheat it needs.

Wheat Production, 1975–1990

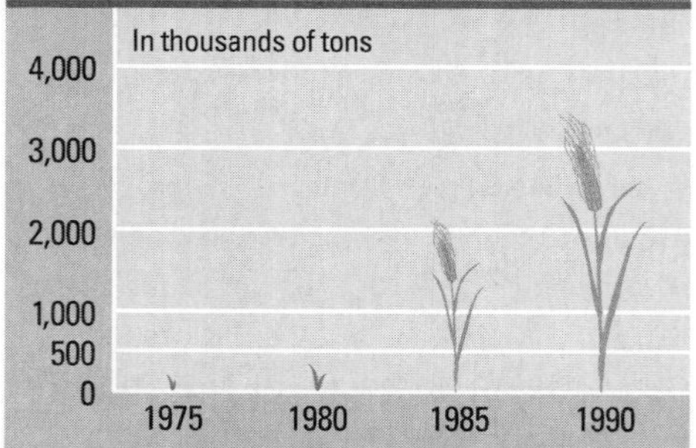

In thousands of tons

4,000
3,000
2,000
1,000
500
0

1975   1980   1985   1990

Source: The Royal Embassy of Saudi Arabia Information Office

The Saud family is trying to develop new sources of income for the country. The Saudis have reopened gold mines. They have started a cement factory, steel mills, and fertilizer plants. Along the coasts they have built plants for the desalination of sea water. The process of **desalination** removes the salt. People can then use the desalinated water for drinking and cooking or for irrigating crops (see the graph).

Need for Workers

Saudi Arabia has only about 16 million people. There simply are not enough people to do the hard work needed to develop the country as quickly as King Fahd wishes.

Workers are needed to build factories and roads, string electric lines, drive trucks, and work in Saudi stores and banks. Nearly 60 percent of these workers now come from other countries.

Foreign workers are not allowed to bring their wives or families with them. They may not become citizens of Saudi Arabia. Although many foreigners may go home on leave, most return. They know they can earn more money in Saudi Arabia than they can at home.

At first, most foreign workers were Muslims from other Arabic-speaking countries. They found it fairly easy to fit into Saudi society. Now, more and more of these workers come from such countries as Sri Lanka, India, Pakistan, and the Philippines. Many of these workers do not speak Arabic. Some are not even Muslims. In time these foreign workers may come to outnumber the native-born Saudi population.

Saudi Arabia has faced many changes in the 60 years it has taken to become a modern nation. In the years to come, the nation may face even greater changes. ■

■ *What major problems does Saudi Arabia face today?*

R E V I E W

1. **FOCUS** How has oil changed life in Saudi Arabia?
2. **BELIEFS** Why did Abdul Aziz have difficulty introducing modern inventions to Saudi Arabia?
3. **ECONOMICS** How do Saudi Arabia and industrial nations such as the United States depend on one another?
4. **CRITICAL THINKING** How would your life change if the world ran out of oil? Where would people get energy?

5. **WRITING ACTIVITY** Coins used in Saudi Arabia bear the words of the Islamic statement of faith: "There is no god but God, and Muhammad is the messenger of God." Examine the sayings found on all U.S. coins. Write a short statement telling what each saying reveals about the United States.

Making Parallel Timelines

Here's Why

Many timelines show you dates from a single culture or nation. Some timelines show links among different groups. They are called parallel timelines because they show parallels among events. For example, some of the events you will read about later in Chapter 21 happened at the same time as some events in this chapter. By using a parallel timeline such as the one below, you can fit together different pieces of history. This will let you compare and contrast the events that happened at the same time.

Here's How

You can follow these steps to make a parallel timeline.

1. **Decide what you want your timeline to do.** You might want to use it to compare the histories of two groups. You might want to show what people were doing when certain events took place. The timeline below shows important dates in technology and Saudi Arabian history.
2. **Decide what span of dates your timeline will show.** The timeline below begins with the year 1930 and ends with 1990. It is divided into 10-year segments.
3. **Gather dates and information about events for your timeline.**
4. **Plot the events near the appropriate dates on the timeline.**

Try It

The list below gives some important inventions that were made after 1930. Copy the timeline below. Add the dates and inventions on the list. Plot the following inventions on the appropriate segment of the timeline.
- 1932, Polaroid glass developed, later used in sunglasses.
- 1938, Ballpoint pen invented.
- 1939, Television shown at the New York World's Fair.
- 1943, First successful electronic computer started operating.
- 1972, Advances made in compact disc technology.

Now, use the timeline you enlarged to answer the following questions.
1. Which invention was made the year Abdul Aziz became king?
2. Which invention helped Saudis keep track of how much oil they produced and sold?
3. Which invention let people in the United States see events as they happened in the Persian Gulf War?

Apply It

Create a parallel timeline. On one part, show events in your life or in your family's history. Use an almanac to find events in U.S. history that happened about the same time.

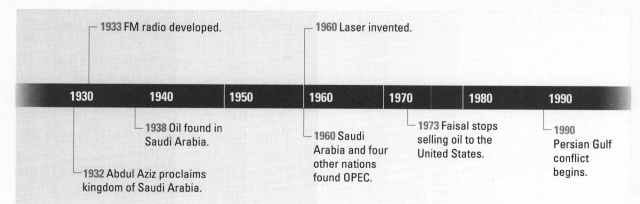

1933 FM radio developed.

1960 Laser invented.

1930 — 1940 — 1950 — 1960 — 1970 — 1980 — 1990

1938 Oil found in Saudi Arabia.

1960 Saudi Arabia and four other nations found OPEC.

1973 Faisal stops selling oil to the United States.

1990 Persian Gulf conflict begins.

1932 Abdul Aziz proclaims kingdom of Saudi Arabia.

199

Chapter Review

Reviewing Key Terms

caliph (p. 189)
caravan (p. 185)
censor (p. 197)
desalination (p. 198)

diagnosis (p. 189)
mosque (p. 186)
oasis (p. 185)
pilgrimage (p. 184)

3. caliph
4. diagnosis
5. censor
6. oasis
7. mosque
8. caravan

A. Imagine you are playing a game with a partner. Your partner tries to guess which key term you are thinking of. For each key term below, think of a phrase you could give to your partner as a clue. Write each phrase on your own paper. An example has been filled in for you.
1. pilgrimage: a religious journey
2. desalination

B. Read each pair of words. Write a sentence telling how the words in each pair are related.
1. caravan, oasis
2. pilgrimage, mosque
3. caliph, censor
4. caravan, pilgrimage

Exploring Concepts

A. In about 125 years, Islam spread from Arabia into Africa, Europe, and Asia. Today this religion has one of the largest followings in the world. Copy and complete the following outline.

I. The Spread of Islam
  A. After Muhammad's death, the caliphs begin spreading Islam beyond Arabia.
  B. Muslims split into two groups of believers.
    1.
    2.
  C. The teachings of Islam appeal to many people.
    1.
    2.
    3.
  D. Muslims make cultural advances.
    1.
    2.
    3.
    4.
    5.

B. Answer each question with information from the chapter.
1. What part does Mecca play in the Islamic religion?
2. Why did an early civilization develop in the the southwestern mountains of Arabia?
3. Why were most Meccans slow to accept Muhammad's message?
4. How did the Islamic religion affect the status of women?
5. Why did so many people come to accept Islam?
6. What role did Muslim scholars play in preserving the ideas of ancient Greek and Roman writers?
7. What were the contributions of Muslim merchants during the golden age?
8. What influence does Islam have on customs in Saudi Arabia?
9. What role did Abdul Aziz play in the development of Saudi Arabia?
10. Why was Operation Desert Storm a turning point in relations between the United States and the Arab nations?

Reviewing Skills

1. Look at the timeline on this page. It shows important dates during the golden age of Muslim culture. Using the timeline, figure out the number of years between the time when the Muslim armies began their conquest of Spain and the date when they were expelled by Christian Spain. Did the Crusaders capture Jerusalem before or after the Muslims began their conquest of Spain?

2. Look at the map on page 190 showing the spread of Islam. Imagine that you are a Muslim traveling in a caravan. Using the map scale, figure out how far it is from Mecca to Damascus. If your caravan traveled at 10 miles per hour, how long would the trip take?

3. Imagine that you are keeping a journal of your travels. What kinds of information would you include in your journal?

600	800	1000	1200	1400	1600	1800

A.D. 711 Muslim conquest of Spain begins.

A.D. 998 Muslim armies conquer northern India.

A.D. 1099 Crusaders capture Jerusalem.

A.D. 1010 Destruction of Christian holy places in Jerusalem ordered.

A.D. 1492 Muslims expelled from Spain.

Using Critical Thinking

1. Islam, Christianity, and Judaism all expanded from the same part of the world. In fact, Jerusalem is a holy city to all three faiths. What might there have been about this region that encouraged the spread of religious beliefs?

2. After 632, as Islam spread to many lands, a golden age of learning developed. Do you think there is a connection? Explain.

3. After Ali and his son Husayn were murdered, the Muslims split into two groups, the Sunnis and the Shi'as. Do you think they could ever be reunited? Explain.

4. In 1973 Faisal stopped shipping oil to nations supporting Israel. When people in the United States looked for ways to use less oil, however, Faisal began to ship oil again. If he had not resumed oil shipments, how might the events of 1990–1991 in the Persian Gulf have been different?

Preparing for Citizenship

1. **COLLECTING INFORMATION** Most of the people living in Saudi Arabia are Muslims. Use an almanac to find and list the names of the major religious groups in the United States. Include the number of members each has.

2. **ARTS ACTIVITY** Muslim artists made writing a form of art. Sometimes, artists in the United States have treated writing as an art form. Collect photographs, pictures, or books that show writing as an art form, or create a work of your own using writing as an art form. Share your collection or your own artwork with the class.

3. **GROUP ACTIVITY** The Qur'an contains rules guiding the lives of all Muslims. In small groups, make a set of rules for your school. What do you think is good school behavior? Display your rules on a poster.

4. **COLLABORATIVE LEARNING** People from other countries come to both the United States and Saudi Arabia to live and work. In small groups, give a presentation on the experience of newcomers to the United States. Brainstorm to create a list of questions you would ask a recent immigrant. As a group, decide how to present your findings to the class.

Chapter 9

Iran

For more than 2,500 years, the Plateau of Iran has been a crossroads for people moving between Asia and the Mediterranean. Here the Persian Empire arose about 550 B.C., and the Zoroastrian religion became important. About A.D. 640 Islam spread to Persia, and 900 years later the Persian ruler turned to the Shi'a branch of Islam. The stage was set for the modern revolution that turned Iran into a republic guided by the teachings of Islam.

Persian artisans were noted for their metalwork. This plate of silver, made about A.D. 350, shows a Sasanian ruler hunting wild boars, a favorite pastime of Persian shahs.

1500	1000	500	B.C.	A.D.

550 B.C. Cyrus the Great forms the Persian Empire.

1500 B.C.

Items like this pear, made of gold set in steel, appeared in Persian markets around 1600, during the rule of Shah Abbas I. Artists often made models of fruit because faithful Muslims are promised they will find abundant fruits in paradise.

Today each Iranian bazaar, or market, is a city within a city. Shopkeepers and clerks meet and talk here. During the revolution of 1979, they helped organize protests against the government.

1502 The first Safavid ruler makes Shi'a Islam the official religion in Persia.

500	1000	1500	2000

c. 642 Islam begins to spread in Persia.

c. 1925 Reza Shah begins attempts to modernize Iran.

Today

LESSON 1

Iran's Land and Traditions

THINKING FOCUS

What is the land of Iran like?

Key Terms

- plateau
- arid

➤ *The Rudbar quake brought down buildings made of concrete as well as houses of dried-mud bricks.*

The clock had just struck midnight in the lonely village of Rudbar. Usually, its farmers and their families were fast asleep. Tonight, however, many of them were awake. They were watching the World Cup soccer match on television. Suddenly, there was a grinding roar. Houses shook. Walls cracked and crumbled. All over the village, roofs crashed down, burying screaming men, women, and children. In less than a minute, almost every building in Rudbar was flattened. With bleeding hands the weeping survivors dug among the rubble, looking for members of their families.

On that June night in 1990, a single earthquake leveled more than 100 towns in northwestern Iran *(ih RAHN)*. As many as 50,000 Iranians were killed, and more than 100,000 were hurt. About 500,000 people were left without homes, food, water to drink, or blankets to protect them from the chilly nights.

The 1990 earthquake was not the first to hit Iran. Find the Caspian Sea on the map on page 205. People living around the Caspian Sea experience dozens of quakes each year. Iran lies right in the middle of an earthquake zone stretching from Europe's Mediterranean shore to the Pacific Ocean. Most quakes in Iran are minor, but some cause as much damage as the one at Rudbar.

Earthquakes are very destructive forces. Yet they are only one of Iran's challenges. Its landforms and climate cause other problems.

The Land of Iran

Iran is a combination of mountains and a huge plateau. A **plateau** is an area of fairly level land that is higher than the land around it. Rising 3,000 to 5,000 feet above sea level, the Plateau of Iran covers more than three-fourths of the country. In its center are two salt deserts, the remains of dried-up lakes.

Iran's Hills and Plains

Most Iranians live on the edge of the plateau, in the foothills and valleys of the mountains. Stretching from northwestern Iran to the Persian Gulf are the mighty Zagros *(ZAG ruhs)* Mountains. In places, rows of these mountains form a wall 150 miles wide. The Elburz Mountains curve along the south shore of the Caspian Sea. They include the highest mountain in Iran, Mount Damavand. More than 18,000 feet high, this mountain's snowcapped peak seems to float above the dusty plateau.

Dust, in fact, is common in this **arid,** or dry, land. Much of the Plateau of Iran gets only a few

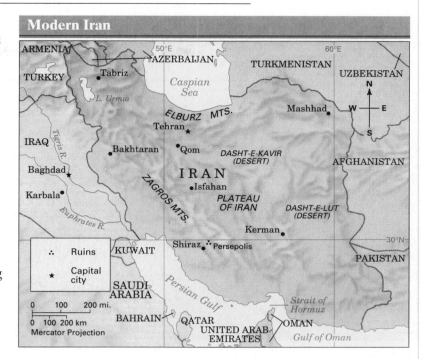

Modern Iran

inches of rain each year. Dry summer winds make the land even more arid. Although forests grow along the Caspian Sea, most of Iran is so arid that crops can be grown only with irrigation.

Finding Water

Farmers get water from the rivers after rains and from the snow melting from the mountains. In some places dams store water for irrigation and electric power.

The Iranians also have a special way of getting water. If you flew over the plateau, you would see a line of large holes. They look like huge, round footprints marching for miles across the plateau. These holes lead to an underground water system. This system was created as many as 2,500 years ago.

The ancient Iranians dug deep shafts that reached 30 to 100 feet below the surface. There they tapped into the water table, the

▲ *Find the dried-up lakes in the Plateau of Iran. How could they make travel across Iran difficult?*

◄ *Tehran, Iran's modern capital, lies at the foot of Mount Damavand.*

moisture that is far below the ground. They built underground canals called *qanats (KAH nahts)* to carry water to the fields. These canals followed the slope of the land. The system worked so well that it is still in use. In the darkness 30 to 100 feet below the surface, water flows silently to villages as far as 50 miles away. ■

Iranians and Their Traditions

▲ *Many Iranian villages nestle in mountain valleys.*

Although Iran is mountainous and arid, it has long been a land bridge linking Asia and the eastern Mediterranean. Herders, soldiers, and traders have moved into and across the Plateau of Iran for many centuries.

Peoples and Languages

About 1500 B.C. small groups of people may have begun to drift south from the region around the Aral Sea. (See the Atlas map on page 682.) This casual southward movement probably went on for hundreds of years. Some of the migrating groups traveled south and east in the direction of India. Other groups moved south and then turned westward into Iran.

The southward-moving peoples spoke several related languages. These languages belonged to the Indo-Iranian group, which is part of the far-flung Indo-European family of languages.

Iran's name comes from the Aryan subgroup of Indo-Iranian languages. For many years, however, people in other nations used the name Persia for Iran. The ancient Greeks took this name from Parsa, the name of an Iranian province. We still speak of the ancient Persian Empire, the Persian language, and Persian art and literature. The name of the modern nation, however, is Iran.

Most Iranians now speak modern Persian, called Farsi, or related languages. Azerbaijanis *(ah zuhr by JAH neez)* are the largest minority group in Iran. They speak Azeri, a language related to Turkish. Like the Farsi-speaking majority of Iranians, the Azerbaijanis are Shi'a Muslims.

Zoroastrianism

Although Shi'a Islam is the major faith in Iran today, traces remain of some very old beliefs. One of the oldest goes back to Zoroaster *(ZAWR oh ahs tuhr),*

➤ *Iranian women have worn head coverings since ancient times. These Baluchi women are baking bread.*

who was born about 628 B.C. His teachings introduced ideas that became important to the religions based on belief in one God.

Zoroaster spoke of a struggle between good and evil. The good, represented by Ahura Mazda, includes light, life, and truth. Opposing good is Ahriman, the lie, a force of evil, darkness, and death. Zoroaster said only Ahura Mazda should be worshiped. He taught that good would finally defeat evil. He made it clear, however, that each person was free to choose between the forces of good and evil. People who lived good lives could expect to go to paradise, or heaven, after they died.

Shi'a Islam

In the 600s Islam reached Iran. Nearly all Iranians today are Muslims, and most of them belong to the Shi'a branch of Islam (see Chapter 8). One of their most important anniversaries each year is Ashura, a time of mourning for the death of Husayn, grandson of Muhammad. During Ashura many Iranians take part in religious plays. These dramas tell the sad story of Husayn's death.

Now Rouz

Muslim and ancient Zoroastrian beliefs can both be found in Now Rouz, the New Year's celebration in Iran. Now Rouz starts on March 21 as the snow is melting and flowers are beginning to bloom.

Weeks before the new year, women begin to clean house, mend clothes, and fix broken household goods. Each family plants seeds of grain in pots inside the house. By March 21 the grain has tender green shoots. Iranians believe that the plants pick up any unhappiness in the home.

Candles or lamps found in each home are a reminder of ancient Zoroastrian beliefs that light stands for good. Each Muslim home proudly shows a copy of the Qur'an, a sign that God comes first in people's lives. When the cannon booms to call in the new year, many Iranians go to the mosque to pray. Others worship at home.

Dressed in new clothes, the Iranians share meals with friends and family. For each person there is a small gift—a toy for a child, a piece of jewelry, scented soap, an article of clothing, or a small plant.

Now Rouz is at least 2,500 years old. One of Iran's greatest rulers even built a city where the New Year's festival could be celebrated. You will read about this city, Persepolis (*puhr SEHP uh lihs*), in the next lesson. ■

Among the things that might be seen in an Iranian home during Now Rouz are fish in a bowl, grain, an apple, and garlic to keep away evil spirits.

■ *What is Now Rouz?*

R E V I E W

1. **FOCUS** What is the land of Iran like?
2. **GEOGRAPHY** What problems do Iranians face because of the natural environment?
3. **CULTURE** How are the people of Iran and India connected?
4. **BELIEFS** What two forces did Zoroaster describe?

5. **CRITICAL THINKING** What evidence is there that some cultural traditions followed in Iran are very old?
6. **ACTIVITY** Now Rouz is a family event. What special events does your family celebrate? Write a paragraph telling about one event and what family members might do.

L E S S O N   2

Iran's Proud Legacy

THINKING
FOCUS

What did different ruling families contribute to Persia?

Key Terms

- shah
- satrap

A soft breeze kicks up a cloud of dust and swirls it across a huge stone platform. Broad, stone stairs rise from the dusty plain to the platform, which is nearly as long as five football fields. Beside the stairway, long rows of marching men are carved in stone. One is tugging at a snorting horse. Two others hold squirming lion cubs. Others march by leading a prize bull, a pair of woolly rams, and a stately two-humped camel from central Asia. There are men carrying elephant tusks from Africa and jars of gold dust from India. Others hold bolts of fine cloth, gold vases with handles shaped like winged bulls, dishes of food, and a bunch of flowers.

The carvings are at the ruins of Persepolis. Here, 2,500 years ago, Persia's king, the **shah,** received tribute during Now Rouz from the peoples he ruled. Horses for the army came from Media, Persia, and Armenia. Arabia supplied more than 6,600 pounds of frankincense each year as tribute, and the Egyptians provided 120,000 bushels of grain.

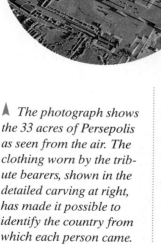

▲ *The photograph shows the 33 acres of Persepolis as seen from the air. The clothing worn by the tribute bearers, shown in the detailed carving at right, has made it possible to identify the country from which each person came.*

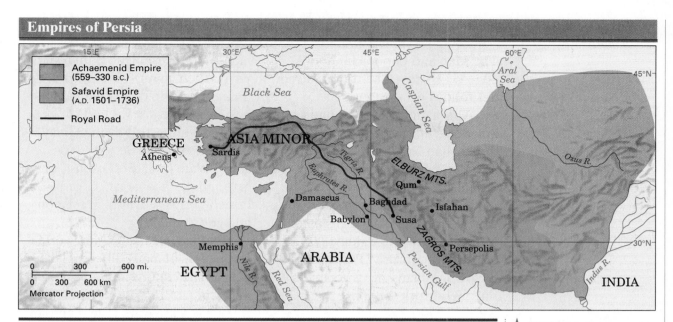

A Glorious Past

Persepolis was built by the Achaemenid *(uh KEE muh nuhd)* family. This family ruled the Persian Empire from 550 to 330 B.C.

The Persian Empire

The Persian shahs were noted for their wise rule. An early shah, Cyrus the Great, built the Persian Empire by conquering other lands. Cyrus let conquered peoples keep their own beliefs and customs, however. Cyrus knew he could turn to his army if any people in the empire challenged his rule.

In 522 B.C., Darius I *(duh RY uhs)* came to the throne. Under Darius, the Persian Empire expanded to two million square miles and may have included 10 million people. Darius adopted some ideas from other peoples, such as laws from the Code of Hammurabi, and used them in the Persian government. To make the empire easier to rule, Darius divided it into 20 provinces. He put a Persian official called a **satrap** *(SAH trahp)* in charge of each province, or satrapy. The satrap collected taxes and tribute for the shah. From time to time, inspectors who were called

"the eyes of the king" visited the satraps to make sure they were being honest.

Each satrapy supplied what grew best there. Peas, onions, apples, cucumbers, apricots, and dates were grown in Babylonia. Pears, lemons (called Persian apples by the Greeks), honey, and pistachio nuts came from Persia itself. Coins made by the Persian government had the same value all through the empire, making it easier for people to buy and sell goods. Banks loaned money and even took checks.

Caravans of merchants moved along the 1,677 miles of the Royal Road built by Darius. It took them about 90 days to travel from Sardis to Susa, the Persian capital (see map above). Relays of the shah's messengers, riding swift horses, traveled the road in about a week.

Conquest and Revival

Even before Darius I died in 486 B.C., some of the satrapies revolted. Persia fought several wars with the Greek city-states (see Chapter 7). In 330 B.C. Persia fell to the army of Alexander the Great.

▲ *Which lands were part of the Persian Empire but were not part of Safavid Persia?*

Across Time & Space

On April 3, 1860, the first pony express riders dashed off with the U.S. mail. They were copying the system Darius I had set up about 2,300 years earlier. "Nothing stops these couriers from covering their allotted stage . . . ," a Greek historian wrote of the Persian messengers, "neither snow, rain, heat, nor darkness." His words are still used by the U.S. Postal Service.

209

Iran

The Map and Globe Handbook, page G12, shows the route Alexander followed.

Although the Greeks had set up kingdoms in Persia, the power of the Persian Empire was gone. In A.D. 224, however, a new family, the Sasanians, tried to revive it. They made Zoroastrianism the only religion in Iran. Scholars translated foreign books into Pahlavi *(PAH luh vee),* the form of Persian spoken by the Sasanians. Artisans made fine metalwork (see page 202).

Arrival of Islam

Despite attacks from the Roman Empire and from India, the Sasanian Empire lasted more than 400 years. Then, in A.D. 637, Muslim armies began to defeat the Sasanians. By 661 Persia was part of the Muslim world ruled by the Umayyads (see the map on page 190). Sunni Islam replaced Zoroastrianism, and the Arabic language became widely used, both in religion and government.

By this time the Muslim world had people of many different languages and cultures. In A.D. 750 the Abbasid *(AHB uh seed)* family overthrew the Umayyads. The Abbasids encouraged trade and learning. They helped bring about the golden age of Islam (see Chapter 8). ■

■ *What threats did the Persians face between 330 B.C. and A.D. 650?*

▼ *The Shah Mosque in Isfahan is noted for its beautiful tiles that form arabesques of blossoms. From its slender columns, called minarets, Muslims are called to worship.*

Safavid Persia

By the mid-900s, local rulers controlled many of the Muslim lands. Various foreign peoples also invaded Southwest Asia. Finally, in 1502 a powerful new family, the Safavids *(sah FAH weedz),* came to the Persian throne.

Safavid Rule

The Safavids ruled Persia from 1502 to 1736. They sought to strengthen Persia and its culture. Their work was important at a time when major changes were occurring elsewhere (see the Minipedia, page 672).

The first Safavid shah proclaimed that Shi'a Islam would be the only religion in Persia. Sunni Muslims who refused to become Shi'as were persecuted. Even today, most people in Iran are Shi'a Muslims. The shah also insisted that the Persian language be used in religion. Many Iranians today speak Farsi (modern Persian).

Persian Culture

The greatest Safavid shah was Abbas I, who became Persia's ruler in 1587. Shah Abbas is best remembered for his capital at Isfahan *(ihs fuh HAHN).* Artists created miniatures like the one in A Closer Look on page 211.

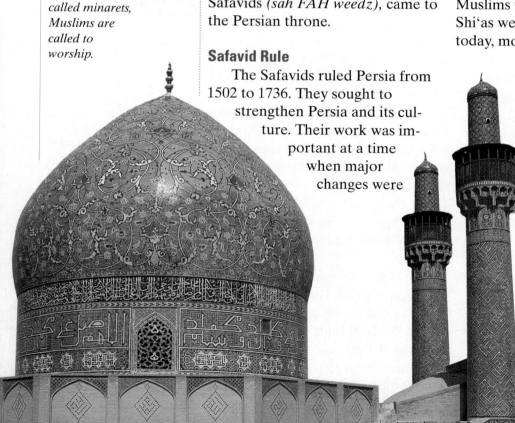

Persian Miniatures

Centuries ago, Persian princes left their palaces to spend months traveling the desert. They took their most treasured paintings with them—bound inside books! Persian miniatures illustrated tales and poems. Some paintings were smaller than this page. Artists began studying in their teens to become master painters. After years of practice, they might be asked to paint the leopards or angels in a landscape, or to fill an entire sky with real gold.

Colors! Artists ground precious stones into a fine powder and mixed it with glue for special colors. A deep, vibrant blue came from lapis lazuli. Malachite created a rich green.

The sad but popular story of young Layla and Majnun is told in this miniature from 1490. They fell in love at school but were kept apart by their feuding families.

Painted cases, like this one, once held the pens of calligraphers. Notice the calligraphy—the ornate script— on the painting.

211

Iran

➤ *This carpet was woven during the Safavid period, the golden age of carpet making. A wool carpet measuring 9 x 12 feet is made of more than seven million knots, as many as 500 to the square inch. A skilled worker can make 10,000–14,000 of these knots per day.*

"If there be a Paradise on earth," exclaimed a Persian poet, "it is here, it is here, it is here!" The word *paradise*, in fact, comes from the Greek word *paradeisos*, meaning "a garden" or "a hunting park." To Persian people familiar with the arid Plateau of Iran, Isfahan did indeed seem a paradise.

Safavid weavers were famous for their fine carpets. One Persian poet compared a carpet with a garden:

Here in this carpet lives an ever-lovely spring;
Unscorched by summer's ardent [burning] flame,
Safe too from autumn's boisterous gales,
Midwinter's cruel ice and snow,
'Tis gaily blooming still.
The handsome border is the garden wall
Protecting, preserving the Park within
For refuge and renewal:
a magic space.

Unknown Sufi poet

A three-mile avenue, shaded by trees, led to the main square in Isfahan. Down a canal in the center of the street flowed water from the river. In a large square at the center of the city, Persians played polo. Troops marched in review as the shah watched from the balcony of his palace. Across the square he could see the heavenly blue tiles of the Shah Mosque.

Shah Abbas brought many artisans to Isfahan. Among them were 300 Chinese skilled in making porcelain and weavers who worked in shops run by the government.

Although Safavid rule ended in 1736, Persia stayed wealthy and powerful until the late 1700s. By 1850, however, it had come under the influence of foreign nations. Great Britain held most of southern Persia, and Russia controlled most of the north. In 1901 Iran agreed to let a British company develop its oil fields located along the Persian Gulf. Persia was on the eve of vast changes. ■

■ *How did the Safavids make Isfahan a center of culture?*

REVIEW

1. **FOCUS** What did different ruling families contribute to Persia?
2. **GOVERNMENT** What did the rulers of the Persian Empire do to make their government strong?
3. **ECONOMICS** How did the Persian rulers meet the costs of governing their empire?
4. **BELIEFS** What part has Islam played in Persian history?

5. **CRITICAL THINKING** Reread the poem above. What does it tell you about the Persian climate? Why do the people cherish gardens?
6. **WRITING ACTIVITY** Imagine you've traveled from a village in Persia to the Isfahan of Shah Abbas. Write a letter home, telling what you've seen. Use the pictures as well as the text to help you write your letter.

LESSON 3

Modern Iran

It's afternoon in Tehran, the capital of Iran. Ali and his friends have been playing soccer. Now Ali glances at his watch and sees that it's time for supper.

As Ali turns to leave, his friend Ahmad grabs his sleeve. "Don't forget," Ahmad whispers. "Call and tell me if you're coming to hear rock tapes tonight."

Ali glances down at his dusty sneakers. Then he looks at Ahmad. *"Basheh,"* he says. "All right. I will."

While eating supper, Ali and his family talk about Ashura. This event, held in memory of the death of Husayn, unites all Shi'a Muslims (see page 190). Ali's village is famous for its religious plays during Ashura.

For a few minutes Ali's memories of Ashura blot out his worries. Then they begin again. He knows his parents don't want him to hear Ahmad's tapes. Iran's government has censored Western rock music. Even so, sometimes tapes are sold secretly. Some of Ali's friends buy these tapes to listen to at home.

Ali doesn't feel comfortable doing something his parents say is wrong. The values he has learned from his family and the teachings of Islam conflict with his friends' values. The choices Ali has to make reflect the clash of values that are faced by many people in Iran today.

(see page 190)

Why did the people of Iran take part in a revolution?

Key Terms

- modernize
- exile
- hostage

◄ *This is one of the giant floats used during Ashura.*

Changes Made by the Pahlavis

Iran has gone through many changes since 1900. In 1906 protests against the shah led to the creation of an elected assembly and a constitution. In 1925 a cavalry officer named Reza Khan gained power, was named shah, and took the name Pahlavi. The new shah insisted that his country be called Iran, instead of Persia.

Modernizing Iran

Reza Shah Pahlavi wanted Iran to be a powerful industrial nation like the United States and Britain. He began to modernize Iran.

213

➤ *Notice that there are two groups of people ranked as lower-class Iranians.*

Society under the Pahlavis

Middle class 23%

Upper class 0.01%

Rural lower class 45%

Urban lower class 32%

Upper class—Pahlavis, army, government office holders

Middle class—shop owners, doctors, office workers, students

Lower classes—farmers, factory workers, unemployed

Source: The Iranian Mojahedin, 1989

▼ *At his coronation the shah and the Empress Farah displayed a fortune in jewels, including a copy of the fabulous Peacock Throne that originally had come from India.*

■ *How did the Pahlavis' policies both help and hurt Iran?*

When a country **modernizes,** it may borrow ideas and ways of doing things from cultures that seem more up-to-date. The shah had factories built to weave cotton and silk, refine sugar, and process food. Roads and power plants were built.

Reza Shah also made social changes. He demanded that Iranians wear Western clothes. The shah built a strong army. He strengthened the school system and tried to weaken the power of Muslim religious leaders.

Not all Iranians liked these changes. Many women felt exposed in Western clothing. Deeply religious Iranians were upset by programs that challenged their Islamic faith. Few benefited from improved farming methods. During the rule of Reza Shah's son, Mohammed Reza, the complaints increased.

Limiting Rights

In 1963 Mohammed Reza set up a plan he called the White Revolution. He used the huge sums Iran was getting for its oil to pay for the changes. Women gained the right to vote, and more Iranians received an education. Between 1956 and 1976, the percentage of people who could read and write tripled, reaching 47 percent.

Although small farmers had gained some land, they did not have the money needed to keep it up. Millions moved to the cities. With fewer people growing crops, Iran had to import the food it needed. The shah had to borrow large sums from the United States. By the 1970s only a small percentage of Iranians were among the rich (see chart above).

When people complained about ties to the United States, among other things, Mohammed Reza censored the newspapers. He outlawed all political parties but his own. With help from the United States, he created SAVAK. This police force used fear to control the people.

In 1971 the shah held a party at Persepolis to celebrate 2,500 years of Iranian history. Heads of state from all over the world were invited. Foreign companies supplied the food and entertainment for the party. However, the event cost the people of Iran about $100 million. Anger at the shah's ties with foreign nations increased. ■

Revolution in Iran

As discontent grew, thousands of Iranians turned to the Ayatollah Khomeini *(koh MAY nee),* the foremost Iranian Shi'a leader. *(Ayatollah* is the title for a Shi'a religious leader.) Khomeini demanded that the shah leave Iran. The ayatollah claimed that modernization was a U.S. plot against Islam. For these views, Khomeini

214

had been forced to leave Iran in 1964. He spent the next 14 years in **exile,** which means he was not allowed to enter Iran. During his exile in Iraq and France, Khomeini used telephones and tape recordings to keep in touch with his supporters.

A Religious Republic

When a newspaper article attacked the ayatollah in 1978, thousands of Iranians poured into the streets, shouting slogans against the shah. Even police bullets did not stop them. By the end of the year, millions of Iranians were taking part in rallies against the shah.

Mohammed Reza had left Iran in January 1979. Two weeks later, millions of wildly cheering Iranians mobbed the streets of Tehran. They joyfully welcomed Khomeini on his return from exile.

A year later voters approved the forming of an Islamic republic. Some officials in the new government were elected. The Shi'a religious leaders, however, were in control. They wanted Islamic laws to be followed strictly. To enforce these laws, they named a Council of Guardians. Women who did not wear proper clothing could be fined or whipped. Western films and music and foreign businesses were outlawed. The amount of oil to be exported was cut back (see graph). People suspected of being enemies of the Islamic government could be jailed or killed.

◀ *Followers of Ayatollah Khomeini used huge banners to win popular support.*

How Do We Know?

HISTORY *Khomeini's followers used posters to stir up feeling against the shah. One poster showed Khomeini confronting the shah, who was being attacked by a dragon beside Persepolis. The caption reads: "Anyone who tries to blow out a lamp lighted by God will burn his beard."*

Oil Production in Iran

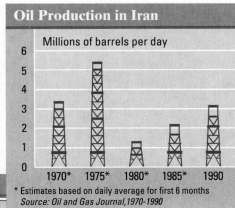

Millions of barrels per day

| 1970* | 1975* | 1980* | 1985* | 1990 |

* Estimates based on daily average for first 6 months
Source: Oil and Gas Journal, 1970-1990

▲ *Under the shah, more than 30,000 tons of crude oil poured into tankers each hour. The Islamic government limited oil production.*

Persian Gulf Oil Production, 1991

ARMENIA
TURKEY
AZERBAIJAN
Tabriz
Caspian Sea
SYRIA
Baghdad
IRAQ
Dezful
Shatt-al-Arab
Abadan
KHARK I.
KUWAIT
Shiraz
Bushehr
SAUDI ARABIA
Dhahran
BAHRAIN
QATAR
UNITED ARAB EMIRATES
OMAN
Gulf of Oman
Muscat

TURKMENISTAN
UZBEKISTAN
TAJIKISTAN
Mashhad
Tehran
Bakhtaran
Qom
IRAN
Isfahan
AFGHANISTAN
Kerman
PAKISTAN
Bandar Abbas
Strait of Hormuz

0   100   200 mi.
0   100 200 km
Lambert Conformal Conic Projection

Oil field
Pipeline
Refinery
Terminal

◀ *Where does the map show that Iranian oil is produced and refined?*

New Problems

The extent of anti-U.S. feeling became clear in February 1979, when armed bands attacked the U.S. embassy in Tehran.

> *Automatic weapons fire started to rip through the upper floors of the building. The windows were shattered, and the walls were riveted with bullets. We all hit the floor.*
>
> Barry Rosen in *444 Days: The Hostages Remember*

▼ *Iranian women are experiencing greater opportunities in many careers. This woman is a television director.*

A more serious problem arose in November 1979, when Iranian students attacked the embassy. They took more than 60 Americans hostage. A **hostage** is someone held captive until certain demands are met. Iranian students demanded the return of the shah, who was in the United States being treated for cancer. They also wanted the Iranian funds in U.S. banks. Although the world condemned the Iranians' actions, the hostages remained captives until January 1981.

In September 1980, Iraq invaded Iran. Iraq feared that Iran's revolution would spread. Iraq also wanted the Iranian oil fields on the Persian Gulf. Iraq's leaders expected a quick victory, for their army was five times the size of Iran's. Later, the United States and some Arab nations backed Iraq.

The Iranians' devotion to their country, however, stopped the Iraqi advance. Iranian boys as young as 13 joined the army. The war lasted until August 1988. More than one million people had been killed or injured on both sides.

Changing Policies

After Khomeini died in 1989, different groups tried to get control of the government. The 1992 elections seemed to be a sign of change. Many of the strictest Islamic leaders were defeated. Nine women won seats in the legislature. Foreign companies were again allowed to do business in Iran.

Today Iranian families enjoy new shopping malls. Iranian factories produce stylish *roupooshes,* housecoats women can wear in place of the *chador.* Iranian folk music is no longer censored. Although the government still censors most Western books, rock music, films, and videos, millions of people enjoy them in private. The big question facing Iran now seems to be: How fast, and how much, should Iran change? ■

■ *What changes have taken place in Iran since the revolution?*

R E V I E W

1. **FOCUS** Why did the people of Iran take part in a revolution?

2. **ECONOMICS** What changes did the Pahlavis make to modernize Iran?

3. **HISTORY** Why did Shah Mohammed Reza choose Persepolis for a major celebration?

4. **HISTORY** Why did Iranian students take hostages?

5. **CRITICAL THINKING** One U.S. foreign policy expert wrote about the protest movements of 1978, "the opposition solidified under the hammer blows of Pahlavi police and military forces." Explain what you think he meant.

6. **WRITING ACTIVITY** Imagine you're a reporter covering Ayatollah Khomeini's return to Iran. Write a story about this moment in history.

216

Making Predictions

Here's Why

When you read a mystery novel, you constantly think about what will happen next. The same thing can happen when you read history. In the beginning of Lesson 3, you read about how Reza Shah tried to modernize Iran. You learned how his son's policies divided the Iranian people. You wondered what would happen next. What might the people do to change the shah's policies? Would they allow Mohammed Reza to continue his rule?

Later in Lesson 3, you found the answer: The shah lost his throne during a revolution. The religious leader, Ayatollah Khomeini, and his followers triumphed and set up an Islamic republic.

Knowing the result of one event can help you predict what might happen later in a similar event. Can you predict how the Iranians might react in the future if the religious leaders of their republic fail to improve conditions?

Here's How

To make predictions as accurately as possible, follow these steps:

1. **Review the stated facts.** In Lesson 3 you read about the changes the Pahlavis made. You read about ways they improved transportation and education. You also read how they failed to make life better for most Iranians. The Iranians' protests turned into a revolution that overthrew Mohammed Reza.

2. **Add other knowledge and experience.** This information may come from your own experience or from something you have read. As you read, Iraq invaded Iran partly because the Iraqis believed that Iran's revolution might spread. On the map on page 205, locate other countries that are neighbors of Iran. How might they feel about the unrest in Iran?

3. **Make a prediction.** Use facts from the text and your additional knowledge to guess what will happen. Will the people of Iran ever again revolt against their government? Give reasons for your prediction.

You might predict that the Iranians will revolt again if the government does not improve conditions for the poor. On the other hand, you may point out that, now that Iran is a republic, the people have the choice of voting against leaders they think are failing to make life better. Either prediction may be true. Only time will tell.

Try It

Reread Lesson 3. Follow the three steps in Here's How to predict whether Ali's values might change as he grows older. Will he choose to live by the strict rules of Shi'a Islam? Will he decide that he can accept some Western ideas? Be sure to support your prediction with information from the chapter.

Apply It

Write a sentence predicting how your classmates might respond to each of the following situations. Use the three steps to make each prediction.

1. You and a friend enter the same essay contest, and you win first place.
2. The school principal decides to cancel the end-of-the-year field trip because too many students have not turned in their assignments.

Iran

Chapter Review

Reviewing Key Terms

arid (p. 205)
exile (p. 215)
hostage (p. 216)
modernize (p. 213)
plateau (p. 205)
satrap (p. 209)
shah (p. 208)

A. Each sentence below has two key terms in parentheses. Choose the key term that is correct, and write it on your own paper.

1. The Iranians built *qanats* to bring water to their (arid, plateau) land.
2. The ruler elected a (shah, satrap) to govern the province.
3. People in the provinces paid tribute to the (hostage, satrap).
4. In his efforts to (modernize, exile) Iran, Reza Shah demanded that the people wear Western clothes.
5. In 1979 Iranian students attacked the U.S. embassy and took (hostages, exiles).

B. Read each pair of words. Write a sentence telling how the words in each pair are related.

1. shah, satrap
2. arid, plateau
3. exile, modernize
4. hostage, exile

Exploring Concepts

A. Important dates in the history of Iran are listed below. Following them is a list of events. Copy the list of dates. Beside each date write the letter of the event that took place on that date.

1. 628 B.C.
2. 522 B.C.
3. 330 B.C.
4. A.D. 224
5. A.D. 637
6. 1502
7. 1925
8. 1979

a. An Islamic republic is set up in Iran.
b. Zoroastrianism becomes the official Persian religion.
c. Darius I becomes shah of the Persian Empire.
d. Zoroaster is born.
e. Muslim armies invade Persia.
f. Reza Shah begins to modernize Iran.
g. Alexander the Great conquers the Persian Empire.
h. Shi'a Islam becomes the official Persian religion.

B. Answer each question with information from the chapter.

1. What makes travel difficult in Iran?
2. How did Iranians solve the problem of bringing water to arid lands?
3. How has Iran been a land bridge?
4. Describe the ideas introduced by the teachings of Zoroaster.
5. What two things made it easy for people in the Persian Empire to trade goods?
6. What changes have taken place in Iran's official religion over the centuries?
7. What major changes were occurring in the world during the period of Safavid rule of Persia?
8. Name at least three crafts at which Iranian artisans have excelled.
9. Why did one poet call Isfahan a paradise?
10. Who were the Pahlavis?
11. What was SAVAK?
12. What accusations did Khomeini make against the shah?
13. Name two values that are in conflict in modern Iran.

Reviewing Skills

1. In the 1980s the United States opposed Iran. Will relations between Iran and the United States get better in the 1990s? Use the three steps in Here's How on page 217 to make your prediction. Be sure to support your prediction with information from the chapter.

2. Iraq invaded Iran in 1980. In Chapter 8 you read about Iraq's invasion of Kuwait in 1990 (page 197). Is it likely that Iraq might attack one of its neighbors in the future? Use the information from Chapters 8 and 9 to make a prediction. Be sure to include information shown on the maps.

Using Critical Thinking

1. Why might the first Safavid shah have changed the official religion of Persia from Sunni to Shi'a Islam?
2. One of the important tasks undertaken both by Darius I and by Reza Shah was building roads. Why was this task important?
3. After the shah left Iran in 1979, Shi'a religious leaders took control. Do you think the average Iranian faced more difficult conditions under the shah or under the religious leaders during the 1980s? Explain your answer.
4. Why might strict Islamic law require women to wear the *chador?*

Preparing for Citizenship

1. COLLECTING INFORMATION Look through newspapers and magazines for stories that answer the following questions about Iran: Is the area still a center of trade? Do the people who live there still borrow ideas from other cultures? What is life like in Iran today? Collect everyone's stories, and display them on a bulletin board under headings such as Trade in Iran Today or Iranian Culture.

2. ART ACTIVITY Persian artisans were skilled metalworkers. One method they used was to cut patterns out of one metal and attach them to another. They also set one metal into another. Use a variation of one of these methods to create a scene from one of the lessons. You might use different colors of foil. As you design and create your scene, think about the talent, materials, effort, and imagination that ancient peoples put into their metalworking.

3. GROUP ACTIVITY Both the Pahlavis and the Shi'a religious leaders of the republic told Iranians what type of clothing they should wear. Imagine that officials at your school want to set up a dress code for all students. Divide the class into two groups. One group can develop arguments supporting a uniform dress code. The second group can develop arguments opposing the dress code. Prepare a debate on the topic, "Resolved, that the school should have a dress code for all students." Two to three students should present arguments supporting each side. Choose one student to act as moderator. Stage the debate for the class and judge the results by a vote on the issue.

4. WRITING ACTIVITY Iran today, unlike the United States, has a state religion. Write three or four paragraphs describing how your life might change if the United States had a state religion.

5. COLLABORATIVE LEARNING The values Iranian youths learn from their families sometimes conflict with the values of their peers. Do the values you learn from your family ever conflict with the values of your classmates? With a few classmates, discuss times when you have faced a conflict of values. Together prepare a short dialogue about one particular conflict of value. Present the dialogue to the class.

Unit 4
Africa

Africa is the birthplace of the human species and of the first spoken language, called proto-World. This East African spice market is a reflection of one of the most vital and most ancient of human activities—the exchange of goods. In a great many African cultures, this activity has traditionally been carried out by women.

332 B.C.

Spice market, Somalia, East Africa

Today

Unit 4 Overview

Africa

Africa is the world's second largest continent. In this vast land are lakes so large that early explorers called them inland seas. Africa is home to the world's longest river—the Nile—and the largest desert—the Sahara. It is the hottest of all the continents. Huge deserts cover much of the land. Grasslands, home to zebras and lions, also spread across wide areas. Africa has many other geographic features too—waterfalls, rain forests, and mountains whose tops are covered with snow all year.

The history of Africa's peoples reaches far into the past. In 1960 scientists Mary and Louis Leakey found pieces of bone in Olduvai Gorge in northern Tanzania. The Leakeys estimated these fragments to be 1.7 million years old—some of the oldest signs of human life found anywhere in the world.

During thousands of years, African peoples settled in every part of the continent. They developed their own customs, languages, and religions. Eventually peoples from other cultures brought new ideas. Sometimes, the meeting of different cultures was peaceful. At other times cultures clashed. Today Africa's peoples blend ancient customs with new ways of life.

▼ *Nairobi, the capital of Kenya, shows the influence of modern architecture in its tall office and apartment buildings. This photo shows the Nyayo Monument in Nairobi's Central Park.*

▲ *Bright colors and bold patterns decorate traditional African clothing.*

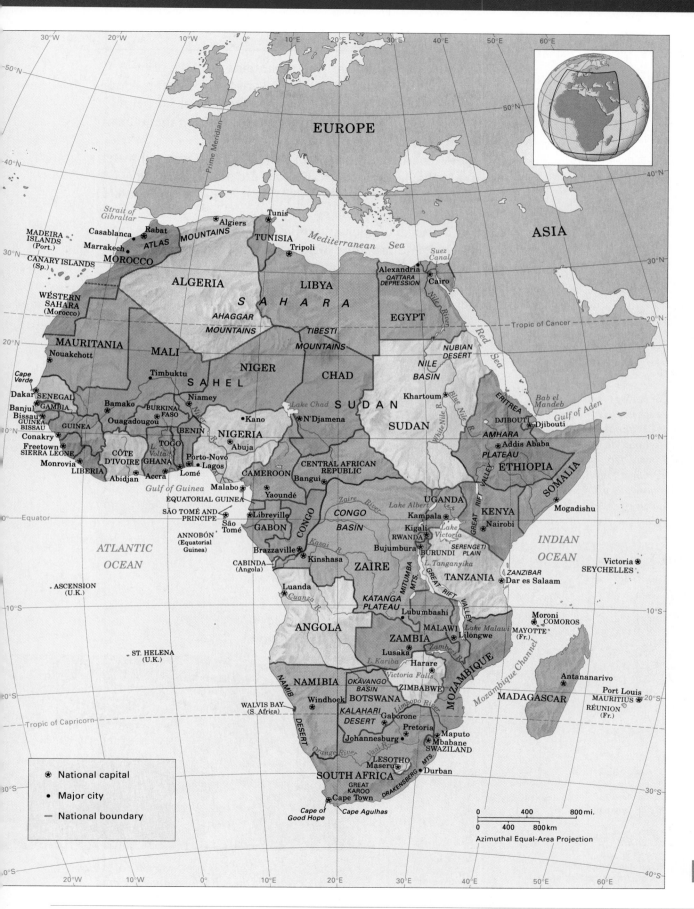

National capital ⊛

Major city •

National boundary —

30°W 20°W 10°W 0° 10°E 20°E 30°E 40°E 50°E 60°E

EUROPE

ASIA

50°N

40°N

Strait of Gibraltar

Mediterranean Sea

MADEIRA ISLANDS (Port.)

Casablanca • Rabat ⊛
Marrakech •

ATLAS MOUNTAINS

Algiers ⊛

Tunis •

TUNISIA

Tripoli ⊛

Suez Canal

Alexandria •

Cairo ⊛

ASIA

30°N

CANARY ISLANDS (Sp.)

MOROCCO

ALGERIA

LIBYA

S A H A R A

AHAGGAR MOUNTAINS

TIBESTI MOUNTAINS

EGYPT

QATTARA DEPRESSION

Nile River

Tropic of Cancer

20°N

WESTERN SAHARA (Morocco)

MAURITANIA

Nouakchott ⊛

MALI

NIGER

CHAD

NUBIAN DESERT

NILE BASIN

Red Sea

Cape Verde

Timbuktu •

S A H E L

Khartoum ⊛

ERITREA

Bab el Mandeb

Gulf of Aden

10°N

Dakar ⊛ SENEGAL

Banjul ⊛ GAMBIA
Bissau ⊛ GUINEA-BISSAU

Bamako ⊛

BURKINA FASO

Niamey ⊛

Lake Chad

N'Djamena ⊛

Kano •

SUDAN

SUDAN

White Nile R.

Blue Nile R.

DJIBOUTI ⊛
Djibouti •

AMHARA

Addis Ababa ⊛

PLATEAU

ETHIOPIA

SOMALIA

Conakry ⊛ GUINEA

Ouagadougou ⊛

BENIN

NIGERIA

Abuja ⊛

Freetown ⊛
SIERRA LEONE

CÔTE D'IVOIRE

TOGO

Porto-Novo ⊛

GHANA

Lagos •

CENTRAL AFRICAN REPUBLIC

Monrovia ⊛
LIBERIA

Abidjan •

Accra ⊛

Lomé ⊛

CAMEROON

Bangui ⊛

L. Volta

0° Equator

Gulf of Guinea

Malabo ⊛

EQUATORIAL GUINEA

SÃO TOMÉ AND PRINCIPE

São Tomé ⊛

Yaoundé ⊛

Libreville ⊛

GABON

CONGO

Zaire River

CONGO BASIN

Lake Albert

Kampala ⊛

UGANDA

Kigali ⊛
RWANDA

Lake Victoria

KENYA

Nairobi ⊛

Mogadishu ⊛

INDIAN OCEAN

ATLANTIC OCEAN

ANNOBÓN (Equatorial Guinea)

Brazzaville ⊛

Kasai R.

Bujumbura ⊛
BURUNDI

SERENGETI PLAIN

Victoria ⊛
SEYCHELLES

GREAT RIFT VALLEY

ASCENSION (U.K.)

CABINDA (Angola)

Kinshasa ⊛

ZAIRE

L. Tanganyika

TANZANIA

Dar es Salaam ⊛

ZANZIBAR

10°S

Luanda ⊛

Quanza R.

KATANGA PLATEAU

Lubumbashi •

MITUMBA MTS.

GREAT RIFT VALLEY

Moroni ⊛
COMOROS

MAYOTTE (Fr.)

ST. HELENA (U.K.)

ANGOLA

MALAWI

Lilongwe ⊛

Lake Malawi

ZAMBIA

Lusaka ⊛

Harare ⊛

Zambezi R.

Antananarivo ⊛

NAMIB DESERT

NAMIBIA

OKAVANGO BASIN

L. Kariba

Victoria Falls

ZIMBABWE

MOZAMBIQUE

Mozambique Channel

MADAGASCAR

Port Louis ⊛
MAURITIUS
RÉUNION (Fr.)

20°S

WALVIS BAY (S. Africa)

Windhoek ⊛

BOTSWANA

Limpopo River

KALAHARI DESERT

Gaborone ⊛

Pretoria ⊛

Maputo ⊛

Mbabane ⊛
SWAZILAND

Johannesburg •

Orange River

Vaal R.

LESOTHO

Maseru ⊛

Durban •

DRAKENSBERG MTS.

SOUTH AFRICA

GREAT KAROO

Cape Town ⊛

Cape of Good Hope

Cape Agulhas

0 400 800 mi.

0 400 800 km

Azimuthal Equal-Area Projection

⊛ National capital

• Major city

— National boundary

50°N

40°N

30°N

20°N

10°N

0° Equator

10°S

20°S

30°S

40°S

Tropic of Capricorn

20°W 10°W 0° 10°E 20°E 30°E 40°E 50°E 60°E

Africa

The Land and People

Most of Africa is a plateau. Tall mountains rise high above the surrounding land in the north and east of the continent. Along the Great Rift Valley in eastern Africa, the land drops far below sea level. This huge gash in the earth's crust is so deep that many Grand Canyons could fit inside it.

Some of Africa's land is changing. Long periods without water have turned some land to desert. Deserts are also expanding where animals have been allowed to overgraze and people have cut down trees to make farmland.

Parts of Africa have rich mineral deposits. These include diamonds, gold, and uranium. Wild animals are also treated as a valuable resource. Some nations, like Kenya, have created parks where animals such as elephants, lions, and giraffes are protected from poachers—people who hunt illegally.

▼ *Long periods without rain cause plants to wither and die. Without plant roots to hold the soil, it blows away. Dry sands take its place. This map shows how this process affects some regions in Africa.*

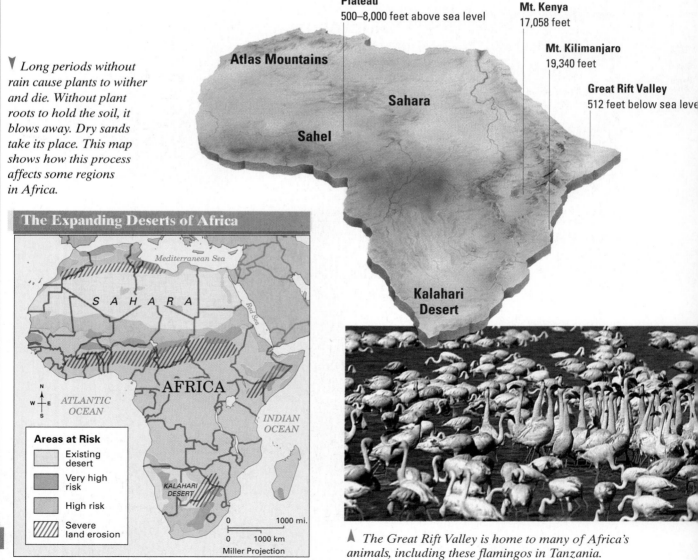

Plateau
500–8,000 feet above sea level

Mt. Kenya
17,058 feet

Mt. Kilimanjaro
19,340 feet

Atlas Mountains

Great Rift Valley
512 feet below sea level

Sahara

Sahel

Kalahari Desert

The Expanding Deserts of Africa

Mediterranean Sea

SAHARA

Red Sea

AFRICA

ATLANTIC OCEAN

INDIAN OCEAN

KALAHARI DESERT

Areas at Risk
- Existing desert
- Very high risk
- High risk
- Severe land erosion

0   1000 mi.

0   1000 km

Miller Projection

▲ *The Great Rift Valley is home to many of Africa's animals, including these flamingos in Tanzania.*

Important Dates in African History

1200	1300	1400	1500	1600	1700	1800	1900

A.D. 1250
Mali becomes the most powerful empire in West Africa.

1497
Navigator Vasco da Gama rounds South Africa's coast.

1670s
Osei Tutu forms the Ashanti Empire.

1914
Europeans colonize all of Africa except Ethiopia and Liberia.

1957
Ghana gains its independence from Great Britain.

TODAY
South Africa works to end racism.

No other continent has more new nations than Africa. For hundreds of years, Africa was home to busy trading empires. Then, during the 1800s, Europeans colonized most of the continent. Africa finally won its freedom from European control after World War II. Today the continent is made up of more than 50 independent nations.

Africa's peoples belong to hundreds of different cultures and speak as many as 1,000 languages. Most Africans live in villages where they work close to the land as farmers or herders. However, millions of people are moving to the cities. Africa's nations are working to create new manufacturing and other industries to provide jobs for their growing populations.

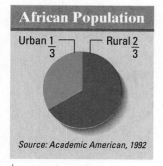

African Population

Urban $\frac{1}{3}$ Rural $\frac{2}{3}$

Source: Academic American, 1992

▲ *More than 200 million of Africa's approximately 700 million people live in cities.*

▲ *Factory workers prepare sisal fibers to make into mats, rope, and baskets. Baskets like those below are often made by hand.*

Chapter 10

Egypt

After the days of the ancient pharaohs, Egypt was ruled by foreigners, such as the clever Greek queen Cleopatra and the Muslim hero Muhammad Ali. All of them changed Egypt, and all were changed by it. After nearly 2,300 years of foreign rule, the people of the Nile took back their country. Today Egyptians seek their own solutions for governing their growing nation.

The Romans, who conquered Egypt in 30 B.C., mixed Egyptian customs with their own. Wealthy Romans in Egypt, like this man, were often mummified in the Egyptian style.

A.D. 395 Egypt becomes part of the Christian Byzantine Empire.

| 500 | B.C. | A.D. | 500 |

332 B.C. Alexander the Great conquers Egypt and founds the great city of Alexandria.

A.D. 639 Arabs come to Egypt, bringing Muslim culture.

332 B.C.

Gamal Abdel Nasser led a revolution in 1952 that established Egyptian self-rule. One of his dreams was to build a dam to tame the floods of the Nile. The Aswan High Dam was completed in 1970.

Feeding the huge population along the Nile is one of the many challenges that Egypt faces today.

1000

1500

2000

A.D. 969 Arab rulers found a new capital, Cairo. In the shadow of the ancient Giza pyramids, Cairo, shown above, reflects the old and new in Egypt today.

Today

LESSON 1

Rulers from the North

Key Terms

- fellahin
- infrastructure

➤ *This stele shows a mixing of traditions that was common among Romans in Egypt. Wealthy Roman families often mummified their dead. They buried the mummies, Roman-style, in underground tombs called catacombs.*

This stele, or stone marker, was carved on the tomb of a little boy who died in Egypt in about A.D. 225. The boy had a Roman name: Julius Valerius. His father served in the Roman army, which occupied Egypt from 30 B.C. to A.D. 639.

If you look closely at the stele, you can see the influence of three cultures in Egyptian history. The writing that describes the boy is both Greek and Latin. "C. Julius Valerius," it

says, "son of C. Julius Severus, a soldier of the second legion Traiana. He lived 3 years." Notice the animals around the boy: At the top are a large bird called a falcon and a type of wild dog called a jackal. They represent Egyptian Gods. At the boy's feet is a creature from Greek mythology called a griffin. After the age of Egypt's pharaohs, three cultures— Egyptian, Greek, and Roman—came together in Egypt, just as they did on the stele of young Julius.

Foreign Pharaohs

Foreigners ruled Egypt most of the time between the fall of the Egyptian pharaohs and modern times. In Chapter 4 you read about the Assyrian invasion of Egypt in 671 B.C. Besides the Assyrians, Egypt was ruled at various times by the Persians and by the Greeks, the Romans, and the Byzantines *(BIHZ uhn teens)*. These groups were followed by many others, including Arabs, Turks, and British.

For most of 2,600 years, foreign rulers controlled Egypt.

Egyptians in towns and cities often accepted the foreigners' Gods, and adopted their languages, weapons, and art. However, foreign rule had less effect on the **fellahin** *(feh lah HEEN)*. They were peasant farmers who lived in villages in the Nile delta and along the Upper Nile. As in ancient times, the *fellahin* planted and harvested according to the yearly Nile floods. Empires came and went, but their lives changed little.

Alexander's Empire

Legend says that Alexander the Great was called to Egypt by a gray-haired man in a dream. "An island lies where loud the billows roar," the old man declared. "Pharos they call it, on the Egyptian shore." Alexander made the dream come true.

In 332 B.C. Alexander entered Egypt without a battle. Egyptians welcomed him as a hero because he freed them from harsh Persian rule.

Alexander made a pilgrimage to the Siwa *(SEE wuh)* Oasis to worship Egypt's sun God, Amon-Re. Pleased that he honored Egyptian Gods, the priests of Amon-Re gave Alexander their blessing. He left Siwa, tradition says, with the godlike powers of a pharaoh.

Ancient Alexandria

After the death of Alexander in 323 B.C., one of his generals, Ptolemy I *(TAHL uh mee)*, ruled Egypt. Ptolemy's dynasty held power for nearly 300 years. Like Alexander, the Ptolemies respected Egyptian traditions. They called themselves pharaohs; they worshiped both Greek and Egyptian Gods.

Ptolemy I completed Egypt's new capital, Alexandria, which Alexander had founded. As the map on page 230 shows, Alexandria lies on the Mediterranean Sea. A lighthouse on the island of Pharos guided ships into the city's harbor. Greeks, Persians, Phoenicians, and Ionians came to settle in Alexandria.

During the time of the Ptolemies, the city also was home to the world's largest Jewish community.

One of the greatest wonders of Alexandria was its library and the "living books," or scholars, who came from all over to study there. Alexandrian astronomers were among the first to suggest that Earth is a sphere that travels around the sun. Mathematicians discovered new laws of geometry based on ideas of the ancient pyramid builders. Sky watchers made the first long-range weather predictions. At all hours, Alexandria's scholars might be called upon to advise Egypt's Ptolemaic rulers.

The first three Ptolemies were strong rulers. The Ptolemies grew weak, however, as the Roman Empire grew strong.

Queen Cleopatra

The last of the Ptolemies may be familiar to you. Her name was Cleopatra VII.

By the time Cleopatra became queen in 51 B.C., Rome had a large role in Egypt's affairs. It was only a matter of time before Egypt became part of the Roman Empire. Yet, by making deals with Roman leaders, the clever Cleopatra kept her throne and Egypt's independence for over 20 years. Finally, in 30 B.C., the Romans defeated Cleopatra's forces. The queen refused to surrender; she later took her own life. Control of Egypt passed to Rome. ■

◄ Cleopatra, the first of the Ptolemies to learn her subjects' language, paid tribute to Egyptian Gods. Here she appears on an Egyptian wall carving and, below, on a Roman coin.

Across Time & Space

In time, the library at Alexandria disappeared. Some scholars believe conquering armies destroyed the library. Others think it died out over time as books began replacing papyrus scrolls.

Today, Egypt is building a new library near Alexandria that will contain thousands of historic books. Computers will let people from all over the world use the library's resources.

■ *Give examples to show how Egypt affected its Greek rulers.*

Major Grain-Producing Areas of the Roman Empire

➤ *Looking at this map, why do you think Rome needed to build up the infrastructure of Egypt and other lands it conquered?*

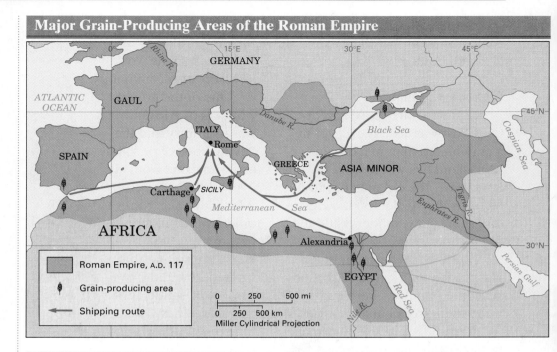

Map legend:
- Roman Empire, A.D. 117
- Grain-producing area
- Shipping route

0   250   500 mi
0 250 500 km
Miller Cylindrical Projection

Roman Times

One ancient historian noted that in the A.D. 200s, Rome gave out free grain to its citizens. The amount of grain needed to feed the city was staggering. It imported 14 million bushels of grain a year. The map on this page shows the role of Egypt in the Roman Empire: to grow grain. For 300 years, until A.D. 300, Egypt sent 150,000 tons of grain a year to Rome.

In some ways, Rome's need for grain helped Egypt. The Romans improved Egypt's **infrastructure,** its system of public services such as roads, harbors, and irrigation canals. New canals helped improve the harvests. Harbors and roads transported grain to Rome. When Roman rule ended, Egypt kept its valuable infrastructure.

Yet some Egyptians suffered under Roman rule. Many wanted to govern themselves, as people in other Roman provinces did, but Rome would not allow it.

Jews, moreover, had fewer rights than other Egyptians under Roman rule. Alexandria's Jews tried to regain rights they had enjoyed under the Greeks. Rome crushed Jewish uprisings so brutally that the Jewish community was almost destroyed. ■

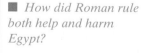

■ *How did Roman rule both help and harm Egypt?*

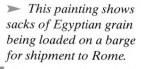

➤ *This painting shows sacks of Egyptian grain being loaded on a barge for shipment to Rome.*

Christianity Spreads

During Roman rule in Egypt, a wave of cultural change swept through the country, affecting both the rich and the *fellahin*. For the first time in 3,000 years, Egyptians adopted a new religion. It was Christianity.

In the A.D. 100s, the followers of Jesus brought Christianity to Egypt. In spite of punishment by some Roman rulers, many Egyptians eagerly accepted the new religion. Gradually, monotheism spread through Egypt and south into Nubia (see Chapter 4).

The Byzantines

Although Roman emperors at first opposed Christianity, they later adopted it. In the A.D. 300s, Christianity became the religion of the Roman Empire. At the same time, the empire split into two parts. Egypt was in the eastern part, the Byzantine Empire. The empire's capital, Constantinople, was the center of the Byzantine Christian church.

Coptic Christianity

In the A.D. 400s, arguments arose among Byzantine Christians. Church leaders in Constantinople and Alexandria did not agree on how to explain Christianity. The Egyptian church broke with the Byzantine church, and a new, Egyptian form of Christianity was born. Its followers were called Copts, from the Greek name for Egyptians. The Copts formed a new written language, Coptic, made up of Egyptian words spelled in Greek letters.

Most Egyptians might be Coptic Christians today, if Egypt had not been invaded yet again. In A.D. 639, however, the Muslim Arabs arrived. ■

◄ *Except for their use of short Coptic phrases, Coptic priests such as these speak mostly in Arabic in services today.*

■ *How did Christianity affect Egypt?*

---

1. **FOCUS** How did the Greeks, the Romans, and the Byzantines affect Egyptian culture?
2. **CULTURE** Who were the *fellahin*?
3. **CULTURE** Explain how Roman rule affected the Alexandrian Jews.
4. **RELIGION** What is the Coptic language?
5. **CRITICAL THINKING** In your opinion, why did Greek rulers of Egypt have themselves crowned as pharaohs?
6. **WRITING ACTIVITY** Pretend you are Cleopatra VII. You have just received a message from Rome demanding the surrender of Egypt. Draft a reply to the emperor.

231

L E S S O N   2

Islamic Egypt

THINKING FOCUS

How did Egypt become an Islamic nation?

Key Terms

- sultan
- isthmus

*I*t is the metropolis of the universe, the garden of the world, the nest of the human species. . . . [It is] the glory of Islam and the orchard of the world.

These words are from the Arab historian Ibn Khaldun *(IHB uhn kal DOON)*. The place he described was a city in the Egyptian desert, al-Qahirah *(ahl KUH hee ruh)*. We know it as Cairo *(KY roh)*.

According to one legend, the birth of Cairo happened this way: In A.D. 969 a group of Shiite Muslims prepared to break ground for a new city. They hired astrologers to tell them when the digging should begin. Workers raised their shovels. The astrologers watched the sky. When the moment arrived, they would give the signal to begin by pulling on a bell rope.

The planet Mars rose in the sky, but before the astrologers could give the signal, a raven landed on the rope and jingled the bells. The new city was named al-Qahirah, Arabic for Mars the victorious.

Whatever the true story of Cairo's founding, the city quickly grew. By the 1300s, Cairo was the greatest city in all of Africa, Europe, and Southwest Asia.

Arab Rule

The Arab Muslims came to Egypt in A.D. 639, when the Byzantines ruled. Like Alexander the Great, the Arabs entered Egypt with little trouble. The Byzantine Empire was too weak to fight. In addition, Egyptian Christians still disliked the Byzantines because of the split with the church at Constantinople.

Arab rule was fairly mild. The Arab ruler, Caliph Umar, did not allow Muslims to take Egyptian land. Instead, Egypt had to pay tribute. "Tribute is better than booty [stolen goods]," Umar said. "It lasts longer."

The Arabs also demanded tribute from Egypt's ancient neighbor, Nubia (see Chapter 4). A treaty made during the mid-600s required Nubia, which

How Do We Know?

CULTURE *The writings of Ibn Khaldun (1332–1406) give a picture of how people lived in old Cairo. An Arabian born in Tunis, Ibn Khaldun used aspects of culture, such as geography and family ties, to understand societies of the past. Before settling in Cairo, he advised rulers in North Africa and Spain.*

was then largely Christian, to do business with Muslim traders, build a mosque, and send 360 slaves to Cairo each year. Yet the treaty also required Cairo to send yearly gifts of food, horses, and cloth to Nubia.

An Islamic Nation

Like Egypt's Greek and Roman rulers, the Arabs allowed the Egyptians to worship as they chose. Although many Egyptians remained Christians, Egypt slowly became an Islamic nation.

The message of Islam, its five basic duties, and the caring community that it provided appealed to the people of the Nile. The practices of Islam were, in some respects, familiar. Like the beliefs of the ancient Egyptian religion and of Christianity, Islam gave Egyptians hope even when the Nile failed. It was the hope of a paradise that worshipers would enter after death.

The Rise of Cairo

Besides a new religion, the Arabs brought Egypt a new culture. Shortly after arriving in Egypt, they built a new capital called al-Fustat *(ahl FUH staht)* on the banks of the Nile. Later a newer capital was built at a site not far from al-Fustat. This new capital was Cairo.

The map on page 685 of the Atlas shows why the Arabs moved the capital from Alexandria. This capital of the Ptolemies bordered the Mediterranean Sea. The Greeks and Romans who had ruled Egypt from Alexandria looked across the sea, toward their homelands in Greece and Italy. The Arabs had little use for a capital that had to be defended from attack by sea. From Cairo the Arabs' ties lay southeast, toward the Muslim holy city of Mecca.

▼ *The Muslim ruler Saladin built this fortress, the Citadel of Cairo, to protect Egypt from Christian invaders.*

■ *Find facts to support this statement: Under Arab rule, the center of Egyptian culture shifted from Alexandria to Cairo.*

Cairo grew busy and famous. Its bazaars were filled with peddlers selling copper pots and silk. Sugar cane from Egypt and coffee, a new beverage in great demand from neighboring Yemen, were shipped from Cairo to markets in Europe and Asia.

Cairo's al-Azhar University became the center of Islamic learning. Muslims, Jews, and Christians lived side by side in the growing city. ■

Ottoman Rule

Arab dynasties brought a Muslim culture that shapes Egyptian life to this day. While Christianity had little effect on Egypt's language or family life, Muslim rule brought dramatic change. Most Egyptians became Muslims. Arabic replaced Coptic as Egypt's written and spoken language. The Arabs also brought new foods and clothing.

New Muslim Leaders

Arab rule lasted nearly 900 years. Then Egypt's foreign rulers changed again. An Asian people, the Turks, under the command of Selim I, invaded Egypt in 1517. Selim, like many other Turkish rulers, was called a **sultan.** The sultan ruled the vast Ottoman Empire (see the map below).

Although the Ottoman Turks were Muslims, they were not Arab. They had their own culture, clothing, and language. Turkish culture did not replace Arab culture in Egypt. Instead, during the roughly 350-year rule, the Turks changed Egypt in small ways. One example is Cairo's Ottoman-style mosques and houses with beautifully carved balconies.

Ottoman control of Egypt weakened in 1805, when the sultan named a new governor of Egypt. His name was Muhammad Ali.

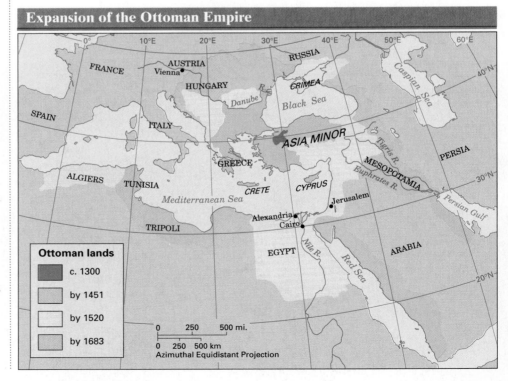

Expansion of the Ottoman Empire

Ottoman lands
- c. 1300
- by 1451
- by 1520
- by 1683

0   250   500 mi.
0 250 500 km
Azimuthal Equidistant Projection

➤ *The Ottoman Empire was named after the empire's founder. On the map, locate the region the Ottomans came from. Find the size of the empire by the year 1520, when it included Egypt.*

234

Ali's Vision

Muhammad Ali is often called the founder of modern Egypt. A great admirer of European countries, he wanted Egypt to become rich and modern.

To reach his goal, Muhammad Ali built ships, canals, and harbors. He founded schools for general and medical education. He hired French experts to teach Egyptians new military techniques. His grandson, Ismail, went even further. "My country is no longer in Africa," Ismail declared, "we now form part of Europe."

Muhammad Ali and his grandson helped Egypt's economy grow. Yet the *fellahin* grew poorer than ever. Muhammad Ali and his family owned much of Egypt's land and industries. The *fellahin* had to grow mostly tobacco, cotton, and other crops to sell on the world market, rather than growing food. ■

▲ *Demand for Egyptian cotton soared when Europe's supply of cotton from the United States was cut off by the Civil War.*

■ *What was Muhammad Ali's goal, and how did he try to reach that goal?*

The Suez Canal

Muhammad Ali's descendants dreamed of a canal that would join the Red Sea and the Mediterranean Sea. The pharaohs of ancient Egypt had made several attempts to link these bodies of water. Yet their efforts did not last. Desert sands blew into the canal and clogged it. In the mid-1800s, however, there were new reasons to solve these problems.

Building the Canal

By this time, Great Britain had a thriving trade with India. Without a canal, British ships had to make a long journey around the continent of Africa. A canal through the Isthmus of Suez would cut 6,000 miles from the trip. An **isthmus** *(IHS muhs)* is a thin strip of land connecting two larger pieces of land.

Egypt's rulers saw that there was money to be made in a new shipping route through the isthmus. France, hoping to compete with England for world trade, wanted the canal dug as well. A French company made a deal with Egypt to build the Suez Canal.

Britain Seeks Control

The canal opened in 1869. Royalty from all over Europe came to celebrate. To house his guests, the Egyptian ruler, Ismail, built the grand Abdin *(ahb deen)* Palace in Cairo. He adorned Egypt's capital in European style, with wide streets and flowering gardens.

▼ *After taking power in 1952, President Gamal Abdel Nasser told a crowd, "The canal will be run by Egyptians, Egyptians, Egyptians!" Nasser kept his promise. He seized control of the Suez Canal from the British in 1956.*

Ismail's heavy spending came just at the time when the price of Egyptian cotton plunged. In addition, Egypt had gone deeply into debt to pay for the Suez Canal. Ismail got large loans from European banks, but he ran out of money to repay them. Egypt had to sell its share of the canal to Great Britain.

The British government sent soldiers into Egypt, saying it was concerned for its property. Yet the move began a new period of foreign control in Egypt. ■

■ *What made the Suez Canal so valuable?*

Egyptians Rule Egypt

In the 1930s Great Britain still controlled Egypt. A descendant of Muhammad Ali, King Farouk, held the throne. Discontent with foreign leaders was growing. In 1935 a 17-year-old Egyptian, Gamal Abdel Nasser *(NAS uhr)* wrote to a friend that Egypt was in a state of "hopeless despair."

*W*ho can remove this feeling? The Egyptian Government is based on corruption and favours. . . . [W]here is . . . the man to rebuild the country so that the weak and humiliated Egyptian people can rise again and live as free and independent men?

As a student at Egypt's Royal Military Academy, Nasser found people who shared his concern. Many Egyptians wanted to be rid of foreign control.

Egyptians Rebel

King Farouk was part of the problem. Egypt's ruler spent most of his time entertaining Europeans in his two palaces or on one of his many yachts. Egyptians resented the king's free-spending ways.

British soldiers protected Farouk. In 1951 the British suppressed four uprisings of *fellahin*— one at the king's country home. In January 1952 an angry crowd set fire to the European section of Cairo. King Farouk watched from Abdin Palace as Cairo burned. Six months later a group of young army officers, led by Nasser, forced Farouk to flee Egypt on his yacht.

Nasser became the nation's new leader. After more than 2,000 years of foreign control, an Egyptian ruled Egypt once again.

War Burdens Egypt

Farouk left Egypt with a warning for Nasser. "Your task will be difficult," he said. "It is not easy to govern Egypt." Farouk was right. President Nasser and his successor, Anwar Sadat *(suh DAHT),* faced great challenges.

Among them was a costly conflict with Israel. Israel had become a nation in 1948. It had been created by the United Nations as a

▼ *Shepheard's Hotel in Cairo was a symbol of the European life of luxury that most Egyptians could never hope to have. On January 26, 1952, Egyptians entered the old hotel and set it afire.*

Jewish state. Egypt and other Arab nations regarded the land that Israel occupied as Arab land. From 1948 to 1973, Israel and Arab nations fought a series of wars in which Egypt lost heavily. By the mid-1970s, President Sadat believed that Egypt would run out of money if it did not make peace.

Israel wanted peace, too. The cost of war, in money and lives, was high. As Sadat's wife, Jihan, wrote to a grieving Israeli woman: "In every soldier who fell in the War . . . there is our son and a part of our soul."

With the help of U.S. President Jimmy Carter, Sadat and Israel's prime minister, Menachem Begin, held peace talks. They signed a peace agreement at Camp David, Maryland, on March 26, 1979. For their efforts, Sadat and Begin won the Nobel Peace Prize.

Questions of Religion and Law

Nasser and the leaders who followed him have tried to help Egypt to support itself. Unlike Ismail, who wanted to make Egypt a part of Europe, they emphasize Egypt's African and Arab heritage.

Today, cultural changes in Egypt are coming not from outside the country, but from inside. Some Egyptians want to do away with their country's European-style democracy. They seek to form a government based on Islamic law, like the government of Iran (Chapter 9).

In the 1970s President Sadat, a Muslim, tried to quiet the growing demand for a new government—a move that angered some Islamic groups. They were further upset when he made peace with Israel. On October 6, 1981, the world was shocked when a member of a Muslim group shot and killed Sadat.

Questions about Egypt's future continue under Sadat's successor, Hosni Mubarak. Many younger people are pushing for a return to Islamic government. College students in Alexandria, for instance, forced their school to make separate classes for men and women.

Changes in government and religion have swept through Egypt many times in the last 2,000 years. Many people wonder if another wave of change is on the way. ■

▲ *Egypt gave the plaque on the left to Israel to celebrate the peace agreement. Shown above, left to right, are Sadat, Carter, and Begin, clasping hands.*

■ *How did Egyptian rulers change Egypt?*

1. **FOCUS** How did Egypt become an Islamic nation?
2. **POLITICAL SYSTEMS** Characterize Arab rule of Egypt and of Nubia.
3. **ECONOMICS** What effect did Ismail have on Egypt?
4. **HISTORY** Why did Egyptians want control of Egypt, and how did they gain control?

5. **CRITICAL THINKING** Contrast the goals of Egyptian leaders Muhammad Ali and Gamal Abdel Nasser.
6. **ACTIVITY** Using the map in the Atlas on page 679, draw a map to show how European ships traveled to India before and after the Suez Canal was built.

237

Evaluating Sources

Here's Why

To learn about the past, we use records and accounts of events left behind. You read in Lesson 2 that in 1978, U.S. President Jimmy Carter invited Egyptian president Anwar Sadat and Israeli prime minister Menachem Begin to Camp David for peace talks. Suppose you want to explore Sadat's feelings and thoughts during those difficult talks. Where would you begin?

Hundreds of books, encyclopedia articles, and newspaper reports have been written about Sadat. Therefore, you must be able to evaluate the sources available to you.

Here's How

First, decide whether you want to get your information from a primary source or a secondary source. To tell if a source is primary or secondary, see if it meets the requirements described below.

To figure out if the source meets the description of a primary or a secondary source, you will need to know the answers to these questions: Who wrote it? When was it produced?

With what you now know about primary and secondary sources, which might you choose to find out about Sadat? Remember, you're trying to find information on his thoughts and feelings during the Camp David talks.

You might try an encyclopedia, but such information is secondary—a secondhand source. Instead, you might try a source such as this:

Every night I called Anwar from Paris. And every night his news was more discouraging. President Carter was meeting . . . with my husband and Begin, trying to [solve] their broad differences. . . .

"You sound so tired, Anwar," I said to my husband two days later. I could hear his sigh all the way across the ocean. "It is exhausting to have to fight so hard for peace," he replied.

The writer is Sadat's wife, Jihan. Her book *A Woman of Egypt* was written nine years after the Camp David meetings. Does her writing qualify as a primary source?

Jihan Sadat's account is indeed a primary source of facts about her husband's experiences. It relates her direct discussion with him—even if only by telephone. Her story seems to be based on her own notes or memories.

A few final questions will help you judge the quality of both primary and secondary sources: What is the purpose of the account—to inform, to describe, or to persuade? Does the writer's background or viewpoint affect the accuracy of the account?

Try It

Would you use Jihan Sadat's book as your only source for a report on the Camp David meetings? Why or why not?

Apply It

The newspapers and books of today are sources that people of the future will use to learn about our times. Find three sources of information about a recent U.S. President. At least one source should be a primary source. Then list what type of information you might look for in each source. Explain your reasoning.

Primary Source
- recorded by someone who participated in the event or who was an eyewitness to it
- recorded at the time of the event, or based on memories or notes from the time of the event

Secondary Source
- uses primary sources for information

L E S S O N 3

A Trip Down the Nile

Every summer, from prehistoric times to modern times, Egyptians watched for the yearly appearance of the star Sirius in the sky. Soon after, they knew, the Nile would flood its banks, providing water for the next year's crop—but how much water?

Low floods meant famine. High floods swept away crops, soil, and the mud-brick homes of the *fellahin.* Egypt, "the gift of the Nile," was at the mercy of the river.

Faced with a growing population that needed more farmland to feed itself, Egypt's President Nasser saw only one answer. He ordered a dam to be built on the Nile at the town of Aswan, near the Nile's First Cataract.

A dam had been built there before, but the new one—started in 1961 and completed in 1970—was much larger. The Aswan High Dam stretched more than two miles across and rose to 364 feet. The huge wall, placed in the river's path, would have amazed even the ancient King Khufu. The dam is 17 times the size of his Great Pyramid.

The dam worked like a giant faucet, allowing a controlled amount of water to flow north to the delta. Without the threat of floods, more land could be irrigated and farmed. Hydroelectricity made by the dam provided power for much of Egypt.

In a land slow to change, the Aswan High Dam brought as much change to Egypt as had all the foreigners who governed it. Like a pebble dropped into a pond, the effects of the dam rippled down the Nile Valley.

THINKING FOCUS

Describe how modern changes are affecting life along the Nile.

Key Terms

- felucca
- silt

◀ *By gradually releasing the water stored in Lake Nasser, the Aswan High Dam irrigates 900,000 acres of what was once desert.*

The Upper Nile

If you traveled the length of Egypt's Nile, you'd find that the dam's effects, both helpful and harmful, have reached into every city, every village, every family. The dam is one of many new changes that have altered Egyptian life forever.

Nubia

To see the effects of the dam, you might start by flying over the region just south of it. The region is now part of Egypt, but it was once the land of Nubia (see Chapter 4). Today, the land has vanished under Lake Nasser. This artificial lake is a reservoir, or body of stored water, which is held back by the dam. The 2,000-square-mile Lake Nasser is one of the world's largest reservoirs.

As water rose behind the dam, it threatened Nubia's ancient monuments. A Closer Look at the rescue of Abu Simbel, on page 241, shows how one historic treasure was saved in the nick of time.

Modern descendants of the ancient Nubians were greatly affected by the dam. Thousands had to leave their homes and move north. Some carried sacks of Nubian soil with them to their new homes.

Aswan

If you head north, as the Nubians did, you come to the town of Aswan. Here, in the shadow of the dam, you can't help but think of how fast Egypt is changing. New hotels look out over palm trees, sand dunes, shimmering water, and the rocks of the First Cataract.

Yet much of Aswan is unchanged. As in ancient days, goods such as animal skins, baskets, and pottery from central Africa make their way to the shops of Aswan.

From Aswan you decide to journey north on an Egyptian sailboat called a **felucca**. Its white sail blows in the wind as you float down the Nile, which now flows quietly year round. In the distance you see the villages where about 60,000 Nubians were relocated after Lake Nasser swallowed their homes.

Along the riverbank, reeds and lilies grow, but the papyrus plant, from which Egyptians once made

▼ *About 99 percent of Egypt's population lives along the Nile. As you can see from the map, the population is very concentrated. In fact, the population density is one of the highest in the world. Many Egyptians are farmers, like the man shown to the right, who still use ancient methods of planting and harvesting.*

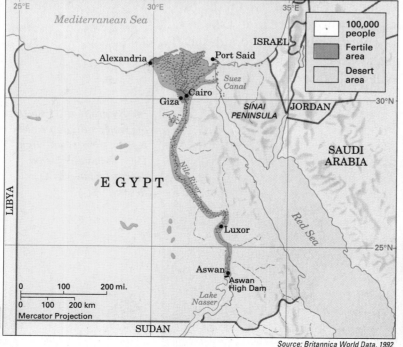

Egypt: Population, 1990

Mediterranean Sea

Alexandria
Port Said
ISRAEL
Cairo
Giza
Suez Canal
SINAI PENINSULA
JORDAN
EGYPT
LIBYA
Luxor
SAUDI ARABIA
Red Sea
Aswan
Aswan High Dam
Lake Nasser
SUDAN

Nile River

100,000 people
Fertile area
Desert area

0 100 200 mi.
0 100 200 km
Mercator Projection

Source: Britannica World Data, 1992

The Rescue of Abu Simbel

Ramesses II built monuments along the Nile to show his power over Nubia. For 3,000 years, huge statues of the pharaoh and his family marked the entrances to two temples at Abu Simbel. In the 1960s, however, Abu Simbel was in danger. Nile waters backed up by the Aswan High Dam would soon submerge the site. Engineers from around the world joined Egyptians to move the ancient monuments to a safe place.

Like a giant puzzle, the fragile sandstone temples were cut into more than 1,000 blocks. Some blocks were as heavy as 18 automobiles.

Sandstone fragments

The new site is shown in this drawing. The temples are higher and set back from the water's edge. The photograph below was taken before Abu Simbel was moved.

The 21-ton face of Ramesses begins the climb to safety. The entire statue stands 67 feet tall.

241

paper, is now hard to find. Here and there, men bathe and women wash clothes in the river. Motorized tourist boats pass by swiftly as you near the next stop.

Luxor

To the ancient Egyptians, the east bank of the Nile was the land of the living, and the west bank was the land of the dead. Today, the city of Luxor celebrates both.

Luxor, on the Nile's east bank, is the place where ancient Thebes once stood. Thebes was Egypt's wealthy capital during the New Kingdom. Today, Luxor attracts wealth from tourism, a key part of Egypt's economy. Here, in the "land of the living," boats and carriages bring visitors. Vendors peddle souvenirs. Tourists cross the

river to see the Valley of the Kings. In this rocky valley, 60 ancient rulers were buried, including the boy king, Tutankhamen.

Even in Luxor, about 135 miles north of Aswan, the dam's effects are felt. Irrigation is swelling underground water supplies. The columns of the Temple at Luxor are damaged by salt from the groundwater.

Near Luxor, *fellahin* live much as their ancestors did when mummies were buried in the Valley of the Kings. Water wheels carry irrigation water from river to canal and from canal to ditch. *Fellahin* life has changed, though, since the dam was built. "We can get three crops a year instead of one," a village elder explains. To do so, he must work three times as hard. Yet Egypt grows only half the food it needs. ■

■ *Describe the contrasts you would see along the Upper Nile.*

The Lower Nile

By steamship, you head north from Luxor, passing endless villages and a few industrial cities. In three days' time an unforgettable view appears in the distance. To the west are Giza's ancient pyramids and the Sphinx of Giza. On the east side, deep-green fields suddenly

give way to a packed, spreading city—Cairo.

Cairo

Cairo is a city of contrasts. Sleek cars and donkey carts wait side by side in snarled traffic. Women in dresses pass those in Muslim robes. Along the river's edge, European tourists and wealthy Egyptians relax in sailboats and cafés. At night they return to large rooms with lovely river views.

Many people in Cairo, however, live four or five to a room. People without homes have built shacks in the city dump.

Cairo is a magnet city. It attracts Muslims to al-Azhar University. It draws young men from the villages who can't find land to farm. *Fellahin* come with crops to sell.

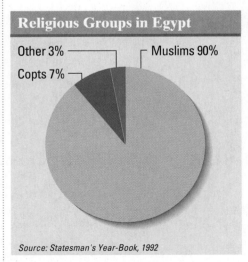

Religious Groups in Egypt

Other 3%
Copts 7%
Muslims 90%

Source: Statesman's Year-Book, 1992

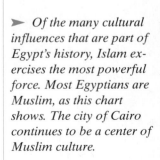

➤ *Of the many cultural influences that are part of Egypt's history, Islam exercises the most powerful force. Most Egyptians are Muslim, as this chart shows. The city of Cairo continues to be a center of Muslim culture.*

242

People in Western and Arab dress appear side by side in Cairo.

In a large open-air market, a delta farmer sells the last of his goods. "Farewell, O oranges!" he cries, taking his baskets home.

The End of the Nile

The map on page 240 shows the delta, where the orange grower lives. This 8,500-square-mile triangle has been called "the greatest vegetable garden on earth." Green fields are planted with wheat, carrots, beans, lettuce, and tomatoes.

A farmer shakes his head when you marvel at the great size of his cauliflower. "Smaller this year than last," he says sadly. Why? "Because of the dam," he replies.

Many people believe that the Aswan High Dam has hurt Egypt's ability to grow food. Before the dam was built, the Nile's floods left a rich substance called **silt** on the land. The silt acted as a natural fertilizer. Now the silt gets caught behind the dam, so farmers must use chemical fertilizers, which pollute irrigation water.

While the dam has caused new problems, Egyptians note that it has saved them from starvation. In the 1980s, when drought brought famine to neighboring Sudan and Ethiopia, Egypt drew on its reservoir of water.

The challenge that faced Egypt in the 1960s, when the dam was built, remains today. Egypt must find a way to feed itself and to protect the river on which it depends. ■

■ *How is life in Cairo different from life in the delta?*

The map on page 240 shows

R E V I E W

1. **FOCUS** Describe how modern changes are affecting life along the Nile.
2. **HISTORY** Why do tourists come to Luxor?
3. **ECONOMICS** What is Egypt's delta region known for?
4. **CRITICAL THINKING** A dam on the Nile could have been built farther south, in Sudan. Then the Nubians would not have lost their homes. Why would Egypt have wanted the dam to be on Egyptian soil?
5. **WRITING ACTIVITY** Imagine you are an archaeologist in the 1960s who wants to help save Nubian monuments from being flooded by the new reservoir. Write a letter to the editor of an Egyptian newspaper explaining the importance of the rescue and asking people to donate money to the project.

243

Egypt

Chapter Review

Reviewing Key Terms

fellahin (p. 228)
felucca (p. 240)
infrastructure (p. 230)

isthmus (p. 235)
sultan (p. 234)
silt (p. 243)

A. Each statement below uses a key term from this chapter. Tell whether each key term is used correctly. Then explain the reason for your answer.

1. The <u>fellahin</u> were scholars who came to study at the library in Alexandria.
2. Under Roman rule, Egypt's <u>infrastructure</u> of roads, harbors, and canals was improved.
3. As <u>sultan</u> of the Ottoman Empire, Selim I appointed Muhammad Ali governor of Egypt.

4. The <u>Isthmus</u> of Suez is a narrow body of water that connects the Red Sea and the Mediterranean Sea.
5. Ancient Egyptians used a type of flat barge called a <u>felucca</u> to float large building stones down the Nile.
6. The Aswan High Dam has prevented <u>silt</u> from being deposited along the banks of the Nile.

B. Use a dictionary to look up the origin of each key term. Make a table listing which words come from Arabic, from Latin, and from Greek. Which word does not come from any of these languages?

Exploring Concepts

A. After the fall of the pharaohs, a long series of foreigners left their mark on Egypt. Copy the chart below, then complete all sections. List the ways in which each set of foreign rulers affected Egyptian culture.

Foreign Rulers	Effects on Egypt
Greeks	
Romans	Improved infrastructure
Byzantines	

B. Answer each question with information from the chapter.

1. What effect did foreign rule have on the *fellahin*?
2. Why were the Arabs able to conquer Egypt with little trouble?
3. Compare and contrast ancient Alexandria and Cairo. Why was location important to each?
4. How did Muhammad Ali attempt to make Egypt into a "European-style" nation?
5. Why was the Suez Canal built? To whom was it valuable?
6. "It is not easy to govern Egypt," King Farouk warned Gamal Abdel Nasser. Give examples to support this statement.
7. How are cultural changes occurring in Egypt today different from those that occurred during ancient times?
8. Why is the Aswan High Dam important to Egypt?
9. Which areas along the Nile have felt the harmful effects of the Aswan High Dam?

Reviewing Skills

1. Read the following passage. Tell whether it is a primary or secondary source, and give reasons to support your answer.

> These were my thoughts about a new war [with Israel]. . . . Such a course would have set us back by more than a century. That is why I chose peace and did not drag my country into war. I found I could achieve the same goals through peace.
>
> Anwar Sadat

2. Many authors—from the Greek historian Herodotus in the 400s B.C. to modern-day magazine writers—have traveled along the Nile and have written accounts of their journeys. Would such accounts be considered primary sources or secondary sources of information about life along the Nile? If you were doing a report on the geographic features of the Nile, would such an account be your first choice for information? Why or why not?

3. Select five important events in this chapter, and show them on a timeline. For each date, write a sentence to describe why you chose this date.

4. Can you explain how a dam works? What kind of drawing would best support your explanation?

Using Critical Thinking

1. Look at the map of Alexander's conquest on page G12 of the Map and Globe Handbook. Trace Alexander's route. How many years did he travel? Now look at the map of Eurasia on pages 682–683, and retrace the route. About how many miles do you estimate he traveled? Make a list of all the things you think Alexander needed to move his armies such great distances.

2. Democracy means government by the people. If a majority of Egyptians vote to replace their democracy with a government based on Islamic law, do you think that change should be made? Support your answer with reasons.

3. Imagine that you are the Great Sphinx of Giza. Most people think that your eyes are sightless, but of course you can see. Describe changes you have witnessed in Egypt over the past 2,000 years.

Preparing for Citizenship

1. WRITING ACTIVITY Think of yourself as a citizen of Egypt today. You are extremely concerned about the environmental problems caused by the damming of the Nile River. What do you think the government should do to help solve these problems? Write a paragraph outlining and explaining your ideas. Compare your ideas with those of your classmates. Which ideas do you think are the most practical?

2. ART ACTIVITY Work in small groups to create a travel poster that would invite tourists to visit Egypt today. Begin by discussing what elements of Egyptian culture you want to include. You may want to show the impact of the many foreign influences on Egypt, or you might decide to focus on purely Egyptian achievements. Display your poster in the classroom. Have a spokesperson from your group explain the reasons for your choice of images.

3. COLLABORATIVE LEARNING Growing enough food has always been a major concern for the Egyptian people. As a class, do research to find out what are the most common foods eaten in Egypt today. Also find out how and where these foods are grown. Does Egypt need to import any of its key foods? Work together to plan a menu consisting only of Egyptian food.

Chapter 11

Mali

Between 1200 and 1600, West African rulers created kingdoms of great size and richness by controlling Africa's trade in gold and salt. Europeans invaded the region in the 1800s and established colonies. The Europeans changed the way the people of West Africa lived. In 1960 the Republic of Mali became independent of French rule. Today people living in Mali value traditions that date back to the early kings.

For centuries people crossing the desert have carried dried fruits for food.

The Sankoré Mosque in Timbuktu is one of the oldest in Mali. The mosque was a center of learning in the 1300s.

Gold dinars from North Africa were made of gold brought from the rich empires of West Africa.

| 1300 | 1400 | 1500 | 1600 |

1324

1324 Mansa Musa, king of Mali, makes a hajj. During his rule from 1307 to 1337, the Mali Empire reaches its greatest extent.

c. 1468 Sonni 'Ali leads the Songhai to victory over the city of Timbuktu, a major center of trade and Islamic learning under Songhai rule.

People in Mali have worn gold necklaces like this since the time of Mansa Musa.

The people of Mali take pride in modern achievements such as the world's first commercial solar energy project in Diré.

1992 Alpha Oumar Konaré is elected president in Mali's first democratic elections.

1700   1800   1900   2000

1894 Seeking to enrich its colonial holdings, France invades Timbuktu. France rules Mali until 1960.

Today

LESSON 1

From Empire to Colony

THINKING
F O C U S

How did the empires of Mali and Songhai come to power in West Africa?

Key Term

• middleman

➤ *This map comes from the Catalan atlas. It was made in the late 1300s. The cartographer drew Mansa Musa holding a golden ball and wearing a golden crown. Can you identify the Atlas Mountains?*

In 1324 the king of the West African kingdom of Mali, Mansa Musa, wanted to fulfill his duty as a follower of Islam. He gave orders to his court to get ready for his pilgrimage to the holy city of Mecca. It was one of the grandest pilgrimages the Islamic world had ever seen.

The king did not travel alone. Thousands of his subjects—officials, his wife, servants, soldiers, and slaves—also made the journey. About 100 camels loaded with gold followed the caravan. They traveled about 3,500 miles across grasslands and desert to reach the holy city of Mecca in what is now Saudi Arabia.

All around the empire, people had helped prepare for the long journey. Leather workers had sewn skin containers to hold water. Servants had loaded camels with gold. Slaves carried huge amounts of food—enough to feed thousands of people for several months.

After months of traveling, Mansa Musa's caravan reached Egypt. They camped near the pyramids for several days before

entering Cairo. The Egyptian ruler let the king from Mali use a palace during his three-month visit. Thankful, Mansa Musa gave away many presents made of gold.

The Egyptians long remembered Mansa Musa's stay. "This man Mansa Musa," one Egyptian recalled, "spread upon Cairo the flood of his generosity: there was no person, officer of the court, or holder of any office . . . who did not receive a sum of gold from him. The people of Cairo earned incalculable sums from him."

Mansa Musa's grand pilgrimage drew the attention of other people living along the caravan routes in North Africa, Southwest Asia, and even Europe. The king's pilgrimage sparked interest from others in the great wealth of West Africa. Mapmakers working at this time started to draw Mansa Musa and the Mali empire on their maps. Once this happened, outsiders began to travel to this great kingdom.

Students in ancient Mali studied the Qur'an by using boards such as these. They memorized sayings from the Qur'an written on the boards.

Mali's Golden Age

Under Mansa Musa's rule the West African kingdom of Mali grew to its largest extent. For about 160 years, from 1240 to 1400, much of what is Mali today was ruled by powerful kings. They brought great wealth to their empires by controlling a lively trade in gold. They held political power in the region through strong armies and a network of ambassadors. These representatives from the king were sent to Egypt, Morocco, and to rival kingdoms.

Mali's first king, Sundiata *(sun dee AHT ah),* was Mansa Musa's great uncle. An epic poem tells how Sundiata united many young Malinke *(muh LIHNG kay)* men under his rule.

The Roots of Mighty Empires

Sundiata conquered many new lands. Mali gained control over the trading centers of Gao *(gow)* and Djenné *(jen AY).* In these cities traders from north and south of Mali met to exchange salt, gold, and other products.

Traders from North Africa brought salt from mines that lay in the Sahara to the north of Mali. Gold traders brought gold mined in locations south of the empire. The kings of Mali became wealthy by taxing the goods traded there.

A Trading Empire

Market towns along the trade routes grew into small cities. Traders passing through the towns needed housing and supplies. People provided what traders needed. Some people offered rooms where travelers

◄ Women in Mali today still wear golden beads such as these. The jewelry shows designs from the Muslim world. Arabic letters cover the metal pendant.

© The Israel Museum, Jerusalem

249

Mali

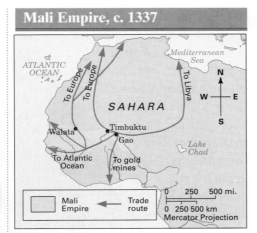

➤ *Songhai leader Sonni 'Ali conquered much of Mansa Musa's empire in the 1400s.*

could stay. Farmers brought crops to market.

Salt traders from the Sahara entered the city of Timbuktu *(tihm buhk TOO)*, their camels bearing huge slabs of salt. Those in charge of the gold mines, south of Timbuktu, did not want the salt traders to see the places where gold was mined. As a result, **middlemen,** people who buy or sell something on behalf of others, ran the trade. The middlemen haggled with the salt and gold traders until they reached a bargain.

Gold and salt were not the only goods traded in ancient Mali. People living there also traded tusks of ivory from elephants hunted in southern grasslands. They traded the ivory for European cloth brought by Arab traders from cities located in North Africa. The Arab traders exchanged the cloth for other items such as kola nuts and bars of copper and iron

offered in Mali's busy trading centers of Gao and Timbuktu.

A Center of Islamic Learning

Sundiata, Mali's first ruler, was not a devout Muslim. Many of the traders who passed through his empire practiced Islam. They brought their religion with them.

Mansa Musa, Sundiata's grand-nephew, was a devout Muslim. He encouraged his subjects to practice Islam too. When he returned from Mecca, the king brought with him Islamic scholars and a well-known Spanish architect. He built large mosques in Gao and Timbuktu.

The Muslim explorer Ibn Battuta visited Mali during the reign of Mansa Musa's grandson. You can find a description of Ibn Battuta in the Biographical Dictionary on page 698. Ibn Battuta praised the people of Mali for, he said, "they are devoted to the prayers and keep praying in congregation, which they impose also on their children. If a man does not come early in the morning to the mosque he will not find a place to pray because of the large crowd."

The Songhai Empire

After Mansa Musa died, his brother ruled Mali. He was

▲ *Today, people trade salt in an open market in the city of Mopti rather than using middlemen to bargain for goods.*

French Occupation, 1924

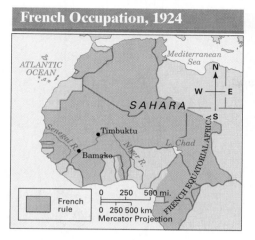

ATLANTIC OCEAN
Mediterranean Sea
SAHARA
Senegal R.
• Timbuktu
Niger R.
L. Chad
• Bamako
FRENCH EQUATORIAL AFRICA

French rule
0   250   500 mi.
0 250 500 km
Mercator Projection

Modern Mali

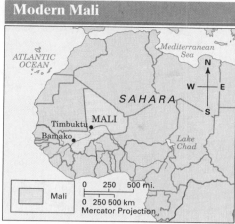

ATLANTIC OCEAN
Mediterranean Sea
SAHARA
MALI
Timbuktu •
• Bamako
Lake Chad

Mali
0   250   500 mi.
0 250 500 km
Mercator Projection

◄ *In the late 1800s, France invaded Mali. How would you compare the area of French occupation to the area of modern Mali?*

How Do We Know?

HISTORY *In 1363, toward the end of his life, Ibn Battuta dictated his memoirs to Ibn Juzayy* (IHB uhn joo ZAH ee). *Ibn Juzayy recorded the stories in the form of a book. Ibn Battuta's stories are valuable sources of information for historians.*

followed by weak kings who could not protect Mali's vast territory. By the late 1300s, the empire faced attack from the east.

The river people of Songhai lived along the Niger River. For years the Songhai resisted Mali's control. In the mid-1400s, under the leadership of Sonni 'Ali *(SOH nee AHL ee),* the Songhai built their own empire. It included parts of the old empire of Mali, as you can see on the Songhai map on page 250.

Timbuktu's fame as a center of trade grew under Songhai rule. People also came to the city because it had

become a great center of Islamic learning. By the 1500s Timbuktu had 50,000 people living there. The large trading town had three Islamic universities. These were religious schools connected to the mosques.

Leo Africanus, a traveler like Ibn Battuta, visited the Songhai Empire in the early 1500s. His writings were the main source of information Europeans had about Islam for 400 years. He praised the Songhai for the high value they placed on learning.

▼ *After each rainy season, the mosque at Djenné requires repairs. It is partly made of earth, which washes away.*

A Mali Metalsmith

8:12 A.M., August 4, 1993
Under a shade tree in Gao, Mali

Jewelry
He finishes a gold earring he will trade today. For generations, traders have sought the finest jewelry from his region. This earring differs little from those made here 200 years ago.

Hammer
He strikes the gold with his hammer. The head of his hammer is made of iron. He crafts iron and other metals besides gold.

Anvil
He treasures his anvil more than any other tool. This one is stable and much harder than the metals he hammers against it.

Files and Pincers
He shares his tools with other smiths who work by the fire. Files smooth jewelry and sharpen blades. Pincers grasp hot metal.

Bellows
In a few minutes, he will take his turn blowing air on the fire's coals with the goatskin bellows. The gusts keep the fire hot so he and the other smiths can soften and shape their metals.

Here in Timbuktu, there are great store of doctors, judges, priests and other learned men, bountifully maintained at the king's cost and charges. And hither are brought divers [different] manuscripts or written books out of Barbary [now Libya], which are sold for more money than any other merchandize.

Leo Africanus

Books were not the only items traded in the markets of Timbuktu. On market days craftspeople set up workshops near the markets. Metalsmiths made hinges and tools of iron and shaped gold into beautiful jewelry. You can find out more about the metalsmiths of Mali in A Moment in Time on page 252.

Like the Mali Empire before it, the Songhai Empire came under attack by outsiders. Moroccan troops rode out of North Africa and attacked the trading cities of Timbuktu and Gao in 1591. The Moroccans were armed with guns. The warriors of Songhai could not succeed against the new weapons.

The vast area that had been the Mali and Songhai empires broke up into smaller states. Various peoples controlled different parts of the old empire from the mid-1700s through the 1800s. Then the French invaded West Africa. ■

■ *What made the rulers of the ancient empires of Mali and Songhai wealthy?*

The French Occupation

In the late 1800s, European nations began to seize huge portions of Africa, including Mali. European nations wanted colonies that could supply raw materials to industries at home. They also wanted colonies to prove they were world powers.

The French wanted to stop the British from grabbing land in West Africa. Look at the first map at the top of page 251. It shows Mali under French rule in 1924. From the mid-1800s to the mid-1900s, France occupied many West African countries that are independent today.

French traders wanted to control a valuable trade in gum arabic. Gum arabic comes from the acacia *(uh KAY shuh)* tree, which grows in the grasslands in southern Mali. In the 1800s, people used gum arabic to dye cloth and starch clothes. The traders asked the French government to set up forts along the Senegal River. The army protected the traders from attack by local

people, who were angered by the French invasion of their lands.

Colonial Rule

The French government did build forts along the Senegal River in the 1850s and slowly gained control over western Mali. The forts

▲ *The French left examples of their architecture as well as their language in Mali, as can be seen in this train station.*

After the French colonies became independent, they created a common currency like this 1,000 franc note used in Mali.

were linked by telegraph. The French also began to build a railroad to connect trading centers. The railroad stretched from Kayes on the Senegal River to Bamako. To protect the lands they had invaded, the French put gunboats on the Niger River.

French officials tried to get local leaders to sign treaties that gave the French control over their land. When the leaders refused to sign treaties, the French used the army to force them to give in. By the late 1800s, France had control over what is Mali today.

A small number of Mali's people benefited from French occupation. The French chose Africans to be leaders of each canton, or government unit. These people had power and responsibility. They collected taxes and rounded up laborers for public works projects. In addition, they represented the government to the local people.

Under French rule very few Africans received a good education. Most people did not attend high school or college. Only a few children were able to attend European-run schools.

■ *What did West Africans gain from French rule?*

The French did not allow people to make their own decisions about their lives. The people of West Africa had not chosen French rule, and they were not given the chance to vote. The French forced many Africans to work on building projects such as the construction of the railroad. Some people were forced to fight for France in time of war.

French officials tried to educate canton leaders, hoping that these leaders would agree that French culture was superior. The plan backfired. Instead of trying to become more like the French, the local leaders held more firmly to their own traditions. African leaders started to resist French laws and policies.

Challenges to France

It was dangerous for Africans to challenge French rule. Yet some people did. Herders in the eastern part of West Africa took up arms against the French in 1914. Koumi Diossé, a Bambara leader, refused to make his people work for the French as porters, people who carry baggage from one place to another. He also led a revolt to protest the French army's taking his people to fight for France in World War I.

However, it took many years for the people of Mali to be free of French rule. Not until September 1960 did Mali become an independent country. Modibo Keita became Mali's first president. Under his rule, Mali broke its political and economic ties with France. ■

1. **FOCUS** How did the empires of Mali and Songhai come to power in West Africa?

2. **BELIEF SYSTEMS** What did Ibn Battuta like about the way of life he had observed in Mali?

3. **HISTORY** What did the French do after they invaded West Africa?

4. **CRITICAL THINKING** How did Mansa Musa change the way the people of his empire lived?

5. **ACTIVITY** Suppose you are a cartographer on Mansa Musa's pilgrimage. Make a map of the trip from Timbuktu to Mecca. Use the text and your best ideas to draw your map.

L E S S O N   2

Mali and Its People

Yassoungo's father is a boatman on the Niger River. He uses a long, flat canoe to bring farm products to open markets. Sometimes, Yassoungo helps his father. They work together, pushing long poles into the muddy river bottom to move the boat.

On this day many people have brought bags of millet and maize to sell at the markets down the river. When his father pulls the canoe close to the river bank, Yassoungo loads the bags onto the boat. The boy listens to the lap of the water against the side of the boat. He looks out across the river and sees many other boats piled high with bags of grain and fresh vegetables.

Yassoungo's father has to turn some people away. There is too much cargo. The boat will get stuck in shallow water if its load is too heavy. In the dry season, the water level in the Niger River falls even farther. Between February and July the water level is so low that large boats cannot travel on the river. At some time during these months, the boy helps his father haul the boat to patch leaks and make new poles.

Most families living along the river catch fish for food. Yassoungo's family also eats vegetables and grains such as rice, millet, sorghum, and maize. They seldom eat meat. Like many other people living in Mali's rural areas, they can't afford it.

THINKING FOCUS

How do the people of Mali use the country's rivers and grasslands?

Key Terms

- landlocked
- Sahel
- drought
- savanna

◄ *Farmers raise crops of maize and rice. This large boat is both house and means of transportation for its owners.*

255

Mali

Land of Mali

Mali is about twice the size of Texas. It is a diverse land. The physical map on this page shows Mali's main vegetation regions. Desert covers the north; grasslands stretch across the south; and a partly arid region lies in between the desert and the grasslands. Most of the people live near Mali's two major rivers.

Mali's Rivers

The Senegal *(sehn ih GAWL)* and the Niger rivers flow through Mali's mostly flat lands. Because Mali is **landlocked,** or enclosed by land, it has no seaports. The Niger is Mali's lifeline to the ocean.

The water from the Niger and Senegal rivers is vital to Mali's population. Without these rivers,

Locate the Sahel region on the map. Why does this Arabic word for shore *fit this region?*

people could not raise enough crops and animals to feed themselves.

The Niger flows in a huge arc of about 1,000 miles through southern and central Mali. The Bani River is a tributary of the Niger River. Together, the Niger and the Bani rivers form part of a large flood plain called an inland delta that covers 40,000 square miles in central Mali.

Mali has a rainy season and a dry season. In the rainy season, the Niger and the Bani swell and overflow their banks onto the surrounding plains. The flooding creates a large lake that stretches almost 200 miles in southwestern Mali.

When the flooding passes and the land starts to dry out, grasses begin to grow along the riverbanks. Then herders bring their goats and cattle to feed on the new grass.

The Sahel

Look at the map of Mali on this page. Find the region called the Sahel *(suh HAYL)*. The **Sahel** is a hot, partly dry region. The word *sahel* comes from the Arabic word meaning *shore* or *coast*. The Sahel is a borderland that lies between the bone-dry Sahara to the north and the wetter grasslands to the south. As the map on this page shows, the Sahel stretches across West Africa, through Mali, and eastward across the continent.

Few plants can grow in this region because at times little or no rain falls there. At other times, too much rain can wash away seedlings. Nevertheless, the Sahel is dotted with scrubby trees and grasses.

Sometimes, there are long periods without rain, or **drought.** During a drought, plants and grasses die.

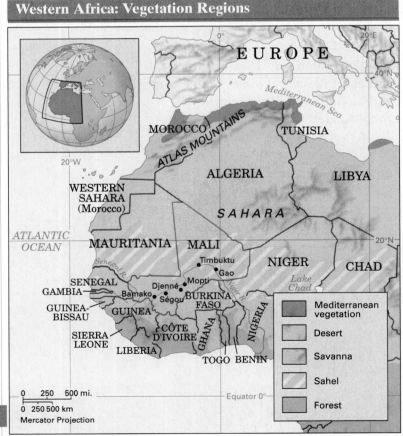

Western Africa: Vegetation Regions

EUROPE

Mediterranean Sea

MOROCCO

ATLAS MOUNTAINS

TUNISIA

20°W

WESTERN SAHARA (Morocco)

ALGERIA

LIBYA

SAHARA

ATLANTIC OCEAN

MAURITANIA

MALI

20°N

Senegal R.

Timbuktu

Gao

NIGER

CHAD

Lake Chad

SENEGAL

Djenné

Mopti

GAMBIA

Bamako

Ségou

BURKINA FASO

GUINEA-BISSAU

GUINEA

Niger R.

SIERRA LEONE

CÔTE D'IVOIRE

GHANA

NIGERIA

LIBERIA

TOGO BENIN

	Mediterranean vegetation
	Desert
	Savanna
	Sahel
	Forest

0   250   500 mi.

0 250 500 km

Mercator Projection

Equator 0°

not find enough food or water, so they migrated elsewhere or died.

Beginning in the late 1960s, Mali has had several droughts. The droughts have caused so much damage to the Sahel that some parts of the land are more like desert.

The Savanna

South of the Sahel lies a region of grasslands and forests called the **savanna**. This region covers southern Mali. Like the Sahel, it extends across West Africa. In the savanna region, a very wet season follows a very dry season. These conditions are ideal for the growth of grasses and certain trees.

Once many elephants, giraffes, and lions roamed the West African savanna. Hunters have killed many of these animals, however. Animals have also been affected by drought. At these times, the animals could

Most of Mali's people live in the savanna in the southern part of the country. These people are farmers. Generally, enough rain falls each year to support crops as well as animals.

Wooded areas also cover the savanna region. Mango trees, first planted by the French, and shea butter trees are common there. However, the people of Mali use their forests to meet most of their energy needs. Cutting trees for firewood for cooking and heating has caused deforestation in some areas. This problem is so serious that Mali has stove police who make sure that people do not waste wood.

Some farmers in southwestern Mali plant mango and papaya trees alongside grains such as millet. The trees enrich the soil and block the dry wind. The tree roots hold soil. In one village a woman grows seedlings that she gives away to other women. Slowly, Mali's people are bringing back their forests. ■

▲ *In Mali's northern desert, temperatures can reach 140°F, and there is barely any rain. (left) The savanna can receive between 20 and 60 inches of rain each year, enough to grow crops.*

◄ *The people of the Sahel get water from wells.*

■ *How are the Sahel and the savanna regions of Mali different and how are they the same?*

257

A Multicultural People

For centuries Mali has been a crossroads of many cultures. Today Mali has a population of about nine million people. The population is made up of eight large ethnic groups and several smaller ones.

The Bambara, who live in the geographic center of the country, are Mali's largest ethnic group. They make up one-third of Mali's total population. They are related to the Malinke, whose ancestors lived at the time of Mansa Musa. The Bambara and the Malinke have benefited from education to help them get top positions in the government and the army. However, 81 percent of all Malians are agricultural workers.

The Songhai are a farming people. They live where the Niger River bends. They grow grain crops such as millet and rice. The Fulani are primarily herders. They live around the flood plain of the river.

Each group of people in Mali speaks its own language. Many people also speak the language of a neighboring group of people. When France occupied Mali, French became the official language of the country. It still is today. Malians write in French and speak it in schools and in the cities.

Mali's many peoples generally cooperate with one another. In spite of their diversity, almost all the population is Muslim. Their shared religious beliefs help them understand one another.

Malians also share their trading heritage from ancient times. Today most people depend on trade among themselves. Different groups of people raise different kinds of food. Bozo fishers can trade their catches for grain grown by Bambara farmers. Fulani herders can trade goats' milk for vegetables raised by the Bambara. The peoples of Mali face the challenges of the future with a spirit of coopera- tion and pride in their cultural traditions. ■

➤ *This Fulani woman comes from one of Mali's many ethnic groups. She wears gold earrings and a necklace. More than 100 years ago men also wore jewelry such as this.*

■ *Name some differences and some similarities among Mali's many peoples.*

R E V I E W

1. **FOCUS** How do the people of Mali use the country's rivers and grasslands?

2. **SOCIAL AND POLITICAL SYSTEMS** Compare the role of the Malinke in the empires of Mali and Songhai with their role in the nation of Mali today.

3. **GEOGRAPHY** In what vegetation region of Mali has the number of wild animals decreased?

4. **CRITICAL THINKING** How do the peoples of Mali cooper- ate with one another?

5. **ACTIVITY** Make a drawing of the regions in Mali. Show details of each region.

L E S S O N   3

Republic of Mali

Imagine a visit to Bamako, Mali's capital. In Mali's cities, you would see a different side of the country than you have read about in Lessons 1 and 2. In the capital, you see streets lined with business buildings and jammed with cars, buses, and motorbikes. Music blasts from open car windows, and engines roar at stoplights. People crowd the streets selling a little bit of everything. Signs in French advertise supermarkets, hotels, movie theaters, a hospital, and a zoo.

Restaurants serve many delicious African foods. One specialty from Mali is a freshwater fish called *capitaine*. Bamako restaurants, like those in other large cities, offer dishes from around the world—pizza, frog legs, or French-fried potatoes.

A visit to the National Museum takes you away from the hustle and bustle of downtown Bamako to earlier times in Mali's history. Here you see displays of about 4,000 pieces of art made by the Bambara and other peoples. Wood carvings of human figures date back to the time of Mansa Musa's empire. Pieces of colorful woven cloth hang near handsome masks.

You listen as a museum guide talks to a group of schoolchildren. She explains how museum specialists restore artifacts in the collection. As you leave the museum and step into the busy streets of Bamako, you leave behind the interesting stories of Mali's past.

THINKING
F O C U S

What challenges does Mali face today?

Key Term

- life expectancy

◀ *Carvings, such as this antelope mask made by the Bambara, form part of the living heritage of Mali.*

◀ *The National Museum is located in busy downtown Bamako.*

Drought and Poverty

The modern nation of Mali faces challenges that its earliest empires could not have imagined. Although the early empire of Mali was one of the richest empires in Africa, today the Republic of Mali is one of the poorest countries in the world. Some of Mali's economic problems date back to the time of French occupation. You read about this period of history in Lesson 1. At that time, the region's farming and trade were controlled by the French for their benefit only.

During the late 1800s, farmers in West Africa grew crops such as peanuts, cotton, and rice. They sold the crops to French merchants, who sent the products to France. Other merchants sold French manufactured goods to the West Africans. In this way money paid to farmers for growing crops came back to France when the farmers bought goods they did not make for themselves. The French took both goods and money from the people of West Africa, leaving very little money in the region for the development of other businesses.

Undeveloped Resources

Mali has deposits of bauxite, copper, iron, nickel, and manganese. Using these mineral resources could bring Mali's people needed money. Mining minerals is expensive. Mali does not have the large sums of money needed to dig mines or to build mills or factories to turn these raw materials into finished goods. The government has had to rely on foreign contributions for this money.

Drought Hinders Farming

As you read in Lesson 2, more than half the population of Mali farm, herd animals, or fish. Farming is hard work everywhere, but especially in Mali. Periods of drought make it hard to grow food or raise animals in the Sahel. Drought affects people, animals, and plants.

When plants don't get enough water, they die. As plants wither, their roots no longer hold the soil. In the Sahel the wind blows the bare soil away. As a result the desert expands into what was once grazing land for animals. Herders

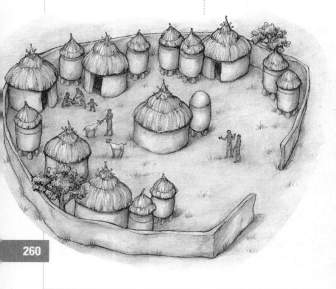

▼ *In rural areas families build mud brick homes made of two or more round buildings. Each building serves a purpose. One is used as a kitchen, another is a bedroom, and still another is a storeroom or a shelter for animals. People use local materials for building—mud bricks and grass roofs.*

move to other areas to find food for their goats and cattle. More and more herders rely on the same area to feed their animals. This over-grazing also kills plants and adds to the loss of soil.

During the 1970s and 1980s, two severe droughts occurred in the Sahel. Crops died. People and animals starved. Herders lost cattle and sheep. A group of herders called the Tuareg suffered especially great losses. Between 1970 and 1974, about 20,000 Tuareg left Mali. In search of food, they went to the neighboring countries of Niger and Algeria. Many other herders and farmers moved from rural areas to cities such as Bamako to look for jobs.

However, most people who moved to the cities could not find work. Neither the government nor private industry has the money to develop businesses that could employ the many people who have come to the cities.

Effects of Drought

People eat whatever is available during times of drought. Often the available foods do not give them enough nutrition to stay healthy.

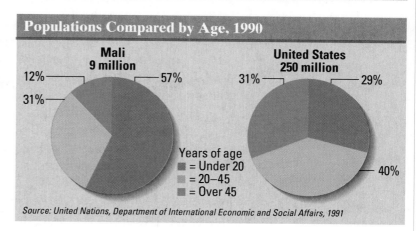

Populations Compared by Age, 1990

Mali
9 million
12%
31%
57%

United States
250 million
31%
29%
40%

Years of age
= Under 20
= 20–45
= Over 45

Source: United Nations, Department of International Economic and Social Affairs, 1991

The average **life expectancy,** or the number of years that people can expect to live in Mali, is about 48 years. Of each 1,000 babies born in Mali, about 175 babies die during their first year. This is one of the highest infant death rates in the world.

Children living in rural areas do not get the medicines they need to prevent or treat diseases such as measles or malaria. Many children do not live to the age of five.

Most doctors and nurses work in the cities where some people have the money to pay for services. Bamako contains more than 50 percent of Mali's doctors, nurses, and medical supplies. Only 8 percent of Mali's people live in Bamako. Most of the rest of the population lives in rural villages in the savanna or in the Sahel, where there are few health care centers. Rural clinics are often staffed by only one nurse who has no stronger medicine than aspirin to help patients who are sick. ■

The population is growing rapidly in Mali. Most of Mali's people are under 20 years old. The government faces the challenge to provide basic health care for the population.

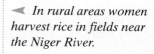

◄ *In rural areas women harvest rice in fields near the Niger River.*

■ *List two effects of drought in Mali.*

261

Mali

Meeting the Challenges

Mali's government must work to meet the challenges of a weak economy and the effects of drought. Like many other nations throughout the world, Mali's government is turning toward democracy. The government held its first democratic elections in 1992. Voters chose Alpha Oumar Konaré *(AL fuh oo MAHR koh NAHR ay)* as president.

President Konaré is looking to other countries to give more money for education. Drought and expanding desert send farmers and herders to the cities to seek work. These people will need to learn to read in order to work in factories and businesses. Today many children go to school only through the sixth grade.

The riches of ancient Mali are gone. However, some of its glorious past still exists in Mali today. Singing storytellers called *djeli (zehl EE)* pass on Mali's history in songs. The *djeli* songs honor the great deeds of Mali's kings and other leaders since the days of great empires.

A hero is born to be a hero.
A numuke [blacksmith] is
   born to be a numuke.
A djeli is born to be a djeli.
If I am poor, still I am a djeli.
If I am rich, still I am a djeli.
If my eyes see, still I am a djeli.
If I am blind, still I am a djeli.
In my heart is the spirit of a djeli.
It puts poetry in my mouth
And my mouth sings poetry.
It puts music in my fingers
And my fingers play my ngoni
   [musical instrument].
When I was poor I said,
"This is not the meaning of
   my life."
When I ruled Jala Bugu I said,
"This is not the meaning of
   my life."
The meaning of my life
Is that I will sing for the
   Traore family of kings.

Harold Courlander and
Ousmane Sako, from
The Heart of the Ngoni

In future years *djeli* may sing of Mali's present leaders. Their songs may tell of great changes in Mali. ■

▼ *Mali's future depends on the education of its people. These students attend college in Bamako.*

■ *Name two of Mali's resources that can help meet the challenges it faces.*

REVIEW

1. **FOCUS** What challenges does Mali face today?
2. **GEOGRAPHY** How are the geography and people of Saudi Arabia and Mali alike? How are they different?
3. **CULTURE** What do you think the following saying means: "When a *djeli* dies, it is as though a whole library dies"?
4. **CRITICAL THINKING** Why is it important to preserve the stories and art of Mali's people in places such as the National Museum?
5. **ACTIVITY** Write a newspaper editorial describing the problems that President Konaré faces, and give suggestions for solving them.

Identifying Supporting Evidence

Here's Why

People often have different points of view about a situation or an event. A writer presents a point of view in the form of an argument. To evaluate a written argument, you need to be able to find supporting facts, or evidence.

There is a growing debate today in Mali about the environmental effects on a part of the Sahel, a flood plain of the Niger River. Locate the Sahel on the map on page 256. Each year the river, overflowing with summer rains, floods the dry, dusty land. This water lets people here farm and fish. It also supports millions of birds that migrate from Europe to this part of the Sahel each year.

Today drought threatens life in the Sahel. What should be done? One argument is that the natural cycle should be allowed to continue. In this way people can continue to work as herders, farmers, and fishers. Others argue for damming the Niger River and creating large-scale irrigation projects. This would allow people to grow rice.

To evaluate the argument, you must be able to understand the ideas and arguments as they are presented. You must ask which ideas are supported by the most evidence.

Here's How

As in most other arguments, there are many opinions about the future of the Sahel. The boxed paragraph offers one opinion. To evaluate the argument, first identify its main point: People should not interfere with the natural cycle of the Sahel.

Now, identify the supporting evidence. Are the facts presented relevant—do they fit the point the writer is making? Statements that do not keep to the point are irrelevant. They weaken the writer's position. Then decide whether the facts are consistent—do they agree with other facts presented?

Try It

Is the statement, "The people of Mali have a rich history of ancient kingdoms," relevant or irrelevant to the writer's point? Explain.

Apply It

You can find an argument presented in the editorial pages of your local newspaper. Choose an editorial argument and identify the writer's main point. Then write a paragraph that evaluates the argument using the steps in Here's How.

People should not interfere with the natural cycle of dryness and flooding in the Sahel. If the area is turned into rice fields, the people have only one way of earning a living—growing rice. In addition, flooding will kill many species of plants and animals. If the cycle is maintained, people can continue to make a living in three ways: fishing, farming, and raising livestock.

Today, because of the decreasing rainfall, people must use the land more wisely. Sometimes animals are lost during windstorms. The number of people who are allowed to farm, raise animals, and fish in the Sahel should be controlled, and only small-scale irrigation projects should be introduced into the area. People and wildlife have lived in the Sahel for thousands of years. Only by taking these measures can they continue to do so.

Main point

Relevant. This emphasizes the main point of the argument.

Irrelevant. This has nothing to do with the main point.

Consistent. This summarizes the argument.

263

Mali

Chapter Review

Reviewing Key Terms

drought (p. 256)   middleman (p. 250)
landlocked (p. 256)   Sahel (p. 256)
life expectancy (p. 261) savanna (p. 257)

A. A compound word or term is made when two smaller words are combined. Three of the key terms are compound words or terms. On your own paper, write a definition for each of the following key terms that relates to ideas in this chapter. Also write what hints about the definition you get from the two smaller words.
1. landlocked
2. middleman
3. life expectancy

B. Answer the following questions regarding selected key terms.
1. What is a drought, and how have droughts affected farming in modern Mali?
2. What is the Sahel? What two types of land does it separate? What is the meaning of the Arabic word sahel, from which it gets its name?
3. What is a savanna? What types of plants might grow in a savanna?
4. What is a life expectancy? How is it affected by the place in which you live?
5. What does landlocked mean? What effect might being landlocked have on a country?

Exploring Concepts

A. Copy and complete this chart to outline key periods in Mali's history. Use the timeline on pages 246–247 and facts from your reading to help you. In the final column, list at least two facts about that period in Mali's history. Some entries have been filled in for you.

Year	Ruler	Government	Events
1250	Sundiata		
1307			
	Sonni Ali	empire, with king	
1894			French becomes official language of Mali
1992			

B. Answer each question with information from the chapter.
1. How did Mansa Musa's grand pilgrimage to Mecca affect Mali's economic growth during his reign?
2. What role did gold and salt have in making Mali a center of trade?
3. Who are Ibn Battuta and Leo Africanus? What information have they provided for people today about Mali's old empires?
4. How did the French use the telegraph and the railroad to gain control of trade in West Africa?
5. Give two examples of French culture that remain in Mali today.
6. What are the people of Mali doing today to bring the forests back to their country?
7. How have Mali's climate and geography created harsh challenges for its citizens today?
8. Describe the major ethnic groups of Mali. In what areas of Mali is each group located?

Reviewing Skills

1. Reread the section entitled The French Occupation on pages 253–254. Imagine that you are a Malian journalist living in 1898. You are writing an editorial. The title of the editorial is The French Have Made Us Suffer! Write a plan for the editorial. Include the following:
   - a sentence stating the main point of your argument
   - a numbered list of sentences containing information that supports your argument
   Use examples from the chapter as your supporting evidence.
2. Look again at the skill feature in Chapter 10, on page 238. Using the techniques given for identifying sources, write an evaluation of the following source: the song of a modern *djeli* about the empire of Mansa Musa.
3. Imagine that you are a *djeli,* planning to write a song about recent accomplishments by the president of Mali, Alpha Oumar Konaré. What would you need to know in order to write your song? What sources might you use to find that information?

Using Critical Thinking

1. You have read that Mali's food supply is threatened by drought and that its people suffer because medical care and educational opportunities are limited. Imagine that you are advising other nations on ways to help Mali. What specific suggestions would you offer?
2. If you were to move to Mali, where would you choose to live—in the capital city, Bamako, or in the countyside? Explain your answer.
3. In many parts of the world, people of different ethnic groups have great difficulty living together in peace. What factors help Malians to work and live together, despite their differences?

Preparing for Citizenship

1. COLLECTING INFORMATION Life expectancy in Mali is only 48 years, and the nation also has one of the highest death rates for babies. Use an almanac to locate the statistics on life expectancy and infant mortality in the United States. Share your research with the class. Then discuss what factors might make the statistics from Mali and the United States vary.
2. WRITING ACTIVITY Imagine that you are a *djeli* in the United States who has been selected to write a song or a poem about the accomplishments of a famous person. It might be, for example, a political leader, a scientist, a historical figure, an athlete, or a musician. Use your imagination. Share your work with the class.
3. COLLABORATIVE LEARNING The National Museum of Mali exhibits beautiful artifacts that provide a glimpse of Mali's rich history. In a small group, plan and create an exhibit that will provide information about Mali's climate and geography. In your group, create three committees, one for each of Mali's regions—the desert, the savanna, and the Sahel. Refer to pages 256–257. Each committee should discuss and summarize the geographic features of their region. Plan an exhibit that combines written material with diagrams, models, or pictures. Then create the exhibit. When you have finished, all the committees in your group should work together to combine and present the three exhibits to the class. Every member of the group should take on a task. After the groups have presented their exhibits, ask them to get together to discuss what aspects of their group work were successful and what group members could have done to improve the final exhibit.

Chapter 12
Ghana

The rain-forest region of West Africa was the home of many different groups. One of them came to be known as the Asante (uh SAHN tee). From their forest home-land, they built the Ashanti (uh SHAHN tee) Empire and gained wealth through trade. After a time as a colony of Britain, Ashanti and neighboring states founded the modern nation of Ghana. Ghana became the first of the former European colonies in Africa south of the Sahara to become an independent nation.

The rain forest of Ghana provides fine wood for carving. Wood-carvers are highly skilled at their traditional craft.

950	1100	1250	1400

1300s Ancestors of Asante migrate into region of today's Ghana.

1482 Portuguese build fort at Elmina.

1340

The Akosombo Dam on the Volta River provides power for industry. It forms the over-250-mile-long Lake Volta, the world's largest artificial lake.

Nana Konadu Agyeman-Rawlings, wife of Ghana's president, Jerry Rawlings, leads the movement to assure rights and opportunities for women in Ghana.

The Black Star monument in Accra, Ghana's capital, is called Independence Arch. The black star symbolizes all those who fought for freedom.

The rain-forest region of Ghana has for centuries been a major producer of gold. Brass weights like these were used to weigh gold dust when it was traded.

1550

1700

1850

2000

late 1600s Osei Tutu forms Ashanti nation.

1820 Height of Ashanti Empire

1957 Ghana becomes independent.

Today

267

L E S S O N   1

The Asante: A People of Tradition

A particular Monday . . . was chosen for the [start] of this ceremony. On that day the reigning King of Ashanti paid a semi-
state visit to the [tombs] at Bantama. . . . The king . . . [addressed the
ancestral spirits] as follows: "The edges of the years have come round,
we are about to celebrate the rites of the odwira; do not permit any
evil at all to come upon us and let the new year meet us peacefully."

Captain R. S. Rattray, *Religion and Art in Ashanti*

THINKING
FOCUS

*What does the Odwira
festival mean to the
Asante?*

Key Terms

- matrilineal
- patrilineal
- kinship
- lineage

Every September the Asante celebrate the great Odwira *(oh DOO ruh)* festival. They give thanks for the yam harvest, honor the spirits of their ancestors, and renew their loyalty to their leader.

Captain Rattray was a British official who witnessed the festival almost a hundred years ago. He also described another part of the ceremony, which takes place 11 days later. This is the royal parade by the Asantehene *(uh sahnt uh HEH nay),* the Asante king. In this parade the Asantehene follows the Golden Stool, the "shrine and symbol of the national soul" of the

Asante. Sheltering the stool is a large umbrella known as "the covering of the nation." Attendants walk alongside the stool, supporting the solid gold bells tied to it. This stool is never used as a seat, and it is treated with great respect.

On the last day of Odwira, Asante chiefs and their attendants once again march to the palace. The Asantehene is carried to the palace in a decorated seat atop his attendants' shoulders. There he awaits the lesser chiefs, who step forward and renew their vow of loyalty. Year after year the Odwira tradition remains unbroken.

➤ *The Asantehene is a
powerful and respected
leader. He maintains order
and justice. His heavy
gold jewelry shows his
wealth and rank as king.*

Land and People

The roughly two million Asante today make up the largest ethnic group in the modern nation of Ghana. They are citizens of Ghana and live in the Ashanti region. The map Modern Ghana on page 282 shows the location of the present Asante homeland in Ghana.

Geography of Ghana

Ghana, a nation in West Africa, borders the Gulf of Guinea. Ghana is about the size of Oregon. Its location, near the equator and at a low elevation, gives much of it a tropical climate. The Atlas map of Africa on page 685 shows where Ghana is located.

Ghana includes a number of different geographic regions. Along its more than 300-mile coast, no natural harbors exist. Tropical swamps and brush-covered plains stretch 50 miles inland in some places. Farther inland lie humid rain forests. The northern two-thirds of Ghana level out and become savanna. Two large rivers, the Black Volta and White Volta, join to form the huge Volta River, which flows into the Gulf of Guinea.

Origin of the Asante

The ancestors of the Asante came from the savanna north of Ghana. They were members of a large Akan-speaking group that migrated south between the 1100s and 1800s. In time they divided into a number of different states. One of these was Ashanti. Its people, the Asante, settled in the rain forest region.

The warm climate, abundant plant life, and mineral resources of the area helped the Asante prosper.

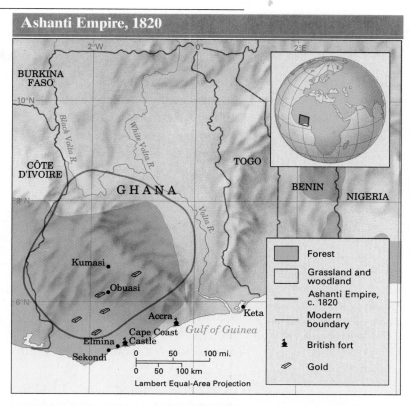

Ashanti Empire, 1820

Forest

Grassland and woodland

Ashanti Empire, c. 1820

Modern boundary

British fort

Gold

Lambert Equal-Area Projection

▲ This map shows the Ashanti Empire at about the time of its first contact with Britain. How large was the Ashanti Empire compared with Ghana today?

◄ The dense, tropical rain forest was the homeland of the Asante.

Besides hunting and gathering, they raised crops in clearings in the rain forest. From the forest they harvested kola nuts and mined gold to sell to traders. They also carried on trade with people of the savanna to the north. ■

■ How did their environment and resources help the Asante prosper?

West African Connections

The Asante are one of many groups who live in West Africa. Some of them, such as the coast-dwelling Fante, are also of Akan descent. Others are of different ethnic and cultural groups. The Dagomba, who live in the north on the savanna, are Muslims.

Patterns of Living

Each ethnic group in West Africa has certain unique traditions. The Odwira is a special festival of the Asante. Asante culture is also **matrilineal** *(mat ruh LIHN ee uhl)*. This means that people trace their ancestry through their mother's side of the family. A chief inherits his position not from his father but from his mother's brother. Most West African cultures, however, are **patrilineal** *(pat ruh LIHN ee uhl)* and trace their ancestry through the father's side.

Women receive much respect in Asante society. Women can own property and carry on trade. Women also influence decisions about government.

► *This young woman is carrying yams to sell at the market in Accra. Market women play an important role in the economy of Ghana.*

UNDERSTANDING KINSHIP

When you have a family gathering, who shows up? Grandparents and grandchildren? Aunts and uncles? First and second cousins, nieces and nephews? All of these people are related to you. All of you share kinship.

Africans value kinship and family as the basis of society. Communities are based on family ties. These ties give people in the community a sense of belonging and of caring for each other.

Within an ethnic group, the main unit of kinship is the clan. This is a very large group of families who long ago shared a special ancestor. This ancestor may have lived hundreds of years ago. Yet the people in the clan still feel linked to that person and to everyone else who is related. Within each clan are smaller groups called lineages, made up of a number of families.

The smallest group within a clan is the family. An Asante family is often very large. Wealthy Asante men may have several wives. The family includes these wives, their children, and their relatives. It also includes aunts, uncles, cousins, and grandparents.

Kinship ties are so strong that people who have died are still seen as belonging to the family. In the same way, future children are already seen as members of the family. The naming of a new baby is a special time. The week-old infant is introduced to the kinship group that will play an important role in its life.

Kinship affects each person's life in many ways. It determines not only a person's role within the lineage but also whom a person may marry. It influences one's position in society and what kind of work one may do.

270

The Queen Mother (the mother of the Asantehene or another close female relative) is the Asantehene's official adviser.

All West African peoples place great value on **kinship,** or relationship through common ancestors. One important aspect of kinship is **lineage** (*LIHN ee ihj*), a group of several families with the same ancestor.

Most people in West Africa believe in one God, who created all things, and in lesser Gods and spirits. People also believe that their ancestors remain a part of the family. People honor their ancestors with prayer and sacrifice. These practices and beliefs reflect people's view of the world. The music, dance, and art of West Africa often express aspects of people's religion.

Traditions of Working

When the Asante had first settled in the rain forest, they lived by hunting and gathering. In time they cleared small areas around their villages and began to farm.

▲ *The houses of an Asante family were built in a circle with low walls between them. The courtyard was a center for family life.*

They raised yams, millet, rice, beans, and cotton. Land belonged to the clan but was divided among the families of each village.

Over time certain kinds of work became the tasks of men or women. Men cleared the land, hunted, mined for gold, or became skilled craftsmen. Men also wove the richly patterned Kente (*KEHN tay*) cloth. Both men and women worked in the fields. Women sold the produce from crops in the market. Women also managed their households and cared for their families. ■

◀ *Nearly every Asante person owned a wooden stool which was a symbol of the person. This is the stool of an Asante king.*

■ *What has been the role of the family in West African society?*

R E V I E W

1. **FOCUS** What does the Odwira festival mean to the Asante?
2. **GEOGRAPHY** Describe the different geographic regions found in Ghana.
3. **CULTURE** What is the role of women in the society and economy of Ghana?
4. **CRITICAL THINKING** The mother of the Asantehene is honored at Odwira. Why do you think this is so?
5. **WRITING ACTIVITY** To the Asante, traditions such as the Odwira festival and symbols such as the Golden Stool and great umbrella gave a feeling of unity. What traditions and symbols does our country have? Write a paragraph explaining why such symbols are important to a people or a country.

271

Ghana

Interpreting Proverbs

Here's Why

People sometimes repeat stories or fables in order to teach wisdom or moral lessons. A proverb is similar to the moral of a story; it is a short saying that expresses a well-known truth. Many proverbs can apply to any place in the world and at any time. Others are more specific and reveal something about a particular culture or historical period.

If you read an African proverb, for example, you may learn something about African culture. You may also learn that Africans share many values with your own culture.

Here's How

The proverbs in the box below originated among the Ewe people of Ghana. The proverb about the blacksmith means that when you go to another place, you must learn

Adinkra cloth, like Kente cloth, is a traditional fabric of the Asante. The designs represent proverbs.

to behave according to the customs of that place. What clues does the proverb provide about African culture? The reference to blacksmiths suggests their importance. Think of a similar saying from your own culture, such as this: You can be a big fish in a small pond or a small fish in big pond.

Now look at the mask on the right of a European from the west coast of Africa. Read the second proverb about the hat. One interpretation of this proverb might be that if a person wants to give you something, you should beware of why the person is giving it to you. The proverb gives you a clue that Africans do not always find people from outside their culture trustworthy. "Beware of Greeks bearing gifts" is a similar saying.

Try It

Examine the last two proverbs. Analyze both of them, asking the same kinds of

questions and using the same kind of thinking you applied to proverbs in Here's How.

Apply It

Your culture has proverbs of its own. Analyze the following proverbs. Discuss how the proverbs provide clues to this culture.

- Haste makes waste.
- A watched pot never boils.
- Anything that can go wrong will go wrong.
- Wisdom is not like money, to be tied up and hidden.

The blacksmith in one village becomes a blacksmith's apprentice in another.

If a [stranger] wants to give you a hat, look at the one he is wearing before you accept it.

You do not become a chief simply by sitting on a big stool.

A stump that stays in a river for a hundred years does not become a crocodile.

Ewe Proverbs, Ghana

LESSON 2

Growth and Change

In the late 1600s, a young Asante chief, Osei Tutu, asked the chiefs of many clans to join him in forming a military union. He and the other chiefs had many interests in common. They all lived in the rain forest, and they spoke languages that were much alike. Osei Tutu led the other chiefs in defeating the Denkyira, the strongest enemy group in the region. After this victory, the other chiefs accepted Tutu as their leader and as the head of the new Ashanti nation. He became the first Asantehene.

The major symbol of the new nation was the Golden Stool. The idea of a stool was not new; by tradition every chief had his own stool. This Golden Stool, however, was different. Tutu said that it held the spirit of the Ashanti nation. It also stood for the power of the Asantehene. So important was the Golden Stool that no one was supposed to sit on it. It became the most important symbol of the Asante people and nation.

Osei Tutu also proclaimed the Odwira a national celebration to honor the Ashanti nation. Finally, he made the city of Kumasi, a trading center, the nation's political and cultural capital. Kumasi is shown on the map on page 269.

Kumasi is shown on the map on page 269.

THINKING FOCUS

How did the Ashanti Empire develop?

Key Terms

- export
- import
- cash crop

◄ *This gilded wood carving, the top for a royal umbrella, shows a king holding an egg. If he holds it too tightly, he will crush it. If he holds it too loosely, it will fall and break. What does this carving show about people's feelings toward royal power?*

The Ashanti Empire

Ashanti rulers who came after Osei Tutu added other states to their kingdom. In time they organized these peoples into an empire. The Ashanti Empire was well run, with strong leadership, military power, and wealth from trade. Ashanti kings respected the traditions of conquered peoples. Local chiefs could still rule their own lands as long as they stayed a part of the Ashanti Empire and accepted the Asantehene as their head of state. All had to pay tribute or taxes to the empire.

Ashanti Rule

The Ashanti Empire lasted for over 200 years. At its peak the empire included more than three million people. It was one of the larger empires in West Africa. The map

273

Ghana

► *The Asante were rich in gold and ornaments made of gold. This gold pendant, representing a mudfish, shows the skill of Asante goldsmiths.*

How Do We Know?

HISTORY *A number of Europeans wrote about their travels among the Asante in the 1800s. The stories told in African oral history also provide a record of events. Today these sources enable historians to study life and events in West Africa at that time.*

▼ *A Dagomba family is shown outside its home in northern Ghana. The Dagomba were a major ethnic group within the Ashanti Empire.*

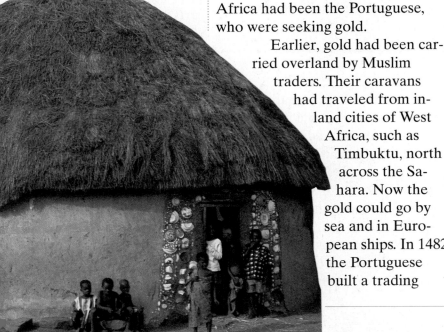

on page 269 shows the empire in 1820.

As it grew, the Ashanti Empire gained the notice of European nations trading in Africa. In 1817 a British trading group visited Kumasi. One of its members, Thomas Edward Bowdich, later described the scene. As the travelers entered the city, Ashanti soldiers saluted them with gunshots. Flag bearers waved British, Dutch, and Danish flags. Soon Bowdich and his friends were led to the royal palace. There they met the Asantehene, whose kindness and dignity impressed Bowdich. "His manners were majestic, yet courteous," Bowdich wrote in his account.

Growth of Trade

Bowdich's visit to Kumasi was one of the first direct contacts between the Asante and British traders. European traders had, however, been active in West Africa for more than 300 years. The first Europeans to reach West Africa had been the Portuguese, who were seeking gold.

Earlier, gold had been carried overland by Muslim traders. Their caravans had traveled from inland cities of West Africa, such as Timbuktu, north across the Sahara. Now the gold could go by sea and in European ships. In 1482 the Portuguese built a trading post and fort, Elmina, to protect their trade. Soon ships from other European nations joined in the rich West African trade.

One West African group that traded with the Europeans was the Fante. Like the Asante, they were of the Akan ethnic group. They lived in the coastal region—the Gold Coast—between the Asante and the Gulf of Guinea. The Fante controlled trade between inland areas and the European trading posts on the coast. The Asante sold their goods to the Fante, who then sold these to the Europeans.

The Asante produced many goods sought by the Europeans. At first these included gold, hardwood, ivory, animal skins, and salt. In return the Asante obtained new food crops such as plantains, peppers, maize, ground nuts, and cassava from the Americas. They traded for iron and copper bars, textiles, and beads. They also bought luxury goods, such as silk, used in making Kente cloth, which is discussed in A Closer Look on page 275.

In time the trade changed as Europeans began to offer guns. In exchange they wanted slaves. This trade in humans was small at first. It grew, however, to meet the demand for workers in the Caribbean and in Latin America. European trading posts in Africa became scenes of terrible suffering and misery. From 1600 until the 1840s, the demand for slaves disrupted life in West and Central Africa.

In time the Asante too became involved in the slave trade. They

Kente Cloth

A proud tradition of weaving continues in West Africa. For centuries Kente (KEHN tay) cloth has been the royal fabric of Ghana, worn by chiefs. Today it is worn by many people in Africa and around the world. Americans of African descent wear it as a sign of pride in their heritage.

Men weave narrow strips and sew them into a large cloth.

This Asante leader wears a Kente cloth robe. Although you may see the cloth used for hats or belts by fashion designers, Africans do not cut the cloth for such purposes.

Each pattern in the cloth has a title. "Belly of the crocodile" is one. Some titles stand for African sayings, such as "I walk alone."

275

Ghana

wanted guns to control their weaker neighbors. To obtain guns, they raided other kingdoms and took captives to sell as slaves.

The slave trade declined by the mid-1800s after a number of European nations stopped buying slaves. At about the same time, church groups in Europe began sending missionaries to spread their religion in Africa. Missionaries built not only churches but also schools where they taught people to read and write. This led in time to new groups of educated people within West African society. However, the teachings of the missionaries questioned traditional African ideas of family and religion.

In those years, British trade with West Africa was increasing. Once again, the kinds of traded goods changed. Along with gold and forest products, the British now sought food crops and raw materials for their factories. Among these products were peanuts, palm oil, cocoa, and cotton. Cocoa, which Asante farmers began to raise in the 1880s, soon became a very profitable crop.

The increase in its trade led Britain to seek control of inland areas in addition to its coastal forts and trading posts. This caused several wars between the British and the Asante, who sought to defend their empire. ■

■ *Why did Europeans trade for slaves, and why did groups like the Asante provide slaves?*

British Colonial Rule

As British power increased in West Africa, Ashanti rule began to weaken. Some groups under Ashanti rule now turned to Britain for support. In 1874, when an Ashanti army invaded lands protected by Britain, an army led by British troops marched on Kumasi. The soldiers burned the city and blew up the royal palace. The Asante remained free, but they lost lands to the British. These lands became part of a new colony, the Gold Coast, set up by Britain. Britain also tried to take over Ashanti trade.

In 1896 the British demanded that the Asante come under British protection. Britain banished the Asantehene and appointed a British governor in his place.

In 1900 Asante chiefs gathered in Kumasi to meet the British governor, Frederick Hodgson. Hodgson greeted the leaders, including Queen Mother Yaa Asantewa. Then he decided to test his power by breaking Asante tradition. He demanded that the Golden Stool be brought to him so that he could sit on it. The Asante leaders, shocked at this show of disrespect for the symbol of their nation, left in silence.

Asante Resistance

That night Asante leaders met to decide what to do. It was Yaa Asantewa who gave the answer. One witness later recalled how she had challenged the men to fight:

> How can a proud and brave people like the Asante sit back and look while whitemen took away their kings and chiefs, and [shamed] them with a demand for the Golden Stool?

▼ *Talking drums like this one are carved out of wood and covered with elephant hide. The Asante used drums to send secret messages.*

▲ Forts like this one, built by the Dutch at Cape Coast (see map, page 269) in 1662, were places where goods were traded and slaves were held before being shipped overseas. The guns protected the ships from raids by ships from other European countries.

Stirred by the Queen Mother's words, the Asante agreed to attack. For four months they trapped the British in the fort at Kumasi. Finally, troops rescued the British and defeated the Asante. In 1901 Britain made the Ashanti kingdom part of Britain's Gold Coast colony.

Colonial Rule

Although they had defeated the Asante, the British did not take away all their rights. Chiefs could still rule, but under British control.

Britain expected to profit from its colonies. One way to do this was to **export,** or send overseas, goods from a colony, and sell them elsewhere for a higher price. Another way was to have a colony **import,** or bring into a colony, goods such as cloth and tools from Britain.

The Asante had many products to export—gold, diamonds, hardwoods, kola nuts, palm oil, and cocoa. Cocoa was an example of a **cash crop,** a crop raised to make money rather than to feed people directly.

Colonial trade brought large profits to the British companies but few benefits to colonial peoples. British traders paid low prices to Asante farmers for the cocoa. Asante farmers, however, paid high prices for products such as food, clothing, cars, and trucks imported from Britain. It was the British traders who profited. Most of the profits went back to Britain.

The Asante hated the British system. They pointed out that it was unfair to local producers and that some of the profits should go to the colony and its people. More and more, they spoke out against British rule. ■

▲ The Queen Mother Yaa Asantewa, shown here dressed for battle, was exiled by the British along with the Asantehene.

■ Why did Britain want to make the Asante part of its Gold Coast colony?

R E V I E W

1. **FOCUS** How did the Ashanti Empire develop?
2. **ECONOMICS** How did the Europeans and Asante become trading partners?
3. **GEOGRAPHY** How did the Asante adjust to the changes in trade in the late 1800s?
4. **CRITICAL THINKING** The British imposed their method of trade on colonial peoples. What does this method reveal about Britain's attitudes toward colonial peoples?
5. **ACTIVITY** Imagine you are an Asante leader at the meeting held after the British governor demanded the Golden Stool. Write a one-minute speech telling what you think your fellow Asante should do.

277

African Jewelry

▲ *Glass beads from Europe were traded in Africa more than 1,500 years ago. These mosaic beads were made in Venice, Italy, the center of European bead manufacturing for hundreds of years.*

Men and women throughout Africa adorn themselves with many styles of jewelry. In some cultures, hair ornaments and bead designs show the wearer's age or wealth. Special beads are worn for magical protection or to bring good luck. By learning about the many uses of African jewelry, you can learn more about different African societies.

Get Ready

Gather books and magazines on jewelry and beadwork in Africa. Does your community have a museum or store that displays African jewelry? Look for beaded necklaces, belts, and hats from Kenya and South Africa. Jewelry from West African countries often includes amber, gold, and bronze. Desert regions favor silver. Search for pictures of jewelry from at least five regions.

Find Out

Take notes on each piece of jewelry. Where is it from? What is it made of? How is it worn? Does the jewelry have a special meaning? Was it made for a chief, a warrior, a child, or someone else?

If beads are used, describe their colors and patterns. Many glass beads were made in Europe and traded to Africans. Cowrie shells were once used for money in some regions. Find examples of jewelry that include beads or shells.

Move Ahead

In class, draw a large map of Africa. Tape each picture of jewelry to the region where it was made. (You can write on the map or make a sketch if your picture comes from a book.) Share your notes. Are there similar uses of jewelry among regions? Do different cultures use the same materials?

You can make your own jewelry with materials of your own. Bring the materials to class, and trade items with classmates. Does your jewelry have a message?

Explore Some More

Many modern craftspeople and artists have been inspired by

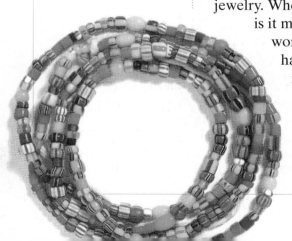

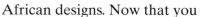

African designs. Now that you are familiar with different styles of African jewelry, look for one-of-a-kind jewelry pieces that are made by U.S. artists.

Find examples that show African influences. Your public library may have magazines and catalogs from museums with photographs of examples.

Do you notice African influences in the patterns and choice of materials in the U.S. jewelry? If possible, bring to class pictures of both African and U.S. examples.

◄ *Because the cowrie shell looks like a human eye, it was thought to have magical powers to ward off evil. These shells have been strung for sale. They will be used in making jewelry or masks.*

◄ *The women in Mauritania braid beads into their hair. The beads are made of glass, silver, amber, and carved stones and shells. Colors have special meaning. Blue stands for the purity of the sky. Violet stands for the dove, which symbolizes love and gentleness.*

▼ *Amber is sap from trees that lived 40 to 60 million years ago. The sap is fossilized, and its hardness and bright color have made it popular for African jewelry for hundreds of years. Many cultures in Africa value carved amber beads for jewelry.*

279

Ghana

L E S S O N   3

A New Nation

Key Terms

- nationalism
- literacy rate

➤ *Kwame Nkrumah was Ghana's first prime minister and, later, president. For state ceremonies he often wore the traditional robe of Kente cloth.*

March 6, 1957, was a day of celebration in Accra, the capital of Ghana. On this day Britain's Gold Coast colony became the nation of Ghana. At midnight, the British flag was lowered. Then the red, green, and gold flag of Ghana was raised in its place.

The nation's leader, Kwame Nkrumah *(KWAH may uhng KROO muh)* spoke to the crowds:

> *At long last the battle has ended! And thus Ghana, your beloved country, is free forever. . . . We are prepared to make it a nation that will be respected by any nation in the world.*

Kwame Nkrumah spent much of his life preparing for this moment. He came from a family of the Nzima in the southwestern Gold Coast. As a youth, he left home to attend Catholic mission schools. In time he became a teacher and considered becoming a priest. Then new ideas changed his thinking.

In 1935 Nkrumah went to the United States to study. He wanted to learn how to help Africans win independence. Ten years later Nkrumah left the United States. He felt he had learned much:

> *I saw the Statue of Liberty with her arm raised as if in a personal farewell to me. "You have opened my eyes to the true meaning of liberty," I thought. "I shall never rest until I have carried your message to Africa."*

Ghana: A Nation

Nkrumah returned to Africa in 1947. During his absence the spirit of **nationalism,** the desire to control one's own nation, had spread in Africa. In the Gold Coast, Nkrumah set up a new political party to work for self-government. He also led strikes and other forms of protest. The British put Nkrumah into jail, but this made him more popular.

In 1951 the people of the Gold Coast elected Nkrumah's political party to power. This forced the British to release Nkrumah from jail to take his place in the Gold Coast Parliament. There, Africans shared in making laws for the colony. Soon Nkrumah became prime minister, or leader of the colony's Parliament.

As prime minister, Nkrumah worked with the British to prepare the Gold Coast for independence. The British expected this change to take many years, but Nkrumah had other ideas. Soon Britain agreed to grant the colony its independence.

A Difficult Beginning

The Gold Coast became the first African colony south of the Sahara to become an independent nation. It was named Ghana after a great ancient kingdom of West Africa.

Ghana hoped to be a model of success that other African colonies could follow. Indeed, Ghana's future seemed bright. It had many resources and a good system of producing and trading goods. However, independence might also bring problems to Ghana. Would new leaders govern wisely? Could the nation's economy prosper in a worldwide market?

Years of Challenge

The new nation soon faced problems. Ghana counted on cocoa as a cash crop to bring money for developing industries, public projects, and social programs such as schools. If prices for cocoa fell, however, Ghana would have few other crops or products to earn money as exports.

During the 1950s prices for cocoa rose, and money flowed into

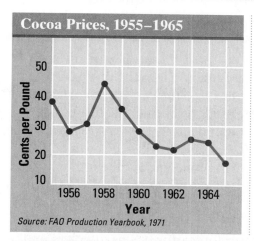

Cocoa Prices, 1955–1965

Cents per Pound

50
40
30
20
10

1956 1958 1960 1962 1964
Year

Source: FAO Production Yearbook, 1971

◀ *This graph shows the decline in the price of cocoa from 1955 to 1965. The fall in prices brought hardship to farmers like these (below). They produce two crops of cocoa a year. Cocoa provides over 40 percent of the money Ghana earns from exports.*

Ghana. The graph above shows, however, that those good times did not last. In the 1960s world prices for cocoa began to fall. Suddenly, the country was earning less money. This made the government cut its spending for schools, health care, and projects important for the future.

The people of Ghana began to lose confidence in Nkrumah. They felt he had spent money too freely and had gained too much power. In fact, he had ruled as a dictator. In 1966 a group of army officers overthrew Nkrumah. They and the military leaders who followed tried—but often failed—to make reforms to help the country. ■

■ *Why did Ghana's economy decline?*

Ghana Today

Across Time & Space

Many Asante now live in New York City. Since they cannot go home to celebrate the Odwira festival, they have brought the festival to New York. Every three years they elect a leader. They pledge their loyalty to him in the same traditional way as in Ghana. The leader helps Ghanaian immigrants in the United States and settles quarrels among local Asante.

Today Ghana is moving more confidently into the future. During the 1980s the economy slowly improved as cocoa prices rose. Unfortunately in the 1990s they began to fall. New exports, however, have earned income for the nation.

Conditions in the government have improved, though slowly. In 1981 Lieutenant Jerry Rawlings, an air force officer, seized power and took control of the government. He promised in May 1992 to allow more than one political party. In November 1992 the people of Ghana elected Rawlings president.

The Asante Today

The nation of Ghana remains rich in its traditions and its different cultures. People still honor the customs and values of their ethnic groups. This is a source of strength in the society.

The government of Ghana is centered at the national level in Accra. Ethnic groups play a part mainly at a regional level, in the 10 units that make up Ghana. These units are shown on the map opposite. Of the 10 units, only one—Ashanti—contains just one distinct group.

All of Ghana's ethnic groups now live in two worlds—traditional and modern. For example, most Asante speak both their traditional language and English, the official language of Ghana. Today's Asantehene is still the traditional leader of the Asante. However, he earns his living as a lawyer.

In the villages, lesser chiefs still play an important part. They help provide for their people's well-being. They also oversee the festivals and other customs of their culture. Thus, they keep traditional ways alive as new changes occur.

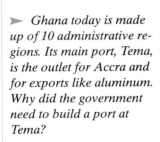

Modern Ghana

Legend:
- ⊛ National capital
- ★ Region capital
- — Administrative Region boundary
- ⊥ Dam

BURKINA FASO
UPPER WEST — Wa ★
UPPER EAST — ★ Bolgatanga
BENIN
NORTHERN — ★ Tamale
TOGO
CÔTE D'IVOIRE — Bui Dam
VOLTA
BRONG-AHAFO
Sunyani ★
Lake Volta
Kumasi ★
ASHANTI
Ho ★
EASTERN — Akosombo Dam
Koforidua ★
WESTERN
CENTRAL
Accra ⊛ — GREATER ACCRA — Tema
Gulf of Guinea
Cape Coast ★
Sekondi Takoradi ★
ATLANTIC OCEAN
Azimuthal Projection
0 50 100 mi.
0 50 100 km

➤ *Ghana today is made up of 10 administrative regions. Its main port, Tema, is the outlet for Accra and for exports like aluminum. Why did the government need to build a port at Tema?*

As the Asante and other groups protect their old ways, they must also adjust to changes. Akuraa, a village of Asante woodcarvers, provides an example of change. Within 20 years its population increased 10 times, as outsiders came to work at a new sawmill. Other strangers made their homes in the village but traveled to Kumasi to work. Suddenly, most villagers were no longer woodcarvers following their traditional craft.

In time the people of the village kept the best of old and new ways. They named a college-educated villager to be the new chief of the community. They also created a new job, chief of the carvers, to see that old traditions were kept.

New Allegiances

Today about one-third of all Ghanaians live in cities like Kumasi and Accra. They have had to learn new ways of living and to deal with new kinds of problems. Many have joined political parties and workers' groups without kinship ties.

Other influences, too, have led to new groups. Public education has raised Ghana's **literacy rate**—the percentage of the population that can read and write. This rising literacy rate benefits everyone. Large numbers of students now attend Ghana's three universities and two medical schools. Some of these students will in time return to the villages of their families. Others will live in cities far removed from family and the support provided by lineage.

Today there is a large group of people working in communications. Ghana has tried to keep a free press, without interference from the government. Hundreds of people work for newspapers, publishing houses, radio, television, and the arts. They bring new issues and ideas to Ghana's 16 million people.

Besides looking to the future, Ghana seeks to preserve its records of the past. Many of its cultural works and treasures did not survive in the villages. Others were lost during the disorder of the slave trade and of colonial rule. The National Cultural Centre at Kumasi works to preserve examples of Asante culture. It also teaches the traditional Asante crafts. Museums in Accra serve the same purposes for the nation as a whole. Traditions of the past are helping the people of Ghana to deal with changes both today and in the future. ■

▲ *Accra, Ghana's capital, is a center for government, education, and business. Crowds of people in modern and traditional dress mingle in the markets and city squares.*

■ *How has Ghanaian society changed since independence?*

R E V I E W

1. **FOCUS** How does Ghana today blend old ways and new?
2. **HISTORY** What problems did Ghana face when it became an independent nation?
3. **ECONOMICS** How do changes in the price of cocoa affect Ghana's economy?
4. **CRITICAL THINKING** Kwame Nkrumah had a major influence on the development of Ghana as a nation. Which do you think was greater, the good effects or the bad effects of his influence? Why?
5. **ACTIVITY** Using the Atlas maps on pages 688-689, find and write out the following information about Ghana: religions, climate, population, and land use.

283

Ghana

The Cow-Tail Switch

Retold by Harold Courlander and George Herzog

In traditional West African villages, storytelling was an important part of village life. Stories taught lessons and brought people together. When telling this story, the storyteller often stopped before reaching the end and would ask the listeners to suggest endings for the story. As you read the story, think about how you would end it. Is your ending the same as the one here? If not, why do you think your ending is better?

Near the edge of the Liberian rain forest, on a hill overlooking the Cavally River, was the village of Kundi. Its rice and cassava fields spread in all directions. Cattle grazed in the grassland near the river. Smoke from the fires in the round clay houses seeped through the palmleaf roofs, and from a distance these faint columns of smoke seemed to hover over the village. Men and boys fished in the river with nets, and women pounded grain in wooden mortars before the houses.

In this village, with his wife and many children, lived a hunter by the name of Ogaloussa.

One morning Ogaloussa took his weapons down from the wall of his house and went into the forest to hunt. His wife and his children went to tend their fields, and drove their cattle out to graze. The day passed, and they ate their evening meal of manioc and fish. Darkness came, but Ogaloussa didn't return.

Another day went by, and still Ogaloussa didn't come back. They talked about it and wondered what could have detained him. A week passed, then a month. Sometimes Ogaloussa's sons mentioned that he hadn't come home. The family cared for the crops, and the sons hunted for game, but after a while they no longer talked about Ogaloussa's disappearance.

Then, one day, another son was born to Ogaloussa's wife. His name was Puli. Puli grew older. He began to sit up and crawl. The time came when Puli began to talk, and the first thing he said was, "Where is my father?"

The other sons looked across the ricefields.

"Yes," one of them said. "Where is Father?"

"He should have returned long ago," another one said.

"Something must have happened. We ought to look for him," a third son said.

"He went into the forest, but where will we find him?" another one asked.

"I saw him go," one of them said. "He went that way, across the river. Let us follow the trail and search for him."

So the sons took their weapons and started out to look for Ogaloussa. When they were deep among the great trees and vines of the forest they lost the trail. They searched in the forest until one of them found the trail again. They followed it until they lost the way once more, and then another son found the trail. It was dark in the forest, and many times they became lost. Each time another son found the way. At last they came to a clearing among the trees, and there on the ground scattered about lay Ogaloussa's bones and his rusted weapons. They knew then that Ogaloussa had been killed in the hunt.

One of the sons stepped forward and said, "I know how to put a dead person's bones together." He gathered all of Ogaloussa's bones and put them together, each in its right place.

Another son said, "I have knowledge too. I know how to cover the skeleton with sinews and flesh." He went to work, and he covered Ogaloussa's bones with sinews and flesh.

sinews tendons, muscles

285

A third son said, "I have the power to put blood into a body." He went forward and put blood into Ogaloussa's veins, and then he stepped aside.

Another of the sons said, "I can put breath into a body." He did his work, and when he was through they saw Ogaloussa's chest rise and fall.

"I can give the power of movement to a body," another of them said. He put the power of movement into his father's body, and Ogaloussa sat up and opened his eyes.

"I can give him the power of speech," another son said. He gave the body the power of speech, and then he stepped back.

Ogaloussa looked around him. He stood up.

"Where are my weapons?" he asked.

They picked up his rusted weapons from the grass where they lay and gave them to him. Then they returned the way they had come, through the forest and the ricefields, until they had arrived once more in the village.

Ogaloussa went into his house. His wife prepared a bath for him and he bathed. She prepared food for him and he ate. Four days he remained in the house, and on the fifth day he came out and shaved his head, because this was what people did when they came back from the land of the dead.

Afterwards he killed a cow for a great feast. He took the cow's tail and braided it. He decorated it with beads and cowry shells and bits of shiny metal. It was a beautiful thing. Ogaloussa carried it with him to important affairs. When there was a dance or an important ceremony he always had it with him. The people of the village thought it was the most beautiful cow-tail switch they had ever seen.

Soon there was a celebration in the village because Ogaloussa had returned from the dead. The people dressed in their best clothes, the musicians brought out their instruments, and a big dance began. The drummers beat their drums and the women sang. The people drank much palm wine. Everyone was happy.

Ogaloussa carried his cow-tail switch, and everyone admired it. Some of the men grew bold and came forward to Ogaloussa and asked for the cow-tail switch, but Ogaloussa kept it in his hand. Now and then there was a clamor and much confusion as many people asked for it at once. The women and children begged for it too, but Ogaloussa refused them all.

Finally he stood up to talk. The dancing stopped and people came close to hear what Ogaloussa had to say.

"A long time ago I went into the forest," Ogaloussa said. "While I was hunting I was killed by a leopard. Then my sons came for me. They brought me back from the land of the dead to my village. I will give this cow-tail switch to one of my sons. All of them have done something to bring me back from the dead, but I have only one cow-tail to give. I shall give it to the one who did the most to bring me home."

So an argument started.

"He will give it to me!" one of the sons said. "It was I who did the most, for I found the trail in the forest when it was lost!"

"No, he will give it to me!" another son said. "It was I who put his bones together!"

"It was I who covered his bones with sinews and flesh!" another said. "He will give it to me!"

"It was I who gave him the power of movement!" another son said. "I deserve it most!"

Another son said it was he who should have the switch, because he had put blood in Ogaloussa's veins. Another claimed it because he had put breath in the body. Each of the sons argued his right to possess the wonderful cow-tail switch.

Before long not only the sons but the other people of the village were talking. Some of them argued that the son who had put blood in Ogaloussa's veins should get the switch, others that the one who had given Ogaloussa breath should get it. Some of them believed that all of the sons had done equal things, and that they should share it. They argued back and forth this way until Ogaloussa asked them to be quiet.

"To this son I will give the switch, for I owe most to him," Ogaloussa said.

He came forward and bent low and handed it to Puli, the little boy who had been born while Ogaloussa was in the forest.

The people of the forest remembered then that the child's first words had been, "Where is my father?" They knew that Ogaloussa was right.

For it was a saying among them that a man is not really dead until he is forgotten.

Further Reading

African Myths and Legends. Kathleen Arnott. These tales are about animals, humans, and superhumans.

Behind the Back of the Mountain. Verna Aardema. These are black folktales from southern Africa.

The Cow-Tail Switch and Other West African Tales. Retold by Harold Courlander and George Herzog. This book contains additional West African tales and legends that have been passed down through oral tradition.

The King's Drum and Other Stories. Harold Courlander. Here are tales from many different peoples of Africa.

The Magic Drum: Tales from Central Africa. W. F. P. Burton. The very short stories in this book are similar to fables. They are favorites in the Congo.

Chapter Review

Reviewing Key Terms

cash crop (p. 277)
export (p. 277)
import (p. 277)
kinship (p. 271)
lineage (p. 271)

literacy rate (p. 283)
matrilineal (p. 270)
nationalism (p. 280)
patrilineal (p. 270)

A. Read each pair of words. Write a sentence telling how the words in each pair are related.
1. matrilineal, patrilineal
2. kinship, lineage
3. export, import

B. Write whether each of the following statements is *true* or *false*. Then rewrite the false statements to make them true. Each new statement should show that you understand the meaning of the key term.
1. By growing <u>cash crops</u>, Gold Coast farmers produced more than enough food to feed their families.
2. Aroused by a spirit of <u>nationalism</u> in the years after World War II, the people of the Gold Coast struggled to remain a colony of Great Britain.
3. When most of its people can read, a country has a low <u>literacy rate</u>.

Exploring Concepts

A. Copy this outline of Chapter 12. Complete the outline with information from the chapter.

   I. The Asante: A People of Tradition
      A. Land and People
         1.
         2. Origin of the Asante
      B. West African Connections
         1.
         2.
  II. Growth and Change
      A.
         1. Ashanti Rule
         2.
      B. British Colonial Rule
         1.
         2.
 III. A New Nation
      A.
         1. A Difficult Beginning
         2.
      B.
         1.
         2. New Allegiances

B. Support each of the following statements with information from the chapter.
1. Traditions helped to unite the Asante people and to give them a sense of belonging to their society.
2. The natural environment helped the Asante to prosper.
3. The Ashanti Empire was one of the larger empires in West Africa.
4. In the beginning, trade with Europeans benefited the Asante.
5. Eventually, trade with the British led to harmful practices.
6. The Asante resisted British expansion in a variety of ways.
7. Kwame Nkrumah gained many new ideas in the United States.
8. Ghana's dependence on one major export crop, cocoa, caused problems for the new nation.
9. The Asante are still an important group in the nation of Ghana.
10. No matter what their ethnic group, today the people of Ghana live in two worlds.

288

Reviewing Skills

1. Explain each of the following proverbs in your own words. What do these proverbs reveal about U.S. culture?
   a. "Time is money."
   b. "Little strokes fell big oaks."
   c. "Heaven helps those who help themselves."
   d. "Haste makes waste."
   Now write a proverb of your own and explain what it means in terms of your own culture.

2. By looking at a flow chart, you can easily see the order of events. Make a flow chart showing the stages by which Britain took control of the Ashanti Empire. The chart should begin in the 1600s and go to 1900.

3. Storytelling is an important part of West African culture. Why is this tradition valuable to historians?

Using Critical Thinking

1. You read in Chapter 12 that "Traditions of the past are helping the people of Ghana to deal with changes both today and in the future." How do you think that keeping traditions helps people deal with changes in their lives?

2. Compare and contrast the role of kinship in a traditional West African culture and in U.S. culture today.

3. Write a "want ad" or a job description for a future leader of Ghana. List all the skills and qualifications you think a new Ghanaian leader should have in order to deal with the people's needs and problems.

4. In this chapter you read that the people spoke out against British rule. In what ways, if any, did British rule help to prepare the people of the Gold Coast for independence?

Preparing for Citizenship

1. **INTERVIEWING** In traditional West African society, a family's history is handed down by word of mouth from one generation to the next in an oral tradition. Interview members of your family to learn as much as you can of your family's history, focusing on events that have occurred in your own lifetime. If you like, share an event or two from this story with your class.

2. **ARTS ACTIVITY** Go to the library to find pictures of the traditional arts of Ghana. Using clay or papier mâché, make a model of a mask or sculpture that you find interesting. Share your work with the class. What can you learn about the people of Ghana from their art?

3. **WRITING ACTIVITY** Imagine that you are Kwame Nkrumah in his role as prime minister of the Gold Coast in about 1955. Write a rousing political speech that you will use to persuade the British to grant independence to your country. In your role, you may draw on your experience in the United States; on colonial resistance to British rule; on feelings of nationalism among your people; and on the advantages of independence. When you have written your speech, give it in front of the class.

4. **GROUP ACTIVITY** After Ghana became independent, national elections chose Kwame Nkrumah to be prime minister. With a partner, debate whether the Asantehene, the leader of the Asante, should have become prime minister. One of you can take the part of Nkrumah and the other the part of the Asantehene.

5. **COLLABORATIVE LEARNING** As a class, decide which are the major events in the history of the Ashanti Empire and Ghana as told in this chapter. Then divide into small groups, and choose one of these events to dramatize. Your group should choose a narrator, rehearse a brief skit about its event, and present the skit to the whole class.

Chapter 13
South Africa

"Blacks and whites must come together," says 12-year-old Edward Diholo. "Violence, when will you stop!!!" writes Nthabiseng Nkole, age 14. These young students live in South Africa, a nation that is home to peoples of many colors who take pride in their roots. Color has deeply divided these peoples, and for generations they have fought bitterly to protect their lands and ways of life. Now blacks and whites are trying to come to agreement.

The Khoisan lived throughout the western part of southern Africa for thousands of years. Bantu speakers in the east lived in farm communities such as the one above.

This wealthy Afrikaner, Gert Maritz, was one of the farmers who made the Great Trek to central southern Africa from 1836 to 1840.

1375

1500

1625

1488

1652 The Dutch settle the African cape and import slaves for farming.

This market is located in Cape Town, one of the first settlements established by Europeans in the 1600s.

Children in this Soweto schoolyard and across South Africa look forward to the day when people of all colors are treated as equals.

1750

1875

2000

1860s Discovery of diamonds brings cities, industry, and waves of English speakers to southern Africa.

1990 Black leader Nelson Mandela is freed from prison. Some unfair laws are repealed.

Today

L E S S O N   1

A Divided Land

What is apartheid, and how does it affect South Africans?

Key Terms

- apartheid
- segregation
- boycott

➤ *Mandela was sentenced to life in prison after a seven-month trial without a jury. In one prison he broke bricks and worked in a mine. His release was celebrated around the world.*

February 13, 1990, Soweto, South Africa: The seats of the South African soccer stadium are full, but people keep coming. Most are black. They are happy and eager. This crowd, however, is not waiting for a soccer match. They have come to see a South African hero.

Joyful chants echo across the stadium. In Xhosa *(KOH sah),* an African language, the voices cry, *"Amandla! Ngawethu!* [Power! It is ours!]" This is the largest crowd in years to gather for a political rally. People in the crowd wave the black, green, and gold flag of the African National Congress (ANC). Only two weeks ago, waving this flag would have been illegal. Two weeks ago, being a member of the ANC was illegal.

Suddenly, the crowd takes up a new chant. "Mandela! Mandela!" rocks through the stadium. Then he appears. Tall, thin, and gray-haired, Nelson Mandela moves with grace. Hand in hand with his wife, Winnie, he walks around the soccer field. They raise their fists in a salute to victory. The crowd goes wild.

Two days after his release from a South African prison east of Cape Town, Mandela has returned to his home in Soweto *(suh WEE toh).* At age 71, Mandela is a free man—almost—for the first time in nearly 30 years.

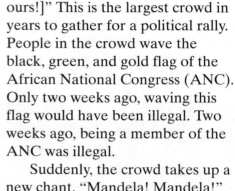

A Whites-Only Government

Nelson Mandela had been put in prison because he had protested policies of his country's government. Why did that government let him out of jail? In a sense, South Africa let Mandela go because it hoped to free itself, too. World opinion had recognized that South Africa was an openly racist country.

The Republic of South Africa, a country roughly three times the size of California, is located on the southern tip of the African continent. The land is rich in natural resources such as gold, diamonds, platinum, uranium, and coal. About 40.5 million people live here, roughly one-half in rural areas.

South Africa's population, like that of most African countries, including its neighbors Namibia, Zimbabwe, Botswana, Mozambique, and Swaziland, is mostly black. Unlike its neighbors, however, South Africa has a minority white population that runs the government. For decades this government has resisted sharing power with the black majority. It has refused to grant basic rights, including voting rights, to blacks. How has the government been able to do this? ∎

▲ *Across the world, supporters of Mandela and the anti-apartheid movement wore buttons such as these.*

∎ *What makes South Africa different from its neighbors?*

Apartheid

Through the early 1990s, the South African government kept its hold on power by creating and enforcing a policy called apartheid *(uh PART hayt).* **Apartheid** was a policy of separation set up in 1948. It defined people in South Africa by color and protected the power of the white government. Apartheid laws labeled every South African white, colored, Asian, or African.

White was supposed to describe people from "pure" European families. *Colored* was a broad term for people of "mixed race" or those who didn't fit any other group. *Asian* was used for people from India as well as for many other Asians. *African* was the term used to describe black Africans.

These terms used by the South African government can be confusing. In this chapter the term *nonwhite* will include the colored, Asian, and African peoples in South Africa. The term *black* will include the African peoples only.

Separate Worlds

Apartheid forced the **segregation,** or separation, of racial groups into two worlds, white and nonwhite. The best schools, hospitals, and public transportation were provided just for whites. There were also separate restaurants, beaches, drinking fountains, train cars, and even park benches. WHITES ONLY signs hung in many public places. Marriage between races was banned.

Apartheid also separated the areas where whites and blacks lived. Large numbers of blacks were crowded into areas called homelands, which were chosen by the government. The map on page 294

▲ *Under apartheid, public facilities were separate and very unequal. For example, nonwhites could use only bathrooms marked for them.*

> *Whites were a small part of the population, but apartheid gave them most of the land, as the chart shows. This land was also the most productive in the country. In contrast, most blacks had to live in homelands. What conclusions might you make about the homelands from looking at the map?*

Population and Land

Population under Apartheid, by Race

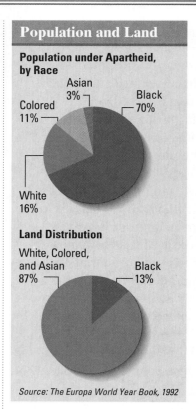

Asian 3%
Black 70%
Colored 11%
White 16%

Land Distribution

White, Colored, and Asian 87%
Black 13%

Source: The Europa World Year Book, 1992

South Africa, 1990

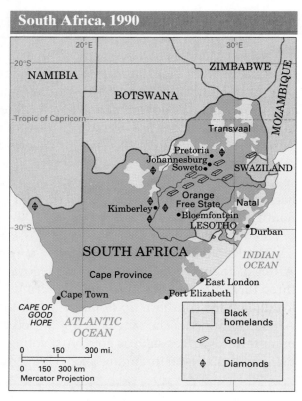

NAMIBIA
BOTSWANA
ZIMBABWE
MOZAMBIQUE
Tropic of Capricorn
Transvaal
Pretoria
Johannesburg
Soweto
SWAZILAND
Orange Free State
Kimberley
Natal
Bloemfontein
LESOTHO
Durban
SOUTH AFRICA
INDIAN OCEAN
Cape Province
East London
Cape Town
Port Elizabeth
CAPE OF GOOD HOPE
ATLANTIC OCEAN

	Black homelands
	Gold
	Diamonds

0   150   300 mi.
0 150 300 km
Mercator Projection

> *All blacks had to carry a passbook like the one on the right. It told personal details of people's lives. These details included information about their past jobs and what employers thought of them.*

shows where the homelands were located. As the chart shows, under the system of apartheid, black people made up 70 percent of the 40.5 million South Africans, but they lived on only 13 percent of the land.

Many blacks needed to live close to the "white" cities, where the government allowed them to work as servants or in other low-level jobs. For these workers, the government set up areas near the cities called townships. In many townships several families lived together in small shacks without electricity or running water.

Mandela Fights for Freedom

In 1964 a white South African court found Mandela and other ANC leaders guilty of trying to overthrow the government. At age 45, Mandela was sent to prison for life. On the day he left prison,

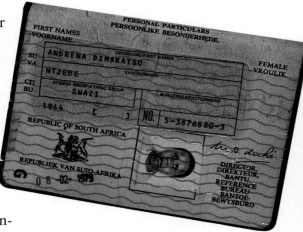

Mandela repeated what he had said at his trial almost 30 years before.

I *have cherished the ideal of a democratic and free society in which all persons live together in harmony and with equal opportunities. It is an ideal which I hope to live for and to achieve. But if need be, it is an ideal for which I am prepared to die.* ■

■ *How did apartheid affect the lives of blacks in South Africa?*

Defeating Apartheid

Nelson Mandela helped make the African National Congress famous throughout the world. Yet the ANC is older than Mandela. In 1912 black leaders from across South Africa formed the group that would become the ANC.

Protests and Responses

For nearly 50 years, the ANC and other anti-apartheid groups led protests and tried to talk to the government. Then in 1960, police fired on a large crowd of protesters in Sharpeville, a black township outside the city of Vereeniging. The police killed 69 people.

Following the Sharpeville Massacre, the government banned the ANC and forced its leaders into hiding. Blacks had found that non-violent protests didn't work.

In June 1976, black students in Soweto marched in the streets to protest a government order. Police fired on the students, killing a 13-year-old boy. The shooting sparked riots. In one week 176 people, mostly blacks, died. People around the world were shocked by the government's attack.

Thousands of young blacks responded to the government's brutality. They began to receive military training in camps in other African countries.

World Pressure

During the 1980s, people throughout the world increasingly spoke out against apartheid. Gradually, South Africa became isolated from the world. Most major nations joined in a boycott of South Africa. In a **boycott,** people refuse to do business with a company, group, or country.

Sports teams boycotted South Africa, too. During the boycott South Africa's famous white rugby, cricket, and tennis teams were not allowed in world tournaments.

How had South Africa become such a racist country? The answer is found in South Africa's long history of struggle between peoples. ■

▲ *Protesters demonstrate in Cape Town, South Africa, just before Mandela's release in 1990. Under apartheid, protest leaders could be jailed for long periods without receiving a trial.*

■ *What methods did people use to fight apartheid?*

REVIEW

1. **FOCUS** What is apartheid, and how does it affect South Africans?

2. **SOCIAL SYSTEMS** Under the policy of apartheid, where were black South Africans legally allowed to live?

3. **HISTORY** In what ways did the South African government respond to the fight against apartheid?

4. **CRITICAL THINKING** Major nations of the world joined in a boycott of South Africa. How would refusing to do business with a country affect the economy of that country?

5. **WRITING ACTIVITY** Can you think of any unfair laws today? Would you be willing to protest these laws in public? Why or why not?

L E S S O N   2

The Fight for Land

THINKING
F O C U S

How was the land of southern Africa important to each group of people who lived there?

Key Terms

* Afrikaner
* trek

➤ *Some rock paintings like the one on this page show the San hunting eland, a type of antelope.*

If you wanted to be a farmer or a rancher today, you would begin by buying a piece of land. Maybe you would put a fence around it or hang a PRIVATE PROPERTY sign.

Not all cultures share the idea that land can be owned as private property. In some places, people have freely

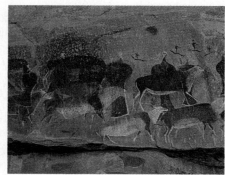

used what land they needed. Still, they haven't thought of it as theirs to fence in, buy, or sell.

For thousands of years, southern Africa was such a place. The spacious veld *(vehlt)*—vast grasslands in the interior of the region—was unmarked by fences or permanent buildings.

Early Southern Africans

The veld was far from empty, however. From very early times, three distinct groups of people occupied southern African land.

Peoples of the Western Region

Thousands of years before Europeans arrived, a people called the San *(sahn)* lived in the dry, rocky western part of southern Africa. The San were hunter-gatherers. They hunted antelope, zebras, and elephants. They also gathered wild fruits, berries, and roots.

The San moved constantly, so they didn't build permanent homes. Instead, they stayed in caves or made shelters out of branches or animal skins.

Living alongside the San were a related people called the Khoikhoi *(KOY koy)*. Besides hunting and gathering as the San did, the Khoikhoi also herded cattle and sheep. They lived in shelters made of branches, twigs, and grass.

Historians sometimes refer to both groups together as the Khoisan *(KOY sahn)*. The map on page 297 shows where the Khoisan eventually settled. The Khoisan were not alone in southern Africa, however.

Peoples of the Eastern Region

To the east of the Khoisan lived groups of taller, darker peoples who spoke Bantu languages. These peoples are known as Bantu-speaking peoples. Many of them lived in southern Africa as early as A.D. 300. They are the ancestors of most people living in southern Africa today.

Bantu-speaking peoples farmed and herded livestock. They made pottery and mined ore to make iron tools and weapons. The Bantu speakers often stayed in one place. They built lasting homes of stone or clay. Individuals owned livestock, but the land the animals grazed on belonged to the whole group.

The lives of the Bantu-speaking peoples and the Khoisan were to change after the 1400s. That is when Europeans found out about their beautiful land. ■

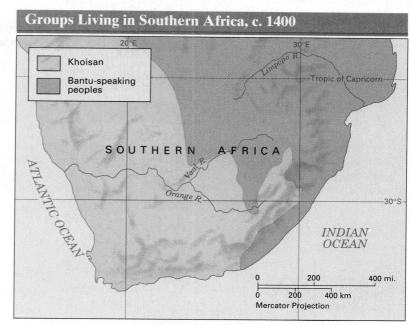

Groups Living in Southern Africa, c. 1400

☐ Khoisan
☐ Bantu-speaking peoples

SOUTHERN AFRICA

ATLANTIC OCEAN

INDIAN OCEAN

Limpopo R.
Tropic of Capricorn
Vaal R.
Orange R.
30°S

20°E   30°E

0   200   400 mi.
0   200   400 km
Mercator Projection

The Arrival of the Europeans

In 1488 Bartolomeu Dias (*DEE uhs*), a Portuguese captain, rounded the southern tip of the African continent. He was searching for a sea route to Asia, the source of much-wanted spices. That southern point came to be called the Cape of Good Hope. It became a regular stop for ships sailing between Europe and Asia. Dias and other early visitors regarded southern Africa as unoccupied and free for the taking.

The Dutch Settle the West

By the 1650s the Dutch had become the leading traders with Asia. In 1652 the Dutch East India Company established an outpost at the cape to supply its many ships with fresh food and water.

The company grew food and traded it with the Khoisan for sheep and cattle. In 1657 the company began giving land on the cape to Dutch settlers to grow food for the fleet. The settlement was known as the Cape Colony.

The land given away had been occupied by the Khoisan for centuries. Not surprisingly, the Khoisan fought to keep their use of the land. European guns and diseases killed many of them. The loss of their lands forced many Khoisan people to work for the Dutch.

The large Dutch farms needed plenty of labor. In addition to hiring Khoisan workers, the colonists brought in slaves from elsewhere in Africa and from Asia. In time the mixing of the Dutch with these African and Asian peoples created a group of Cape Colony residents whom the settlers much later began to call "Cape coloreds."

As more Europeans—especially the Germans and French—joined the Dutch at the Cape Colony, they all began to call themselves **Afrikaners.** The British, who came later, called them Boers. *Boer (bohr)* is the Dutch word for "farmer." The mix of many languages spoken in the colony slowly influenced the Dutch that the Afrikaners spoke.

▲ *Referring to the map, explain how geography affected the early peoples who lived in southern Africa.*

■ *Find two facts in the text that support this statement: The Khoisan and Bantu-speaking peoples were well established in southern Africa centuries before the Europeans arrived.*

➤ *The Bantu speakers planted grains such as sorghum (shown here and on the opposite page) as well as melons, squashes, beans, and yams.*

297

South Africa

Creation of Modern South Africa

1835–1840s Afrikaners expand north and east, battling Bantu-speaking peoples. This painting depicts Afrikaners on the Great Trek.

1840	1850	1860

1840 Mpande becomes head of the Zulu Kingdom, founded by Shaka in the early 1800s.

1860s Diamonds are discovered west of the Orange Free State. The Kimberley diamond mine is pictured on the right.

▲ *Modern South Africa emerged from centuries of conflict and wars over the land and its resources. The timeline above records some of the events that shaped South Africa from 1835 to 1912.*

➤ *The map shows routes that many Afrikaners took on the Great Trek and the Afrikaner and British territories that were created soon afterward. Why did the trekkers move north and east rather than north and west?*

Over the years, Afrikaans *(af rih KAHNS)*, a new language, emerged.

The Cape Colony began to grow. In search of new farmland, large numbers of Afrikaners headed east and invaded the lands of the Bantu-speaking Xhosa people. In the late 1700s, the Xhosa fought the Afrikaners to defend their homelands.

The Great Trek

By the early 1800s, Great Britain, a rising world power, had taken over the Cape Colony from the Dutch. As British settlers, merchants, and government officials arrived, the new rulers began to make changes. English, not Dutch, became the official language. In the 1830s, slaves in all the British colonies, including the Cape Colony, were freed.

These changes angered many Afrikaner settlers. From 1835 to about 1840, some 6,000 Afrikaner men, women, and children fled British rule. They loaded their belongings, including slaves and servants, into ox-drawn wagons and set off with their slaves and livestock in search of new lands.

The migration became known as the Great Trek. The **trek,** or journey, was long and dangerous. The Afrikaners crossed steep mountains and the huge veld. Most Afrikaners were members of the Dutch Reformed Church and felt guided by their religious beliefs as they made the trek. They believed that God had chosen them to occupy new lands and to rule non-Christian peoples. The Afrikaners saw southern Africa as their rightful home.

The powerful Xhosa blocked the Afrikaners' trek to the east, so the Afrikaners pushed northward.

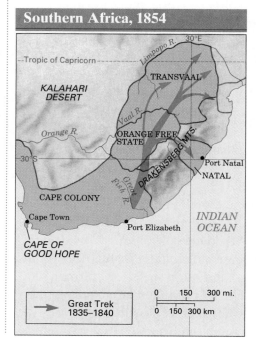

Southern Africa, 1854

- Tropic of Capricorn
- Limpopo R.
- 30°E
- TRANSVAAL
- KALAHARI DESERT
- Vaal R.
- Orange R.
- ORANGE FREE STATE
- DRAKENSBERG MTS.
- 30°S
- Great Fish R.
- Port Natal
- NATAL
- CAPE COLONY
- Cape Town
- Port Elizabeth
- INDIAN OCEAN
- CAPE OF GOOD HOPE
- Great Trek 1835–1840
- 0 150 300 mi.
- 0 150 300 km

1880s Waves of whites and non-whites come to the Transvaal during the gold rush.

1893 Mohandas Gandhi arrives in South Africa, where he will lead nonwhites in a movement of non-violent protest.

1899–1902 British defeat Afrikaners in South African War.

1910 Former British and Afrikaner republics join to become the Union of South Africa. The stamp above is issued, with King George V of England on its face.

1912 African National Congress founded.

1880   1890   1900   1910

The map on page 298 shows the routes they took. Yet the northern regions were the farmlands and pastures of other Bantu speakers.

Even before the Great Trek, many Bantu-speaking peoples had faced tremendous hardship. In the early 1800s, a Bantu-speaking warrior named Shaka had conquered much of the region and formed the Zulu kingdom. Shaka's Zulu army had fought fierce wars of conquest. These wars had killed or uprooted other Bantu-speaking peoples throughout southern Africa. The widespread destruction and scattering of the Bantu-speaking peoples is known as the Mfecane *(uhm fuh KA nay).*

Because of Shaka's wars, the Bantu-speaking peoples were so scattered that they could not unite to defeat Afrikaner and, later, British invaders. By the late 1800s, the Bantu speakers had lost most of their land. ■

■ *Why did many Afrikaners make the Great Trek?*

A Century of Change

In the 1830s and 1840s, the Afrikaners and Bantu-speaking peoples fought many battles over the land. By 1854 the Afrikaners had won control and had created two new Afrikaner republics, the Transvaal *(trans VAHL)* and the Orange Free State. In these republics, only white men could vote, and slavery was practiced.

Diamonds and Gold

In 1867 diamonds were discovered along the Orange and the Vaal rivers west of the Orange Free State. Settlers found gold in the Transvaal.

Thousands of prospectors from Great Britain, other European countries, the United States, Australia, and elsewhere in Africa poured into the Orange Free State and the Transvaal. Blacks also joined the rush to the mines. Many of them had lost their farmlands to white settlers. Now they were forced to work as laborers in the mines to feed their families. A Closer Look on page 300 tells about life in South Africa's diamond and gold mines today.

By 1896 about 44,000 white miners lived in the Transvaal. With their arrival a new city, Johannesburg, was born. Today Johannesburg is South Africa's largest city.

Across Time & Space

One of the first leaders of the movement for fair treatment in South Africa was Mohandas Gandhi (GAHN dee). Gandhi, an Indian lawyer who lived in South Africa from 1893 to 1914, led Asians in nonviolent protests against unjust laws. Protesters would break laws intentionally to call attention to the injustice. Later, protesters around the world would use Gandhi's methods.

Mining in South Africa

Over the past century, almost half of the world's gold has come from South African mines. Diamonds, silver, platinum, coal, and other metals and ores are also mined there. More than 340,000 workers go underground each workday. The dangers they face include extreme heat, poisonous gases, falling rocks, and explosions.

A solid-gold Krugerrand, minted from South African gold, weighs one ounce. Other countries buy South African gold to mint their own coins.

Some mines tunnel two miles below the earth's surface. As many as 10,000 miners work in narrow shafts with heavy machines.

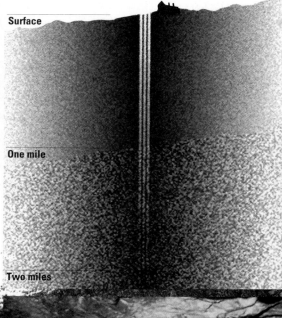

Surface

One mile

Two miles

Of the miners who bring the riches out of the ground, black miners have traditionally earned the lowest wages.

Afrikaners Battle the British

As the Cape Colony expanded, the Afrikaner and British settlers disagreed more and more about which group should control the government. In 1899 the Afrikaners and the British began to fight. Both sides recruited blacks to help them. By the end of the South African War (also called the Boer War), thousands of blacks and whites had been killed, and much farmland had been ruined.

The war ended with a British victory in 1902. Bitterness remained for generations, however, between the blacks, the Afrikaners, and the British.

A New Nation

In 1910 the two British colonies, the Cape Colony and Natal *(nuh TAL)*, joined with the Afrikaner republics, the Orange Free State and the Transvaal. Together they formed the Union of South Africa. The timeline on pages 298 and 299 shows some of the events that led to the founding of the union. This new nation, with a strong central government, became part of the British Empire. Refer to the map on page 672 of the Minipedia to locate other nations that were part of the British Empire during this time period.

Blacks, Asians, and coloreds made up most of the population of the new nation. However, under a new constitution, few nonwhites could vote. A former Afrikaner general, Louis Botha *(BOH tuh)*, became prime minister of an all-white government. ∎

Afrikaner Power

As mining grew, whites and blacks continued to rush to the mines from the countryside. Many whites became diggers in the mines. Blacks, however, often found jobs only as whites' assistants.

More cities sprang up as workers settled near the mines. Gradually, South Africa's economy shifted from farming to industry and from the country to the city. As more and more people moved to the cities, however, jobs became harder and harder to find. Whites began to pass laws that further limited the freedom of nonwhites.

Growing Discrimination

In 1911 South Africa set aside the best jobs at the mines—and the best pay—for whites only. Soon white miners were earning about

▼ *Some Asians were originally brought to South Africa as slaves. The photo below shows a Malayan family long after slavery had ended. Other Asians came as laborers. On the left, Indians arrive in Durban on their way to Natal in the late 1800s.*

10 times more than black miners. Blacks formed unions to protest their low wages. Yet the mine owners, supported by the government, refused to recognize the unions.

Whites limited blacks' power in still other ways. The Natives Land Act of 1913 made it hard for black South Africans to buy or rent land outside areas set aside for them. These areas, called reserves, quickly became crowded. Thousands of men had to leave their families on the reserves while they worked at white-owned mines and farms. Blacks also needed a pass, or permit, just to go from the reserves to the cities to look for work. These reserves later became homelands under the apartheid policy.

Asians, too, faced new hardships. The British had begun bringing Asians to South Africa in the 1860s to work in the sugar cane fields of Natal. South Africa now passed laws to stop Asians from entering the country and limited the places where they could live.

"A White Man's Land"

Beginning in the early 1900s, some Afrikaners wanted to separate themselves even more from blacks and English-speaking whites. On the one hand, the Afrikaners feared the growing influence of English-speaking whites in both government and business. By the 1930s they were twice as wealthy as Afrikaners. On the other hand, Afrikaners worried about job competition from blacks.

During the 1920s Afrikaners worked to protect white privileges. Afrikaans, along with English, became an official language of South Africa. In 1934, Afrikaners formed the Purified National Party. The party leader said it was the Afrikaners' duty to "make South Africa a white man's land."

The National Party won control of South Africa in 1948. To maintain its power and prevent blacks from gaining equality, the National Party began the policy of apartheid, which means "apartness" in Afrikaans. More than 40 years of apartheid government would follow. ■

■ *Find evidence in the text to support this statement: Laws limiting nonwhites' rights began long before the government set up apartheid.*

R E V I E W

1. **FOCUS** How was the land of southern Africa important to each group of people who lived there?

2. **CULTURE** Compare the ways of life of the Khoisan and the Bantu-speaking peoples before Europeans arrived in South Africa.

3. **HISTORY** Why did the government of South Africa pass laws that limited the freedom of nonwhites?

4. **CRITICAL THINKING** Why did the Dutch, Germans, and French in South Africa call themselves Afrikaners?

5. **ACTIVITY** Draw your own Moment in Time that illustrates the culture of one of these groups: the San, the Khoikhoi, or the Bantu speakers.

Recording Information

Here's Why

To make the most effective use of sources such as books, magazines, and newspapers, develop the skill of taking and organizing notes. Suppose you have to prepare a report about life under apartheid. How would you take notes and organize them for your report?

Here's How

As you begin to gather information for your report, write down questions you want your report to answer. For example, you might ask: What were the laws of apartheid? What effect did apartheid have on people's lives?

Once you've written your questions, begin the note-taking process. Write your notes on index cards. On each card, write notes about just one major point. This way you can keep track of information and organize it to prepare for writing your report.

As you take notes, paraphrase what you have read. That is, write the notes in your own words. You may want to shorten this information into brief phrases as shown on the cards below.

Copy the exact words from a source only if you want to use them as a quotation. Make sure to copy the spelling, punctuation, and grammar exactly as it appears in your source. Also, put quotation marks at the beginning and the end of the quotation. This way you can tell it from your paraphrased notes.

Write the source information on each card. Source information includes the author or editor, title, publisher, and date of the source and the page number on which you found the information. You'll need to know this information if you have to go back to the source to check your notes or take more notes. You will also need to name the source if you use any of the information from it in your report.

Using information in a report without naming its source can get you into trouble with your teacher and even with the law. It is against the law to steal other people's ideas and words.

Try It

Now turn to Lesson 2, page 298. Write a note card paraphrasing the information about the Great Trek. Record this book as your source.

Apply It

Suppose you are writing a report about Nelson Mandela. Write three or four questions you want to answer, and write two note cards on the material you find for one of the questions.

To protect their power, Afrikaners developed a policy called apartheid. In Afrikaans, the word *apartheid* means "apartness." Apartheid was a complex set of laws designed to bring about total segregation and white domination. For example, people of different races could not eat together, go to the same schools, or ride in the same train cars.

Apartheid
— Apartheid keeps black and white people apart in their daily lives.

Apartheid
— Apartheid means "apartness."

Apartheid
— Complicated laws set up by South Africans so white people could keep power.
Source: *South Africa*, p. 8

303

South Africa

LESSON 3

A New South Africa

Two African women rounded the last lap of the 10,000-meter race. With a final burst of speed, Ethiopia's Derartu Tulu pulled ahead to win the Olympic gold medal. Elana Meyer came close behind to take the silver medal for South Africa.

This moment at the 1992 Olympic Games was thrilling for South Africans. Since 1964 South Africa had been banned from the Olympics. Since 1968 almost no country in the world had played against South African sports teams.

The international sports boycott began to ease when South Africa started changing its policies. In 1991 the International Cricket Council readmitted South Africa as a full member. With the repeal of some of the cruelest apartheid laws, South Africa was allowed to participate in the 1992 Olympics.

After the race Tulu and Meyer hugged each other. Then the two Africans—one black, one white—held hands and ran around the track. Did this scene symbolize a more peaceful future for blacks and whites in Africa? Meyer was hopeful. Later she said of her silver medal, "This is for the new South Africa."

New Problems, New Progress

By the late 1970s, some white South Africans saw that their country had to change. Yet supporters of apartheid wanted more than ever to prevent the black majority from gaining power. Many South Africans—white and black—began to think that apartheid would end only with a violent war. Others still hoped that the government and the anti-apartheid movement could agree on a peaceful change. What kind of change would solve the country's problems?

Government Reforms

In 1978 the National Party elected P. W. Botha as prime minister. Under Botha's leadership, the government abolished some apartheid laws. Yet it refused to consider demands for equal participation of blacks in government.

Anti-apartheid groups renewed their protests. Police and other officials often met these protests with violence. Nearly 900 people were killed as a result of political violence in 1985 alone. In 1986 Botha declared a national state of emergency. This decree strengthened the power of the police.

More and more whites began to think that, violently or nonviolently, blacks would one day take control of the government. Many thought the best way to prevent a violent takeover was to listen and talk to black leaders. Important white business leaders met with ANC leaders in 1985 to begin talking about how to end apartheid peacefully.

In 1990 a new president, F. W. de Klerk, promised to end apartheid. He abolished many apartheid laws, made the ANC legal, and freed Nelson Mandela. De Klerk also agreed to meet with anti-apartheid leaders to work on forming a new government in which all races would share power fairly.

In 1991 people from all racial groups began holding talks about making a new government and writing a new South African constitution. Many wanted a whole new set of laws to bring about **social justice,** or fairness for people of all races, levels of income, and ways of life. You

can read more about social justice on page 306.

Most whites supported the talks with black leaders. Some Afrikaners opposed the talks, though, and said that they would use violence, if needed, to keep whites in power.

Most nonwhite South Africans also supported the talks. They wanted to make sure that they would be fairly represented in any new government that resulted from the talks. This was especially true of the Inkatha Freedom Party (IFP). The IFP was led by Mangosuthu Buthelezi *(boo tuh LEH zee),* chief of the Zulu. Some blacks, however, felt that talking had gone on too long already, with little change in the government's apartheid policies.

▲ *This school in Johannesburg is one of the many schools that became integrated in the early 1990s.*

▼ *As apartheid laws were abolished, the hated* WHITES ONLY *signs in Durban, South Africa, began to come down.*

Tension among members of all these groups rose. It flared into ongoing violent attacks against both whites and blacks. These attacks continued through the early 1990s.

Signs of Progress

Some observers said that South Africa had come a long way in the early 1990s. The laws that had given high-paying jobs only to whites were cancelled. The hated pass laws were gone. Some white schools were taking nonwhite students. People of all races could legally marry each other and live in the same areas. Restaurants, beaches, and other public places were open to all races. A new constitution was being discussed.

Other observers, however, pointed out that apartheid had not disappeared. Many apartheid laws remained in force. Some people expressed fear that strong apartheid laws could be put back into effect unless nonwhites shared power in the government soon.

The effects of apartheid also had not disappeared. The fear of violence prevented many nonwhites from moving to white areas or from marrying a person from another race. Most blacks still lived in the homelands. There were not enough houses or jobs for blacks. Schools and health care in black areas were still poor.

The most important change of all was also yet to come. The white government still did not share power with the black majority. Blacks like Nelson Mandela still could not vote. ∎

■ Name two major problems and two major improvements in conditions in South Africa today.

UNDERSTANDING SOCIAL JUSTICE

Do you think it is fair when most of the people in a country cannot vote? Is it fair to allow only white players on a rugby team? Most people would answer no. Under apartheid, though, that is how things were in South Africa. People around the world criticized the country for its lack of social justice.

What Is Social Justice?

Social justice is the idea that a society ought to treat all its members fairly—not just a lucky few. It stems from the idea that all members of a society are equal. Thus, social justice is related to political issues such as fair representation in government and the right to vote. Legal issues, such as the right to proper treatment by police and to a fair trial, are also involved.

Yet social justice cannot be achieved through political and legal action only. Economic and social equality are also needed. No member of society should be excluded from education, jobs, or health care. It is hard, however, to make sure that people who hire workers or give health care are treating all people fairly.

Achieving Social Justice

The changes South Africa made in the early 1990s were a step toward bringing about social justice. However, people's minds and attitudes must also change. That can take a long time.

It is important to remember that South Africa is only one country where achieving social justice is difficult. People all over the world must work to assure everyone of an equal place in human society.

South Africa and the World

The boycotts of many countries in the 1980s began to do great damage to South Africa's economy. Following de Klerk's reforms in the early 1990s, many nations ended their boycotts of South Africa. Still, the country's economy was slow to recover. In addition, continued violence in the townships hurt many South African businesses.

As South Africa looked to the future, many important questions remained unanswered. Would the government continue to talk with black leaders about extending democracy to the nonwhite majority? Would the ANC and other nonwhite groups be able to agree among themselves about how the new government should be formed?

Instead, would talks between the white government and non-white groups break down? Would the country be engulfed in a bloody civil war? Would other countries become involved? Would the land and the economy of South Africa be completely destroyed before the white minority shared power equally with all its citizens? South Africans considered these questions as they prepared for change.

In the early 1990s, South Africans faced an uncertain future. Despite the uncertainty, however, young people expressed great hope

for their country. In 1992 Jane Mogase *(moh GAH seh)*, a 13-year-old student in Johannesburg, wrote about her dreams.

*I*n a new South Africa we want to help each other and love each other and we want violence to be stopped. . . . We want to do things together and we want to have equal rights and no more war in the world. We want white people to live in our areas and white kids to come to our schools, and we want peace between blacks and whites. ■

▲ *To build harmony and cooperation among racial groups, South African opponents of apartheid planned events like the Open City Walk in Cape Town in June 1989.*

■ *What possible outcomes can you think of for South Africa's future?*

---

1. FOCUS What are some of the changes that took place in South Africa beginning in 1978?

2. CULTURE Why was South Africa able to participate in the 1992 Olympics?

3. HISTORY How did whites and blacks feel about talks between the South African government and black leaders about forming a new government?

4. CRITICAL THINKING What items in a new South African constitution would help guarantee the rights of people in all racial groups?

5. ACTIVITY Make a chart comparing the viewpoints of some of the political groups who want a say in forming a new South Africa.

307

Chapter Review

Reviewing Key Terms

Afrikaner (p. 297)
apartheid (p. 293)
boycott (p. 295)

segregation (p. 293)
social justice (p. 305)
trek (p. 298)

A. In each statement below, a key term has been used incorrectly. Rewrite each sentence using the correct key term.

1. <u>Afrikaner</u> was a policy of separation set up in 1948 in South Africa to protect the power of the white government.
2. Unfair laws enforced the <u>boycott</u> of races into separate and unequal groups.
3. <u>Trek</u> is a name that Dutch, German, and French settlers took to distinguish themselves from Europeans who arrived later in South Africa.
4. To protest its unfair policies toward non-white residents, many nations joined in a <u>segregation</u> of South Africa.

B. Answer the following questions regarding selected key terms.

1. What is <u>social justice</u>, and how does it differ from <u>apartheid</u>?
2. Which key term is a synonym for *journey*?
3. Which key term is a synonym for *separation*?
4. If you and your classmates agreed to <u>boycott</u> a store or a company, what would your agreement mean?

Exploring Concepts

A. Copy and complete the timeline below to summarize key events in the history of apartheid and the African National Congress (ANC). On your timeline, place these events at their correct dates:

1. ANC leader Nelson Mandela is sentenced to life in prison for trying to overthrow the government.
2. The Afrikaners' Purified National Party wins control of South Africa and sets up the policy of apartheid.
3. Black leaders form a group that comes to be called the African National Congress.
4. The South African government bans the ANC.
5. President F. W. de Klerk frees Nelson Mandela and lifts the ban on ANC membership.

B. Support each of the following statements with information from the chapter.

1. The San and Khoikhoi peoples, sometimes together referred to as the Khoisan, were both alike and different in their ways of life.
2. South Africa's geographic location and farmland were major features that attracted European traders and settlers.
3. European settlers showed a shocking lack of respect for black South Africans.
4. In South African history, diamonds and gold made a few people rich, but many people in the country remained poor.
5. Violence has played a terrible and continual role in the history of South Africa since the 1650s.

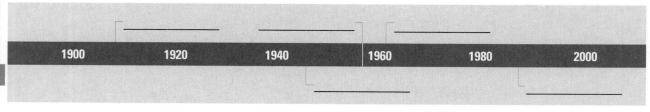

Reviewing Skills

1. In the Atlas, look at the climate map on page 688 and the land use, land, and ocean resources map on page 689. Use the maps to make a chart comparing the climates, land uses, and natural resources of the western and eastern regions of South Africa. Then use your chart to answer these questions:
   • How did the ways of life of the early Khoisan and Bantu-speaking peoples reflect the features of their separate regions?
   • What features led the Afrikaners to migrate to the eastern and northern regions of South Africa during the Great Trek? Why were they seeking these features?
2. Refer to Recognizing Patterns on page 107. Next, reread the first section on page 304. Then, follow these directions:

   • Write a paragraph to summarize the end of the Olympic race and what happened just after the race. Use a chronological pattern. Use clue words to make the pattern clear.
   • Then write a brief paragraph to explain why international sports teams have lifted their boycott of South African teams. Use a cause-and-effect pattern. Use clue words to make the pattern clear.
3. Look again at Understanding Note Taking on page 303. Imagine that you are going to write an article about President F. W. de Klerk's plans to end all of South Africa's apartheid laws. Tomorrow you will interview him. What questions should you ask him to get all the information you need for your article?

Using Critical Thinking

1. In a brief paragraph, explain how each slogan and sentence on the poster on page 307 expresses the goals and dreams of anti-apartheid groups. What other slogans and sentences might you put on an anti-apartheid poster? Explain your answers.
2. Imagine that you are at a conference of international leaders. Your collective goal is to help South Africa grow economically and to enable its citizens to attain full social justice. What suggestions might you offer to the conference? Explain how each suggestion might help the people of South Africa.
3. As the Germans and the French joined the Dutch in South Africa, they all began to call themselves Afrikaners. Why do you think they chose that specific name?

Preparing for Citizenship

1. COLLECTING INFORMATION Nelson Mandela's release from prison was celebrated all over the world. Page 292 shows a front-page headline in one U.S. newspaper. How did your local paper report his release? How did local residents react to the news? Do some research at a library. Then interview family members and neighbors. Find out their reactions to Mandela's release. Report your findings to the class.
2. WRITING ACTIVITY On page 307 you read about the dreams that one student in South Africa has for her country. What dreams do you have for your country? Write a paragraph that describes those dreams.
3. COLLABORATIVE LEARNING In a small group, reread the description on page 292 of the stadium scene. Discuss the feelings people might have had that day, the sounds and sights, and so on. Then work together to create a television news broadcast of the event. Two members of the group should act as reporters on the scene, who explain the events for viewers around the world. Two members should portray Nelson and Winnie Mandela. Other members should portray people in the stadium. Present your broadcast to the class.

Asia

The quiet beauty of this Indonesian rice field captures the ancient rhythms of life in rural Asia. For centuries, Asian artists, thinkers, and priests have been fascinated by such beauty, which was created by human interaction with the land. This is only part of Asia's long history. For almost 10,000 years, Asia has also seen the rise and fall of many high civilizations and mighty empires. Because Asia contains about three-fifths of the human race, what happens here today will affect the world's future.

A.D. 250

Rice field on the Indonesian island of Bali

Today

Unit 5 Overview

Asia

Asia can boast some of the greatest contrasts of geography and climate of any continent—volcanoes and plains, deserts and rain forests. The tallest mountain range in the world, the Himalayas, forms a huge arc north of India. One Asian city is one of the wettest places on earth. An average of more than 100 inches— almost 9 feet—of rain falls each June on Cherrapunji, India.

China and India rank first and second as the most populous countries in the world. Although Asia is home to some of the world's oldest cultures, much of it is also quite modern. Today many Asian nations are among the world's fastest-growing industrial nations.

➤ *Bicycles are an important means of transportation in Asia. This bicyclist carries Chinese lanterns.*

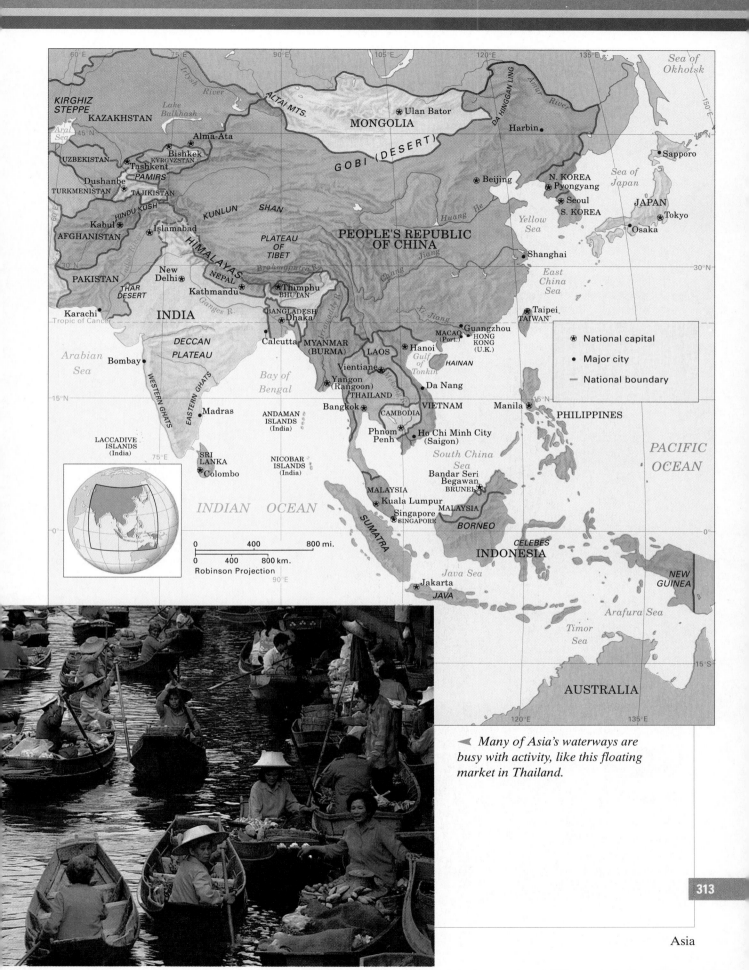

KIRGHIZ STEPPE

KAZAKHSTAN

Aral Sea

Lake Balkhash

Alma-Ata

UZBEKISTAN

⊛ Bishkek
KYRGYZSTAN
⊛ Tashkent

TURKMENISTAN

Dushanbe ⊛

PAMIRS

TAJIKISTAN

HINDU KUSH

Kabul ⊛

AFGHANISTAN

⊛ Islamabad

KUNLUN

SHAN

ALTAI MTS.

Irtysh River

MONGOLIA

Ulan Bator ⊛

GOBI (DESERT)

DA HINGGAN LING

Harbin •

Amur River

Sea of Okhotsk

• Sapporo

⊛ Beijing

Huang He

N. KOREA
• Pyongyang ⊛
⊛ Seoul
S. KOREA

Sea of Japan

JAPAN

• Tokyo
Osaka •

PEOPLE'S REPUBLIC OF CHINA

PLATEAU OF TIBET

HIMALAYAS

Brahmaputra R.

Chang Jiang

Shanghai •

Yellow Sea

East China Sea

PAKISTAN

THAR DESERT

New Delhi ⊛

NEPAL
⊛ Thimphu
Kathmandu ⊛ BHUTAN

Ganges R.

BANGLADESH
• Dhaka ⊛

Karachi •

Tropic of Cancer

INDIA

DECCAN PLATEAU

Arabian Sea

Bombay •

WESTERN GHATS

EASTERN GHATS

Calcutta •

MYANMAR (BURMA)

Irrawaddy R.

Xi Jiang

MACAO (Port.)

⊛ Guangzhou
HONG KONG (U.K.)

Taipei •
TAIWAN ⊛

LAOS

Hanoi •

Gulf of Tonkin

HAINAN

National capital ⊛

Major city •

National boundary —

Madras •

ANDAMAN ISLANDS (India)

Bay of Bengal

Vientiane ⊛

Yangon (Rangoon) ⊛
THAILAND

Bangkok •

Da Nang •

VIETNAM

Manila •

PHILIPPINES

LACCADIVE ISLANDS (India)

CAMBODIA

Phnom Penh ⊛

Ho Chi Minh City (Saigon) •

SRI LANKA
• Colombo

NICOBAR ISLANDS (India)

South China Sea

PACIFIC OCEAN

INDIAN OCEAN

MALAYSIA

⊛ Kuala Lumpur
Singapore ⊛
SINGAPORE

SUMATRA

Bandar Seri Begawan ⊛
BRUNEI

MALAYSIA

BORNEO

CELEBES

INDONESIA

NEW GUINEA

0   400   800 mi.
0   400   800 km.
Robinson Projection

Java Sea

Jakarta ⊛
JAVA

Arafura Sea

Timor Sea

AUSTRALIA

◄ *Many of Asia's waterways are busy with activity, like this floating market in Thailand.*

313

Asia

The Land and People

In much of Asia, the climate is dry in winter. During the rest of the year, rain falls almost every day. Monsoon winds bring these changes in climate. In winter the monsoons blow from the northeast, bringing dry air. In summer the winds pick up moisture from the warm Indian Ocean. When these winds move over land, they drop heavy rains.

Among Asia's most dramatic geographic features are its mountains. Few people have made the difficult climb to the top of Mount Everest in the Himalayas, the highest point on the earth. Each year, though, thousands of people climb Japan's Mount Fuji. This cone-shaped mountain—once an active volcano—stands high above the surrounding land. To many Japanese, Mount Fuji is a symbol of their nation's beauty.

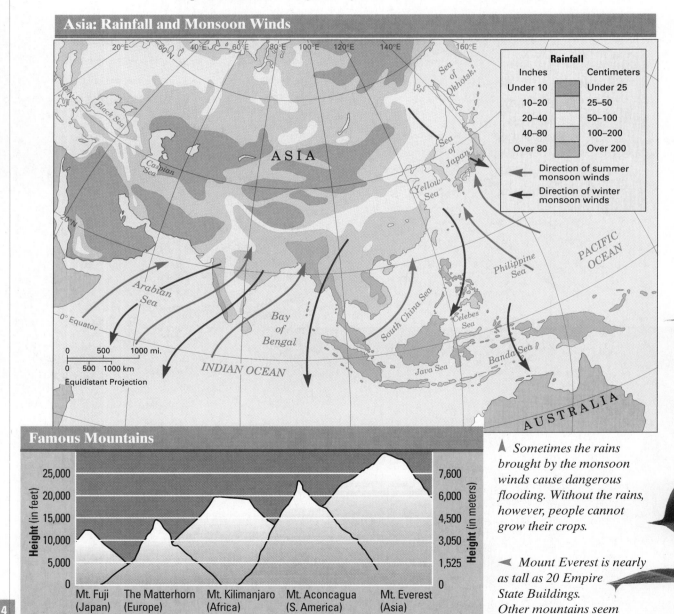

Asia: Rainfall and Monsoon Winds

Rainfall

Inches	Centimeters
Under 10	Under 25
10–20	25–50
20–40	50–100
40–80	100–200
Over 80	Over 200

← Direction of summer monsoon winds

← Direction of winter monsoon winds

0   500   1000 mi.
0   500   1000 km
Equidistant Projection

Famous Mountains

Height (in feet): 25,000 / 20,000 / 15,000 / 10,000 / 5,000 / 0

Height (in meters): 7,600 / 6,000 / 4,500 / 3,050 / 1,525 / 0

Mt. Fuji (Japan)   The Matterhorn (Europe)   Mt. Kilimanjaro (Africa)   Mt. Aconcagua (S. America)   Mt. Everest (Asia)

Source: Encyclopaedia Britannica, 1992

▲ *Sometimes the rains brought by the monsoon winds cause dangerous flooding. Without the rains, however, people cannot grow their crops.*

◄ *Mount Everest is nearly as tall as 20 Empire State Buildings. Other mountains seem small by comparison.*

314

Asia's people belong to many ethnic groups and speak many different languages. Although other peoples have brought new customs, Asia has kept its own rich traditions—including music, dance, and theater. A popular form of Indian music, for example, is played on a stringed instrument called a sitar. The traditional Japanese forms of drama—Noh and Kabuki—are still performed today.

The economies of many Asian nations bordering the Pacific Ocean are growing rapidly. This region, called the Pacific Rim, includes Japan, South Korea, Singapore, and other East Asian nations as well as Australia and nations on the west coast of North and South America. These nations trade actively among themselves as well as with other nations.

Pacific Rim Trading Partners

Key: Machinery, Clothing, Oil, Office machines, Electronics, Clocks, Watches, Textiles

Country	Import Partner	Export Partner	Main Exports
Japan	United States	United States	Machinery, Office machines
Philippines	Japan	United States	Machinery, Clothing
Singapore	Japan	United States	Office machines, Oil
Indonesia	Japan	Japan	Oil
South Korea	Japan	United States	Machinery, Textiles
Hong Kong	China	United States	Clothing, Clocks, Watches, Textiles

Source: Europa World Yearbook, 1991

▲ *Great changes are taking place in world trade patterns.*

▲ *Kabuki actors use colorful costumes and heavy makeup to bring characters to life. Scenery, music, and pantomime enliven their performances.*

▼ *Much of the world's natural rubber comes from rubber trees grown in Malaysia and Indonesia.*

▼ *Asian cities are some of the most densely populated in the world.*

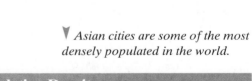
City Population Density

City	
Hong Kong	
Dhaka, Bangladesh	
Jakarta, Indonesia	
Bombay, India	
Ho Chi Minh City, Vietnam	

0   100,000   200,000   300,000
Density per Square Mile

Source: World Almanac and Book of Facts, 1992

Chapter 14

India

The earliest Indian civilization arose about 4,500 years ago. Gradually, other ancient peoples moved to India. Over the centuries the people blended old and new customs and beliefs into uniquely Indian forms. This wondrous mixture of religious and social traditions continues in India today.

This storekeeper sells powdered dyes and incense to be used during Hindu religious ceremonies.

A.D. 320–550
During India's Gupta dynasty the Hindu religion prospers. These coins were made from gold imported from Rome.

| 250 | 600 | 950 |

A.D. 320

1001–1027 Mahmud of Ghazna arrives and establishes a Muslim presence in northern India.

A turban ornament like this one, decorated with many jewels, was a Muslim symbol of high rank.

In India today the old and the new exist side by side. This young woman is dressed in traditional clothing. In the cities she walks with people in western clothing.

Under British rule thousands of miles of railroad tracks were built. Today the railroad continues to link the people of India.

1300

1650

2000

1600–1858 The English East India Company lays the foundation for the British Empire in India.

1947 India becomes an independent nation. Its first prime minister is Jawaharlal Nehru.

Today

LESSON 1

A Hindu Empire

Why is the period of the Gupta Empire called India's Golden Age?

Key Term

• epic

They were probably some of the world's first exchange students. They came from China, Tibet, and as far away as Japan. During the fourth century, students from all over Asia filled the classrooms of the University at Nalanda. It was a long trip to northern India, but worth it.

The students came to study subjects such as religion, agriculture, art, architecture and medicine. Their teachers at Nalanda and other Indian schools were making amazing discoveries.

Even today these ancient Indian thinkers affect students everywhere. In fact you can thank them for your math homework tonight. Indian mathematicians invented the number system you use today. It is based on nine digits, the zero, and the decimal.

India's Golden Age

The University at Nalanda had eight colleges and three libraries. It blossomed in India during the reign of the Guptas *(GOOP tuhz)*. The Guptas ruled northern India from A.D. 320 to about 550.

➤ *The Guptas began as rulers of a small kingdom in northeast India. By A.D. 400, Gupta lands covered most of northern India. Find the Ganges River. Was the Ganges River in Gupta territory?*

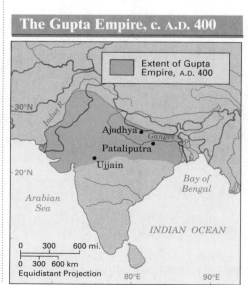

The Gupta Empire, c. A.D. 400

Extent of Gupta Empire, A.D. 400

30°N

Indus R.

Ajodhya•
Pataliputra• *Ganges*
•Ujjain

20°N

Arabian Sea

Bay of Bengal

INDIAN OCEAN

0   300   600 mi.
0   300 600 km
Equidistant Projection   80°E   90°E

The founder of the Gupta Empire started as the ruler of a small Indian kingdom. At that time, India had suffered through hundreds of years of invasions. After the Guptas took control, they protected India's borders. For the next 200 years, India was safe from invaders. This was India's Golden Age, a time of learning and great advancement.

Discoveries in Science

Aryabhata *(ah ree ah BAHT uh)* was just one of the many scientists who made important discoveries during Gupta times. He knew that the earth was round and rotated on its axis. In Europe some people still hadn't accepted that fact more than 1,000 years later, when Columbus set out to sea.

Great medical advances were also made. Doctors learned to set broken bones and used plastic surgery to fix scars. They also developed many medicines and knew the importance of cleanliness in stopping the spread of disease.

In the crafts the Guptas made beautiful metalwork. They also improved cloth making. Later, Indian cloth-making methods would be borrowed by the Arabs and by the Europeans. Calico, chintz, and cashmere are all fabrics that were first woven in India.

Achievements in the Arts

Gupta rulers lived in beautiful palaces bustling with activity. The arts flowered under their rule. People throughout Asia, and later in Europe, enjoyed Indian fables and fairy tales. Especially popular was the *Panchatantra (puhn cha TUHN trah),* a collection of fables in which animals speak and act like people.

Before the days of the Guptas, Indians learned about Hindu Gods, myths, and religious duties through two epics. **Epics** are stories told in the form of long poems.

These epics were called the *Mahabharata* and *Ramayana.* People learned them by heart from their elders. Then they taught them to the next generation. In Gupta times, these epics were at last written down in the old Sanskrit language of India. (See the Minipedia for more on early alphabets.)

Booming Trade at Home

Wealthy Gupta merchants supported the advances made in science and the arts. Gupta trade routes hummed with activity. Ox-drawn carts loaded with goods for market bumped along the overland trails. The trade routes crossed through desert, forest, and rain forest.

Trade in Indian towns was busy. Food filled the markets and people crowded the cobblestone streets. Most shoppers walked through the markets buying rice, wheat, and sugar. Wealthy people were carried in chairs called litters. They might buy some of the more expensive fruits such as mangoes, melons, pears, and peaches.

Trading Outside India

Trade outside India thrived, too. Westward, Gupta trade routes led to Rome as well as to Africa. Eastward, trade was carried on with China, Southeast Asia, and what is now Indonesia.

Goods coming into the Gupta Empire included gold from Rome, silk from China, and horses from Arabia and Central Asia. In other countries, merchants eagerly bought the Guptas' expensive exports. These exports included gems, pearls, pepper, red dye, ginger, cinnamon, fine cotton cloth, wood such as teak, and perfumes. ■

How Do We Know?

ART *The art from the Gupta Empire gives us a picture of what court life was like during this period. It shows palaces filled with servants, music, and artists.*

▼ *The Guptas exported pearls and imported gold from Rome.*

◄ *In the* Ramayana, *the God Vishnu comes to earth as Rama. In this picture Rama is shown carrying the bow and arrow he uses to save his wife.*

■ *How did trade contribute to advances in arts and science during the Gupta Empire?*

319

India

Hindu Way of Life

As learning and trade grew in India during the Gupta Empire, the Hindu religion grew, too. Most of Hinduism's main teachings reached final form in the Gupta period. In towns and villages workers built Hindu temples. Hinduism spread throughout both the north and the south of India. Hinduism became India's largest religion, and the number of Buddhists in India grew very small.

These Hindu people are bathing in the holy Ganges River. Hindu people may travel hundreds of miles to bathe in the river.

Indian Society

As you read in Chapter 5, the Aryans divided people into four social groups: priests, warriors, merchants and peasants, and servants. These social classes slowly divided into more than 3,000 castes. Children inherit their father's caste.

Caste rules stated whom you could marry and how you could earn a living. In ancient days these castes gave Hindus a sense of security. It was the duty of each caste to care for its members.

At the bottom of the caste system were the untouchables. They were called untouchables because it was said that even their touch could pollute or dirty you. As a result, untouchables were excluded

from village life. They were not allowed to drink from the village well. Hindu doctors would not treat their illnesses.

Even today castes remain an important part of life in India. Arranged marriages remain common. Your caste still determines what you can eat. For example, some castes will not eat meat or fish but will eat eggs.

Village Life

The ancient villages of India were usually made up of mud and straw huts. Most people were poor farmers who worked small fields outside the village. Women cooked the family's meals on fires outside the home.

Some villages were made up of members of only one caste. In other villages, members of many castes lived together.

For most Hindus the home was the center of worship. Upper caste families called in priests for ceremonies. In lower caste homes, women performed many of these religious rituals.

Caste councils in each village took care of religious matters. If a

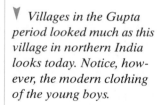

Villages in the Gupta period looked much as this village in northern India looks today. Notice, however, the modern clothing of the young boys.

caste member broke a religious law, council members decided the punishment. The worst punishment a person could suffer was to be made an untouchable.

Villages were governed by the *panchayat (puhn CHAH yuht)*, a council of five elected people. The members of the council were usually rich farmers or from the higher castes. They collected taxes, ordered the building of roads and wells, and settled fights between feuding villagers.

Today there are some places where village life still looks much as it did in ancient India. Women conduct many of the old rituals, and caste councils are still important. However, changes have slowly taken place.

Villages are still governed by *panchayats*, but they are very different from those of the Guptas. Today there are hundreds of thousands of *panchayats* in India. They work together with the national and state governments to improve village life.

Decline of the Gupta Empire

An eyewitness account of India's golden days comes to us from Faxian *(fah shee AHN)*, a Buddhist monk from China. He kept a diary while traveling through India in the early A.D. 400s. He

wrote that "the people are numerous and happy." His diary tells, too, that there was little crime, and in certain areas hospitals gave free care to the poor and helpless.

About 50 years after Faxian's travels, the Gupta Empire began to decline. Invaders called White Huns swept down from Central Asia. Their attacks weakened the empire, causing it to break up into small kingdoms. By A.D. 467, India's Golden Age was almost over. ■

An Indian woman is shown here spinning silk. For hundreds of years, traders from all over the world have eagerly bought fine Indian silk.

■ *What is the caste system in India?*

R E V I E W

1. **FOCUS** Why is the period of the Gupta Empire called India's Golden Age?
2. **CULTURE** Identify an achievement in science and another in the arts during the Gupta period.
3. **SOCIAL SYSTEMS** Who were the untouchables? Why were they given that name?
4. **CRITICAL THINKING** Meeting someone, falling in love, and choosing your own marriage partner is common in Western countries. How would you feel if your parents told you they had picked a spouse for you? What would you tell them?
5. **ACTIVITY** Imagine you are in charge of bringing foreign students to the University at Nalanda during Gupta times. Using the information in the lesson, create a poster encouraging students to come to study at Nalanda.

321

India

L E S S O N 2

Foreign Rulers

THINKING FOCUS

How did the Mughals and the British affect Indian culture?

Key Terms

- Mughal
- imperialism
- civil disobedience

➤ *This finely crafted household object is made of gold. It was probably made in a palace workshop.*

*T**he whole country of India is full of gold and jewels, and of the plants which grow there are those fit for making apparel, and aromatic plants and the sugarcane, and the whole aspect of the country is pleasant and delightful. Now, since the inhabitants are chiefly infidels and idolaters, by the order of God [Allah] and his Prophet it is right for us to conquer them.*

Turkish Sultan Mahmud of Ghazna

Seventeen times Mahmud *(mah MOOD)* and his soldiers invaded India between 1001 and 1027. They terrorized Hindu and Buddhist priests, tore down religious shrines, and plundered palaces. Riding on horses, Mahmud's troops defeated the Indians. Hinduism had been the center of Indian life for hundreds of years. Now it was under attack.

Muslim Rule

Mahmud of Ghazna was one of many Muslim invaders who entered India between A.D. 711 and the 1500s. As Muslims spreading the holy word of Islam to unbelievers, they thought their invasions were just. Arab, Turkish, and Mongol armies entered India through the Khyber Pass in the Himalayas.

As you read in Chapter 8, Muslims worship one God. In this way they differ from Hindus who may worship many Gods. Also, the Islamic religion has no caste system. Muslims believe that all people are equal before God. Individuals can change their social status with hard work and luck.

These basic differences in religion and society led to conflict between neighboring Hindu and Muslim states. Some Muslim rulers tried to force Hindus to convert to Islam. In spite of the pressure, many Hindus refused to change their religion or their way of life. The bitterness between Muslims and Hindus that started during this time still divides the Indian people today.

Akbar the Ruler

In 1519, Muslim Turks from Central Asia invaded northern India. They founded the Mughal (*MOO gahl*) Empire. The word **Mughal** comes from the Persian-Indian word for Mongol.

The Mughals built a large and rich empire. Look at the map of India on page 324. Compare it to the map on page 333. What parts of present-day India did the Mughal Empire control?

The greatest Mughal leader was Akbar (*AK bahr*). He came to power when he was only 13 years old and reigned for 49 years (1556 –1605). Akbar showed great tolerance and respect for other religions. He did not try to make Hindus become Muslims. Akbar saw himself as the ruler of all India's people.

During Akbar's reign, the Mughal court became one of the world's leading centers of culture. Akbar invited artists, poets, and musicians to his court. They produced great paintings and other works of art. The Mughals would have a lasting effect on Indian arts and architecture.

◄ *Miniature painting reached great heights under the Mughals. The subject of this painting is Akbar. He is in the center of the picture, holding court.*

Mughal Rule Ends

The last important Mughal ruler was Aurangzeb (*AWR ehng zehb*). He ruled from 1658 to 1707. Unlike Akbar, he tried to force Hindus to become Muslims. He forbade the building of new Hindu temples and put a tax on non-Muslims. This caused many rebellions. Many Indians refused to accept Mughal rule.

Look at the map of rebellions on page 324. Locate the Hindu

▼ *The Taj Mahal glimmers through the mist behind the boaters. This outstanding example of Mughal architecture took more than 20,000 laborers and 22 years to build. Caravans brought rare, colorful gems from around the world so that the flower designs inside would be the right colors.*

➤ *The map shows areas of resistance to Mughal rule. The Sikhs were followers of a new faith that blended Islam and Hinduism. Name the two centers of Hindu resistance.*

▼ *This Hindu temple is found in southern India. Its style is very different from the Mughal architecture of the Taj Mahal.*

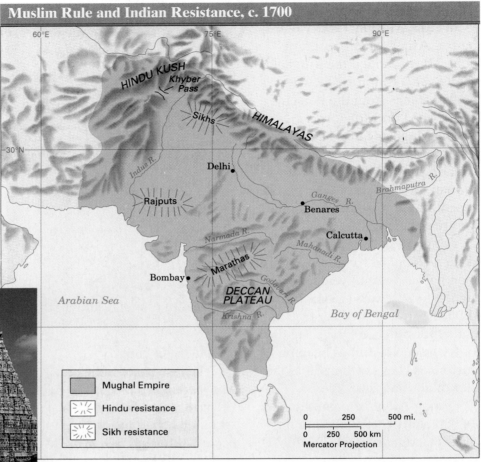

Muslim Rule and Indian Resistance, c. 1700

HINDU KUSH
Khyber Pass
Sikhs
HIMALAYAS
Delhi
Rajputs
Ganges R.
Benares
Brahmaputra R.
Indus R.
Calcutta
Narmada R.
Mahanadi R.
Marathas
Bombay
Godavari R.
DECCAN PLATEAU
Krishna R.
Arabian Sea
Bay of Bengal

Mughal Empire
Hindu resistance
Sikh resistance

0   250   500 mi.
0 250 500 km
Mercator Projection

■ *In what ways did Muslim rule affect India?*

Rajputs. The Rajputs successfully fought Mughal rule and are said to have saved Hinduism in northern India.

The Mughal Empire began to break apart. Once again, India was a collection of kingdoms and small states. Stories of India's splendor and the Mughals' growing weakness spread. Without the Mughals to fear, European nations began to invade by sea. ■

British Rule

For many centuries, Great Britain and other European nations had been attracted by the tea, spices, sugar, indigo, silk cloth, and other products of India and Asia.

It was the Portuguese explorer Vasco da Gama *(VAHS koh dah GAH muh)* who opened the sea route from Europe to India in 1498. Soon trading ships from England, Denmark, and France began arriving in India's harbors.

British East India Company

In the 1600s the ships of the British East India Company anchored in Indian waters. The company built trading posts and forts in Calcutta, Bombay, and Madras. When the Mughal Empire began to fall apart, the East India Company saw the chance to spread its reach.

Step by step the company—a privately owned business—grasped control of more territory. By the mid-1700s, the British East India Company had become India's most powerful ruler.

When the company's Indian soldiers rebelled, the British government became alarmed. They took over the job of governing India. In 1877 Queen Victoria was crowned empress of India.

The Jewel in the Crown

By the 1800s Britain had become the world's greatest imperial power. It had an empire with colonies all around the world. The colonies supplied Britain, the imperial nation, with raw materials and cheap labor. Usually, the colonies also had to buy goods from Britain. This system in which one nation takes control of another one and makes it a colony is called **imperialism.**

For example, India supplied British textile factories with cotton to be woven into cloth. The cloth was then shipped back to India and sold. British manufacturers made huge profits. The British called India the "Jewel in the Crown" because it was the most valuable colony in the empire. Meanwhile British imperialism was destroying India's own industries.

To keep India running, the British did make improvements. They built railroads, highways, and a telegraph system. They improved irrigation and introduced a postal service. They also allowed some Indians to be educated in Britain. However, the improvements were made on Britain's terms. ■

◄ *The British in India lived well above the means of the average Indian. In British neighborhoods signs were often posted that said* FOR EUROPEANS ONLY.

■ *In what ways did India change under British rule?*

The Move Toward Independence

Many Indians began to say that the British were stealing India's wealth and discriminating against India's people. Indian opposition to British rule grew.

Those Indians who had traveled to England for schooling led the movement to end British rule. While in England, they saw that they did not have the same rights or opportunities as British citizens. When they went home, it did not matter that they had college degrees. The British would not allow them to hold high-ranking jobs in the Indian Civil Service.

Angry at how they were being treated, Indians began organizing. Peasant protests helped to increase the pressure on the British. The cry for independence was picked up across India.

Mohandas Gandhi

In 1915 an Indian leader by the name of Mohandas *(moh HAHN dahs)* K. Gandhi was gathering a following. Gandhi was a Hindu who had attended law school in Britain. After becoming a lawyer, he spent 21 years in South Africa fighting discrimination against Indians living there. In 1915 he returned to India.

Four years later, the British passed a new series of laws designed to put a stop to Indian demands for more independence. Gandhi told Indians not to obey these laws.

Shortly thereafter, more than 10,000 unarmed Indians held a protest meeting in a town called Amritsar. To break up the meeting, British soldiers were ordered to fire into the crowd. When the rifle shots stopped, about 400 Indians lay dead, and another 1,200 were wounded. After Amritsar, Gandhi became the most well known leader in the fight for Indian independence.

Gandhi didn't believe in war or the use of violence. Yet he did believe in fighting for what was right. The method he used to push the British out of India is called civil disobedience. **Civil disobedience** is the refusal to cooperate or to obey laws that you believe are unfair. You realize that by breaking the law, you may have to go to jail.

Gandhi urged Indians not to buy British goods or pay certain taxes. Across India, Indians refused to work for the British or go to British schools. Millions joined the campaign for independence.

Gandhi was arrested and put in prison many times for his actions. He grew thin from hunger strikes. With each hunger strike, more and more Indians joined the protests.

In 1947 the long independence campaign finally paid off. After World War II, the British decided that the cost of maintaining colonial rule was too high. Britain agreed to give India its independence. With victory in sight, problems between

Gandhi wore simple homespun cloth as a symbol of resistance to British rule. Following his lead, millions of Indians refused to buy British-made cloth.

This 1930 photograph is of a demonstration encouraging Indians not to buy British-made goods. Notice the line of women demonstrators on the right side of the street.

Hindus and Muslims surfaced. Many Muslims were worried that the Hindu majority would treat them unfairly. Riots broke out when Muslims asked for their own independent country.

To end the violence, Britain divided India. In the northeast and northwest, where Muslims made up a majority of the population, the British created the Muslim nation of Pakistan. Five months after independence, Gandhi was shot and killed. His assassin was a Hindu who thought Gandhi was too tolerant of Muslims.

A New Nation

One of Gandhi's followers was a young man named Jawaharlal Nehru (juh wah hur LAHL NAY roo). On the eve of independence, Nehru stood ready to become India's first prime minister. As the hands on the clock approached 12, Nehru spoke to the crowd.

A t the stroke of the midnight hour, when the world sleeps, India will awake to life and freedom. A moment comes, which comes but rarely in history, when we step out from the old to the new, when an age ends, and when the soul of a nation, long suppressed, finds utterance. . . .

On August 15, 1947, India became an independent nation. Huge gatherings cheered with parades and spectacular fireworks. At the same time, millions of Hindus and Muslims fled their homes for religious reasons.

As the Independence Day celebrations faded, India's leaders set about forming a government. India was organized as a democratic republic. In India, every man and woman who had reached the age of 21 was given the right to vote. India was now the world's largest democracy. ■

Across Time & Space

Pakistan was formed as a nation made up of two parts separated by more than 1,000 miles. The government was located in West Pakistan. The people of East Pakistan felt the government discriminated against them. In 1971 civil war broke out. In the same year East Pakistan declared its independence. The new nation was called Bangladesh.

◄ *Indira Gandhi was prime minister of India from 1966 to 1977 and from 1980 to 1984. Her father, Jawaharlal Nehru, is on the poster behind her.*

■ *How did Mohandas K. Gandhi help India gain independence?*

R E V I E W

1. **FOCUS** How did the Mughals and the British affect Indian culture?

2. **POLITICAL SYSTEMS** Compare Akbar's rule of India with the rule of Aurangzeb.

3. **ECONOMICS** Why did the British call India the "Jewel in the Crown"?

4. **HISTORY** How did Indians peacefully protest British rule?

5. **CRITICAL THINKING** Do you think Gandhi's method of civil disobedience could be used to change laws in the United States? Why or why not?

6. **ACTIVITY** Imagine you could meet Mohandas Gandhi. What would you like to know about his life and his beliefs? Make a list of five questions.

Using the *Readers' Guide*

Here's Why

To find current information about a topic, you need to use references other than encyclopedias and books. Magazines and other periodicals can provide recent information about events.

Suppose that you want to find more information about life in India today. How would you find the periodicals?

Here's How

The *Readers' Guide to Periodical Literature* is a set of reference books. It lists articles by topic and year. The boxes below contain entries from the 1991 *Readers' Guide*.

To find an article about life in India today, look under the topic "India." There you will find cross-references, such as "Americans—India."

These references tell you that more articles about India today can be found under these headings. What kind of information might you expect to find under the "Americans—India" heading?

Notice that there are also several subheadings under the topic India. One or more articles are listed under each subheading.

Look at the box to your right. It is a key that tells you what kind of information you can find in each entry. Each entry always includes the name of the article, the periodical that published it, and the date. What other information is sometimes given?

Once you find entries that interest you, write the information on a sheet of paper. Look for those magazines

and newspapers in the periodicals section of the library.

Try It

Look again at the *Readers' Guide* entries. In what magazine can you find an article about the Hindu-Muslim conflict in India? What is the title of the article? Who wrote it?

Apply It

Think about a holiday or tradition that is part of your ethnic background. Use the *Readers' Guide* to make a list of articles about this topic.

1. Title
2. Cross-References
3. Subject heading
4. Author
5. Illustrations, portraits, maps
6. Periodicals, volume, page numbers, date

INDIA 1

See also 2

Americans—India
Bhopal poisonous gas disaster, India, 1984
Calcutta (India)
Environmental policy—India
Grand Trunk Road (India and Pakistan)
Ladakh (India)
Motion pictures—India
Public welfare—India
Securities—India
Wildlife conservation—India
Women—India

Commerce
Russia (Republic)
3 Russian sale of rocket engine to India [statement, May 11, 1992] R. Boucher. *US Department of State Dispatch* 3:386 My 18 '92

Economic policy
India after the Gandhis. *The Wilson Quarterly* 16:7–8 Spr '92

Foreign relations
India after nonalignment. R. C. Thakur. 4 bibl f *Foreign Affairs* 71:165–82 Spr '92
United States
See United States—Foreign relations—India

History
British occupation, 1765–1947—Historiography
Marxism and modern India. D. Chakra-
5 barty. il *History Today* 42:48–51 Mr '92

Nationalism
Marxism and modern India. D. Chakra-
barty. il *History Today* 42:48–51 Mr '92
Storm over India [Hindu-Muslim conflict]
E. W. Desmond. il (*The New York Review of Books* 39:37–40 My 14 '92) 6

L E S S O N   3

Modern India

The monsoon rains were late. In the cities, air conditioners hissed to a halt. Movie houses were limited to one showing a day. Neon signs were turned off, and factories were silenced. In the countryside temperatures rose to more than 110°F, and several people collapsed and died from the heat. Only the arrival of a healthy monsoon could bring relief.

In India the monsoon rains are of great concern, and not only to India's millions of farmers. India's engineers and politicians also worry about them. A good deal of India's electricity is made by water power. If the rains do not come, the cities may lose lights and power. When this happens, India's politicians know they will be blamed for the country's problems. It will be a bad year for those holding elected office.

THINKING FOCUS

How has India progressed since independence?

Key Term

- subcontinent

India's Geography

Monsoons are only one part of India's fascinating geography. (For more on monsoons, see A Closer Look on page 330.) India has everything from snow-capped mountains to burning desert sands. It also has tropical rain forests and wide river plains that make an ideal place for people to settle. India is truly a country of many different environments.

A World Apart

In the north, two jagged mountain ranges separate India from the rest of the Asian continent. In the south the Indian Ocean and the Arabian Sea separate it. Because the mountain ranges and oceans form natural barriers around India, geographers call India a subcontinent. A **subcontinent** is a large landmass

◄ *In the mountains of northeast India, the Ganges River swells during the monsoons.*

329

India

Monsoons

May to September is summer monsoon season in India. Strong monsoon winds carry rain to a parched, hot land. When the first rains fall, people celebrate! They will have water to drink, and their crops will survive. Yet the sudden changes in weather can be dangerous. People must look out for mudslides, broken dams, and fierce swirling wind-storms called cyclones.

Before the monsoon, dry winds blow dust and grit across the plains. If the monsoon comes late, crops and animals may die in the sweltering heat.

Once it rains, farmers hurry to plant in the wet soil. Fields that were brown and barren become lush with plentiful crops.

Wading through flooded streets or even flooded houses and offices, city people are also joyful for the life-giving rains.

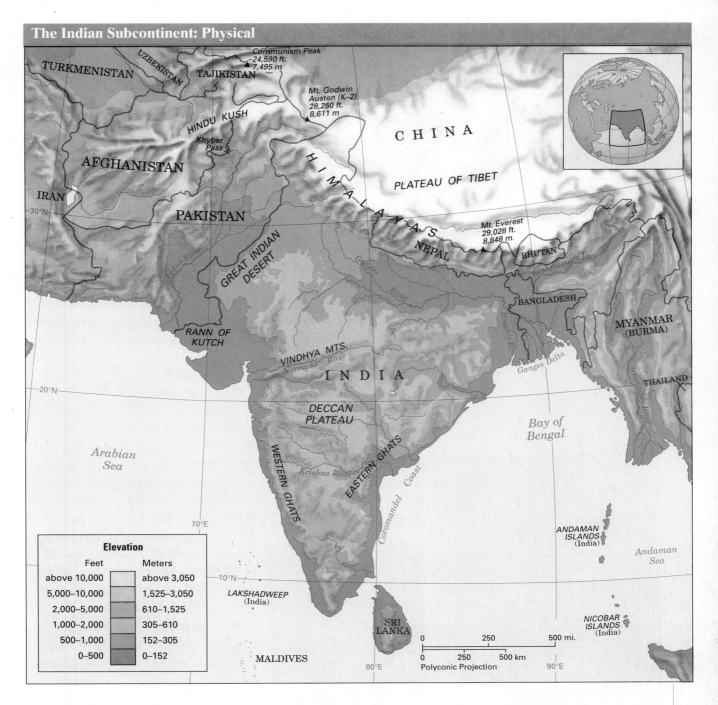

TURKMENISTAN

UZBEKISTAN

TAJIKISTAN

Communism Peak
24,590 ft.
7,495 m

Mt. Godwin
Austen (K–2)
28,250 ft.
8,611 m

HINDU KUSH

Khyber
Pass

AFGHANISTAN

IRAN

30°N

PAKISTAN

CHINA

PLATEAU OF TIBET

H I M A L A Y A S

Mt. Everest
29,028 ft.
8,848 m

NEPAL

BHUTAN

Indus River

GREAT INDIAN
DESERT

Ganges
River

Brahmaputra R.

BANGLADESH

RANN OF
KUTCH

VINDHYA MTS.

Narmada River

I N D I A

MYANMAR
(BURMA)

Hooghly R.

Ganges Delta

THAILAND

20°N

DECCAN
PLATEAU

Bay of
Bengal

Irrawaddy River

Arabian
Sea

WESTERN GHATS

Krishna River

EASTERN GHATS

Coromandel Coast

70°E

ANDAMAN
ISLANDS
(India)

Andaman
Sea

Elevation

Feet		Meters
above 10,000		above 3,050
5,000–10,000		1,525–3,050
2,000–5,000		610–1,525
1,000–2,000		305–610
500–1,000		152–305
0–500		0–152

10°N

LAKSHADWEEP
(India)

SRI
LANKA

NICOBAR
ISLANDS
(India)

MALDIVES

80°E

0   250   500 mi.

0   250   500 km

Polyconic Projection

90°E

that is somewhat separate yet still part of a continent.

Find the Himalayas and the Hindu Kush mountains on the map above. What is their elevation? (See the Map and Globe Handbook on page G9 if you need help on how to read physical maps.)

During India's long history, people from all over Asia and Europe have settled in India. Because of its geography, these people are said to have formed a world unto themselves.

New Borders

After independence new maps of India had to be drawn. Important parts of what was once considered India were now gone. These parts became the nations of Pakistan and later Bangladesh.

These changes made many Indians unhappy. Much of the Indus

▲ Look at the physical map of India. Using the elevation legend, describe northern and southern India. If you were a farmer, where in India would you settle?

331

River Valley region was now a part of Pakistan.

The leaders of India, however, agreed to the new borders. They felt that it was time to begin building a new nation. Still, conflict between India and Pakistan continued. In some territories they could not agree on who should have control. Sometimes, this led to war.

Indian leaders decided to divide India into states. When the new map was drawn, it showed 25 states and 7 territories. For the first time in its history, India was governed by a central Indian government. ■

■ *How did the map of India change after independence?*

A Multicultural Nation

India is a blend of the different people who have settled there over the centuries. Some came as invaders. Others came to trade or to search for a new home.

Each group brought the language, religion, and customs of its homeland. Over time, the majority of these people became Hindus. Today, sharing the Hindu religion helps Indians live together in peace. Yet all Indians are not Hindus, and not all Hindus are alike.

People of different cultural backgrounds don't always get along well. All of India's leaders and people have had to find ways to solve these disagreements. This task has not been easy.

Languages and Peoples

Language has been a hotly debated issue for many years. More than 800 languages and dialects are spoken in India. When Hindi was chosen as the national language, many people protested. More than half of all Indians do not speak Hindi. Many did not want to learn a new language.

Those who protested argued that if they gave up their own languages, an important part of their cultural heritage would disappear. In an effort to be fair, the government gave official status to 15 languages. For now, English is considered an additional official language. It is used a great deal in government and business.

▼ *India is a land of many different peoples and cultures.*

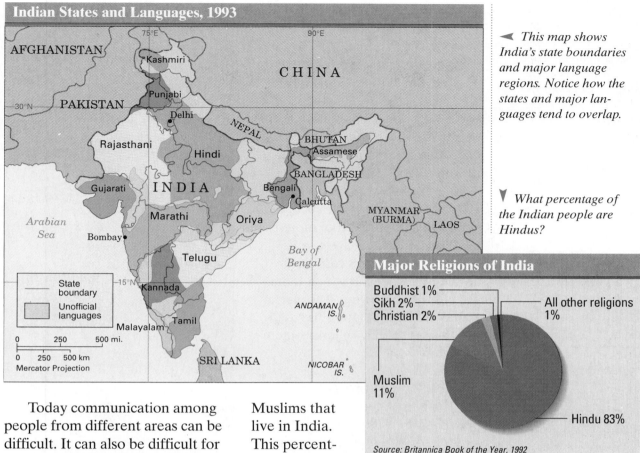

Indian States and Languages, 1993

AFGHANISTAN
Kashmiri
PAKISTAN
Punjabi
Delhi
CHINA
Rajasthani
Hindi
NEPAL
BHUTAN
Assamese
BANGLADESH
Gujarati
INDIA
Bengali
Calcutta
Arabian Sea
Marathi
Oriya
MYANMAR (BURMA)
LAOS
Bombay
Telugu
Bay of Bengal
State boundary
Unofficial languages
Kannada
ANDAMAN IS.
Malayalam
Tamil
0 250 500 mi.
0 250 500 km
Mercator Projection
SRI LANKA
NICOBAR IS.

◄ *This map shows India's state boundaries and major language regions. Notice how the states and major languages tend to overlap.*

▼ *What percentage of the Indian people are Hindus?*

Major Religions of India

Buddhist 1%
Sikh 2%
Christian 2%
All other religions 1%
Muslim 11%
Hindu 83%

Source: *Britannica Book of the Year, 1992*

Today communication among people from different areas can be difficult. It can also be difficult for the government. India has so many peoples and so many languages that governing it is more like governing the United Nations than a country.

Look at the map at the top of the page. Find where the majority of Hindi-speaking people live.

Religious Differences

After independence many Muslims stayed in India rather than moving to Pakistan. Look at the graph of India's major religions at the right. Notice the percentage of Muslims that live in India. This percentage totals more than 95 million people. Many live in the area where the Mughal Empire first began.

The bitter feelings between Hindus and Muslims can still be felt in India. In the north, fighting sometimes breaks out between the two groups. Muslims say that the Hindu majority discriminates against them in business and government. Like other minority groups in India, they also fear they will lose their culture. ■

■ *What are some of India's cultural challenges?*

Social Progress

As a new nation, India faced many serious problems. Hunger and disease were common, its people were poorly educated, and the future looked difficult. Since 1947 India has worked hard to make a better life for all of its people. Its leaders have struggled to end the grim poverty under which millions live. Programs have been started to improve the economy, health care, and education.

333

India

The modern city of Delhi is divided into Old Delhi and New Delhi. This is a photograph of Old Delhi. It is where most of the people live and work. New Delhi is the capital of India.

A Growing Population

Life has gotten better in India, but its growing population makes progress difficult. Today nearly one-sixth of all the people in the world live in India. Between 1950 and 1990, India's population grew by about 490 million people. This is almost twice as many people as now live in the United States. In 1990 India's population was about 850 million. By the year 2000, India will have a population of more than 1 billion people.

Improved health care has increased the speed at which India's population is growing. The size of India's large population has made progress in solving other problems very slow.

A Higher Living Standard

The British left India a very poor nation. It did not produce enough food to feed all its people, and it had few industries. Also, in general, the Indian people were poorly educated.

Education in India has improved. Look at the line graph below. Literacy is

In rural areas such as this, school may be held outdoors or in very simple buildings.

the ability to read and write. The improving literacy rate gives you a good idea of how much education has improved in India. What percentage of boys could read in 1991?

To help grow more food, farmers began to use better methods of irrigation and more fertilizers. Indian farmers now grow enough food to hold off famine even when the monsoons fail.

India's industries also have grown. In the villages carpets are made by hand for sale all over the world. Around the cities, factories now produce goods such as appliances and cars.

India has slowly moved forward in the areas of agriculture, industry, and education. Yet there still is much to be done to end poverty.

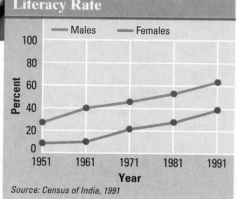

Literacy Rate

— Males — Females

Source: Census of India, 1991

This graph shows two literacy rates, one for boys and one for girls. Why do you think more boys can read and write than girls?

334

Equality for All

One notable feature of the Indian constitution is its goal of full equality for all people. Following in the footsteps of Gandhi, the Indian constitution rejects the caste system and bans laws against untouchables, now called Scheduled Castes.

The constitution requires universities to admit them as students. It also tries to change basic Hindu and Muslim traditions by giving women equal rights with men. It gives women the right to own property. Today Indian women and Scheduled Castes are legally free to pursue careers in government, education, and medicine. In their daily lives, however, equality is still a long way off.

India Today

In India today the old and the new exist side by side. In many villages, there are few modern conveniences. Some houses have electricity, but women still carry water to their homes from wells.

In other villages change is slow, but it is noticeable. It is not unusual to hear the news blaring from a radio or to see a tractor plowing a field. Even the caste system faces challenges from the government and women's groups.

As people move to the cities, modern ways often replace old traditions. In India's crowded cities, office buildings share the sky with ancient temples. Flashy billboards advertise new movies. Men and women in suits and jeans walk side by side with people in traditional clothing. People of different castes and religions mix together.

Modern India is a nation of many people and cultures. With all of its struggles, it moves ahead as the world's largest democracy. ■

▼ *Along with the United States and Japan, India is one of the world's largest film producers.*

■ *How has life in India improved?*

R E V I E W

1. **FOCUS** How has India progressed since independence?
2. **GEOGRAPHY** Describe some of India's different landforms and climates.
3. **SOCIAL SYSTEMS** Why did Indians disagree over their national language?
4. **CRITICAL THINKING** Like India, the United States is also a multicultural nation. How are the United States and India similar, and how are they different?
5. **ACTIVITY** If you could visit India, where would you like to go? Draw a map of India, and mark the places you would like to visit. Tell why you would like to visit these places.

Chapter Review

Reviewing Key Terms

civil disobedience (p. 326)   Mughal (p. 323)
epic (p. 319)   subcontinent (p. 329)
imperialism (p. 325)

A. Write whether each of the following statements is *true* or *false*. Then rewrite the false statements to make them true.

1. Information about the Hindu religion can be found in long poems called epics.
2. The Mughals spread the Buddhist religion in India.
3. Under imperialism, Britain allowed India to govern itself.
4. Civil disobedience means refusing to obey laws that you believe are unfair.
5. India is called a subcontinent because it has a hot climate.

B. Write two sentences for each of the words below. Your sentences should show how each word applies to the Hindu religion or to India.

1. epic
2. Mughal
3. imperialism
4. civil disobedience
5. subcontinent

Exploring Concepts

A. Use the chart below to help you summarize the influence of the Gupta, Mughal, and British empires on the history of India. Copy the chart and fill it in with two facts from the chapter about each empire's influence.

Empires	Influences on India
Gupta	There were advances in astronomy, mathematics, and medicine. They include the following: knowledge that the earth rotates on its axis, plastic surgery, and the development of a number system.
Mughal	
British	

B. Support each of the following statements with information from the chapter.

1. Many scientific advancements were made in India during the Gupta period.
2. Most Hindu people still follow a rigid social order.
3. Hindus and Muslims have different religious beliefs.
4. For Great Britain, India was "the Jewel in the Crown."
5. In leading the fight for India's independence from Britain, Mohandas Gandhi used nonviolent methods.
6. India faced many challenges after it had gained independence in 1947.
7. India is a land of many different environments.
8. Language is a hotly debated issue in India.
9. The size of India's population is a matter of concern.
10. One goal of the Indian government is to bring equality to all of India's people.
11. In India today the old and the new exist side by side.

Reviewing Skills

1. Imagine you are writing a report about the challenges facing modern India. Would you try to find books about India in the *Readers' Guide to Periodical Literature*? Explain your answer.
2. Review the *Readers' Guide* material on page 328. Write the name of the cross reference that would give you more information on India's movie industry.
3. Use the information in Lesson 2 to complete this flow chart, entitled "The Road to India's Independence." The flow chart starts with Queen Victoria's being crowned empress of India in 1877 and ends with India's independence in 1947. Copy the flow chart onto a separate sheet of paper. List the important events that occurred between these two dates. Make sure that you list the events in the order in which they happened.

Queen Victoria crowned empress ⇒ ⇒ ⇒ ⇒ ⇒ ⇒ India gains Independence

Using Critical Thinking

1. The Gupta Empire, India's Golden Age, was a time of great advancement. Think about the term *golden age*. What characterizes a society during a golden age? Do you think that future historians will use that term to describe the United States today? Why or why not? Give reasons for your answer.
2. Some Mughal leaders encouraged religious tolerance during their rule in India. Other Mughal rulers did not. How did religious freedom benefit Mughal rule? What happened when religious freedom was denied?
3. Mohandas Gandhi once wrote, "No people exists that would not think itself happier under its own bad government than it might really be under the good government of an alien [foreign] power." In this statement does Gandhi support or reject imperialism? Explain your answer.
4. Why would teaching people to read and write be a basic goal of a government trying to improve the standard of living of its citizens?

Preparing for Citizenship

1. **COLLABORATIVE LEARNING** Both India and the United States fought British rule and became independent nations. As a class, compare and contrast India's and the United States' fight for freedom. Divide into small groups. Each group should research a different topic, gathering information on both India and the United States. Some possible topics include (a) the feelings of the colonists toward independence, (b) tactics used by the colonists to gain support for their cause, (c) important Indian and U.S. leaders, (d) important British leaders, and (e) events that led to independence. Be sure to look at the maps in the Atlas to locate where the United States and India are in relation to Great Britain. You may also want to collect quotes and writings from the time. As a class, put the information together in a bulletin-board display entitled "Fighting for Freedom."
2. **WRITING ACTIVITY** Mohandas Gandhi believed in *satyagraha*. *Satya* is a Sanskrit word meaning "truth," and *agraha* means "force." *Satyagraha* can therefore be roughly translated as "truth weapon." In what ways can ordinary citizens use truth as a "weapon" to change government policy?

337

Chapter 15

China

For thousands of years, powerful emperors ruled China. They thought their right to rule came from heaven. During the 20th century, however, China has undergone extraordinary changes. The Communist party came to power in 1949. It took over farms and industries, creating a new society. It changed many ancient traditions. Today China struggles to adapt to the modern world.

The Forbidden City, located in Beijing, includes the palaces where China's emperors once lived. Only members of the emperor's household and certain high officials were allowed to enter the Forbidden City without permission.

1000	1200	1400

1200

1280 Kublai Khan becomes the first Mongol ruler of China. Mongol rulers, like the emperor pictured above, are the first outsiders to control China.

1368 The Mongols are thrown from power. Under the Ming emperors, China makes advances in education and the arts.

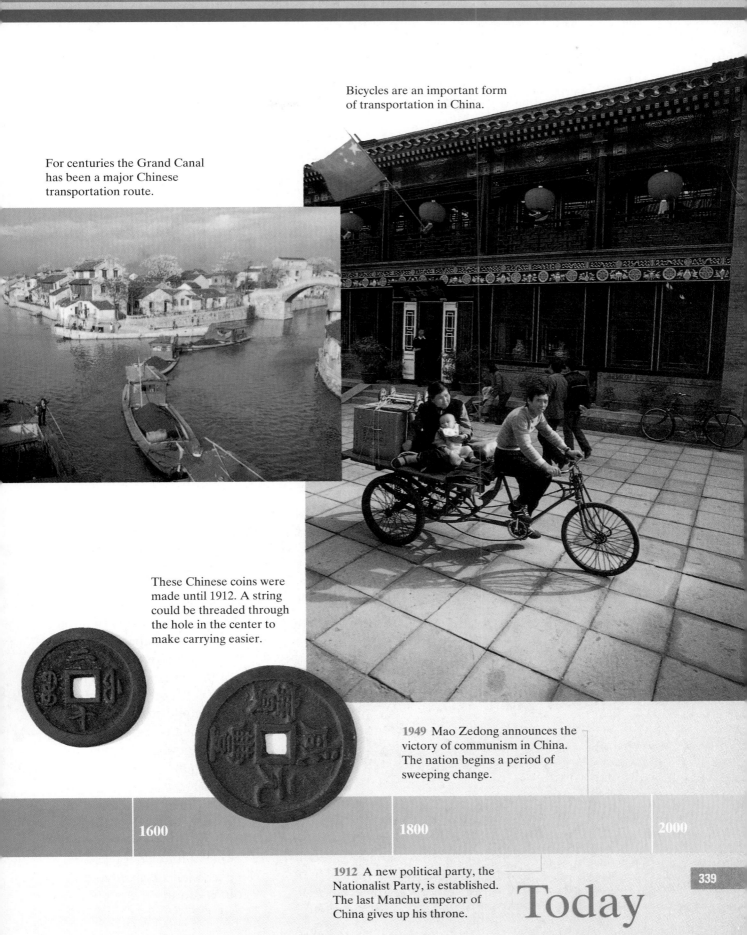

Bicycles are an important form of transportation in China.

For centuries the Grand Canal has been a major Chinese transportation route.

These Chinese coins were made until 1912. A string could be threaded through the hole in the center to make carrying easier.

1949 Mao Zedong announces the victory of communism in China. The nation begins a period of sweeping change.

1600

1800

2000

1912 A new political party, the Nationalist Party, is established. The last Manchu emperor of China gives up his throne.

Today

L E S S O N   1

Mandate of Heaven

How has the hope for peace and order guided the Chinese people and their rulers?

Key Terms

- famine
- communism

➤ *The dragon was the symbol of the emperor's great power.*

"T he iniquity [evil] of the Shang is full. Heaven commands me to destroy it," declared King Wu, the first ruler of the Zhou *(joh)* dynasty (1122–256 B.C.).

According to that story, Wu described the evil ways of the Shang emperor, Di-xin *(dih shihn)*. Di-xin, he said, had wasted the empire's wealth on palaces, towers, ponds, and pavilions. He had not cared for the temples of his ancestors, nor had he protected the harvest. Di-xin had even "burned and roasted the loyal and good." Therefore, Wu and his followers threw out the Shangs and beheaded Di-xin.

To justify their rule, the Zhous began preaching a new idea. It was called the Mandate of Heaven. The king claimed that his power came from heaven. According to this idea, the king himself was the Son of Heaven.

According to the Mandate of Heaven, a ruler must be just and virtuous and live a moral life. He must also take care of the well-being of the people. If the ruler was not just, did not show proper concern for the people, or lived immorally, heaven would take away his right to rule.

The Mandate of Heaven continued to influence China long after the Zhous lost their power. Years of hunger or unrest might end an emperor's rule. To the people, such troubles showed that their ruler had lost the support of heaven. Without the support of heaven, a ruler had no right to rule. Thus, the people could stop obeying their emperor. They could revolt and take a new ruler, who would bring back peace and order.

The Chinese thinker Mengzi (or Mencius) taught this idea of the right to revolt. A well-known follower of Confucius, Mencius lived in the fourth century B.C.

Mongol Invaders

As you learned in Chapter 5, the Chinese feared invaders entering from the north. For hundreds of years, the Great Wall had protected China from these outsiders. In the early 1200s, however, Mongols from central Asia came around the wall. They burned and looted villages. In 1206, their leader was declared the Genghis Khan *(JEHNG gihs kahn)*, or "Universal Ruler." For the first time, an outsider would control parts of China.

Kublai Khan's Rule

Kublai Khan *(KOO bly kahn)*, a grandson of Genghis Khan, started the Yuan dynasty in 1271. A capable ruler, he rebuilt parts of northern China and repaired the Grand Canal. This transportation route, built in the early 600s, unified China. It connected rivers in the north and south. Each year the canal carried millions of tons of grain.

Trade grew under Kublai's rule.

Yak and camel caravans carried goods over the Silk Road. Early Europeans valued silk so much, it was said to be worth its weight in gold.

Most Mongols did not adopt Chinese ways. They had special rights. They did not pay taxes. Mongols were favored over Chinese for government posts. The Chinese resented the Mongols. In fact, China's dislike of foreigners lasted for hundreds of years.

Mongol Rule Challenged

In time, the Chinese challenged Mongol rule. Terrible drought and famine added to the unrest. During a **famine** food is very scarce. More than seven million people starved in the famine. ■

▲ *The Mongol invaders were expert riders. They rode small, sturdy horses like the one above.*

◄ *In the 1200s the Mongol Empire extended far west into Russia and parts of eastern Europe.*

The Mongol Empire in China, c. 1294

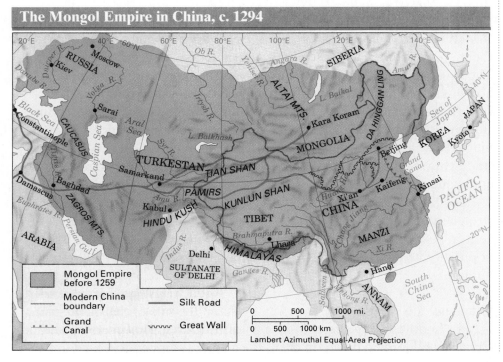

Mongol Empire before 1259

Modern China boundary

Grand Canal

Silk Road

Great Wall

0 500 1000 mi.
0 500 1000 km
Lambert Azimuthal Equal-Area Projection

■ *How were the Chinese people treated under Mongol rule?*

341

China

The Ming Period

In 1368 Chu Yüan-chang led a successful revolt against the Mongols. Chu was a poor farmer, who once begged for food. As founder of the Ming dynasty, he took the reign title Hung-wu.

Early Ming rulers brought peace and order to China. They made new laws. They reformed local government. They built new schools and printed many books.

To increase trade, the Ming expanded the canal system. Cotton, tea, silk, timber, and iron pans called woks could now be shipped to all parts of China.

To protect China, the Ming repaired the Great Wall. They also added on to the old walls. Most of the Great Wall that is seen today was built under the Ming.

To encourage art, the first Ming ruler built a painting academy. Tapestry, calligraphy, and Ming porcelain—known to the outside world as china—also thrived.

Sometimes artists lived in the Ming court. However, one artist, Dai Jin (1388–1462), was sent away from court. He angered the emperor with his painting of a fisher wearing a red jacket. Red was not supposed to be worn by people of the common class.

Famines in the 1620s led to revolts. Once again, the rulers seemed to have lost the Mandate of Heaven. ■

■ *How did China fare under the Mings?*

The Last Dynasty

The Manchus took over the weakened Ming Empire. They came from Manchuria in the northeast. In 1644 these new rulers founded the Qing (*chihng*) dynasty.

The Manchus were different from the Mongol invaders before them. They adopted Chinese ways. The Manchus spoke Chinese. They accepted Confucian ideas of how to rule. Manchus and Chinese worked side by side in the Qing government. Once again, learning, art, and trade grew. Some great libraries contained over 36,000 volumes.

The Manchu Empire now stretched from the east coast to central Asia in the west. China's population tripled, reaching 430 million.

China and the West

For hundreds of years, the Chinese had looked down on the outside world. From the Mongols, they had learned not to trust foreigners. What's more, other countries seemed to have little to offer China.

During the 1800s, the West went through huge changes. Western nations developed great factories that produced many new goods. They also built fleets of ships and powerful new weapons. Merchants from France, Great Britain, and the United States hoped to trade their goods for China's tea, porcelain, and silk.

The Chinese were not as interested in opening trade with Western countries. In response, British merchants began smuggling opium into China.

The Chinese government tried to stop the sale of this habit-forming drug. However, the amount of opium shipped to China grew

How Do We Know?

HISTORY *Historians have used local census records for taxes to estimate China's population under the emperors. However, people who did not want to pay taxes often avoided being counted. This led census recorders to report too few people in a village. Historians take these factors into account when they estimate population.*

The Voyages of Zheng He

While Europeans searched for a sea route to the East, Chinese ambassador Zheng He was exploring the West. His emperor sent Zheng He to display the splendor and power of China and to collect presents along the way, such as beautiful pearls. Under these orders, Zheng He sailed on seven expeditions to southeastern Asia, India, Arabia, and Africa in the early 1400s.

Zheng He, detail from a woodcut by Lo Mou-teng, 1597

Pearls

Fine porcelain and silk were brought along on Zheng He's trips to show off China's wealth.

Zheng He's fleets included more than 300 vessels and carried more than 27,000 men.

Ming vase

Zheng He brought back animals the Chinese had never seen before, including zebras and ostriches. The African kingdom of Malindi sent a giraffe to the Chinese emperor.

The Tribute Giraffe with Attendant *by artist Shen Tu, c.1414*

343

China

European flags fly over the docks of Guangzhou, a port city in southern China. Before the Opium War, the Chinese allowed Westerners only a limited space in which to carry on trade.

■ *Why do you think the Manchus enjoyed such a long rule in China?*

➤ *Japanese bombing caused death and destruction in many areas of China before and during World War II.*

off the southern coast of China, to Great Britain. It also opened five ports to British trade. Soon other Western nations also forced China to give them new trading rights and land.

Angered by this treatment, many Chinese called for change. Some wanted to adopt Western ways. They hoped to use Western technology to protect China. However, others feared the loss of Chinese traditions.

The ruling Manchus were blamed for China's troubles. The Manchus made some efforts to reform. Many Chinese, however, held little hope for real change under the elderly Empress Dowager. At that time she held power for her young nephew.

In 1911 there was a revolution. China was declared a republic. One year later, China's last emperor, Pu Yi, gave up his throne. He was six years old. Thus ended 267 years of Manchu rule. ■

from 200 chests in 1729 to 30,000 chests in 1839.

The Opium War

In 1839 China and Britain went to war. This Opium War ended in humiliating defeat for China. British ships and weapons easily overwhelmed China's military forces. An 1842 peace treaty gave the island of Hong Kong, located

Struggle Toward a New China

The head of the new republic was Sun Yat-sen. Sun wanted to build a Chinese government based on Western democracy.

There was never much chance to try out Sun's ideas. Uniting China proved difficult. Local leaders took control of many areas. Fighting broke out. After Sun's death in 1925, Chiang Kai-shek *(chang ky shehk)* became leader. For a time, he controlled much of China.

One group in Chiang's party pushed for even greater change. Its members believed in communism. Under **communism** the government owns and controls all property and businesses. Chiang feared

and fought these Communists. Many were killed. Others fled to the mountains of southeastern China.

344

The Rise of Mao

In 1931 Japan invaded Manchuria. Then the Japanese moved deeper into China. They dreamed of conquering China and becoming the most powerful nation in the Pacific area. This dream came to nothing.

In 1934, meanwhile, Chiang finally forced the Communists out of the mountains. Mao Zedong *(mow dzuh dahng)* helped lead the Communists in what is called the Long March. For a year, Mao's Red Army fought and marched for 6,000 miles.

In 1945 Japan signed a peace treaty that ended World War II. Japanese troops then left China. The war had exhausted China's resources. Prices were high. Many Chinese had lost faith in Chiang. Fighting

◄ *At the height of his power, Mao held huge rallies where he addressed his followers.*

UNDERSTANDING COMMUNISM

The idea of communism is an old one. Many people have dreamed of a society that fostered equality. In such a society, everyone would share the land, the factories, the businesses, the wealth.

No country based on the idea of communism existed before 1917. In that year, Communist revolutionaries came into power in Russia. They turned the country into a Communist state.

After a long civil war, the Chinese Communists, under Mao Zedong, took power in 1949. For thousands of years, a small number of people had held most of China's power and wealth. Communism offered the promise of prosperity and equality for all.

In practice, Chinese communism turned out to be different from the idea of communism. The Communists did take over land and factories. They built collective farms where farmers worked together. Production increased.

However, a small number of people still controlled the government in Communist China. Only one party, the Chinese Communist party, was allowed. Many who did not conform to the ideas of the Chinese Communist party were sent to work camps.

Today the Chinese Communist party is still China's only party. The Chinese people have no right to vote, to speak their minds freely, or to practice their religions. What's more, there are still serious economic problems in China that communism has not solved.

China

Following the Cultural Revolution, artists were encouraged to create works illustrating the successes of Communist society. This 1978 painting shows that many women entered the work force after the Communists came to power.

■ *Why were many peasants attracted to communism?*

between Chiang's army and the Communists continued.

By 1949 the Communists had captured Beijing, the capital city. To a cheering crowd in Tiananmen *(tyahn ahn mehn)* Square, Mao declared, "Never again will the Chinese be an enslaved people."

Mao Changes China

In the past, strong emperors had held China together. Now Mao united the country. Posters of Mao hung on public buildings everywhere.

Life for many Chinese improved under Mao. The government built new schools. They repaired railroads, riverways, and roads. Doctors were sent to small villages. Women achieved greater equality.

Over time, public ownership of farms, factories, businesses, and stores replaced private ownership. The people worked together in groups known as collectives. Small farms were turned into larger farms of 20 to 30 families. On a farm collective, people shared their work as well as their harvests. These

new groups produced more food and goods.

Mao wasn't satisfied. He wanted more rapid change. In 1958 he designed a new economic plan. It was called the Great Leap Forward. As part of this plan, collectives were united into giant communes. Each one included about 5,000 households. The Communists also organized worker groups. They built bridges, canals, and roads using little more than muscle power.

The Great Leap Forward was mostly a failure. The people became overworked and exhausted. No matter how much they produced, they still received the same pay. To make matters worse, poor harvests and drought led to massive food shortages throughout China.

Many people criticized Mao. His answer to these critics was the Cultural Revolution of 1966. He aimed to destroy old Chinese customs and ideas. He hoped to create a whole new society. The result was 10 years of bloodshed and disorder, much of it caused by students in Mao's "Red Guard." Schools closed. Art treasures and books were destroyed. People were killed if they criticized what was going on. Others were sent to work camps in the countryside where many more died. ■

1. **FOCUS** How has the hope for peace and order guided the Chinese people and their rulers?
2. **HISTORY** Beginning with the Zhous, how did new rulers justify overthrowing a poor or corrupt emperor?
3. **POLITICAL SYSTEMS** How was Manchu rule of China different from Mongol rule?
4. **CRITICAL THINKING** What positive and negative effects did Mao's rule have on the people of China?
5. **WRITING ACTIVITY** Imagine you are a peasant whose farm became part of a collective after the Communist victory in 1949. Now you must work with a group and share the harvest. Write a letter to your sister who lives at another collective. Describe this new situation and how you feel about it.

L E S S O N   2

China after Mao

Changes have come to China since Mao's death in 1976. Moderates took over the government. They favored gradual change instead of the excesses of the Cultural Revolution. Over time, private enterprises came to operate side by side with state-owned businesses. In 1979, two sisters in China planned their future.

So when we heard about the government policy relaxing a bit on private enterprise, the two of us sat up half the night working out how we could open up a restaurant. We did a rough financial estimate and figured it could make money.

They showed their plan to local officials. Before long, the sisters got a license. Now they had a chance to run the first privately owned restaurant in all of China.

These two women were pioneers of the marketplace. Like other pioneers, they faced hardships. They had to deal with competition from other restaurants. They had to face the rising costs of seafood. In the end, the two sisters merged with a state-run restaurant.

Their story shows the benefits and difficulties of **free enterprise** in China. Under free enterprise the government does not control prices or decide how people earn or spend their money. Businesses compete with each other. The best-run businesses survive. Others fail.

THINKING
FOCUS

How has Deng's government responded to China's problems?

Key Terms

- free enterprise
- ideology
- dissident

▼ *After Mao, Western styles became popular with many young people. Many older people, however, continued wearing the style of the Mao years.*

Steering a New Course

"It does not matter whether a cat is black or white, as long as it catches mice," said Deng Xiaoping *(duhng shyow pihng)*.

Deng succeeded Mao in the late 1970s. Mao had never turned from his strict Communist ideals. To Mao, **ideology,** a set of ideas and beliefs, was most important. However, his ideology did not lead to higher production. Deng was more concerned with finding workable solutions to China's problems.

Economic Reforms

Deng understood that people would produce more if they could make a profit from their work. So Deng introduced some free enterprise in China. A few people were permitted to start their own businesses. At the same time, government loosened its control over prices.

Deng also offered opportunities to farmers and factory workers. He got rid of the communes created under Mao. He set up the "responsibility system." Under this system, farmers had to produce a specified amount. If they produced more, they could sell their extra crops for profit. Deng introduced new technology to help make industry more productive. Factory workers who performed with excellence could also earn extra pay.

Social Changes

Deng also tackled the problem of population control. China has the largest population of any country in the world. Over 1.1 billion people live in China. Such a huge population requires vast amounts of food, water, and other supplies. Famines were once a problem in China. Deng wanted everyone to have enough. In 1979 the government began to give bonuses to one-child families. It fined families with more than one child. ■

▼ *China is home to over one-fifth of the world's population.*

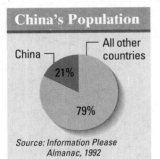

China's Population

China — 21%
All other countries — 79%

Source: Information Please Almanac, 1992

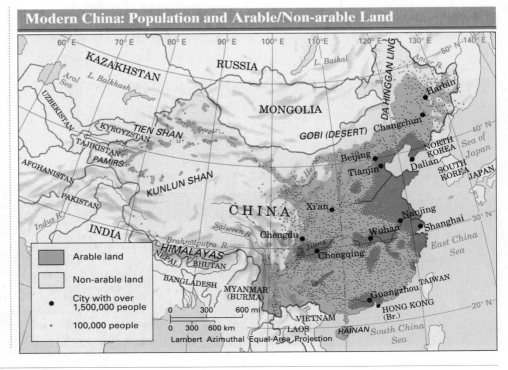

Modern China: Population and Arable/Non-arable Land

Arable land
Non-arable land
● City with over 1,500,000 people
· 100,000 people

0   300   600 mi
0   300   600 km
Lambert Azimuthal Equal-Area Projection

➤ *Much of China's land is mountainous or desert. Most of its people are crowded into the eastern third of the country. This area enjoys a mild climate, plenty of rainfall, and good soil.*

■ *What reforms did Deng Xiaoping introduce to China?*

348

New Conflicts

Deng's reforms improved China's economy. At the same time they caused some problems. After the government loosened economic controls, rising prices became a problem. Goods and supplies cost more. Another problem was unemployment. Many people moved to the city after the breakup of the huge farming communes. Some could not find jobs.

Under Mao's strict Communist system, everyone was supposed to "eat out of the same pot." All people would be equal. To reach this goal, the government had controlled the economy. Under Deng, China moved toward limited free enterprise. Some Chinese thought that Deng's reforms undermined the ideals of communism. Some people had bad feelings toward those who were earning more under the "responsibility system." There was also anger at those officials who had grown rich from bribes. For these reasons some people opposed Deng's reforms.

Other Changes

To bring China into the modern world, Deng looked to the West for help. He encouraged Western companies to build factories in China. He let Chinese students study overseas. He invited scientists from other countries to teach in China.

This contact with the West has helped to bring change to China. Many people can now afford consumer goods, such as televisions and watches. What's more, they want to earn more money, like workers in the West. Some Chinese have also started asking for the same rights that people enjoy in Western democracies.

New Questions

For China, change has led to many questions.
• Can Chinese ways survive the influences of the West?
• Can the Communist system survive if China keeps moving toward free enterprise?
• Can China have economic freedom without political freedom? ■

▲ *Deng's economic reforms brought more consumer goods to China, including radios, watches, and appliances. This Chinese girl is waiting outside with a new rice cooker and microwave oven.*

■ *What problems came with Deng's reforms?*

The Democracy Movement

Deng's reforms raised people's hopes for more political freedom. Many Chinese, especially students, called on Deng to bring democracy to China.

Student Protest

The democracy movement came to a head in 1989. Thousands of students gathered in Beijing's Tiananmen Square. They came to

In 1986 and 1987 Chinese students protested for democracy at more than 100 universities. One student poster echoed Dr. Martin Luther King, Jr., the African American civil rights leader of the 1960s. It said: I HAVE A DREAM OF DEMOCRACY. I HAVE A DREAM OF LIFE ENDOWED WITH HUMAN RIGHTS.

➤ Student protesters in Tiananmen Square built a "goddess of democracy" as part of their protest for greater freedom. Chinese soldiers later attacked the protesters and crushed the democracy movement.

■ What did the protesters in Tiananmen Square want?

demand free speech, free press, and the right to hold demonstrations. A protester's poem in a shop window urged people to

O verthrow the old system
Return power to the people
Elect good people to office
And impeach the rotten ones.

The **dissidents,** or protesters, were led by students. Thousands of Chinese citizens joined the protest.

The government appeared uncertain about what to do. Newspeople from around the world were reporting on the events. The government seemed to be worried about world opinion. The protests lasted more than six weeks. Finally, the government ordered the army to surround the square. Some dissidents left. Many others built a statue of the "goddess of democracy." It stood for their dream of greater freedom.

A Brutal Response

On June 4 Chinese troops opened fire in the square. Hundreds of unarmed students were killed. Others fled as tanks took over the square. The democracy movement was forced into hiding. Some protesters were sent to prison. Others left the country. Because of its actions against the students, Deng's government lost the respect of many nations.

These events suggest China is moving toward a free enterprise economy without democracy. Although people are freer to earn money, they do not have the right to speak their minds. Nor can they elect their leaders. ■

REVIEW

1. **FOCUS** How has Deng's government responded to China's problems?

2. **ECONOMICS** Reread the story about the two women who opened China's first privately owned restaurant. What difficulties did they face?

3. **POLITICS** What policy has China's government adopted to control the size of its population?

4. **CRITICAL THINKING** How has Deng's approach to economic problems differed from Mao's?

5. **ACTIVITY** Imagine that you were a student during the time of the Tiananmen Square protests. A protest leader asked you to join the demonstration. Tell how you responded. Explain why.

LESSON 3

China Today

China is a vast and varied land. Daily life is different from place to place. In the city or in the country, life in China means hard work. Here's a look at the lives of two Chinese women.

The first, Meng Maying, describes her job as a weaver. She lives in the busy port city of Shanghai, in eastern China. She works in a textile factory. For 22 years she has held this job.

For the eight-hour shift, we're on our feet all the time walking up and down the rows of machines. . . . We cannot sit for a moment for fear that there'll be broken ends somewhere. I've never tried to count how far I've walked in the workshop all these years. But I think I've walked a much longer distance than the Red Army's. . . Long March.

As a result, my feet are always swollen after a work shift. We all wear flat soled cloth shoes in the workshop.

The second woman, Xiao Wenxin, lives in rural Hebei *(hoh bay)* Province in northern China. She has taught third and fifth grades for over 20 years. The classrooms in her school are nothing more than clay huts.

By the time Xiao starts her job each day, she has already cooked her meals, taken care of her pigs and chickens, and fed her two children.

I arrive at school before 8 o'clock. Four classes in the morning. Go home after 12 o'clock. Three classes in the afternoon. Go home again at 5 o'clock. Then back to the school at 6:30 and coach the students to review or correct homework, or prepare lessons for tomorrow.

THINKING FOCUS

How is life in China today a mix of old and new ways?

Key Term

- work unit

◄ *Children at school wear red scarves, part of the standard uniform from the time of Mao.*

351

China

Rural Life, Urban Life

Feeding China's huge population requires thousands of tons of food and millions of farmers. Cities have grown rapidly since the Communists came to power in 1949. The countryside, however, is still home to most Chinese. Farming is the most common way of life.

A Farm Family

Meet the Kuos. They farm 10 acres of land on China's southeastern coast. Their life is a blend of old ways and modern changes.

Three generations live together in the Kuo household, as Chinese families have done for thousands of years. Following tradition, the Kuos' son brought his bride to live with his family when he married. But unlike Chinese families of old, the son has only one child, a boy. After all, China has a policy of fining families that have more than one child. The boy's name is Vu. Vu is one of China's "little emperors" who get lots of attention.

While Vu is in school, his parents and grandparents do the farm work. They plant their fields with cotton, corn, rice, and wheat. After the harvest, they sell their crops to the government. Under Deng's new policy, they raise another small crop for cash.

The Kuos are far from rich, but their life is comfortable. Many of the Kuos' relatives live nearby. The Kuos' courtyard is often filled with people. Family is important in modern China, as it was in earlier times. People share chores, such as cooking and laundry. There is a washing machine to help, but it can only be run at night. Rural factories use all daytime electricity.

Meals are an important time for families to get together. Family meals usually include soup, rice, vegetables, and fish. Much of the family's food comes from the market in the Kuos' village. Markets in China are often outdoors. They always include large displays of vegetables.

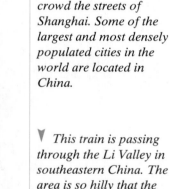

► *Hundreds of people crowd the streets of Shanghai. Some of the largest and most densely populated cities in the world are located in China.*

▼ *This train is passing through the Li Valley in southeastern China. The area is so hilly that the farmers build terraces in order to grow their crops.*

Life in the City

China's cities bustle with people and bicycles. Many houses and apartments have only two or three rooms. Furniture is simple. Posters and family pictures may decorate the walls. Because indoor space is tight, people like to spend time outside. In city parks, they can play games and listen to singers and storytellers. They can also practice *tai chi chuan (ty chee chwahn)*. It is an ancient form of slow-motion exercise.

A worker's life is controlled by the *danwei*, or **work unit.** Everyone in China belongs to a work unit. A work unit might include, for example, all the workers in a certain factory.

The work unit takes care of all the family's needs. It provides housing and medical care. It may even throw dance parties or show a movie. It also takes care of schooling for young people.

Over time, a typical factory worker can earn enough to buy a refrigerator or a washing machine. An unskilled worker's family may have to make do with a tiny concrete apartment. The family may have to share a kitchen and toilet with other families. But a skilled worker can move into roomier quarters.

For typical factory workers, the day starts at 6:00 A.M. The factory loudspeaker begins broadcasting music and announcements. Then it is time for breakfast—perhaps fried dough and sweet soup. Most workers ride to the factory on bicycles. They return home for lunch, then go back to the factory until 4:00 P.M.

After work, young people may listen to Chinese rock 'n' roll on their tape decks. Or they may play video games set up on the street. Grownups may watch television or go to a teahouse or a restaurant. ■

▲ *Like the Kans from Beijing, many Chinese families have parents, grandparents, and one child.*

◄ *The streets in China's villages are busy with activity. This woman is selling noodles, a popular meal in the wheat-growing regions of northern China.*

■ *How does life in rural China compare with life in the city?*

353

China

China Looks to the Future

China's population is the largest in the world. It is also one of the youngest. About 750 million Chinese are younger than 35 years of age. The future belongs to them.

China's Youth

What direction will this future take? This question is hotly debated between young and old in China. Older people remember Mao's revolution. They recall the struggle to build a fairer society. They grew up believing that everyone should work for the common good. For many older people, obeying a ruler is a part of their tradition. They have trouble understanding some of the young people who want "too much" freedom. They don't accept the "get rich quick" attitude of some of China's youth.

Many young people, on the other hand, think the older generation is out of touch with the world. These young people have learned about the West from films and television. They've picked up Western styles of clothing. They've absorbed Western attitudes about money and freedom.

But will these young Chinese be able to put their new ideas into practice? That question is yet to be answered.

Hong Kong

Another big question for China today concerns what will happen to Hong Kong in 1997.

China had to give up the island of Hong Kong to the British in 1842. Since then Hong Kong has become one of the richest markets in Asia. Each year thousands of ships load and unload goods at Hong Kong's busy docks. Hong Kong is also an important manufacturing center. Its factories make textiles, clothing, and appliances.

Hong Kong returns to Chinese control in 1997. China has promised to let Hong Kong keep its free enterprise market. However, after what happened at Tiananmen Square, many people in Hong Kong wonder whether Deng's government will keep its word.

People in China and Hong Kong have questions about their future.
• Will the Communist party extend its tight control over Hong Kong?
• Will mainland Chinese get more freedom, like people in Hong Kong? ■

▼ *Hong Kong is busy, crowded, and prosperous. Double-decker buses are just one sign of British influence.*

■ *What questions face China as it approaches the 21st century?*

R E V I E W

1. **FOCUS** How is life in China today a mix of old and new ways?
2. **CULTURE** What role does the work unit play in the lives of China's workers?
3. **POLITICS** What are some important questions facing China today?

4. **CRITICAL THINKING** Would you rather be a farmer or a factory worker in China? Give reasons.
5. **WRITING ACTIVITY** Imagine that you could have a pen pal who is your age in China. What would you tell your pen pal about your life? What questions would you like to ask your pen pal? Try writing such a letter.

Presenting Information

Here's Why

Writing a report is a good way to add to your knowledge and to share information with others. Look at the map. It shows some of the different dialects of the Chinese language spoken in China today.

Suppose you were asked to write a report about the many Chinese dialects. Would you know what to do? Where would you begin?

Here's How

Here are six basic steps for writing a good report.

1. **Explore your topic.** Make a list of five things you want to know about your topic. Consider narrowing your topic to one of the five questions.
2. **Do research.** You can find general information about China in Chapters 5 and 15, but you should use other sources such as encyclopedias, books, and magazines to help you find information about the Chinese language.
3. **Take notes.** As you read, record information on note cards. Write a different idea on each note card. When you finish taking notes, group the cards according to the main ideas.
4. **Write an outline.** Look at the beginnings of an outline below. The biggest ideas from the note cards become the main points, shown by Roman numerals. Somewhat smaller ideas become subtopics, shown by capital letters. Details are then added, shown by Arabic numerals, and then small letters.
5. **Write a first draft.** Use the items with Roman numerals in your outline as paragraph topic sentences in your report. Use the subtopics as supporting details. Write in complete sentences and paragraphs.
6. **Revise, proofread, and publish.** After completing the first draft, read it over to see how you can improve it and to correct any mistakes you may find. Then prepare the final copy.

Try It

Follow the first four steps of writing a report. Use this topic: What changes occurred in China under Mao before the Great Leap Forward?

Apply It

Use the first three steps of writing a report to learn more about a hobby of interest to you. Then make an outline.

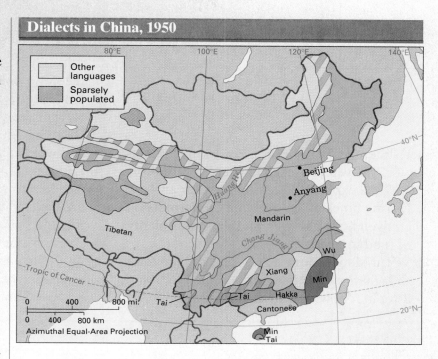

Dialects in China, 1950

Other languages
Sparsely populated

Beijing
Anyang
Mandarin
Tibetan
Chang Jiang
Wu
Xiang
Min
Tai
Hakka
Cantonese
Min Tai
Tropic of Cancer
Hwang Ho
80°E 100°E 120°E 140°E
40°N
20°N

0 400 800 mi.
0 400 800 km
Azimuthal Equal-Area Projection

I. Dialects are like distinct languages.
   A. Many different dialects are spoken in China today.
      1. Mandarin, the northern dialect, is the official language.
      2. Southern China contains many more dialects than the north.
         a. Most Chinese in the United States speak the Cantonese dialect.

355

China

Chapter Review

Reviewing Key Terms

communism (p. 344)
dissident (p. 350)
famine (p. 341)

free enterprise (p. 347)
ideology (p. 348)
work unit (p. 353)

Each statement below uses a key term from this chapter. Tell whether each key term is used correctly. Then explain the reason for your answer.

1. During times of <u>famine</u>, Chinese farmers enjoyed huge harvests, and there was plenty of food for everyone.
2. When Mao Zedong's programs did not lead to higher production, he continued to believe in following a strict Communist <u>ideology</u>, or set of beliefs.
3. Under the <u>free enterprise</u> system, the government controls the economy by setting prices and deciding what farmers will grow and what factories will manufacture.
4. <u>Dissidents</u> in China have always had the freedom to speak their minds because they are the traditional supporters of the government in power.
5. Everyone in China today belongs to a <u>work unit</u>. The work unit is responsible for its members' housing, medical care, education, and even for some leisure activities.

Exploring Concepts

A. Important dynasties and events in Chinese history, from the Mongols to modern times, appear on the timeline below. Copy the timeline on a separate sheet of paper. From the following list, fill in on the timeline the items connected with each dynasty or event:

- Great Wall repaired
- Chinese ways adopted
- Grand Canal repaired
- The arts encouraged
- Five ports opened to western trade
- Pu Yi gives up throne
- Manchus defeat Mings
- Collectives united into communes

B. Answer each question with information from the chapter.

1. Why were the attempts by Mao to create a new society in China costly failures?
2. What is Deng Xiaoping's "responsibility system"?
3. Why does the Chinese government want to limit population growth?
4. Why and how did Deng seek contact with the West?
5. What was the purpose of the demonstrations at Tiananmen Square in 1989? What was the result?
6. What problems will Hong Kong face in 1997?

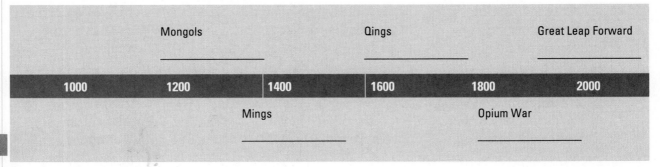

Mongols   Qings   Great Leap Forward

1000   1200   1400   1600   1800   2000

Mings   Opium War

Reviewing Skills

1. Reread the sections Steering a New Course, New Conflicts, and The Democracy Movement on pages 348–350. Make a list of five questions you might want to explore if you were writing a report about communism in China today.
2. Choose one question from your list for your report. Explain why you chose it. Which step in the process of presenting information have you completed?
3. Copy the flow chart below and fill in the missing steps.
4. List three sources of information you might look at in the second step of this process.

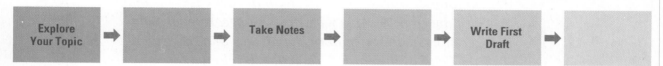

Explore Your Topic → [ ] → Take Notes → [ ] → Write First Draft → [ ]

Using Critical Thinking

1. For centuries the Chinese looked down on other cultures and shut themselves off from the world. In what ways might China have developed differently if it had been open to exchanges of ideas and trade with other countries?
2. Compare life in a Chinese city with life in a U.S. city. What are some important differences? What similarities can you find?
3. "Throughout the history of China, a single strong leader has been a key to stable government." What evidence from the chapter can you find to support this statement?
4. Why do you think that Deng's reforms raised students' hopes for greater freedom in China?

Preparing for Citizenship

1. **WRITING ACTIVITY** Imagine that a Chinese student is coming to study at your school. Write a short essay describing aspects of life in the United States that will be new to him or her. If you like, illustrate your essay with drawings or magazine pictures. Also describe ways you might help the student adapt to your school and your community.
2. **GEOGRAPHY ACTIVITY** Find "50 largest cities of the world" on page 664 of the Minipedia. How many of these cities are in China? Construct a bar graph showing the four countries with the largest cities. What does this graph tell you about China's population?
3. **COLLABORATIVE LEARNING** Who should lead China after Deng Xiaoping? Imagine that Genghis Khan, Hung-wu, Mao Zedong, and Deng Xiaoping came together to discuss what kind of person the new leader should be. Divide the class into four groups. Each group should decide on recommendations that one of these people might make, based on what the group knows of that person's policies and impact on Chinese life. Use reference works or other library books for more information about each leader. Discuss these questions: (1) What values and qualities should the new leader have? (2) What should be the new leader's highest priorities? (3) What kind of leadership style should this person have?

   A speaker from each group should report the leader's recommendations to the class. Is there a class consensus among the leaders about what qualifications China's next leader should have? Then, as a class, imagine that you are Chinese supporters of democracy. How would your recommendations differ from the suggestions of the four leaders listed in the collaborative activity?

Chapter 16

Japan

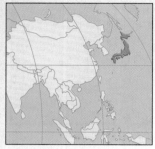

How can one explain the success of the Japanese people in today's world? A small chain of rocky islands that dot the coast of Asia with miles of ocean separating it from its nearest neighbor, Japan was once considered the "end of the earth." Yet it has developed into an economic giant with one of the world's unique and exquisite cultures.

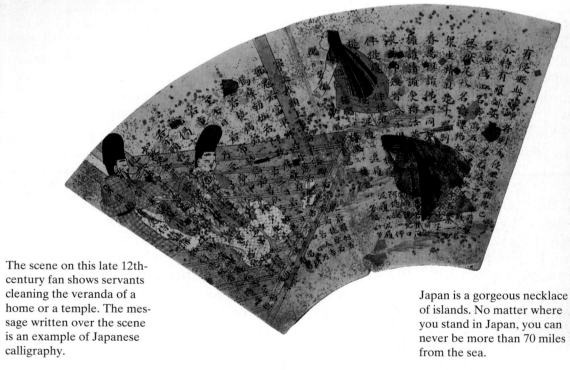

The scene on this late 12th-century fan shows servants cleaning the veranda of a home or a temple. The message written over the scene is an example of Japanese calligraphy.

Japan is a gorgeous necklace of islands. No matter where you stand in Japan, you can never be more than 70 miles from the sea.

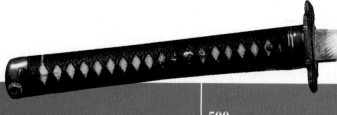

125	500	875

A.D. 250

A.D. 250–710 Under the rule of the Yamato, Japan is unified, and China becomes its cultural model.

At this company in Asahikawa, workers start the day by exercising.

These beautiful sword guards, made in the 1700s, separated the sword handle from the blade. The smaller of the two sword guards pictures Buddha and Confucius standing under a pine tree.

1952 The U.S. occupation of Japan ends. Japan continues the rebuilding of its war-torn cities and eventually becomes one of the world's leading economic powers.

| 1250 | 1625 | 2000 |

1192 Shogunate begins. Samurai of this period often wore steel swords like the one above made in the 1100s.

1603–1867 The Tokugawa shogunate closes Japan to Western nations. Laws forbid Japanese subjects from leaving the country without permission.

Today

Island Culture

➤ *The Gods Izanagi and Izanami are shown in this painting. According to a Japanese myth, they created the islands of Japan.*

In the beginning there was chaos. Then heaven and earth divided, and the Lord of Heaven sent two young Gods, Izanagi and Izanami, to create beauty. Izanagi threw a spear into the ocean. As he pulled the spear out, drops fell and formed the islands of Japan.

This is how the world began, according to Japanese mythology. Today scientists say that volcanoes erupted millions of years ago forming mountains on the floor of the Pacific Ocean. These mountains pushed up out of the ocean and created the islands of Japan.

With its rocky coastlines and forest-covered mountains, Japan is a land of great beauty. Perhaps this is why the Japanese have always shown such an appreciation for the wonders of the natural world.

Land of the Rising Sun

In total area Japan covers a little less land than the state of Montana. As you can see from the map on page 361, Japan has four large islands: Hokkaido *(hah KY doh),* Honshu, Shikoku, Kyushu *(kee OO shoo),* and thousands of smaller islands. These islands stretch about 1,500 miles from north to south. If the islands were placed next to the east coast of the United States, they would reach from Maine to Florida.

The Japanese people do not call their country Japan. They call it either Nihon or Nippon. We get the name Japan from the Chinese pronunciation of Nippon. The word *Nippon* means "where the sun has its origin." This is why Japan is often called the Land of the Rising Sun.

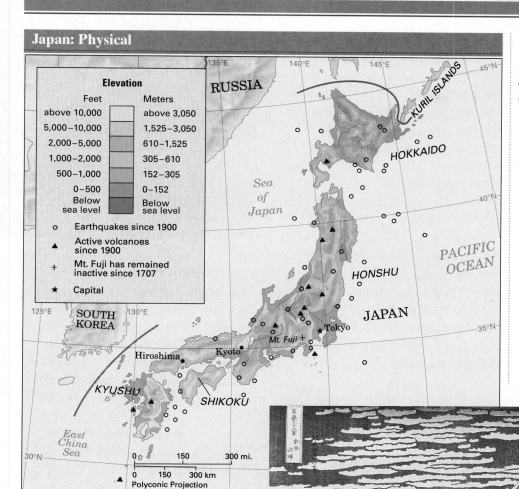

Japan: Physical

Elevation

Feet		Meters
above 10,000		above 3,050
5,000–10,000		1,525–3,050
2,000–5,000		610–1,525
1,000–2,000		305–610
500–1,000		152–305
0–500		0–152
Below sea level		Below sea level

○ Earthquakes since 1900

▲ Active volcanoes since 1900

+ Mt. Fuji has remained inactive since 1707

★ Capital

RUSSIA

KURIL ISLANDS

HOKKAIDO

Sea of Japan

HONSHU

PACIFIC OCEAN

JAPAN

SOUTH KOREA

Mt. Fuji + ★ Tokyo

Kyoto

Hiroshima

KYUSHU

SHIKOKU

East China Sea

0   150   300 mi.

0   150   300 km

Polyconic Projection

◄ *Which of Japan's four major islands is the farthest north?*

Earthquakes and Volcanoes

Japan lies in an area that has some of the earth's most dramatic forces. Each year Japan has about 1,500 earthquakes. Though most are mild, some cause serious damage. At times earthquakes shake the ocean floor near Japan. These cause tidal waves that smash into the coast, destroying homes and killing people.

Japan also has more than 150 major volcanoes—60 of which are still active. Violent ocean storms sometimes visit Japan. Their heavy winds and rains batter Japan's coasts and flood its valleys.

Natural Resources

Mountains and hills cover most of Japan. Less than 20 percent of the land is suitable for farming. Because of Japan's mild climate and plentiful rainfall, most of this land is used for growing rice. In addition to rice, Japanese farmers grow crops such as soybeans, vegetables, and barley.

The sea has provided another source of food. For centuries fish has been an important part of the Japanese diet. A traditional dinner often includes seafood, such as fish, squid, and octopus, with rice.

▲ *Mount Fuji is the tallest of Japan's volcanoes. It stands almost 12,390 feet high. Each year thousands of people climb to the Shinto shrine on its peak.*

361

Japan

➤ *The "wedded rocks" of this Shinto shrine are linked by a straw rope. In the Shinto religion, the rocks are associated with the Gods who created the islands of Japan.*

Other than its mild climate, ample rainfall, and the sea, Japan has few natural resources. There is little coal, iron, oil, or other minerals. Yet this has not stood in the way of Japan's development into a prosperous nation.

Living with Nature

A deep appreciation of nature and its beauty runs through the Japanese way of life. For example, **Shinto,** the original religion of the Japanese, is a form of nature worship. Shinto teaches that the world is filled with divine spirits that are seen in nature. These spirits may be found in a beautiful waterfall or a colorful sunset.

■ *How does traditional Japanese housing reflect Japan's geography?*

Though nature can be harsh, the Japanese have long believed in living in harmony with the natural world. For example, the traditional Japanese home is built to adapt to Japan's hot and humid summers and short, cold winters. It is built off the ground to let it catch cooling breezes. It is made of wood instead of stone, because wood is cooler in summer and warmer to the touch in winter. Also, wood can better absorb the shocks of earthquakes. The tile roof has overhangs to provide protection from the sun and the rain.

The traditional Japanese home welcomes the outside world. Inner walls are often lightweight paper screens that can be slid back to open up onto a courtyard garden or closed for privacy. ■

▲ *Most rooms in a traditional Japanese home have little furniture. Straw mats called* tatami *cover the floor. At night cotton mattresses called* futons *are rolled out for sleeping.*

Island People

Archaeologists tell us that the first people to live in Japan came from Korea and northeast Asia more than 100,000 years ago. Find South Korea on the map on page 361. Notice how close it is to Japan.

The flow of people into Japan continued into the eighth century A.D. Then it stopped. After this, Japan's seas acted as a natural barrier keeping Japan in **isolation,** or setting it apart. For about the next thousand years, Japanese society grew with little influence from other countries except China.

Early Cultures

In about 4000 B.C., the Jomon *(JOH mahn)* society developed in Japan. The Jomon were fishers and

hunter-gatherers. In about 200 B.C., the Jomon were replaced by a new group called the Yayoi *(yah YOY).* The Yayoi taught the Japanese how to cultivate rice in water. They also brought metal tools to irrigate and level the land. The Yayoi changed the Japanese to farmers.

Later the Yayoi were replaced by another culture called the Yamato. Under the Yamato rule (A.D. 250–710), Japan became a unified nation. For a short time during the fourth and fifth centuries, the Yamato were powerful enough to gain control of Korea.

From China to Japan

In Korea the Japanese came in contact with Chinese civilization and a new religion, Buddhism. As you read in Chapter 15, China was considered the most advanced civilization in the world at this time. The more the Japanese learned about China, the more they admired what they saw.

When Prince Shōtoku became the ruler in A.D. 593, he sent students to China to learn more about its culture and government. He also welcomed Chinese scholars and artists to Japan. They brought Chinese language, arts, mathematics, and agricultural techniques to Japan.

This cultural borrowing continued for many centuries and deeply affected the way the Japanese thought and lived. Japanese music, architecture, sculpture, and painting went through enormous changes.

Between 794 and 1185, the emperor's court was in the city of Heian *(HAY ahn),* later called Kyoto *(KYOH toh).* During this time, called the Heian period in Japanese history, a culture of refinement and luxury came into being. The Chinese influence could still be seen in this culture. Yet it had been changed into something new and uniquely Japanese.

A good example of how the Japanese adapted Chinese culture is the writing system. Since the Japanese had no writing system of their own, they used the Chinese system. Yet because the languages are very different, some of the Chinese symbols could not express Japanese words or feelings. Over time the Japanese created their own symbols to better express their own language.

Poetry was the favorite form of writing among Japanese courtiers. Courtiers were finely dressed men and women who took part in the social life of the court. After poetry, diaries were the favorite form of writing. Women wrote some of the greatest literature of the age. ■

Across Time & Space

The Japanese imperial line of rulers was started in the fifth century by the Yamato clan. Akihito, who occupies the emperor's throne today, is one of the clan's descendants. Since 770, only males have been allowed to succeed to the throne. Before that time several women ruled Japan as empresses.

■ *How did the early culture of Japan develop?*

R E V I E W

1. **FOCUS** How did Japan's geography affect the development of its culture?
2. **CULTURE** What contributions did the Jomon and the Yayoi peoples make to Japanese civilization?
3. **BELIEF SYSTEM** What is the Shinto religion?
4. **CRITICAL THINKING** What are some advantages of a country's developing in isolation from the outside world? Can you think of any disadvantages?
5. **ACTIVITY** Find Japan on the map on page 689 of the Atlas. What does the map tell you about land use in Japan? What else does the map tell you?

Japanese Poetry

Written by Sanpū, Bashō, and Gokason

Japanese poets sometimes use special forms of verse that must have a certain number of lines and syllables. The first three poems on these pages are haiku, which you may have read (and written) in language arts. They are translated by Kenneth Koch. The others, given in both Japanese and English, are senryu, short poems that are usually about everyday events and thoughts.

As you read in Lesson 1, writing poetry has been a popular and well-respected art form in Japan for many centuries.

May rains!
Now frogs are swimming
At my door.
—*Sanpū, 1647–1732*

mallow a flowering plant

Beside the road
Mallow flowers bloom—
Now eaten by my horse!
—*Bashō, 1644–1694*

How cool it feels
To take a noonday nap
With my feet against a wall!
—*Bashō, 1644–1694*

The kite with a
full stomach
flies high in the sky.

Hara no ii
tombi kōkū ni
takaka mai

—*Gokason*

kite a large bird, member of the hawk family

When I think it's mine,
how light this big bundle is.

Waga mono to
omoeba karushi
ōzutsumi

—*Gokason*

Wondering
where they're going,
the clouds disappear.

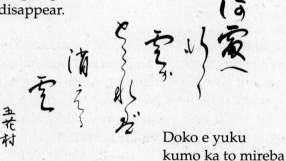

Doko e yuku
kumo ka to mireba
kieru kumo

—*Gokason*

Further Reading

In the Eyes of the Cat: Japanese Poetry for All Seasons. Selected and illustrated by Demi, these delightful short nature poems in a variety of Japanese styles come from different countries.

Valley of the Broken Cherry Trees. Lensey Namioka. An unemployed young samurai and his friend solve a mystery in 16th-century Japan.

History of Japan

THINKING FOCUS

Why did the Japanese view the outside world with suspicion?

Key Terms

- shogun
- samurai
- feudalism
- westernize

▼ *White Heron Castle near Kyoto was completed in 1609 by a Tokugawa. To reach it, an enemy would have had to pass through 11 barricades. However, the castle was never attacked.*

*T*omoe galloped into their midst, rode up alongside Moroshige, seized him in a powerful grip, pulled him down against the pommel of her saddle. . . . She discarded armor and helmet and fled toward the eastern provinces.

Anonymous, from
The Tale of the Heike

The passage you just read is from a collection of Japanese tales about war in the 1100s. It was a dangerous age, one in which men— and even a few women, as this description shows—won fame as warriors. It was a time when many swords clashed.

As Japan's nobles closed themselves away in the Kyoto court, warriors rode across the countryside. Inside the luxurious court, well-mannered nobles talked of music and poetry. Outside the court in Kyoto, there was a dangerous situation growing. Slowly the emperor was losing control of Japan.

Shoguns Gain Control

In the 1100s lawlessness was spreading throughout the provinces. People fought for land and power. Looking for help, the court at Kyoto asked nobles in the provinces to help them stop the fighting.

A fierce war broke out between the Taira and Minamoto warrior families. After a long battle, the Minamoto won control. Led by a man called Yoritomo, they set up a new government.

In 1192 the emperor gave Yoritomo the title **shogun,** meaning "the emperor's general." Yoritomo let the emperor and his court remain at Kyoto. The emperor was still called the ruler of Japan. In reality, however, the shogun now ruled Japan.

For about the following 700 years, Japan was ruled by military governments called shogunates. To keep order the shoguns tried to control almost every part of Japanese society and life. Shogunate rule was often cruel.

The Samurai

The shogun was supported by nobles who had large estates in the provinces. These nobles were known as *daimyo (DY mee oh)*. Each daimyo relied on warriors called **samurai** *(SAM uh ry)* to wage battle against rival clans.

As a reward for their help, the samurai were given small pieces of land or official positions. This system in which people exchange land or services for protection is called **feudalism.** See Understanding Feudalism below.

The samurai became a new class in society. They lived by a code of behavior called *bushido,* or "the way of the warrior." The code called for strict obedience to one's superiors. A samurai was expected to give up his life if his lord wished it. If a samurai failed, he sometimes felt so humiliated that he would kill himself.

Samurai values, such as loyalty, honor, and hard work, spread to people of every class. They became a part of Japanese society. Today these are still values that the Japanese people respect.

From Wars to Unity

In spite of military rule, fighting continued for many centuries. By the mid-1400s, Japan was divided into hundreds of warring states.

Out of the chaos appeared a strong leader in the late 1500s. Oda Nobunaga was a powerful and smart

◄ *Samurai armor is made of steel, silk, and bronze. This armor was made between 1338 and 1573.*

UNDERSTANDING FEUDALISM

You can think of a Japanese samurai in much the same way as you think of a European knight in armor. Both kinds of warriors were part of a political system known as feudalism. In Europe, feudalism began in the 700s and lasted until the 1400s. In Japan, the system began in the 800s and lasted into the 1800s.

What Is Feudalism?

Under feudalism, people exchange land in return for service or military protection. The word *feudalism* comes from the Latin word *feodum,* which means "fief," or "estate." A lord gave a fief to a warrior in return for a pledge of loyalty and military service.

Feudalism Develops

In both Europe and Japan, feudalism developed at a time of political chaos. As governments became weak, people needed a way to protect themselves. In Chapter 18 you will read more about the growth of feudalism in Europe. In Japan, landowners in the provinces depended on samurai warriors to protect their estates and to wage war against rival clans.

Life under Feudalism

In both Europe and Japan, feudal society was divided into separate social classes. Landowners, priests, and warriors were at the top. At the bottom were the peasants who farmed the land.

Most people stayed in the class into which they were born. Each class obeyed rules of behavior, and change was frowned upon.

How Do We Know?

HISTORY *For warriors in medieval Japan, the ritual and ceremony of the battle were as important as the battle itself. Stories describing heroism in battle were popular.* The Tale of the Heike, *for example, tells about battles between the Taira and Minamoto clans in the 1100s.*

▼ *Proper clothing for a samurai family often consisted of beautiful, long flowing robes for both the men and the women.*

leader. Instead of swords and arrows, he armed his troops with muskets from Portuguese traders. With his modern army, Nobunaga soon controlled almost half of the country of Japan.

Still more power struggles followed Nobunaga's death. Finally, Nobunaga's assistant general succeeded in unifying Japan under one government. He was succeeded by Tokugawa Ieyasu *(ih yeh YAH soo)*, who was named shogun in 1603. The Tokugawa shogunate would last until the 1860s.

The Tokugawa shoguns created thousands of laws limiting what peasants could and could not do. Some laws forbade peasants to leave the land or ride a horse. Other laws described the clothes and hairdos that peasants could wear. These laws were meant to uphold a strict class system. Outside of work, the classes rarely mixed except, perhaps, at a tea ceremony. For more on tea ceremonies, see A Moment in Time on page 369.

At the top of the social classes were the *daimyo* and samurai. Samurai had the freedom to enforce the laws as they saw fit. The following order by Tokugawa Ieyasu makes clear that it was dangerous not to obey a samurai.

> *Farmers, craftsmen and merchants may not behave in a rude manner towards samurai. The word for a rude man is "other-than-expected-fellow" and a samurai is not to be interfered with in cutting down a fellow who has behaved to him in a manner other than is expected.*

Closing the Doors

The Tokugawa shogunate was determined to keep Japan unified. For this reason, the Tokugawas decided to rid Japan of all outsiders. They did not want foreigners introducing new ideas that might lead to rebellion.

Soon after Portuguese traders reached Japan in 1542, Catholic missionaries began to visit Japan. As the number of Japanese who became Christians grew, the shogunate began to see the missionaries as a threat. The Tokugawas feared the missionaries might weaken the loyalty of the Christians. They also feared that *daimyo,* who became rich from foreign trade, might rebel.

A Tea Master

Noon, October 3, 1992
A tearoom in Kyoto, Japan

Ladle *(Hishaku)*
With a graceful gesture, he dips the bamboo ladle. For years he has practiced each movement of the ceremony.

Kettle *(Kama)* **and Brazier** *(Furo)*
Hot coals in a brass *furo* heat water in his cast iron kettle. The sound of water in the *kama* reminds him of wind blowing through trees. Tea masters have heard this sound for centuries.

Tea Scoop *(Chashaku)*
He gives his bamboo scoop a special name—*akatonbo*. This is the name of a red dragonfly common in autumn. His tea ceremony honors the fall season.

Whisk *(Chasen)*
He rinses his whisk before stirring thin tea for his guests. Purity is important in sharing tea.

Tea Powder Container *(Natsume)*
Earlier this morning he poured green tea powder into his *natsume* to resemble a mountain. His guests appreciate the image from nature.

Tea Bowl
His tea bowls are simple and imperfect, as things are in nature. His favorite bowl has a faint crack shaped like an old vine in his garden.

369

In the early 1600s, the shogunate outlawed Christianity, cut down on European trade, and expelled foreigners. No Japanese person was allowed to leave the country. The Tokugawas began a period of forced isolation. For more than 200 years, Japan had almost no contact with the outside world.

Business Booms

Japan did not stand still during this long period of isolation. Life in the cities was busy. More merchants were hired to bring food, cloth, and other goods to the capital city of Edo—which is now called Tokyo. Merchants became rich from their trade and their political power grew.

During the 1600s, education spread to all classes, and the economy boomed. The samurai learned to read, and many became government officials. By the 1800s Japan was a prospering nation.

Lured by the hope of new trade, Dutch, French, British, and U.S. ships tried to dock in Japanese harbors. Time and time again, the Tokugawas' answer was the same— "Go away!" The Japanese feared that they might fall under the rule of these powerful foreigners. ■

■ *Why did the Tokugawa shogunate close off Japan to outsiders?*

Japan Faces the West

In 1854, eight U.S. warships commanded by Captain Matthew C. Perry steamed into Edo Bay. Perry was determined not to leave empty-handed. He wanted a trade agreement with Japan. Japan could not keep the foreigners out any longer. Faced with the warships' threatening cannons, Japan gave Perry the treaty he wanted.

Soon the Japanese signed similar trade treaties with other Western nations. These treaties all seemed to put the interests of the foreigners ahead of the interests of the Japanese. One treaty went so far as to make foreigners exempt from Japanese law.

Many Japanese people grew very angry. Soon rebels who wanted to overthrow the Tokugawa shogunate made their voices heard all over Japan.

Meiji Restoration

The rebellion was led by a group of young samurai. In 1867 the rebels overthrew the Tokugawa shogunate. Then in 1868 they declared the restoration, or return, of the emperor's rule. This rule was called the Meiji *(MAY jee),* which means "enlightened rule."

The Meiji leaders felt that the best way to protect Japan from foreigners was to **westernize.** The

During the Meiji Restoration, Japan went through a rapid modernization. This print of Yokohama in 1883 shows a trolley car and the city's first electric streetlight.

word *westernizing* means adopting the ways of developed countries in Europe and North America.

Thousands of Japanese students were sent to Germany, France, the United States, and Britain—just as Japan had sent students to China more than 1,300 years earlier. They studied Western business, military science, government, and education. Also, more than 3,000 Western teachers were hired to teach in Japan.

The government began building railroads and telegraph lines. By the end of the Meiji period in 1912, Japan was a modern nation with growing industries. It had a new constitution, compulsory education, and several universities.

Japan in World War II

Japan also wanted to build up an empire of its own. This led to war with China (1894–1895) and Russia (1904–1905). In 1910 Japan took control of Korea and in 1931 seized Manchuria from China.

By 1939 war was raging in both Europe and China. Japan had sided with the United States during World War I, but it joined Germany and the other Axis powers in World War II. Then, on December 7, 1941, without declaring war, Japanese planes attacked U.S. warships in Pearl Harbor, Hawaii. The United States declared war and joined the Allied fight against Germany, Italy, and Japan.

The Allies first defeated Germany and Italy and then turned to Japan. In 1945 the United States dropped atomic bombs on the Japanese cities of Hiroshima and Nagasaki. The Japanese surrendered within a week—on August 14, 1945. A treaty was signed in September.

Recovery

Japan's cities were in ruins, and more than one million Japanese had died. The United States decided that the best way to build a peaceful future was to help the Japanese rebuild their country.

The U.S. Army occupied—controlled—Japan for seven years after the war. Under the leadership of General Douglas MacArthur, the U.S. Army helped rebuild Japan.

During the occupation, Japan adopted a democratic constitution. It gave women the right to vote and outlawed the military forces. Then the United States poured technical know-how and money into rebuilding Japan's industries. By the end of the occupation in 1952, the groundwork had been laid for Japan's booming future. ■

◄ *This watch was found in the ruins of Hiroshima. It reads 8:15 A.M.—the exact time the atomic bomb exploded. After Japan surrendered, the U.S. Army helped the Japanese rebuild Japan. In the photograph below, plans are being made to rebuild the Industrial Arts Building in Hiroshima.*

■ *How did Japan's attitude toward the West change after the Meiji Restoration?*

| R | E | V | I | E | W |

1. FOCUS Why did the Japanese view the outside world with suspicion?

2. GOVERNMENT Describe shogun rule in Japan.

3. CULTURE What was *bushido*?

4. CRITICAL THINKING What advantages did Japan gain by being occupied by the United States after World War II?

5. ACTIVITY Use the information in the lesson to make a timeline that traces Japanese relations with other countries. Include dates from the Tokugawa shogun era to the end of the U.S. occupation in 1952.

371

Japan

Interpreting Symbols

Here's Why

Maps can show statistical information, such as population, rainfall, or resources, in many ways. For example, mapmakers may choose to use a standard map base and then add thematic information, which is explained in a map key. Mapmakers can also use cartograms.

Cartograms are chartlike maps that present statistical information through size. They rarely try to show the actual shape of a country or region. On a cartogram the sizes of real geographic areas are made smaller or larger according to the statistical information. Cartograms allow you to see information at a glance and make comparisons between countries quickly.

Suppose you want to compare Japan's petroleum resources with those of other major industrial nations of the world. Most industrialized nations depend heavily on petroleum for many purposes. Petroleum, often called crude oil, is the source of gasoline and kerosene. It can also be refined and made into products such as paints, plastics, synthetic rubber, soaps, medicines, and explosives. A cartogram can help you learn which countries have the most petroleum and which countries have the least.

Here's How

Look at the maps on these pages. Read the titles. Then find out how each map shows information.

The map below is a political map. It shows the countries of the world. Look carefully at the map. You can use this map as a basis for understanding the cartogram on the next page.

Now look at the cartogram on page 373. Notice that it has no scale of miles. The sentence at the bottom of map tells you that the size of each country is related to the amount of petroleum resources found in each country. The cartogram distorts

World: Political

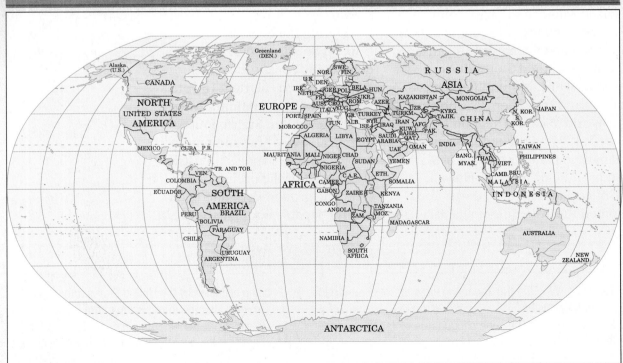

Chapter 16

the actual size and shape of countries to show how their natural resources compare.

Find Japan on the map on page 372. This map shows Japan's actual size. On the cartogram, however, Japan looks tiny because of its lack of petroleum resources. Now look at other major industrial countries such as the United States, Germany, and the United Kingdom. How do they compare with Japan in terms of actual size and in terms of petroleum resources?

Try It

Compare the cartogram on this page with the cartogram on page 375. What information does this cartogram show? Now find Japan on each cartogram. On which cartogram is Japan larger? What do these cartograms tell you about the relationship between Japan's economy and its petroleum resources? How does the Japanese economy compare with the economies of the United States, Germany, and the United Kingdom?

Apply It

Find Japan on the World Population Cartogram on page 689. How does the population of Japan compare with the population of the United States?

World: Petroleum Resources

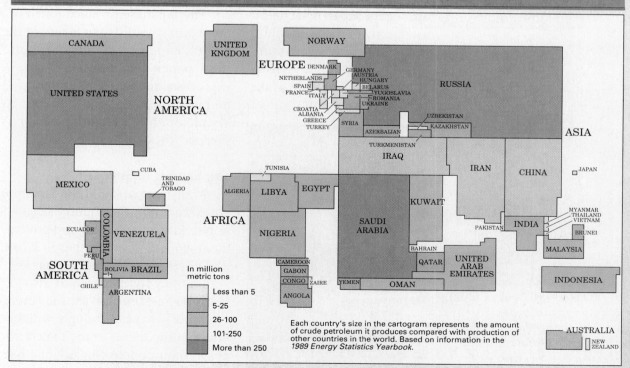

In million metric tons

Less than 5
5-25
26-100
101-250
More than 250

Each country's size in the cartogram represents the amount of crude petroleum it produces compared with production of other countries in the world. Based on information in the *1989 Energy Statistics Yearbook*.

373

Japan

L E S S O N 3

Japan Today

THINKING FOCUS

What factors have led to Japan's economic success?

Key Terms

- gross national product
- standard of living
- homogeneous
- trade imbalance

In 1946 about 20 people started a small electronics company. They used a burned-out building in the rubble of downtown Tokyo. There they made the first tape recorders and transistor radios in Japan.

Today this Japanese company—Sony—is one of the biggest companies in the world, with yearly sales of billions of dollars.

Like Sony, the Japanese people and their government also went to work after the war. As part of a national effort, they cleared bombed-out cities and turned them into thriving industrial centers. They bought the newest and most advanced machinery to equip their newly rebuilt factories. Today Japan stands as a leading economic power in the world.

The Japanese Miracle

Take a quick look at worldwide business facts, and you will see Japan's amazing success. Japan is second only to the United States in gross national product (GNP). **Gross national product** is the total value of all goods and services produced yearly by a nation. You can see this on the cartogram on page 375.

The Japanese produce much of the world's steel. Japan is one of the world's largest producers of robots, ships, paper, computers, cameras, videocassette recorders, and automobiles. The list goes on and on. People often call Japan's postwar success "the Japanese miracle."

The Secrets of Success

Many people credit the Japanese government for the country's economic success. Business and government work closely together in Japan. The government helps companies with money for research. It also helps businesses plan for the future.

Most Japanese, though, will tell you that the secret to their success lies in their people. Since Japan has

Camera Production

Millions (y-axis: 0, 2, 4, 6, 8, 10, 12, 14, 16, 18)

Year (x-axis: 1930, 1950, 1970, 1990)

Source: *Through Japanese Eyes, V. 1, 1974; Japan Statistics Yearbook, 1991*

➤ *By 1960, Japan's economy was taking off. Look at how camera production grew. This photograph shows an assembly line worker in a camera plant.*

World: Gross National Product

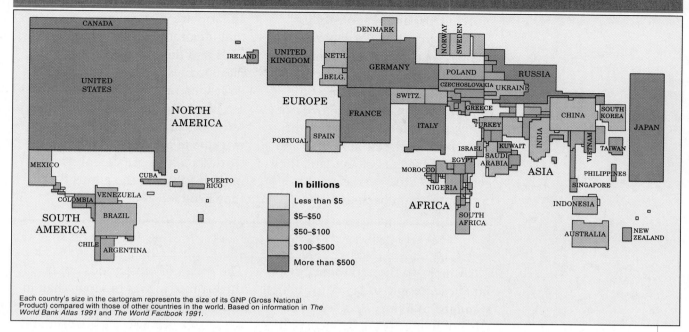

Each country's size in the cartogram represents the size of its GNP (Gross National Product) compared with those of other countries in the world. Based on information in *The World Bank Atlas 1991* and *The World Factbook 1991*.

In billions
- Less than $5
- $5–$50
- $50–$100
- $100–$500
- More than $500

very few natural resources to fuel its industry, it relies on its human resources. In Japan the key to the future has been education.

The Role of Education

One very important reason for Japan's economic success is its highly educated work force. The nation has one of the world's highest literacy rates—99 percent of the Japanese people can read and write. In the United States, this number is about 85 percent.

In addition to being highly educated, the Japanese people share a set of values that make them extremely good workers. Cooperation, hard work, and loyalty are all very important to the Japanese. Children first learn these values at home and then at school.

They are also taught a sense of shared responsibility. Shared responsibility means that everyone pulls together to get a job done. In school or at work, you succeed as your classmates or work mates succeed (see Exploring Japanese and U.S. Schools on pages 380–381).

Today these cultural values have made the Japanese people some of the most productive workers in the world. Like Japanese schools, Japanese companies put great stress on working hard and being part of the group.

From School to Work

As a new workday begins at Matsushita, a Japanese electronics company, the workers gather to recite the company motto. The motto includes the lines, "Alone we are weak, together we are strong. We

▲ *This cartogram shows that Japan has the second highest GNP of any nation in the world—an amazing achievement for a small country with few natural resources.*

▼ *Japanese mothers are often called "education mamas," because they spend a great deal of time helping their children with their schoolwork.*

shall work together as a family in mutual trust and responsibility."

Working at one of Japan's giant companies is often very demanding. In order to get ahead, some male white-collar workers spend little time with their families. One young man's schedule is to arrive home from work between 11:00 P.M. and midnight. He eats, sleeps, and then gets up at 7:00 A.M. to catch his commuter train back to work.

"For the Japanese worker, life and job are so closely interwoven that it cannot be said where one ends and the other begins," says one Japanese writer. In Japan's largest companies, most employees are hired for life. This has created a sense of company loyalty among workers at all levels. As a result, workers take a great deal of pride in their jobs and the goods that they produce. ■

■ *Why is education very important in Japan?*

Living in Japan Today

Thanks to the economic boom, Japanese people today enjoy a high **standard of living.** People's standard of living is usually measured by how comfortable their lives are. In Japan's cities the standard of living is high but costly.

Tokyo, which has a population of more than 12 million people, is Japan's largest city. About 25 percent of the Japanese population lives in the area surrounding Tokyo. It is a modern city filled with high-rise buildings and crowded subways. Most of Japan's best universities are located in Tokyo. Its main shopping district, the Ginza, is famous throughout the world.

Living in Tokyo is expensive.

The prices of most goods are nearly three times higher in Japan than in the United States. Food is also very expensive because the government helps Japan's farm families by keeping the price of farm goods high.

In large cities like Tokyo, the cost of owning a home is expensive. Along with the rising standard of living came a demand for better houses. So many people live in the cities, however, and land prices are so high, that few middle-class families can hope to own their own homes. A rather ordinary home, about one hour from downtown Tokyo, costs $500,000.

Family Life

Before World War II, two or three generations of a family often lived together. The oldest son stayed at home and brought his wife to live with him. Today most couples and their children live in small apartments of their own.

Japanese women are still expected to care for the home and the children. Yet it is becoming more common to find women working outside the home. As in the United States, a woman's salary is far below a man's salary. Also,

▼ *Tokyo is Japan's political, economic, and cultural center. Once a small fishing village called Edo, it is now one of the world's largest and most sophisticated cities.*

men are far more likely to get the best jobs. Most Japanese women are hired as office workers or at various low-level jobs.

Slowly the traditional attitudes toward Japanese women are changing. One reason for this change has been the impact of the women's rights movement in Western countries. The Japanese government is aware of world opinion and does not want to appear out of step with other modern countries. This has helped strengthen Japan's own feminist movement.

Also, many Japanese companies realize that women are a highly educated resource. In new areas like biotechnology, Japanese women are making progress.

Baseball to Kabuki

In Japan life is more than just going to work and school. The Japanese entertain themselves in many ways. Their choices range from the traditional to the modern.

Sumo, a sport that dates back over 2,000 years, attracts thousands of spectators. Sumo is like wrestling. Huge men, sometimes weighing more than 500 pounds, face off in a ring. They throw, trip, and shove each other. The loser is the first to be forced out of the ring or to touch the ground with any part of his body besides his feet.

In August baseball fever grips Japan as the high school baseball tournaments are played. Today baseball is Japan's most popular spectator sport. The Japanese have professional baseball teams, with names like the Buffalos, the Braves, and the Tigers.

Much like people in the West, the Japanese enjoy many kinds of outdoor recreation. Hiking, skiing, golf, tennis, gardening, and fishing are popular. The Japanese also enjoy indoor sports such as basketball, volleyball, bowling, judo, chess, table tennis, and karate.

In addition to sports, a Japanese family might entertain themselves by going to the Kabuki theater. Kabuki theater goes back hundreds of years to feudal Japan. Kabuki plays range from tales of samurai adventures to stories based on

▲ *This little girl and her grandmother are on a shopping trip. Until the 1950s, it was customary for several generations of a Japanese family to live together.*

◄ *These two little girls await the first pitch. Like their U.S. counterparts, they may also enjoy collecting baseball cards. These baseball cards give the batting statistics of two players for the Yomiuri Giants—a very popular team in Japan.*

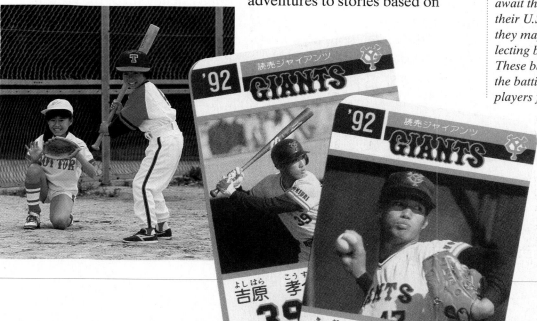

Japan

current gossip. Singers and dancers wear fancy costumes and have colorfully painted faces. The "good guys" have white faces, and the "bad guys" have red faces.

Traditional forms of entertainment such as painting and dance continue to be enjoyed by the Japanese. However, Japan has become very westernized. In Tokyo you will see people enjoying many of the same things as you do. Rock music concerts, Western movies, operas, and plays are all popular. ■

■ *How can you tell that the Japanese enjoy a high standard of living?*

▼ *These people seem to be enjoying their retirement years, but many of Japan's elderly face a difficult future.*

▼ *Japan's bullet trains travel at speeds of more than 100 miles per hour.*

Future Challenges

In spite of its economic success, Japan does face challenges in the coming years. The high standard of living that the Japanese people enjoy has come at a price. At home and in foreign countries, there are environmental and political issues that must be faced.

Environment

In their rush to develop industries, the Japanese created serious overcrowding in their cities. Pollution also became a problem. During the 1970s, children went to school wearing face masks to protect themselves from the smog. Industrial waste also flowed into Japan's rivers, poisoning many people.

The Japanese government has attempted to clean up the air and the waterways. By 1990, Japan had some of the toughest environmental protection laws in the world.

Dealing with Others

Japan has also had problems dealing with others, both at home and in foreign countries. At home Japan must face its treatment of minority peoples.

Japan has a very homogeneous population. **Homogeneous** *(hoh muh JEE nee us)* means "the same." The homogeneous nature of the Japanese people has both advantages and disadvantages. On the plus side, it has given the Japanese a strong feeling of unity. On the minus side, many Japanese people do not relate well to people who are not Japanese.

For example, in Japan the Korean population is not treated very well. More than 600,000 Koreans live in Japan. Although most were born in Japan and speak Japanese, they are not treated equally. The same can be said of the growing number of foreign workers living in Japan. Like the Koreans, they face a great deal of discrimination.

Another group, the *burakumin,* are also social outcasts. They are descendants of butchers and leather workers, jobs that were once thought to be unclean. Although Japanese laws ban discrimination against minorities, it is still quite common.

Perhaps Japan's greatest challenge lies in its relationships with people from other countries. Japan's relationship with its trading partners has become a problem in recent years.

Japan sells enormous numbers of cars and high technology products in other countries. However, it limits the amount of goods other countries can export for sale in Japan. This creates a **trade imbalance.** In other words, Japan sells more goods to other nations than it buys from other nations. This is good news from the Japanese point of view. It is bad news for those countries that buy more goods from Japan than they sell to Japan.

Many nations, including the United States, want Japan to fix this trade imbalance. They have asked Japan to allow more foreign goods into the country for sale—which Japan has done. Yet many think that Japan should do more.

The Japanese feel that they are simply being blamed for the economic problems of other countries. They point out that some countries, like the United States, also have favorable trade imbalances—just not with Japan.

Role in the World

In 1945 a U.S. newspaper reporter looked at the bombed-out nation of Japan and predicted that Japan would return to being a small, self-contained nation. Take one look at modern Japan, and you will realize that this reporter was very wrong.

Today other nations expect that Japan will become a leader in world affairs. They want it to play a bigger role in areas such as keeping world peace. So far the Japanese have not decided what their role should be. Still, Japan's future seems bright. Relying on its people and proud heritage, Japan's economic success is likely to continue. ■

▼ *Japan has a number of foreign aid programs. In this photograph, South African students are participating in a program designed to teach new ways of increasing agricultural production.*

■ *What problems do the Japanese face in their relations with trade partners?*

R E V I E W

1. **FOCUS** What factors have led to Japan's economic success?
2. **CULTURE** What is it like to work for one of Japan's large companies?
3. **ECONOMICS** Why does a strong economy rely on a good school system?
4. **CRITICAL THINKING** What might other nations do if Japan does not try to correct its trade imbalance?
5. **ACTIVITY** Many Japanese companies think of their employees as family members. In what ways does your classroom work as a family? Make a chart that compares your family with your classroom. Compare such things as goals, decision making, relationships, and so forth.

Japanese and U.S. Schools

*Y*ou can learn a great deal about another country by finding out about its schools. Education is one way in which a society passes its values and knowledge to the next generation. What is school like in Japan?

Find Out

Look for answers to each of your questions. If an answer gives you an idea for another question, add it to your list.

Divide your information into two groups: ways in which U.S. and Japanese schools are alike and ways in which they are different. Did you find more similarities or more differences?

▲ *Who cleans your school? In Japan the students themselves sweep the floors of their classrooms daily.*

➤ *This is the cover of a seventh-grade textbook popular in Japan. Japanese seventh graders spend more time on social studies than on any other subject except Japanese.*

Get Ready

You'll need a notebook, a pen, and some books or magazines with information about schools in Japan.

Make a list of questions you want to answer: What time does school begin and end for Japanese students your age? Do they have dress codes? What about after-school sports? Do students move from class to class? Does one teacher handle all subjects? What subjects do Japanese schools teach? How much homework do teachers give?

新編 **新しい社会**(地理)

Move Ahead

Tape a large sheet of paper to the wall of your classroom. Each student should mention a question that he or she asked. Use the questions to create categories on the chart. For instance, some people may have asked about school hours. If so, a student might write on the chart: Hours in School per Day (or Week).

Do everyone's answers agree? If not, find out where the information came from. Is one magazine or book more recent than another? Does one author have more experience than another?

When the chart has been completed, discuss the information. What Japanese ideas would you like U.S. schools to adopt? Why?

Explore Some More

Choose another area of life in the United States, one you're very familiar with. It might be sports, games, crafts, music, art, or some current concern—animal welfare, the environment, or political campaigns, for instance.

Find out if any Japanese share your interest. If so, do they pursue it in the same way? If not, can you find out why not?

▲ *The symbol of the carp—a fish that swims against river currents—is often flown on Children's Day. It inspires boys and girls to face life's difficulties with courage.*

◄ *Dolls' Day is a school holiday in Japan celebrated on March 3rd. On Dolls' Day young girls display their dolls and hold tea parties where they serve little cakes iced with peach-blossom frosting.*

Chapter Review

Reviewing Key Terms

feudalism (p. 367)
gross national product
   (p. 374)
homogeneous (p. 378)
isolation (p. 362)
samurai (p. 367)

Shinto (p. 362)
shogun (p. 366)
standard of living (p. 376)
trade imbalance (p. 379)
westernize (p. 371)

A. Use a dictionary to find the origins or the definitions of the following words. Then explain how the meaning of each word applies to the history or culture of Japan.

1. homogeneous
2. isolation
3. Shinto
4. samurai
5. shogun

B. Each statement below contains one or more key terms from the chapter. Decide whether the statement is correct or incorrect. Give reasons to support your decision using information in the chapter.

1. In <u>westernizing</u> Japan, the Meiji leaders adopted many ideas from China.
2. During its period of <u>isolation</u>, Japan carried out a brisk trade with foreign nations.
3. Food in Japan is expensive because the Japanese people have such a high <u>gross national product</u>.
4. Like Japan, the United States has a <u>homogeneous</u> population.
5. The current <u>trade imbalance</u> with Japan has caused problems for the United States.

Exploring Concepts

A. Feudalism began in Japan in the 800s and lasted into the 1800s. Copy the following outline and fill in all the blank spaces.

  Feudalism in Japan
    I. What feudalism is
      A.
      B. Laws uphold a strict social order
        1. Shogun
          a. controls almost every part of Japanese life
          b.
        2. *Daimyo*
          a.
          b.
        3. Samurai
          a.
          b.
        4. Peasants
    II. Why feudalism developed
      A.
      B.

B. Answer each question with information from the chapter.

1. What influence did Prince Shotōku and the Heian period have on Japanese culture?
2. What influence did the samurai have on Japanese values? How have these values contributed to Japan's economic success in recent years?
3. How did Japanese society change during the period of isolation in the 1600s and 1700s?
4. What changes occurred in Japan during the Meiji Restoration?
5. How were the Heian and Meiji periods similar?
6. What is it like to live in Japan today?
7. How has the role of women changed in modern Japanese society?
8. What evidence exists today of Western influence in Japan?
9. What challenges does Japan face in the coming years?

Reviewing Skills

1. Look at the World Population cartogram on page 689. Compare the population of Japan with the populations of India and China. Compare this cartogram with the cartogram on page 375. What do these cartograms tell you about the relationship between Japan's economy and its population?
2. Look at the painting on page 360. What was the artist's purpose in painting this picture? Who are the figures in the painting? What are they doing? What does this painting tell you about the Japanese people?
3. What information would you need in order to compare the location of Tokyo with that of Washington, D.C.? Where would you find that information?

Using Critical Thinking

1. Other than its mild climate, ample rainfall, and the sea, Japan has few natural resources. How has this fact influenced the course of Japanese history?
2. Both the Tokugawas and the Meiji leaders feared that Japan might fall under the rule of powerful foreigners. Yet, each government reacted very differently to the threat. How did each government try to protect Japan? Why do you think the policies were so different?
3. Japanese schools and companies put great stress on working hard and on being part of the group. Do you think this is true of schools and companies in the United States today? Give some examples to support your answer.
4. Today, other nations in the world look to Japan to become a leader in world affairs. So far, the Japanese have not decided what their role should be. Why do you think Japan may be reluctant to become a leader in world affairs?

Preparing for Citizenship

1. WRITING ACTIVITY The Japanese have shown an appreciation for the beauties of the natural world throughout their history. They often express their appreciation through poetry, such as haiku. A haiku is a Japanese lyric poem of a fixed, 17-syllable form. The first line contains words that equal five syllables. The second line contains words that equal seven syllables. The third line contains words that equal five syllables. Haiku poetry is usually simple, and it usually captures a mood about a scene in nature or a season. Write a haiku poem. Choose your words carefully to stir the reader's imagination.
2. ARTS ACTIVITY The traditional Japanese home was built to adapt to Japan's hot, humid summers and short, cold winters. Design a home that is well suited to the region where you live. Share the drawing with your classmates.
3. GROUP ACTIVITY Japanese people value cooperation, hard work, and loyalty. Working in small groups, make a list of the values that are important to you and your group. Then try to think of ways to foster these attitudes in your classmates. Share your ideas with the class.
4. COLLABORATIVE LEARNING After World War II, many people in the United States believed that the best way to build a peaceful future was to help Japan rebuild. In small groups, debate the following proposition: "Resolved, that the United States' decision to help rebuild Japan has helped build world peace." Two or three students should present arguments in support of the proposition that a healthy Japan was more likely to be a friend than an enemy. Two or three others should present arguments against the proposition that the Japanese should assume full responsibility for rebuilding the nation. Another student should act as moderator. Hold the debate for the class.

383

Chapter 17

Southeast Asia

Gold, silks, spices, and precious gems lured the traders and explorers who made their way to Asia. The mainland and islands of Southeast Asia—including Vietnam, the Philippines, and Indonesia—lie at the southern doorway of Asia, surrounded by oceans. As people from Southwest Asia and Europe braved the unknown seas ever more boldly, they discovered that the region between China and India had treasures of its own.

Shadow puppets like these have entertained the people of Indonesia for centuries. They may be used today to tell an ancient Hindu legend or to instruct the people about a government policy.

This Buddha is part of Borobudur, the largest Buddhist temple in the world. Located on the island of Java, it was built in the 700s and 800s.

500	800	1100

700

c. 700–1250 Arab traders set up trading routes to India, China, and Southeast Asia. They bring Islam to the area.

Supporters of former Philippine president Corazón
Aquino celebrate her victory over Ferdinand Marcos
at Camp Crane in the Philippines.

The many religious festivals in the Philippines
reflect the people's Christian heritage. Carved
wooden masks are worn each year to act out
the Easter story.

1898 The United States defeats Spain
in the Spanish-American War.

1400

1700

2000

1521 Ferdinand Magellan claims what
is now the Philippines for Spain and
brings Christianity to the area.

1957–1975 The Vietnam War is fought
between Communist North Vietnam
and U.S.-backed South Vietnam.

385

Today

LESSON 1

The Geography of Southeast Asia

THINKING FOCUS

How has Southeast Asia's geography affected its cultural history?

Near the shores of a lovely land
Where waves splatter on sand
And foam spreads in white bands
The green sea sprouts islands

Covered with noble mountains,
Islands set in the ocean like fountains
Of beauty: my home, my Indonesia.

Mohammad Yamin

With these words an Indonesian poet describes the beauty of his homeland in Southeast Asia. In this lesson you will learn how the ocean and geography of this region have played a key role in its history.

Key Terms

- archipelago
- typhoon

▼ *Beautiful Komodo, an island in southern Indonesia, is home to the Komodo dragons—the largest known lizards.*

A Region Bounded by Ocean

Southeast Asia lies to the south of China and to the east of India. It includes two different land areas: mainland and island Southeast Asia.

The Mainland and the Islands

Mainland Southeast Asia is on an Asian peninsula. Rugged, tall mountain ranges and a series of rivers run from north to south.

River valleys along these rivers have rich, moist soil ideal for growing crops. Similar to the river valleys of Egypt, India, and China, the rivers and their floodplains here support life and civilization. The rivers also provide water highways for travel, trade, and the shipment of goods. Vietnam, Thailand, Myanmar (once called Burma), Cambodia, Laos, and Malaysia make up mainland Southeast Asia today.

Indonesia, the Philippines, Singapore, and Brunei are islands or parts of island groups. These island groups are called

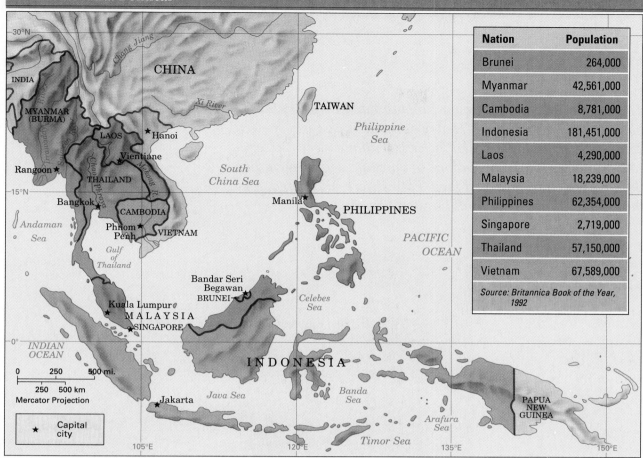

Nation	Population
Brunei	264,000
Myanmar	42,561,000
Cambodia	8,781,000
Indonesia	181,451,000
Laos	4,290,000
Malaysia	18,239,000
Philippines	62,354,000
Singapore	2,719,000
Thailand	57,150,000
Vietnam	67,589,000
Source: Britannica Book of the Year, 1992	

archipelagoes *(ahr kuh PEHL uh gohz)*. Most of the islands were formed by volcanoes, some of which are still active. You can read about a recent eruption of a volcano in the Philippines in A Closer Look on page 388.

Climate and Resources

Most of Southeast Asia has a wet, hot climate. The average daily temperature is 80°F, and the average annual rainfall is 60 inches. This climate supports the growth of rain forests. In May, strong, moist monsoon winds blow in from the sea. Although the monsoons can cause drastic floods, their rains are needed for the growing of rice, the major food crop.

The dry season begins when the monsoons switch direction in October. When these winds shift, violent storms called **typhoons** *(ty FOONZ)* often occur. They are similar to the hurricanes that strike the United States in autumn. Typhoons can result in huge damage and loss of life.

The climate of Southeast Asia is ideal for growing spices such as the cloves found in the Moluccas *(muh LUHK uhz),* or Spice Islands, of eastern Indonesia. Long ago, spices such as pepper, cinnamon, nutmeg, and cloves were extremely valuable. They were used to flavor and preserve foods, and even as medicines. So nations competed to get these spices.

Early traders came to the region for other resources, too. These included gold and gems such as sapphires and diamonds. Today, tin, crude petroleum, teak, and rubber are major resources of the region. ■

▲ *The chart above lists each nation of Southeast Asia with recent population figures. Find each nation on the map. Which nation has the lowest population?*

■ *How are mainland and island Southeast Asia alike and different, in terms of physical geography and climate?*

Volcanoes

The 5,770-foot cone of Mount Pinatubo in the Philippines blew up on June 15, 1991. Heavy ash and thick gases spewed 25 miles high and blackened the sky. Within a week, 26 separate eruptions rained down tons of volcanic debris, including pumice, which is hardened lava. Farms were smothered, and thousand of homes and buildings collapsed.

Quiet for 600 years, Mount Pinatubo showed signs of an eruption in time for scientists to alert nearby people. Many safely left the area.

Like these fields in Bali, farmlands near Mount Pinatubo will become fertile again. Ash enriches the soil, but it may take hundreds of years.

Volcanic pumice

A Crossroads of Many Cultures

Since ancient times the sea has linked Southeast Asia with the rest of the world. This region is located halfway between the major trading centers of India and China. Thus, Southeast Asia became a busy intersection of ocean trade and exploration. For centuries traders and seafarers from many parts of the world have sailed in and out of its ports. Many have left cultural influences on the region.

India and China

Four thousand years ago, very advanced civilizations existed along the Indus River in India and the Chang Jiang (or Yangtze River) in China. You read about these civilizations in Chapter 5.

Indian and Chinese traders traveled to Southeast Asia in search of riches. After finding out how valuable the resources of the region were, some of these traders settled in Southeast Asia. Wealthy from trade profits and well educated, they gained power. They married native Southeast Asians and started families. They brought their own cultures to the region, including the religions of Hinduism and Buddhism. Indian and Chinese languages, literature, art, and architecture also became part of the culture of Southeast Asia.

Soon other traders from distant lands discovered that Southeast Asia was a region of riches and a convenient stop between China and India. Beginning in the eighth century, Arab traders from the Middle East established trading colonies in India, China, and Africa. They also set up profitable trading centers in Southeast Asia itself. Today most people of Malaysia and Indonesia practice Islam, the religion that the early Arabian traders brought with them many centuries ago.

East Meets West

In the 1400s, European traders arrived from the West. The Portuguese set up trading bases in the Spice Islands. The Dutch, English, and French came, too. Wanting to share in the riches, Spain sent the explorer Ferdinand Magellan to stake claims. As you will read, Magellan's arrival in 1521 changed forever the history and culture of the Philippines. ■

The vinta boat above is one of a large variety of small, wooden boats used for fishing and inter-island transportation. They continue to sail the oceans of Southeast Asia much as they have for hundreds of years.

■ *How did Southeast Asia's geography and natural resources lead other cultures to the region's door?*

R E V I E W

1. **FOCUS** How has Southeast Asia's geography affected its cultural history?

2. **GEOGRAPHY** What role have rivers played in the development of Southeast Asian civilization?

3. **ECONOMICS** What attracted traders from Europe, the Middle East, and other parts of Asia to Southeast Asia?

4. **CRITICAL THINKING** Compare the benefits of living along river valleys in Southeast Asia today with the benefits of living in ancient river valley civilizations.

5. **MAPPING ACTIVITY** Draw a map to show the routes that early Chinese and Indian traders may have taken to and from Southeast Asia.

LESSON 2

The Philippines

What factors shaped Philippine history?

Key Terms

- circumnavigate
- galleon
- mestizo
- martial law

➤ *The portrait at right is of Ferdinand Magellan. The first circumnavigation of the world, completed by Magellan's crew after his death, added greatly to the world's geographic knowledge.*

It is 1519. You are sailing on one of five wooden ships—all smaller than modern-day tugboats. The fleet captain is Ferdinand Magellan, a Portuguese explorer. King Charles I of Spain has sent Magellan to find a western route to the Spice Islands.

The voyage drags on for almost two years. Often the ships are damaged by rough seas. The food runs out, so you eat rats, sawdust, and boiled leather straps. The drinking water is dirty and full of bugs. You watch many of your shipmates die. You are thin, tired, sick, and almost without hope.

Then one morning, you spy mountain peaks on the misty horizon. Soon your small fleet reaches the rocky, palm-fringed coast of an island. You see many other islands dotting the calm waters. You are able to get rice, fruit, and fresh water at one of these islands. At last, you are saved!

Exploration and Colonial History

Magellan and his crew planted the Spanish flag on the shore of what is now the Philippines. One month later, Magellan was killed when he took sides in a war between local peoples. However, his 18 surviving crew members completed the westward voyage back to Spain. They were the first Europeans to **circumnavigate** *(sur kuhm NAV ih gayt),* or sail around, the world.

Magellan's arrival led to three centuries of Spanish control of the Philippine archipelago. It soon became a Spanish colony named Islas Filipinas *(EEZ lahs fee lee PEE nahs),* or

the Philippine Islands, in honor of the king of Spain, Philip II.

Spanish Colonial Rule

The first Spanish settlement in the Philippines was founded in 1565 on the island of Cebu *(seh BOO).* Then, in 1571, the colonial capital was established in Manila on the western coast of the island of Luzon. A governor-general, appointed by the king of Spain, ruled the colony.

Spanish priests traveled throughout the islands converting the Filipinos to Catholicism, the religion of Spain. Church leaders and

Manila Galleon Trade Routes, 1565–1815

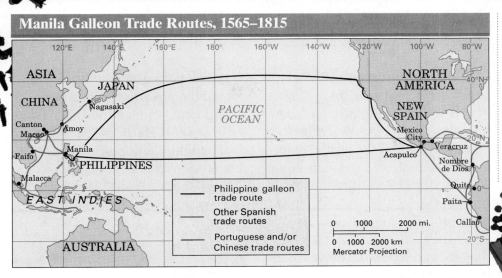

◀ A round trip for the Manila galleons usually took about a year. About how many miles was the voyage from Mexico back to the Philippines?

▲ Spices like the cinnamon sticks, nutmeg, and peppercorns shown above were part of the galleon shipments.

other Spaniards took control of the land. Soon the Spanish colonizers forced the native people to work for them and to pay taxes to Spain.

Filipino laborers were used, for example, to build galleons for the Spanish. **Galleons** were large three-masted sailing ships used mostly for trade. The galleons built in the Philippines became known as the Manila galleons because Manila was the major port through which goods flowed from east and west. For 250 years, these Spanish galleons sailed the trade route shown on the map above.

Chinese traders brought silks, spices, gems, and items created by Chinese artists to Manila. In Manila, these and other goods from Southeast Asia were loaded onto galleons bound for Mexico and the coast of what is now California. There the goods were traded for silver, which the Chinese desired as payment. Then the galleons returned to Manila to load up with goods again. From Mexico, many of the goods were shipped across the country to the Gulf of Mexico, then across the Atlantic Ocean to Europe.

As a rich trading center, Manila attracted a large group of wealthy Chinese merchants. Many of these merchants married Filipino women, and their children became known as **mestizos** (mehs TEE zohs). The mestizos became a new, well-educated, wealthy middle class.

This powerful new middle class rebelled and started a revolution against the Spanish colonial government in 1896. When a truce seemed near, however, the United States came on the scene.

The United States was trying to help Cuba, a Caribbean colony of Spain. Cuba is a large island about 90 miles off the southern coast of Florida. In 1898 the United States declared war against Spain and won the war in four months. As part of the treaty at the end of the Spanish-American War, Spain gave Cuba its independence. Spain gave control of Puerto Rico, Guam, and the Philippines to the U.S. for $20 million. Thus, the Filipinos' fight for independence was ignored. Instead, the Philippines became a colony ruled by the United States.

U.S. Colonial Rule

The Filipinos rebelled against their new colonial masters—the United States. By the time the

391

Southeast Asia

United States crushed the rebellion, about 200,000 Filipinos had died in the fighting.

Colonization eventually led to improved health services, police departments, military forces, and schools. However, at first many Filipinos disliked the use of English in their schools and the increasing influence of U.S. culture.

In 1934 leaders of the Philippines and the United States made an agreement. During a 10-year period, the Filipinos would take control of the government. Then in 1941 Japan bombed the U.S. naval base at Pearl Harbor in Hawaii and invaded the Philippines. Thus, the United States and its Philippine colony entered World War II. ■

■ *In what specific ways did the cultures of Spain, China, and the United States affect the history of the Philippines?*

➤ *Colorful new "jeepneys" used as taxis are now made in the Philippines. Filipinos made the first jeepneys by adapting jeeps left behind by the United States after World War II.*

World War II and the Postwar Years

U.S. and Filipino troops fought together in the Philippines against Japan. The U.S. general Douglas MacArthur led these combined forces. In April 1942, Japanese troops defeated the U.S. and Filipino forces on the Bataan *(buh TAN)* Peninsula. Victorious, Japan declared the Philippines free of U.S. colonial rule.

Japanese Occupation

Japan set up an "independent" Philippine republic. However, the Japanese military leaders retained strict control.

In 1944 General MacArthur and U.S. troops returned to the Philippines to fight again. In August 1945, the United States dropped two atom bombs on Japan. Japan surrendered and World War II was over.

On July 4, 1946, the Philippines gained total independence at last. The United States provided aid to rebuild after the war. Much of the old colonial relationship continued.

Many wealthy Filipinos, who had cooperated with the Japanese, became the leaders of the new nation. The poor had openly resisted Japanese control during the war. This created a split between the rich and the poor that continued long after the war. When the people

rebelled, Filipino leaders used military force to control unrest.

In 1965, when Philippine army officer Ferdinand Marcos was elected their president, the people believed that the pattern would change. Marcos promised economic reforms to help the poor. He also promised to change treaties to limit the influence of the United States in the Philippines.

From Marcos to Aquino

Ferdinand Marcos kept few of his promises. Seven years after he became president, he declared a state of **martial law.** That is, he placed the country under the rule of the military forces. Marcos claimed that only under martial law could he maintain democracy and strict law and order.

Under martial law, Marcos had tremendous power. He and his wife Imelda became very rich, while most Filipinos remained poor. Thousands who opposed Marcos went to jail or "disappeared." In 1983 Senator Benigno Aquino *(beh NEEG noh ah KEE noh),* an important opposition leader, was killed.

His murder horrified and united many Filipinos. In February 1986 they tried to get rid of Marcos through a presidential election. Their candidate was Aquino's widow, Corazón "Cory" Aquino. Even though the election was proved to be a fraud, the government still declared Marcos the winner.

Filipinos were angry, and some of Marcos's own officials were, too. Army Deputy Chief of Staff Fidel Ramos and Defense Minister Juan Ponce Enrile *(ahn REEL ay)* quit. They formed a resistance movement to try to get rid of Marcos.

On February 22, 1986, Marcos sent army tanks to defeat Ramos and Enrile. In response, the Roman Catholic cardinal of Manila spoke on the radio. He urged all citizens to support and protect the resistance leaders.

What happened next became known as the People Power uprising. Nuns and priests, teachers and students, farmers, police officers, business leaders, and mothers with little children formed a barrier across the road leading to the resistance camp. Most wore a yellow ribbon, the symbol of Aquino. The nuns knelt down at the front of the crowd. The tanks hurtled toward them but then stopped. For four days the courageous, nonviolent crowd held off the military forces of Marcos. His soldiers never got through the barrier to the resistance camp.

The People Power uprising succeeded in toppling the corrupt government of Ferdinand Marcos. He and his wife fled the Philippines, and Corazón Aquino became president.

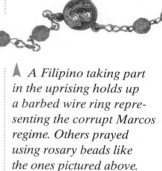

▲ *A Filipino taking part in the uprising holds up a barbed wire ring representing the corrupt Marcos regime. Others prayed using rosary beads like the ones pictured above.*

◄ *Under the watch of armed soldiers sent by Marcos, a crowd of Aquino supporters, including several nuns in the foreground, listens to a priest during the uprising.*

393

Southeast Asia

The Philippines Today

It is up to you to bring to the life you are entering, to the state you must help to form, an energy of true religious faith.

Pope Pius XII

Corazón Aquino had selected these words to appear in her high school yearbook. As president, she put them into action to try to restore civil rights, reform the government, and encourage economic growth. However, she faced many problems, including continued resistance from rebel groups.

In 1992 the first peaceful election in over 25 years took place in the Philippines. The Filipinos chose a new president, Fidel Ramos—the man who had helped to defeat Marcos. He is trying to improve the economy. In recent years, lack of jobs has led to the migration of thousands of Filipinos to the United States and other nations. Land reform is also needed to allow more Filipinos to own their own land.

Approximately 62 million people live in the Philippines today. One of every eight people lives in or around Manila, the center of the government and the economy.

About two-thirds of all the country's industries are located there.

The educational system is strong in the Philippines, and the literacy rate is high. According to 1990 figures, about 90 percent of the population aged 15 and over can read and write.

Almost 70 native languages and dialects are spoken in the Philippines. The most widely spoken language is Pilipino *(pihl uh PEE noh)*. It is based on Tagalog, one of the earliest languages. English is also widely spoken.

Today's Filipinos are a people of many different heritages. Malay, Spanish, Chinese, Arab, Japanese, and U.S. influences reflect the nation's history. The Philippines is the only Asian nation that is mostly Christian. ■

➤ *Filipinos today are proud of their heritage. These girls from the Philippine island of Mindanao are wearing traditional, brightly colored, beaded outfits.*

■ *Beginning with World War II, what are the events in Philippine history that led to independence?*

R E V I E W

1. **FOCUS** What factors shaped Philippine history?
2. **CULTURE** Describe the trade route between China, the Philippines, and North America under Spanish colonial rule.
3. **SOCIAL SYSTEMS** What did the Filipinos do to bring down the government of Ferdinand Marcos?
4. **CRITICAL THINKING** Imagine that you are a Filipino student. You have studied your nation's history and ways in which the United States both aided and controlled the Philippines. How do you feel about the United States? Explain why some Filipinos may be pro-United States and others may not be.
5. **WRITING ACTIVITY** Imagine that you are one of the participants in the People Power uprising. Write two or three journal entries describing everything that you saw and heard and the people whom you met. Tell what feelings and beliefs led you to oppose Ferdinand Marcos and to join Cory Aquino's followers.

LESSON 3

Singapore, Indonesia, and Vietnam

An Asian legend tells of a seventh-century Sumatran prince exploring an island off the Malay Peninsula. From offshore, he sees a black-faced tiger. Thinking it is a lion, he names the island Singa Pur, meaning "lion city" in the ancient language of Sanskrit.

In 1857 alone, wild tigers roaming Singapore's tropical forests carried off 300 human victims! Today, tiny Singapore is known as one of the Four Tigers of Asia because of its startling, recent economic success. How did a tiny, tiger-filled rain forest become a major center of business and trade?

THINKING FOCUS

How do Singapore, Indonesia, and Vietnam reflect the wide variety of cultures in Southeast Asia today?

Singapore: A Thriving City-State

In 1819 the East India Company, a large British trading firm, sent Sir Stamford Raffles to Southeast Asia. He selected Singapore as an ideal location for storing and shipping Asian goods. Singapore, lying halfway between India and China, had just the wide, deep harbor that Raffles sought.

In 1824 when Singapore became part of the British colonial empire, about 11,000 people lived there. By 1911 its population had grown to more than 250,000.

In 1965 Singapore became an independent republic. Today its population of about 2.8 million people are packed into an area of about 242 square miles—less than one-fifth the size of Rhode Island.

Today Singapore is a bustling city and one of the world's busiest ports.

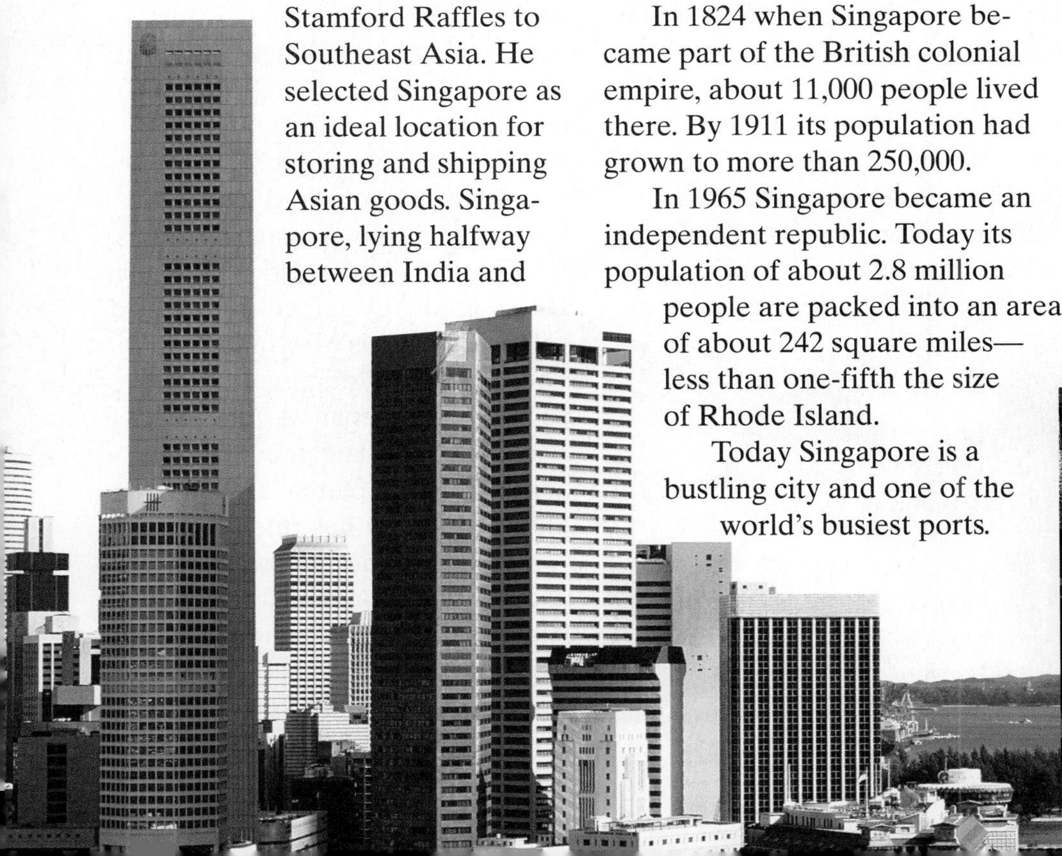

Key Term

- embargo

▼ *Below, at the left, modern high-rises in Singapore look out over the harbor waters. At the right, a woman sells fish at an open-air market.*

It is also a leading center for oil refining, shipbuilding, and manufacturing—including computer parts.

The population is a varied mix of cultures and religions. About 76 percent of the people are Chinese. They are mostly Confucianists, Buddhists, or Taoists. About 15 percent of the people are Malay Muslims. About seven percent of the people are Indian, and they are mostly Hindu.

The government of Singapore has a great deal of control over the lives of its citizens. Singapore, however, is a peaceful, well-ordered society. Most of the people of Singapore enjoy a high standard of living. The government is committed to religious and ethnic tolerance. Singapore, like its larger neighbor Indonesia, has been working to create unity out of a great diversity of peoples and cultures. ■

■ *How did Singapore's location and natural features help it to attract workers and to become a thriving nation?*

How Do We Know?

HISTORY *In 1891, Dutch scientist Eugene Dubois found a human fossil on Java. It was found in stream deposits on the Solo River. He named it Java man. Some scientists have concluded that Java man lived between 500,000 and 1 million years ago.*

▼ *This famous mosque in Banda Aceh, Indonesia, combines elements of style from Arabia and India.*

Indonesia: A Varied Nation

With a population of about 190 million people, Indonesia is the world's fifth largest country. However, its people are divided by geography. The country is made up of more than 13,600 islands, spread out across 3,000 miles of sea. So, from east to west, Indonesia covers about the same number of miles as the distance from northern Maine to southern California. More than half of the people live on the island of Java where Jakarta, the nation's capital city, is located. Many of the other islands are not inhabited.

Beginning thousands of years ago, people from diverse cultures brought many religions to Indonesia. From India came Buddhism and Hinduism. From the Middle East came Islam. From Europe came Christianity. Today about 87 percent of the people practice Islam, making Indonesia the world's largest Muslim nation.

Today the nation is committed to tolerance of its many religions, including those that combine religious practices. Many people, for example, practice a religion that combines Hinduism, Buddhism, and local customs.

The large number of ethnic groups and languages also reflect the nation's cultural diversity. There are more than 300 distinct ethnic groups in Indonesia. About 25 languages and about 250 different dialects are spoken. The national language is Bahasa Indonesia, which has its roots in Malay, the language of early Sumatran traders.

From 1619 to World War II, the Dutch gradually gained control and colonized what is now Indonesia. Then, like the Philippines, it was conquered by Japan. After World War II, Indonesia gained independence from the Dutch. Since 1967 a military dictator has ruled there.

Today Indonesia joins Singapore as a growing economic force in the Pacific Rim area of the world (see the Atlas map of the Pacific Rim region on page 684). Indonesia is a

world leader in the production and export of natural gas, petroleum, and tin. The nation is a major supplier of rubber, coffee, tea, and spices including cloves and nutmeg. Major industries process agricultural and mineral products. The nation is also a leading manufacturer of shoes. Working with Singapore, Indonesia has developed the island of Batam into a thriving industrial park. Several international companies have built manufacturing plants there. ■

▲ *The Indonesian* hudoq *dancer in the foreground is a Christian performing a traditional ceremony to protect the rice crop. A terraced rice field is shown in the background.*

■ *In what specific ways is Indonesia a nation of diversity?*

Vietnam: A War-Torn Nation

Vietnam is a narrow, S-shaped country on the eastern side of the peninsula of Indochina. It is smaller than California but has a population of about 70 million, about twice the population of California.

Throughout much of its history, Vietnam has fought fiercely to maintain its independence. About 2,000 years ago, China conquered Vietnam. Chinese settlers flooded into the region, bringing their religions and cultural influences including Buddhism and Confucianism. In A.D. 939, the Vietnamese drove out the Chinese, but conflicts with China continued for hundreds of years.

Vietnam became a French colony in 1883. Then, like many of its neighbors, it was taken over by Japan during World War II. France tried to regain its colony after the war. A Communist group called the Viet Minh, led by Ho Chi Minh *(hoh chee mihn),* defeated the French colonial power in 1954. Vietnam was divided in half by the terms of the peace treaty. A Communist government ruled North Vietnam. An anti-Communist

government supported by the United States ruled South Vietnam. Afraid that the Communists would win, the United States opposed elections that might have unified the country.

In 1957 Ho Chi Minh went to war to unite North and South Vietnam. Communist nations such as China and the former Soviet Union aided North Vietnam. The United States, France, and South Korea later sent troops to aid South Vietnam. Warfare killed hundreds of thousands of people, and much of Vietnam was in ruins. North Vietnam won the Vietnam War in 1975. Communists then reunited North and South Vietnam into one

▼ *Rice is transported along the Mekong River in Vietnam.*

In Ho Chi Minh City, where bicycles remain a major means of transportation, hopes are high for better days. The price of property has gone up in expectation of renewed relations with the West.

■ *What is life like for the people of Vietnam today?*

country. Other Communist governments took control of the neighboring nations of Laos and Cambodia.

Almost 50 years of waging war have made Vietnam one of the poorest nations in the world. Thousands of craters made by bombs dropped during the Vietnam War remain. Many buildings built by the French still stand in its two major cities, Hanoi and Ho Chi Minh City (formerly Saigon). Yet the buildings are now shabby, and few new ones have been built since the Vietnam War. There are few factories, and many city residents do not have jobs. The nation brims with natural resources, including coal, oil, and timber. However, the government

does not have the funds to build processing plants to make use of these resources.

About 75 percent of the Vietnamese live in small villages. They raise rice in the wet, fertile river valleys of the Red River and the Mekong River. Under communism, some Vietnamese work together on large farms called "collectives." They give most of their crops to the government, which distributes them to the people. Recently, the government has allowed the people to keep their crops and sell them privately. Thus, Vietnam has begun to shift to a limited market economy.

The government of Vietnam is trying to improve the economy by renewing trade with the West. However, the United States has had an **embargo,** or a ban on trade, with Vietnam. The United States wants Vietnam to end military involvement in Cambodia. Vietnam must also provide all the facts it has about U.S. military personnel missing in Vietnam since the Vietnam War. In October 1992, Vietnam began to release photos and new information about these U.S. soldiers. This action will help lead to an end to the U.S. trade embargo and to improved relations between the two nations. ■

REVIEW

1. **FOCUS** How do Singapore, Indonesia, and Vietnam reflect the wide variety of cultures in Southeast Asia today?

2. **GEOGRAPHY** Refer to the map of Southeast Asia on page 387. Compare the geography of Indonesia with the geography of Vietnam. How has their geography affected the history of these two countries?

3. **ECONOMICS** Compare and contrast the economic conditions in Singapore with those in Vietnam. Explain

the reasons for the differences.

4. **CRITICAL THINKING** You read that Singapore is extremely crowded. What problems do you think overcrowding in a city can cause? Suggest reasonable solutions for solving these problems.

5. **WRITING ACTIVITY** Imagine that you are Sir Stamford Raffles. Write a letter to the East India Company explaining why you chose this location and describing what you saw there.

Analyzing Elevation Maps

Here's Why

If you plan a bicycle route to avoid hills or to go around a lake, you are showing that you understand topography—the natural surface features of the land.

Studying topography gives you more than information about possible routes. Understanding topography can also help you find out more about the land, its people, and its wildlife. For example, understanding topography can help you study the animals in any given place.

Here's How

Imagine you are a naturalist looking for the Sumatran rhinoceros, an animal that is close to extinction. From your study, you know that the Sumatran rhinoceros feeds on bamboo and fruit. On the island of Sumatra, this rhinoceros lives only in highlands and mountain forests.

How would you plan a trip that would take you across the island of Sumatra in search of this rhinoceros? You might begin by looking at the map and the diagram on this page.

The map uses color to show different ranges in elevation, or height, above sea level. The key shows the elevations represented by each color. The diagram below the map shows the elevation of one route across the island of Sumatra.

Study both the map and the diagram. Based on what you know about the rhino and the information on the map, would you expect to find the Sumatran rhinoceros along this route? Why or why not?

Try It

Your friend is a naturalist studying the clouded leopard, another endangered animal living in Sumatra. According to her information, the clouded leopard lives in evergreen forests that range from sea level to a height of 6,600 feet. Your friend wants to study the clouded leopard in the wild. Would you invite your friend to join you on your route? Would this leopard be likely to live at the top of Mount Kerinci?

Apply It

Research an animal found in your state. At what altitudes does it live? Find a topographic map of your state in an atlas. Use the map to pinpoint areas in your state where the animal would most likely be found.

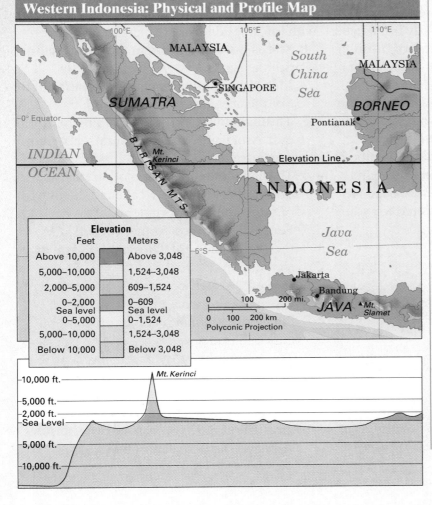

Western Indonesia: Physical and Profile Map

Elevation

Feet		Meters
Above 10,000		Above 3,048
5,000–10,000		1,524–3,048
2,000–5,000		609–1,524
0–2,000 Sea level 0–5,000		0–609 Sea level 0–1,524
5,000–10,000		1,524–3,048
Below 10,000		Below 3,048

Southeast Asia

Chapter Review

Reviewing Key Terms

archipelago (p. 387)
circumnavigate (p. 390)
embargo (p. 398)
galleon (p. 391)

martial law (p. 392)
mestizo (p. 391)
typhoon (p. 387)

A. Answer the following questions regarding selected key terms.
1. What is a <u>galleon</u>? What is a <u>typhoon</u>? What might happen to a galleon caught in a severe typhoon?
2. What is meant by the term <u>martial</u> <u>law</u>? Under a system of martial law, what jobs could a nation's ruler give to soldiers?
3. What might occur if the United States declared an <u>embargo</u> on Indonesia?
4. What two cultural groups intermarried to create the first <u>mestizos</u> in Southeast Asia? What success did the <u>mestizos</u> gain?

B. Write a brief definition of the following key terms. Then draw a labeled diagram or picture to illustrate the term's meaning.
1. circumnavigate
2. archipelago

Exploring Concepts

A. Throughout history, the cultures of Southeast Asian nations have been greatly influenced by outside factors. Summarize a few of those outside influences by copying and completing the chart below. The first column lists specific cultures that came to Southeast Asia. Fill in the second column by listing a Southeast Asian nation that shows a lasting influence from that culture. Fill in the final column with a specific example of what the outside culture brought, built, or established in the Southeast Asian nation. The first line has been completed for you as an example.

Outside Culture	Nation	Influence
Spain	Philippines	Roman Catholicism
China		
England		
Arabia		
United States		

B. Support each of the following statements with information from the chapter.
1. Spices were important in the early history of Southeast Asia.
2. Monsoons are both helpful and harmful to Southeast Asia.
3. Throughout its history, the region of Southeast Asia has been a busy intersection for ocean trade.
4. The Japanese occupation of Southeast Asia during World War II weakened the power of the colonial governments.
5. Ferdinand Marcos, former president of the Philippines, ruled his nation with tremendous power.
6. Peaceful resistance by the Philippine people drove Marcos from office.
7. Singapore is a major center of world business and trade.
8. The geography of Indonesia has contributed to the existence of many different languages, religions, ethnic groups, and cultures.
9. The nation of Vietnam has suffered throughout much of its history because of wars and the destruction they caused.

Reviewing Skills

1. Look at the map at the right. Construct a vertical profile of the land at 16°N. What is the highest elevation shown on your vertical profile? What is the lowest elevation shown on your vertical profile?

2. Look at the top photo on page 393. Explain what the barbed wire and yellow ribbon symbolized to the People Power uprising. In your opinion, why did they choose barbed wire as a symbol? Why did they choose a yellow ribbon?

3. Imagine that you are building a museum exhibit that will represent the diversity of Southeast Asia—its land features, its resources, and its ethnic and cultural groups. How would you gather, plan, and organize your ideas and materials?

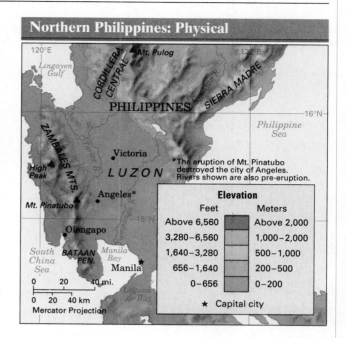

Northern Philippines: Physical

*The eruption of Mt. Pinatubo destroyed the city of Angeles. Rivers shown are also pre-eruption.

Elevation

Feet	Meters
Above 6,560	Above 2,000
3,280–6,560	1,000–2,000
1,640–3,280	500–1,000
656–1,640	200–500
0–656	0–200

★ Capital city

0   20   40 mi.

0   20   40 km
Mercator Projection

Using Critical Thinking

1. Describe the "collective" system of farming that has been practiced by many Vietnamese rice growers. How does this system differ from farming in a free market economy? In your opinion, what are the benefits of collective farming? What are the drawbacks?

2. Magellan's ships were severely damaged during the long voyage that led to the Spaniards arriving at the Philippines. How might the history and modern-day culture of the Philippines have been different if Magellan's ships had never reached their destination?

3. To keep the streets clean, the government of Singapore does not allow people to chew gum. Do you think this is a fair law, or is it too strict? Suggest other ways that the government might solve the problem. Explain why your ideas might be better.

Preparing for Citizenship

1. **COLLECTING INFORMATION** Gather articles and photographs from current newspapers and magazines about recent events and daily life in the nations of Southeast Asia. Include any information you can find about politics, economics, or any other interesting topics. Share your information with the rest of the class.

2. **WRITING ACTIVITY** Imagine that you are the new leader of Indonesia. Write a plan of at least three steps you would take to try to unify the peoples of your diverse nation.

3. **COLLABORATIVE LEARNING** In your community there may be people who have first-hand information regarding past or present events in Southeast Asia. With a partner, brainstorm for ideas concerning individuals you might interview together. You might talk with an Asian who emigrated to the United States, or with a soldier who served in World War II or the Vietnam War. With your partner, prepare your questions. During the interview, listen carefully. Then work together to present your findings to the class. If you cannot conduct an interview, do research with your partner to answer the questions, and then present your findings to the class.

Europe and Russia

Past meets present everywhere one looks in Europe. As this Renaissance painting by Raphael shows, the past can be inspiring. However, the past can also serve as a haunting reminder. As the Spanish-born philosopher George Santayana warned, "Those who cannot remember the past are condemned to repeat it." European history has been bloody. In this century, two world wars started here and only ended after the deaths of tens of millions of people. Today, Europeans struggle to overcome their conflicts from the past. Can they find common ground on which to build a peaceful future?

A.D. 476

School of Athens, *a fresco painted by the Italian artist Raphael between 1508 and 1511*

Europe and Russia

Europe is the smallest continent of the world except for Australia. Hundreds of islands and peninsulas make Europe's coast rough and jagged. Away from the coast, however, much of Europe is a wide, fertile plain reaching far into Russia. Yet Europe also has high and beautiful mountains—including the Alps. Great rivers serve as major transportation routes.

Beginning in England in the 1760s, people turned from farms to factories to make their living. New machines helped people make goods much more quickly than in the past. People flocked to where the factories were—in the cities. Today in some nations more than 90 percent of the people live in cities. Europe is a world leader in industry. European goods include machinery, automobiles, and steel.

▲ Most Europeans live in city neighborhoods where shops and markets are within walking distance.

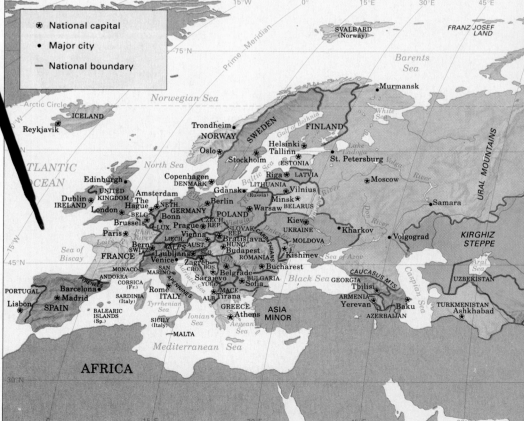

Moscow, the capital of the former Soviet Union, lies in a part of Russia that has short summers and long, cold winters. Those who go to Red Square today can still see the Kremlin, once the center of government.

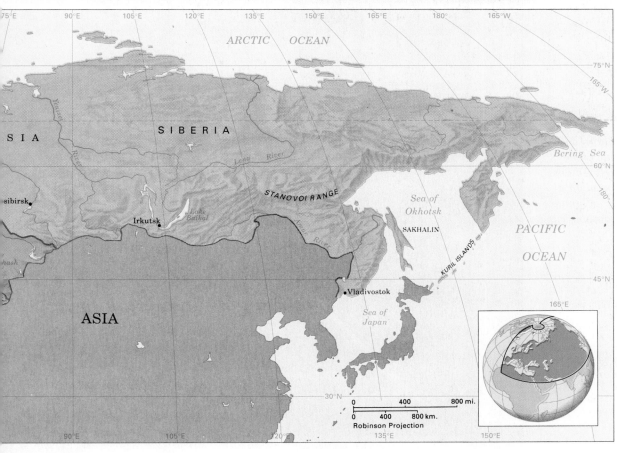

ARCTIC OCEAN

75°N

SIBERIA

Bering Sea

60°N

STANOVOI RANGE

Sea of Okhotsk

PACIFIC

OCEAN

SAKHALIN

Irkutsk

Lena River

Lake Baikal

sibirsk

S I A

hash

ASIA

Vladivostok

45°N

KURIL ISLANDS

Sea of Japan

165°E

30°N

0   400   800 mi.

0   400   800 km.

Robinson Projection

405

Europe and Russia

The Land and People

French, Spanish, Romanian, Dutch, Greek, Russian—these are some of the many languages spoken in Europe. From the Mediterranean to the Bering Sea, the people of Europe and Russia speak many languages. They also follow many different traditions.

Europe and Russia's many cultural groups have often found it difficult to feel united. Europeans have fought many wars among themselves. Today, most Europeans hope that people from across the continent can work together to solve problems involving the environment, trade, and ethnic conflict.

➤ *Acid rain is formed when gases released by burning oil, coal, and gas mix with water vapor in the air. These acids can be carried hundreds of miles. Acid rain can damage trees and buildings.*

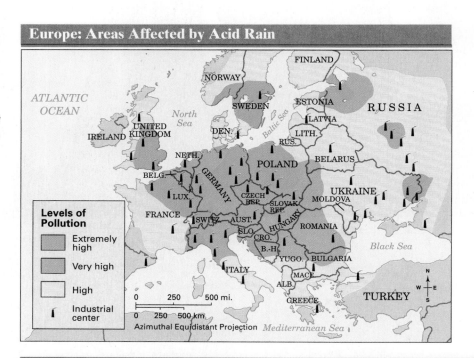

Europe: Areas Affected by Acid Rain

Levels of Pollution
- Extremely high
- Very high
- High
- Industrial center

0   250   500 mi.
0   250   500 km
Azimuthal Equidistant Projection

➤ *The alpenhorn dates back to the time of the Roman Empire. Herders and villagers used the instrument for communication and entertainment.*

➤ *Edelweiss grows throughout Europe's alpine region.*

European artists have contributed great literature, music, and painting to the world. Some of the world's most valuable art is housed in the Louvre in Paris. The Louvre was once a palace, home to the kings and queens of France. Today, it is one of the world's largest museums.

Another important European contribution to the world is the British system of government. Great Britain's representative form of government provided an ideal for its colonies throughout the world. When they became independent, many of these colonies adopted Britain's system of government. The most important branch of the British Parliament is the House of Commons, which holds most of the government's power.

▲ *Both old and new architecture greet visitors to the Louvre.*

▲ *The queen of England, Elizabeth II, opens Parliament in the spring of 1992.*

▼ *England and France have cooperated to build a huge tunnel under the English Channel. Sometimes called the Chunnel, the new tunnel will help unify Europe.*

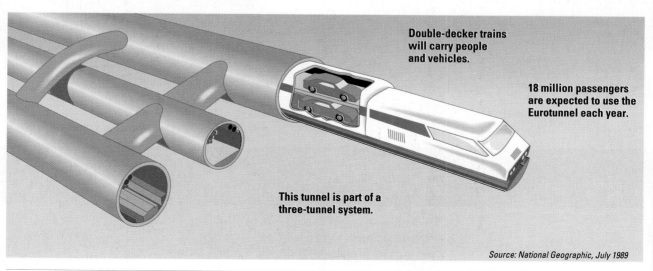

Double-decker trains will carry people and vehicles.

18 million passengers are expected to use the Eurotunnel each year.

This tunnel is part of a three-tunnel system.

Source: National Geographic, July 1989

Chapter 18
The Making of Europe

After the fall of the Roman Empire in A.D. 476, another great power rose from its ruins—the Christian church. People of Europe turned to the Church for protection and guidance. For more than 1,000 years, the Church towered over Europe. It was Europe's most powerful institution. Then, the rise of new ideas changed the way Europeans viewed themselves and the world.

In this painting from the Middle Ages, peasant life looks peaceful and happy. In reality, it wasn't. Most European peasants had a hard life and usually died by their thirties.

This gold and silver container shows domes that are typical of Byzantine architecture.

800–1054 After years of conflict, the Christian church splits into an eastern and a western branch—the Roman Catholic church and the Eastern Orthodox church.

450	625	800	975

476

800 Charlemagne is crowned "Holy Roman Emperor" by Pope Leo III. Much of western Europe is briefly united under Charlemagne.

This Renaissance painting uses perspective to create a sense of depth. It fools the human eye by making objects in the background smaller, which makes them seem farther away.

This sculpture by the German sculptor Adam Kraft is a self-portrait that dates back to the late 1400s.

1347 The plague, a disease carried by fleas on rats, spreads through Europe. Although millions die, Europe begins a cultural rebirth soon after—the Renaissance.

1517 Martin Luther calls for the Catholic church to reform. His ideas lead to a religious revolution in Europe—the Reformation.

1150

1325

1500

1675

Traders brought tulips to Europe from Constantinople in the 1500s.

1650

LESSON 1

The Power of the Church

Name two or more ways the Church influenced daily life in Europe during the Middle Ages.

Key Terms

- clergy
- monastery
- tithe

➤ *After the fall of the Roman Empire, many European cities fell into ruins. Even Rome itself, shown here, was nearly deserted. Some historians have called the Middle Ages the Dark Ages.*

After the fall of Rome in A.D. 476, Germanic tribes, or *volks,* roamed western Europe. They burned cities. They destroyed bridges. To the Romans, it seemed like the end of the world. Where the Roman Empire once had kept peace, now there was war. Orientus, a Roman poet who lived in the 400s, wrote:

See how swiftly death comes upon the world, and how many people the violence of war has stricken [hit]. Some lay as food for dogs; others were killed by the flames that licked their homes. In the villages and country houses, in the fields and . . . on every road— death, sorrow, slaughter, fires.

The fall of Rome marked the end of the ancient Roman world. It also marked the beginning of a new era in Europe. Historians call this new era the Middle Ages, or the medieval period. The Middle Ages lasted from about A.D. 476 to 1450.

For much of the Middle Ages, the Germanic *volks* divided Europe into many pieces. Each tribe obeyed its own laws and followed its own customs. Many of these

tribal differences still exist in Europe today.

Even so, most Europeans of the Middle Ages shared a common faith—Christianity. They belonged to the Church, headed by the Pope in Rome. Europeans looked to the Church for salvation, or the promise of life after death. They did not question the Pope, nor did they expect life to improve.

One Church, One Faith

During the Middle Ages, the Church was the center of the community. It was the heart of religious life, the center of learning, and a major political force.

The **clergy** were the priests, archbishops, bishops, and cardinals who served the Church. The main duty of priests and bishops was to conduct the worship service, the Mass. Other men who served the Church were called monks. These men lived in a religious community, or **monastery.** Monks led ordered lives. At set times each day, they had to work, pray, study, and teach. Monks also copied the Bible by hand for people to read.

The Church set up religious communities, or convents, for women, too. Women who agreed to follow the convent rules were called nuns. Like monks, nuns spent most of their day working and praying. Nuns also treated people who were ill or dying. However, only a few nuns studied or copied the Bible. In general, most women of the Middle Ages were not taught how to read and write.

Daily Life and the Church

In every village and town, the Church shaped the lives of the common people. Church bells rang when it was time to work, eat, sleep, and go to Mass. People turned to their local priest to bless marriages, baptize babies, comfort the sick, and pray for the dead.

To support the Church, people paid a tithe *(tyth)* each year. A **tithe** equaled one-tenth of a person's income. People could pay their tithes in money, crops, or labor. Church leaders used this income to care for the ill and help the poor. They also used tithes to build huge churches, or cathedrals *(kuh THEE druhls)*.

Cathedrals and Religious Art

Cathedral spires, or tall steeples, towered over many towns during the Middle Ages. Cathedrals were designed to fill people with wonder at the power of God.

Stained glass windows filled the cathedral interiors with beautiful light. Since most people couldn't read, these windows took the place of books. They told stories from the Bible, using colorful pictures that all could understand.

Building a cathedral took a great deal of time and money. Hundreds of workers were needed to cut stone, build walls, and perform other tasks by hand. It could take more than 100 years of hard work to finish a cathedral. Many workers never lived to see one completed. ■

▼ *The cathedral at Chartres, France, was built in less than 30 years. Towering over the city, it shows the power of the Church and the faith of its believers during the Middle Ages.*

■ *What were some of the duties of the clergy, monks, and nuns during the Middle Ages?*

A Divided Empire, a Divided Church

Across Time & Space

What is the only city located on two continents? It's Istanbul, Turkey, which spans Europe and Asia. Before 1930 Istanbul was called Constantinople after the Roman emperor Constantine.

▼ *This map of Constantinople was drawn about 1420. Can you find a dome-roofed cathedral? Compare it with the one on page 411.*

In Chapter 7 you read that the Roman Empire split into two parts: a western empire and an eastern empire. This division would also split the Church.

The Eastern Empire

Germanic tribes invaded the western part of the Roman Empire. The eastern part, called the Byzantine *(BIHZ uhn teen)* Empire, stayed rich and powerful. Constantinople *(kahn stan tuh NOH puhl)*, the Byzantine capital, filled western visitors with wonder. It was a city of riches, unlike any city in western Europe. While Rome stood dark at night, Constantinople glowed with streetlights.

The Byzantine Empire differed in other ways from the western empire. The Byzantines took pride in their Greek heritage. Greek was their common language. Priests in the Byzantine Empire spoke Greek during the worship services. Byzantine Christians could understand what their priests said and what they read from the Bible.

In western Europe, priests often did not use the people's everyday language. They spoke mainly Latin, which was the language of the ancient Romans. After A.D. 1000, few people in the West could understand Latin.

The Church Divides

At the core of the differences between East and West was this question: Who ruled the Church, and who ruled the empire? In the East the Byzantine emperor ruled both church and state. In the West the Pope ruled the Church while kings and queens ruled the land.

When Pope Leo III crowned King Charlemagne *(SHAHR luh mayn)* "Holy Roman Emperor" in 800, Byzantine Christians were angry. What right had Pope Leo III to name him emperor? Charlemagne had united western Europe, as the Roman emperors had done centuries before. However, to the Byzantines, the Pope was not head of the Church. To them, the only true leader of the Church was the Byzantine emperor.

For years, these differences caused many disputes in the Church. Finally, in 1054, the Church split in two. The western church became

Division of the Christian World, c. A.D. 950

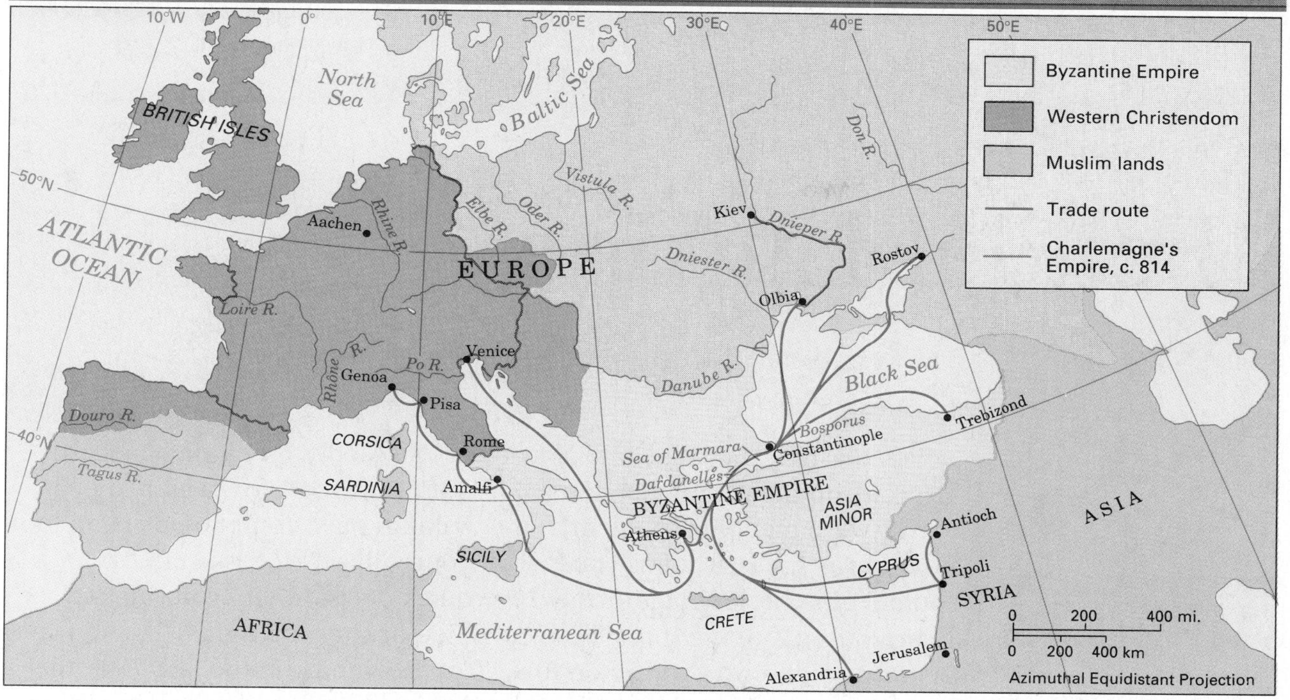

Map legend:
- Byzantine Empire
- Western Christendom
- Muslim lands
- Trade route
- Charlemagne's Empire, c. 814

Azimuthal Equidistant Projection

East vs. West: Church and Culture

	Religious Center	Religious Leader	Church Language	Ruler	Economy	Settlement Patterns	Cultural Influences
East	Constantinople	Emperor, Patriarch	Greek	Emperor	Farming, trade	Rural and urban	Greek, Roman
West	Rome	Pope	Latin	Kings, queens, nobles	Farming	Mostly rural	Roman, Germanic

the Roman Catholic church. The eastern church became the Eastern Orthodox church. As the map and chart above show, two separate Christian cultures developed during the Middle Ages.

After Charlemagne's death in 814, his western empire crumbled. Western Europe was again divided into pieces. The Byzantine Empire, however lasted until 1453. It survived many attacks before it fell to the Ottoman Turks.

During the Middle Ages, western Europe was often in turmoil. War, violence, famine, and disease were common. In the next lesson, you'll read about how the people of Europe tried to protect themselves during these dangerous times. ■

▲ Study the map and the chart above. How did the location of Constantinople help to support a trading economy?

■ How did the language used in the eastern church differ from the one used in the western church?

REVIEW

1. **FOCUS** Name two or more ways the Church influenced daily life in Europe during the Middle Ages.

2. **HISTORY** Most Europeans of the Middle Ages could not read or write. However, most monks and clergy could. Did the ability to read and write give monks and clergy power over people? Why or why not? If you could not read or write, how would your life be different?

3. **CULTURE** What differences led to the split between the eastern church and the western church?

4. **CRITICAL THINKING** Why did Europeans pay tithes?

5. **ACTIVITY** Learn more about church architecture during the Middle Ages. Research a cathedral or a monastery such as one found on the map above. Draw a diagram or sketch of the building. Use the Minipedia on pages 662 to 663 to label some of the building's most interesting features.

413

The Making of Europe

B.C. A.D.
450
700
1400
1500
1675

LESSON 2

Feudal Europe

Describe daily life in feudal Europe.

Key Terms

- manor
- vassal
- serf
- crusade
- knight
- plague

S plash! What was that? You drop the fishing net you were mending. A silent, gray fog surrounds you. You peer into it, looking for the square sails of Viking ships. You see only ocean mist. You listen for the roar of the Viking battle cry. You hear only the waves.

This fog hides all other sights and sounds. You try to convince yourself that what you heard was just a seagull diving for a fish. Sitting down, you pick up the net and start sewing.

The cold air stings your face and numbs your fingers as you work. You laugh at your fright. The rest of your village still sleeps. All is quiet again. Then you hear that splashing sound again.

Suddenly, a dragon head rises out of the fog. Now a ship appears. Vikings have come to burn and loot your village! You must make a quick decision: Do you run and hide or stay and fight?

Beginning in the late 700s, the Vikings sailed from their homes in Scandinavia, which is now Sweden, Norway, and Denmark. Because of a growing population, they sought new lands to conquer and settle.

Vikings were skilled sailors and shipbuilders and ruthless pirates and warriors. They were also farmers, fishers, and traders. Over time, Vikings—who were also called Norsemen or Northmen—settled in what is now Great Britain, Ireland, France, and Russia.

For about 250 years, Vikings plundered, or raided, European towns, monasteries, and cathedrals, especially those along sea-coasts and rivers. No one, not even rulers with armies, felt safe from Viking attacks. In England people prayed, "From the fury of the North-men, deliver us, O Lord."

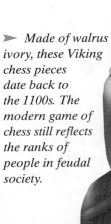

➤ *Made of walrus ivory, these Viking chess pieces date back to the 1100s. The modern game of chess still reflects the ranks of people in feudal society.*

414

Daily Life in Feudal Europe

During the Middle Ages, feudalism developed out of people's need for protection. Feudalism is a social, political, and economic system. European feudalism was like the Japanese feudalism you read about on page 367.

Life on the Feudal Manor

The people of Europe looked to strong rulers—usually kings and queens—for protection. In return the people promised to be loyal to their monarch.

As a reward for loyalty, kings and queens granted land to trusted warriors. Castles, farms, villages, and people usually were included in this grant, or gift. The land and everything on it was a **manor.** In exchange for a manor, a warrior agreed to become the subject, or **vassal** *(VAS uhl)*, of the ruler. Vassals promised to protect and obey their monarch.

Under the feudal system, women had to obey their husbands or fathers. Although women ran the day-to-day affairs of the home, they had few rights. However, noblewomen often were in charge of the entire manor. Some were political and military leaders, such as Queen Margaret I of Denmark. In the late 1300s, she united Denmark, Norway, and Sweden into one Scandinavian state. Others were writers or artists. Marie de France, for example, won fame for her poems, which use some of the legends of King Arthur of England.

Serfs: Backbone of Feudalism

Few people of the Middle Ages were kings or queens. Most were poor peasant farmers.

Some peasants were free, but most were **serfs.** Although serfs were not free, they were not slaves either. Serfs belonged to the land. They could not be bought or sold, unless the land was also. Serfs could leave the land only with their lord's permission or by buying freedom.

Most serfs and free peasants had to pay rent to their manor lord. Most paid rent by working three or more days a week for their lord. Often, serfs and free peasants also had to pay money or crops. ■

▲ *During the Middle Ages, families depended on clay pottery to keep food and drink cool as well as safe from pests such as rats.*

▼ *The pictures on this page were taken from a French book of prayers. The scenes show some of the activities of the farm year.*

Medieval Life: Serfs and Lords					
	Land Owned	**Food**	**Clothing**	**Housing**	**Income**
Serf	Zero to 20 acres	Bread, eggs, poultry, some meat and vegetables	Wool, animal skins, linen	Mud and straw huts; wood and stone houses	A few animals, crops from a few strips of land
Lord	Hundreds to thousands of acres	Meat, game, fish, pastries, spices, vegetables	Wool, silk, linen	Stone and wood castles	Rents, taxes, and services from serfs and peasants

◄ *Use this chart to compare the life of a serf with that of a lord.*

■ *How did the feudal system protect the people of Europe during the Middle Ages?*

The Crusades

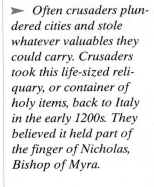

Church leaders used such words to inspire kings and peasants to fight the crusades.

Conflict over the Holy Land

The **crusades** were a series of religious wars that took place from 1095 to 1291. Christians and Muslims fought over the Holy Land, which includes modern Israel. Both wanted to control the holy city of Jerusalem, a sacred place to Jewish, Christian, and Muslim believers.

For most of the Middle Ages, Muslims ruled the Holy Land. Early Muslim rulers allowed all believers to worship in Jerusalem. However, in 1085 the Seljuk Turks captured Jerusalem. Christian pilgrims no longer felt safe.

When the Seljuks also threatened to take Constantinople, the Byzantines asked for help. Christians in Europe resolved to protect the pilgrims and Byzantines— and to capture the Holy Land.

Those who vowed to "take up the cross" in battle became known as crusaders.

Going on a Crusade

Nearly 30,000 crusaders left western Europe in 1096 to fight in the First Crusade. About 4,000 were knights. A **knight** was an armed soldier on horseback. To learn more about the knights of the crusades, read A Moment in Time on the next page. Most crusaders were not knights, but peasant foot soldiers. Women and priests also traveled with the crusaders.

People had several reasons for going on the crusades. First, Church leaders promised salvation for anyone killed on a crusade. Second, crusaders hoped for economic gain. The Holy Land was thought to be full of riches.

The crusades did not turn out to be exciting adventures. Instead, they were bloody wars. Thousands of Muslims and Christians were killed. Jews were often attacked and killed as well. When the crusades ended in the late 1200s, Muslims still ruled the Holy Land. ■

➤ *Often crusaders plundered cities and stole whatever valuables they could carry. Crusaders took this life-sized reliquary, or container of holy items, back to Italy in the early 1200s. They believed it held part of the finger of Nicholas, Bishop of Myra.*

▼ *On the map, trace the route of the First Crusade. What city was its destination? How is the power of the Church shown on this map?*

■ *Why did Christians go on the crusades?*

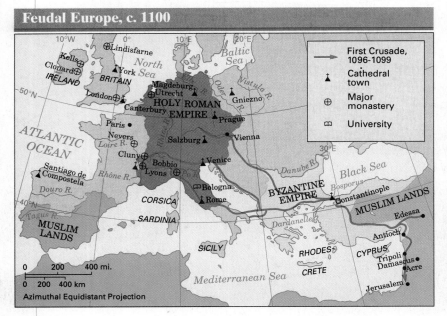

Feudal Europe, c. 1100

First Crusade, 1096–1099
▲ Cathedral town
⊕ Major monastery
▥ University

A Crusader

3:32 P.M., October 20, 1192
In a field outside Vienna, Austria

Sword
His heavy sword is useful for fighting on foot. But his chain mail makes swinging the sword difficult.

Chain Mail
His protective chain mail covers him head to toe. Chain mail is made of interlocking metal rings. It is heavy, hot, and hard to keep clean.

Pebble
In his pouch is the stone he picked off the floor of the Church of the Holy Sepulchre in Jerusalem. He keeps it as a good luck token.

Shield
Like the symbols on his tunic, his shield shows a design that identifies him to friend or foe on the battlefield.

Spices
These gifts will delight his friends in England. Black pepper is uncommon in his region, and sugar is a rare treat.

Quilted Body Suit
He wears a cloth suit under his chain mail to keep it from scraping his skin. He has not washed or removed his body suit in many months.

Bandage
The crusader's arrow wound is dressed with a sophisticated healing ointment, applied by an Islamic doctor.

417

Europe at the End of the Middle Ages

➤ *This painting shows Death riding on horseback, striking down people with the plague.*

After the crusades, international trade increased. Peace treaties helped open up new trade routes among Europe, Asia, and Africa. Italian cities such as Venice, Florence, Milan, and Genoa grew rich and powerful. Skilled shipbuilders, merchants, and bankers lived in these Italian cities. They helped supply wealthy Europeans with the foreign goods they demanded —spices, herbs, fine cloth, maps, and jewels.

However, trade ships brought more than just rare goods to Europe. They also carried rats infected with the **plague** (*playg*), a deadly disease. Fleas living on these rats carried the germs that caused plague. When the trade ships docked in the ports of Europe, the infected rats raced to shore.

Around 1347 the plague—known as the Black Death—swept across Europe from Asia. All over Europe, people tried to fight it. Yet nothing cured the plague or stopped it from spreading. In less than 10 years, about 25 million Europeans died from this deadly disease. The plague continued to strike Europe and the rest of the world for centuries. In 1525 Michael V. Behaim, a German teenager, wrote this to his cousin:

There has been a terrible plague throughout the land. More than a hundred thousand people have died, men, women, and children. . . . You may well wonder how I survived.

To learn more about the spread of the plague, read Making a Hypothesis on the opposite page.

For survivors of the Black Death, the future may have looked bleak. People may have felt helpless. Could a new society come about from the ruins of the past? ■

▲ *Rats helped spread the plague across Europe.*

■ *How did trade ships bring the plague to Europe?*

R E V I E W

1. **FOCUS** Describe daily life in feudal Europe.
2. **HISTORY** How was feudalism in Europe similar to feudalism in Japan?
3. **ECONOMICS** How did increased trade after the crusades have positive and negative effects on Europe?
4. **CRITICAL THINKING** Did the crusades fail? Explain.

5. **ACTIVITY** Write a short story for young children about life during the Middle Ages. Describe the events of one day in the life of a queen, knight, peasant, or crusader, for example. The setting for your story could be a castle, farming village, or seaport.

Making a Hypothesis

Here's Why

You have just finished reading about the plague. Perhaps you want to learn why it spread so quickly through Europe from 1347 to 1350. How would you find the answer? You could ask your teacher, or you could do what many scientists do. You could make a hypothesis.

A hypothesis is an educated guess that can be tested. It is based on facts you know from reading, observing nature, or experimenting. Before a hypothesis can be useful, it must be tested.

To test a hypothesis, scientists set up experiments and collect data. However, hypotheses about events in history—such as the plague—cannot be tested by experiment. They can be tested by collecting data from maps, books, and other historical sources. In fact you can use the map on this page and information from Lesson 2 to make and test a hypothesis about the spread of the plague.

Here's How

To make and test a hypothesis of your own, follow these steps:

1. **Define the question.** You could ask: Is there any connection between trade routes and the spread of the plague?
2. **Gather evidence.** Study the map, and review page 418. List the facts that might support your idea. Your list might look like this:
   - From the map it appears that the plague affected Europe in a wavelike pattern.
   - The port cities shown on the trade routes were among the first places affected by the plague.
   - Fleas found on rats carried the disease. These rats lived on many of the ships traveling the trade routes.
3. **Make a hypothesis.** Based on the evidence, your hypothesis might be: Though the development of trade routes helped people to exchange goods and ideas, these routes also helped spread the plague.
4. **Test the hypothesis.** You can test your hypothesis by learning more about the plague in a book, magazine, or another source. If you learn new facts about the plague, change your hypothesis to account for the new information.

Try It

Now use the map to form another hypothesis. For example: Why were the northernmost areas on the map the last areas affected by the plague? Use the four-step process to make and test your hypothesis.

Apply It

Make a hypothesis that answers this question: Why do some students make excuses about late homework assignments? Again, use the four-step process.

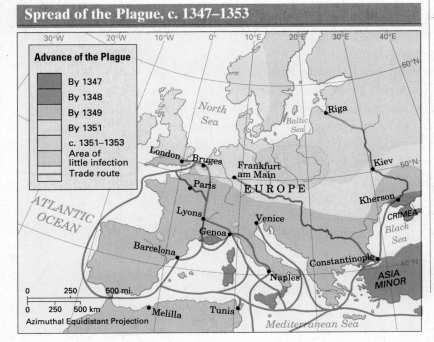

Spread of the Plague, c. 1347–1353

Advance of the Plague
- By 1347
- By 1348
- By 1349
- By 1351
- c. 1351–1353
- Area of little infection
- Trade route

30°W 20°W 10°W 0° 10°E 20°E 30°E 40°E

North Sea
Baltic Sea
Riga
London Bruges
Frankfurt am Main
Paris
EUROPE
Kiev
ATLANTIC OCEAN
Lyons
Venice
Kherson
Genoa
CRIMEA
Black Sea
Barcelona
Constantinople
Naples
ASIA MINOR
Melilla Tunis
Mediterranean Sea

0 250 500 mi.
0 250 500 km
Azimuthal Equidistant Projection

60°N
50°N
40°N

419

The Making of Europe

Valentine & Orson

*Re-created as a folk play in verse and paintings by
Nancy Ekholm Burkert*

In Lesson 2 you read
about the feudal world of
medieval Europe. This
story presents the flavor
of the period when kings
employed knights to
protect their kingdoms.

Europe during the Middle Ages was a continent divided into many kingdoms. King Pepin led the Franks between 751 and 768 A.D. The fanciful tale below is chapter six of a long poem that recounts an adventure of King Pepin, his sister Bellicent, and her twin sons, Valentine and Orson. The twins were separated at birth by a strange series of happenings. Bellicent was accused by her husband, Emperor Alexander, of unfaithfulness. He ordered her to leave his realm. During her return to France, she gave birth to twins while traveling through a forest. A bear took one of the babies and raised him in the wild. This earned the child, Orson, the nickname Wild Man because his appearance resembled that of a bear. King Pepin himself found the other child, Valentine, and raised him at the royal court. Valentine and Orson became good friends and learned that they were brothers only after sharing many adventures together. As you read this narrative poem, ask yourself why Valentine agrees to fight the Green Knight.

Aquitaine a region in
southwestern France

predicament difficult
situation

infamous having a
bad reputation

The good Duke Savary
Ruled in Aquitaine
And was King Pepin's friend.
I shall explain
How he was caught
In a predicament
That for our tale
Is most significant!
A brother of the giant Ferragus,
Renowned as the "Green Knight," and infamous,
Laid siege against the Duke and all his land.
He held him hostage, with but one demand:
"Give me your daughter, Fezon, for my wife,
Or I will burn your land and take your life!
I shall depart, if you can find a knight
To challenge and defeat me in a fight!"
Duke Savary sent letters everywhere.
But in King Pepin's court no one would dare
To undertake the cause, save Valentine,
Who in his heart had never ceased to pine
For knowledge of his own nativity.

nativity birth

This was a splendid opportunity
To search in realms outside of France, and find
Some tidings of his birth to ease his mind.
He felt obliged, moreover, to defend
The noble man who was King Pepin's friend.

Wild Orson ran beside him, on the route
Toward Aquitaine, and all the world ran out,
Amused to see a man so like a bear,
All rough, and nearly naked. He could hear
Their laughter but the Wild Man paid no heed.
However, Valentine could see his need
And found an armorer nearby who made
A coat of mail, in finest steel. He bade
That Orson pull it on, and ever thence,
The Wild Man had a prouder countenance!

They journeyed on, two fellows glad to be
Companions on the road, and soon could see
The spires of Aquitaine, which rose on high.
By chance, or fate, an aged man passed by
Who had a long white beard and the attire
Of a pilgrim. Actually, he was a squire
On his way from Portugal to France, carrying
A noble lady's message to the King.
He warned them not to enter Aquitaine,
Where forty knights were overcome and slain.
They could be seen, afar, hanging from a tree.
And then, as they were parting company,
Valentine was strangely drawn to this old man,
Who was, as you have guessed, good Blandyman.

They ventured on and soon arrived before
The Duke and his fair daughter. Gathered there
Were fourteen other knights from foreign lands,
To challenge the Green Knight and his demands.
Valentine spoke reverently to Fezon:
"Right dear Lady, I have come from Pepin,
Mighty King of France, and with me, here,
The bravest man on earth. He has no peer."
The maiden gazed upon the simply clad
And rugged Orson. Ah, we hear it said
That when the heart is dealt a blow, no love
Is less than beautiful. And, friends, above
All others, Fezon set her heart on Orson!
"A thousand thanks to both of you," said Fezon.
"Too many noble knights were slain for me.

mail flexible armor

countenance
appearance

Blandyman the
queen's loyal squire

I beg you not to put your lives in jeopardy!"
But Orson placed his hands across his heart,
And Valentine insisted, for their part.

Thus on the morrow, sixteen men in all
Took counsel with each other in the hall.
The two who asked that they be first to fight
Were soon defeated by the fierce Green Knight,
Who hung them without mercy from the tree.
Now Orson shook his fists ferociously,
But Valentine was next, and when he rode
Onto the field, the evildoer crowed,
"Ha, Knight! On yonder rowan tree, you see
A green shield hanging. Bring it here to me!"
Valentine retorted, "Why? Do I observe
That you have servants? Why not let them serve!"
The villain shouted, "You shall fetch the shield,
Or by my law, we shall not take the field!"
So Valentine complied in fear his foe would try
To use this lame excuse, but could not pry
The shield away. "Now you will understand,"
The villain jeered, "this shield from Fairyland
Will not come loose unless you are the one
Predestined as my conqueror, the son
Of royal rank, but nourished well without
A woman's milk!" "What you have said I doubt
Is true of me," lamented Valentine, "yet
I shall fight!" "Such folly reaps regret,"
The Green Knight said and spurred his horse.
The two fought back and forth along the course
So fiercely all their weapons broke apart.
They stopped as darkness fell, but vowed to start
When it was day. They had sore wounds to tend.
The Green Knight kept a magic balm to mend
His injuries, but this he kept concealed.
Poor Valentine was not so quickly healed.
When he had dressed his wounds, he tried to rest,
But could not sleep as he reviewed his quest
To learn the truth about his origin.
He thought of the enchanted shield, or Orson;
Was he by chance or by a jest of fate
Somehow descended from a high estate?

At dawn, it could be seen that Valentine
Was in a melancholy state of mind.
He gathered all his armor for the fight,
But, friends, imagine Orson's wild delight

---

jeopardy   risk

retorted
replied sharply

lamented   said sadly

balm   a soothing oil

quest   search

melancholy   sad

When Valentine came forth to place it all
Into his hands! Orson, prancing round the hall,
Made signs that he preferred a club of wood
To other weapons, but he understood
The reason he must pose as Valentine.
The shining armor made him look so fine
That all who saw him clapped and cheered, except
His wounded friend, who was forlorn and kept
An anxious watch as Orson rode away,
And prayed for his return, unharmed, that day.

Further Reading

Adam of the Road. Elizabeth J. Gray. Searching for his minstrel father and his dog, Adam wanders through 13th century England. He meets jugglers, minstrels, pilgrims, and nobles on his journeys.

Life in a Fifteenth Century Monastery. Anne Boyd. The author provides a detailed look at the daily life of monks in an English monastery.

A Proud Taste for Scarlet and Minevar. E. L. Konigsberg. This historical fiction brings to life the adventures of Queen Eleanor of Aquitaine.

The Road to Camlann. Rosemary Sutcliff. This book retells the adventures of King Arthur's court and all its colorful figures, including Sir Lancelot and Queen Guenevere.

The Merry Adventures of Robin Hood. Howard Pyle. The book retells the legend of a man who robs from the rich and gives to the poor peasants.

L E S S O N   3

The Renaissance

What were some of the major achievements of the Renaissance?

Key Terms

- Renaissance
- patron
- classics
- humanist

➤ *Note the rich colors and religious themes in this Raphael painting. Raphael (1483–1520) was called "the prince of painters" for his mastery of the Renaissance style.*

*T*ake pains and pleasure in constantly copying the best things which you can find done by the hand of great masters [the best painters]. And if you are in a place where many good masters have been, so much the better for you. But I give you this advice: take care to select the best one every time, and the one who has the greatest reputation.

Cennino Cennini, from
The Craftsman's Handbook, 1437

Cennini's book gave practical advice for the beginning artist. He wrote about how to mix paint, prepare a canvas, and protect one's hands.

Yet Cennini's book was not just a how-to-paint manual. Cennini also gave advice about life: what to eat, wear, and study, and how to act in public. After the horrors of the Black Death, Europeans were eager to read books such as Cennini's.

A new way of living and thinking took hold in Europe after the Black Death. People of the late 1300s and 1400s wanted to know more about the world. Although religious, they hoped to gain great wealth and lasting fame.

A new era had begun. It was called the **Renaissance** *(rehn ih SAHNS)*, from a Latin word meaning "rebirth" or "revival." The Renaissance was a time of renewed interest in both the arts and sciences of ancient Greece and Rome. It was a rebirth of learning. The Renaissance began in northern Italy during the late 1300s, then spread through Europe.

Italy: Birthplace of the Renaissance

Renaissance Italy was not a unified country. Instead it was made up of individual city-states. Like ancient Athens and Sparta, each Italian city-state ruled itself and the surrounding countryside.

Wealthy families, not kings or queens, ruled the Italian city-states. Often these rulers fought for control of the Mediterranean Sea trade. Their thirst for power led to many murders, riots, and feuds.

In spite of these dangers, Italian cities thrived during the 1400s and 1500s. Italy's location made it a crossroads between Europe, Africa, and Asia. Venice, Florence, Milan, and Genoa were centers of international trade and banking. Their wealth would fuel the rebirth of Europe—the Renaissance.

City Life

In these bustling Italian cities, people were divided into social classes, or ranks. The lower classes were made up of unskilled workers, such as boat workers and peddlers. In spite of the wealth in Italian cities, most people of the lower classes were poor. They had no say in running either the government or the powerful guilds, which were like unions.

The middle class was made up of shop owners, carpenters, blacksmiths, and other skilled workers. Each one belonged to a guild. Guilds set prices and quality standards. They decided who could or could not join.

Patrons of the Arts

At the top of the social classes were the wealthy nobles,

merchants, and businesspeople. They ran the most powerful guilds. These major guilds included cloth manufacturers, merchants, bankers, and doctors. Wealthy families, such as the Medici *(MEHD uh chee)* family in Florence, ran their cities like personal kingdoms.

The Medicis also used their wealth to enjoy leisure, or free time. Like many other wealthy families of the Renaissance, the Medicis were **patrons,** or supporters of the arts and learning. Patrons hired artists to fill their homes with beautiful paintings and sculptures. They bought rare books and paid scholars to teach their children.

Just as these families competed in business, they competed in the arts and learning. Patrons spent huge sums of money bidding for the services of the best artists and teachers. They also competed with the richest patron of them all— the Catholic church. ■

▲ Note how this Renaissance painting by Ambrogio Lorenzetti (c. 1290–1348) gives you a sense of depth—some people and buildings appear close, while others appear far away.

◄ To keep their dresses from dragging in dust or mud, Italian women often wore platform shoes, like the one shown at left.

■ *Describe the people who made up the different classes of Renaissance Italy.*

A Flowering of Arts and Learning

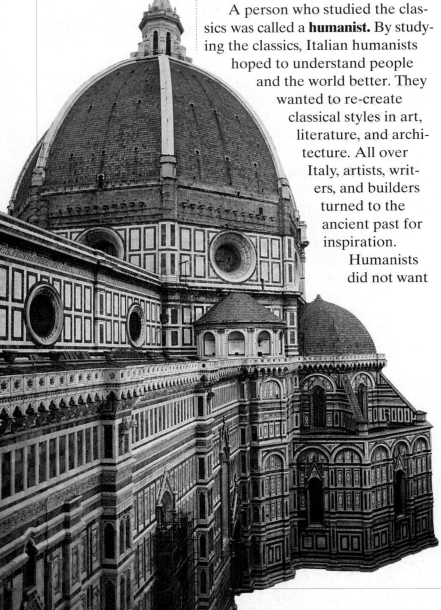

Compare Brunelleschi's dome on the Florence cathedral, shown here, with the Byzantine domes on page 412. Brunelleschi's most famous work took 16 years to build. He is buried there.

Trade did more than just increase the wealth of the Italian cities. It also brought the Italians into contact with people from all over the Mediterranean world. Just as goods were traded, so too were ideas.

Looking Forward to the Past

Trade brought the Italians into greater contact with Arab and Byzantine scholars. These scholars were experts in the **classics**—the works of ancient Greece and Rome.

A person who studied the classics was called a **humanist.** By studying the classics, Italian humanists hoped to understand people and the world better. They wanted to re-create classical styles in art, literature, and architecture. All over Italy, artists, writers, and builders turned to the ancient past for inspiration.

Humanists did not want simply to copy ideas from the past. They hoped to use old ideas to create something new—and better.

Age of the Artist

One such humanist was Filippo Brunelleschi (*broo nuh LEHS kee*), an architect and engineer who lived from 1377 to 1446.

Brunelleschi left his home in Florence to study ancient ruins in Rome. Since ancient times no dome had been built in Europe. After years of study, he built a dome for the Florence cathedral. Another architect of the time, Leon Battista Alberti, wrote of Brunelleschi's dome that "it was probably unknown and unthought of to the ancients."

Another famous Renaissance artist designed a dome about 100 years after Brunelleschi had designed his. You may think of Michelangelo (*my kuhl AN juh loh*) only as a painter or sculptor. However, he wrote hundreds of poems. He also designed the dome of St. Peter's cathedral in Rome.

Many of Michelangelo's works, such as his dome, were paid for by one patron—the Catholic church. In 1508 Pope Julius II asked Michelangelo to paint biblical scenes on the ceiling of the Sistine Chapel in Rome. Michelangelo worked while squatting on shaky boards high above the marble floor. Paint splattered into his eyes. His back always ached. Often he grew dizzy and would almost faint.

Finally, in 1512, Michelangelo finished. In all he had painted more than 300 figures from the Bible and classical times. One visitor at the time wrote that "all Rome admired it and crowded to see it."

The Renaissance Man

During the Renaissance, well-educated men were expected to do many things well. They collected art, wrote poetry, played music, and learned Greek. They also took part in politics, were skilled at sports, and could fight if necessary.

Perhaps the most famous Renaissance man was Leonardo da Vinci. Leonardo began his career as a teenage apprentice, working for a master painter in Florence. By 1478, Leonardo had left his master to set up his own workshop.

Leonardo's fame grew—and not just for his painting. Leonardo was in demand for his great knowledge and engineering skills. In Italy and France, patrons such as the Medicis bid for his services. Only after his death were many of his inventions discovered, such as the one shown on page 429.

The Renaissance Woman

Unlike the Renaissance man, the Renaissance woman was not encouraged to develop her abilities. One male writer gave Renaissance women this advice:

> *I*t does not befit [suit] women to handle weapons, to ride, to play tennis, to wrestle, and to do many other things that befit men. . . .
>
> Baldassare Castiglione,
> *The Book of the Courtier,* 1528

Some Renaissance women ignored this advice. Some became writers or artists. Others became skilled workers or shop owners. A few held political power.

Two exceptional Renaissance women were Isabella d'Este *(DEHS tay)* and Christine de Pizan

◄ Leonardo da Vinci made this drawing of Isabella d'Este in 1500.

(pee ZAHN). During the late 1400s, d'Este helped her family rule the Italian city-state of Mantua. She was also a patron to many gifted Renaissance artists.

Christine de Pizan was born in Venice in the late 1300s but spent most of her life in France. She studied the arts and sciences, then married and had children. After her husband died, de Pizan wrote poems and essays to support her family. ■

© Nippon Television Network Corporation Tokyo 1991

How Do We Know?

HISTORY *In 1980 art experts began cleaning the dirt from Michelangelo's paintings on the ceiling of the Sistine Chapel. In 1989 the experts finished their work. With the dirt removed, the paintings seemed to come alive with color and light.*

◄ Cleaning and restoring Michelangelo's paintings on the ceiling of the Sistine Chapel took nine years—more than twice as long as it took Michelangelo to paint them.

■ *Compare the life of a Renaissance woman with that of a Renaissance man.*

The Spread of the Renaissance

➤ *This painting,* The Renaissance Classroom, *shows people's thirst for learning during the Renaissance. By 1500 about six million books had been printed in Europe. As more people learned to read and write, demand for books grew.*

The rebirth of the Italian cities attracted visitors from all over Europe. Clergy and pilgrims flocked to Rome. Merchants and bankers hoped to make their fortunes in the Italian city-states. Artists and students sought knowledge, fame, and fortune.

When these travelers returned home, they brought Renaissance ideas—and newly printed books—with them. In the 1450s a German named Johannes Gutenberg (*GOOT n burg*) had developed a new printing press. Gutenberg's press used movable type—individual letters made into small, metal blocks. This movable type was easy to arrange and rearrange into words. Instead of having to be copied by hand, books could be printed quickly, in larger numbers, and for less money than ever before.

By the late 1400s, printers used movable type to print everything from the Bible to cartoons. This explosion of print helped spread the Renaissance north.

Northern Renaissance Ideas

As in Italy, humanists in northern Europe focused on the individual. However, their style of writing and painting was very different from that of the Italians.

England's William Shakespeare may be the best-known northern Renaissance writer. Born in 1564, Shakespeare was a poet, an actor, and a playwright. His plays showed the strengths and weaknesses of all

➤ *This painting by Pieter Bruegel is called* The Peasant Dance. *Bruegel tried to tell the stories of everyday people in his paintings. Notice the different expression each figure has.*

people—past and present. Shakespeare's characters included Roman emperors, British kings and queens, and Italian teenagers. Because his plays mixed slapstick humor with drama, audiences flocked to see them.

The Dutch painter Pieter Bruegel *(BROY guhl)* also wanted to show people as they really were. Many of his paintings showed peasants working, dancing, and eating. Although he had studied Italian painting, Bruegel developed his own style. Compare Bruegel's painting on the previous page with Raphael's on page 424.

Rebirth of Science in Europe

Interest in the past led to a new age of science in Europe. The first modern European scientists studied science and philosophy from Greece, Egypt, and India. They performed experiments to test their own ideas. The Scientific Revolution had begun in Europe.

The Polish astronomer, Nicolaus Copernicus *(koh PUR nuh kuhs),* was one of its earliest leaders. Copernicus began his studies in 1491—just one year before Columbus's first voyage. Copernicus read ancient scientific works. He also observed the planets, stars, and moon. Finally, he used math to conclude that the sun was the center of the solar system.

For centuries, the Catholic church had claimed that the sun revolved around the earth. Although the Pope approved of his findings, others did not. Copernicus did not publish his work until just before his death in 1543. Turn to page G8 in the Map and Globe Handbook to see how Copernicus's ideas helped to explain the seasons.

While Copernicus explored the night sky, Andreas Vesalius *(vih SAY lee uhs)* roamed French cemeteries. Vesalius was searching for dead bodies. Ancient texts about human anatomy were wrong, Vesalius thought. By studying dead bodies, he hoped to learn how the human body really worked. Vesalius's book, *On the Structure of the Human Body,* helped improve the practice of medicine.

Copernicus and Vesalius questioned long-held beliefs about the world. Other Europeans began to question the teachings of the Catholic church. As you will read next, the Church—and the world— would never be the same. ■

◄ *Leonardo da Vinci drew this design for a parachute in one of his many notebooks around 1485. The first air-to-ground jump wasn't made until 1797—over 300 years later.*

■ *How did the ideas of the Renaissance spread through Europe?*

R E V I E W

1. **FOCUS** What were some of the major achievements of the Renaissance?
2. **GEOGRAPHY** How did Italy's location contribute to its role as birthplace of the Renaissance?
3. **CULTURE** What did humanist artists and builders try to teach or show?
4. **CRITICAL THINKING** What role did the printing press play in the spread of the Renaissance through Europe?
5. **ACTIVITY** Study a work of Renaissance art from this chapter or another book. Research the artist's life, and make a report to your class. What ideas from the past influenced this artist? Did he or she influence other artists? How? Illustrate your report with a painting or drawing of your own.

429

LESSON 4

The Reformation

Key Terms

- indulgence
- Protestant
- Reformation
- Inquisition

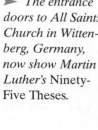

➤ *The entrance doors to All Saints Church in Wittenberg, Germany, now show Martin Luther's* Ninety-Five Theses.

On October 31, 1517, Martin Luther marched to All Saints Church in Wittenberg *(VIHT n behrk),* Germany. Luther was a Catholic priest, and he was angry. He held up the paper he carried. Bang! Bang! Bang! Quickly Luther nailed his challenge to the church doors for all to see. Luther marched back home in silence.

Meanwhile, outside Wittenberg, a noisy crowd had gathered around another man of the Catholic church. People eagerly bought the slips of paper this monk, Johann Tetzel *(TEHT suhl),* offered. Tetzel was selling indulgences. Issued by the Pope, **indulgences** were pardons, or forgiveness, for sins.

The sale of indulgences had angered Luther. "How could the Catholic church sell forgiveness?" he wondered. Luther felt that only God could forgive sins. In the paper he had nailed to the church doors, Luther protested that the Church had become too worldly. Luther's writings, called the *Ninety-Five Theses,* pointed out the problems he saw:

> *Why doesn't the pope build the basilica of St. Peter [the pope's church] out of his own money?. . . He would do better to sell St. Peter's and give the money to the poor folk who are being fleeced by the hawkers of indulgences.*

Luther's *Ninety-Five Theses* called for a debate. He hoped people would openly discuss his ideas and think about reforming the Church. Luther did not expect anything more than that. Yet in his lifetime, Luther's writings split the Catholic church and rocked the thrones of kings.

The Reformation Begins

Within a year, printing presses had helped to spread Luther's ideas all over Europe. People debated his ideas. Many agreed with Luther. They began to question the Catholic church: Were its teachings and practices still true to the Bible?

The Church's critics were soon called **Protestants**. Like Luther, they protested what they saw as abuses by the Church. Their protest movement became known as the **Reformation**. These Protestants wanted to reform, or change, the Church from within.

In 1518, Pope Leo X ordered Luther to stop his attacks. Luther refused, so Pope Leo asked the Holy Roman Emperor, Charles V, to bring Luther to trial. Standing before a huge crowd, Luther again refused to take back his words:

I do not accept the authority of popes and councils, for they have contradicted each other—my conscience is captive to the Word of God. I cannot and I will not recant [take back] anything, for to go against conscience is neither right nor safe. God help me. Amen.

Charles then declared Luther an outlaw. Anyone could arrest him. Luckily for Luther, he had a powerful friend. Frederick the Wise, Prince of Saxony, hid Luther.

While in hiding, Luther translated the Bible into German. For the first time, Germans could read the Bible for themselves. Many felt they no longer needed priests to read and interpret it.

Luther's teachings inspired many people to break away from the Catholic church. Some called themselves Lutherans. They based their religious beliefs on Luther's ideas. Soon more people would become Protestants. ■

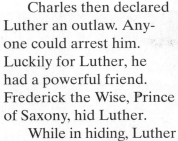

▲ *Martin Luther felt that the clergy should be allowed to marry. Luther is shown here with his wife, Katherina von Bora, a former nun.*

◄ *Johann Tetzel sold so many indulgences that some people made fun of him in a popular rhyme, "As soon as money in the box rings, The soul from Hell's fire springs."*

■ *Why did Luther object to the sale of indulgences?*

The Making of Europe

The Reformation Spreads in Europe

▲ *This illustration comes from one of Luther's printed Bibles.*

Across Time & Space

Martin Luther and Martin Luther King, Jr., share more than a name. Both led reform movements that changed the way people live and think. King's policy of civil disobedience promoted racial equality in the United States during the 1950s and 1960s. Under his leadership, the civil rights movement helped reform U.S. society.

The printing press helped to spread Luther's ideas quickly. His teachings were translated from German and printed in English, Dutch, and other languages. As more people read or heard Luther's ideas, the Reformation grew throughout northern Europe.

Other Protestant Movements

In addition to Luther, the Reformation had many other leaders. Because the Catholic church did not change, many reformers decided to leave it and form their own churches.

John Calvin of Switzerland agreed with much of what Luther thought. However, Calvin taught that God had already chosen a special group for heaven. These believers, Calvin thought, could be recognized during their lifetime.

Calvin's followers were called Calvinists. Their church services were plain. No images of saints hung on the walls. No organ played as people sang. Nothing distracted the people from solemn prayer, reading the Bible, or listening to sermons.

Calvinists also followed strict rules outside of church. By the time Calvin died in 1564, his beliefs had taken root in Scotland, the Netherlands, and many other places.

In England during the 1500s, King Henry VIII made himself, rather than the Pope, head of the Church of England, or Anglican (*ANG glih kuhn*) church. King Henry split from the Catholic church because he wanted to divorce his wife, Catherine of Aragon.

Catherine and Henry had only one living child, Mary Tudor. Henry wanted a son to rule after him. He feared a civil war would break out after his death if he did not have a son to take over the throne. Henry thought that a new wife would give him this son. However, the Pope refused to grant him the divorce from Catherine.

In response to the Pope, King Henry took over most of the Church's property in England. He still kept many of the practices of the Catholic church, but he would not obey the Pope.

The Catholic Church Responds

Throughout Europe more and more people joined Protestant churches. Finally, in 1545, Catholic leaders decided to make some important changes.

The reforms were expressed in different ways. New rules were made to help rid the Catholic church of any abuses. New religious orders were made up of believers who agreed to follow special rules, like the monks of the Middle Ages. One such order was the Jesuits. They took vows of poverty and swore to obey the Pope. Jesuits focused their efforts on education and missionary work.

The Catholic church also tried to stop the spread of Protestantism with the Inquisition *(ihn kwih ZIHSH uhn)*. An **Inquisition** was a Catholic church court. People suspected of being heretics, or nonbelievers, were brought to trial. Many Jewish and Muslim believers were tried as well. Those who were believed to be guilty but refused to admit their wrongdoings were sometimes tortured or sentenced to death. However, no reforms or harsh measures could stop the spread of Protestantism.

Europe Is Divided

During the late 1500s and early 1600s, religious beliefs began to divide the people of Europe. In the north, England, Denmark, Sweden,

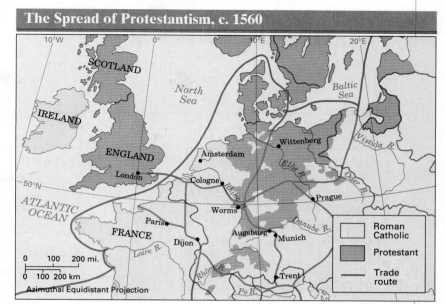

The Spread of Protestantism, c. 1560

and parts of Germany and the Netherlands became Protestant. In the south, Spain, France, and Italy remained Catholic.

Use the map on this page to see how religion divided Europe. Then compare this map with the Atlas map of religions today on page 688.

Loyalty to the state often meant having the same religion as the ruler. In Spain, England, Russia, and elsewhere, religious differences would lead to violent conflict. You will read about some of these conflicts in the next chapter. ■

▲ *This map shows how religious beliefs divided Europe. Which countries were mostly Protestant in 1560? Which were mostly Catholic?*

◄ *Turn this woodcut portrait upside down to see what Luther's enemies thought about him.*

■ *Why did the Reformation spread?*

REVIEW

1. **FOCUS** What were the causes and the effects of the Reformation?

2. **HISTORY** What role did the printing press play in the Reformation? How does this compare with its role in the Renaissance?

3. **BELIEF SYSTEMS** Why did Martin Luther want to reform the Catholic church? How did the Catholic church respond to the Reformation?

4. **CRITICAL THINKING** Why did the Reformation divide Europe?

5. **ACTIVITY** Think of something you would like to reform or change in your community. For example, should your community recycle more than it does? Write your ideas on the topic and post them on a bulletin board. As in Luther's time, invite other students to debate you and exchange ideas.

Chapter Review

Reviewing Key Terms

classics (p. 426)
clergy (p. 411)
crusades (p. 416)
humanist (p. 426)
indulgence (p. 430)
Inquisition (p. 433)
knight (p. 416)
manor (p. 415)
monastery (p. 411)

patron (p. 425)
plague (p. 418)
Protestant (p. 431)
Reformation (p. 431)
Renaissance (p. 424)
serf (p. 415)
tithe (p. 411)
vassal (p. 415)

A. Use a dictionary to find the origins of the following words. Write down the earliest origin given. Then, write a sentence or two explaining how the meaning of each word applies to the medieval Catholic church.

1. clergy
2. monastery
3. tithe
4. crusades
5. indulgence
6. Inquisition

B. Read each pair of words. Write a sentence telling how the words in each pair are related.

1. knight, vassal
2. serf, manor
3. humanist, classics
4. Protestant, Reformation
5. Renaissance, plague
6. patrons, Renaissance

Exploring Concepts

A. From 476 to 1600, a series of momentous events rocked Europe. Copy the following chart. Then, complete it by writing the cause(s) or effect(s) for the events listed. Use the time-line on pages 408–409 to help you.

Cause(s)	Effect(s)
	The Church becomes very powerful.
Byzantine Christians disagree with the western church on many issues.	
	Feudalism develops in Europe.
The Seljuk Turks capture the Holy Land.	

B. Support each of the following statements with information from the chapter.

1. During the Middle Ages, the Church was the center of the community.
2. The eastern church split from the western church because of several disagreements.
3. Because of people's need for protection, feudalism developed in Europe.
4. Serfs were the backbone of feudalism.
5. Many Christians in Europe were eager to join the crusades.
6. Trade brought many new things to Europe, some good, some bad.
7. Learning about the ancient past helped inspire the Renaissance.
8. The Renaissance had little effect on the lives of people in the lower classes.
9. Wealth, and competition among the leading families in Italy, helped to fuel the Renaissance.
10. The Renaissance changed the way some Europeans looked at their life and their place in the world.
11. Reformers questioned the teachings and practices of the Catholic church.
12. The printing press helped spread the ideas of the Renaissance and the Reformation all over Europe.

Reviewing Skills

1. Write a hypothesis that answers these questions: Why did the Catholic church punish Martin Luther? Why wasn't there an open discussion of his ideas? Use the four-step process on page 419 to test your hypothesis.
2. Reread the passage from Martin Luther's *Ninety-Five Theses* on page 430. What is Luther's main idea, or most important point? Which statements, in the passage or from your reading, support Luther's main idea?
3. Imagine that you are writing a report about various Protestant groups. What information would you include in your report? What topics would you select to compare the different groups?

Using Critical Thinking

1. During the Middle Ages, building a cathedral took a great deal of time and money. Why might people have devoted so much time and energy to the project?
2. The word *renaissance* means "rebirth." In what ways was the Renaissance both a rebirth of classical learning and a rebirth of interest in new ideas? Give examples from your reading.
3. During the Renaissance, a middle class of shop owners and skilled workers emerged. Do you think this was an important development? Explain.
4. Wealthy patrons, many of whom were rulers of Italian city-states, supported artists during the Renaissance. Do you think the government should support the arts today? Give several reasons to support your response.
5. In the 1500s Martin Luther and other reformers hoped to change the Catholic church for the better. Today, many reformers hope to improve governments, businesses, and other institutions around the world. Name two reformers who are active today. What are their goals? Compare these reformers with Luther. How are they alike and how are they different?

Preparing for Citizenship

1. **WRITING ACTIVITY** Michelangelo, Leonardo da Vinci, and Christine de Pizan excelled in the arts. Who do you think is an excellent writer, artist, or builder today? Write a review of the person's work. Be sure to include details that support your opinions about him or her.
2. **COLLECTING INFORMATION** During the Renaissance, Europeans read books by authors such as Cennino Cennini. Europeans wanted to learn all they could about good manners, human achievement, and personal growth. What people do you turn to for advice about life? Make a list of the people and the resources that are available to you. Share the list with your classmates.
3. **ARTS ACTIVITY** In many of his paintings, Pieter Bruegel told stories of everyday life. Create a painting, a sculpture, or a collage that shows a part of everyday life in your community. Write a title for your work. Display your work of art in your classroom.
4. **COLLABORATIVE LEARNING** During the Renaissance, carpenters and other skilled workers belonged to guilds, or unions. Form small groups. Have each group give a presentation on a modern labor union. Divide the following tasks among the members of each group: (a) research the history of the union, (b) find out about the benefits the union offers workers, (c) investigate the problems the union faces today, and (d) interview one or more members of the union (or a similar union in your community). Then, as a group, present your report to the class.

Chapter 19

The Rise of Spain, Great Britain, and Russia

The period after the Reformation was a stormy time in Europe. Catholics and Protestants fought for their beliefs. Kings and queens plotted against their enemies. Spain, Great Britain, and Russia each built enormous empires. Meanwhile, European explorers sailed across uncharted waters and claimed new lands. The New World was colonized and a "revolution" began to change the old one.

Christopher Columbus set sail from Spain and landed in the West Indies in 1492. This painting shows Columbus and King Ferdinand of Spain kneeling at the feet of the Virgin Mary as she blesses them and their ships.

800	1040	1280

800

988 Kievan Prince Vladimir I becomes an Orthodox Christian. He begins a tradition of deep religious devotion among the Russian people. The Church of the Annunciation (above), built in the 15th century, is a lasting symbol of Russia's religious heritage.

At the height of its empire, Great Britain became known as the workshop of the world. Goods and resources flowed between Britain and the rest of the world through busy ports like this one in Bristol, England.

The Industrial Revolution affected all aspects of life, including the way people kept track of time. This 18th-century British watch shows how workers, who once measured their labor in terms of crops and seasons, adapted to the strict schedule of the modern workday.

1588 The Spanish Armada is defeated by the English navy and unfavorable winds in the English Channel.

1770 James Cook of the British navy sights and explores Australia.

1891 Work begins on the Trans-Siberian Railroad in Russia.

1520

1760

2000

Plants and animals such as the Australian emu were unfamiliar and fascinating to European explorers.

1867 Russia sells Alaska to the United States.

Today

LESSON 1

Spain: The First Modern Empire

THINKING

FOCUS

What did the Spanish people gain and lose by building an empire?

Key Terms

- conviso
- Reconquista
- colonialism
- Columbian exchange

➤ *The marriage of Ferdinand and Isabella was the first step toward Spain's becoming an empire.*

It is an October morning in 1469. Eighteen-year-old Princess Isabella of Castile *(kas TEEL)* and seventeen-year-old Prince Ferdinand of Aragon are about to make history. They will soon be married against the wishes of Castile's King Henry IV, Isabella's half brother.

King Henry has ideas of his own about whom Isabella should marry. He wants her to choose between Charles, the brother of the king of France, and Alfonso, the king of Portugal.

However, Isabella has no interest in either of these men. She does not want her kingdom controlled by either France or Portugal. Nor does she want to marry an older man, especially one as old as King Alfonso. He merely wants a queen to bear his children—most important, a male heir. Isabella wants to be a ruler herself. She has

made sure of that by drawing up a marriage contract that protects all of her rights as a ruler. Alfonso would never allow it. Ferdinand has already agreed to her terms.

If Isabella marries Ferdinand, they can unite their two kingdoms. One day she hopes to unite all the Spanish peninsula to create one of the strongest crowns in Europe.

Although Isabella is young and inexperienced, she is also intelligent and strong willed. She knows that her choice of a husband is very important; kingdoms are united and allied through royal marriages.

Isabella succeeded in the first step of her plan. She married Ferdinand before her brother could halt the wedding. The question remained, however, as to what kind of a kingdom she and Ferdinand would create and who would be allowed to live in it.

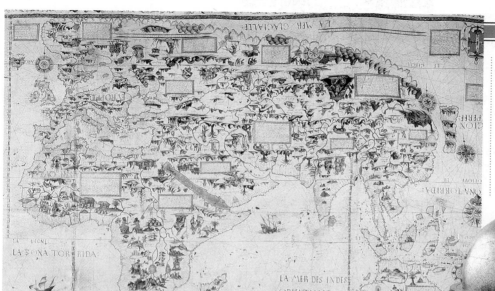

Uniting Spain

Isabella and Ferdinand were determined to make Spain a completely Catholic, united state. To do this, they needed to wrest the kingdom of Granada, to the south, from the control of the Muslims from North Africa. Spain also wanted to drive all Jews, Muslims, and **conversos,** Jews who had converted to Christianity, out of Spain.

The Reconquista

Isabella and Ferdinand needed to capture Granada, the last Muslim stronghold in Spain. They led their armies in the **Reconquista,** or reconquering of the peninsula.

Finally, in 1492, the Spanish rulers captured Granada.

The Spanish Inquisition

Some Christians worried that the *conversos* were a threat. They thought some *conversos* had converted only so they could hold offices that were barred to Jews. In reaction to this fear, Isabella and Ferdinand set the Spanish Inquisition in motion. People who were suspected of being non-Catholic were examined. Suspects were sometimes tortured. Several thousand *conversos* and many Muslims who claimed to have converted were persecuted.

In 1492 Ferdinand and Isabella drove out all Jews who refused to be baptized. More than 100,000 Spanish citizens left the country. However, many Jews remained in Spain and became Catholics. Many others returned to Spain later and converted.

By 1492 Isabella's dream of a unified Spain was becoming a reality. For the first time in centuries, efforts to make Spain a unified Catholic state were beginning to show results. ■

▲ *Muslims made many valuable contributions to Spain and Spanish culture. This 12th century celestial globe was made in Persia and aided the Spaniards in their explorations.*

◄ *Before the Inquisition, many Spanish Jews were successful merchants, doctors, and scholars. In this picture a wealthy Jew distributes food to the poor.*

■ *What did Ferdinand and Isabella do to unify Spain?*

The Rise of Spain, Great Britain, and Russia

Building an Empire

With the conquest of Granada, Ferdinand and Isabella concentrated their energies on overseas expansion. They wanted to catch up with rival Portugal, which now led the European world in trade, navigation, and exploration. If Spain could match Portugal's successes, Spain would have to seek its own trade routes and establish its own overseas contacts and colonies. Read Understanding Colonialism below to discover more about colonies.

➤ *Spanish explorers followed Columbus to the Americas to seek their fortunes, to claim land for the Spanish Crown, and to spread Christianity.*

The Voyages of Columbus

Shortly after the defeat of the Muslims, the Italian seaman Christopher Columbus reached an agreement with Queen Isabella. Columbus would sail west and seek a shorter route to Asia. The Spanish monarchs would fund his expedition. As payment for a successful

UNDERSTANDING COLONIALISM

Spain, Portugal, France, England, and the Netherlands were all once great colonial powers. They had colonies in North, South, and Central America as well as Asia, Africa, and the islands in the Pacific.

What Is Colonialism?

Colonialism means that one country occupies another and controls its people, politics, and economy. Colonies were not free to make their own decisions.

Why did the European powers seek colonies? Is colonialism practiced today?

Reasons for Colonialism

Colonies gave the European powers added territory, natural resources, and cheap labor. Since colonies were under a European nation's control, the land, the resources, and the labor of the colonists were used to benefit the ruling country rather than the colony itself.

Most colonial powers believed they were helping the people they had colonized by bringing them Christianity or ideas of Western civilization. However, this view also served to justify their often cruel or unjust treatment of the colonized peoples.

Colonialism Today

Nearly all the colonies of European nations have now won their independence and are recognized as nations themselves. Some made this transition without violence; others had to fight for it. Colonialism is considered wrong today, but many of the economies of less developed countries are still controlled by the industrialized nations. In this way colonialism is still occurring throughout the world.

voyage, Columbus would receive a title, knighthood, and a share of any wealth that he discovered.

In 1492 Columbus reached the West Indies. Upon his return to Spain, rumors spread that the lands he had explored were rich with gold. This news attracted many Spanish fortune seekers to the Americas.

The Empire Grows

Armed adventurers and colonizers poured out of Spain. Most were from poor families. They claimed most of the Caribbean Islands, Panama, Florida, Mexico, Peru, and then much of South America for Spain. In less than 50 years, these explorers had seized for Spain territories that were about the size of the Roman Empire at its height.

The Spanish monarchs did not trust all of these adventurers. These bold fighters were very likely to set up governorships of their own. Colonists and administrators were quickly sent to make sure the new conquests remained under the Crown's control and were well run. Plantations were set up to grow sugar cane and other crops for export to Europe. With native labor, they built cities, towns, and churches in the Spanish style. By 1540 the first printing presses and universities in the Western Hemisphere were quickly established in Santo Domingo and Mexico City.

By the middle of the 1500s, Spain's empire included wide holdings in North, Central, and South America. The map of Spain's empire below shows the full extent of Spanish colonization. Spain also controlled what is now the Netherlands and Belgium as well as parts of France, Italy, Austria, and Germany. ■

▲ *These coins, called pieces of eight, were made in Mexico for use in Asia. They show the vastness of the Spanish Empire in the 16th and 17th centuries.*

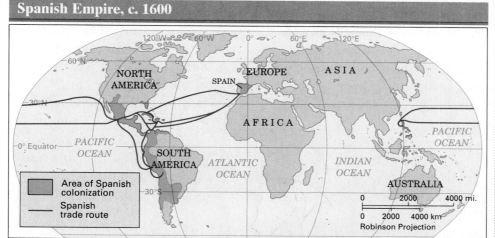

Spanish Empire, c. 1600

Spanish Empire, 1492–1898

Reasons for Empire	Imports from Spanish Colonies
Seek private profit, increase national wealth, spread Christianity	Silver, gold, copper, grain, tobacco, cocoa beans, hides, sugar

◄ *In what regions did most of Spain's overseas trade activity take place?*

■ *What was the extent of Spain's empire by the end of the 1500s?*

441

The Rise of Spain, Great Britain, and Russia

The Columbian Exchange

People, goods, culture, and ideas were exchanged between Spain and its colonies, and with the rest of the world. Soon five continents were involved in the trade: North and South America, Europe, Asia, and Africa. Everything from religion to potatoes traveled back and forth across the Atlantic. This vast movement has become known as the **Columbian exchange.**

The Columbian Exchange

"I believe there are many plants and trees here that would be very much appreciated in Spain," wrote Columbus, as he surveyed the island of Hispaniola *(hihs puhn YOH luh)*. In time, the Americas provided Spain with a number of new foods and other products. Maize, or corn, and chocolate made their way to Europe, along with avocados, beans, tomatoes, tobacco, and timber. Foods such as corn became important crops in Africa as well.

The Spanish brought many foods to their colonies. The chart below shows some of these items. In addition, they introduced horses, cows, pigs, and sheep to the Americas.

Africans brought with them to the Americas their cultures, including African languages and beliefs. The Spaniards brought European beliefs to many parts of the Americas. They also brought their language and Christianity to the colonies.

The Cost of Exchange

Much of Africa's involvement in the Columbian exchange was tragic. Vast numbers of Africans were shipped to the Western Hemisphere as slaves to work on the plantations. In general they were inhumanly treated.

The arrival of the Europeans and slaves from Africa brought death to many Native Americans. Fatal diseases, overwork, and slavery accounted for untold losses.

Measles, smallpox, typhus, and other diseases rapidly spread through the hemisphere. The native peoples had never before been exposed to these illnesses from Europe and Africa. They had no way to fight them off.

Many Spanish explorers and

▲ *This 15th-century cross was found on La Isabella, one of the islands in the West Indies that Columbus visited.*

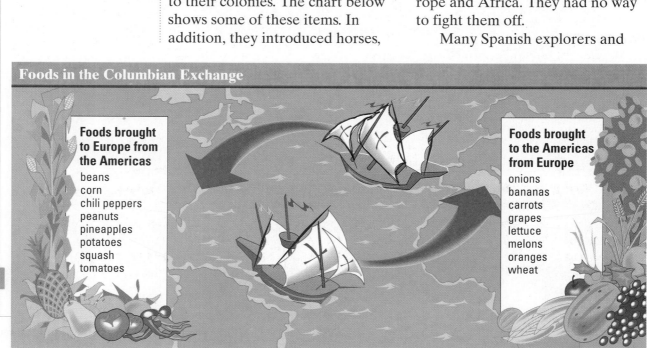

Foods in the Columbian Exchange

Foods brought to Europe from the Americas

beans
corn
chili peppers
peanuts
pineapples
potatoes
squash
tomatoes

Foods brought to the Americas from Europe

onions
bananas
carrots
grapes
lettuce
melons
oranges
wheat

settlers treated Native Americans cruelly. They forced them to work on plantations or to mine precious metals. Yet a few Spaniards, such as Bartolomé de las Casas *(bahr toh loh MAY day lahs KAH sahs)*, a planter who had become a priest, objected to this mistreatment. In his *History of the Indies,* he describes "the mild and pacific [peaceful] temperament [personality] of the natives" and comments, "but our work was to exasperate, ravage, kill, mangle, and destroy."

Spain's Empire in Decline

Spain's rulers started to rely on shipments of silver and gold from the Americas to solve their financial problems. The flood of precious metals caused prices at home to rise, which created a need for even more wealth. Only a small part of the riches was invested in the country's economy or people. The silver and gold were instead used to pay for the Crown's expenses and for the Spanish armies fighting Protestants in Europe.

Spain experienced a large outflow of population while building its empire. Many of its brightest citizens, most of whom were adventurous young people, went to Spanish America to look for riches.

When Philip II, Isabella and Ferdinand's great-grandson, took the throne in 1556, he wanted to spread Catholicism throughout the world. His desire to convert England back to Catholicism led in 1588 to an unsuccessful attack on England by the so-called Invincible [unbeatable] Armada, a fleet of 130 Spanish galleons. The defeat of the Armada was the beginning of the decline of the Spanish Empire. ■

Although they outnumbered the English, Spanish ships were big and slow. English ships were faster and easier to handle.

How Do We Know?

HISTORY *Although the journal Columbus kept during the voyage has been lost, we know much of what he said in it. Bartolomé de las Casas used it to write his* History of the Indies *in the 1500s. It is one of our most important sources of information about the 1492 voyage.*

■ *What was the Columbian exchange?*

R E V I E W

1. **FOCUS** What did the Spanish people gain and lose by building an empire?
2. **ECONOMICS** What did Spain receive through the Columbian exchange? What did Spain's colonies receive in return?
3. **HISTORY** Why is 1492 such an important date in Spanish history?
4. **CRITICAL THINKING** Why did Spain and other European nations seek colonies in this period?
5. **ACTIVITY** One of modern Spain's great artists was Pablo Picasso. One of his contributions to art was his development of the collage. Use pictures from magazines or travel brochures to create a collage about Spain.

LESSON 2

Great Britain's Sea Empire

THINKING FOCUS

What inspired Great Britain to build an empire?

Key Terms

- Industrial Revolution
- trade union
- raw materials

➤ *One of the lasting marks of Britain's worldwide empire is the tradition of afternoon tea.*

Y*ou could hardly see the sea. The Spanish fleet was stretched out in the form of a half moon. . . . The masts and rigging, the towering sterns and prows which in height and number were so great that they dominated the whole [scene], caused horror mixed with wonder and gave rise to doubt whether that campaign was at sea or on land. . . .*

This eyewitness account of the Spanish Armada describes the enormous invasion force Spain sent to attack England. It had been called the Invincible Armada by the Spaniards. Never before had such a military force been put together. The English navy faced an enemy like no other.

Outnumbered, English sailors outwitted the Spanish navy. With the aid of the weather, the English successfully turned the armada away. Spain's navy and spirit were all but destroyed.

Much more was won than just a military victory, however. Spain's power and prestige throughout the world were shaken. As you have read, Spain's empire quickly declined after the defeat of the armada.

Out of the smoke of the battle, a new world power appeared. This power would be known as the British Empire.

Building the British Empire

At its peak, Britain's empire spanned the globe. The British boasted that "the sun never sets on the British Empire." The map below supports this claim. The process of building this empire, however, was a long one.

The Rise of the British Empire

The early stages of empire building began with the failure of the Spanish Armada. English merchants and sailors became eager to compete with the Spaniards around the world.

Abundant fish and the fur trade first had attracted British ships to the Americas. By 1670, colonies were established in North America. Settlements were also built in Bermuda, Honduras, Antigua, and Barbados.

Spices had attracted ships to India in the early 1600s. As you read in Chapter 14, by the mid-1700s England had become the true ruler of India.

In 1707 the Kingdom of England and the Kingdom of Scotland approved the Act of Union. England had already united with Wales. The entire island was now under a single government. This union was called Great Britain.

Competition with France

With Spain in decline, Britain found itself competing with France for economic control of North America, the West Indies, and India. Several armed conflicts between the British and the French took place. The conflict between them finally boiled over in the French and Indian War.

Begun in 1754, this war was fought in North America. Each side allied itself with Native American peoples and fought throughout the hemisphere. Two years later the

▲ Among the world's greatest explorers was the British navigator James Cook. This drawing of one of Cook's ships was made by a member of his crew.

◄ On how many continents did Great Britain have colonies?

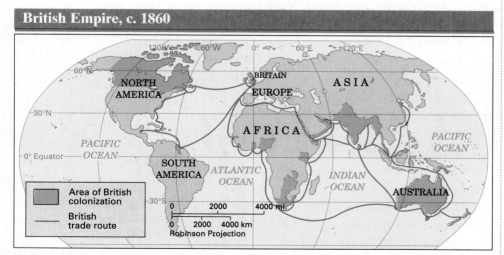

British Empire, c. 1860

Area of British colonization

British trade route

2000   4000 mi.

0   2000   4000 km
Robinson Projection

Great Britain's Empire, 1600–1931

Reasons for Empire	Imports from British Colonies
Expand trade, improve defense, increase power	Sugar, oil, palm oil, ivory, gold, nuts, cocoa, cotton, copper, tea, spices

The Rise of Spain, Great Britain, and Russia

conflict spilled over into Europe and was called the Seven Years' War.

Britain emerged victorious and gained French territories throughout North America, including Canada.

The Empire Suffers Setbacks

Britain sought to pay for the expansion and control of its empire by taxing the colonies. The burden of supporting Britain's growth was too much for many colonies.

Taxes such as those on stamps and tea were put into effect in North America. Eventually, the 13 original North American colonies broke away to form the United States. Britain, however, continued to colonize Canada, which it prized for its fur and timber. The chart on page 445 shows more about the empire and the goods it valued.

India's rulers and their peoples struggled with the British taxes. Many Indian rulers revolted. However, India for the time being was unable to break away from Britain. India was too important for Britain to lose.

The cost of fighting France in the Americas and throughout Europe had severely drained the British treasury. In Great Britain itself colonialism was becoming increasingly unpopular. ■

■ *How did Britain become a great colonial power?*

▲ *Isambard Kingdom Brunel was one of Britain's greatest engineers. He is shown standing in front of the launching chains of the ship* Great Western *in 1857.*

➤ *Street scenes like this one in 19th-century London were common during the Industrial Revolution.*

The Industrial Revolution

In 1769 James Watt, a poor Scottish instrument maker, built a steam engine that was fast and efficient. A few years later he began manufacturing his engine. Eventually, it powered many different types of machines. Watt's invention helped bring about a revolution—the **Industrial Revolution.**

From Farm to Factory

The Industrial Revolution greatly changed the way workers lived and did their jobs. It caused a dramatic increase in the amount of work human beings could get done in a day.

People who had once made thread or cloth at home by hand now went to work in factories. There they used steam-powered machines to spin thread and weave it into cloth. A 19th-century textile worker using steam-powered machines could make 50 times as much cloth as a worker in the previous century.

As the Industrial Revolution expanded, more and more factories sprang up in Britain's cities. Many people left the countryside for good. They exchanged their old ties to the land for a new and often troubling life.

New Machines and Ideas

Many technologies of today can be traced back to this era. For example, in the 1830s William Henry Fox Talbot produced the first photographic negative in Britain. Inventions and discoveries of all sorts changed ordinary life.

A scientific approach to solving problems was behind these inventions. That approach had its roots in the Enlightenment of the 1600s and 1700s. Enlightenment thinkers believed that humans could understand and explain the laws that governed the universe.

In the 1800s some artists, writers, and musicians rebelled against that way of thinking. They valued emotions and nature over science and machines. Their movement was called Romanticism.

Technology Changes Daily Life

Industrialization made life harder for workers. Early factory working conditions were miserable. People who had once made their own decisions about when to work now had to work when the factory boss told them to. Instead of setting their own pace, workers had to match their pace to a machine's.

Yet the growth of industry opened up many new opportunities. People no longer needed large amounts of land to be wealthy. Through hard work, shrewd investing, and luck, they could improve their standard of living and even become rich. More and more people entered the middle class.

Cries for Reform in Great Britain

Britain's House of Lords was still controlled largely by the rich, landowning nobility. The middle class demanded a larger voice as it grew and prospered. In 1832 middle-class males won the right to vote.

Also successful, in the long run, were efforts made by workers themselves. They formed societies and eventually **trade unions** to fight for better working conditions and better pay. Unsafe conditions injured, disabled, and killed many workers, who worked up to 15 hours a day. Gradually, in the face of great opposition, the unions rolled back the worst problems. Eventually, over several decades, pressure from the voters and the unions led to changes such as the 10-hour work day, child labor laws, and required schooling.

No one—rich or poor—could escape the filth caused by the Industrial Revolution. Pollution affected the land, the air, the rivers, and the lakes everywhere. Inadequate sewer systems, polluted water, and dirty streets led to the spread of dangerous diseases. As the 19th century progressed, social reformers pressured the British government to improve sanitation. ■

◄ *The camera was one of the most important inventions of the 19th century.*

■ *Who benefited most from the Industrial Revolution? Explain your answer.*

447

Expanding the British Empire

The astonishing increase in Britain's wealth brought on by the Industrial Revolution now fueled the growth of the empire. Britain soon dominated world trade.

The Empire Expands

Britain's growing middle class could not buy all the goods that were being produced. By the middle of the 1800s, Britain's workers and machines produced more than 1.75 billion yards of cotton a year. Britain's production of iron made up nearly half the global output.

Because Great Britain had a small population, it had to seek more buyers for its goods all over the world. The British believed that an expanding empire would create markets for their goods.

Britain's own supplies of coal and other important raw materials were too small. **Raw materials** are the basic materials from which industrial goods are produced. Raw materials poured into Britain from its colonies. Manufactured goods were shipped out. All of these exchanges were carried on merchant vessels that were protected around the world by the British navy.

By the close of the 19th century, Britain had established settlements or colonies throughout the world. The map on page 445 shows the extent of Britain's empire.

British Influence Worldwide

As their empire grew to include more distant regions, many Britons grew curious about these lands. Like the Spaniards, some Britons thought they were helping people by bringing them Christianity and Western civilization. Rudyard Kipling captured much of the romance of the British Empire in his poetry. He expressed its best and worst side in his poem "The White Man's Burden."

*T*ake up the White Man's
burden–
  Send forth the best ye breed–
Go, bind your sons to exile
  To serve your captives' need

Not everyone in Britain thought that foreigners needed to be "civilized." A few naturalists and anthropologists wanted to study the cultures, plants, and wildlife of distant parts of the empire. Marianne North and Charles Darwin are examples of this.

▲ *Great Britain reached the height of its power during the reign of Queen Victoria. The period of her rule is often called the Victorian age.*

▼ *The costs of maintaining an empire were very high. The British soldiers below are the 93rd Highlanders, on duty in India in the 1890s.*

Britain, Transplanted

Wherever the British went during the days of their empire, they took along their way of life. They packed their trunks with Victorian clothing and games. Tropical heat in foreign lands would force most people indoors at noon—but not the British. Some newcomers even drank hot tea every day at teatime. Most tried to live as if they were still in England.

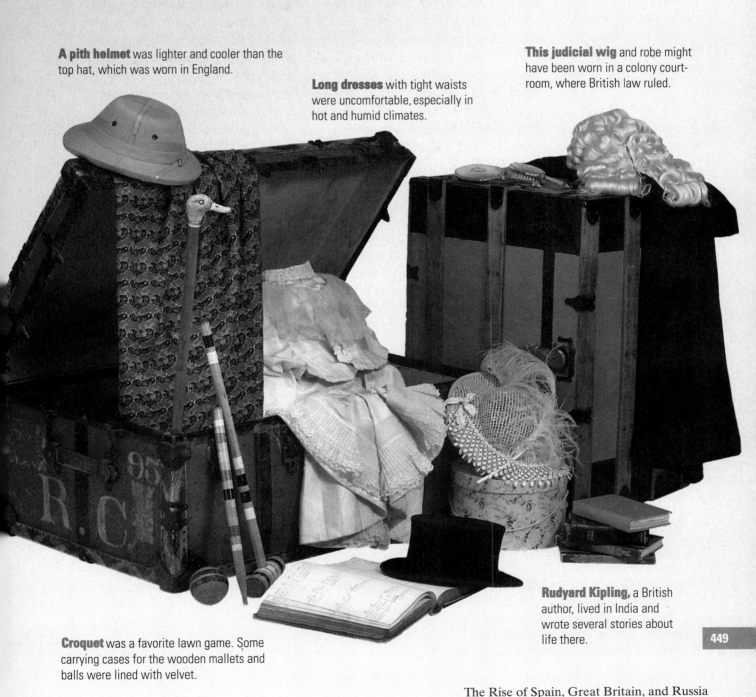

A pith helmet was lighter and cooler than the top hat, which was worn in England.

Long dresses with tight waists were uncomfortable, especially in hot and humid climates.

This judicial wig and robe might have been worn in a colony court-room, where British law ruled.

Croquet was a favorite lawn game. Some carrying cases for the wooden mallets and balls were lined with velvet.

Rudyard Kipling, a British author, lived in India and wrote several stories about life there.

449

North traveled throughout the empire and the world, painting the flowers and other plants of various regions. Her paintings are displayed at London's botanical gardens.

Darwin sailed around the world, observing plants and animals. His notes from his journey were the basis for his theory of natural selection, or how he believed life had evolved on the earth. Darwin's theory was considered at the time to be one of the 19th century's most important contributions to science.

At about the same time, a German philosopher named Karl Marx wrote *Das Kapital* in Great Britain. In this work he analyzes the economics of capitalism. His ideas served as the basis for the theories of communism.

The Empire Dwindles

Although it had taken centuries to build, Britain's empire declined in just a few decades. A whole generation of British people were killed or ruined by World War I. The war exhausted the British economy. After the war, independence movements arose in many British colonies. One of the most famous was the non-violent campaign for India's independence, led by Gandhi. You read in Chapter 14 about his role in India's struggle for independence.

The costs of World War II ended Britain's role as a world power. It was now utterly unable to maintain an empire. Britain withdrew from the Middle East and most of its Asian colonies between 1945 and 1948. In the early 1960s, most of Britain's African colonies won their independence, some after violent struggles.

The Influence of British Culture

Like Spain, Great Britain brought its language and its religion, Protestantism, to its colonies. Today, English is the second most widely spoken language in the world. This language has in turn been enriched by all the peoples who have spoken it. For example, the word *pajamas* comes from India, as does the word *loot*. Read A Closer Look on page 449 to discover more about British culture and Britain's relationship with its territories. ∎

▼ *Traces of British culture can be found around the world in everything from the use of the English language to the popular sport of badminton.*

∎ *Why were Britain's colonies important to its industrial expansion?*

R E V I E W

1. **FOCUS** What inspired Great Britain to build an empire?
2. **SOCIAL SYSTEMS** How did the Industrial Revolution change British society?
3. **ECONOMICS** How did the Industrial Revolution contribute to the growth of the British Empire?
4. **POLITICAL SYSTEMS** How did the Industrial Revolution affect the government of Great Britain?
5. **CRITICAL THINKING** Do you think that the Industrial Revolution made life better or worse for people in Britain? Explain your answer.
6. **WRITING ACTIVITY** Imagine you are the editor of a small newspaper in Britain during the Industrial Revolution. Write a positive or negative editorial commenting on an aspect of life that has changed in your town in recent decades.

Comparing Graphs

Here's Why

Graphs can help you organize information. They can help you see patterns and make comparisons. Some kinds of graphs are best used to present certain kinds of information.

Suppose you want to understand how world trade increased as a result of the Industrial Revolution in Europe. You can use graphs to analyze this information.

The graphs on this page present information on world trade. The graphs show trade information in two very different ways.

By comparing two graphs, you can get more information than you can from one graph. Also, by understanding what each graph does best, you can learn which type of graph to choose to present your own information.

Here's How

The graph on the left is a bar graph; the other is a pie graph. The bar graph shows change over time. The bar graph at the lower left shows how world trade increased from the year 1780 through the year 1820. The amount of trade is measured in British money, called pounds (£).

You can see that in 1780 world trade was valued at approximately £186 million. By 1820 this figure had risen to about £350 million.

Suppose you want to know what countries were involved in most of the trade at one particular time. You could use a pie graph for this information.

A pie graph shows how something is divided into parts. Each part is a fraction, or a percentage, of the whole. For example, if you made a pie graph of your class, you might show how the class is divided into boys and girls.

The pie graph below shows what countries took part in world trade in the year 1820. Each piece of the pie shows how the amount of trade from one country or region relates to the total world trade. You can see that Great Britain was involved in 22 percent of the total world trade.

Try It

Now try making your own graphs with the following information. Suppose that in 1840 world trade dropped by £100 million. What would your new bar graph look like? Suppose that in 1840 France decreased its trade by 4 percent because of trade barriers. France's loss was split evenly between Germany and Russia. Trade in all the other countries remained the same. What would your new pie graph look like?

Apply It

Keep track of how you spend your free time after school for a week. Your activities might include studying, reading, and playing. What would be the best way to present this information? Draw the graph you have chosen and be prepared to present it to the class.

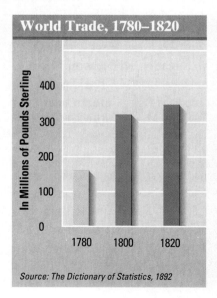

World Trade, 1780–1820

In Millions of Pounds Sterling

400 300 200 100 0

1780 1800 1820

Source: The Dictionary of Statistics, 1892

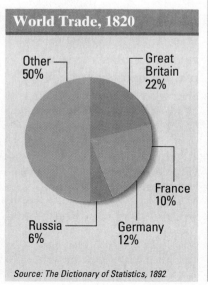

World Trade, 1820

Other 50%
Great Britain 22%
France 10%
Germany 12%
Russia 6%

Source: The Dictionary of Statistics, 1892

451

LESSON 3

Russia's Land Empire

How did the Russian Empire grow?

Key Terms

- steppe
- czar

➤ *Saint Basil's Cathedral in Moscow's Red Square was built during the reign of Ivan IV. He celebrated the empire's growth during his reign by having it built.*

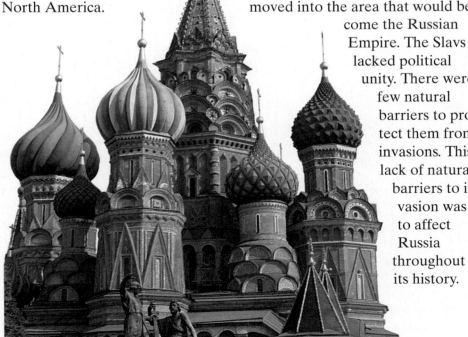

To the distant east, far from Spain and Great Britain, another empire was growing. For most of this empire's history, wild horses stampeded across the plains and wandering peoples herded cattle. It was a vast land of great beauty.

What did this land look like? Imagine a broad, rolling plain covered with tall, greenish gold grasses higher than your head. Purple, blue, and golden wildflowers dot the grass. The sea of grass goes on for several thousand miles in every direction. This is the **steppe**—a huge grassland like the Great Plains of North America.

North of the steppe is a thick forest. The windy steppe and thick, northern forests dominate the land.

Even today, thick forests cover much of the land. In the north the trees are evergreens. Other forests include oak, birch, and beech trees.

Several large rivers cross this land. They run generally from north to south, many between the Baltic Sea and the Black Sea. Rivers provided the easiest way to travel across the wild land.

People eventually settled in valleys near the rivers. They worshiped statues and figures that they believed controlled the forces of nature and life.

Later, Eastern Slavs *(slahvz)* moved into the area that would become the Russian Empire. The Slavs lacked political unity. There were few natural barriers to protect them from invasions. This lack of natural barriers to invasion was to affect Russia throughout its history.

The Rise of Russia

By the 800s, Slavic groups had established towns in the western portion of Russia known as the Ukraine. Before long two powerful forces dominated these peoples.

The First Russian State

Probably early in the 800s, the first invading group, the Vikings, discovered that the rivers of Russia were a good trade route. The route ran from the Baltic Sea to Constantinople, one of the main cities of the Byzantine Empire. Vikings took slaves, furs, amber, honey, and beeswax to trade for the Byzantines' gold, silver, and silk.

To protect trade the Vikings fortified their trading posts of Kiev *(KEE ehv)* and Novgorod *(NAWV guh rawd)*.

Vikings soon ruled Kiev and Novgorod. Kiev became a rich trading center due to its position on the Dnieper River, which is between the Baltic Sea and the Black Sea. The ruler of Kiev came to be known as the *grand prince* and ranked above all other Russian princes. Kiev's rulers greatly admired Byzantine culture. In about 988, Prince Vladimir I and all of his subjects became Orthodox Christians.

The Mongol Invasion

Disaster came suddenly to Kievan Russia. Weakened by civil wars and lacking strong leadership, the area fell to the Mongols. This second group of invaders were

▲ *A mid-16th-century Russian crown made of engraved gold set with jewels and fur trimming.*

◀ *What were the last regions to become part of the Russian Empire?*

Across Time & Space

Only about 55 miles of water separate Siberia, in easternmost Russia, from the State of Alaska. Russian expeditions sent by Peter the Great landed in Alaska in the 1700s, and a rich fur trade grew there. Russians made the first settlement in 1784, and a joint Russian-U.S. company ran the territory. Russia sold Alaska to the United States in 1867, for $7,200,000.

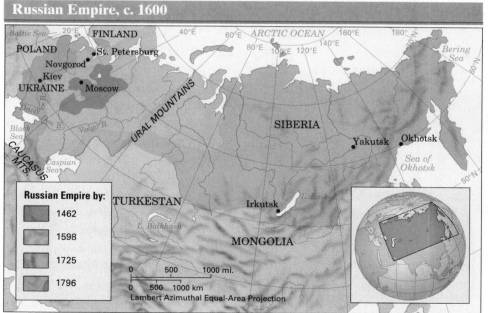

Russian Empire, c. 1600

Russian Empire by:
- 1462
- 1598
- 1725
- 1796

Russian Empire, 1462–1917

Reasons for Empire	Imports from Russian Colonies
Protect borders, gain seaports, increase trade, add natural resources	Timber, iron ore, gold, fur, grain

fierce warriors from Asia who came galloping in from the plains to the east.

By 1240 Russia had become part of the immense Mongol Empire. The Mongols did not rule the region directly. Instead, they required tribute and troops from the Slavic princes. Paying high taxes to the Mongols kept Russia poor.

The Rise of Moscow

Deep in the forest, the town of Moscow was becoming strong and rich. Its rulers were clever and ambitious. They took over neighboring lands and fought to escape Mongol control.

In 1480 Ivan III, called "the Great," stopped paying tribute to the Mongols. He declared himself the leader of Russia and defender of its church. He took the title **czar,** from the Latin word for emperor.

Ivan's grandson, Ivan IV, conquered lands along the Volga River. Called "Ivan the Terrible" for his cruelty, he limited peasants' freedoms. Over the centuries Russian peasants became serfs, bound to the land they worked. ■

■ *Did the Vikings or the Mongols better rule the people of Russia? Why?*

Russia Becomes a World Power

After Ivan IV died in 1584, wars and revolts swept over Russia during the Time of Troubles. In 1613 a new ruling family, the Romanovs, came to power. The Romanovs would remain in power for the next 300 years until the February Revolution of 1917. You will read about the end of Romanov rule in Chapter 20. The map on page 453 shows the Russia that the Romanovs would rule.

Peter the Great Looks to the West

The reign of Peter the Great was a turning point for Russia. Peter, a Romanov, became czar in 1682. He wanted Russia to catch up with Western Europe's skills, technology, and culture.

Disguised as an ordinary traveler, Peter had explored much of Western Europe before he took power. As czar, Peter began to modernize and westernize Russia. He encouraged the building of modern factories and schools. Peter made changes in the government and improved the quality of the army.

Peter also wanted to enlarge Russia's borders and build an empire. To help him achieve these goals, he began a massive shipbuilding program. He went to war against the Ottoman Empire and against the Persians. His victories allowed Russia to extend south, to the shores of the Caspian Sea.

To gain land and a seaport on the Baltic Sea, Peter went to war against Sweden in 1700. He defeated Sweden and opened up a

➤ *Peter the Great desperately wanted to westernize Russia. He even wanted Russia's nobles to cut off their beards to look more like the upper classes of Europe. A nobleman could keep his beard if he paid a special tax to obtain a beard license like the one above.*

"window to the West," a needed passageway to the Baltic Sea. Peter then built a brand-new capital city, St. Petersburg, near the Baltic coast.

Imperial Russia

Russia's empire grew most of all during the reigns of Catherine the Great and the two czars who came after her. Catherine, a German princess, became empress in 1762, after her husband was deposed. She ruled until 1796 and made Russia a great power. Land in Poland and Turkey became part of the empire.

Like Peter, Catherine admired the culture of Western Europe. She corresponded with the great thinkers of her time. She encouraged schools and the arts, including ballet. Yet although Europeans were discussing new ideas such as the rights of ordinary people, Catherine did nothing to help the peasants in Russia.

Russia Expands Its Empire

Once Russia was a great power, it had to fight to keep and expand its position. Unlike Spain and Great Britain, Russia continued to look around its own borders for room to expand, as China had done before.

Russia fought the Ottoman Empire, Britain, and France, losing the Crimean War in 1856. Russia then moved eastward toward the Pacific Ocean. It won territories from China and in central Asia.

Life under the Czars

From the time of the first czars, there had been a huge gap between the Russian upper classes and ordinary people. Nobles and wealthy families lived in glittering luxury, often following Western European customs. Russian peasants simply tried to survive.

Some czars after Catherine were truly interested in democratic ideas. They did not want to give up power, however. Writers and young nobles who demanded reforms often faced prison or exile.

In 1861 Czar Alexander II gave the serfs their freedom and some land. Unfortunately, the lives of ordinary Russians did not improve much. As you will read in the next chapter, the growing gap between rich and poor would eventually tear Russian society apart. ■

▲ *Russian writer and novelist Leo Tolstoy, pictured here telling a story to his grandchildren in 1909, lived through much of Russia's expansion. A veteran of the Crimean War, he later gave up all his wealth to live and write among peasants.*

■ *How did Peter the Great and Catherine the Great modernize Russia?*

R E V I E W

1. **FOCUS** How did the Russian Empire grow?
2. **GEOGRAPHY** How did Russia's physical environment play a role in its history?
3. **HISTORY** What changes did Peter and Catherine begin in Russia?
4. **HISTORY** Why was the reign of Peter the Great considered a turning point in Russia's history?

5. **CRITICAL THINKING** What do you think was the greatest difference between Russia's empire and the empires of Spain and Great Britain?
6. **ACTIVITY** Imagine you are living in Russia during the 800s. Give an eyewitness account of the arrival of the Viking raiders. Where did they come from? How do they treat you and your family? What do they want?

455

The Rise of Spain, Great Britain, and Russia

Chapter Review

Reviewing Key Terms

colonialism (p. 440)
Columbian exchange
   (p. 442)
converso (p. 439)
czar (p. 454)
Industrial Revolution
   (p. 446)

raw materials (p. 448)
Reconquista (p. 439)
steppe (p. 452)
trade union (p. 447)

A. Read each pair of words. Write a sentence telling how the words in each pair are related. Be sure to use the terms themselves in each explanation.
1. Reconquista, converso
2. Industrial Revolution, trade union
3. colonialism, raw materials

B. Write the key term that is described by each sentence below.
1. The Mongols crossed a broad, rolling plain of tall grasses and conquered Kievan Russia.
2. People, goods, culture, and ideas flowed between North and South America, Europe, Asia, and Africa.
3. Ivan the Great created a new title for himself that came from the Latin word for emperor.

Exploring Concepts

A. In this chapter you have read about the Columbian exchange. Copy and complete the table below to show what was brought to the Americas and what was sent to Europe. List at least two items in each box.

Items Exchanged	To the Americas	To Europe
Food plants		
Animals and other plants		
Other		

B. Answer each question with information from the chapter.
1. Why did Princess Isabella want to marry Prince Ferdinand instead of someone like King Alfonso of Portugal?
2. What were Isabella and Ferdinand's main goals for Spain?
3. In the 1400s, what country was Spain's main rival for leadership in trade and exploration throughout the world?
4. On what continents did Spain hold territories by the mid-1500s?
5. In what ways did building an empire weaken Spain?
6. Why was the English navy able to turn the Spanish Armada away from England's shores?
7. What kingdoms were united in 1707 to form Great Britain?
8. In what ways did Britain and France compete during the 1700s?
9. Explain two ways in which the Industrial Revolution changed how goods such as cloth were made.
10. How did the Industrial Revolution increase Great Britain's need to build an empire around the globe?
11. What three outside groups influenced the development of Russia before the 1400s?
12. What were Peter the Great's main goals for Russia?
13. As the Russian Empire expanded, where were the new lands that it acquired?
14. What social reform did Czar Alexander II put into effect in Russia?

456

Reviewing Skills

1. The table below tells how many millions of tons of coal were used in Great Britain at the height of the British Empire. Would you use a bar graph or a pie graph to show this information?

Year	Coal (in millions of tons)
1890	132
1900	155
1910	168
1913	177
1920	193

2. On your own paper, create a graph using the figures from the table. Make the kind of graph you chose in Question 1.
3. The end of Lesson 3 makes this prediction: "The growing gap between rich and poor would eventually tear Russian society apart." Reread the lesson to find facts and statements on which this prediction is based. From what you have read, would you make the same prediction?
4. The Industrial Revolution greatly increased the variety of goods made in Britain's factories. What graphing method would best show the different types of goods made during this period?

Using Critical Thinking

1. Finding gold and silver was a major goal of Spanish explorers and conquerors in the Americas. How did these new riches prove harmful for Spain? Could Spain's rulers have prevented these problems?
2. When a Spanish official received land and the Indians living on that land, he was expected to provide something in return: to care for them and teach them Catholicism. Based on what you have read in this chapter, did most Spanish officials fulfill their part of this agreement?
3. If the Industrial Revolution had taken place in Russia in the 1800s, how might the country's history have been different?
4. At the close of the 19th century, Great Britain was known as the "workshop of the world." Explain why.

Preparing for Citizenship

1. COLLECTING INFORMATION The growth of the empires discussed in this chapter was the result of the efforts of a number of individuals. Choose someone mentioned in a lesson or feature and do research on this person. Prepare a short speech to present to the class about what you have learned about this person's life and work.
2. ARTS ACTIVITY The Romantic movement in art and literature began after the Industrial Revolution. English Romantic poets, such as William Wordsworth, Samuel Taylor Coleridge, and William Blake, wrote about nature. Find one or two short poems by one of these writers that you like. Read what you have chosen to the class, or draw a picture that illustrates the poem's meaning.
3. COLLABORATIVE LEARNING Working with your classmates, make an illustrated map of the Spanish or the British empire at its height. Some students might work together and draw a large-scale copy of the map of Spain's Empire (page 441) or the map of the British Empire (page 445). Other students could look in magazines for pictures of some of the goods that passed between each empire and its colonies as part of the Columbian exchange. Place each map on the bulletin board and use ribbons and thumbtacks to connect each picture with the right location.

457

Chapter 20

Europe: 1900 to the End of the Cold War

As the 20th century began, Europeans felt that technology would improve their lives. However, Europeans used gains in technology to build modern weapons. Triggered by nationalism, two world wars exploded in Europe. After World War II, Europe lay in ruins. An "iron curtain" then divided Europe—until the curtain came crashing down, peacefully.

Two world wars destroyed entire cities, such as Warsaw, Poland, shown here. World War I recruiting posters served to raise troops for the war.

YOU ARE THE MAN I WANT

1860	1880	1900	1920

1871

1914–1918 More than eight million people die in World War I, the most destructive war to date.

Berliners celebrate the fall
of the Berlin Wall in 1989.
One year later, East and
West Germany would re-
unite. Below, a Lithua-
nian worker sweeps off
the toppled statue of
the once-feared Soviet
ruler, Josef Stalin.

Mother Russia carries the
hopes of the Russian people
for their revolution of 1917.

1940

1960

1980

2000

1939–1945 About 50 million people die
in World War II—six times as many as
died in World War I. After the war, the
United Nations is formed, and the Cold
War begins.

1961 The East German government
builds the Berlin Wall to prevent its
people from fleeing to the West. The
wall is a grim symbol of the deep division
between Eastern and Western Europe.

1991

L E S S O N   1

World War I

THINKING FOCUS

What were the causes and outcomes of World War I?

Key Terms

- jingoism
- alliance

*W*e don't want to fight,
   But, by jingo, if we do,
We've got the ships,
We've got the men,
We've got the money too!

British music-hall song, 1878

During the late 1800s, the people of Europe were extremely proud of their countries. As this song shows, the British were proud of their world empire. The French took great pride in their country as did the Germans in theirs. What these people felt was nationalism—that loyalty to one's country was more important than individual, family, or global interests.

In Europe, nationalism also meant belonging to the same ethnic group. For example, most of the citizens of France considered themselves to be one ethnic group. They shared the same customs and language. Nationalism united the French as it did the Germans and other Europeans.

However, nationalism also divided Europe. Reread the song on this page. It introduced the word *jingo.* In the late 1800s, European nationalism often turned into **jingoism,** or warlike nationalism. "Jingoes" believed their nation could beat anyone at anything.

As a result, France, Germany, Great Britain, and Russia competed for world power. First, they raced to modernize their industries. Second, they competed for control of trade routes, raw materials, and markets around the world. Third, Germany, Great Britain, and France fought to set up colonies in Africa and Asia.

Finally, these nations competed in an arms race. They built up great armies and huge supplies of weapons.

➤ *Before World War I, using new technologies to build a dirigible, or airship, made Europeans proud of what their modern nations could accomplish. This airship's hull, or main body, held hydrogen gas, which made it lighter than air.*

Europe in Conflict

Look at the map on page 462 to see where the people of Europe lived in the early 1900s. Notice where Austrians and Hungarians lived. Find the region of southeast Europe surrounded by the Black Sea and the Mediterranean known as the Balkan peninsula, or simply the Balkans. What groups of people did this region include?

Europe's Powder Keg

Nationalism turned the Balkans into Europe's powder keg. Since the late 1400s, the Ottoman Turks had ruled most of the Balkans. Then, in 1867, the Austrians and Hungarians formed the Austro-Hungarian Empire, which was also known as Austria-Hungary.

This empire soon ruled over much of the Balkans. Turn to the map again to see which peoples they ruled. From the map you can see that many Serbs lived in the Austro-Hungarian Empire. Serbs are one of the Slavic peoples you read about in Chapter 19.

By 1878 most of the Serbs had formed an independent country, Serbia. Yet not all Serbs lived in Serbia. Many still lived in areas ruled by Austria-Hungary. Serbia wanted to expand its borders to include all Serbs. Austria-Hungary was determined not to lose any part of its empire.

The Alliance System

In the 1870s, Europeans began forming alliances to try to keep peace in Europe. An **alliance** *(uh LY uhns)* is an agreement among nations to advance a common interest.

Europeans trusted alliances to keep conflicts between nations from leading to war. Germany, Italy, and Austria-Hungary formed one alliance. Great Britain, France, and Russia formed another. Russia also promised its support to Serbia.

This alliance system was thought to be foolproof. For example, attacking Serbia meant probably having to fight Russia, too. Then, if Russia fought, Great Britain and France might back up Russia. After all, they belonged to an alliance. No country would dare attack one that had an alliance—or would it? ■

Huge factories owned by the Krupp family of Germany produced tons of steel and weapons in both World War I and World War II.

■ *Explain why the Balkans were known as the powder keg of Europe.*

▲ *This cultural map shows the ethnic groups of Europe before World War I. How does it help explain nationalism as a cause of World War I? For help in using a cultural map, see page G14 of the Map and Globe Handbook.*

"The War to End War"

On the morning of June 28, 1914, Serbs in Sarajevo *(sar uh YAY voh)* watched as a parade of six cars passed. The day was their national holiday. As part of their celebration, Archduke Francis Ferdinand rode through their city. The archduke was the future ruler of Austria-Hungary. This empire still ruled Sarajevo against the Serbs' wishes.

Suddenly, shots rang out, killing the archduke. Austria-Hungary blamed Serbia for his death. It then declared war on Serbia.

Since Russia had promised to support Serbia, it prepared its soldiers to fight Austria-Hungary. As Russian soldiers readied for war, so did the German troops. France and Great Britain also prepared for war. Instead of preventing war, the alliance system was now dragging nations into one.

As armies moved into position, European leaders were not able to back down from the fight. Remember that jingoism was a common feeling in Europe then. Each country believed that its modern armies and navies meant victory.

The First Modern War

On August 4, 1914, World War I began. Germany, Bulgaria, Turkey, and Austria-Hungary fought on one side as the Central Powers. France, Russia, Great Britain, and seven other European countries formed the Allied Powers, or Allies.

Before the war, few Europeans knew the destructive power that modern industry could produce. During the war, railroads quickly

moved huge armies to the war zones. Then machine guns, artillery and poison gas were unleashed, killing millions of soldiers.

For several years neither side could defeat the other. In 1917 Russia began peace talks with Germany, which you'll read about in the next lesson. That same year the United States joined the Allies. After losing several major battles, German leaders asked for peace. On November 11, 1918, in a railroad car in France, they signed a truce. World War I was over.

The Costs of War

World War I was the most destructive war up to that time. In all about 8.5 million soldiers died, and another 21 million were wounded. This enormous loss of life drained Europe of a generation of workers,

artists, scientists, and new leaders.

Revenge shaped the peace terms that ended the war. The Treaty of Versailles *(vuhr SY),* signed in 1919, divided Europe in new ways. To see how, compare the map on the opposite page with the Atlas map on page 682.

The Allies divided Austria-Hungary among seven countries. They took away some of Germany's land and all its colonies. They ordered Germany to admit its "war guilt." Germany was forced to pay huge sums of money for war damages to the Allies.

Many Europeans believed that World War I would be "the war to end war." French army marshal Ferdinand Foch *(fosh)* disagreed: "This is not a peace treaty. It is an armistice [cease-fire] for twenty years." ■

◄ *To support the war effort at home, many women on both sides worked in their country's weapons factories.*

HISTORY *Before television, newsreels helped people see current events. These short films first appeared in movie theaters about 1897. During World War I, efforts were made to produce newsreels that showed battle scenes from Europe, but people didn't get a very good idea of what the war was like. It was not until World War II that newsreels became an effective source of war news.*

◄ *For months at a time, soldiers fought from—and lived in—trenches, or deep ditches. Modern weapons made trenches essential for protection.*

■ *Explain why World War I was so destructive.*

R E V I E W

1. **FOCUS** What were the causes and outcomes of World War I?

2. **HISTORY** Give two examples of how nationalism divided the people of Europe before 1914.

3. **POLITICAL SYSTEMS** Why did European countries form alliances? Did the alliance system work? Explain why or why not.

4. **CRITICAL THINKING** What does this slogan mean to you: "My country, right or wrong." Explain how this slogan

points out the positive and negative aspects of nationalism.

5. **ACTIVITY** Research the changes in communications technology after 1850 and before World War I. Read pages 666–667 in the Minipedia to learn what some of these changes were. Use the library to find more information about a topic that interests you. Then report your findings to your class.

Russia Becomes the Soviet Union

THINKING
F O C U S

How did life under the czars compare with life under Lenin and Stalin?

Key Terms

- revolution
- dictator
- propaganda

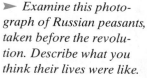

➤ *Examine this photograph of Russian peasants, taken before the revolution. Describe what you think their lives were like.*

Arctic winds blasted the women marching through the streets of Petrograd on March 8, 1917. "Bread! Bread! Bread!" they chanted. Russian soldiers stood by, unsure of what to do. Confused, the soldiers let the women march.

The winter of 1916–1917 was a bitter one for the Russian people. Not only was it extremely cold, but fuel and food supplies were low. Worse, World War I showed no signs of ending. Already hundreds of thousands of Russians had been killed.

At first most Russians had supported the war. Like other people in Europe, they believed it would result in an easy victory for their country. However, Russia was far less modernized than most of Europe. Most Russians were still peasant farmers. Russian soldiers had poor equipment and little training.

As a result, one disaster followed another, both on the battlefield and at home. By March 1917 the Russians had had enough fighting. In Petrograd, formerly St. Petersburg, Russians took to the streets in protest. They demanded peace, land, and bread from their ruler, Czar Nicholas II.

Soon rioting spread throughout Russia. How would the czar respond?

These Russian children stand next to a toppled statue of Czar Alexander III, Nicholas II's father. After the Russian Revolution, statues of the czars were replaced with those of Lenin and other Communist leaders.

The Russian Revolution

In the past, soldiers had shot protesters out of loyalty to the czar. Now, Russian soldiers—cold, hungry, and angry—joined the protests. On March 15, 1917, the protesters forced Nicholas to give up his throne. To learn more about Czar Nicholas and his family, read A Closer Look on the next page.

Lenin Takes Control

News of this **revolution,** or overthrow of a government, swept through Russia. Peasants seized land. Workers took over factories. Lacking a strong ruler, Russia soon erupted in chaos, or disorder.

One Russian, known as Lenin, believed communism was Russia's best hope for the future. He called for Russians to own all land and industry in common. Lenin won support by promising "Peace, Land, and Bread."

In November 1917 Lenin and his supporters took control of the weak Russian government by force. Lenin divided farmland among the peasants. Then he signed a peace treaty with Germany to end Russian fighting in World War I.

The Russian Civil War

Many Russians did not support Lenin. In May 1918 his opponents started a civil war in Russia.

Lenin's supporters called themselves the Red Army. Those who opposed Lenin were called the Whites. Some Whites wanted a new czar. Others fought for democracy. Still others were non-Russians, such as Ukrainians, who wanted to form separate countries.

By the end of 1920, the Red Army had defeated the Whites. Lenin set up governments in the separate republics, or states. In 1922 Lenin united these republics, forming the Union of Soviet Socialist Republics, or Soviet Union.

According to Communist ideals, workers were to run the cities, farmers the countryside. Instead, only Lenin and his supporters ruled. ■

Russian Communists used posters such as this one to win support for their revolutionary goals. The dolls, symbols of children, are shown demanding fresh milk, fresh air, and healthy parents.

■ *What were the causes of the Russian Revolution?*

465

The Last Czar

Czar Nicholas II lived in lavish palaces with his wife, the empress Alexandra; their daughters Olga, Tatiana, Marie, and Anastasia; and their young son Alexis, heir to the monarchy. In his royal, protected world, the czar was out of touch with the Russian people. Communists killed him and his family in 1917, after his government was overthrown.

Worry tormented Nicholas and Alexandra. Alexis, shown here in 1914 in front of his mother, had hemophilia—a painful and dangerous condition in which blood fails to clot normally.

Rasputin! He posed as a holy man, but his unholy behavior caused many Russians to despise him. Yet Nicholas and Alexandra trusted him because he eased Alexis's suffering.

Fantastic eggs were crafted for the czar by Carl Fabergé and his jewelry firm. This egg is like a cuckoo clock. Inside another egg, a miniature train runs on tiny tracks.

Building the Soviet Union

World War I and the civil war left the Soviet Union in ruins. Lenin tried to rebuild the country. In 1921 he allowed peasants to sell some grain for private profit, rather than at set prices to the government. Given a chance to earn a profit, people worked harder. The Soviet Union began to recover.

Stalin's Five-Year Plans

After Lenin died in 1924, Josef Stalin took over the Soviet government. Like Lenin, he ruled as a **dictator,** or ruler who holds total power. Stalin wanted to industrialize the Soviet Union. He forced peasants to work on huge collective farms run by his government. He ordered factories to produce only basic goods such as steel.

Stalin set out his goals for the Soviet Union in Five-Year Plans. In some ways his plans were successful. Soviet factories grew quickly in the 1930s. Yet the Soviet people paid a terrible price for Stalin's plans. Collective farms failed to supply enough food for the country. Drought made the famine worse. Millions died from starvation.

A Life of Fear

Stalin held complete power over the Soviet people. He arrested anyone suspected of disloyalty. Many were sent to labor camps in Siberia or were killed by his secret police.

To stay in power, Stalin also used **propaganda** (prahp uh GAN duh), or information spread to advance one's cause or ideas. All newspapers, radio stations, and schools were run by the Soviet government. They could print, air, or teach only propaganda that praised Stalin and his plans. Stalin also controlled artists and writers. By the late 1930s, the Soviet Union was a world power again. However, under the dictator Stalin, millions of Soviet people had no say in their government. ■

◄ *Millions of Soviet peasant farmers, such as the woman shown here, moved to cities to work in heavy industry—steel, cement, and tool factories.*

■ *What were Stalin's economic plans?*

R E V I E W

1. **FOCUS** How did life under the czars compare with life under Lenin and Stalin?
2. **HISTORY** Why did the Russian people revolt against Czar Nicholas II?
3. **ECONOMICS** Communism in the Soviet Union had many negative effects. Describe at least one negative effect.
4. **CRITICAL THINKING** Explain why Lenin's slogan, "Peace, Land, and Bread," gained the support of the Russian people. Was Lenin's slogan an example of propaganda? Explain why or why not.
5. **ART ACTIVITY** Design a propaganda poster. You may want to design one that Lenin or Stalin might have used. Or, design a poster that opponents of Lenin or Stalin might have used.

L E S S O N   3

World War II and the Cold War

What were the causes and outcomes of World War II?

Key Terms

- genocide
- Holocaust
- superpower
- iron curtain
- Cold War

➤ *Hitler is shown here inspecting his Nazi troops. Notice the swastika, or cross with bent arms, on the flags, uniforms, and helmets. Nazi Germany used the swastika for its national symbol.*

Thousands of Germans gathered for a rally in the city of Nuremberg in 1933. "*Sieg heil!* [Hail to victory!]" they shouted. Everyone saluted the *führer (FYUR uhr),* or leader—Adolf Hitler.

Hitler's success grew out of the German people's despair. In the early 1920s, Germany struggled to pay the millions of dollars it owed the Allies for World War I. German money, the *mark,* became almost worthless.

Then, in 1929, a worldwide depression struck. This economic downturn put more than six million Germans out of work. Many Germans were angry and afraid. They wanted a strong leader to restore order and German pride. They turned to Hitler and his political party, the National Socialist German Workers' Party, or Nazis.

Germany under Nazi Rule

Hitler promised that the Nazis would create new jobs and make Germany a strong military power again. He vowed that Germany would win back all the land it had lost in World War I—and more.

Hitler ruled Germany as a dictator. His goal was "one state, one people, one leader." Like Stalin, Hitler used propaganda and fear to control people. "Storm troopers" and secret police arrested, beat up, or killed anyone viewed as a threat to Hitler.

Hitler preached hatred for the Jews. Germany's troubles, he said, were caused by a "Jewish world conspiracy." Many Germans also wanted someone to blame for their suffering. They shared Hitler's ideas.

The Night of Broken Glass

On the night of November 9, 1938, Nazis began smashing and burning Jewish stores, homes, and synagogues all over Germany. Afterward, the streets of Germany were littered with broken glass. This night was named *Kristallnacht* —the night of broken glass.

Kristallnacht was Nazi Germany's first official large-scale attack on Jews. Although they had committed no crimes, about 30,000 Jews were arrested that night. The Nazis split up Jewish families and seized their property. However, the worst was yet to come.

Germany's Road to War

Hitler built up Germany's military strength. Then he began to take back what he saw as Germany's rightful territory. In 1938 Hitler forced Austria into his new German Reich, or empire. Then, from 1938 to 1939, he took over Czechoslovakia piece by piece.

Other European leaders tried to ignore Hitler. They did not want to risk another major war by opposing him. They hoped Hitler would stop after Czechoslovakia. Then, on September 1, 1939, Hitler ordered German troops to march again— and invade Poland.

European leaders finally realized that only force could stop Hitler. Two days after the invasion of Poland, France and Great Britain declared war on Germany. World War II had begun.

On one side were the Axis Powers: Germany, Italy, and Japan. On the other side were the Allies, which included France and Great Britain. Later Canada, the Soviet Union, and the United States joined the Allies. ■

Across Time & Space

Between 1936 and 1939, Spain fought a civil war that resulted in General Francisco Franco becoming dictator. Franco ruled Spain until his death in 1975. Germany and Italy used the Spanish Civil War to test modern tanks and warplanes in preparation for a future war.

■ *What events led to World War II?*

World War II

German tanks rumbled down the muddy roads leading to Poland's capital, Warsaw. Modern German airplanes bombed Poland's cities and countryside. The Polish army fought back, often with soldiers on horseback. However, in just 17 days, Germany conquered Poland.

◄ *Hundreds of thousands of Polish people were forced to flee from their homes after Germany invaded their country in 1939.*

1901 Queen Victoria of Great Britain dies.

1912 Conflict flares in the Balkans.

1917 The Russian Revolution begins.

1933 Hitler comes to power in Germany.

1900	1910	1920	1930	1940

1905 "Bloody Sunday" in St. Petersburg results in nationwide strikes.

1914–1918 World War I

1922 USSR is formed.

1939–1945 World War

▲ *Londoners shown here used their subways, or "the tube," as air raid shelters when German warplanes bombed Great Britain from 1940 to 1941.*

➤ *Nazis in Poland forced Jewish men, women, and children into a crowded ghetto, or restricted area, of Warsaw. Later, as this photograph shows, they were sent to concentration camps.*

Hitler's "Lightning War"

In the first year of the war, German armies waged a *blitzkrieg (BLIHTS kreeg)*, or "lightning war." After Germany defeated Poland, it conquered Denmark, Norway, the Netherlands, Belgium, and Luxembourg by the spring of 1940. Then Germany forced France to surrender. A proud Hitler made French leaders sign a truce in the same railroad car where the truce ending World War I was signed.

Great Britain was the only western European power left fighting Hitler. Winston Churchill, Britain's new prime minister, proclaimed, "We shall go on to the end; . . . we shall never surrender."

The Resistance

In countries conquered by the Nazis, people tried to fight back in secret. Others helped Jews escape or smuggled secrets to the Allies.

This movement to fight the Nazis was called the Resistance. Resistance groups formed in many of the countries Germany had defeated. One member of a Jewish resistance group wrote, "Our watchword was: Live and die with dignity!"

The Holocaust

In 1942 Hitler began to carry out his "final solution to the Jewish problem." His "final solution" was **genocide,** or the planned killing of an entire race or ethnic group. Nazi soldiers rounded up all the Jews they could find. Some were killed; others were sent to prison camps.

Many Jews tried to hide in cellars, attics, and barns. Anne Frank, a teenager, hid with her family in an attic in Amsterdam, the Netherlands. She wrote:

The Germans ring at every front door to inquire if there are any Jews living in the house. If there are, then the whole family has to go at once. If they don't find any, they go on to the next house. No one has a chance of evading them unless one goes into hiding.

1961 Berlin Wall is built.

45 United Nations is formed;
ld War begins.

1989 Berlin Wall falls.

1950   1960   1970   1980   1990

1986 Chernobyl nuclear power plant explodes near Kiev, USSR.

1991 USSR breaks up and the Cold War ends.

1957 Common
Market begins.

If caught, Jewish families were sent to prison camps in Poland or Germany—the Nazi concentration camps. Prisoners were often beaten and tortured in the concentration camps. The healthiest were forced to work as slave labor. Most of the rest—the old, the sick, and the young—were killed.

Some camps, such as Treblinka and Auschwitz *(OWSH vihts),* became "death camps." Jews, Gypsies, and other prisoners were brought there and worked to death, or killed. About six million Jews, and several million others—Gypsies, Slavs, Poles, and political prisoners—died in these Nazi camps.

Nazi Germany's murders of Jews and others in Europe is now known as the **Holocaust.** The word *holocaust (HAHL uh kawst)* means "great destruction by fire." To learn more about genocide and the Holocaust, read Understanding Genocide on this page.

UNDERSTANDING GENOCIDE

Genocide is an attempt to kill all the people or members of a certain group. Why would one group of people want to completely destroy another group of people?

The Roots of Genocide

One reason a group of people commits genocide is hatred. In Nazi Germany, Jewish people were blamed for the country's problems. Hitler accused them of being evil. These false beliefs resulted in the Holocaust.

A second reason one group commits genocide is to gain land. During World War I, Turks forced Armenians to leave Turkey. About 600,000 Armenians died or were killed on this forced march. A group may also commit genocide to stay in power. In Kampuchea (Cambodia), in the 1970s, the Pol Pot regime stayed in power by killing about two million Khmer people.

The UN Resolution of 1948

In 1948 the United Nations declared genocide "a crime under international law." This UN resolution tried to prevent another Holocaust from happening.

471

Europe: 1900 to the End of the Cold War

This picture of Churchill, U.S. President Franklin D. Roosevelt, and Stalin is from the Yalta Conference, held in 1945 to settle differences as World War II neared an end.

■ *How did World War II damage Europe?*

Turning Points of the War

By 1940 Hitler had gained control of much of western Europe. He then tried to defeat Great Britain by bombing its cities. When these air attacks failed, he turned east. In the summer of 1941, Hitler attacked the Soviet Union, which then joined the Allies.

These German attacks—and above all, the Japanese attack on Pearl Harbor—led the United States to join the Allies. On December 8, 1941, the United States declared war on Japan. By the end of the year, the United States was also at war with Germany and Italy.

In 1943 Soviet troops defeated a large German army at Stalingrad (now Volgograd). Soviet troops then pushed the German troops out of the Soviet Union. Next, they moved across eastern Europe and began to attack Germany. Meanwhile, in western Europe, Allied forces defeated Italy in 1943. After the secret invasion known as D-day, on June 6, 1944, the Allies freed France and Belgium in 1944. Finally, the Allies invaded Germany.

The Costs of World War II

On May 8, 1945, Germany surrendered. However, World War II did not end until September 2, 1945, with the surrender of Japan, which you read about on page 371.

About 50 million people, including 35 million civilians, died in World War II. More than 40 million people were left homeless. Bombs had reduced much of Europe to rubble. ■

The Cold War

➤ *This East German border guard was never seen again after disobeying orders. He let a boy cross back from West Berlin to East Berlin.*

For centuries western Europe had controlled much of the world. However, after World War II, two new superpowers emerged: the United States and the Soviet Union. A **superpower** is a military, political, and economic giant. For the next 45 years, the United States and the Soviet Union would dominate world affairs.

The peace treaties ending World War II divided Europe almost in half. In fact, Germany was split in two, as you can see from the map on page 473. Notice, too, how Germany's capital, Berlin, was also divided. This division was made even more dramatic in 1961. That year, East Germany built a wall separating East and West Berlin.

An iron curtain fell upon Europe. **Iron curtain** was the term used to describe how Eastern Europe was isolated from the West. Many democratic countries of Western Europe aligned with the United States. However, most countries

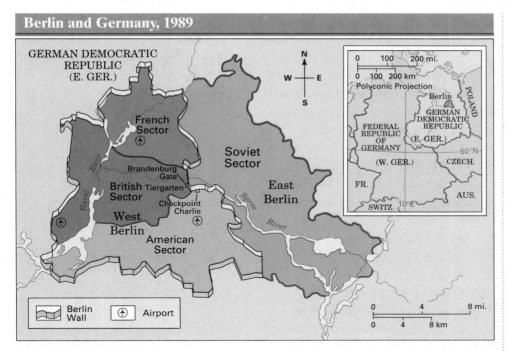

Berlin and Germany, 1989

GERMAN DEMOCRATIC REPUBLIC (E. GER.)

French Sector

Brandenburg Gate

British Sector — Tiergarten

Checkpoint Charlie

West Berlin

American Sector

Havel River

Soviet Sector

East Berlin

Spree River

FEDERAL REPUBLIC OF GERMANY (W. GER.)

GERMAN DEMOCRATIC REPUBLIC (E. GER.)

Berlin

POLAND

CZECH.

FR.

AUS.

SWITZ.

50°N

10°E

0   100   200 mi.
0   100   200 km
Polyconic Projection

Berlin Wall   Airport

0   4   8 mi.
0   4   8 km

◄ *This map shows East and West Germany, and a divided Berlin. Why were West Berliners called "islanders"?*

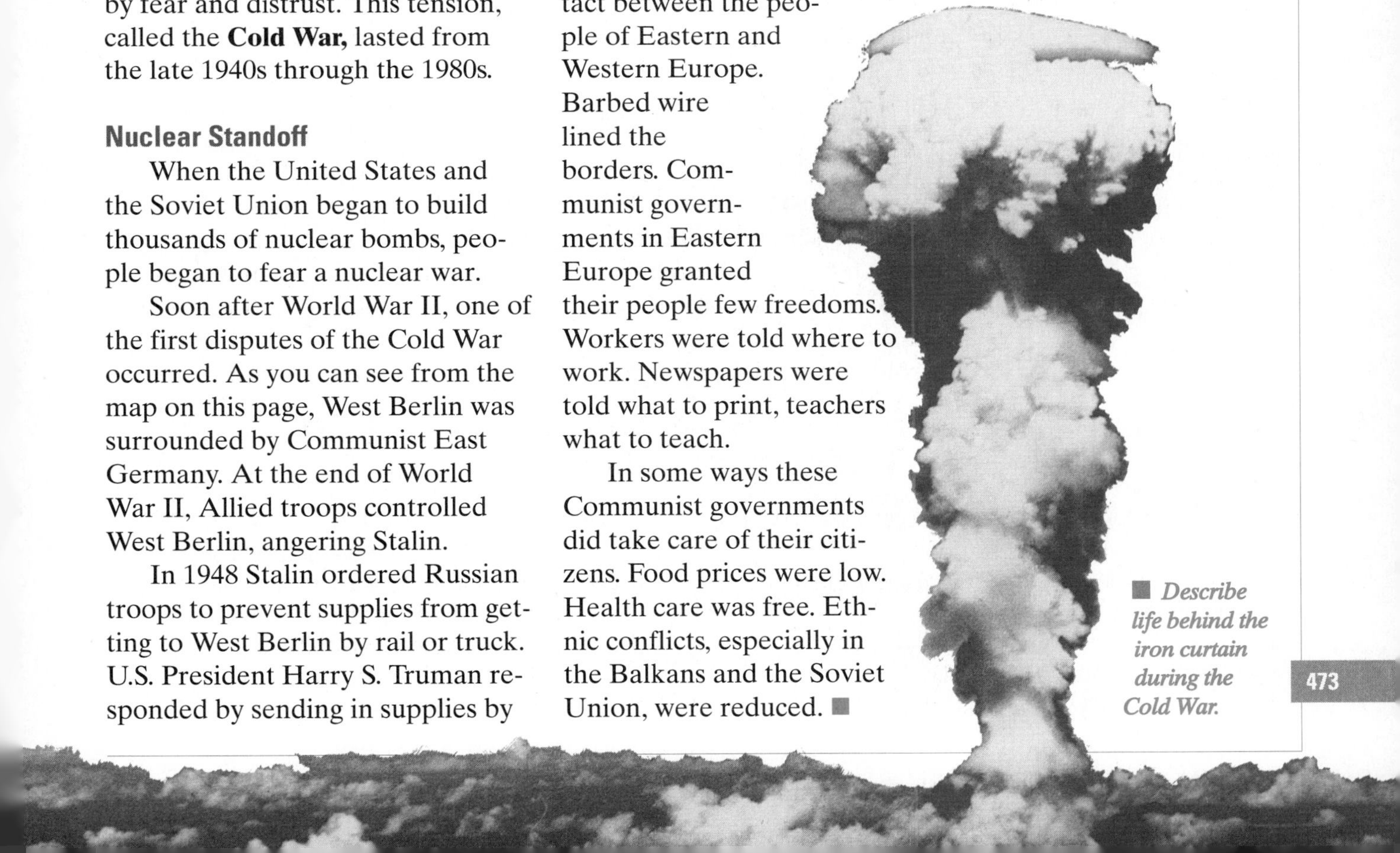

▼ *News of nuclear weapons tests, such as the one shown here in the Pacific Ocean, frightened people around the world during the Cold War.*

in Eastern Europe became part of the Soviet bloc. Soviet troops had freed them from the Nazis. After the war, the Soviet government turned them into Communist states and controlled their governments.

Once more Europe was divided by fear and distrust. This tension, called the **Cold War,** lasted from the late 1940s through the 1980s.

Nuclear Standoff

When the United States and the Soviet Union began to build thousands of nuclear bombs, people began to fear a nuclear war.

Soon after World War II, one of the first disputes of the Cold War occurred. As you can see from the map on this page, West Berlin was surrounded by Communist East Germany. At the end of World War II, Allied troops controlled West Berlin, angering Stalin.

In 1948 Stalin ordered Russian troops to prevent supplies from getting to West Berlin by rail or truck. U.S. President Harry S. Truman responded by sending in supplies by airplane. After 277,264 flights, Stalin gave in and let West Berlin exist as a democratic "island" in East Germany.

Life Behind the Iron Curtain

The iron curtain cut off contact between the people of Eastern and Western Europe. Barbed wire lined the borders. Communist governments in Eastern Europe granted their people few freedoms. Workers were told where to work. Newspapers were told what to print, teachers what to teach.

In some ways these Communist governments did take care of their citizens. Food prices were low. Health care was free. Ethnic conflicts, especially in the Balkans and the Soviet Union, were reduced. ■

■ *Describe life behind the iron curtain during the Cold War.*

473

The Collapse of Soviet Communism

The Cold War "thawed" in the early 1970s as the two superpowers discussed arms control. The United States and the Soviet Union agreed to limit the number of nuclear weapons they kept.

Even bigger changes happened when Mikhail Gorbachev *(GAWR buh chawf)* took power in the Soviet Union in 1985. He began to give Soviet citizens more freedom. For instance, he let non-Communist candidates run for office. Gorbachev also hoped to reform the Soviet economic system. The Cold War era had not improved life for most people in the Soviet Union.

Gorbachev also said that Soviet soldiers would no longer crush protests against Communist governments in Eastern Europe. Without Soviet support, Eastern European Communist governments began to collapse in 1989. Some republics within the Soviet Union demanded independence as well.

On August 18, 1991, some Soviet Communist party leaders tried to overthrow Gorbachev. They wanted to stop Gorbachev's reforms. They sent tanks into the streets of Moscow to enforce their takeover. Yet thousands of Russians blocked the tanks in protest. Many soldiers and police joined

➤ Mikhail Gorbachev, shown at right, tried to reform the Soviet government. The people were unhappy with the slow pace of his reforms, however. They preferred the plans of Russian Republic President Boris Yeltsin. These plans called for greater—and quicker—changes.

■ *Why did Gorbachev try to reform the Soviet Union?*

the protesters, just as they had in the Russian Revolution of 1917.

Gorbachev returned to power in just three days. However, the Russian people no longer trusted Gorbachev or feared the Communist party. They wanted greater changes. Boris Yeltsin, newly elected president of the Russian Republic, won their trust by ending Communist rule. "When I heard they had outlawed communism, I felt like a man freed from jail," one Soviet man said. In the next chapter, you will read about what happened to the Soviet Union—and to all of Europe—after the Cold War. ■

REVIEW

1. **FOCUS** What were the causes and outcomes of World War II?
2. **HISTORY** Explain why Hitler's ideas appealed to so many Germans.
3. **HISTORY** What was the Holocaust? Give another example of an attempt at genocide.
4. **CRITICAL THINKING** Why did the United States and the Soviet Union fight the Cold War?
5. **WRITING ACTIVITY** There are many excellent books about World War II. Some, such as *Anne Frank: The Diary of a Young Girl,* are personal accounts of people's wartime experiences. Ask your teacher or librarian for title suggestions. Then write a journal entry based on your reading.

Interpreting Political Cartoons

Here's Why

Reading political cartoons can be an amusing way to learn how people feel about certain events. By making dramatic, often funny drawings, political cartoonists make strong statements that reflect their feelings or those of their readers.

Suppose you wanted to know more about how people feel about economic reforms in Russia, formerly part of the Soviet Union. Looking for political cartoons in a newspaper or magazine would be a good place to start.

Here's How

Look at the cartoon below, drawn by a Russian artist. Use the following steps to understand it.

1. **Read the captions.** Identify the action and people in the cartoon. The action of this cartoon is easily seen: People in a car are going over a cliff. Who are the people? Boris Yeltsin, the president of Russia, and another Russian leader are the drivers. We can assume the people in the back of the car are the Russian people.

2. **Identify the symbols in the cartoon.** Symbols are objects or people that are used to represent an idea. The cartoonist has used the car as a symbol of the Russian economy. The steep cliff represents the danger that the Russians face as they try to get to the reforms on the other side.

3. **Try to understand the cartoonist's message.** On one hand, the cartoonist may be saying that despite people's fears, the Russian economy will land safely and the reforms will get the economy rolling again. On the other hand, the cartoonist may be saying that the Russian economy will crash, as will Yeltsin and his group of reformers. What do you think the cartoonist is trying to say?

Try It

Examine the cartoon again. What might the cartoonist think life will be like after the reforms? How can you tell?

Apply It

Find a political cartoon in a newspaper or magazine. Write a short paragraph explaining what the cartoonist is trying to say. Be sure to identify the people and symbols in the cartoon.

475

Chapter Review

Reviewing Key Terms

alliance (p. 461)
Cold War (p. 473)
dictator (p. 467)
genocide (p. 470)
Holocaust (p. 471)

iron curtain (p. 472)
jingoism (p. 460)
propaganda (p. 467)
revolution (p. 465)
superpower (p. 472)

A. Each statement below uses a key term from this chapter. Tell whether each key term is used correctly. Then explain the reason for your answer.

1. Because France and Great Britain were part of an alliance before World War I, they fought each other when war began.
2. Lenin and Stalin, the first two leaders of the Soviet Union, did not establish democracy but ruled as dictators.
3. The 1917 revolution in Russia strengthened the government of the czar.
4. Jews, Slavs, Poles, and gypsies were victims in the Holocaust.
5. Both Stalin and Hitler used propaganda and fear to rule their countries.

B. Use the text or a dictionary to write the meaning of each of these terms in your own words. Then explain how each word was related to the history of Europe after 1900.

1. Cold War
2. genocide
3. iron curtain
4. jingoism
5. superpower

Exploring Concepts

A. Copy this chart of cause-and-effect relationships in World War I. Then supply what you think is the main cause for each effect. One cause has been filled in.

Cause	Effect
Modern industry develops in the late 1800s.	More destructive weapons of war are built.
	Austria-Hungary attacks Serbia.
	World War I begins.
	German leaders ask for peace.
	Austro-Hungarian Empire is divided.

B. Answer each question with information from the chapter.

1. In what ways did Germany, France, and Great Britain compete before World War I?
2. What were some of the ethnic groups living within Austria-Hungary?
3. How did the terms of the Treaty of Versailles affect Germany?
4. In the early 1900s, how was Russia different from its allies France and Britain?
5. What groups of Russians were involved in the 1917 revolution against the czar?
6. What were Stalin's goals for the Soviet Union? How did he try to reach those goals?
7. What were the effects of Germany's "lightning war" in Europe in 1939 and 1940?
8. When and why did the United States become involved in World War II?
9. Why was Berlin a symbol of the Cold War?
10. What were some of the reforms begun in the Soviet Union by Gorbachev?

Reviewing Skills

1. Political cartoons can make a strong statement in a simple, amusing way. Study this cartoon. Identify the people, symbols, and actions it shows. Then write an explanation of what you think the cartoon means. Do you think the cartoonist is sympathetic toward events in the Soviet Union or not?

2. Events in Europe and Russia in the 20th century were related. To show this, make a timeline for the years 1910 to 1950. Divide your timeline into decades, or 10-year periods, starting with 1910. From the chapter find at least two events that occurred in each decade. Write them in the correct position on the timeline. Place events in Russia (and the Soviet Union) above the timeline. Place events for the rest of Europe below the timeline.

3. Suppose you want to compare the number of civilian and military casualties suffered by different European countries in World War I and World War II. What would be the best way to show this information? Explain your response.

Using Critical Thinking

1. What events after World War I led the German people to support Hitler and his Nazi party's rise to power?

2. Should the leaders of a country encourage people's feelings of nationalism? What are the advantages and dangers of doing so?

3. How do you think dictators such as Hitler and Stalin manage to stay in power for many years? What do people gain and what do they lose when ruled by a dictator?

4. Why did Hitler try to destroy the Jews of Europe? Do you think that genocide could ever become a reality in the United States? Explain your response.

Preparing for Citizenship

1. COLLECTING INFORMATION During the first half of the 20th century, many Europeans influenced history, for better or worse. Choose a person mentioned in the chapter or another European from this time period. Use the encyclopedia or other library sources to research his or her life. Then give a biographical report to the class.

2. WRITING ACTIVITY Imagine that you are a U.S. newspaper reporter in Germany during the late 1930s. Choose an event such as *Kristallnacht* or a Nazi rally, and write a news story for your paper. Remember that your readers at home may not be aware of what is going on in Germany.

3. INTERVIEWING Many people have emigrated from, or left, the former Soviet Union and Eastern Europe. If possible, interview someone from the former Soviet Union or Eastern Europe. Ask why he or she came to the United States. What does he or she miss most? Report your interview to your class.

4. COLLABORATIVE LEARNING Imagine you live in a European village about to be taken over by the Nazis during World War II. Divide into groups and discuss the reasons for and against joining the Resistance. After your group discussion, share your ideas with the entire class. As a class, vote on whether your village will join the Resistance.

477

Chapter 21
Europe and Russia Today

As the 20th century neared its end, change swept through Europe. Western Europeans debated whether a "United States of Europe" was a realistic goal. In Eastern Europe, people freed themselves from Communist dictatorships and one-party rule. What would happen as a result? The Soviet Union fell apart. What would take its place? No one knew the answers to these questions.

Russians celebrate independence from the Soviet Union in Moscow's Red Square in 1991.

A record-setting group of 150 skydivers joins together over Belgium.

1988 Lech Walesa leads workers on a strike against Poland's Communist government.

1990 Germans celebrate the reunification of their country.

1980	1984	1988

1984

1984 Sarajevo, Yugoslavia, hosts the Winter Olympics.

1989 Playwright Vaclav Havel leads a peaceful "Velvet Revolution" that topples Czechoslovakia's Communist government.

Muslim girls study the Qur'an in a mosque in Tajikistan, which was a Soviet republic until 1991. Under Soviet rule, freedom of religion did not exist until 1990.

France and Great Britain cooperated to build the Concorde, a supersonic jetliner.

Civil war erupts in Yugoslavia in 1991. Carrying all she owns, this woman leaves her home near the Croatia-Serbia border, heading to an uncertain future.

1993 Czechoslovakia divides into two countries.

1992	1996	2000

1992 Violence continues in many of the former Soviet republics. Elsewhere, thousands die in Bosnia, Croatia, and Slovenia—former republics of Yugoslavia.

Today

L E S S O N   1

Europe Today

THINKING
FOCUS

Why is Europe such a productive region?

Key Terms

- marine climate
- continental climate
- Mediterranean climate

I n a speech he made while he was still leader of the Soviet Union, Mikhail Gorbachev quoted a famous French writer:

A day will come when you, France; you, Russia; you, Italy; you, Britain; and you, Germany—all of you, all nations of the Continent [Europe] will merge tightly. . . . A day will come when markets, open to trade, and minds, open to ideas, will become the sole battlefields.

Victor Hugo, 1802–1885

When Hugo wrote this passage more than 100 years ago, Europe was a continent of ancient conflicts. Its peoples were divided and often at war.

However, many Europeans such as Hugo hoped for greater unity within Europe. Hugo never saw his dream for a united Europe come true. Yet in your lifetime, a united Europe may become a reality.

Barriers to peace and unity still divide Europe, however. The effects of the iron curtain continue to split Europe into eastern and western halves.

The Land of Europe

The East-West division in Europe is based mainly on political and ethnic differences, not on geography. That is, no natural borders such as mountains or rivers separate Eastern Europe from Western Europe. What continues to divide Europeans today are their ethnic differences and history of conflicts. From the map on the opposite page, you can see how Europe is divided between East and West. Note that no natural borders mark this political division.

The Land Regions of Europe

Take a closer look at this same map. Two mountain systems, one in the north, the other in the south, divide Europe into three land regions: northern, central, and southern Europe.

Northern Europe is marked by a series of mountains that cover northern Great Britain and most of Norway and Sweden. The Alpine

▼ *The Alps, stretching across southern Switzerland, give that country a distinct natural border.*

NORWAY
FINLAND
SWEDEN
EST.
DENMARK
LAT.
North Sea
Baltic Sea
LITH.
IRELAND
RUS.
RUSSIA
UNITED KINGDOM
BELARUS
NETH.
GERMANY
POLAND
ATLANTIC OCEAN
BEL.
Vistula R.
Don R.
LUX.
CZECH REP.
UKRAINE
Dnieper R.
Seine R.
LIECH.
SLOVAK REP.
MOLDOVA
Loire R.
FRANCE
SWITZ.
AUSTRIA
HUNGARY
CARPATHIAN MTS.
ALPS
SLO.
ROMANIA
Po R.
CRO.
Black Sea
AND.
BOS. H.
Danube R.
PORTUGAL
PYRENEES
MONACO
ITALY
YUGO.
BULGARIA
SPAIN
MACE.
ALB.
TURKEY
GREECE
Mediterranean Sea

Legend:
- Formerly a Communist country or region
- Formerly a republic of the Soviet Union
- Formerly East Germany

0   250   500 mi.
0   250   500 km
Azimuthal Equidistant Projection

mountain system separates central from southern Europe. These mountains run between France and Spain, across northern Italy, and into the Balkans.

The Great Plain of Europe

Between these two mountain systems lies central Europe. At the heart of this region is the Northern European Plain. This plain stretches from the west coast of France to the Ural Mountains in Russia.

In the past, this plain was a battleground. Many of Europe's ethnic groups fought over its land and resources. Today, this region is home to much of Europe's population, agriculture, and industry.

The Northern European Plain has rich farmland. There, European farmers grow wheat, barley, oats, potatoes, and rye. They raise hogs, cattle, and sheep. Using the plain's rich supplies of iron and coal,

Europeans also produce steel, cars, airplanes, textiles, and chemical products.

A Productive Land

In spite of being the world's second smallest continent, Europe is an agricultural and industrial giant. Its almost 700 million people are well educated. Much of Europe's wealth results from its people's productivity.

Throughout history, Europeans have made great use of their resources and geographic location. Europe's timber, oil, coal, and other resources are raw materials for its factories. Europe's rivers serve as important shipping routes. European farmers produce most of the food the people of Europe need. They also export their products all over the world. ■

Notice on the map above how the European plain grows wider west to east. What countries are part of this plain? Below the map, this Greek fisherman sorts a catch of sponges. Many Europeans depend on the sea for their livelihood.

■ *Where is Europe's great plain located?*

481

The Climates of Europe

If you look at the Atlas map on page 680, you can see that most of Europe is farther north than the Great Lakes. Yet most of Europe has a temperate, or mild, climate. Why is this so?

The Winds of Europe

Europe's climate is mainly determined by three prevailing winds, or air masses that blow in a certain pattern. First, moist winds from the Atlantic blow across western Europe. These winds are warmed by the Gulf Stream, a warm ocean current that starts in the Gulf of Mexico and flows to Europe.

➤ *In spite of Spain's dry climate, Spanish farmers export food all over the world. Modern irrigation and farming methods made this land in Spain a productive olive grove.*

■ *Give two reasons why most of Europe has a mild climate.*

As a result, most of western Europe enjoys a **marine climate** because its winds form over the ocean. A marine climate has fairly constant, mild temperatures.

Second, the Gulf Stream winds cool as they move across the European plain. Because land cools these winds, most of eastern Europe has what is called a **continental climate.** Summers are warm and short while winters are long and cold.

Third, in southern Europe, hot, dry winds blow across the Mediterranean Sea from North Africa. These winds give much of Spain, Portugal, Italy, and Greece mild winters and hot, dry summers, or a **Mediterranean climate.**

A Longer Growing Season

Since much of Europe has a mild climate, many farmers in southern and western Europe can grow crops for much of the year. In eastern Europe, however, the continental climate greatly reduces the length of the growing season.

In the past, Europeans went to war, seeking control of land and resources. In recent years, ethnic conflicts continue to divide eastern Europe. Western Europe, as you will read in the next lesson, is trying to resolve its past conflicts and unite. ■

R E V I E W

1. **FOCUS** Why is Europe such a productive region?
2. **GEOGRAPHY** What mountain system divides southern from central Europe?
3. **GEOGRAPHY** What are the differences between a marine climate, a Mediterranean climate, and a continental climate?
4. **CRITICAL THINKING** In what ways does the mild climate benefit European farmers?

5. **ACTIVITY** Europe's ethnic differences, not its geography, still divide its peoples. One such difference is Europe's many languages. Study the English alphabet chart on page 660 in the Minipedia. Then research one of the other languages of Europe. Make a chart of its alphabet similar to the one in the Minipedia. Compare your chart with those of your classmates. How are they alike and different?

Resolving Conflicts Peacefully

Here's Why

Disagreements or conflicts are part of life. After all, not everyone shares the same values, beliefs, or goals. However, people can choose to resolve conflicts positively or negatively. Too often people around the world have gone to war to settle their differences. The results, as you know from reading Chapter 20, have been millions of deaths and widespread destruction.

What if someone calls you names, makes fun of you, or "puts you down"? What if someone hits you? You may be angry and hurt. You may want to strike back with words—or fists. However, striking back in anger often leads to more angry words or more violence.

Resolving conflicts peacefully is difficult. Yet it is an essential skill for getting along with others. Do you know how to resolve your conflicts without violence or name-calling?

Here's How

Suppose the members of your class disagreed about where to go on a class trip.

Some students wanted to go to an amusement park. Others wanted to go hiking in a state forest. Here's one way to resolve this conflict:

1. **Define the problem.** Have people from both sides answer this question: What is the problem? The class members disagree about where to go on a trip. Try to understand the reasons for both points of view. Some students may rarely get a chance to go to an amusement park. Others may rarely get a chance to explore nature. You may find areas of common concern. For example, how much money each trip will cost may worry both sides.
2. **Brainstorm for solutions.** Think about solutions— the ways this problem can be resolved. As a class, talk over all the possible solutions. Be sure to give everyone a chance to speak. Don't reject any ideas— the goal is to think up as many solutions as you can together. You do not have to choose one solution at this step.

3. **Choose the best solution.** Aim for the solution that lets both sides feel the resolution is fair. For example, your class may agree to go to the state forest. To be fair to both sides, your class may also decide to raise money and take a trip to the amusement park another time.
4. **Evaluate the solution's success.** If both sides feel good about your solution, it was probably the right one. However, if anyone is still angry or upset, your class may need to talk about it some more. Consider asking your teacher or another adult for advice.

Try It

Reread the solution to this conflict. What are the strengths of the solution? What are the weaknesses?

Apply It

Try using the steps listed above to resolve a conflict at home, in school, or with a friend. What do you think will be the most difficult step in resolving your conflict peacefully?

Define ➡ **Brainstorm** ➡ **Choose** ➡ **Evaluate**

L E S S O N   2

Western Europe Today

THINKING
F O C U S

Is the dream of a united Europe coming true? Explain why or why not.

Key Terms

- common market
- tariff
- customs check

➤ *Lighting this beacon in London, above right, helped mark the beginning of closer unity in Western Europe.*

CORPORATION OF LONDON

Just before midnight on New Year's Eve, a crowd of people gathers at the Acropolis in Athens. There, where the Parthenon stands, they wait in the cool night air. Other crowds wait near the Eiffel Tower in Paris and at a park in Dublin. Crowds gather at other sites all across Western Europe. Together they will celebrate a historic event in the coming new year of 1993.

At midnight, the first of 1,000 beacons is lit in Athens. This chain of signal lights stretches hundreds of miles across Western Europe. These beacons blaze in Europe's quiet villages and bustling cities.

In the past, Europeans lit beacons out of fear or to spread news. The ancient Greeks used them to signal victories or to warn of attack. In 1588 the English lit beacons to warn of the approach of the Spanish Armada.

However, Europeans lit the 1,000 beacons to celebrate a new era. These beacons signaled the beginning of a new economic union in Western Europe. Nearly 350 million Europeans would now be able to work, trade, and move more freely across national borders.

On the morning of January 1, 1993, thousands of Europeans were on the move. For the first time in their lives, most did not have to stop at national borders. These Europeans took steps toward greater unity—and perhaps a lasting peace.

Western Europe Moves to Greater Unity

During the Cold War, Western Europeans formed an economic union, or a **common market.** Europeans created a common market to increase trade and cooperation among countries. If Europeans became economic partners, maybe

they would not become enemies again—and all could profit.

Building the Common Market

In 1957 Belgium, France, Italy, Luxembourg, the Netherlands, and West Germany signed the Treaty of

Per Capita Income in Europe and the United States

1990 Average Income (in dollars)

	Czecho-slovakia[1]	Denmark	France	Germany[2]	Great Britain	Greece	Ireland	Italy	Poland	Spain	Switzer-land	United States

Source: World Development Report, 1992 1. Income before country was divided 2. West Germany's income before unification

Rome. This treaty created the European Economic Community (EC), or the Common Market.

The Common Market made trade easier among these six countries. For example, it reduced **tariffs,** or fees a country charged for imported goods. Tariffs raised the price of those goods. Higher prices discouraged people from buying imports and slowed the economic growth of all countries.

By 1986 Great Britain, Ireland, Denmark, Greece, Portugal, and Spain had also joined the Common Market. As trade increased among these countries, their economies all grew and their standards of living rose. Study the chart above to learn more about average personal, or per capita, incomes in Europe.

Still, barriers to trade remained. For example, goods and people still had to pass through a **customs check,** or border inspection. A customs check required a person to have certain papers, such as a passport, in order to enter another country. If someone wanted to work in another country, he or she also had to have a work permit. Truck drivers had to stop at each border, fill out forms, and have their goods inspected. Customs checks slowed movement and trade within the Common Market.

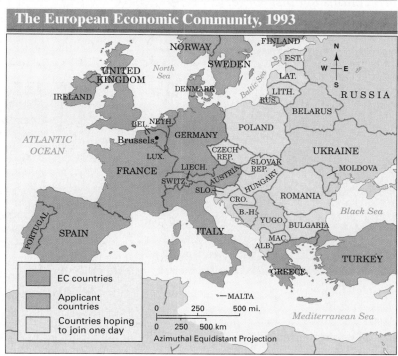

The European Economic Community, 1993

Toward Greater Economic Unity

Starting in the late 1980s, Europeans set new goals for the Common Market. Europeans hoped to form a single economic market, like the one in the United States. As in the United States, they would be free to trade, work, and live anywhere within the Common Market.

The lighting of the 1,000 beacons celebrated this new economic union in Western Europe. Customs checks and trade barriers were removed or greatly reduced. Could economic union lead to a "United States of Europe"? ■

▲ *The European Economic Community, or Common Market, includes most of Western Europe. Which Western European countries are not part of this union? Use the chart above to compare the per capita, or per person, income of the United States with that of several European countries.*

■ *What is the Common Market?*

485

European Currency

Most European nations may share a single currency by the year 2000. Today, each nation mints and prints its own money. Special papers and inks and hidden patterns and symbols prevent forgers from making false money. Dutch bank notes, or guilders, include images of a shorebird, astronomer, sunflower, and lighthouse—each with unusual protections against forgery.

Magnifier and design tools

A printed fingerprint hides in this Dutch guilder, which is shown among the guilders at the bottom of this page.

The lighthouse includes part of a poem, which would be difficult to copy. In a one-guilder note, a rabbit is visible only with a filter.

At this exchange booth in Paris, people can buy and sell French francs, Spanish pesetas, British pounds, or Italian lire, among other currencies.

Western Europe Faces Its Future

During the 1980s and early 1990s, Europeans worked on a new treaty. They called it the "Maastricht *(MAHS trihkt)* Treaty" since it was signed in the town of Maastricht, Netherlands. This treaty was a plan for a more united Europe.

The Maastricht Treaty

One of this treaty's most important goals was to create a single currency for Europe. To learn more about currency in Europe, read A Closer Look on the opposite page.

In 1992 Europeans voted country by country on whether to approve the Maastricht Treaty. However, Europeans still held strong feelings of nationalism and ethnic pride. Many feared losing their national identity, or their sense of who they are as a people, if they voted yes.

In Denmark, voters said no. In France, the treaty barely passed. As a result, European leaders decided to revise the Maastricht Treaty and to put it to a new vote.

Challenges to Unity

Feelings of nationalism also led to outbreaks of violence in Germany, France, and other European countries. For instance, a few Germans formed groups inspired by Hitler's Nazis. These "neo-Nazis,"

or new Nazis, attacked immigrants to Germany.

Anti-immigrant feelings also arose in other Western European countries. Many immigrants to Western Europe were Muslims from Southwest Asia searching for better jobs. When Europe's economy stumbled in the early 1990s, millions of people lost their jobs. Some Europeans blamed immigrants for their economic troubles.

Western Europe also faces the challenge of how best to help Eastern Europe. Should it get involved in Eastern Europe's ethnic conflicts and economic problems? In the next lesson, you will read about the challenges of Eastern Europe. ■

▼ *Not everyone in Europe wants free trade. These French farmers protested the removal of trade barriers by dumping their apples in Paris.*

■ *What was a goal of the Maastricht Treaty?*

R E V I E W

1. **FOCUS** Is the dream of a united Europe coming true? Explain why or why not.
2. **HISTORY** What was the Treaty of Rome?
3. **ECONOMICS** The Common Market formed a single market in 1993. What were three of its goals?
4. **CRITICAL THINKING** Denmark rejected the Maastricht Treaty in 1992. France barely passed it. Suggest some reasons why so many Europeans opposed this treaty.
5. **ROLE-PLAYING ACTIVITY** Form groups of three to five students. Act out what you think it was like to cross national borders in Europe when customs checks were required. Then act out what crossing national borders without customs checks might be like today.

Voting For or Against a United Europe

Free trade between countries

▼ *Just a few years ago, the London district of Notting Hill, shown here, was the site of riots between ethnic groups. As diversity increases throughout Europe, many wonder how it will affect European unity.*

I don't want a United States of Europe. There would be no Denmark. . . . We Danes are less than two percent of the community [the Common Market], and we'll lose everything. Denmark will be just a patch of Europe attached to Germany.

Kim Jensen, glassware artisan, near Copenhagen, Denmark

I am 16 and live in a small village in Greece. My country is not wealthy and I come from a very poor region. Yet I feel like a true European and my dream, like so many others in Europe, is of final union to benefit all Europe's citizens. . . . If Europeans want to unite, then we must start thinking together as one.

Aristides H. Liakopoulos, Kendrico, Greece

Background

In the early 1990s, Western Europeans debated the idea of a united Europe. As you read in the previous lesson, much of this debate focused on the Maastricht Treaty. This treaty was a plan to form a "United States of Europe" that would be somewhat similar to the way the states of the United States form a union. Although states have their own laws, they are also subject to higher, federal laws.

The Maastricht Treaty had several goals, including:
1. a single currency and a central bank
2. a more powerful European Parliament to make laws
3. a more powerful European Court of Justice

4. European citizenship for residents of the Common Market
5. a common foreign and defense policy.

The terms of the Maastricht Treaty would become law for all the countries of a united Europe. In other words, some laws of a united Europe would override, or overpower, laws of individual countries.

Concerns about a United Europe

Some Europeans—such as the young man from Greece (page 488)—support the idea of a united Europe. They feel it would ensure future peace and economic growth. To compete in a global economy, they say, would require European countries to join together for greater economic strength.

However, other Europeans—such as Kim Jensen of Denmark (page 488)—do not support the Maastricht Treaty. Many Danes think of themselves as Danish first and European second. Other Europeans feel the same way about their countries. Danes voted to reject the Maastricht Treaty, fearing loss of their national identity.

Some Europeans also fear losing their jobs if Europe is united. They worry that increased competition would force many companies to go out of business.

Partly as a result of the Danish vote and these economic worries, the Maastricht Treaty—and its plan for a united Europe—is being revised.

Can Europeans preserve their national identities in a united Europe? Can the many national groups of Europe get along as one people? Would a united Europe reduce the ethnic tensions within countries? Should creating a united Europe take place before the end of this century? These are just a few of the difficult questions Europeans face as they decide whether to form a united Europe.

Environmental protection

Free travel between countries

Scientific cooperation

Decision Point

1. What are the benefits of a united Europe? What are the costs? (Consider these questions with regard to having one currency, one law-making body, and one supreme court.)
2. What goals and values would cause Europeans to support a united Europe? What goals and values would cause them to reject the idea?
3. Suppose the United States, Mexico, and Canada agreed to form a "United States of North America." Would you support this idea? Explain your response.
4. Collect information from newspapers and magazines about current events in Europe. Discuss how these events could lead to greater unity—or division—in Europe.

▲ *These illustrations reflect some of the benefits of a united Europe. Think about what is not shown—the costs of a united Europe.*

489

L E S S O N   3

Eastern Europe Today

What are two challenges facing Eastern Europe?

Key Terms

- command economy
- market economy

➤ *These women register to vote in Warsaw. The first free election to Poland's parliament was held in November 1991.*

For families in Sarajevo, the last night of 1992 passed quietly. No bombs crashed into their city. No gunfire sounded. The war between the Serbs and the Muslims of Bosnia-Herzegovina *(BAHZ nee uh hehrt suh goh VEE nuh)*, once part of Yugoslavia, had not ended. Yet fighting had stopped this cold winter night during a brief cease-fire.

For warmth, families huddled together under piles of blankets. Homes in Sarajevo lacked electricity, heat, and running water. For dinner, most people had only a few pieces of bread to eat.

Meanwhile, in Czechoslovakia people counted down the last minutes of 1992. At midnight, Czechoslovakia would split into two separate countries: the Czech Republic and the Slovak Republic. Unlike people in the former country of Yugoslavia, Czechs and Slovaks did not go to war. Their leaders chose to part peacefully. However, Czechs, Slovaks, and many other East Europeans worried about their futures.

Progress in Eastern Europe

Until recently, Communist dictators ruled Eastern Europe. Today, East Europeans are building democratic governments. They are inexperienced with democracy, however, having lived under one-party rule for so long.

East Europeans are also changing from a command economy to a market economy. In a **command economy,** the government owns all farms and factories. It decides what to produce and sets all prices. Under communism, Eastern Europe had a command economy, as in the Soviet Union. In a **market economy,** as in the United

States, farms and factories are privately owned. Owners decide what to produce and set their own prices.

East Europeans hope a free-market economy will help to improve their lives. However, they face ethnic conflict, unemployment, and lack of security. Many are making choices that they have never before had.

Czechoslovakia Divides

When Czechoslovakia split into two separate nations, the two sides split up their assets, or property and equipment, fairly. They agreed to share the same currency.

The Slovak Republic is poorer and less industrialized than the Czech Republic. Many of its factories were used to build weapons during the Cold War. Converting them to other uses will be costly. However, Slovaks are determined to build their own modern country. One of their first goals is to create their own national currency.

Most Czechs wanted to remain as one country with the Slovaks. However, they too feel they can stand on their own. Many Czechs are well educated. With many modern factories, Czechs hope to build a thriving market economy quickly.

Success in Poland

The 1980s saw Poland in turmoil. Its Communist government was losing control over the country. Hundreds of thousands of workers went on strike. From these strikes, a new leader arose in Poland, Lech Walesa *(wah LEHN sah)*.

Walesa led the unions in toppling Poland's Communist government in 1989. Then he worked to transform Poland into a democracy with a market economy. Poland has suffered from high unemployment and rising prices. However, economists now expect Poland's economy to grow.

A New Germany

East and West Germany reunited in 1990. For the first time since World War II, Germans were one people and one country. Germans celebrated this union. Some other Europeans did not.

Many feared a united Germany. They worried that Germany would once again try to rule over Europe. Their fears were not of military power, but of economic power. ■

Prague, the capital of the Czech Republic, is noted for its rich cultural life, especially in music and literature.

How Do We Know?

HISTORY *When events change as quickly as they are changing in Eastern Europe, how do people there make sense of them? In Warsaw, Poland, for example, one way people stay up to date on current affairs is by reading several of the city's 15 newspapers. Just a few years ago, Poland had only one official newspaper.*

■ *Why did East Europeans want to change from a command economy to a market economy?*

491

Old Conflicts Rise Anew

Across Time & Space

Religious differences have divided Serbs, Croats, and Bosnian Muslims—who speak the same language—for centuries. Charlemagne converted the Croats to western Christianity. Later, Byzantines converted the Serbs to eastern Christianity. After being invaded by the Ottoman Turks in the 1300s, many Bosnians converted to Islam.

▲ *Despite the dangers in Sarajevo, these men must cook their meals outdoors.*

■ *Why are Serbs, Muslims, and Croats at war in Bosnia?*

After the collapse of one-party rule, violent ethnic conflicts broke out in many regions of Eastern Europe. The worst of these conflicts arose in parts of what was once Yugoslavia.

The Breakup of Yugoslavia

Until 1991, Yugoslavia included the republics of Bosnia-Herzegovina (or Bosnia), Macedonia, Slovenia, and Croatia. Today, Yugoslavia is made up of only two republics: Montenegro and Serbia.

Turn to the map on page 481 to see what Yugoslavia and its former republics look like today.

Several ethnic groups live in Yugoslavia and its former republics. For the most part, each ethnic group calls one republic its home. For example, mostly Eastern Orthodox Serbs live in Serbia. Croatia is home to mainly Roman Catholic Croats. However, Muslims, Serbs, and Croats all live in Bosnia.

Civil War in Yugoslavia

In mid-1991 civil war broke out when Croatia and Slovenia declared independence from Yugoslavia. Serbs fought to keep Yugoslavia together. After months of war, Slovenia and Croatia made peace with the Serbs. Then Bosnia declared its independence. As a result, Serbs fought Muslims and Croats for control of Bosnia. The Serbs tried to kill or drive out all the non-Serbs from Bosnia. They hoped to make Bosnia part of Yugoslavia again.

Thousands of people, mostly civilians, died in the fighting. Hundreds of thousands of others fled their homes, becoming war refugees. The city of Sarajevo lay battered.

Serbs were accused of "ethnic cleansing," or genocide, for trying to rid Bosnia of everyone who was not a Serb. Serbs were blamed for horrible war crimes, including attacks on women and children and the use of death camps.

Peace talks between the United Nations and leaders of all sides began in mid-1992. The United Nations also sent a small military force to Bosnia to supply people with food and medicine.

Ethnic tensions are also creating problems in the former Soviet Union. The next lesson describes some of the political, economic, and environmental challenges the former Soviet Union is facing. ■

R E V I E W

1. **FOCUS** What are two challenges facing Eastern Europe?

2. **ECONOMICS** What problems do Eastern European countries face in trying to shift from a command economy to a market economy?

3. **GEOGRAPHY** Name the republics that seceded from Yugoslavia in the early 1990s.

4. **HISTORY** What ethnic groups were fighting in Bosnia?

5. **CRITICAL THINKING** Why are some people afraid that war in Bosnia may spread throughout Europe?

6. **ACTIVITY** Compare the Atlas map of modern Europe on page 682 with the cultural map of Europe in 1914 on page 462. Then make a chart showing some of the ways Europe today differs from Europe in 1914.

L E S S O N   4

Russia and the Former Soviet Republics

THINKING FOCUS

What are two challenges facing the former Soviet republics today?

Key Terms

- entrepreneur
- commonwealth

▲ *The Kremlin is the heart of Moscow and the center of government. Next to it is Red Square, home to kiosks, such as this one.*

Vladislav Vasnev owns one of the first private businesses in the former Soviet Union. Vasnev and his partners run a chain of kiosks *(KEE ahsks),* or booths, near Red Square in Moscow. From their kiosks, they sell a variety of goods from video equipment to shoes.

Russian shoppers crowd around Vasnev's many kiosks. Only a few have enough money to buy something there. Still, Vasnev's business continues to grow. Elsewhere in Russia, other **entrepreneurs** *(ahn truh pruh NUHRS),* or people who start businesses, are trying to realize their dreams. However, Russian entrepreneurs risk losing their investments—and businesses.

Although Russians are building a democracy and a market economy, what if they fail? As Vasnev says, "There were never any guarantees, and there still aren't any. We are still at risk, even today."

After the Breakup of the Soviet Union

In Chapter 20 you read how Communist officials tried to overthrow Gorbachev in August 1991. Afterward Gorbachev returned as president of the Soviet Union. His goal was to reform the Soviet Union slowly. However, many people demanded quicker reforms.

493

The Caspian and Aral Seas—or Deserts?

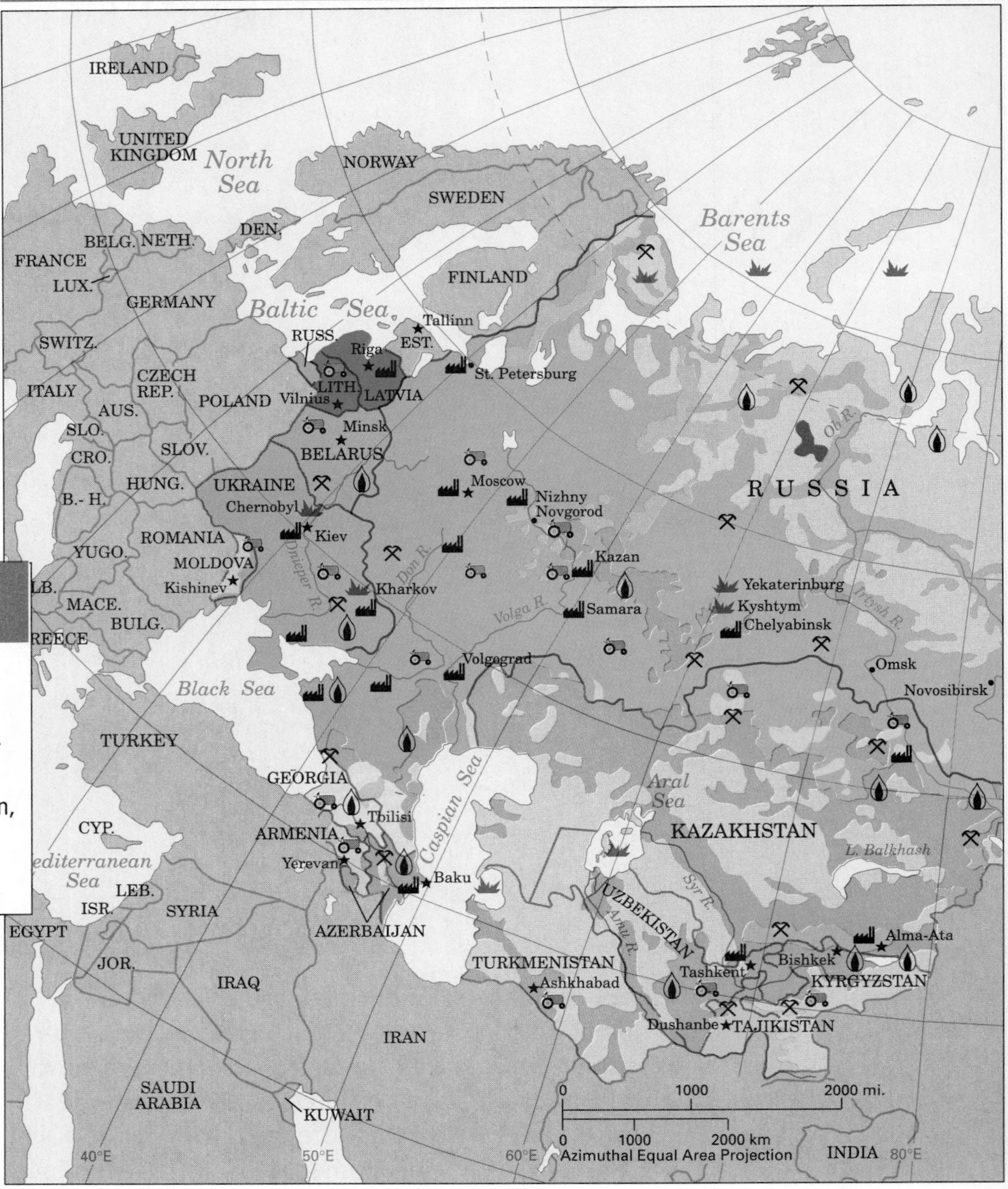

Rivers supplying fresh water to the Caspian and Aral seas are being diverted to grow cotton. As a result, these two inland seas are drying up—and becoming deserts.

Ethnic Conflict in the Caucasus

Christian Armenia and Muslim Azerbaijan are fighting over Nagorno-Karabakh. This region is located in Azerbaijan, but its people are mostly Armenians.

➤ Study this map of Russia and the other former Soviet republics. Why might ethnic conflict become a major problem in these republics?

The Soviet Union Falls Apart

Fear of Soviet troops had kept the 15 republics from breaking away from the Soviet Union. After the failed takeover, however, people no longer feared Soviet troops.

During the autumn of 1991, the republics took the final steps to become independent countries. Gorbachev was powerless to stop them from leaving the Soviet Union. He could not depend on the loyalty of the Soviet troops. People no longer trusted the slow pace of his reforms.

As a result, the Soviet Union broke apart. Gorbachev resigned as Soviet president. At the end of 1991, the Soviet Union ceased to exist.

Fifteen New Countries Emerge

All of the 15 republics of the Soviet Union were now independent countries. To learn more about these 15 new countries, see the map on this and the opposite page.

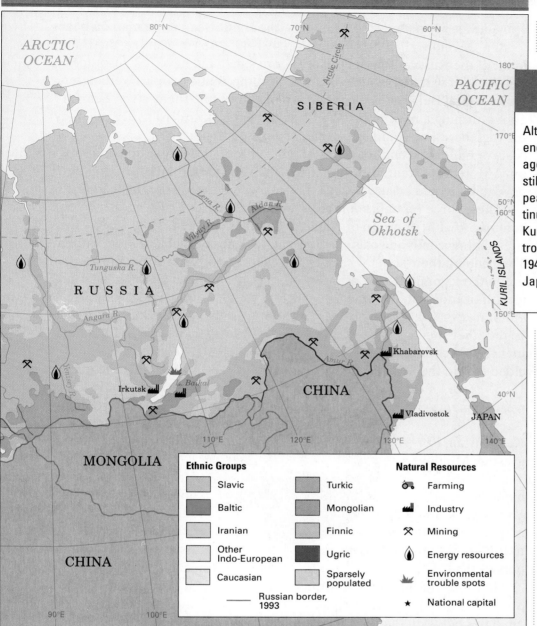

ARCTIC OCEAN

PACIFIC OCEAN

SIBERIA

RUSSIA

Tunguska R.

Lena R.

Aldan R.

Vilyuy R.

Angara R.

Yenisey R.

Sea of Okhotsk

L. Baikal

Irkutsk

Amur R.

Khabarovsk

Vladivostok

CHINA

JAPAN

KURIL ISLANDS

MONGOLIA

CHINA

Ethnic Groups

- Slavic
- Baltic
- Iranian
- Other Indo-European
- Caucasian
- Turkic
- Mongolian
- Finnic
- Ugric
- Sparsely populated
- — Russian border, 1993

Natural Resources

- Farming
- Industry
- Mining
- Energy resources
- Environmental trouble spots
- ★ National capital

Friction Between Russia and Japan

Although World War II ended almost 50 years ago, Russia and Japan still have not signed a peace treaty. They continue to argue over the Kuril Islands—controlled by Russia since 1945, but ruled by Japan for centuries.

The Siberian Tiger: Soon to Be Extinct?

The last 300 or so Siberian tigers on earth are in danger of losing their home—and disappearing forever. Their home, the world's largest forest in Siberia, is being cut down for timber.

Like many Eastern European countries, these 15 new countries faced many challenges. Most attempted to form democratic governments. Most struggled to change from a command economy to a market economy.

In the past, the Soviet government controlled the local economies and local governments. Now, the 15 former Soviet republics are in charge of both. Nickolai Karanko, a Ukrainian teenager, said:

Five years ago, we had to do what the government wanted. Now, they have to do what we want. That's democracy.

Still, people in the former Soviet republics worried about the future. People still had to wait in line for food. Worse, unemployment and prices were rising. Could they survive without the Soviet Union?

The Soviet Union was home to many ethnic groups, such as Ukrainians and Georgians. For years, Russians had ruled these ethnic groups with czars and later with Communist dictators. Then, in 1991 the Soviet Union broke up, and some of these peoples were free to govern themselves.

➤ *Russian President Boris Yeltsin, shown here, wants to move quickly toward a market economy. However, other government leaders do not.*

■ *Give two reasons why Russia and several other republics formed the C.I.S.*

The C.I.S. Is Formed

On December 7, 1991, the president of the Russian Republic, Boris Yeltsin, met with the leaders of Ukraine and Belarus. They talked about forming a new union. Working together, they could share the costs of building a market economy. More important, they hoped a new union would ensure peace.

These three republics formed a **commonwealth,** or group of countries sharing common goals. They named their new union the Commonwealth of Independent States, or C.I.S. Eight other former republics decided to join the C.I.S. These were Armenia, Azerbaijan, Kazakhstan, Kyrgyzstan, Moldova, Tajikistan, Turkmenistan, and Uzbekistan. Study the map on pages 494–495 to find the 11 original members of the C.I.S.

Tensions throughout the former Soviet Union have already weakened ties between the republics. Azerbaijan and Armenia, for example, are fighting over territory.

The Baltics Struggle Alone

To locate the Baltic countries of Estonia, Latvia, and Lithuania, find the Baltic Sea on the map on pages 494–495. As you can see, the Baltics are small and have few resources. Yet the Baltic peoples were determined to rule themselves. Fearful of being controlled by Russia, they refused to join the C.I.S.

Free for the first time in more than 50 years, the Baltic peoples expected a good life. Instead of quick success, however, the Baltic peoples suffered. They faced shortages of fuel and food. Prices rose. Many people lost their jobs and could not find work. Angry at the lack of progress, people in Lithuania elected a Communist government back into office.

More troubling, Russian soldiers still remained in all three countries. In fact, almost two million Russians call the Baltics their home. However, the Baltic peoples view Russians as their former rulers. Estonia and Latvia passed laws making it difficult for Russians to become citizens there. As a result, ethnic conflict in the Baltics increased.

Just a few years after independence, the high hopes of the Baltic peoples were fading. They wondered if they would survive as independent countries. ■

Challenges for the Future

People in the other former Soviet republics also expected their economies to improve quickly. However, as in the Baltics and Eastern Europe, they did not. Prices and unemployment rose, while many factories closed. In Russia, organized crime greatly increased. People wondered if economic reforms were worth these costs.

In Russia, President Yeltsin and several former Communist leaders agreed to slow down the change to a market economy. For example, they decided to control the prices of milk, pasta, and bread.

Many of the other former republics also tried to slow their reforms. Some people approved of these slowdowns. Others, however, feared a return to communism.

Reducing Nuclear Weapons

Almost all Soviet nuclear weapons had been placed in Russia, Ukraine, Belarus, and Kazakhstan. What would happen to these weapons now?

In 1993 Russian President Yeltsin and U.S. President George Bush signed a new treaty, called START II (Strategic Arms Reduction Treaty). Both leaders agreed to destroy many of their country's nuclear weapons. Belarus, Kazakhstan, and Ukraine had signed an earlier treaty to reduce nuclear arms with the United States and Russia. That treaty quickly ran into trouble, however. Some Ukrainians wanted to keep their nuclear weapons to protect the country against Russia. Ukrainian officials asked for more aid from

the West. U.S. President George Bush offered millions of dollars to help Ukraine disarm.

Cleaning Up the Environment

Turn back to the map on pages 494–495. Note the locations of some environmental trouble spots facing the former republics today. Cleaning up their air, land, and water will cost billions of dollars. However, these new countries do not have enough money to pay these costs.

Perhaps the greatest challenge facing the former Soviet republics is living with so much uncertainty. Will life improve? Will a Communist dictator again seize power? Only in the future will the answers be known. ■

▲ *These Soviet bombers once carried nuclear weapons. After agreeing to arms control treaties with the United States, Russian officials cut off the tails to prove that these planes no longer posed a nuclear threat.*

■ *Why do some Russians and others in the former republics want to slow their economic reforms?*

R E V I E W

1. **FOCUS** What are two challenges facing the former Soviet republics today?
2. **HISTORY** Explain one reason for the breakup of the Soviet Union.
3. **ECONOMICS** Why were the Baltic peoples disappointed in the years following independence?
4. **CRITICAL THINKING** Russia and the former republics need investments to help them succeed. What kind

of investments might benefit Russia and the former Soviet republics? Explain how the United States might benefit from making investments there.
5. **ACTIVITY** Imagine you are a Russian entrepreneur, such as Vladislav Vasnev. What would you say to Russian leaders to persuade them to keep your kiosks open and to continue to build a market economy? Write a letter that Vasnev might write on this topic.

Chapter Review

Reviewing Key Terms

command economy (p. 490)
common market (p. 484)
commonwealth (p. 496)
continental climate (p. 482)
customs check (p. 485)
entrepreneur (p. 493)

marine climate (p. 482)
market economy (p. 490)
Mediterranean climate (p. 482)
tariff (p. 485)

A. Write a short paragraph explaining how the terms in each of these groups are related. Be sure to use the terms themselves in your explanation.
1. marine climate, Mediterranean climate, continental climate
2. command economy, market economy

B. Answer the following questions, using the key term in parentheses.

1. How did Western European nations hope to increase economic cooperation during the Cold War? (common market)
2. What happens when goods and people cross a country's borders in Europe? (customs check)
3. How might a country whose factories make shoes protect its shoe industry from cheaper imported shoes? (tariff)
4. What was one result of the economic and political changes taking place in Russia? (entrepreneur)
5. What kind of organization brought together some of the former republics of the Soviet Union? (commonwealth)

Exploring Concepts

A. Copy the timeline below. Place these events in their proper positions.
- Czechoslovakia divides in two.
- Germany reunites.
- Civil war erupts in Yugoslavia.
- Poland's Communist government falls.
- Three former Soviet republics form the C.I.S.
- Europeans vote on the Maastricht Treaty.
- Gorbachev resigns as Soviet leader.

B. Answer each question with information from the chapter.
1. Where are the mountain systems of Europe located? What regions do they separate?
2. How has the Northern European Plain contributed to Europe's prosperity?

3. What causes Europe's marine climate?
4. Name at least three of the founding members of the European Economic Community.
5. What were some of the original goals of the European Economic Community?
6. Why did some Europeans oppose the first version of the Maastricht Treaty?
7. Who were the targets of Germany's neo-Nazi groups? Why were they targets?
8. What change occurred in Czechoslovakia at the end of 1992?
9. What were the main causes of the breakup of Yugoslavia?
10. When the Soviet Union fell apart, what became of its former republics?
11. What countries formed the C.I.S.?

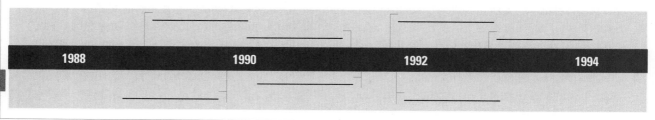

1988   1990   1992   1994

Reviewing Skills

1. Suppose that you and a friend or family member want to watch different television shows that are on at the same time. Applying the steps on page 483, describe the first step you would take to resolve this conflict. How might you reach a solution that satisfies both of you?

2. One of the major changes in Europe in the 1990s was the split of Czechoslovakia into two nations. Reread the section of Lesson 3 that discusses this change. From those paragraphs, what predictions would you make about the future of the Slovak Republic and the Czech Republic? Explain the reasons behind your predictions.

3. Study the chart below. If a Russian worker earned 350 rubles a month, how much would he or she have left over after buying one gallon of milk, two loaves of bread, one-half pound of sausage, and one pound of butter?

Basic Food Costs in Russia		
Food	**Before Price Reforms**	**After Price Reforms**
Milk (1 quart)	.69 Rubles	2.1 Rubles
Bread (1 loaf)	.60 Rubles	2.63 Rubles
Butter (1 pound)	4.5 Rubles	20.35 Rubles
Sausage (1 pound)	35 Rubles	50 Rubles

Note: The average salary is 350–500 rubles ($3.15–$4.50) a month.
Source: Facts on File, 1992

Using Critical Thinking

1. Why would the members of the Common Market want lower tariffs? How do tariffs benefit the people of a country that charges tariffs? How might tariffs hurt those people?

2. Some planners hope for a "United States of Europe." How might this be harder to achieve than a United States of America?

3. In many countries of Eastern Europe, people have never lived under a democratic government. What things about democracy do you think would be surprising or difficult for Eastern Europeans to accept?

Preparing for Citizenship

1. COLLECTING INFORMATION Working with one or two classmates, choose one European nation to study. From newspapers, news magazines, and TV or radio reports, gather information about ongoing events in the nation you have chosen. Make a scrapbook of articles, pictures, and notes for that country. Then use this information to prepare a short report that will bring your classmates up to date on events in the country you have studied.

2. WRITING ACTIVITY Imagine that you have a pen pal in Russia, Poland, the Baltic states, or the Czech or Slovak republics. Your friend has written you about problems resulting from changes in the government and the economy. Write a letter to your friend in which you describe the good things about democracy and a market economy—the things you feel will make the changes and difficulties worthwhile.

3. COLLABORATIVE LEARNING Working with your classmates, make a large-scale illustrated map of modern-day Europe. Use the map on page 481 as a guide. Then look in used magazines or newspapers for pictures you may cut out that show the land and people of Europe. Include pictures of art and handicrafts, as well as your own drawings. Use ribbons and thumbtacks to connect the pictures to the map.

The Caribbean, Central and South America

Wrapped in a hammock, a man is carried off for burial. Hanging above the body are food and prized possessions that will accompany him into the afterlife. This story, told in this brightly colored cloth panel called a mola, reveals part of traditional Kuna culture. Native Americans, such as the Kuna of Panama, are the descendants of Asians who first came to the Americas perhaps 50,000 years ago. Native Americans developed agriculture, complex belief systems, and civilizations that scientists and historians today are still learning about.

1492

A mola (fabric made from stitched pieces of cloth) from the San Blas Islands, Panama, c. 1965

Today

Unit 7 Overview

The Caribbean, and Central and South America

The islands of the Caribbean stretch for more than 2,000 miles. Many are part of a vast underwater mountain chain. Some islands are the tops of volcanoes that erupted long ago. Other islands are made of coral that was formed during thousands of years from the skeletons of tiny sea animals.

A funnel-shaped ribbon of land forms Central America. This narrow strip is crisscrossed by steep mountains and volcanoes. The region is often shaken by earthquakes. At its southern end, Central America meets South America, the world's fourth largest continent.

Native American cultures had prospered in this region long before Columbus sailed into the hemisphere. Spanish and Portuguese sailors began to arrive in the late 1400s and found highly developed civilizations. The explorers overpowered the Indians, took their lands, and forced them to work on farms and in mines. Later, Africans and Asians were brought to the region to work for European plantation owners.

The people of the Caribbean and Central and South America are descendants of Indians, Europeans, Africans, and Asians. Their music, dance, literature, art, and religion all show the influence of many different cultures.

▼ *Mountains covered with snow rise high above Peru's Lake Titicaca.*

▲ *This young girl's Incan ancestry is revealed in her style of dress.*

90°W   80°W   70°W   60°W   50°W   40°W

Gulf of Mexico

⊛ Nassau
BAHAMAS

Havana ⊛
CUBA

Tropic of Cancer

20°N

Santiago de Cuba
CAYMAN
ISLANDS
(U.K.)   JAMAICA
Port-au-Prince
HAITI   DOMINICAN
REPUBLIC   PUERTO
RICO
(U.S.)   VIRGIN
ISLANDS (U.S., U.K.)
ANGUILLA (U.K.)
Kingston   Santo
Domingo   ANTIGUA AND BARBUDA
ST. KITTS   GUADELOUPE (Fr.)
AND NEVIS   DOMINICA
MARTINIQUE (Fr.)
ST. LUCIA
ST. VINCENT AND
THE GRENADINES   BARBADOS

BELIZE
GUATEMALA   Belmopan
HONDURAS
Guatemala   Tegucigalpa
City
San Salvador
EL SALVADOR   NICARAGUA
Managua   MOSQUITO
Lago de Nicaragua   COAST

Caribbean Sea

NETHERLANDS
ARUBA (Neth.)   ANTILLES
(Neth.)
GRENADA

ATLANTIC

San José   ISTHMUS
COSTA RICA   OF PANAMA
PANAMA   Panama
City
Gulf of
Panama   Barranquilla
Cartagena   Maracaibo   Caracas   TRINIDAD AND
TOBAGO

OCEAN

10°N   10°N

Medellín   LLANOS   VENEZUELA   Georgetown
Angel Falls   GUYANA   Paramaribo
Bogotá   GUIANA HIGHLANDS   SURINAME   Cayenne
FRENCH
GUIANA
(Fr.)

MALPELO
(Colombia)   COLOMBIA

Rio   Negro

Equator   0°   0°

GALAPAGOS
ISLANDS
(Ecuador)   Quito
ECUADOR
Guayaquil
Gulf of
Guayaquil   Iquitos   AMAZON   Manaus   Amazon
River   Belém

BASIN   Solimões   River
Tapajós River
Xingu River   Fortaleza

Trujillo   Madeira   River
PERU   Tocantins River
A   BRAZIL   Recife
Lima   N   São Francisco River
Cuzco   D   BRAZILIAN
10°S   E   PLATEAU OF   10°S
Arequipa   S   Lake Titicaca   MATO GROSSO   Brasília
La Paz   HIGHLANDS
BOLIVIA   Salvador
ALTIPLANO   Sucre

PACIFIC   Belo Horizonte
GRAN CHACO
OCEAN   A   PARAGUAY   Paraguay River   Paraná River
N   São Paulo   Rio de Janeiro
Antofagasta   D   Asunción   Santos
ATACAMA DESERT   E
SAN FÉLIX   SAN AMBROSIO   S   Salado River   Paraná River
ISLAND   ISLAND
(Chile)   (Chile)

Tropic of Capricorn   20°S   20°S

Pôrto Alegre
Córdoba
JUAN FERNÁNDEZ   CHILE   Rosario   URUGUAY
ISLANDS   Valparaíso   Buenos Aires   Montevideo
(Chile)   Santiago   Rio de la Plata   30°S
ARGENTINA   30°S
Concepción   PAMPAS
Colorado R.   Bahía Blanca
Valdivia

Gulf of San Matías

ATLANTIC
OCEAN   40°S   40°S

PATAGONIA   Comodoro Rivadavia
Gulf of San Jorge

⊛ National capital

0   400   800 mi.   • Major city
0   400   800 km   National boundary
Azimuthal Equal-Area Projection

Strait of   FALKLAND
Magellan   ISLANDS
(U.K.)
TIERRA
DEL FUEGO
Cape Horn   SOUTH GEORGIA
(U.K.)
110°W   100°W   90°W   80°W   Drake Passage   60°W   50°W   40°W   30°W   20°W   50°S

The Caribbean, and Central and South America

The Land and People

Much of the Caribbean and Central America have a tropical climate and rain forest vegetation. As you might expect in so large an area, South America is a land of great variety. South America is home to soaring mountains and wide, grass-covered plains. The vast Amazon rain forest is the largest forest in the world. Thousands of kinds of plants and animals live in this rain forest. These include one of the world's longest snakes, the anaconda—and the largest rodent, the capybara.

▼ *South America's climate ranges from the tropics in the north to the polar regions of the south.*

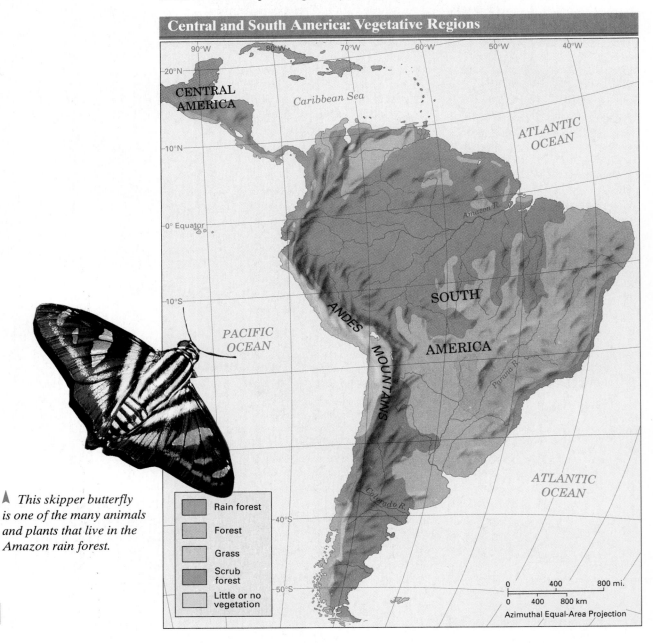

Central and South America: Vegetative Regions

Rain forest

Forest

Grass

Scrub forest

Little or no vegetation

0   400   800 mi.

0   400   800 km

Azimuthal Equal-Area Projection

▲ *This skipper butterfly is one of the many animals and plants that live in the Amazon rain forest.*

504

Central and South America separate the Caribbean Sea and Atlantic Ocean from the Pacific Ocean. At one time, people had to sail around South America to get from the Atlantic to the Pacific by ship. In 1904, however, the United States began to build a canal in Panama that would link the oceans. To dig a passage through the rain forest took thousands of workers. Many lives were lost from disease and landslides. Most African Americans who live in Central America today descend from those who came to the region to build the Panama Canal.

When Portuguese and Spanish explorers arrived, many were looking for gold. They had heard tall tales of El Dorado, a ruler so rich that he covered himself in gold. Some did return home with riches. More important, they brought their languages and religion. Today Spanish and Portuguese are the region's major languages. Roman Catholicism is the main religion.

Much of the region's culture is a blend of traditions, however. The festival of Carnival, for example, began with the Catholic custom of feasting before Lent. Today, the people of the region bring their own cultural traditions to Carnival's music, dance, costumes, and parades.

➤ *Spanish and Portuguese sailors returned to Europe with gold and jewels. They transported their treasure in heavy wooden ships called galleons.*

Comparing the World's Canals

Chesapeake and Delaware Canal U.S.A. 1927	27 feet deep
Panama Canal Panama 1914	41 feet. deep
Suez Canal Egypt 1869	36 feet. deep

Miles	0	50	100
Kilometers		31.25	62.5

Source: Information Please Almanac, 1992

⬆ *Shippers depend on the world's canals to transport their goods. The canals on the chart above are three of the world's longest and most important ones.*

➤ *The festival of Carnival in Trinidad and Tobago reflects its European, African, Indian, and Asian heritage.*

Chapter 22

The Caribbean

From Cuba to Guadeloupe to Trinidad and Tobago, the tropical world of the Caribbean is a region of diversity. Different cultures have met and influenced one another, and they all have been shaped by the history of colonialism. Although different ethnic traditions have been kept, a unique Caribbean culture has been produced.

The tropical beauty of the islands, admired long ago by European explorers, continues to draw people to the Caribbean today.

This woodcut shows Arawak women baking cassava bread. Cassava, a starchy root, is still used today in Caribbean cooking.

1492 The images of Ferdinand and Isabella adorn the Spanish coin shown above. Columbus gives coins like these to the Native Americans of the Caribbean.

1375	1500	1625

1492

1502 Santo Domingo, the first permanent European settlement in the Americas, is established by Spaniards.

These children enjoy their leisure time after school under the warm sun of the Bahamas.

This colorful Carnival mask from Puerto Rico shows how people of the Caribbean celebrate Spanish cultural traditions.

1804 Haiti is the first country in the Caribbean to gain independence from colonial rule.

1750

1875

2000

1952 After years under U.S. control, Puerto Rico is established as a commonwealth. Though its residents are U.S. citizens, Puerto Rico is a self-governing island.

Today

L E S S O N   1

Geography of the Caribbean

THINKING
F O C U S

Describe the land and the people of the Caribbean islands.

Key Term

• tropical

We started driving down into a beautiful valley. The sea sprang up all around. It was sparkling like a blue Carnival costume. The waves were smacking the rocks with big kisses and then ducking back into the sea. The trees were green and spread out wide like fans. Even the rocks looked different here. They jutted out from the land like big, brown fishermen waiting to catch fish.

Writer Lynn Joseph knows all about the beauty of the Caribbean *(kar uh BEE uhn)*. Joseph grew up on the island of Trinidad, one of the thousands of islands in the Caribbean Sea. In the passage above from her book *A Wave in Her Pocket,* she describes a special trip to Toco, a beach on the northeastern tip of Trinidad. This passage reveals some characteristics common to Caribbean geography.

➤ *This painting reveals Caribbean artist Frané Lessac's view of an island fishing scene.*

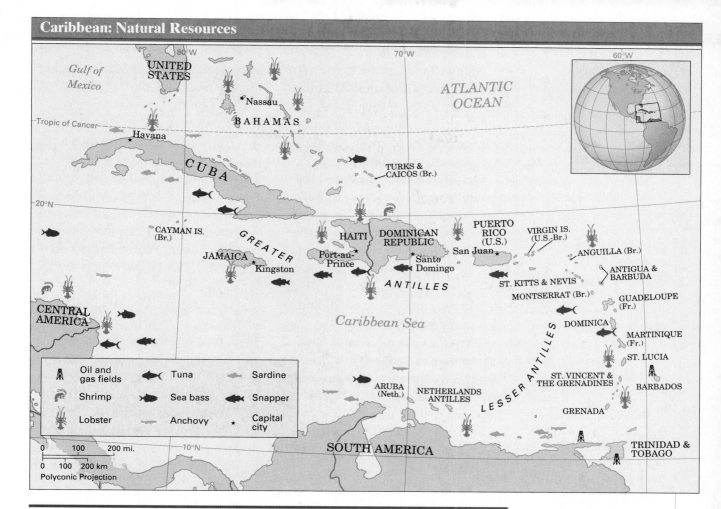

Map legend:
- Oil and gas fields
- Shrimp
- Lobster
- Tuna
- Sea bass
- Anchovy
- Sardine
- Snapper
- ★ Capital city

0   100   200 mi.
0   100   200 km
Polyconic Projection

A Chain of Islands

Find Trinidad on the map above. It is one of the southernmost islands in the Caribbean Sea. The Caribbean refers to a chain of islands in the Caribbean Sea that stretches from Florida to South America.

People often call the Caribbean region the West Indies. When Christopher Columbus bumped into a Caribbean island in 1492, he thought he had reached islands in Asia called the Indies. Later, people began calling the Caribbean islands the West Indies, to tell them apart from the East Indies.

Look again at the map. Find the islands of the Bahamas off the tip of Florida. South of the Bahamas are the largest islands of the Caribbean. This group, called the Greater Antilles *(an TIHL eez),* includes Cuba, Jamaica, Puerto Rico, and Hispaniola. The island of Hispaniola is split into two countries: Haiti and the Dominican Republic.

To the south and east of Puerto Rico is a group of islands called the Lesser Antilles. At the end of the chain are Barbados, Trinidad and Tobago, the Netherlands Antilles, and Aruba, off the coast of South America.

A Tropical World

Many islands in the Greater Antilles are the tips of huge, underwater mountains in the Caribbean Sea. Large islands such as Jamaica or Cuba have rugged mountains and lush, green rain forests.

▲ *(above) Colorful fish thrive in the warm Caribbean Sea. (top) Study the map. Some kinds of marine life are considered natural resources. Name the kinds that are caught in the waters around the Greater Antilles.*

509

The Caribbean

Many islands in the Lesser Antilles are the tips of ancient, underwater volcanoes. Other islands, such as tiny Barbuda, were formed by large masses of coral, the skeletons of small sea animals.

On any Caribbean island, the climate is normally warm to hot. The islands are near the equator, the hottest, or **tropical** part of the earth. Surrounding waters help to cool the land, however. Therefore, temperatures stay at about 81°F in the summer and between 70 and 75°F in the winter.

Most Caribbean islands have a rainy season and a dry season. Sometimes, the rainy season brings with it terrible hurricanes. The heavy rains and violent winds often cause much damage and many deaths.

The Tropical Land

The warm and humid climate of most islands is ideal for certain crops. Caribbean markets are filled with stands stacked with fruits—juicy pineapples, tart limes, and sweet mangoes, to name just a few.

Some islands have special crops. Spices such as nutmeg gave Grenada the nickname Spice Island. In Antigua people grow fine sea-island cotton. Other important export crops throughout the Caribbean are bananas, citrus fruits, coffee, tobacco, and sugar.

The warm islands are also home to a variety of tropical wildlife. Throughout the islands tiny hummingbirds with feathers of blue, green, or yellow fly from flower to flower. They look like big, colorful bugs. Brilliant green parrots and bright red flamingos live on the islands, too.

The seas are also full of life. Sharks, tuna, marlin, and sailfish swim in the waters. You can see where some of this marine life is found on the map on page 509. Many types of fish are caught and sold in the local markets.

The Greater Antilles are rich in minerals. Cuba has deposits of iron, copper, manganese, and chrome. In Jamaica bauxite is mined to make aluminum. Trinidad, in the Lesser Antilles, has oil and oil refineries.

On many Caribbean islands, however, the greatest natural resources are the climate, sea, and landscape. Like birds flying south each winter, more than eight million tourists flock to the Caribbean to enjoy the beauty around them. ■

▼ *Shipping ports such as this one in the Dominican Republic hold goods ready for export. Hurricanes frequently lash West Indian islands, badly damaging their economies.*

■ *What are some of the most valuable natural resources in the Caribbean?*

A Multicultural Past

Callaloo is the name of a special soup served in the Caribbean. It is made from a tasty mixture of soft-shell crab, coconut, curry, taro leaf, and hot peppers. As one writer remarked, "The more diverse the ingredients, the sweeter the soup."

Like callaloo, the people of the Caribbean are a diverse group. Among their ancestors are Native Americans, Africans, Europeans, and Asians. Although their family backgrounds are different, the people share a common history.

A Shared Colonial Past

The story of the Caribbean is one of colonialism. European nations fought for land and control in the Caribbean. Today many islands are independent nations. Yet a few are still associated with France, Great Britain, the Netherlands, or the United States.

On all the islands, you can see the remains of this colonial past. People speak a wide variety of languages in the Caribbean—from English in Jamaica and French in Martinique to Spanish in the Dominican Republic. Governments vary too. Jamaica, for example, has a British-style, elected government. Guadeloupe and Martinique are overseas departments of France. Their people are French citizens.

A Special Caribbean Culture

The people of the West Indies have combined their backgrounds into a shared Caribbean culture. You can see the influence of different traditions in many ways.

In Haiti the people speak French Creole, a language influenced by African languages and French. In Trinidad thousands of people gather for a huge Carnival celebration each year. Carnival was introduced by European settlers. Trinidadians, however, have made Carnival a celebration of their own culture. Through this blend of traditions, people of the Caribbean seem to embody the national slogan of Jamaica, "Out of Many, One People." ■

▲ *This Carnival band called China the Forbidden City shows how Trinidadians celebrate their Asian origins.*

■ *In what ways can you find evidence of a colonial past in the Caribbean?*

R E V I E W

1. **FOCUS** Describe the land and the people of the Caribbean islands.
2. **HISTORY** Why are the Caribbean islands also called the West Indies?
3. **GEOGRAPHY** Why are the Caribbean islands warm to hot all year round?
4. **CRITICAL THINKING** Why is it important for people of the Caribbean to preserve the beauty of the natural landscape?
5. **ACTIVITY** Use the map on page 509 to make a chart of the Caribbean islands and their major natural resources. You may want to illustrate your chart with drawings or photographs.

511

The Caribbean

LESSON 2

The Caribbean: Cradle of the Americas

I swam closer to get a better look and had to stop myself from laughing. The strangers had wrapped every part of their bodies with colorful leaves and cotton. Some had decorated their faces with fur and wore shiny rocks on their heads. Compared to us, they were very round. Their canoe was short and square, and, in spite of all their dipping and pulling, it moved so slowly. What a backward, distant island they must have come from. But really, to laugh at guests, no matter how odd, would be impolite, especially since I was the first to meet them. If I was foolish, they would think they had arrived at a foolish place.

THINKING FOCUS

What was the impact of European arrival on Caribbean history?

Key Terms

- indentured servant
- triangle trade
- emancipation

➤ *Doña Carmen is a Cuban descendant of the Arawaks, one of many groups who once lived in the beautiful Dominican Republic, shown below.*

You have just read a passage from *Morning Girl,* a book of fiction by Michael Dorris. The book tells about the arrival of Christopher Columbus in the Caribbean. As the passage above shows, Dorris's story is unusual. It is told from the point of view of a young Native American girl.

The visitors whom Morning Girl saw were Columbus and other explorers from Spain. When these Europeans stepped onto the islands, they changed the lives of the people who lived there—the Arawaks, Caribs, and Ciboneys. The Spaniards brought back accounts of the islands and the Caribbean peoples. Soon other Europeans also sailed to this so-called New World.

The Arrival of the Europeans

Wading ashore on an island in the Bahamas, Columbus thought he had found a new route to the gold and spices of Asia. After a few days on the island, Columbus and his men explored Cuba and Hispaniola.

Returning to Spain, Columbus got a royal welcome. He also received orders to colonize Hispaniola. On this second voyage, he took 17 ships and more than 1,000 men. They founded Santo Domingo, the first permanent European colony in America.

Columbus made two more voyages to the Caribbean. His travels touched off enormous changes on three continents. Europeans would soon be scrambling for land and riches in the Americas. Africans would soon be captured and forced to work on plantations there. Also, Native Americans were already dying as a result of contact with Columbus's men.

Many of these Native Americans were killed in battle. Others died of measles, smallpox, and other diseases brought from Europe by the explorers. Many others died of overwork in the mines or on plantations that the Spaniards set up. Millions of Native Americans died within 50 years of Columbus's arrival.

Competing for Gold

Spanish explorers did not intend to remain only on the islands. They used them as stepping stones to the treasures of Aztec and Inca societies in Mexico and Peru.

At first the English and the French were too busy with problems at home to try to get riches from the Americas. However, individual Frenchmen like François (*frahn SWAH*) le Clerq (*luh KLAIRK*) and English sailors like Francis Drake became pirates in the Caribbean. Their ships attacked Spanish trading vessels carrying gold from Mexico and Peru.

Some pirates worked for themselves. Others, like Francis Drake, worked for their monarchs. Drake stole so much gold from Spain that he was knighted by Queen Elizabeth I in 1581 despite Spanish protests.

European Settlement

Like the Spaniards before them, English and French colonists began building settlements on some Caribbean islands in the 1620s. The Dutch did the same in the 1630s.

The settlers grew tobacco, indigo, and spices. At first they depended on indentured servants from Europe to do the work. **Indentured servants** were people who signed contracts to work without pay for three to seven years. Their life on the Caribbean plantations was one of hard, physical labor and abusive conditions. The few who survived the hard work and terrible treatment usually became farmers. ■

▼ *This engraving depicts the* Santa María, *Columbus's flagship on his first voyage to the Americas. The ship lasted the voyage but ran aground off Haiti on December 25, 1492, and was lost.*

■ *Why did European countries want to control the Caribbean islands?*

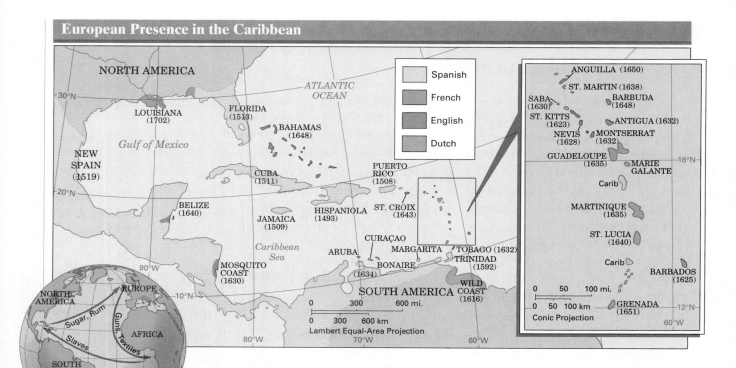

NORTH AMERICA

ATLANTIC OCEAN

	Spanish
	French
	English
	Dutch

ANGUILLA (1650)
ST. MARTIN (1638)
SABA (1630)
BARBUDA (1648)
ST. KITTS (1623)
ANTIGUA (1632)
NEVIS (1628)
MONTSERRAT (1632)
GUADELOUPE (1635)
MARIE GALANTE
Carib
MARTINIQUE (1635)
ST. LUCIA (1640)
Carib
BARBADOS (1625)
GRENADA (1651)
60°W
Conic Projection
0 50 100 mi.
0 50 100 km
16°N
−12°N

LOUISIANA (1702)
FLORIDA (1513)
BAHAMAS (1648)
Gulf of Mexico
NEW SPAIN (1519)
CUBA (1511)
PUERTO RICO (1508)
BELIZE (1640)
HISPANIOLA (1493)
ST. CROIX (1643)
JAMAICA (1509)
Caribbean Sea
CURAÇAO
MARGARITA
TOBAGO (1632)
ARUBA
BONAIRE (1634)
TRINIDAD (1592)
MOSQUITO COAST (1630)
SOUTH AMERICA
WILD COAST (1616)
0 300 600 mi.
0 300 600 km
Lambert Equal-Area Projection
30°N
20°N
10°N
90°W
80°W
70°W
60°W

NORTH AMERICA
EUROPE
Sugar, Rum
Guns, Textiles
Slaves
AFRICA
SOUTH AMERICA
ATLANTIC OCEAN

▲ *European countries claimed the Caribbean islands as their territories. The circular map shows the triangle trade.*

➤ *The business of growing, harvesting, and processing sugar cane shaped the history of the islands.*

■ *What was the triangle trade system developed by the Dutch, and what were its consequences?*

The Development of Plantations

Sugar was becoming popular in Europe. The English and the French quickly took advantage of this popularity. By the 1650s, Caribbean sugar plantations and mills brought their owners large profits. This profit was mainly due to the low cost of labor. To lower their costs even further, the planters replaced the indentured servants with persons in bondage for life, or slaves. African people were brought in for this purpose.

The Slave Trade

This was not the first appearance of slavery in the Caribbean. Spanish explorers had brought in Africans as slaves when the local Native American population died.

It was the Dutch, however, who developed the **triangle trade** system. Through this system, they exchanged European goods for enslaved Africans. African men, women, and even children were taken to prisons on the coast of Africa where they spent months waiting for the ships. As the map on this page shows, the enslaved people were then exchanged for the sugar, salt, and other island products that Europeans wanted.

The Middle Passage

The number of Africans who died on the Middle Passage, the second leg of the triangle, is unknown. Thousands suffocated, packed in the holds of ships. Many died of disease.

Those who survived faced more abuses on the plantations. The planters split up families. They prevented the enslaved Africans from being educated. African men, women, and children were forced to work in the fields for 12 or more hours a day. They often had to work under the hot sun with little to eat or drink. ■

Resistance and Revolution

In spite of the planters' efforts, the enslaved Africans began to organize. Many rose up against the plantation owners and escaped.

In August 1791 the largest and most successful slave rebellion in human history took place. It happened in the French colony of Saint Domingue, now known as Haiti. Boukman, a slave from a northern plantation, had held secret meetings all summer. At these meetings, the slave leaders sang political songs with words such as "We swear to destroy the whites and all that they possess; let us die rather than fail to keep this vow."

After attracting more than 10,000 slaves to his cause, Boukman planned a revolt for the night of August 22. Carrying pruning hooks, sugar cane knives, and torches, the slaves surrounded the homes of planters, killed most of them, and set fire to the plantations. As one survivor wrote:

The most striking feature of this terrible spectacle was a rain of fire composed of burning cane-straw which whirled thick before the blast like snow and which the wind whipped, now toward the harbor and ships, now over the houses of the town.

The rebellion spread like wildfire throughout the colony. The revolution was taking hold. A new leader emerged named Toussaint L'Ouverture (too SAN loo vehr TUR). With Toussaint's leadership and military knowledge, the former slaves took over the countryside within a few weeks. This rebellion marked the beginning of the end of slavery throughout the Caribbean. ■

This portrait of Toussaint L'Ouverture was painted by Gerard, a Haitian artist.

■ *How did blacks forge a path to freedom and leadership in the Caribbean?*

The End of Colonialism

Emancipation, the act of freeing people from slavery, came at different times to each of the Caribbean islands. Slavery ended in 1794 in Saint Domingue, in 1833 in the British colonies, and as late as 1886 in Cuba.

The Cost of Slavery

Emancipation was the result of many forces. First was the great resistance of the enslaved Africans. As slave rebellions became more frequent, European investors lost property, and sugar production fell.

The costs of maintaining slavery grew even more when European governments sent armed forces to the islands to stop the revolts. In addition, many Europeans were beginning to think that slavery was wrong. These different pressures ended slavery in the Caribbean.

Many former slaves left the plantations and became farmers and fishers. Others went to the Latin American mainland. The Africans who stayed on the plantations demanded more money and better working conditions.

515

The Caribbean

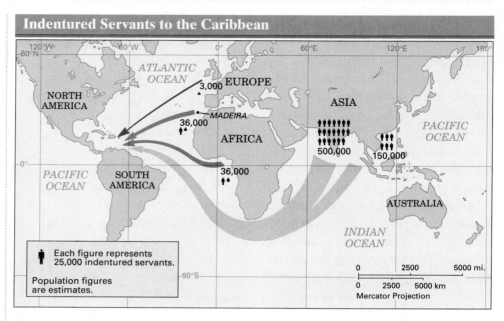

Indentured Servants to the Caribbean

Each figure represents 25,000 indentured servants.

Population figures are estimates.

Mercator Projection

➤ *After the end of slavery, hundreds of thousands of people were brought to the Caribbean as indentured servants. Where did most of these people come from?*

The plantation owners, however, still wanted a cheap work force. As a result, they brought in hundreds of thousands of people from India and other places in Asia as indentured servants.

Struggle for Independence

After emancipation, people living on some islands demanded self-government. As a result, colonialism in parts of the West Indies began to come apart.

The French colony of Saint Domingue, under the leadership of Toussaint L'Ouverture until his death in 1803, was the first to gain independence. Following years of warfare, the colony declared its independence in 1804. It was renamed Haiti, its original Arawak name. Other colonies would not gain independence until much later.

Although most Caribbean islands are independent nations today, some remain politically tied to other countries. For example, the Cayman Islands is a British dependency, and Puerto Rico is a U.S. commonwealth.

As you can see, much of Caribbean history has been brutal, marked by terrible conflict. Throughout this history, however, Caribbean peoples have built a culture that is complex, creative, and proud. This culture has shown its ability to stand up against abusive situations. It has flourished in the face of great hardships. ■

■ *Why did slavery end in the Caribbean, and what events followed emancipation?*

R E V I E W

1. **FOCUS** What was the impact of European arrival on Caribbean history?
2. **ECONOMICS** In what ways did the plantation system support colonialism, the triangle trade system, and slavery?
3. **HISTORY** What conditions made it difficult for the Africans to organize and rebel when they were first brought to the Caribbean?
4. **CRITICAL THINKING** What are some advantages and disadvantages of a small Caribbean island nation remaining tied to a large political power?
5. **WRITING ACTIVITY** Suppose you are someone living in the early 1800s who is against slavery. Write a speech or an editorial in which you describe the Middle Passage or life on a plantation. Persuade your audience to take action against slavery.

Using Constructive Criticism

Here's Why

We have all had our feelings hurt because of something critical someone said to us. Perhaps the criticism was well-intended, but it hurt because of the way it was said.

In school you and your classmates are often asked to present your work to the rest of the class. How can you comment on other people's work without hurting their feelings? Learning to give constructive criticism will help you.

Here's How

If you try hard enough, you can usually find something good to say about anyone's presentation. Suppose you are listening while another student presents a report. Listen carefully, and try to comment on what the student has done well. If you can't think of anything constructive to say, consider the questions in the box on this page.

Sometimes, to be truthful, you need to point out something that is wrong with another person's work. Perhaps a good friend asks you to read a report before turning it in. How do you handle this?

Always remember to criticize the work, not the person. Also, give your good comments first. If you start with something positive, then your criticism won't be so difficult to hear. Your friend will probably thank you for your help.

Try It

Take your turn at presenting to the class the speech you wrote against slavery. (See Lesson 2 Review, Question 5.) Review the presentations of your classmates. Listen carefully to each student, and pay attention to how each speech is presented. Use the suggestions in the box, or use your own words to say something positive about each speech.

Apply It

Keep a diary during a 24-hour period at home and at school. Make a note every time you say something constructive about a person. What reactions did you get? Were your family and friends pleased? Did your constructive criticism help others?

Evaluating a Presentation
1. Were the facts accurate?
2. Did the presenter speak clearly, without hesitation?
3. Did the presenter look directly at the audience while speaking?
4. Were the ideas creative and original?
5. Did the presentation really work for you?

L E S S O N   3

The Caribbean Today

THINKING FOCUS

What is life like in the Caribbean today?

Key Terms

- monocrop
- labor-intensive

▼ *Cricketers play in Queen's Park, known as the Savannah, in Trinidad. All ages and social groups enjoy cricket.*

Dressed all in white, the player slams the hard, maroon ball with a paddle-shaped bat. Crack! The ball sails over the far wall, and the crowd roars. It's a 6—cricket's version of a home run.

Under the hot sun, people crowd together in the Jamaican stadium to watch the best cricket players in the West Indies take on Great Britain's team. Since the 1960s the West Indians, with their expert, hard-hitting play, have ruled the sport.

A British game, cricket is a favorite sport on the islands once ruled by Great Britain. The West Indians take great pride in their teams. "Whatever we are, we are cricketers," wrote one West Indian.

What cricket is to the former British islands, baseball is to the Spanish-speaking Caribbean. There are thousands of baseball fans in Cuba, Puerto Rico, and the Dominican Republic. These places have produced some of the best players in the world, including the great Roberto Clemente from Puerto Rico, and Manuel Lee from the Dominican Republic. Sports such as baseball and cricket help unite the different peoples of the Caribbean.

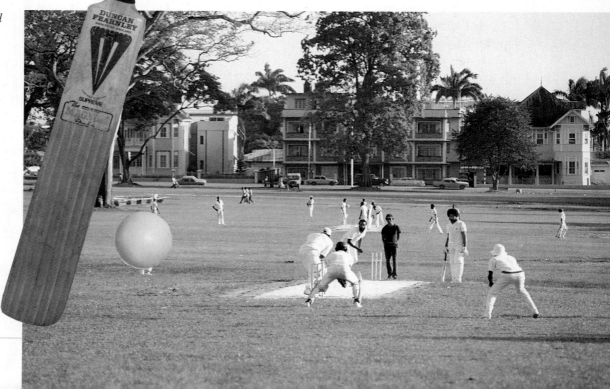

Life in the Caribbean

On many Caribbean islands, most people live in small rural villages. Villages might include small homes, a police station, a church, a post office, and a school.

Life in the Countryside

In the villages, school children play cricket, baseball, or soccer. Their families live in small houses. Many of the houses are built of brightly painted wood with tin roofs.

When colonial rule ended, many West Indians left the huge plantations to farm small plots of land. The people grow vegetables and raise chickens, cows, and goats. Today, fewer than half the people in the Caribbean still make their living this way. Many people fish in small boats. What their families don't eat, the fishers sell in the local markets.

To earn extra money, some family members may look for seasonal or part-time work on the large, mostly foreign-owned sugar and coffee plantations. Others find jobs related to tourism as waiters, drivers, hotel staff, and guides.

Life in the Cities

Throughout the islands, you'll also find cities bustling with activity. San Juan, the capital of Puerto Rico, is a lively mix of modern life and Spanish heritage.

When Spain first ruled the island, the city's name was *Puerto Rico,* or "rich port." Here ships loaded with treasure set sail for the trip back to Spain. Although the name has changed to San Juan, the city is still a rich port, one of the busiest in the Caribbean.

In "Old San Juan," you'll find Spanish-style houses and shops

with tiled roofs and floors. El Morro, a fortress built in 1539 to guard the port from pirates, still stands. Another old Spanish fort serves as the governor's palace.

Outside Old San Juan lies the modern-looking part of the city, complete with tall apartment buildings and offices, factories, large stores, and a luxurious shopping mall. Traffic fills the streets. San Juan and its suburbs are home to about one-third of Puerto Rico's population.

In Caribbean cities the rich and the very poor live near each other. Many cities are overcrowded. Rural people who move to the cities often cannot find work. Thousands live just outside the city in crude shacks in shantytowns, without any running water or electricity.

No matter where you are, in the country or in the city, in the poorest or the richest areas, you'll hear the distinctive sounds of Caribbean music. Through their music West Indians are able to express many political and social views.

▲ *(top) These women are sewing lace in front of their home in Saba, one of the islands of the Netherlands Antilles. (bottom) These children are eating conch salad, a favorite dish on many of the islands.*

519

The Largest Caribbean Islands

	Country	Area/Population	Language	Government
	Cuba	42,804 square miles 110,862 square kilometers 10,700,000 people	Spanish	One-party Communist republic
	Dominican Republic*	18,704 square miles 48,443 square kilometers 7,320,000 people	Spanish	Republic
	Haiti*	10,714 square miles 27,749 square kilometers 6,617,000 people	French, Creole	Temporary military-dominated government
	Jamaica	4,244 square miles 10,992 square kilometers 2,500,000 people	English	Parliamentary republic
	Puerto Rico	3,515 square miles 9,104 square kilometers 3,500,000 people	Spanish, English	Self-governing commonwealth of U.S.A.

*shares island of Hispaniola

Source: Britannica Book of the Year, 1992

Flowers decorate many of the Caribbean islands.

Two Islands in Contrast

Puerto Rico and Cuba have some things in common. Both Caribbean islands were once Spanish colonies, and both were occupied by the United States. These two neighbors, however, have developed differently.

After a war with Spain in 1898, the United States gained Puerto Rico. Today it is a self-governing commonwealth in free association with the United States. Puerto Ricans are U.S. citizens, but island residents can't vote for President.

After Cuba gained independence from Spain in 1899, the island went through periods of U.S. occupation, rule by presidents, and rule by dictators. In 1959 Fidel Castro and a small band of rebels took over the government. Soon Castro turned Cuba into a Communist state. It remains so today.

The two islands today differ economically as well. Once sugar cane was the heart of Puerto Rico's economy. Now it is industry. Since the 1950s, thousands of factories have opened all over Puerto Rico. Puerto Ricans manufacture textiles, clothing, medicines, metal products, processed foods, and chemicals.

Cuba, on the other hand, still depends largely on agriculture and especially on growing and refining sugar cane. In the past the Cuban economy was heavily supported by the Soviet Union. Since the Soviet breakup, the Cuban economy has suffered greatly.

For both islands, the future is uncertain. Puerto Ricans heatedly debate whether their island should remain a commonwealth, become the 51st state, or seek independence from the United States. (See the Making Decisions feature in Chapter 27.) Cubans wonder whether their nation will withstand its economic problems. They also wonder whether their country will continue to be Communist after Fidel Castro passes from the scene.

Caribbean Connections

The West Indies have never been politically unified. However, between 1957 and 1962, most British colonies briefly joined together in the West Indies Federation. The federation collapsed when the islands of Jamaica and Trinidad decided to withdraw from the group. The leaders of these larger, more industrialized islands did not want to support the smaller, poorer islands in the region.

Look at the chart on page 520 and you can see just how varied the islands are. Still, a common West Indian spirit is found on some of the islands. This spirit is expressed in different forms—including music and the popular Carnival celebrations that are held throughout the islands. A Closer Look (below) examines one kind of music.

Moving Around the Islands

West Indians form ties when they migrate or move from island to island in search of jobs. People usually travel from small, mostly agricultural islands such as Grenada to islands such as Trinidad with more industry. There they might find jobs in construction or factories.

Farm workers move from island to island to harvest crops. In this way the people of different islands build connections. ■

■ *What unites the people of the West Indies, and how are these bonds expressed?*

A CLOSER LOOK

Steel Drums

Music of the Caribbean islands often relies on drums for strong dance rhythms. You may have heard calypso and reggae music. Steel drums got their start at Carnival in Trinidad in the 1930s and 1940s, when drummers beat large oil barrels. Before long, they refined the barrels into steel drums, which are called pans.

Steel bands, which play and compete at festivals, may include more than 100 drummers.

The top of the drum is hammered into a dish shape. Dips are chiseled around the inside rim to create a range of high and low tones.

Pan sticks have rubber ends, which add to the special sound of the drums.

Economic Challenges

Today people throughout the Caribbean must respond to many economic challenges. Most of these problems can be traced back to one crop: sugar cane.

Relying on Sugar

European landowners in the Caribbean had one interest—making money by exporting sugar cane. Sugar cane became a **monocrop,** or the only major crop in the region. This reliance on sugar led to a number of problems on the islands.

The sugar industry created a surplus of unskilled workers on the islands. Growing and processing sugar cane is **labor-intensive.** That is, it requires huge numbers of people. In some places machines can do much of the harvesting, but hilly fields of cane still must be cut by hand.

In the past the sugar industry kept the number of sugar workers high by importing slaves and indentured servants. With the introduction of modern medicine and the decline in infant deaths, the result was overpopulation. Today the islands have more people than they can support with their present economies. Unemployment is very high, and wages are very low.

Creating New Businesses

Many Caribbean islands are creating jobs for their people in assembly plants. These factories offer the people jobs, but the wages are usually low. The workers perform simple tasks and do not develop skills for better-paying jobs.

Haiti, for example, is the world's largest producer of baseballs. The companies pay women low wages to stitch baseballs all day. Yet since most of these factories are owned by people in other countries, they add little wealth to the local economy.

In recent years tourism has boosted the economies of the islands. Tourism, however, has become a "monocrop" on some islands. When tourism slumps, for reasons such as a hurricane, the economy is hurt badly.

Tourism presents other problems. It, too, is labor-intensive. It calls for many unskilled workers who are often poorly paid. Foreign owners often reap most of the profits from the large hotels and resorts. In some areas the building of hotels and resorts threatens the beauty that brings people to the Caribbean. ■

▼ *The shantytowns of San Juan contrast greatly with the rest of the city. This sight is common in many cities throughout the islands.*

➤ *The currency of the Dominican Republic and Barbados reflects European influence in the Caribbean.*

■ *What economic problems did growing sugar bring to the Caribbean islands?*

Spread of Caribbean Culture

Every summer in Toronto, Canada; Brooklyn, New York; and London, England, people from the Caribbean organize huge Carnival celebrations. These are people who have left the islands in search of better-paying jobs and a higher standard of living for their families.

Moving Throughout the World

Many islanders have moved to Europe and Canada, but the highest number have come to the United States. By the mid-1980s, about one million West Indians were living in the New York City area alone. More than one million Cubans live in the United States, the majority in Florida.

These islanders bring their culture with them. Caribbean culture can be seen not only at Carnival, but in radio shows, restaurants, and food shops in cities everywhere. There are many Caribbean writers and artists at work throughout the world as well. In 1992 Caribbean poet Derek Walcott was awarded the Nobel Prize in Literature. Walcott, born in St. Lucia, lives in both Trinidad and Massachusetts.

Maintaining Close Ties

Caribbean immigrants keep close ties to their island homes. West Indian doctors, taxi drivers, nurses, and postal workers living in North America and Europe send money back to their relatives. The money helps island families buy houses or land. It also benefits the whole economy as tens of millions of dollars are sent back to the larger islands each year.

West Indians often return to the islands to visit. They bring consumer goods such as clothes, radios, and furniture for babies, which help improve the standard of living of their families.

One group of West Indian doctors returns regularly to give free medical care to the island people. As one Jamaican woman now living in the United States said, "You never really leave the islands; they're always with you in your heart." ■

▼ *A Caribbean-style Carnival is held every year in Brooklyn, New York.*

■ *In what ways is Caribbean culture spread throughout the world?*

---

1. **FOCUS** What is life like in the Caribbean today?
2. **ECONOMICS** How did most people in the Caribbean earn a living after the end of colonialism?
3. **CULTURE** How do West Indians keep their culture alive in other countries of the world?
4. **CRITICAL THINKING** Why is it difficult to build a strong economy based on unskilled workers?
5. **ACTIVITY** Review the chart on page 520. With a partner, record the population density, or the number of people per square mile, for each island listed. Which of the islands has the highest population density? Form groups to make a class graph.

Chapter Review

Reviewing Key Terms

emancipation (p. 515)   monocrop (p. 522)
indentured servant (p. 513)   triangle trade (p. 514)
labor-intensive (p. 522)   tropical (p. 510)

A. Use each word below in a sentence that shows what the word means. Write your sentence as if it were the beginning of a story.
1. tropical
2. indentured servant
3. triangle trade
4. emancipation
5. monocrop
6. labor-intensive

B. Write whether each of the following statements is *true* or *false*. Then rewrite the false statements to make them true.
1. Tropical areas have dry seasons and rainy seasons.
2. Indentured servants had to work for a plantation owner for a certain period of time before they were free to work where they wanted.
3. The triangle trade refers to trade between three European countries.
4. The act of emancipation freed people from slavery.
5. Sugar cane was called a monocrop because one person owned all the sugar plantations.
6. Labor-intensive industries are those that require small numbers of people for a long time.

Exploring Concepts

A. The cause-and-effect chart below lists facts about the Caribbean. Copy the chart. Then fill in a sentence to the right of each cause that tells an effect. The first one has been done for you.

Cause	Effect in Caribbean
Christopher Columbus thought he had reached the East Indies in Asia.	He called the Caribbean the "Indies."
The Caribbean islands were colonies of different European countries.	
Sugar growers in the Caribbean wanted to increase their profits by lowering the cost of labor.	
Enslaved blacks organized themselves and rebelled against their slave masters.	
After emancipation, the sugar growers wanted to find another source of cheap labor.	
Today, tourism is a monocrop on many Caribbean islands.	

B. Support each of the following statements with information from the chapter.
1. Geography and climate have been important influences on Caribbean culture.
2. The people of the Caribbean must be careful to safeguard their environment.
3. There are many diverse cultural influences in the Caribbean.
4. The desire for freedom and independence has been very important to the development of the Caribbean nations.
5. The sugar cane plant shaped the history of people in the Caribbean.
6. The people of the Caribbean are unified in a number of ways.
7. Cities in the Caribbean are very much like cities in the rest of the world.
8. Caribbean culture has spread to countries all over the world.
9. Tourism is important to the economies of many Caribbean nations.

Reviewing Skills

1. Imagine that you and your classmates are going to evaluate the oral reports that students give in social studies class. You have been asked to create a form that your classmates will fill in with constructive criticism after they listen to each oral report. Review the suggestions about constructive criticism on page 517. Use these suggestions to create the one-page form.
2. Look at the map on page 509. What kind of prediction could you make about the future success or failure of the economies of the Caribbean nations if the seas around these islands were to become severely polluted?
3. Reread the description of the slave revolt in Haiti on page 515. Is this a primary source or a secondary source? Explain your reasoning.
4. Reread the literature excerpt on page 508. What kind of organization pattern did author Lynn Joseph use to write her description—chronological, cause-and-effect, or spatial order? How can you tell?

Using Critical Thinking

1. Why can the Caribbean region be called a true "melting pot" of cultures? Support your answer with at least two cultural examples.
2. In 1973 a Native American named Adam Nordwall flew to Italy on an airplane. When he stepped off the plane onto the ground, Nordwall "claimed" Italy for the Indian people "by right of discovery." What point was Adam Nordwall trying to make with this action?
3. What factors have kept the nations of the Caribbean from unifying into one political nation? Support your answer with both historical and cultural information.
4. In what ways does the sugar economy continue to hurt the Caribbean economy today?

Preparing for Citizenship

1. **WRITING ACTIVITY** Today many people disagree about whether or not Christopher Columbus should be honored as a hero, considering the fate of Native Americans after his arrival in the Caribbean. Columbus once wrote about the Native Americans, "They are completely defenseless . . . and so they are fit to be ordered about and made to work. . . ." Imagine that you have been asked to write a guest column in a local newspaper about the following issue: Is Christopher Columbus a U.S. hero? Write a rough outline for your column. Be sure to support your opinions with concrete facts.
2. **COLLABORATIVE LEARNING** Many different types of governments exist in the West Indies, from the Communist government of Cuba and the temporary military-dominated government of Haiti, to the parliamentary government of Barbados and the commonwealth status of Puerto Rico. As a class, find out more about different governmental systems. Divide into small groups, with each group choosing a different Caribbean island country to research. Use the chart on page 520 as a starting point for your research. Each member of a group should research different aspects of the island government. Questions to investigate include: Who is allowed to take part in the government? How are the people of the country represented? Who are their leaders? How are government decisions made? How did this type of government develop in this island country? Together your group should prepare and present a government fact sheet that answers these questions.

Chapter 23

Central and South America

An Andean woman weaves a rich tapestry with the secret symbols of her ancient culture. Dancers swing to the rhythms of the rumba, a dance of African origin. A visitor thinks of Spain as he walks on cobblestone streets, past courtyards and red-tiled roofs. These scenes of Central and South America have their roots in the past—in the cultures of Native Americans, Africans, and Europeans. Together these people will shape the future of the region.

Many explorers wore armor such as this Spanish helmet.

A sign on a storefront symbolizes the ethnic origins of the people of Venezuela—Africans, Europeans, and Native Americans.

1498 Columbus lands in South America, the first European explorer to arrive there.

1475	1550	1625	1700

1498

1600s Most of Central and South America is under Spanish or Portuguese control.

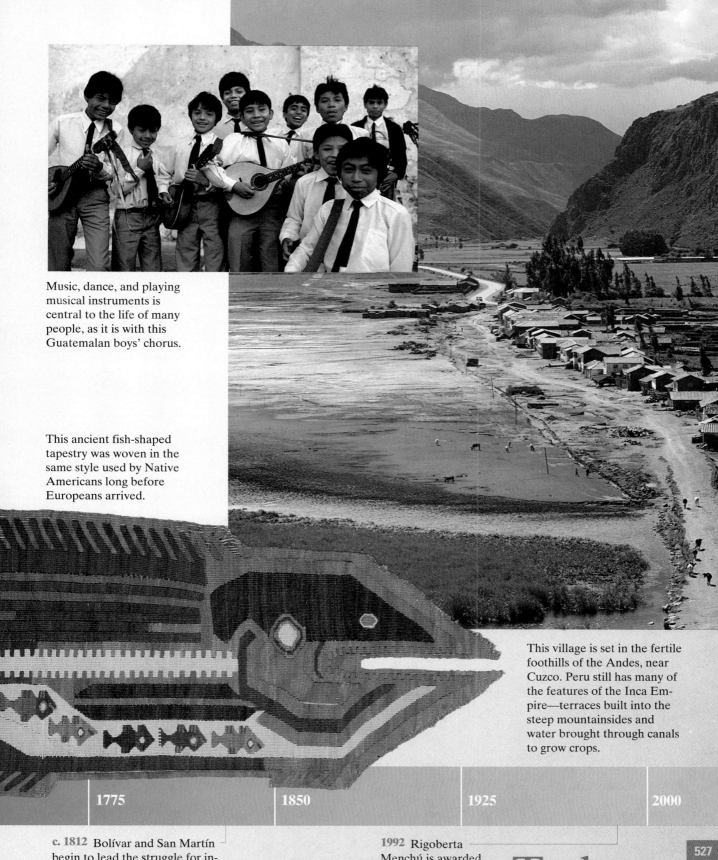

Music, dance, and playing musical instruments is central to the life of many people, as it is with this Guatemalan boys' chorus.

This ancient fish-shaped tapestry was woven in the same style used by Native Americans long before Europeans arrived.

This village is set in the fertile foothills of the Andes, near Cuzco. Peru still has many of the features of the Inca Empire—terraces built into the steep mountainsides and water brought through canals to grow crops.

1775	1850	1925	2000

c. 1812 Bolívar and San Martín begin to lead the struggle for independence for South America.

1992 Rigoberta Menchú is awarded the Nobel Peace Prize.

Today

LESSON 1

The Land and Its History

What are the physical and cultural features of Central and South America?

*A*ll grass and sky, and sky and grass, and still more sky and grass, the pampa stretched . . . a thousand miles away. . . .

Well did the ancient Quichuas name the plains, with the word signifying "space," for all was spacious—earth, sky, the waving continent of grass, the enormous herds of cattle and of horses, the strange effects of light, the fierce and blinding storms and, above all, the feeling in men's minds of freedom, and of being face to face with nature. . . .

These words by R. B. Cunninghame Graham in the 1800s describe the Argentine **pampas**, the grassy plains. You will learn about other features of Central and South America and the region's history.

Key Terms

- pampas
- basin
- vertical zone

Land of Variety

Central and South America is a land of extremes. The region has the world's longest mountain range— the Andes *(AN deez)*. It has the highest waterfall— Angel Falls—and the world's largest river—the Amazon.

The map on page 529 shows that Central America is the region stretching south from the border of Mexico through the narrow strip of Panama. Pear-shaped South America extends nearly to Antarctica.

Mountains and Rivers

A long chain of majestic mountains runs along the western region of South America. This range, called the Andes, curves northward for about 5,500 miles. Many peaks are more than 20,000 feet high. Only a narrow coastal plain lies between the Andes and the Pacific Ocean.

The land under the Andes is restless and unstable. Active volcanoes and earthquakes shape these mountains.

The Andes affect all of South America. They cut through the region,

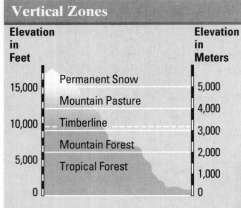

Vertical Zones

Elevation in Feet		Elevation in Meters
15,000	Permanent Snow	5,000
	Mountain Pasture	4,000
10,000	Timberline	3,000
	Mountain Forest	2,000
5,000	Tropical Forest	1,000
0		0

Source: Elements of Physical Geography, 1989

▲ *These vertical zones are found on the eastern side of the Andes in Peru, where llamas (right) are used for transportation, food, wool, and hides.*

creating borders and making communication difficult. The Andes also form a divide, from which the rivers flow east or west.

East of the Andes and south of the Guiana Highlands is the Amazon River. The river forms a huge basin covering about 2.7 million square miles. A **basin** is an area drained by a river and its tributaries. The Amazon basin is the largest in the world.

Four-fifths of Central America is hilly or mountainous. Most people live in these cool highlands rather than in the tropical coastal lowlands. Destructive earthquakes and volcanoes are common.

Climates

Because Central and South America extend over a vast region, the climate varies greatly. Yet many areas are tropical in climate.

The equator crosses South America near the continent's widest point. South of the equator in the Southern Hemisphere the seasons are opposite from those in the Northern Hemisphere.

If you have ever climbed a mountain, you know that the air gets colder as you go higher. The climate and vegetation at different altitude levels make up **vertical zones.** As

the chart on page 528 shows, you can begin your climb in tropical forests and end in snow!

Farming in the Andes depends on the climate in these vertical zones. It is difficult to grow bananas at high altitudes or to grow wheat in the tropical forest zone.

Rain Forests

Heavy rains—150 inches or more a year—fall in parts of tropical South America. Dense tropical rain forests cover much of the Amazon Basin, coastal Brazil, the Pacific coast of Colombia, and much of the eastern lowland area of Central America.

The trees provide timber and protect the soil. Even more important, the rain forest contains types of plants and animals that exist nowhere else on earth. ■

Central and South America: Climate Regions

Legend:
- Tropical wet (hot and rainy all year)
- Tropical wet and dry (hot, with rainy and dry seasons)
- Humid subtropical (hot, rainy summer and mild, rainy winter)
- Desert (dry, either hot or cold)
- Semiarid (short rainy season)
- Mediterranean (hot, dry summer and mild, rainy winter)
- Marine (cool and wet)
- Highland (climate varies with elevation)

0   500   1000 mi.
0 500 1000 km
Mercator Projection

◄ *What regions of Central and South America do not have a tropical climate?*

▲ *Central and South America have climate extremes. A tropical climate is found in Panama (top). Appliqué mola art is on display in this picture. A cold climate is typical at the southern tip of Argentina (bottom). In the distance is Upsala Glacier.*

■ *How do the land forms affect the climate in Central and South America?*

529

Looking at the People

The charts on pages 530 and 531, show that most of the people of Central and South America are *mestizos*. In fact, two-thirds of Central Americans are of mixed Spanish and Native American ancestry. Until the early 1800s, immigration from Europe to Central America was limited to citizens of Spain, except in present-day Belize. Many people in Belize are of African and European ancestry. In South America, only Spaniards and Portuguese were admitted to their

Central America

Country	Percent Urban	Largest Ethnic Group	Official Languages	Percent Adult Literacy
Belize	52	Creole	English	93
Costa Rica	54	European	Spanish	93
El Salvador	44	Mestizo	Spanish	73
Guatemala	35	American-Ladino	Spanish	60
Honduras	40	Mestizo	Spanish	73
Nicaragua	60	Mestizo	Spanish	74
Panama	53	Mestizo	Spanish	88

Source: Britannica Book of the Year, 1992

▼ *A wooden folk mask from Guatemala is worn by this boy during a dance festival.*

▼ *Hand-carved painted toys like this one from El Salvador capture children's imaginations.*

colonies until the end of the colonial period.

The native peoples of Central and South America influenced the populations that settled there later. Today Peru, Bolivia, Ecuador, and Guatemala—which once had dense native populations—now have many descendants of these native peoples. As the charts show, large European populations are found in Argentina and Costa Rica, which are areas that had fewer native peoples. Along the coast of Brazil, and in Belize, Honduras, and Nicaragua, people of African ancestry are a significant part of the population. ■

South America				
Country	Percent Urban	Largest Ethnic Group	Official Languages	Percent Adult Literacy
Argentina	86	European	Spanish	95
Bolivia	51	Mestizo/Quechua	Spanish, Aymara, Quechua	78
Brazil	75	European	Portuguese	81
Chile	81	Mestizo	Spanish	93
Colombia	67	Mestizo	Spanish	87
Ecuador	55	Mestizo/Quechua	Spanish	69
Guyana	28	East Indian	English	96
Paraguay	46	Mestizo	Spanish	90
Peru	69	Mestizo/Quechua	Spanish, Quechua	87
Suriname	65	Indo-Pakistani	Dutch	95
Uruguay	86	Mixed Spanish-Italian	Spanish	95
Venezuela	84	Mestizo	Spanish	91

Source: Britannica Book of the Year, 1992

▲ *Red-hot peppers or chilies, a very hot seasoning, come from a tropical plant. Chilies may first have been grown by native peoples in South America.*

■ *What countries in Central and South America have the highest literacy rates?*

➤ *Weddings like this one in Peru, family gatherings, and other local traditions are an important part of the culture of Central and South America.*

Colonialism to Independence

In Chapter 6 you read that many Native American cultures flourished in Central and South America before Europeans first arrived in the late 1400s. Here you will learn how the colonial era changed this region.

Native Peoples and Europeans

The years following the arrival of the conquistadors brought disease and disaster to Native Americans. Many were killed in warfare. Millions more died of diseases, such as measles and smallpox, brought by the Europeans and enslaved Africans. The Native Americans were forced to farm the land and work in the mines for the Spaniards. Many died because of the harsh working conditions.

Yet some Native Americans in Central and South America continue to live in groups that have great cultural influence. In Paraguay, for example, the original language, Guarani *(gwah ruh NEE),* is spoken as widely as Spanish. In Peru one of the official languages is Quechua *(KEHCH wuh),* the language of the ancient Inca.

Revolution and Independence

By the 1600s Spain and Portugal controlled nearly all of Central and South America. Then, in the late 1700s, the spirit of freedom swept through the Western Hemisphere.

British colonists in North America declared their independence in 1776. Haitians rebelled against the French monarchy in 1804.

The idea of independence led the peoples of South America to demand their freedom. The leader of the fight for independence from Spain was the wealthy Venezuelan general Simon Bolívar *(boh LEE vahr).* By 1822 his armies had won major victories. José de San Martín *(san mahr TEEN)* led the fight for independence in Argentina, Chile, and Peru. In 1821 Peru declared its independence. By 1826 most of South and Central America was free of Spanish rule.

A Mix of Peoples

In the colonial period and later, Native American peoples mingled with people from Europe and Africa. Most of the early European settlers spoke Spanish and Portuguese, which are Latin-based languages (see charts on pages 530 and 531). Therefore, Central and South America, along with Mexico and the Spanish- and French-speaking islands of the Caribbean, are often called Latin America.

Spanish colonial society in Central and South America was divided into distinct classes. These social groups were ranked according to race and wealth. At the top, holding much of the wealth and power, were

➤ *In the 1800s Simon Bolívar led the movement for liberation from colonialism. He hoped to unite all of South America but failed in his attempt.*

How Do We Know?

HISTORY *Quechua Indians hold on to their past by weaving and wearing traditional clothes. Women have brightly colored shawls; men wear ponchos. Nearly everyone wears patterned hats. Archaeologists have found looms and textiles of early Andean peoples. By studying these artifacts, we learn the origin of some of the patterns, symbols, and weaves that are used today.*

a few officials and merchants born in Spain.

Creoles made up the next class. They were born in the Americas to Spanish or Portuguese families. Although many *creoles* were wealthy and owned large pieces of land, they had little political power. Many leaders—such as Bolívar and San Martín—were *creoles*.

Much of the population was of mixed ancestry. These people were a blend of Spaniards, Portuguese, Africans, and Native Americans.

At the bottom of the social ladder were Native Americans and enslaved Africans. In the 1500s, Africans were brought in as slaves to replace the dying Native American population. By the 1850s, most African slaves, except those in Brazil, had been freed.

Independence changed Central and South American society. Being Native American, African, or of mixed ancestry affected a person's class and culture. It did not necessarily keep the person from rising to a higher class, however.

Ability and education as well as race and family background continue to be important today. Yet there are still more Europeans at the top and more Native Americans and mixed peoples at the bottom of the social ladder.

Urban and Rural Life

Today less than one-half of the people of Central America live in rural areas. The percentage of people who live in rural areas in South America is even less.

Most of the people live in cities, where rapid growth has led to pollution, crime, job and housing shortages, and poverty. On the edge of the cities, the poorest people often live in shacks. The cities are working to solve these problems.

Throughout Central and South America modern architecture blends with ancient native structures and old Spanish buildings. Many people enjoy a rich cultural life. Many of the oldest universities in the Western Hemisphere are located here. The oldest, founded in 1551, is in Lima, Peru. ■

▲ *Peruvian women display their produce at the marketplace. The styles of their colorful clothes and straw or felt hats represent different social status.*

■ *What were the main ethnic groups in colonial Central and South America?*

R E V I E W

1. **FOCUS** What are the physical and cultural features of Central and South America?

2. **GEOGRAPHY** What effect do the vertical zones in the Andes have on vegetation in the region?

3. **POLITICAL SYSTEMS** How did the colonists in North America affect the movement for independence led by Bolívar and San Martín in South America?

4. **SOCIAL SYSTEMS** How did the ethnic background of the people and their place of birth affect social classes in colonial South America?

5. **CULTURE** In what ways are the countries of Central and South America centers of culture today?

6. **ACTIVITY** The Andes have affected many areas of life in South America. Choose one aspect of the Andes to research in the library: for instance, animal life, plant life, products grown, people who live in the area. Then either write a short description or draw a detailed picture of this feature.

The Captive

Scott O'Dell

As the Spaniards began to explore and settle the Caribbean islands and Central and South America, they brought with them Christian missionaries. These representatives of the Church were intent on bringing Christian beliefs to the peoples living in the Western Hemisphere in the 16th century. Scott O'Dell tells a gripping tale of a young seminary student, Julian Escobar, who stands up to the leaders of an expedition when they enslave the island people and force them to mine gold. As you read the excerpt from The Captive, *try to answer this question: Why was Julian angry about the happenings on the island?*

In Lesson 1 you learned that the people of Central and South America today are descended from a blend of many cultures. This story tells of the early contact between Native Americans and the Spanish explorers and missionaries.

ruffian tough and rowdy

marauding raiding

encomendero Spanish agent

By noon Señor Guzmán had collected his band, six in all, as well as the lone Indian who knew where his tribe had hidden in the past and where they were apt to hide now, and Esteban, our translator. At the last minute, though he thoroughly mistrusted me, Guzmán decided that I should also go along.

Don Luis and I were standing at the head of the lagoon, watching members of the crew empty the storehouse. He had decided to move the gold onto the *Santa Margarita* in case the camp was overrun by the Caribs. There was danger in this, because the ruffian crew could take it into their heads to sail off with the treasure while we were ashore. But it seemed to be less than the danger from marauding Caribs. There was another and more important reason as well. The *encomendero* who now owned the island might appear and, finding the shed overflowing with gold, rightfully claim it.

Señor Guzmán came up with his band. "We need you," he said, laying a hand on my shoulder. "The savages will believe what you tell them."

"And what will that be?"

"Say that the Caribs have been vanquished, so it's safe to return to their village."

"The Caribs haven't been vanquished," I replied.

Guzmán went on as if I hadn't spoken.

"Say we regret that it was necessary to do away with the cacique."

"It was not necessary."

cacique (kah SEEK) Indian chief

534

"I gave him fair warning."

"Why should you warn him? It's his island and his people. Why should you order him to do anything? You are not a king."

Guzmán's mottled face grew pale.

Don Luis said, "We need the men and the women also. We can't mine without them."

Guzmán swallowed hard but went on, "Say that we forgive them for running away. That we'll share the gold they mine; share and share alike."

"You're a friend. They'll listen to you," Don Luis said.

"I have nothing to tell them."

"Say what Guzmán has told you to tell them."

"I would have trouble speaking the words."

"Then say that we need them." He was growing impatient. "Go. Every moment counts."

I did not move.

"You want the Indians back as much as I do."

I spoke slowly so that there would be no doubt about what I was saying. "The truth is, sir, I don't wish them back. I wish them to stay where they are. Wherever it is, they are far better off than here."

Guzmán held in his hand the musket he had used upon the Caribs. He glanced at Don Luis, as if asking his permission to use it at that moment upon me. He had large white teeth, and his drawn-back lips showed that they were clamped tight together.

musket gun

The young Indian who had given him information about the tribe's whereabouts was watching. He sat huddled on the ground. Around his neck from ear to ear I saw that he wore a thin red welt.

I listened in silence as Don Luis repeated his request.

"You are a member of this expedition," he said. "I, Don Luis de Arroyo, Duke of Cantavara y Llorente, am its leader. I have asked you to accompany us on a mission of great importance. You give me evasive answers."

evasive indirect

"What makes you think that our Indians will return to their village if only I speak to them? They have been worked close to death. Some, close to a dozen, have died. Many more have sickened from hard work. And now their chieftain has been cruelly slain. They trust neither you nor Guzmán. They shouldn't trust *me*."

"But they do trust you."

"That, sir, is the point. They trust me, and I will not betray them."

Further Reading

The Forty-Third War. Louise Moeri. A war story about a fictional Central American country where a 12-year-old boy fights for his survival.

L E S S O N 2

South America

Key Terms

- caudillo
- nationalize
- coup
- guerrilla

▼ *Venezuelan houses on stilts reminded Amerigo Vespucci of the houses along the canals in Venice, Italy.*

> **W**e discovered a very large population, who dwelt in houses having foundations that had been built in the water, like Venice, with much ingenuity.
>
> From the writings of Amerigo Vespucci

Amerigo Vespucci *(vehs POO chee)*, an Italian explorer, may have named the place in South America where he landed in 1499. Because it reminded him of Venice, Italy, it became known as Venezuela, or "little Venice."

Several years later, a mapmaker suggested that all the newly discovered lands in South America be called America after Amerigo Vespucci. Later, the name was extended to include North America.

This lesson examines two South American countries—Venezuela and Argentina. Both are wealthy nations, yet their people, history, and resources are quite different.

Venezuela: Land of Liquid Gold

In 1498, on his third trip to the Caribbean, Christopher Columbus landed in Venezuela in South America. It seemed to him like an earthly paradise.

A Blend of Cultures
Venezuela was one of the first South American lands to be colonized by Europeans. Yet it was ignored for many years because it lacked the natural resources of other colonies. The Spaniards who settled there raised cattle and grew cacao and tobacco. These products, however, did not interest Spain nearly as much as gold and silver.

The colonists forced the Native Americans to work the land for them. When many died from the harsh working conditions, Africans were brought in as slaves to work on the plantations. Today most Venezuelans are a blend of European, Native American, and African descent.

Striking Oil
In the early 1500s, Spanish explorers saw Native Americans using a gooey black substance in their

canoe-making. Yet no one realized until about 400 years later that this substance, oil, was valuable.

By the early 1900s, industries in the United States and Europe needed oil for fuel in factories. In 1913 European companies began to drill for oil in Lake Maracaibo. U.S. companies joined in and by the 1920s, the oil business in Venezuela was booming.

Suddenly Venezuela changed from a quiet farming country into a major world oil producer and exporter. Good wages drew thousands of farmers and other workers from rural areas to the oil fields and the cities. Venezuela now had to import food it once had grown.

When the drilling began, Venezuela was ruled by a military dictator, or **caudillo** *(kaw DEE yoh)*. The *caudillo* encouraged foreign oil companies to set up drilling rigs. Under the *caudillo,* most of the profits went to government officials. Few oil profits went to improving health or schools.

Although the country's leaders were rich, most Venezuelans remained poor. Discontent grew until a group overthrew the dictator and changed the government. In 1958 Venezuela held democratic elections. Rómulo Betancourt, a political reformer, became president.

Betancourt launched programs to help Venezuelans. In 1960 the government passed a law that gave land to small farmers. Betancourt also used oil profits to fund education and health programs.

Effect of Oil on Venezuelan Life

Foreigners from Europe and from other South American countries poured into Venezuela to work in the oil industry. These jobs provided a way for many people to become part of the middle class. Today the country has a prosperous, educated middle class.

To distribute the wealth, Venezuela sought to gain ownership of, or **nationalize,** its most valuable resource—oil. In 1976 the government nationalized the oil industry.

Oil is a risky business, however. Prices go up and down. When oil prices dropped in the 1980s, many people lost their jobs. As a result, Venezuelans recognized the need for other industries. The discovery of iron ore deposits and the growth of the steel and aluminum industries have helped the economy. ■

Across Time & Space

In 1960 it was Venezuela that took the lead in forming OPEC, the Organization of Petroleum Exporting Countries (see Chapter 8, page 196). OPEC meets to set world oil prices. Although most OPEC members are Arab states, other members include nations in Asia, Africa, and Latin America.

▼ *Oil pumps operate near Lake Maracaibo (left) in Venezuela. The oil wealth of the country is evident in downtown Caracas (below).*

■ *How did the oil industry change Venezuela?*

A Gaucho

7:20 A.M., December 21, 1893
Pampas near the Rio Colorado, Argentina

Poncho

Last night he slept on his wool poncho on the ground, his usual bed under summer stars. Proud and rugged, he scorns the comforts of town life.

Leather Belt

Wearing his best belt, he leaves his grazing cattle and heads for today's fiesta. Since the last fiesta, he has sewn more coins on his belt. He enjoys praise for the large silver buckle.

Pants
(Bombachas)

Miles of high pampas grass brush against these tough baggy pants as he herds his cattle. He knows the land well. From the taste of grass shoots, he can tell whether water is nearby.

Saddle

Thick cloth padding under the leather protects his horse. The gaucho rides all day, working in the saddle. He shows off his expert riding skills in fiesta contests.

Argentina: European Influences

Like Venezuela, Argentina was a disappointment to Spanish colonists because it lacked silver and gold. Even so, in 1860 *Argentina,* a Latin word for "silver," became the official name of the country. Today Argentina is one of South America's wealthiest nations, with resources such as iron ore, oil, and natural gas.

Buenos Aires *(BWAY nuhs AIR eez),* the capital of Argentina, is an important cultural center in South America. The city has a distinct European flavor, with spacious parks and tree-lined avenues. About 80 percent of Argentina's people live in or near a city.

Immigrants from Europe

The racial and ethnic character of Argentineans is different from that of other South American peoples. In the colonial period, there were a few Spaniards, many *mestizos,* and a small population of Africans and Native Americans. Then in the late 1800s and early 1900s, about six million Europeans moved to the farms, ranches, and factories of Argentina.

The government lured Europeans to Argentina to work as farmers and ranchers. The largest number of immigrants came from Italy and Spain. Swiss, German, and British settlers also arrived.

After the 1930s many people immigrated to Argentina from Eastern Europe. European Jews came to escape the Nazis. After World War II, more Europeans arrived. Today

nearly 85 percent of the people are of European descent. Only a small number are *mestizo,* Native American, or of African descent.

Cattle, Grain, and Industry

The wealth of Argentina comes mainly from the pampas, the fertile grasslands. This flat plain is much like the prairies of North America. Gauchos, or Argentinean cowhands, work the open range (see A Moment in Time, page 538). Grains are also grown here. During the late 1800s, Argentina exported meat and grain to Europe. Beef, corn, and wheat are still important exports. Look at your shoes or billfold. The leather may come from cattle raised on the pampas.

Industry also has thrived in Argentina. Refrigeration, invented in the 1870s, made meat processing and the shipment of meat safer. Mills were built to make flour. Factories turn out cars and machinery.

From Dictatorship to Democracy

By the mid-1800s, Argentina set up a constitutional government modeled after that of the United States. One of its first presidents,

▲ *The capital and main port in Argentina is Buenos Aires. Notice the ornate European-style buildings with balconies.*

▼ *A gaucho rides the range, herding beef cattle on the Argentine pampas. Most of the country's cattle and wheat come from this region.*

▼ Mothers and grand-mothers of the "disap-peared ones" protest. Carrying photographs, they demand to know what has happened to their children.

■ How does the population of Argentina differ from that of most other South American countries?

Domingo Sarmiento, created the public education system. For the first time, Argentina opened its schools to women. As the country thrived, foreign investors poured money into trade and business.

A period of conflict followed, however. Argentina faced economic and political crises. In 1930 a group of army officers staged a **coup** *(koo),* or takeover of the government. After this coup, a series of undemo-cratic governments held power.

One military officer became a leader who would change Argentina's history. In 1946 Juan Domingo Perón *(puh ROHN),* an army officer, was elected president. Perón's policy, called *peronismo,* helped poor city workers. He gave the workers higher pay and pro-vided other benefits.

The workers backed Perón and adored his gifted wife, Eva Duarte de Perón, a former actress, better known as Evita *(ay VEE tuh).* She helped women gain the right to vote in 1947. She also set up a foundation to aid the poor.

Perón was less popular after Evita died in 1952. As opposition grew, he became ruthless. He banned political parties and shut down newspapers that disagreed with him. Then in 1955 he was driven from power. Although Perón returned to power in 1973, he died soon after.

A time of violence and terror followed. In 1976 new military lead-ers took over. **Guerrillas** *(guh RIHL uhz),* or small groups of fighters, organized against the government. However, the government forces crushed the guerrillas and arrested, tortured, or killed thousands. Some people have never been found; they have simply "disappeared."

In 1982 Argentina suffered a humiliating defeat by Britain in the Falklands War. The military gov-ernment resigned, and in 1983 a new president was elected. The democratic leaders who followed have faced problems of debt and high prices. Argentina's recovery depends on the wise use of its natu-ral resources and its well-educated population. ■

R E V I E W

1. **FOCUS** How do the ethnic groups and the sources of economic wealth of Venezuela and Argentina differ?

2. **ECONOMICS** Why did Venezuela face economic prob-lems in the 1980s?

3. **GEOGRAPHY** Describe the geographic feature in Ar-gentina that is similar to one in the United States. In what other ways are the two countries similar?

4. **POLITICAL SYSTEMS** What kind of rulers did Argentina

have between the 1930s and the early 1980s?

5. **CRITICAL THINKING** Why do you think Argentina has a large European population but Venezuela does not?

6. **ACTIVITY** Imagine you are a European farmer who migrated to Argentina around 1900. Write a letter home telling your family about your new country and your way of life. Persuade them to join you in South America.

540

Presenting Information

Here's Why

Oral reports are one way to share information with others. Suppose you were assigned to give an oral report about the role of Eva Duarte de Perón in gaining women's rights and aiding the poor. How would you do it?

Here's How

In Chapter 15, you read about preparing a written report. Use those steps and the steps below to prepare an oral presentation on the social programs of Eva Perón.

1. **Identify your audience.** How much does your audience already know about Eva Perón and Argentina? How much background information do they need?
2. **Identify the time limit for your presentation.** Five or ten minutes may seem like a short period of time, but if you're not prepared, five minutes in front of the class can seem like forever.
   Try reading your information aloud. How long does it take to get a sense of how much information you have? Cut back or add information so that you're close to your time limit.
3. **Create note cards to help you as you speak.** You won't be reading directly from the note cards. They will serve as guides. Try not to write long sentences on your note cards. Instead, write key words and phrases. Below are some student note cards about Eva Perón.
4. **Sharpen your memory.** The best speakers look directly at their audiences. Try to memorize as much of your information as possible, so you won't have to look at your notes as often. Eye contact holds the listeners' attention.
5. **Practice your report.** Speaking in front of people may make you nervous. Practice is the best way to help you get past your fear. At first practice your report alone. Remember these public speaking hints:
   - Keep eye contact with your audience.
   - Stand up straight.
   - Speak loudly and clearly.
   - Avoid saying "um" and "you know."

Later, practice in front of a friend. Ask your friend to evaluate your presentation. The more you practice your report, the easier it will be to give it in class.

Try It

Imagine you have been assigned to give an oral report on the political situation in a country in Central America, such as Honduras. Your audience will be your classmates. Think about your audience. What do they already know about politics in Central America? What do they know about Honduras?

Apply It

Use the steps above to prepare an oral report about a special hobby or interest you may have. You might want to give a report about a political leader whom you admire.

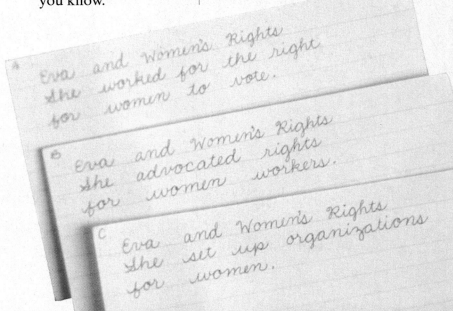

a. Eva and Women's Rights
She worked for the right for women to vote.

b. Eva and Women's Rights
She advocated rights for women workers.

c. Eva and Women's Rights
She set up organizations for women.

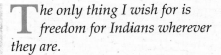

L E S S O N   3

Central America

THINKING FOCUS

What common challenges do many countries of Central America face?

Key Terms

- migrant worker
- negotiate

▼ *This 11-year-old girl is part of a guerrilla unit in El Salvador.*

> The only thing I wish for is freedom for Indians wherever they are.
>
> Rigoberta Menchú, 1992 Nobel Peace Prize winner

Rigoberta Menchú of Guatemala expressed this hope for her people after she was awarded the Nobel Peace Prize in 1992. It was given in honor of her work for the rights of Native Americans.

Menchú is a Mayan Indian of the Quiché *(kee CHAY)* group. Her father organized groups to protest the unfair treatment of Indian farm laborers. As a result, her parents and brother were tortured and killed by government forces in Guatemala.

Death squads killed thousands of others who rebelled against the government. Fearing for her safety, in 1981 Menchú fled to Mexico.

Countries in Turmoil

The seven countries of Central America—Guatemala, Belize, Honduras, El Salvador, Nicaragua, Costa Rica, and Panama—lie in the narrow land bridge connecting North and South America (see Atlas, page 686). Although they have much in common, each nation has its own history and faces its own problems.

In recent years some of these problems have exploded into violence. Civil wars and revolutions have torn apart El Salvador and Nicaragua. Dictators in Guatemala and Panama have ruled by terror. Many young people have lived with war all their lives. Why is this region so troubled?

Influence of History

Most of Central America—like South America—was part of Spain's empire. By the early 1800s, most countries had gained independence. Yet centuries of colonial rule had set the stage for conflict.

As in South America, a small group of people in Central America controlled most of the land and wealth. The rest of the people lived in poverty. The class system remained rigidly in place. Today a deep division between rich and poor still exists in most of these Central American nations.

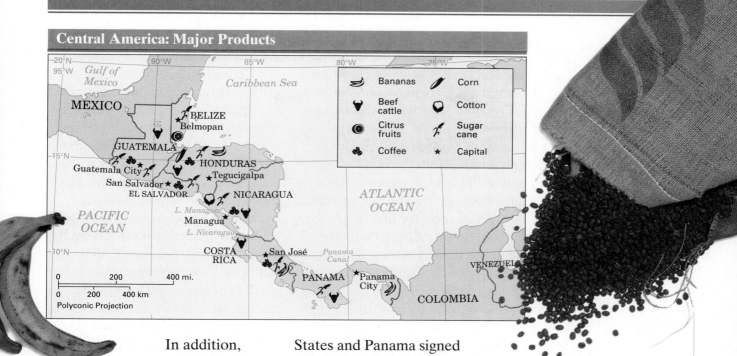

Central America: Major Products

Bananas
Beef cattle
Citrus fruits
Coffee
Corn
Cotton
Sugar cane
Capital

MEXICO

BELIZE
Belmopan

GUATEMALA
Guatemala City
San Salvador
EL SALVADOR

HONDURAS
Tegucigalpa

NICARAGUA

L. Managua
Managua
L. Nicaragua

COSTA RICA
San José

PANAMA
Panama City

Gulf of Mexico
Caribbean Sea
ATLANTIC OCEAN
PACIFIC OCEAN

Panama Canal

VENEZUELA
COLOMBIA

0   200   400 mi.
0   200   400 km
Polyconic Projection

In addition, these countries have often depended on one crop. If prices for that one crop went down, the country's economy was in trouble.

The United States has long had a close connection with Central America. By the 1930s U.S. companies owned huge tracts of land there, mostly banana plantations. Two large U.S. fruit companies had the power to influence local laws.

To protect U.S. business interests, the government has sent troops to Central America many times. As recently as 1989, U.S. troops landed in Panama. They removed Manuel Noriega, the corrupt military ruler, from power. However, sending in the army has often caused bad feelings toward the United States.

The Panama Canal is another reason for U.S. involvement in this region. Built by the United States, the canal is a vital link for ships between the Atlantic and Pacific oceans. Since 1903 the Canal Zone, the land on either side of the canal, has been controlled by the United States. Then in 1977 the United States and Panama signed treaties agreeing to turn over control of the canal to Panama on December 31, 1999.

A Land-Based Economy

Crops like coffee, cocoa, and bananas, along with sugar and cotton, grow well in Central America. Coffee became a valuable export as early as the 1830s. Many workers are needed to pick plantation crops. Often they are **migrant workers,** workers who move from place to place as crops ripen.

Tropical crops have become important exports for Central America because these crops cannot be grown in cool climates. The profits from these crop sales are used to buy manufactured goods.

Many Central Americans have moved to the cities. However, about half the people of the region make their living in some way from the land. Some work in factories making wood products or processing food.

Conflicts and Civil Wars

In the past 20 years, much of Central America has been caught

▲ *Exporting agricultural products is essential to the economies of Central American countries. Bananas and coffee beans are some of the most valuable exports in Central America. Which countries produce coffee and bananas?*

543

up in violence. Most Central American nations do not have a tradition of democracy. For years they have been ruled by dictators and dishonest officials. Political conflicts have often been settled by violence. Demands for land reform and for better conditions for middle-class and working-class people often have been ignored or met by force.

El Salvador, for instance, had been ruled by military dictators since the 1930s. By the 1970s protests by peasants and labor unions had led to limited land reforms. Landowners and army officers violently opposed these reforms.

Civil war followed in El Salvador. At least 70,000 Salvadorans died in the war. Finally, in 1992, after 12 years of civil war, the government and the opposition groups signed a peace agreement and agreed to disarm.

Central America is a small region, and turmoil in one country can spill over into nearby nations. Wars in El Salvador and Nicaragua were a threat to peace in neighboring Honduras and Costa Rica. Thousands of refugees escaped to more peaceful regions, such as Mexico, the United States, Canada, and other Central American countries. About 20 percent of all Salvadorans left their country.

By the early 1990s, there was an uneasy calm in Central America. In Guatemala, government and guerrilla groups reached a truce and began to **negotiate,** or discuss the issues. Civil war was over in El Salvador. In Nicaragua, voters democratically elected a new leader. ■

■ *How has geography affected the economies of Central American countries?*

▼ *Many army barracks were converted into schools after Costa Rica replaced the standing army with a civil guard.*

Costa Rica

Unlike governments in other Central American nations, Costa Rica's government is politically stable and democratically elected. Wealth and land have been more evenly divided than elsewhere in the region. As a result, the country has a large middle class. Costa Rica has stayed out of its neighbors' wars. In fact, it has not had an army since 1949. A civil guard keeps order.

In Central America, Costa Rica is the most Spanish in character. The people of Spanish descent have kept much of their culture.

Democratic Tradition

The roots of democracy in Costa Rica were formed during the colonial period. The land held no gold or silver. No large Native American population existed. As a result, the colonists owned small family farms. Early in the 1800s, Costa Ricans began to grow coffee beans. It was by exporting coffee that the country first became prosperous.

Costa Rica held its first free democratic elections more than 100 years ago. Except for two short periods, the nation has maintained democracy since then.

Oscar Arias Sánchez

Oscar Arias Sánchez *(AH ryahs SAHN chez)* became president in 1986. He not only kept his country out of war, but he also negotiated a peace in the region.

In 1987 Arias persuaded the leaders of Guatemala, El Salvador, Honduras, and Nicaragua to sign a peace plan. Soon after, he was awarded the Nobel Peace Prize.

Looking Forward

The people of Costa Rica enjoy a fairly high standard of living. With a stable economy, the government has established far-reaching educational and social programs.

However, the country still depends on imports, such as wheat, corn, beans, and oil. It has had to borrow money to pay for these goods. In addition, Costa Rica's

wealth depends largely on world coffee prices.

Costa Rica's population is growing rapidly. Retired people from North America have moved there because of the climate and the political stability. The civil wars of the 1980s have led many refugees from other Central American countries—especially from El Salvador and Nicaragua—to settle there. These newcomers strain the country's economy and resources.

When Arias received the peace prize, he said, "It has been given to a magnificent country and to the values we share: freedom, peace, and democracy." ■

◄ *Oscar Arias Sánchez of Costa Rica is greeted warmly by his enthusiastic supporters.*

▼ *The Pan American Games—like this one between Costa Rica and Brazil—build good relations among the nations of Central, South, and North America.*

■ *What features make Costa Rica different from other Central American countries?*

R E V I E W

1. **FOCUS** What common challenges do many countries of Central America face?

2. **ECONOMICS** Why has depending on one crop for export caused problems for Central American countries?

3. **HISTORY** Why has the United States been involved in the politics and economies of many Central American countries?

4. **SOCIAL SYSTEMS** How is the social structure in most Central American countries different from that in Costa Rica?

5. **CRITICAL THINKING** Why do you think Costa Rica developed a tradition of democracy while other Central American countries did not?

6. **ACTIVITY** You have read about two people who won the Nobel Peace Prize. Imagine you are a member of the committee that awards this prize. Write two or three paragraphs describing the things you would look for in choosing a person for the Nobel Peace Prize. If you think of any specific people, name them.

Chapter Review

Reviewing Key Terms

basin (p. 529)
caudillo (p. 537)
coup (p. 540)
guerrilla (p. 540)
migrant worker (p. 543)

nationalize (p. 537)
negotiate (p. 544)
pampas (p. 528)
vertical zone (p. 529)

A. Use each of the following key terms in a sentence that shows clearly what the word means.
1. caudillo
2. coup
3. nationalize
4. negotiate

B. Answer the following questions regarding selected key terms.
1. Which three key terms are related to the geography of Central and South America? Write a sentence that uses each term correctly and shows that you understand its meaning.
2. Which two terms refer to people? For each term, write a sentence that describes the role of those people in events that have occurred in present-day Central and South America.
3. Compound terms are discussed on page 264. Which key terms here are compound terms?

Exploring Concepts

A. On a separate sheet of paper, copy and complete the chart below to compare three countries of Latin America.

Country	Population Makeup	Important Products	Government
Argentina		beef, corn	
Costa Rica			
Venezuela		oil	

B. Answer each question with information from the chapter.
1. What are the major geographic features of Central and South America?
2. What river forms a huge basin in South America?
3. Why is the climate in Central and South America generally tropical? What factors influence the continent's climate?
4. Why are the rain forests so important?
5. What European colonial powers controlled Central and South America in the 1800s?
6. What three ethnic groups are blended in almost all Latin American populations?
7. What kind of changes did the oil industry bring to Venezuela?
8. What different reasons brought immigrants to Venezuela and to Argentina in the 20th century?
9. How has Argentina's geography influenced its history and economy?
10. What makes Costa Rica unusual among Central American countries? Explain differences fully.

Reviewing Skills

1. Imagine that you are planning an oral report on someone who has been important in the history of Latin America, such as Simon Bolívar, Domingo Sarmiento, or Eva Perón. First, list five questions you want to answer in your report. Then list the places where you might look for this information.

2. Put the following steps for preparing an oral report in the right order:
   - Create note cards as guides.
   - Identify your audience.
   - Practice giving your report.
   - Memorize as much as you can.
   - Test your time limit by reading your information aloud.

3. Look at the Atlas map on pages 680–681. Different colors show elevation, or height above sea level. The map key shows the elevation range represented by each color on the map. Looking at South America, answer these questions: (a) At about what elevation are the highest parts of the two "highlands" regions? (b) Where are the highest parts of the Andes? (See also the political map on pages 678–679.) (c) What is the elevation of the pampas region?

4. Suppose you want to show the amount of oil exported by Venezuela between 1920 and 1990. What would be the best way to show this information?

Using Critical Thinking

1. From your reading, which country in Central or South America do you think is most like the United States? What qualities do you think make the two countries alike? How are they different?

2. How has the history of Central and South America led to deep divisions between the rich and the poor in this region? Do you think it is better for a society when most people are in the middle class rather than being very rich or very poor? Or do you think that very wealthy people would be able to look after the rest of the population? Explain your answer.

3. Depending on one crop or product—such as coffee or oil—has caused economic problems for some Central and South American countries. What would you predict these countries will do? Give evidence from the text to back up your prediction.

Preparing for Citizenship

1. **ARTS ACTIVITY** Choose any country in Central or South America and make a poster for it. Either draw your own pictures or use pictures cut from magazines to create a collage. The poster can show people, landscapes, works of art, or anything else you believe represents the country you have chosen.

2. **INTERVIEWING** If possible, talk to someone who has come to the United States from a country in Central or South America. What does this person see as the country's future?

3. **COLLECTING INFORMATION** Find and bring to class a tape cassette of music from the Andes or another part of Central or South America. Look in an encyclopedia or in library books for information about the flutes, pipes, drums, and other musical instruments that are used on the tape or played elsewhere in the region. Give a report to the class about your findings.

4. **COLLABORATIVE LEARNING** Working with your classmates, plan a meal for your class that includes foods typical of Central and South America. Your local supermarket, for example, is likely to have bananas, mangoes, papayas, and other tropical fruits and fruit juices. If anyone in your class has friends or relatives from the region, ask them for suggestions about typical and easy-to-make dishes.

Chapter 24
Brazil

Brazil is a vast and modern industrial nation with busy cities, high technology, and many natural resources. Like other South American countries, however, Brazil has had to face the challenges of poverty, crime, and political corruption. As the 20th century draws to a close, the Brazilian people are striving to fulfill their country's motto: "Order and Progress."

When the Portuguese sailors landed in Brazil in 1500, they may have met the ancestors of this Indian boy. Many Indian groups, such as the Tupí, retreated to the Amazon rain forest to escape slavery.

When the Indians could not provide enough labor, Africans were brought in to work on the big sugar cane and coffee plantations, like the one shown above.

1375	1500	1625

1492

1500 Pedro Alvares Cabral lands on the Brazilian coast and claims the region for Portugal.

Famous for its beautiful beaches and large harbor, Rio de Janeiro, settled in 1555, is the cultural capital of Brazil.

This folk art sculpture shows migrant workers from the northeast region of Brazil.

1750

1875

2000

1822 Brazil becomes independent.

1888 Slavery is abolished in Brazil.

1992 Earth Summit on world environmental problems held in Rio de Janeiro.

Today

L E S S O N   1

The History of Brazil

THINKING FOCUS

How did Brazil gain its independence?

Key Terms

- Line of Demarcation
- convert

➤ *Prince Henry the Navigator was the driving force behind Portuguese explorations. This portrait of the prince appears in a book titled* The Chronicle of the Discovery and Conquest of Guinea, *written in the mid-1400s.*

In the 1400s Portuguese explorers sailed the Atlantic Ocean on small ships called *caravels.* Their sails were marked with a red-bordered cross, a symbol of the Catholic church. They were searching for new lands and new trade routes.

When they visited a land unknown to them, the Portuguese claimed it for their king. Stone markers, called *padrões (pa DROENS),* were placed on the ground for everyone to see. The Portuguese believed that this land now belonged to them.

Prince Henry the Navigator (1394–1460), the son of the king of Portugal, supported the search for new lands. He started a school for sailors in 1419. Prince Henry's school trained sailors to find a sea route to Asia. He also wanted Portugal to profit from the gold found in West Africa. Sailors at his school learned to read maps and use the compass. They made voyages farther and farther south along the African coast.

Spain was also interested in trade. Over the years competition between Portugal and Spain grew fiercer. Soon the Pope had to step in to keep peace between these two Catholic powers.

In 1492 and 1493, Pope Alexander VI drew a **Line of Demarcation** that split the non-Christian world in two. Spain could have the lands on the west side of the line. Portugal could have the lands on the east side of the line. As a result, most of Brazil was placed in Portugal's half of the world.

Portuguese Exploration and Settlement

Vasco da Gama made the long ocean trip from Portugal around Africa to India and back, from 1497 to 1499. Thus, nearly 40 years after Prince Henry's death, Portugal had a sea route to Asia. The Portuguese explorer Admiral Pedro Álvares Cabral began another trip to India in the spring of 1500. On the way south, he sailed off course to the west. He reached a land the Portuguese had not visited before and named it *Terra da Vera Cruz*—the Land of the True Cross.

Later explorers found trees there that could be used to make a red dye. The Portuguese called the trees brazilwood. Soon people began to call the land *Terra do Brasil (TEHR rah du brah ZEEL)*, the Land of the Brazilwood. This was later shortened to Brazil.

Making Contact

The Tupí Indians had lived and worked in Brazil for thousands of years before Cabral. The Indians' first meeting with the Portuguese

Brazil: Geographic Regions

This map shows Brazil's five different regions. Which regions might the Brazilians have settled first? Why?

was described in a letter to King Manuel in Portugal.

They carried in their hands bows with their arrows. All came boldly towards the boat, and Nicolau Coelho made a sign to them that they should lay down their bows, and they laid them down. . . . He gave them only a red cap and a cap of linen, which he was wearing on his head, and a black hat. And one of them gave him a hat of long bird feathers with a little tuft of red and grey feathers like those of a parrot.

From the letter of Pero Vaz de Caminha to King Manuel, written at Porto Seguro, Brazil, May 1, 1500

These good feelings didn't last long. The Portuguese soon began to enslave the Indians as a source of cheap labor for their plantations.

This detail from an early Portuguese map shows the brazilwood trees that gave the country its name. What product came from the brazilwood trees?

551

Brazil

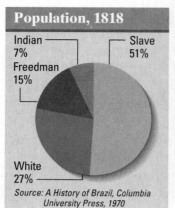

Population, 1818

- Indian 7%
- Freedman 15%
- White 27%
- Slave 51%

Source: A History of Brazil, Columbia University Press, 1970

Slavery and Settlement

About two to five million Indians lived in Brazil in 1500. In less than a century, two-thirds of the Indians were dead. Hundreds of thousands died working for the Portuguese as slaves.

The first permanent Portuguese colony was founded in 1532 at São Vicente, near the present-day city of Santos. Other Portuguese colonists settled what are now the cities of Salvador, São Paulo *(sown POW lu)*, and Rio de Janeiro *(REE u dee zhuh NAI ru)*.

Along with the first Portuguese settlers came Jesuits. They tried to make the Indians **convert,** or change, from their own religions to Catholicism.

While the number of Indians in Brazil grew smaller and smaller, Portuguese landowners there still wanted people to work on their large plantations. The Portuguese began to use slaves from Africa. They brought about three and one-half million Africans to Brazil during more than three centuries of slave trading. ■

Brazilian Independence

The American Revolution gave Brazilians the idea of rebelling against their Portuguese rulers. In 1789 the rebels were led by a cavalry officer and part-time dentist called Tiradentes *(tee ruh DEHN tees)*, the Tooth Puller. The rebels failed, and Tiradentes was put to death.

From Colony to Country

In the early 1800s, the French ruler Napoleon Bonaparte had conquered much of Europe. In 1807 he turned his armies toward Portugal. To escape Napoleon, the Portuguese royal family fled to Brazil. There Prince Dom João *(dahm zhwown)* took over the government. He made changes that made Brazil more independent. Brazil became the center of the Portuguese Empire.

In 1821 things changed. To stop unrest in Portugal, Dom João, now king, had to return there to rule. João's son, Dom Pedro, stayed to govern Brazil. In Portugal, parliament tried to undo most of

João's reforms. The Brazilians became angry with Portugal.

Dom Pedro took the side of the Brazilians. When an order came for him to return to Portugal, he refused to go. On September 7, 1822, with the words "Independence or death!" Dom Pedro declared Brazilian independence. Unlike many other South American countries, Brazil had become free with little bloodshed.

Pedro I ruled Brazil for only a short time, but his son, Pedro II, ruled for 49 years. Pedro II's long reign improved farming, trade, and business. He also worked to keep political unity. However, slavery was still legal.

The government had been slowly working to end slavery. In 1850 the slave trade became illegal. In 1871 a law was passed that freed all children born to slaves. However, Pedro II needed the help of the big plantation owners to stay in power. The plantation owners used slaves to keep their plantations running.

In 1888, while Pedro II was on vacation in Europe, his daughter Princess Isabel was left in charge. She signed the Golden Law. This law freed all the slaves in Brazil. The landowners were angry because they were not paid for the loss of their slaves. They stopped supporting Pedro II, and the next year he was overthrown.

Movement Toward Democracy

When Pedro II's rule ended, Brazil became a republic. It has had several constitutions, some modeled on the Constitution of the United States. However, dictators have ruled Brazil until recently.

This pattern seemed to change with the election of Fernando Collor de Mello (*COH lawr dee MEHL lu*) as president in 1990. He was popular with the people of his country when first elected. Improving trade with other countries and helping Brazilian businesses to grow were just two of his important achievements. He also stopped Brazil's nuclear bomb program, helped the Indians, and started to save the rain forest.

In the fall of 1992, however, the government discovered that the president had broken the law. He was legally removed from office. This peaceful change in government gave Brazilians hope that they finally had a real democracy. ■

▼ *Some farmers, like this woman, are very wealthy and live in fine homes on their plantations.*

■ *Why do many Brazilians have hope for a democratic government?*

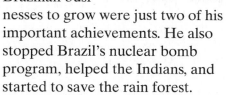

| R E V I E W |

1. **FOCUS** How did Brazil gain its independence?
2. **CULTURE** Why did Prince Henry the Navigator start his school for sailors?
3. **HISTORY** What effect did the arrival of the Portuguese have on the Native American population of Brazil?
4. **CRITICAL THINKING** Pedro II was afraid to abolish slavery because he needed the support of big landowners to stay in power. After his daughter Princess Isabel abolished slavery in 1888, the empire was overthrown. Do you think that Isabel was right or wrong to abolish slavery? Explain your answer.
5. **WRITING ACTIVITY** Imagine you are Princess Isabel and you have just signed the Golden Law. Write a letter to your father, Pedro II, explaining why you signed the law in spite of the anger of the landowners.

Recognizing Assumptions

Here's Why

Suppose you are in charge of ordering food for a special after-school event. You choose to serve pizza. Your decision has been made based on an assumption: most students like to eat pizza.

An assumption is an idea that is accepted as fact without proof or demonstration. Most assumptions can be proved either true or false, depending on the facts.

Correct assumptions can help you make sound decisions quickly when you aren't able to gather all the facts. Incorrect assumptions, on the other hand, can cause you to make poor and even harmful decisions.

Here's How

Suppose you want to identify some of the assumptions made by the Portuguese when they first came to Brazil. You can use the following steps to help you identify and evaluate their assumptions.

1. **Put the assumption into words.** In Lesson 1 you read about the Portuguese treatment of the Brazilian Indians. What assumptions do you think the Portuguese settlers made about the Indians? You might say the Portuguese assumed that the Indians had no rights to the land.

2. **Identify the basis of the assumption.** Think about why people hold certain assumptions. Many assumptions are based on experience. Others are an unquestioned part of a culture or set of beliefs. Portuguese assumptions were based on their cultural beliefs.

3. **Check assumptions for accuracy.** Always try to test assumptions against accurate information. In Lesson 3 you will read many facts about the Brazilian Indians. You will read about the many ways in which they helped the Portuguese adapt to life in a tropical climate. These facts show that the Indians had a dynamic culture and held strong beliefs about the land.

Try It

Many people are concerned about resources. What assumption might you have made about the people who are trying to protect the rain forests of Brazil? Follow the three steps listed in Here's How to identify and test your assumption.

Apply It

Write a sentence or two identifying the assumptions that might have led to each situation listed below. Explain the basis of each assumption.
1. The radio announcer says it is going to rain tonight. You decide to leave your windows open anyway.
2. You are going camping at a campground you've never been to before. It's the middle of summer. You decide to bring insect repellent.

LESSON 2

The Geography and Economy of Brazil

A group of men struggle through a dense forest. Parrots cry in the branches overhead. An Indian slave stops to listen. African slaves carry heavy loads of supplies.

The men leading this group are called *bandeirantes (bahn dee RAHN tehs)*. *Bandeirantes* means "flag bearers" in Portuguese. They are named after soldiers who carried banners, or flags, into battle.

Many of these men were once soldiers in São Paulo. They have tired of barracks life and poor pay. They hope to get rich quickly in the areas of Brazil that Europeans have not yet explored. They are often cruel, but their raw courage is undeniable. They are making trails that other, more respectable settlers will follow later:

> Sometimes they fell upon the land and sometimes upon man. Sometimes they went in search of gold and sometimes in search of slaves. But one thing they did do was to discover huge tracts of land—land which they did not cultivate and which, it might be, they left more of a desert than it was before. . . .
>
> Euclides da Cunha,
> *Rebellion in the Backlands*

THINKING FOCUS

Why does Brazil have serious economic problems in spite of its many exports and natural resources?

Key Terms

- boom-and-bust
- capital
- inflation

◄ *Brazil is a huge country with a variety of terrains. What are some physical features of Brazil visible in this picture?*

555

Brazil

The Geography of Brazil

Brazil is the largest country in South America. It is the world's fifth largest country, stretching across nearly half of South America. Brazil can be divided into five regions: the northeast, the south, the southeast, the north, and the central west. (See the map on page 551.)

The Northeast

The population of the northeast is largely African Brazilian. The 1,800-mile São Francisco River is the major source of water for the region. Today areas of dry land called *sertão (SEHR town)* cover the region. Most of the *sertão* is flat and dry, with few trees, and it is hard to make a living here. Some people do raise cattle. Others work on the cocoa and sugar cane plantations along the Atlantic coast. These large farms created Brazil's first big cash crop—sugar.

Times of drought and flooding have made this region one of the poorest in the country. For example, in 1984 a drought that had lasted for more than five years ended with heavy floods. These natural disasters forced thousands of people in the northeast to move to Brazil's crowded cities.

Although poor, northeastern Brazil is known for its history and culture. Cities like Recife *(reh SEE fe)* and Olinda *(oh LEEN dah)* reflect Brazil's rich past. These cities are filled with art treasures and historic churches.

The South and Southeast

The south is the smallest of Brazil's five regions. It is also the only region that has four seasons. Many people from Europe moved to this region because of its mild climate. Today southern Brazil

➤ There is a large and thriving community of Japanese in Brazil. They came to Brazil in search of a better life. How does education help people advance economically?

▼ São Paulo is one of Brazil's fastest growing cities. It is also the largest. What makes São Paulo a good industrial city? See the Minipedia, pages 660–673, for the worldwide ranking of Brazil's cities.

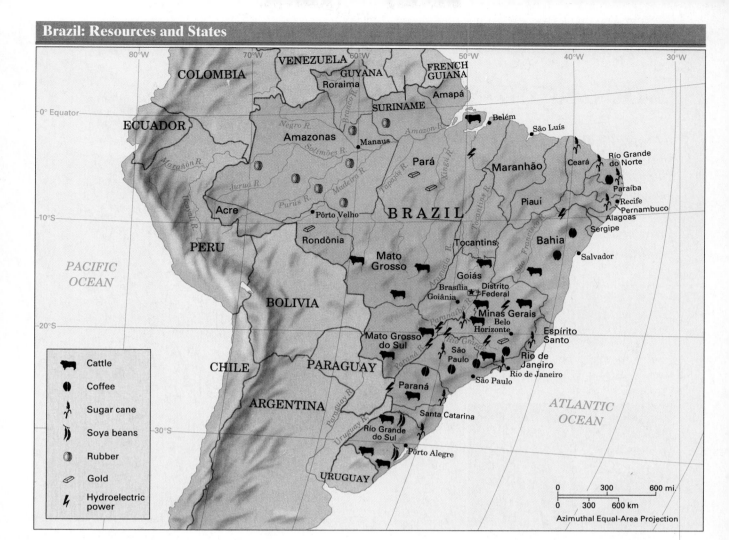

shows traces of Germany, France, Poland, Italy, and Switzerland in its buildings, food, and music.

The major landforms in the south are a low mountain range covered with evergreen forests and a flat grassland called the pampas. Most of Brazil's cattle are raised on the pampas. The south is also the site of the world's largest hydro-electric plant.

The southern regions are the engines that drive Brazil's economy. São Paulo, Rio de Janeiro, and Belo Horizonte (*BAY loh hawr ah ZAHT ee)* are here. They are the country's three largest cities. Most of Brazil's businesses are based here. Much of the world's coffee grows in the rich, red soil of São Paulo state. The southeast is rich

in minerals and gems. Forty-four percent of Brazil's population now lives in this region. The state of São Paulo has the largest Japanese population outside Japan.

The North and Central West

Brazilians view their northern and western regions as the land of the future. The north includes Amazonia, a land of rain forests and rivers. The Amazon is the largest river in Brazil and, indeed, the largest on the earth. Along with the rain forest the river is a very important natural resource. It holds about one-fifth of the earth's fresh water. (See A Closer Look at the Amazon River on page 558.)

The central west region on the Central Plateau is covered with

As this map shows, Brazil is a nation rich in resources. What are the three most common resources in Brazil? Where are they found?

The Amazon River

The Amazon begins as a stream high in the Andes. It flows across Brazil, transporting more water than any other river on the earth. Every hour it empties more than 170 billion gallons of water into the Atlantic Ocean. The river winds through rain forests, where the Indians grow many crops, including yams, corn, manioc, and medicinal herbs. Their ancient farming methods renew, rather than destroy, the forests.

Wildlife by the millions thrives in the river and forests—insects, birds, monkeys, frogs, eels, water snakes, fish, and more.

On dugout canoes, hollowed out of tree trunks, the Indians travel the river and its tributaries.

558

brush and small trees. It has rich, red soil that is good for farming. To encourage Brazilians to move to this region, the government began building a new city, called Brasília *(Brah ZIL yah)*, there in the 1950s. In 1960 it became the capital of Brazil.

In the 1950s the government also built the Belém *(beh LEHM)* Brasília Highway to connect the northeast to Brasília. The Trans-Amazonian Highway was built in the 1970s to cross the Amazon rain forest at Brazil's widest point.

The Panatal is a low swampland off the Central Plateau. Between October and April, heavy rains flood this area. More than 350 kinds of fish and exotic plants can be found in this isolated region. ■

■ *Which of Brazil's five regions drives the economy? What features give it this power?*

The Economy of Brazil

Thousands of settlers poured into Brazil's interior in search of riches, after gold was discovered there in 1722. A century later the gold was gone. The gold boom had gone bust.

A Boom-and-Bust Economy

The gold rush is only one example of the **boom-and-bust** pattern of the Brazilian economy. In a boom-and-bust cycle, a new product first brings high profits. People and businesses rush to invest in the new product. Often, they borrow money to do so. When the product stops bringing in big profits, many people lose all their money and the economy is weakened.

In the 1500s and 1600s, there was a sugar boom in Brazil. Brazil was the number one exporter of sugar in the world. Then Caribbean plantations began to produce sugar more cheaply than Brazilian plantations. The Brazilian sugar market failed, or crashed.

In the late 1800s, there was a sudden boom in Brazilian rubber. Then rubber trees were planted in British colonies in Asia. Rubber from countries such as Malaysia quickly won the largest share of the world market. By 1913 the price of rubber was less than one-fourth of what it had been in 1910. Many Brazilian rubber merchants went bankrupt. Wealthy communities in the Amazon became ghost towns.

Coffee was also an important crop and major export in the 19th century. The families who controlled Brazil's coffee crop also controlled its land and politics. Thus, changes in world coffee prices affected not only Brazil's economy but also its politics.

Industrial Development

From the 1930s on, Brazil's leaders worked to end the ups and downs of a boom-and-bust economy. Although sugar, rubber, coffee, and gold mining had promised a better future, the dreams had not come true.

◀ *Rubber tappers like this worker took part in the great rubber boom of the late 19th century.*

559

Brazil

▶ *Because Brazil has little oil and no coal, the government has built dams, which use the power of water.*

The economy needed to be made stronger. Brazil's leaders decided to industrialize. If the people of Brazil built their own businesses and factories, they could create their own products and services. They could also export finished goods instead of raw materials.

São Paulo seemed like the perfect place to start building. It was the center of the coffee industry and had the capital needed for

UNDERSTANDING INFLATION

*I*nflation occurs when the prices of many goods and services in a country or a region rise. Why should we worry about rising prices? Let's look at a personal example.

What Is Inflation?

Suppose you have just earned $2 for selling a birdhouse you made to your neighbor. What can you do with your money? You can save it in the bank and earn interest (a payment the bank makes to you), or you can spend your money for goods and services. For example, with $2 you can buy an ice cream cone and one of your favorite magazines.

What would happen if the prices of ice cream, magazines, haircuts, gasoline, bicycle tires, and lots of other prices in your region increased? Your $2 just wouldn't go as far as before.

With rising prices, or inflation, your money might buy only an ice cream cone. To continue buying an ice-cream cone and a magazine, you might be tempted to raise the price of your birdhouses.

Pushing the Price Up

If you raise the price of your birdhouse, you have just contributed to inflation. The price of the birdhouse also depended on the cost of making it. You had to buy lumber, glue, and plastic. If there is a shortage of lumber, the price of wood will increase, and so will the cost of producing your birdhouse. Think about the raw materials, human skills, and machinery needed to make the products you see around you. What would happen to your birdhouse business if the costs of all these materials increased?

Pulling the Price Up

Sometimes, people have so much money to spend on goods and services that producers cannot supply all the goods people want to buy. Then people are willing to pay more for these goods and services. When this happens, producers can raise prices. Thus, prices rise as a result of the actions of both producers and consumers. This causes inflation.

Inflation can cause problems for individuals and for a country. People with low or limited incomes suffer because their money doesn't go as far as it went before. The prices of exports increase along with other prices. People from other countries buy fewer of the exported products. Thus, the economy of the exporting country is hurt because fewer of its goods are sold on the global market.

560

Rare plant and animal species that rely on the unique habitats found in rain forests become extinct.

The slash and burn method pollutes the air and may contribute to the "greenhouse effect," the gradual warming of the earth's atmosphere.

The livelihoods of native people, such as those who extract material from rubber trees for making rubber, are destroyed.

When logging operations clear vast areas, topsoil is washed away, so nothing will grow.

When the roots of trees and plants that soak up water are removed, flooding can result.

business growth. **Capital** is money that is used to start businesses. The city was also well located. It was near mines that could provide raw materials. It was also near farms that could produce food for a growing population. It had a network of roads and railroads for bringing goods into the factories.

Industry grew in São Paulo and other cities. By the early 1990s, Brazil had the world's eighth largest economy. It exported the most coffee and orange juice concentrate in the world. Soybeans, cocoa, metal ore, gold, and military weapons are other important products of Brazil.

Yet Brazil paid a high price for this development. The government had borrowed money—too much money. Money that should have gone to improve the country had to go to other countries to pay off loans. This debt caused **inflation,** or a general increase in prices. ■

Cutting down trees for lumber and other wood products and clearing the land for farming helps Brazil's economy. Still, what are the long-term effects of destroying the country's rain forests?

■ *Why did the Brazilian government decide to industrialize the country?*

R E V I E W

1. **FOCUS** Why does Brazil have serious economic problems in spite of its many exports and natural resources?
2. **GEOGRAPHY** How did the geography and climate of the northeast region force thousands of people into the cities?
3. **ECONOMICS** Why has the government of Brazil encouraged people to settle in the western regions?
4. **CRITICAL THINKING** Can you think of examples of boom-and-bust economies in other countries?
5. **ACTIVITY** Locate the regions, features, and cities you read about in this lesson on a map of Brazil. Mark rivers in blue, cities in red, and regions in green.

L E S S O N   3

Brazil Today

T H I N K I N G

F O C U S

What are some of the problems facing the people of Brazil today?

Key Term

- favela

➤ *Although Brasília was built to symbolize the unity of the people, it also highlights their differences.*

The capital city of Brasília was built in the 1960s. Yet the idea for this city is much older. More than 100 years ago, in 1891, a large area of land was set aside for the new capital. This area, called the Federal District, was modeled after the District of Columbia, the capital of the United States.

However, not all the citizens of Brazil were included in the plans for this city of the future. Indians living in the area lost land to the new development. The poor people who came looking for work had no homes built for them. That is why there are **favelas** *(fuh VEH luhz),* poor communities made up of shacks, all around the city.

Problems and Solutions

Some people think that developing the rain forests will solve Brazil's economic problems. Others believe that developing the rain forests may harm Brazil and the world (see page 561). Many scientists think that the rain forests help control the earth's temperature and protect its atmosphere.

Chico Mendes *(SHEE ku MEHN dehz)* was one of the most

famous protectors of the Amazon rain forest. He worked as a rubber tapper. When developers began to destroy millions of acres of trees, Mendes organized nonviolent protests called *empates (ehm PAH tees).* The *empates* saved up to three million acres of forest. Chico Mendes was murdered in 1988 by ranchers who wanted to stop him.

Mendes believed that the forest could be saved by sustainable development, or using natural resources in a way that doesn't harm them or use them up. Harvesting forest products that will grow back, such as rubber and nuts, are examples of sustainable development.

Scientists have learned a great deal by studying Indian farming methods. The Kaiapó *(kay ah POH)* live in the Amazonia region of northern Brazil. They clear circular fields and mix crops so that the fragile rain forest soil is not harmed.

In 1992 Brazil hosted an Earth Summit. People from all over the world met to talk about different ways to protect the world's environment.

◄ *Conservationist Chico Mendes, shown in the painting, made his living tapping rubber trees, like the man in the photo on page 559.*

Brazilians, like people everywhere, do not want other nations telling them how to use their natural resources. However, with help from other countries, Brazil might find a way to meet the needs of its citizens without destroying its natural treasures. ■

■ *Why have scientists and concerned citizens of other countries criticized Brazil's efforts to develop its rain forests?*

Brazilian Life

Brazil's cities are lively and modern. However, many city-dwellers are very poor, living in shacks without running water or electricity. About 40 percent of the people of Rio de Janeiro live in *favelas*.

More than half the workers in Brazil earned less than $170 a month in 1990. Perhaps as many as eight of every ten children living in the northeast suffer from hunger. In the southeast, nearly one-fifth of São Paulo's children are homeless. Many of them were forced out of their homes because their parents couldn't feed them. In spite of their problems, Brazilians struggle to survive and hope for better days.

There are few African Brazilians or Indians in the government. This is starting to change. Benedita da Silva became the first African Brazilian woman in Brazil's congress in 1987. In 1992 she

almost won the race for mayor of Rio de Janeiro.

City-dwellers enjoy simple pleasures. Many Brazilians live a short bus ride from a beach. Soccer matches are also popular events in Brazil. Soccer players are big stars, like football players in the United States. African Brazilian Edson Arantes do Nascimento, known as Pelé *(pay LAY),* is said to have been the greatest soccer player of all time. He may even run for president sometime in the future. ■

▼ *Thousands of poor people live in* favelas *on the edges of the modern capital city. In this respect, Brasília is just like Brazil's older cities.*

■ *Describe some of the problems facing people living in Brazil today.*

The Culture of Brazil

It is almost 500 years since Cabral reached the shores of Brazil. In the years following his arrival, Portuguese and African people came to the country. They joined the Indians already living there, and as these people mixed, so did their cultures.

The Historic Blend

The Portuguese brought their language, religion, legal system, and noble families to Brazil. They set up the government, plantations, and other institutions that have shaped Brazil's economy and society.

The Indians taught Portuguese settlers traditional skills and showed them local foods and materials. They taught the Portuguese to eat manioc *(MAN ee ohk),* made from the cassava plant, instead of bread. The Indians also taught them how to build dugout canoes and rafts.

The methods used by African slaves improved Brazilian mining, farming, cattle ranching, and iron working. African cooks added red peppers, okra, and ginger to European and South American foods. African music, stories, and games are part of the lives of all Brazilians.

Most Indians and Africans in Brazil became Catholics. For other Brazilians, however, many old and new beliefs have been brought together. For example, *candomblé (kuhn dawm BLEH)* is an important Brazilian

religion. It honors African Gods, called *orixás (aw ri SHAS)*. However, the *orixás* are sometimes given the names of Catholic saints, such as Saint Anthony or the Virgin Mary.

Modern Brazilian Culture

Music is an important part of Brazilian culture. The music of Brazil is based on a blend of Indian, Portuguese, and African influences. Perhaps Brazil's most famous musical export is the samba rhythm.

The samba comes from what is now the African country Angola. The samba is a major part of the Carnival of Brazil. Carnival is a four-day festival that marks the beginning of the Christian Lent.

Thousands of Brazilians belong to neighborhood groups called samba schools. During Carnival the samba schools perform in the parades for big cash prizes. Today Brazilian musicians like Milton Nascimento and Gilberto Gil use Indian, Portuguese, and African-based music to create popular music that has a special Brazilian sound.

Brazil's artists and writers have learned much from the different traditions found there. For example, landscape architect Roberto Burle Marx uses native Brazilian plants to create gardens and parks around the world. Brazilian writers, such as Euclides da Cunha and Abdias do Nascimento, have based their works on the real lives and culture of their fellow Brazilians. ■

◄ *A wild mix of color and music, Carnival is the last celebration before the Christian season of Lent. Samba schools, whose members have been rehearsing, planning, sewing, and building since last year's Carnival, compete against one another in Carnival parades for big cash prizes.*

■ *How has Brazil's popular music been affected by Brazil's cultural mix?*

R E V I E W

1. **FOCUS** What are some of the problems facing the people of Brazil today?
2. **SOCIAL AND POLITICAL SYSTEMS** What is the importance of the election of Benedita da Silva to Brazil's Congress in 1987?
3. **CULTURE** What were the cultural contributions of different ethnic groups in Brazil?
4. **CRITICAL THINKING** At one time most African and Indian Brazilians were slaves. Yet Brazil's religion, food, and music have been strongly influenced by African and Indian culture. How do you explain this?
5. **WRITING ACTIVITY** Arbor Day, a holiday for planting trees, is celebrated in some U.S. communities. For an Arbor Day celebration in your city or town, write a brief speech about the importance of preserving rain forests using what you have read about Brazil.

565

Rain Forests: Preserve Them? Use Them?

We simply cannot replace this invaluable resource once it is gone. The rain forests . . . once lost, can never be regained. Every second of every day, we are losing a tropical forest the size of a football field.

Hon. John E. Porter
U.S. Representative, Illinois

How can Brazil be expected to control its economic development, [Brazil's President José Sarney] asks, when it is staggering under a $111 billion foreign-debt load? By what right does the U.S. . . . lecture poor countries like Brazil on their responsibilities to mankind?

Time, September 18, 1989

Background

From the air Brazil's great forests look like a giant, green cushion. Once the earth nourished many such rain forests. Now only a few remain. The loss of these rain forests affects the entire world.

How? Like all plants, the huge trees of the forest take in carbon dioxide from the air. They use this gas to make their food. In the process, they release oxygen into the atmosphere. The enormous forests, therefore, help balance the carbon dioxide and the oxygen in the earth's atmosphere. When the trees are cut down, we reduce the amount of carbon dioxide taken from the air. At the same time, we are burning more gasoline and other fossil fuels,

releasing more carbon dioxide into the air. Some scientists predict that this buildup of carbon dioxide in the atmosphere will cause the world's climates to grow warmer and warmer. We cannot foresee all the results of this global warming. One possibility, though, is that fertile farmland could someday become barren desert.

A close look at the rain forests reveals bare patches, some as big as Connecticut. Other effects of deforestation are more difficult to see. When trees go, so do mammals, plants, insects, and birds. Species as unique as the frogs shown here may also become extinct if this trend continues. Such extinctions could have far-reaching effects. For example, many of our

566

medicines come from plants. What if a plant growing in a rain forest today contains a cure for a form of cancer? What if the plant becomes extinct as the forest shrinks?

Roots of the Problem

If you look only at the effects of this loss of the rain forests, the solution may seem clear: Put a stop to it. To see how complicated the problem really is, you have to study the causes—the reasons for clearing the rain forests.

As you have read, Brazil has a large and rapidly growing population. Providing jobs and housing requires space. Some forests are cleared to build homes, factories, roads, and bridges.

Like most other countries, Brazil wants to keep a balance of trade. This means that Brazil tries to sell to other nations as much as it buys from them. Brazil imports steel and other products. It exports beef, rubber, and lumber. Forests are cleared to provide grazing land for cattle. Lumber, of course, comes from the forests.

In addition, Brazilian miners bring 70 tons of gold a year out of the rain forests. Some areas of the forests are cleared to give the miners room to work.

Brazilians want to raise their standard of living. If the rain forests can be useful, why shouldn't they benefit the nation in which they grow?

Decision Point

1. After reading about the problem of the rain forests, what questions do you have?
2. Where would you look for more information about global warming? About Brazil's economy?
3. Are there ways to both preserve and use the rain forests? How can you find out?
4. Choose one topic related to the rain forest problem. What more do you need to know about it? Find the information in newspapers and magazines.
5. Discuss the new information you and your classmates found. Based on this limited information, what ideas and alternatives can you suggest?

Chapter Review

Reviewing Key Terms

boom-and-bust (p. 559)
capital (p. 561)
convert (p. 552)

favela (p. 562)
inflation (p. 561)
Line of Demarcation (p. 550)

A. Write whether each of the following statements is *true* or *false*. Then rewrite the false statements to make them true.

1. The Line of Demarcation is the boundary between the countries of Portugal and Spain.
2. Jesuits tried to make Indians convert, or change from their own religions, to Catholicism.
3. In a boom-and-bust cycle, a product first brings high profits, then it stops bringing much profit at all.
4. São Paulo lacked the capital to create businesses in Brazil.
5. Inflation causes a general decrease in prices.
6. Most of Brasília's wealthy population lives in *favelas*.

B. Write sentences according to the directions below. Your sentences should show your understanding of each term.

1. Write two sentences about the future of Brazil's cities using the term <u>favela</u>.
2. Write two sentences about Brazil's economy using the term <u>boom-and-bust</u>.
3. Write two sentences about Brazil's history using the term <u>convert</u>.

Exploring Concepts

A. Copy and complete the chart below. Fill it in with three to four major ideas from the chapter.

Brazil Fact Sheet	
Brazil's Colonial History	
Government of Brazil	
People of Brazil	
Modern Economic Challenges	development causes inflation and environmental problems

B. Answer each question with information from the chapter.

1. Why was Prince Henry interested in sea travel?
2. How did Pope Alexander VI settle a dispute between Spain and Portugal in 1493?
3. Why did conflict arise between the Indians of Brazil and the Portuguese?
4. Why were Africans brought to Brazil?
5. When did Brazil gain its independence from Portugal?
6. In which of Brazil's five regions is the Amazon River located?
7. What products fueled Brazil's boom-and-bust economy?
8. How did Brazil's leaders hope to stabilize their economy?
9. What were the *empates*?
10. Name at least two contributions made by the native Indians and the Africans to the culture of Brazil.

Reviewing Skills

1. What is an assumption? Why is it important to always test an assumption against facts? What types of assumptions do adults make about young people today? Do you think that their assumptions are true? Why or why not?

2. Look at the graph on page 552. What kind of graph is this? What kind of graph would you use if you want to show the shrinking Indian population in Brazil from the 1500s to today? Explain your answer.

3. Imagine that you have been asked to write an essay about the importance of preserving the rain forest in Brazil. What types of supporting evidence found in this chapter could you use in your essay?

4. As you write your essay, you realize that you would like more information about efforts to preserve the rain forest. Where would you find a list of magazine articles about the rain forest that were written during the past year?

Using Critical Thinking

1. Compare the histories of the Caribbean and Brazil. In what ways are they similar? Think about each region's colonial experiences, including their economies, the Europeans' treatment of Native Americans, the types of people who were brought into or came to each area, and the blend of cultures in each region.

2. Why did the development of Caribbean sugar plantations in the 1500s and 1600s result in problems for Brazil's economy?

3. Why do Brazilians view their northern and western regions as the land of the future? Why are some people opposed to this way of thinking?

4. You have read about many nations that are trying to combat poverty. Based on your readings, how can nations such as Brazil hope to bring their people a better standard of living?

Preparing for Citizenship

1. **WRITING ACTIVITY** When Princess Isabel signed the Golden Law freeing Brazil's slaves in 1888, she angered the landowners of Brazil. In this case, Isabel went against their wishes in order to do what she thought was right. Think about leaders in the United States. Is it ever right for an elected U.S. representative to act against the wishes of the people to do what he or she thinks is right? Why or why not? Give reasons to support your answer.

2. **ART ACTIVITY** Make a map of the landforms, climate, and major geographic features of the community in which you live. You may want to use the map of North America: Political and Physical in the Atlas on page 686. Do geography and climate affect the ways that people in your community make a living? Do the people in your community share environmental concerns similar to those of the Brazilian people?

3. **INTERVIEWING** Every community has people working to improve the environment. Some people are active in cleaning up polluted streams or lakes. Others are concerned about the future of endangered animals. Find a person to interview in your community who is active in environmental issues. They may be employed by an environmental organization. Or, they may volunteer in their spare time to help protect our environment. You may find a suitable person who is willing to come and discuss their work with your class.

4. **COLLABORATIVE LEARNING** As a class, create a Community Environmental Report. Your report may include maps of your area showing places of concern to environmentalists, and clippings from local newspapers about environmental issues.

North America

Over millions of years, great upheavals of earth and vast movements of ice and water formed the huge mountain chains of North America. The first humans reached these mountains from Asia perhaps 50,000 years ago. Around 500 years ago, explorers and conquerors came from Europe. They were followed by waves of settlers from many parts of the world.

1400

The San Juan Mountains in Colorado

Today

North America

North America stretches "from sea to shining sea." The continent measures 3,300 miles at its widest point—from St. John's, Newfoundland, to the Pacific coast. From Alaska to Mexico, the continent extends 4,900 miles. Unlike Europe, which is made up of many small nations, North America is composed of only three large nations: Canada, the United States, and Mexico.

The earliest North Americans crossed the Bering Strait from Asia thousands of years ago. Over time, groups of people settled in every part of the continent. Each group created its own culture and way of life. The Zuni hunted and herded in the southwestern desert. The Inuit adapted to the frozen, snowy climate of what is now Canada and Alaska.

In time North America came under the control of the English, French, and Spaniards. The arrival of Europeans greatly changed Native American culture. Many place names, including New York City, San Francisco, and Montreal, show their European origins. Today people from almost every country in the world make their home in North America.

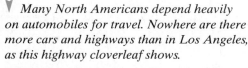

▼ *Many North Americans depend heavily on automobiles for travel. Nowhere are there more cars and highways than in Los Angeles, as this highway cloverleaf shows.*

▲ *Today, the people of North America share a rich heritage of many ethnic and national traditions.*

572

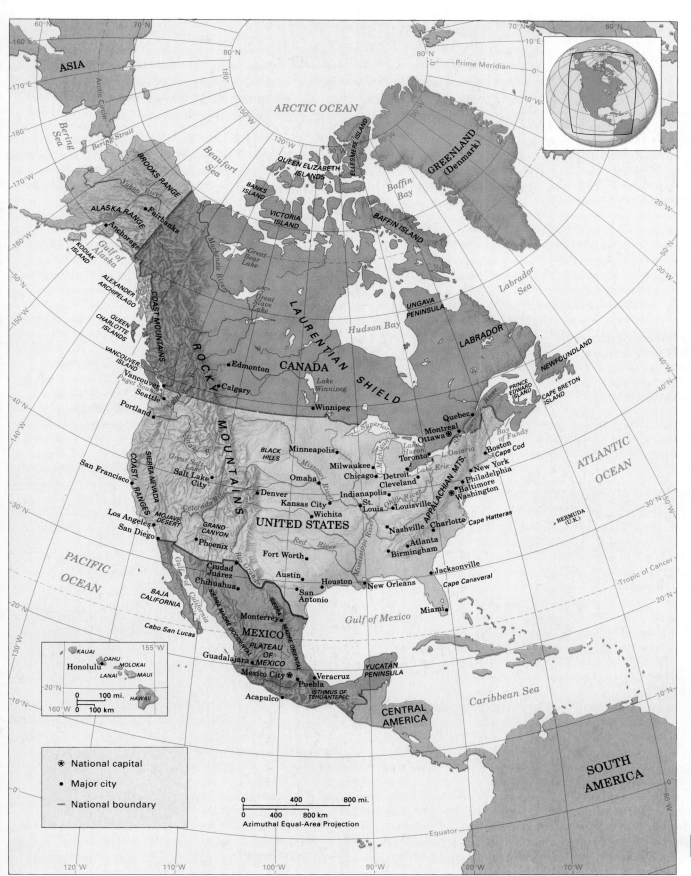

ASIA

ARCTIC OCEAN

Bering
Sea

Beaufort
Sea

BROOKS RANGE

BANKS
ISLAND

QUEEN ELIZABETH
ISLANDS

ELLESMERE ISLAND

GREENLAND
(Denmark)

Baffin
Bay

VICTORIA
ISLAND

BAFFIN ISLAND

ALASKA RANGE

Fairbanks

Anchorage

Gulf of
Alaska

KODIAK
ISLAND

Yukon River

ALEXANDER
ARCHIPELAGO

QUEEN
CHARLOTTE
ISLANDS

Mackenzie River

Great
Bear
Lake

Great
Slave
Lake

LAURENTIAN SHIELD

Hudson Bay

UNGAVA
PENINSULA

Labrador
Sea

LABRADOR

COAST MOUNTAINS

VANCOUVER
ISLAND

Edmonton

CANADA

NEWFOUNDLAND

Vancouver

Calgary

ROCKY

Lake
Winnipeg

PRINCE
EDWARD
ISLAND

CAPE BRETON
ISLAND

Puget Sound

Seattle

Portland

Winnipeg

Quebec

Montreal

Bay
of Fundy

Columbia River

BLACK
HILLS

Minneapolis

L. Superior

Ottawa

St. Lawrence River

Boston

Cape Cod

San Francisco

COAST RANGES

SIERRA NEVADA

Salt Lake
City

Great Salt
Lake

Snake River

Milwaukee

Lake
Huron

Toronto

L. Ontario

Chicago

Detroit

Lake Erie

Cleveland

New York

Philadelphia

ATLANTIC
OCEAN

Omaha

Missouri River

MOUNTAINS

Denver

Indianapolis

St.
Louis

Baltimore

Washington

Los Angeles

MOJAVE
DESERT

Kansas City

Ohio River

Louisville

APPALACHIAN MTS.

San Diego

GRAND
CANYON

Colorado River

Wichita

Nashville

Charlotte

Cape Hatteras

BERMUDA
(U.K.)

Phoenix

UNITED STATES

Atlanta

Fort Worth

Red River

Birmingham

PACIFIC

OCEAN

Ciudad
Juárez

Chihuahua

Austin

San
Antonio

Houston

Mississippi River

New Orleans

Jacksonville

Cape Canaveral

Tropic of Cancer

BAJA
CALIFORNIA

Monterrey

Gulf of California

Gulf of Mexico

Miami

Cabo San Lucas

SIERRA MADRE OCCIDENTAL

SIERRA MADRE ORIENTAL

MEXICO

PLATEAU
OF
MEXICO

KAUAI

OAHU

MOLOKAI

155° W

Honolulu

LANAI

MAUI

Guadalajara

Mexico City

Veracruz

YUCATÁN
PENINSULA

0   100 mi.

HAWAII

0   100 km

Puebla

Acapulco

ISTHMUS OF
TEHUANTEPEC

Caribbean Sea

CENTRAL
AMERICA

SOUTH
AMERICA

⊛ National capital

• Major city

— National boundary

0   400   800 mi.

0   400   800 km

Azimuthal Equal-Area Projection

Equator

ASIA

Arctic Circle

Bering Strait

Prime Meridian

573

North America

The Land and People

North America might be called a land of fire and ice. Huge glaciers—great rivers of ice—covered much of North America thousands of years ago. Glaciers act like giant bulldozers, scooping up rocks and soil as they move over the land. Sometimes, glaciers pile up rocks in narrow ridges. They also carve out U-shaped valleys between mountains.

The western coast of North America is part of the Ring of Fire—the region of earthquakes and volcanoes that circles the Pacific Ocean. In 1985 one of the largest earthquakes of the 1900s destroyed part of Mexico City. Major earthquakes have badly shaken California and Alaska.

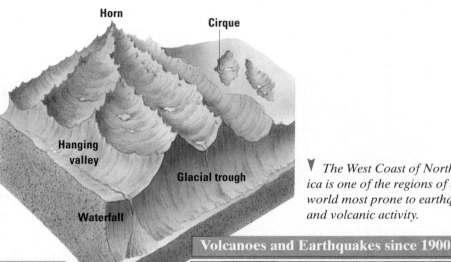

Horn

Cirque

Hanging valley

Glacial trough

Waterfall

➤ *When glaciers melt, they leave behind a changed landscape. The Great Lakes and many smaller lakes were formed by glaciers.*

▼ *The West Coast of North America is one of the regions of the world most prone to earthquakes and volcanic activity.*

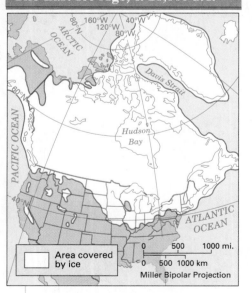

The Last Ice Age, c. 16,000 B.C.

Area covered by ice

0   500   1000 mi.

0   500 1000 km

Miller Bipolar Projection

▲ *Ice covered one-third of the earth's surface 20,000 years ago. This is more than three times the area covered by today's glaciers.*

Volcanoes and Earthquakes since 1900

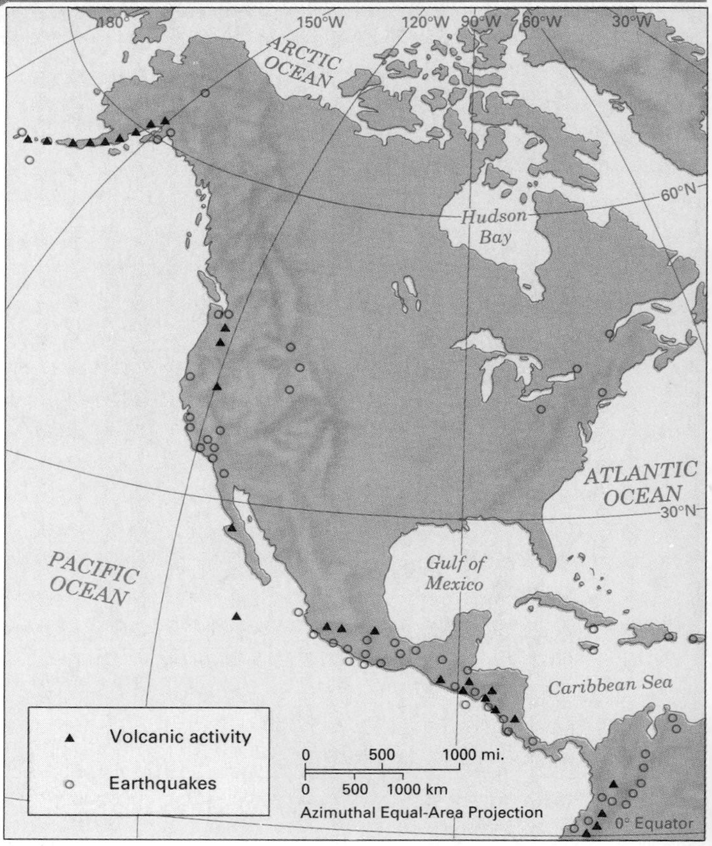

▲ Volcanic activity

○ Earthquakes

0   500   1000 mi.

0   500 1000 km

Azimuthal Equal-Area Projection

North America is rich with minerals. Its other natural resources include vast forests and a large supply of fresh water and fertile soil. North America uses its many natural resources to produce about one-third of the world's manufactured goods. The United States and Canada also are major exporters of agricultural products.

Most North Americans live in cities. Each of these cities has been enriched by the traditions of the peoples from all over the world who settled there.

Holidays reflect each nation's geography, history, and traditions. During long, cold winters, Canadians create amazing shapes from ice and snow.

➤ *The jaguar symbol has been used in ceremonies and festivals throughout Mexico for hundreds of years. Masks such as this one are still worn in parades and ceremonies today.*

➤ *On the first Thanksgiving, the English Pilgrims who settled in Plymouth cooked Native American foods. These included squash, wild turkey, and corn.*

Chapter 25

Mexico

Mexico's culture, formed through the meeting of Spanish and ancient Indian civilizations, has kept traditions from both. In recent history, Mexico and the United States have had a close relationship. Mexicans are a proud people who honor their past as they look toward the promising future of North American unity.

The patterned fabric sold in a Mexico City market reveals the influence of both Spanish and Indian designs.

Before the arrival of the Spaniards, Indians had never seen people wearing armor or riding horses. This figure of Santiago (Saint James) was made by a Mexican artist during the colonial period.

1500	1600	1700

1519

1521 Spaniards conquer Tenochtitlan, the capital of the Aztec Empire.

Mexico City spreads over a high plateau surrounded by mountains. In the foreground is the Palace of Fine Arts, which contains many murals by Mexico's most famous painters.

Thick tortillas and meat and sausage flavored with chilies are being served at this market stand.

1800

1900

2000

1810 Struggle for independence begins.

1910 Mexican Revolution begins.

1988 President Salinas is elected.

577

Today

LESSON 1

The Forming of Mexico

**THINKING
FOCUS**

*What were the major
causes of Mexico's fight
for independence?*

Key Terms

- conquistador
- hacienda
- peon

➤ *At their first meeting
with Cortés and his men,
the Aztecs were amazed
at the horses and the iron
armor of the Spaniards.*

ontezuma, the Aztec
emperor, was worried.
For some time mes-
sengers had told him
of floating mountains in the water
offshore and of bearded men who
rode deerlike animals (horses) and
had weapons such as the Aztecs
had never seen.

Montezuma feared that the
leader of these men might be a
God who had come to reclaim his
kingdom. On November 8, 1519, he
let Hernán Cortés and his followers
into the city of Tenochtitlan.

Colonization of Mexico

Two years later the Spaniards
and their Native American allies
conquered the city. Tenochtitlan
had been the political, religious,
and marketing center of the Aztec
Empire. Under Spanish rule, the
city was rebuilt and became Mexico City, the capital of New Spain.

Setting Up a Spanish Colony

After the conquest two urban
civilizations blended. The Spaniards
took over the Aztecs' centralized
system of government. Through this
system, tribute from all over the empire had poured into Tenochtitlan.

The **conquistadors**—the new Spanish overlords—allowed the local
lords and chiefs to keep their titles,
gather tribute payments, and recruit
free labor.

After the conquest the
Spaniards recruited Indian craftworkers to rebuild the city destroyed by warfare. New cities
blended Spanish and traditional
Indian styles.

Most Spanish settlers stayed in
the cities. Here they mixed with the
Indians and had children with Indian women. These children were
the first Mexican *mestizos*.

◀ *The Spaniards and the peoples of the Americas loved gold. Examples of this love are the detailed golden ceiling of this Spanish church and the ceremonial cup (below) created by people of northwest Peru.*

Following the conquistadors, missionaries from Spain arrived to convert the Indians to Catholicism. The friars learned Indian languages and set up schools and missions.

Some Indians believed the God of the Christians had defeated their Gods. As Indians came to accept Christianity, they often blended the new religion with their old beliefs.

Sometimes, Indian workers hid images of their Gods in the new churches they built. Thus Indians could secretly continue to honor their Gods while worshiping in Christian churches. You can read more about this in Understanding Historical Evidence on page 583.

Extracting Wealth from Mexico

The conquistadors brought many other changes to Mexico. They imported sheep, pigs, horses, and cattle and let them roam freely over Indian land. They brought in wheat, barley, and a variety of vegetables.

As new settlers came from Spain, more food was needed for the cities. Spanish settlers formed large estates called **haciendas** *(hah see EHN duhz)*. Many took over part of the communal lands owned by Indian villages.

Many Indians who had lost their lands became **peons,** or peasants. Often they received pay in advance from their employers, whom they could not repay. The peons would then lose the freedom to leave their masters' *haciendas.*

Spanish settlers had been dazzled by the Aztecs' gold and silver and were eager to find more for themselves. The Native Americans had practiced surface mining, but now the Spaniards opened underground silver mines. Some Indians were forced to work in these mines. Soon the Spaniards needed more workers. They brought enslaved Africans to do this work.

When the conquistadors arrived, about 21 million Indians lived in central Mexico. By 1700 just over one million remained. Most died from diseases brought by the Spaniards or enslaved Africans. Many others died from bad treatment and overwork. ■

Across Time & Space

English colonists arrived in New England with their families and tended to establish colonies separate from the Indians. Most early Spanish settlers, on the other hand, came without wives or families. They tended to marry Indian women.

■ *How did life change for the Indians after the Spanish conquest?*

579

Mexican Independence

The rulers of Mexico were often sent from Spain. They were called *peninsulares,* after the peninsula where Spain is located. The children of Spaniards who settled in Mexico were called *creoles.* In the 1800s the *creoles* came to resent the new *peninsulares* who ruled Mexico.

Fighting for Independence

In 1810 the parish priest of the town of Dolores was a *creole* called Miguel Hidalgo y Costilla. He felt that the Indians had been treated unjustly by the Spaniards. With *creole* friends he planned a revolt against the government.

On September 16, 1810, Hidalgo heard that their plot had been discovered. Quickly he had the church bells rung, calling his people to church. With the now-famous *Grito de Dolores,* "the cry of Dolores," he told them to rise up against their Spanish rulers:

> My children: . . . Will you free yourselves? Will you recover the lands stolen three hundred years ago from your forefathers by the hated Spaniards? We must act at once. . . . Long live our Lady of Guadalupe! Death to the Spaniards! . . .

Heading an army of poor Indians and *mestizos,* Hidalgo marched to Mexico City. There his army was defeated. Later, he was executed.

Ten years later, a group of *creoles* succeeded in making the break from Spanish rule. For *mestizos* and Indians, little was gained. The *creoles* were now their masters.

Defending Independence

Soon Mexico faced new dangers. In 1836 Texas fought against Mexico and won its independence. Ten years later the United States went to war with Mexico and, in 1848, seized over half of its territory. The map on this page shows how much land Mexico eventually lost to the United States. Even today some descendants of families from

▼ *How did Mexico lose Texas? When did the United States take over the territories of northern Mexico?*

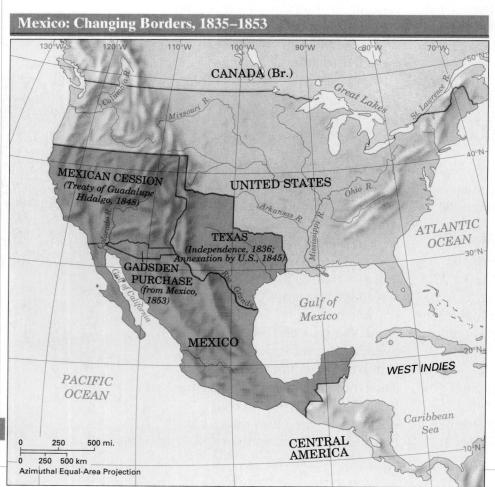

Mexico: Changing Borders, 1835–1853

CANADA (Br.)

Columbia R.

Missouri R.

Great Lakes

St. Lawrence R.

50°N

UNITED STATES

MEXICAN CESSION
(Treaty of Guadalupe Hidalgo, 1848)

Colorado R.

Ohio R.

Arkansas R.

40°N

Mississippi R.

ATLANTIC OCEAN

TEXAS
(Independence, 1836; Annexation by U.S., 1845)

30°N

GADSDEN PURCHASE
(from Mexico, 1853)

Gulf of California

Rio Grande

MEXICO

Gulf of Mexico

20°N

PACIFIC OCEAN

WEST INDIES

Caribbean Sea

CENTRAL AMERICA

10°N

0   250   500 mi.

0   250   500 km

Azimuthal Equal-Area Projection

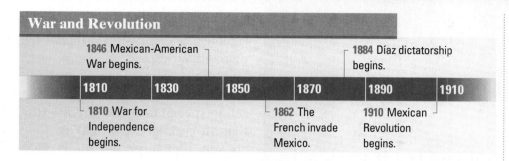

War and Revolution

1846 Mexican-American War begins.

1884 Díaz dictatorship begins.

| 1810 | 1830 | 1850 | 1870 | 1890 | 1910 |

1810 War for Independence begins.

1862 The French invade Mexico.

1910 Mexican Revolution begins.

◄ *How many wars did Mexicans fight in the 1800s?*

Mexico's lost territories still think of these as Mexican lands.

In 1862, France tried to expand its empire by attacking Mexico. Mexicans defeated the French at the Battle of Puebla on May 5, 1862. Mexicans continue to celebrate this victory every Cinco de Mayo (fifth of May).

Their victory did not last. The French again invaded. This time they chose an emperor. Three years later the French were forced to withdraw, and Mexico was free. ■

■ *How did the fight for Mexican independence begin?*

Social and Economic Revolution

As an independent nation, Mexico wrestled with problems dating back to the Spanish conquest. New leaders, some Indian and some *mestizo,* came to power.

New Leaders

Benito Juárez, a Zapotec Indian, had been president before the French invasion. He became president again. During his rule he encouraged the building of railroads. He also supported free education for young children.

In 1876 Porfirio Díaz, a *mestizo* general, took control and ruled first as president and later as dictator. He encouraged foreign investment and built thousands of miles of railroads. Now trains whisked cotton, iron ore, and other raw materials to factories throughout Mexico.

In spite of these improvements, many Mexicans resented Díaz. The profits from industry went to foreigners and enriched few Mexicans. Díaz also let big landowners take over *ejidos (ay HEE dohs)*, the communal native lands. Many Indians were now forced to work for others on what had been their own property.

Revolution and Land Reform

By 1910 simmering anger exploded into revolution against Díaz. Fighting began in the north and spread throughout Mexico. Leaders formed bands of armed peons.

One of these leaders was Emiliano Zapata, a *mestizo* from southern Mexico. A few months after the revolution had begun, Zapata called on local villagers to join the fight. He commanded fierce loyalty from the peasants because of his demand for *Tierra y Libertad!*—"Land and Liberty!"

Zapata turned the landless peasants of his region into a tough army that swooped down on the haciendas. When a hacienda surrendered, he divided the land among the peons who had worked on it.

▲ *Porfirio Díaz, in the center of the photo above, resigned the presidency of Mexico in May 1911. He then went into exile.*

581

Mexico

José Clemente Orozco, a famous painter from the time of the revolution, painted this mural of Mexican peasants in revolt.

When the revolution finally ended in the 1920s, its ideals were written into a new constitution. However, land reform didn't begin until Lázaro Cárdenas, a *mestizo,* became president in 1934.

Cárdenas turned 50 million acres of hacienda land into *ejidos*. He also encouraged workers in the cities to organize. In 1938, when the foreign-owned oil companies had refused to increase workers' pay, Cárdenas decided that the government should take over the oil companies. In a rush of national pride, thousands of Mexicans gave whatever they had to pay off the foreign owners.

Modernizing Mexico

World War II brought about many changes in the Mexican economy. For years Mexico had exported raw materials and imported consumer goods. Now the United States, Mexico's main supplier, was busy producing arms for war. Mexicans responded by developing their own industries.

After the war the government encouraged growing industries. It set up special taxes on imports so that Mexican goods would be cheaper than imported goods. The government also built roads, railroads, and dams to provide electricity. Large foreign corporations, mostly from the United States, opened branches in Mexico where wages were low. The Mexican government also encouraged tourism.

At this time the government ended its program of land reform. It began large irrigation projects that increased the amount of farmland. Its policies favored large farms that could grow huge amounts of cotton and winter vegetables for export. Many small farmers could not keep up and went to the cities to find jobs.

Profits from the booming economy still went mostly to foreigners. However, the increased number of jobs did help many Mexicans rise into the middle class. At the same time, government spending on health care reduced infant deaths and helped adults live longer. Mexico's population increased rapidly.

Mexico—called the "Mexican Miracle" by many—became Latin America's greatest success. During this time Mexico's economy became more closely tied to U.S. markets and capital. ■

■ *What were the goals of the Mexican Revolution?*

---

1. **FOCUS** What were the major causes of Mexico's fight for independence?
2. **POLITICAL SYSTEMS** Did Indians and *mestizos* gain much from independence before the French invaded?
3. **ECONOMICS** How did events in World War II affect Mexico's economy?
4. **CRITICAL THINKING** Why might Spain have kept important government positions for the *peninsulares*?
5. **ACTIVITY** Write and deliver a one-minute speech supporting or opposing Díaz's modernization plans.

Interpreting Artifacts

Here's Why

In Chapter 4, you read about examining art to get a better understanding of how people live. You also can learn from artifacts, or the things that people made and used in their daily lives, to understand people of the past.

Artifacts you might examine include weapons, clothes, pots and pans, tools, furniture, and even toys. The list is endless. How these things were made and used can shed light on what was important in people's lives.

In this chapter you read about the meeting of the Aztec and Spanish civilizations. Artifacts of the time can reveal the way people's beliefs changed or adapted.

Here's How

Here are some steps you might take to learn from the artifact on this page.

1. **Study the artifact carefully.** What does it look like? What is it made of? Does it have any decorations? What do they represent? You see that the artifact is a block of stone, wider and flatter on one side. It looks like the base of a column lying on its side. It has a carving on the flat side. An archaeologist might tell you that this carving represents the Aztec God Tlaltecuhtli, lord of the earth. The carving was made to face the earth; it is the underside of the artifact.

2. **What is already known about the artifact?** Where was it found? How was it used? This stone came from an ancient Aztec temple. It was reused by Indian workers to build a church. They shaped the stone into a column base, with the carving facing down.

3. **What does this information tell us?** Why was it used this way? Did it have a special meaning for those who used it? By using this ancient carving as a column base for a Christian church, Indian builders secretly placed their God within the church building.

As they prayed to the God of the Spaniards, they could also continue to worship their own God.

Try It

This artifact is an excellent example of the cultural *mestizaje (mehs tee ZUH hay)*, or the blending of Indian and Spanish cultures. Explain why.

Apply It

Your entire bedroom is filled with artifacts that tell about the daily life of a student living in the United States! Imagine you are a historian examining an artifact from your room, such as a tape player or a pair of jeans. Write a paragraph describing your "artifact" and what it could tell about its user.

L E S S O N   2

Regions and Resources

THINKING
F O C U S

*What natural resources
have helped Mexico's
economy grow?*

Key Term

• border

▼ *It is harvest time in the
high Valley of Toluca, central Mexico. Maguey
plants grow in the fore-
ground. Their tough fiber
is used to make mats.*

Emperor Charles V,
Spain's ruler during the
conquest of Mexico,
never saw his new colony.
When a messenger arrived to report on Mexico, Charles V asked,
"What is the land like?"

The messenger took a sheet of
paper and crushed it in his hand.
Then opening his palm, he showed
the crumpled paper to the emperor.
"It is like this, sire," he said.

Like the messenger's crumpled
paper, two-thirds of Mexico's land
is folded into huge, ragged mountains. The rest is made up of high
plateaus and coastal plains.

The forces that shaped the land
of Mexico are still at work. In
1943 and again in 1982, volcanoes
erupted, and seas of lava swallowed
up land and crops. In 1985 a terrible earthquake shook and damaged
Mexico City.

The Land and Its Resources

Look back at the map on page
580. You can see that Mexico lies
between the United States and
Central America. In the past, agriculture supported a limited population.
The minerals and oil discovered in
later times are Mexico's greatest
natural resources. These and the
labor of its growing population are
the main assets of Mexico today.

Diversity of Land and Climate

Mexico's mountains divide the
land into six very diverse regions.
The largest is the high, dry plateau
of Mexico. It is ringed by high
mountains often crested with snow.
Most of Mexico's cities and half of
its population are on the plateau.
Mexico's five other regions surround this area.

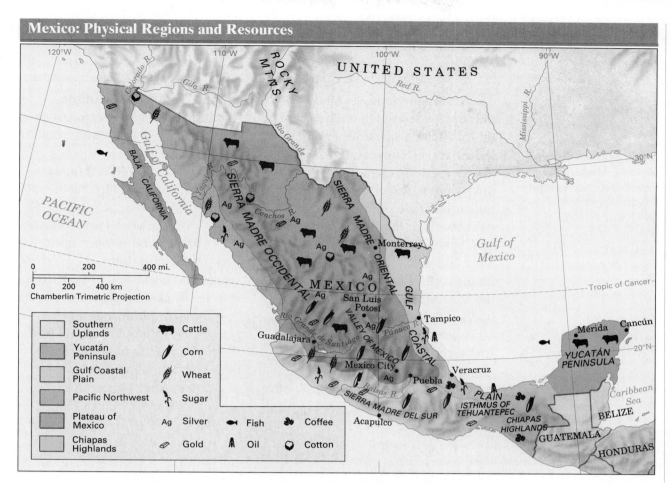

Within each region the mountains create areas with very different climates and vegetation. The mountains also isolated the valleys, so people in each valley often had their own culture.

Agriculture

By some estimates only one-third of Mexico's land can be farmed. Today much of Mexico's best land is divided into large, irrigated farms and ranches. Their products are mostly for export: winter vegetables and fruits, cotton, coffee, and cattle. Most of these are sold to the United States.

By contrast, most of the *ejidos* that were given to the Indians were small, dry pieces of land. Since these small farmlands cannot produce enough food to feed the growing population, Mexico imports corn and wheat.

Mexico's coastal waters are an important source of food and export. Each year Mexico's fisheries catch large amounts of shrimp, tuna, sardines, and oysters.

Mining and Oil

Mexico's rugged land may be poor for farming, but it holds a treasure of minerals. Mexico is the world's largest producer of silver. It is also a major producer of 14 other minerals including lead, zinc, copper, gold, and iron. Exports of these minerals earn millions of dollars for Mexico's economy.

In the 1970s, drillers found huge oil reserves in Mexico, giving the country the fourth largest oil supply in the world. Soon Mexico gained billions of dollars from oil exports. It used this income to develop and improve its roads and industries. ■

▲ *Which is the largest of Mexico's regions? Which crops are grown only on low-lying plains?*

■ *How do Mexico's mountains affect the lives of Mexicans?*

585

Growing Industries

➤ In 1993 the Mexican Finance Ministry began circulating a new peso. Today three of these pesos are equal to one dollar in the United States. Before 1993 it took 3,000 pesos to equal one dollar.

Although money from oil exports provided much needed capital for Mexico's developing industries, U.S. investment also helped Mexican industry grow. Eager to take advantage of low-paid Mexican labor, U.S. businesses have opened plants south of the U.S.-Mexican border. A **border** is an area or line that separates two regions or nations. The importance of borders, particularly in the case of the United States and Mexico, is explained in the feature below.

From Miracle to Crisis

In the late 1960s, Mexico appeared to be prosperous. However, to pay for industries, roads, and other programs, the government had borrowed money from foreign banks. It planned to pay its debt by exporting oil.

For a time high oil prices kept Mexico going. Suddenly, oil prices started to drop, and Mexico found

UNDERSTANDING BORDERS

Mexico and the United States share a 2,000-mile border. It stretches from the Pacific Ocean to the Gulf of Mexico.

Kinds of Borders

A border can be formed by a physical barrier such as a river or a mountain range. As you can see by the map on page 585, the Rio Grande (a river called the Rio Bravo del Norte in Mexico) forms part of the border between Mexico and the United States.

A border can also be cultural. For instance, the Mexican-U.S. border separates two societies with very different histories and cultural roots. Mexico's culture is the result of a unique mix of Spanish-Catholic influence and Indian traditions. The United States is mostly Protestant in religion and English in language.

Borders are also economic. The U.S.-Mexican border is one of the few places in the world where two countries with very different economic systems and resources meet.

The Role of Borders

Borders are lines that both separate and join. People divided by a border are almost sure to have contact.

In spite of their differences, Mexico and the United States depend upon and influence each other. Of the world's countries, Mexico is third in the value of goods it buys from the United States. It is about fourth in the value of goods it sells to the United States. U.S. investments were crucial in Mexico's industrial development. On the other hand, U.S. businesses have drawn heavily on Mexican labor and raw materials.

As you cross the border, differences between the two countries strike you immediately. However, the mixing of people and exchange of goods that take place create a region where U.S. and Mexican cultures blend.

586

itself in trouble in the early 1980s. It was $80 billion in debt with no money to repay its loans.

The Mexican Miracle quickly fell apart. The government cut its support to industry and stopped some major construction projects. Tens of thousands of people lost their jobs. The value of the peso, the Mexican unit of currency, dropped. As a result, inflation soared. The price of a hamburger that once cost 10 pesos zoomed to 100 pesos.

Today Mexico is recovering from these problems. The government has cut spending. It has cut back on protecting Mexican industry and has sold many state-owned businesses to private owners. Forced to compete, these businesses have become more profitable.

Mexican Industry Today

Today Mexico's industries produce about one-fourth of the national income. Many products such as cars, chemicals, electrical products, and processed foods are made for export, mostly to the United States. As you can see on the graph above, exports of manufactured goods have become very important.

Most of Mexico's factories are located in the central plateau

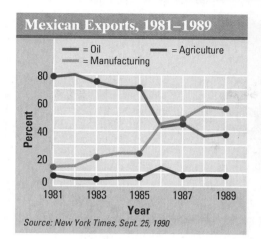

Mexican Exports, 1981–1989

— = Oil   — = Agriculture
— = Manufacturing

Percent (y-axis: 0, 20, 40, 60, 80)
Year (x-axis: 1981, 1983, 1985, 1987, 1989)

Source: New York Times, Sept. 25, 1990

region. Mexico City alone has half of the nation's industries. Monterrey is a major steel manufacturing center. Puebla and Guadalajara are two of Mexico's major industrial centers.

Many U.S. manufacturing plants have been opened in Mexico. These plants, called *maquiladoras (mah kee lah DAW rahs)* in Spanish, import parts to be assembled at low cost by Mexican workers. Today the number of *maquiladoras* is growing, and their workers are often highly skilled technicians.

Tourism is also a growing source of jobs and income for Mexicans. More than six million tourists visit Mexico each year.

Although expanding, Mexico's industry cannot provide work for the 800,000 workers who join the labor force each year. As a result, thousands slip across the U.S. border to look for work. ■

▲ *(left) As oil prices fell, Mexican oil exports became less important than manufacturing exports. (right) Many women find work in the* maquiladora *assembly plants.*

■ *What are Mexico's major industries, and what is their importance to the economy?*

R E V I E W

1. **FOCUS** What natural resources have helped Mexico's economy grow?
2. **GEOGRAPHY** What geographic features dominate Mexico's landscape?
3. **ECONOMICS** How has oil affected Mexico's economic growth?
4. **CRITICAL THINKING** How do you think Mexicans feel

about the *maquiladoras*? Explain the reasons for your opinion.
5. **ACTIVITY** Imagine that you have been traveling around the Mexican countryside. Write a letter to a friend describing the scenery, farming, and industry you have seen. What route did you travel? What places did you visit?

587

Mexico

A Blending of Cultures

THINKING
FOCUS

How does Mexico blend traditional and modern ways?

Key Terms

- fiesta
- trade agreement

▼ *This Parachico dancer is from Chiapas. He wears a mask and uses a rattle. This dance recalls events of the Spanish conquest.*

Hardly a week passes in Mexico without a fiesta. A **fiesta** is a religious or patriotic festival. It may be a village celebration for the local saint. Or it may be a feast day observed all over Mexico such as Independence Day or Día de los Muertos (Day of the Dead), described on page 592.

Sometimes, pilgrimages are part of a fiesta. Then thousands travel from all over Mexico to honor saints at shrines like that of the Virgin of Guadalupe. Tourists also flock to these festivals.

Mexican fiestas are outpourings of emotion and color. As Mexican writer Octavio Paz explains, fiestas release deep feelings:

Thanks to the fiesta the Mexican opens out, participates, communes [shares thoughts] with his fellows and with the values that give meaning to his religious or political existence. And it is significant that a country [like] ours should have so many and such joyous fiestas. Their frequency, their brilliance and excitement, the enthusiasm with which we take part, all suggest that without them we would explode.

Daily Life

Age-old traditions come alive in fiestas in the countryside. Isolated Indian villages in particular have preserved their way of life. Although Spanish is spoken throughout Mexico, many native groups in the rural areas still speak their own language. In the fast-moving cities, however, signs of the past are changing.

Rural Family Life

Many villages and small towns reflect Mexico's past. The plaza at the center, with its church and town hall, is typically Spanish. The open market is an Indian tradition as you read in Chapter 6.

For villagers, life centers around the extended family. Such a family includes the immediate family, as well as aunts, uncles, cousins, and godparents. Children get a set of godparents for every ceremony that marks a new stage in their lives. Godparents are trusted friends and advisers of the entire family.

The father is the head of the family and its main provider. The

mother takes care of the home and children and controls the money. She may also earn money by growing vegetables or raising chickens. Some women weave cloth or make pottery. Their products bring in good money at the local market.

Traditionally, parents expect their sons to be tough and independent. Daughters learn to be reserved and dependent. They share in household chores and prepare for their future duties as wives and mothers.

Village houses, often made of adobe, or sun-baked clay, are centered around a courtyard. The courtyard usually is full of color from flowering and green plants. Here the family gathers for meals and social occasions.

Religion is the most important influence in the lives of villagers. Religious rituals mark every important event of their lives. In addition to a village church, each neighborhood has a roadside chapel for its favorite saint. These are often built in places the Indians considered holy. Homes also have shrines for the family's favorite saint. People pray to the saints for good health or a plentiful harvest.

Urban Living

For 70 percent of all Mexicans, daily life involves skyscrapers, traffic, crowds, and industries in the cities. Each year more families leave the countryside to seek jobs in the growing urban areas.

Most Mexican cities can't keep up with these newcomers' needs for housing and jobs. Those who are lucky enough to find jobs often receive low pay. To make ends meet, newcomers tend to move in

Middle-class households in the city usually have modern kitchens with the latest appliances.

589

Mexico: Population, 1990

UNITED STATES

Mexicali
Ciudad Juárez
Chihuahua
Monterrey
MEXICO
PACIFIC OCEAN
Gulf of Mexico
León
Mérida
Guadalajara
Mexico City
Puebla
BELIZE
GUATEMALA

N
W E
S

0   250   500 mi.
0   250   500 km
Azimuthal Equal-Area Projection

• 50,000 people

Source: Britannica World Data, 1992

What are the four largest population centers shown on this map? How do you know?

How Do We Know?

SOCIAL SCIENCE *Population figures are gathered by the government through a process called census taking. Mexico's households answer questionnaires about who lives there, their gender, age, occupation, and other information. A census is usually taken every 10 years.*

➤ *Suburban neighborhoods in Mexico are often modern and colorful.*

■ *How does rural life differ from middle-class urban living?*

with family members. Others live in shacks outside the city close to people from the same town or village.

People do whatever they can to earn a living. They may work as household servants, shoe shiners, or vendors on busy downtown streets. No matter how hard life is for these Mexicans, the family continues to be a source of strength.

Middle-class families in the city lead very different lives. Many live in modern houses in the suburbs. Both men and women may hold jobs outside the home. They may work in offices in government and business, or they may be professional people such as doctors, lawyers, and teachers. Some even own their own small businesses. Many women in this class are well educated. They tend to be more outgoing and independent than women in the villages. In some middle-class households, children go to private schools, and there are servants who live with the family.

In the cities Mexicans use many U.S. products. They enjoy fast food, rock music, U.S. films, and even baseball. Those that can

afford it dress in styles that are popular in the United States.

The Largest City in the World

The rapid growth of cities has caused big problems in Mexico, especially in the capital. Mexico City has a population of around 20 million, and it is growing very fast. You can compare it with other large cities in the Minipedia on page 664.

Because Mexico City is surrounded by mountains, pollution from about 30,000 factories and three million motor vehicles hovers overhead. When the pollution level is too high, the government closes schools, limits driving, and closes some factories until the air clears.

In spite of its problems, Mexico City is an exciting place. Glass skyscrapers and fancy hotels, fashion shops and restaurants line its wide streets. Mexico City's university, founded in 1551, is the second oldest in North America. Historic churches, splendid museums, and theaters provide a rich cultural life. Find some of these places in the Map and Globe Handbook on page G3. You will also see that the city is dotted with plazas and parks. ■

Folk Traditions

Even as Mexico modernizes, its heart and soul stay linked to its cultural traditions. Religious and historic celebrations and traditional arts express the deepest feelings of Mexican people.

Food, Music, and Dance

As you read earlier, Mexicans love fiestas. At these lively gatherings, there is usually plenty of good food, music, and dance that have their own ancient traditions. One traditional fiesta food is *mole (MOH lay)* sauce. It is made from hot chilies and chocolate and is often served with turkey.

Dances are an important part of most festivals. Some, like the *quetzal* dance—also called the Bird Dance—are reminders of Aztec rituals. Huge, feathered headdresses make the dancers appear to be twice their height. Other dances tell stories from the time of the Spanish conquest. Dancers wear masks to play the roles of saints, heroes, or animals.

Musicians accompany the dances. Sometimes they play the *concha*, a stringed instrument made from the shell of an armadillo. Trumpets, drums, rattles, and flutes are also used. Then there are the famous *mariachi* bands. These musicians wear big *sombreros* (hats) and dark suits with silver trim. A young man might hire a *mariachi* band to play for his favorite woman friend.

Folk Art

Mexico's folk art remains deeply rooted in its Spanish and Indian traditions. Each region, and often each village, has its own specialty.

Some folk artists make practical items such as clay bowls, colorful woven rugs and shawls, and cotton embroidered clothing. Patterns used to decorate these are often old Indian designs.

Other craftworkers make religious objects such as carved masks and figures of saints. Still others make toys, games, or perhaps figures of playful skeletons or devils. Each feast day has its own traditional candies or baked goods. You can see some of these in A Closer Look, Día de los Muertos, on page 592. Papier-mâché figures and puppets also change with the seasons. Huge puppets are sold around Easter. They are made to be destroyed by fireworks or burnt on the streets the day before Easter. ■

◄ *The jaguar mask worn by this boy goes back to an Aztec jaguar-warrior tradition.*

■ *How do fiestas and folk art link Mexicans to their culture?*

Día de los Muertos

Many Mexicans honor their ancestors on November 1, All Saints' Day, and November 2, All Souls' Day or the Day of the Dead. This is a happy event. In many places All Saints' Day is spent at home honoring children who have died and are believed to have become saints. Families prepare the favorite foods and drinks of their ancestors. They decorate tables with flowers and candles. In the evening they bring the food and decorations to the graves of their ancestors. The souls of the dead are believed to enjoy the pleasures of life again. The celebration usually continues into the following day, the Day of the Dead.

This ancient tradition is celebrated differently from region to region. In some communities, the people decorate their churches.

Sugar treats, fruits, tamales, special breads, and other foods are offered for souls to savor.

The Aztecs considered marigolds the favorite flowers of the dead. Here the flowers are displayed to guide souls to their feasts.

Public Life

As Mexico faces the 21st century, changes are being made in government and trade. These offer great promise.

Mexican Government

For the past 10 years, Mexicans have struggled through hard economic times. Many citizens have asked for reforms.

Since 1929 every Mexican president and state governor has been a member of the Institutional Revolutionary Party, or PRI. A change came in 1988. For the first time, candidates other than those of the PRI had a chance of winning. Carlos Salinas de Gortari, the PRI candidate, had a difficult fight to win the presidency. Two other political parties won many seats in the congress.

Mexico and the World

During this century Mexico has developed strong economic ties with the United States. It has become Mexico's biggest trading partner and a major source of loans. Some Mexicans feel that their country has become too dependent on the United States.

In Latin America, however, Mexico has acted on its own. In the mid-1980s, it presented a peace plan for war-torn Central America.

Mexico suggested ways to settle conflicts between Central American countries and the United States.

Balancing independence and economic needs remains a challenge for the people of Mexico. This is especially true of the North American Free Trade Agreement that President Salinas strongly supports. In a **trade agreement,** different countries agree on rules about exchanging goods. According to the new trade agreement, goods and money will move freely among Mexico, the United States, and Canada. Those who favor the agreement hope that many Mexican workers will find work at home instead of having to emigrate to the United States. ■

▲ *In October 1992 the North American Free Trade Agreement was signed. The representatives of each signing nation (from left to right, standing at lecterns) were President Carlos Salinas of Mexico, President George Bush of the United States, and Prime Minister Brian Mulroney of Canada.*

■ *How is Mexico both dependent on and independent of the United States?*

R E V I E W

1. **FOCUS** How does Mexico blend traditional and modern ways?
2. **CULTURE** How does modern tourism help keep Indian and Spanish traditions alive?
3. **CULTURE** Why are fiestas and folk art very important to Mexican culture?
4. **CRITICAL THINKING** How do you think the North American Free Trade Agreement will affect Mexico's relations with the United States and Canada? Give reasons for your opinion.
5. **ACTIVITY** Imagine you are preparing a fiesta for a holiday such as Thanksgiving, the Fourth of July, or some other holiday of your choice. What food, costumes, masks, music, or rituals might you use? How would these remind you and your friends of the traditions of this special day?

593

Chapter Review

Reviewing Key Terms

border (p. 586)
conquistador (p. 578)
fiesta (p. 588)

hacienda (p. 579)
peon (p. 579)
trade agreement (p. 593)

A. Be sure you understand the meanings of the key terms. Use each of the words below in a sentence that gives a specific fact about Mexico.
1. conquistador
2. peon
3. border
4. trade agreement

B. Write whether each of the following statements is *true* or *false*. Then rewrite the false statements to make them true.
1. Baskets and clay pottery were used to decorate large rooms in the hacienda.
2. The United States, Mexico, and Canada agreed to limit the size of their armed forces in a recent trade agreement.
3. A border between two nations can be a cultural, economic, or physical barrier that separates them.
4. Fiestas are held throughout Mexico on Independence Day.
5. The peons owned enormous farms where they grew cotton, tobacco, and a variety of vegetables.

Exploring Concepts

A. Mexico and the United States are separated by different kinds of borders. Three types of borders are listed on the following chart. Copy and complete the chart. List at least two examples of each kind of border that separates Mexico and the United States.

Types of Borders	Characteristics
Cultural	
Economic	
Physical	

B. Answer each question with information from the chapter.
1. What happened to Tenochtitlan after the arrival of the Spaniards?
2. Why did the Spaniards form haciendas?
3. Why did some Indians come to accept Christianity?
4. Who did Mexico fight in the 1800s?
5. What territories did Mexico lose to the United States in 1848?
6. In what ways did Porfirio Díaz improve Mexico as a nation? How did he hurt Mexico?
7. What changes did Lázaro Cárdenas make in Mexico after he became the nation's president?
8. What are the greatest assets of Mexico today?
9. Why do U.S. businesses open manufacturing plants in Mexico?
10. Why did Mexico find itself in economic trouble in the early 1980s?
11. What role does the institution of the family play in Mexico?
12. What is the most important influence on the lives of Mexico's villagers?
13. What effect has Mexico's growing population had on the nation?
14. Why is air pollution a major problem in Mexico City?

Reviewing Skills

1. Find a photograph of an artifact from Mexico's colonial period. For sources look in an encyclopedia or in books on Mexico's history at your local library. Study the artifact carefully. Then write a paragraph describing the artifact. Tell what it looks like, what it is made of, where it was found, how it was used, and why it was used in this way.

2. Find Mexico on the political map of the world on page 372 of your text. Then find Mexico on the cartogram of world petroleum resources on page 373. How do the United States, Canada, and Brazil compare with Mexico in terms of actual size? How do they compare with Mexico in terms of petroleum resources?

3. Imagine you are a naturalist studying the armadillo. What information about this animal would you need in order to pinpoint areas in Mexico where the animal could be found? What type of map would be most useful to you?

Using Critical Thinking

1. After the conquest of Tenochtitlan, how were the Spaniards able to extend their control over the peoples living in the rest of Mexico?

2. Throughout Mexico's history, governmental policies concerning foreign investment have frequently changed. Describe some of these changes.

3. Today government policies favor large farms that contain Mexico's best land. By contrast, the *ejidos* given to the Indians are often small, dry pieces of land. What has been the effect of these policies? Do you think the government should continue to favor large farms? Why or why not?

4. In his office, President Carlos Salinas de Gortari displays only two figures from Mexico's past. One is a painting of Benito Juárez and the other is a bronze statue of Emiliano Zapata. What do you think these choices reveal about Salinas?

5. Each year more and more families leave the countryside to seek jobs in urban areas. Today, about 70 percent of all Mexicans live in the cities. What effect has this shift in population had on Mexico? How do you think this trend will affect the future of Mexico?

Preparing for Citizenship

1. **WRITING ACTIVITY** Imagine you are a Mexican whose business failed when the Mexican Miracle fell apart. Write a letter to a friend describing what has happened to your country. Who do you blame for the decline of the economy? How can Mexico recover?

2. **INTERVIEWING** The North American Free Trade Agreement has stirred debate in the United States between those who favor the treaty and those who oppose it. Interview one or two adults in your community to discover how they feel about the agreement. Report your findings to the class.

3. **ARTS ACTIVITY** Tourism is an important part of Mexico's economy. Create a travel poster that encourages people to vacation in Mexico. What is there to do? What places should people visit? Be prepared to present your poster to the class.

4. **GROUP ACTIVITY** Benito Juárez has often been compared to Abraham Lincoln. With a classmate, find out more about Juárez. Compare the lives of these two leaders.

5. **COLLABORATIVE LEARNING** Mexicans have many fiestas. In small groups, plan a Mexican-style fiesta. Have one group prepare some traditional Mexican dishes. Have another group research Mexican music and dances to play and perform. Have another group design and make costumes and masks.

Chapter 26
Canada

Like a chilly giant, Canada sprawls across the top of North America. Canada's massive land area stretches from the Pacific coast to the Atlantic coast, and extends to the Arctic. Its landforms include lofty mountain ranges, fertile plains, and frozen tundra. Only about one-fifth of this huge nation has been settled. Immigrants from many nations have joined the Native Americans living there to create Canada's cultural pattern.

The bright red maple leaf, part of Canada's flag and its national symbol, is painted on barn doors in Saskatchewan.

A portion of a map drawn in 1655 shows part of the east coast of North America. From what is now Massachusetts, the coast stretches northward into Canada.

1497 Giovanni Caboto (John Cabot) claims Newfoundland for England.

| 1300 | 1400 | 1500 | 1600 |

1400

1608 Samuel de Champlain establishes the first permanent French settlement.

These colorful fabrics represent a few of the many cultures present in Canada. From left to right are typical patterns of Scotland, India, the West Indies, and Asia.

The beautiful coastline of Cape Breton in Nova Scotia remains much as it appeared to the first European explorers.

The Inuit people of Canada, including this mother and child, will have their own official territory in 1999.

1992 The Canadian government and Canadian citizens agree to the plan for the Nunavut Territory.

| 1700 | 1800 | 1900 | 2000 |

1756–1763 The Seven Years' War is fought between Great Britain and France. Great Britain is the victor.

Today

LESSON 1

Geography and Native Peoples

THINKING
FOCUS

What are the geographic regions of Canada, and how did its early native peoples adapt to each region?

*T*he air was fresh and crisp, and little smoke-blue mists curled through the valleys and floated off from the hills. Sometimes the road went through woods where maples were beginning to hang out scarlet banners; . . . sometimes it wound along a harbor shore and passed by a little cluster of weather-gray fishing huts . . .

L. M. Montgomery, *Anne of Green Gables*

These words of a Canadian author describe autumn on Prince Edward Island, a province of Canada. Canada is the world's second largest nation—covering about seven percent of the earth's surface. Each region has its own features and natural beauty.

Canada's Regions, Climate, and Resources

Canada's political regions are made up of two northern territories and ten provinces to the south.

On the Atlantic coast are the four Atlantic Provinces, or the Maritimes: Nova Scotia, New Brunswick, Prince Edward Island, and Newfoundland. Long ago, moving glaciers there ground out rocky islands and peninsulas. Resources of these provinces include rich Atlantic Ocean fishing grounds,

Key Term

• permafrost

▼ *The majestic Canadian Rockies in Alberta (below) and the golden wheat fields of the Saskatchewan prairies (right) display some of the varied beauty of Canada.*

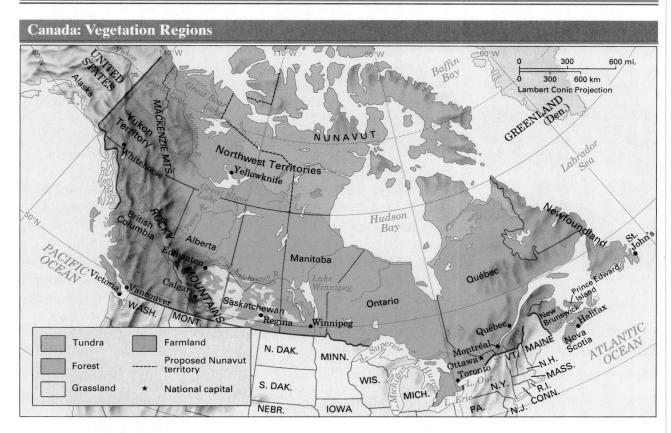

Tundra

Forest

Grassland

Farmland

Proposed Nunavut territory

★ National capital

Lambert Conic Projection

dense forests that are an important source of pulpwood for paper, and abundant iron and coal.

West of the Maritimes are the St. Lawrence River and Great Lakes lowlands, the southern parts of the provinces of Ontario and Quebec. The St. Lawrence River flows from Lake Ontario to the Atlantic Ocean. This southern, warmer region of Canada is the most populated.

Ontario and Quebec stretch north to the remote shores of chilly Hudson Bay. Here ancient glaciers shaped the Canadian Shield, a vast wilderness plateau filled with thick forests, fast-flowing rivers, glacial lakes, and rich deposits of gold, silver, and copper. The shield curves around Hudson Bay and into Newfoundland and the Northwest Territories.

The flat grasslands of the Great Plains are west of the shield. Here lie the Prairie Provinces of Manitoba, Saskatchewan, and Alberta. Spring rains and dry autumns have helped make this region a major producer of wheat and other grains. Resources include large amounts of oil and natural gas.

West of the plains rise the Rocky Mountains, part of the eastern border of the province of British Columbia. The Coast Mountains lie along Canada's western border near the Pacific Ocean. Here warm, moist air makes the climate mild. Between the mountain ranges are wide valleys with forests, orchards, and vineyards.

The Northwest Territories and the Yukon Territory lie farthest north. They cover 40 percent of Canada's total area. Chilled by the arctic winds, most of the area has **permafrost**; all the soil, except the top few feet, is permanently frozen. Summers are cool and brief; winter is long, dark, and icy. ■

▲ *This map of Canada shows the provinces and territories, including a proposed territory called Nunavut. Which provinces have most of Canada's farmland?*

How Do We Know?

HISTORY *We know that ancient moving glaciers formed much of the geography of Canada through the study of glacial geology. By analyzing the age, types, and layers of rock and land formations, scientists can recreate the movement of glaciers that melted years ago.*

■ *How do the landforms and climate of Canada's regions differ?*

599

The Native Peoples of Canada

Native peoples already living in Canada when Europeans arrived include the Haida *(HY duh)* and the Tsimshian *(CHIM shee uhn)* of Canada's Pacific coast. When the English explorer, James Cook, arrived there in the late 1780s he noted that these people were "ingenious sculptors." From cedar trees they built longhouses. They also made 70-foot dugout canoes for hunting whales and seals and carved tall, beautiful, wooden totem poles.

The Algonquin were hunters, so they did not build permanent settlements. Instead, they moved through the northern forests, following moose, herds of caribou, and other animals.

In contrast, the Iroquois *(IHR uh kwoy)* were farmers. They built permanent farming villages along the St. Lawrence River and lower Great Lakes. Many of their villages united with other Native Americans to form the League of the Five Nations. Each member nation sent a representative to a council that decided issues by voting.

The Assiniboine *(uh SIHN uh boyn)*, Blood, Cree, and Ojibwa *(oh JIHB way)* hunted the buffalo that roamed the Great Plains of Canada. From the buffalo they obtained food and clothing, as well as materials for shelters and weapons.

The ancestors of the Inuit *(IHN yoo iht)* probably first arrived in Canada about 1,000 years ago. Some lived in ice houses, or igloos, but most lived in homes of matted soil called sod. They hunted whales and seals for food and clothes and made tools from the animals' bones.

Native peoples thrived for thousands of years in Canada. Yet, their lives changed drastically when Europeans sailed to their shores. ■

▲ *Inuit children expect to have their own territory, Nunavut, in 1999.*

➤ *Restored totem poles carved by native peoples of Canada's northwest stand in Stanley Park in Vancouver.*

■ *Describe the way of life of three Native American groups in Canada before Europeans arrived.*

R E V I E W

1. **FOCUS** What are the geographic regions of Canada, and how did its early native peoples adapt to each region?

2. **GEOGRAPHY** Refer to the map of Canada on page 599. Why do you think most Canadians live in the St. Lawrence and Great Lakes lowlands?

3. **GEOGRAPHY** Look at the map of North America in the Atlas on page 686. Compare the overall physical geography of Canada with that of the United States.

4. **CRITICAL THINKING** The European explorers took the name Canada from the Native American word *kanata*, which means "settlement." Why might they have chosen that name?

5. **WRITING ACTIVITY** The sacred tales of Native Americans explained their world. Choose a natural event such as a rainstorm. Write a myth using animal characters that explains the natural event.

L E S S O N 2

History of Canada

Imagine that the year is 1536 and you are a Native American living along the St. Lawrence River. Your people have met a man called Jacques Cartier (ZHAHK kahr tee AY) who has come with ships and men from France. All of these strangers want to reach a place called China.

You have shown Cartier and his crew your homes and villages. You have filled their longboats with loaves of bread made from corn. You have welcomed them to your hearths and treated them to feasts of beans, soup, fish, and broiled meat. You have shown them where to fish and hunt. Still, they ask if your rivers lead west to another land of riches.

THINKING
F O C U S

How have France and Britain influenced the history of Canada?

Britain and France Vie for Power

Before Cartier, Giovanni Caboto—called John Cabot by the English—had sailed across the Atlantic. He reached Canada in 1497. Yet neither man ever found an ocean route west to Asia and its riches of silks and spices.

However, they did find other riches—a wealth of fish and furs to sell to Europeans and a beautiful land. Cabot claimed Newfoundland for England; Cartier claimed lands around what is now called the St. Lawrence River for France. On this river in 1608 Samuel de Champlain established the first permanent French settlement in Canada. The French named the settlement Quebec, from an Algonquin word meaning "narrowing of waters."

By the mid-1700s, France had claimed about half of Canada and the Mississippi River valley. Britain had established colonies along the Atlantic coast. In 1756 fierce competition for lands and profitable trade finally led to the Seven Years' War. In North America that war is called the French and Indian War.

Both England and France received help from Native Americans during the war. They taught the French new fighting strategies.

Key Terms

- confederation
- dominion

▼ The Death of General Wolfe *by Benjamin West shows the British commander dying during the successful British battle for Quebec in 1759.*

However, many Native Americans fought at the side of the British.

In 1758 the British won a key battle when they defeated the French with the siege of Louisburg. From then on, British victories increased. In 1763 the British won the war. In defeat, the French gave up control of Canada and nearly all of North America east of the Mississippi River.

In 1774, to avoid possible revolt, the British agreed to let the French people of Quebec keep their civil laws, religion, and customs. Then, after the American Revolution broke out in 1775, thousands of Loyalists—colonists loyal to Britain—fled from the American colonies to Quebec. Although they wanted British rule, they did not want to live according to French laws and customs. Thus, in 1791, the British split Quebec into Upper Canada and Lower Canada. Most British Loyalists lived in Upper Canada—today, the province of Ontario. Most French Canadians lived in Lower Canada—today, the province of Quebec. ■

■ *How did Britain become the dominant power in Canada?*

Westward Expansion and Immigration

▼ *Below is a portrait of the famed Canadian explorer Alexander Mackenzie. Trace his routes in 1789 and 1793 on the map to the right. Locate the Mackenzie River. Why did he first name it the River of Disappointment?*

Much of Britain's huge new territory remained uncharted. The task of exploring and mapping it fell to the "Nor'Westers," explorers and fur traders from the North West Company. They were greatly helped by Native American guides.

"From Sea to Sea"

"Thus I have fully completed the survey of this part of North America from sea to sea," wrote David Thompson in 1811, "and . . . have determined the positions of the Mountains, Lakes and Rivers, and other remarkable places. . . ."

More than any other early surveyor and mapmaker, Thompson deserves credit for the first accurate map of western Canada. He took two years to complete it after many years of exploration.

Thompson was not the first Nor'Wester to venture into Canada's vast western lands. One of the most successful was Alexander Mackenzie. In 1789, almost 300 years after John Cabot had tried to find a route to Asia, Mackenzie set off to do the same. He was looking for an inland waterway to the Pacific Ocean.

For many weeks, he and his guides paddled canoes down an icy, unknown river. The land they passed through was frozen. Finally, they reached the ocean. However, it was filled with floating ice; obviously, it was not the Pacific.

Mackenzie's Explorations

Mackenzie's Explorations in:
→ 1789
→ 1793

Mackenzie had found a route to the Arctic Ocean. Still, Mackenzie was determined to find an inland waterway to the Pacific Ocean. The feat would gain him fame and a large reward offered by the British Parliament.

So, in 1793, he set off on a different route west. This time he traveled in a 25-foot canoe with French explorers, Native American guides, and a dog. The river took them to the Rocky Mountains. They scaled the steep river banks on foot, carrying the canoe and all their supplies. Then Native Americans they met told them which river would lead to the Pacific.

After weeks of dangerous passage through raging waters, they finally reached the Pacific Ocean. Mackenzie had become the first European in the far north to reach the Pacific Ocean by inland waterway.

Others followed Mackenzie's route, and Thompson would eventually map the western wilderness. These explorers opened the way for Canada's westward expansion and settlement.

Expansion and Unity

By 1821, there were six colonies in Canada—Newfoundland, Prince Edward Island, New Brunswick, Nova Scotia, Upper Canada (now Ontario), and Lower Canada (now Quebec). In the 1830s the British government considered uniting the colonies. Later, Canadians drew up plans for a **confederation**—a unified state in which power is shared between

the national and local governments. Fears of U.S. expansion convinced many that confederation was necessary.

On July 1, 1867, many Canadians celebrated when the confederation became a reality. The provinces of New Brunswick and present-day Ontario and Quebec had voted to unite to form the dominion of Canada. Nova Scotia also became part of the dominion. Becoming a **dominion** of Great Britain meant having self-rule. Canada was ruled by a governor general appointed by the British crown and a Parliament made up of the House of Commons and the Senate. In 1873 the dominion had grown to include Prince Edward Island, British Columbia, and Manitoba.

To keep law and order during westward

An Inuit husband and wife add information to a chart for the British explorer Captain John Ross aboard his ship in 1830.

The quadrant was an instrument used by the early European explorers to measure altitudes.

Immigrants in Canada in the late 1800s included a railroad crew of Chinese workers in British Columbia (left) and Russian women sorting grain on the prairies (right).

■ *How did exploration, expansion, and immigration cause Canada to spread "From Sea to Sea"?*

expansion, Canada created the North-West Mounted Police in 1873. Known today as the Royal Canadian Mounted Police, or "Mounties," this force of men and women continues its work.

The Immigration Boom

Before British Columbia would join the dominion in 1871, it insisted that a railroad be built to connect the nation from east to west. The government agreed. It encouraged people from other countries to help build the railroad

and to settle along its route.

Thousands of immigrants came. Canada's western plains promised rich farmland and natural resources. Meanwhile, the Canadian Pacific Railway promised work. People came from as far away as China to build the railroad. When it was completed in 1885, many of those workers stayed. Between 1900 and 1911, Canada's population increased by nearly two million. Many immigrants came from Britain, Russia, Germany, and India. Some settled in the Prairie Provinces to grow wheat and other crops. Others settled farther east in Ontario and the Maritime Provinces. They brought many new languages and religious traditions and added to Canada's cultural diversity. ■

From Dominion to Independence

Canadians had considerable power over the workings of their government. However, as a dominion of Britain, they could not enjoy total independence.

Many English-speaking Canadians felt closely connected to Great Britain. For example, when Britain went to war in South Africa in 1899, some English speakers demanded involvement in the fight. French speakers, on the other hand, were against participation. In a compromise, Canadian volunteers served under British command in that war. Yet French Canadians continued to resent many aspects of British control of their lives.

Steps to Independence

World War I erupted in 1914. Hundreds of thousands of Canadians volunteered to fight. At first they fought under British command. Then, in 1917, a Canadian officer took command of Canadian forces. These units became the first truly independent Canadian groups in the eyes of the world. Following the war, Canada signed the peace treaty and joined the newly formed League of Nations, another move toward independence.

In 1931 Great Britain agreed to cut another major tie. With the Statute of Westminster, Britain declared Canada an independent nation, but kept control over the amendment process of the Canadian constitution.

Canada fought with the Allies in World War II. In 1949, Canada joined the North Atlantic Treaty Organization (NATO). In 1982, Britain completed the final step of Canada's peaceful transition to total independence. It gave up its power to change or influence the Canadian constitution in any way.

British Influence Today

Today Canada is a politically independent nation. However, many effects of British rule remain.

In many ways Britain's influence has served Canada as the wise advice of a favorite teacher might serve a student. The Canadian government is based on the British parliamentary system. The laws of Canada, like those of the United States, are based firmly on the principles of British law. The province of Quebec is the exception, with a legal system based on its French origins.

On its dollar bills, Canada continues to print the picture of the ruling king or queen of Britain and Canada. Yet the legacy and influence of Britain does not rest well with all Canadians. As you will read in the next lesson, sharp tensions continue to separate many English-speaking citizens from French-speaking citizens. Groups of native peoples are also seeking new rights. ■

▼ *The image of Britain's Queen Elizabeth II appears on many Canadian coins and bills. Although she is Canada's queen, she does not govern Canada.*

◄ *On July 1, 1967, Canadians celebrated the hundredth anniversary of the creation of the dominion of Canada.*

■ *What were the major steps that led to Canadian independence from Britain?*

R E V I E W

1. **FOCUS** How have France and Britain influenced the history of Canada?
2. **GEOGRAPHY** Why was it important to the people of British Columbia that Canada build a transcontinental railroad?
3. **HISTORY** How did the building of the railway contribute to the diversity of Canada's population?
4. **CRITICAL THINKING** How might the history of Canada have been different if the French had won the Seven Years' War instead of the British?
5. **WRITING ACTIVITY** Imagine that you are Alexander Mackenzie on his first trek, which would lead to the Arctic Ocean. Write three diary entries describing his experiences and feelings. The first entry is for June 3, 1789, just before Mackenzie sets off. The second is on July 12, 1789, when ice is spotted. The final entry is on September 13, 1789, a day after Mackenzie has returned to his camp.

Reading a Process Diagram

Here's Why

The St. Lawrence Seaway is a very important transportation route for both Canada and the United States. It is a 2,350-mile inland route that makes it possible for ocean-going vessels to travel from the Atlantic Ocean to the Great Lakes and into the heart of Canada.

Look at the diagram on this page. It is a process diagram. A process diagram usually uses pictures to explain the steps of an entire process more clearly. For example, instructions for assembling a bike are likely to include a process diagram.

A process diagram can help you understand how the St. Lawrence Seaway works. Much of the waterway depends on locks that raise and lower ocean-going vessels so they can travel from one body of water to another.

Here's How

Now look at the process diagram more carefully. The numbers tell you how to follow each part of the diagram. For example, the first part of the diagram shows the ship entering the lock from the higher level.

The second part of the diagram shows that after the gates have been shut, water is let out of the lock through openings. What are these openings called?

In the third part of the diagram, you see that as the water passes to the lower level, the water level and the ship are lowered. Now look at the fourth part of the diagram. When are the gates to the lock finally opened?

Try It

See if you can use the diagram to write a paragraph that explains why the gates to the lower channel aren't opened after the vessel first enters the lock.

Apply It

Find a process diagram in your science textbook or another source. Explain each step of the diagram.

How a Lock Works

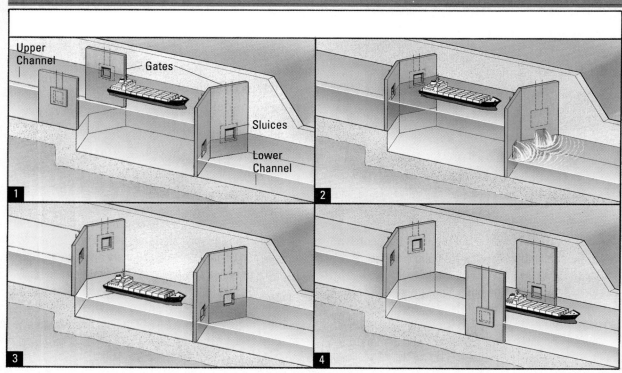

L E S S O N   3

Canada Today

O Canada! Our home and
native land!
True patriot love in all thy sons
command.
With glowing hearts we see
thee rise,
The True North strong and free!
From far and wide, O Canada,
We stand on guard for thee.

These lines from Canada's national anthem express the pride and commitment its peoples of many different cultures feel for their "home and native land." Modern Canada is indeed a multicultural nation. In fact, Canadians were among the earliest users of the term **multicultural**, which means "of many cultures."

THINKING FOCUS

What factors make modern Canada a prosperous, multicultural nation?

A Multicultural, Bilingual, Urban Nation

In 1991 there were more than 27 million people living in Canada. Of these, about 60 percent are English-speaking and about 24 percent are French-speaking. About 20 percent have other international roots. Native peoples including the Inuit make up about 1.5 percent of Canada's total population.

A Cultural Quilt

Canada's many ethnic groups are like the pieces of a patchwork quilt. Instead of blending,

separate pieces combine to make one nation.

For example, most people in Newfoundland are of British heritage, while most people in the province of Quebec are of French heritage. Saskatchewan has Ukrainian, French, German, and many other ethnic communities. A large community of Asian people lives in British Columbia.

Cultural identity and pride are, of course, important to each group.

Key Terms

- multicultural
- bilingual
- separatism

◄ *Members of the Parti Québecois rally to gain support for a separate Quebec. The* fleur-de-lis *painted on the woman's face (far left) is a symbol of French culture.*

607

Canada

▼ Caribana *is a joyous two-week Caribbean festival enjoyed by the people of Toronto. It boasts a parade with elaborate, colorful costumes.*

Canada's government has tried to help by supporting all cultures. The Multiculturalism Act of 1988 states that every citizen, regardless of origin, has equal rights.

People speak several languages in Canada. Canada's constitution states that it is a **bilingual** nation. That is, it has two official languages, English and French. Many Canadians are bilingual, speaking two languages with ease.

The discontent of Quebec's French Canadians with English-speaking influence led to the growth of separatism in the 1960s. Supporters of **separatism** believe that if French Canadian culture is to survive, Quebec must become an independent nation. A separatist party called Parti Québecois *(pahr TEE keh beh KWAH)* came to power in Quebec in 1976. Then a new law made French the only official language of the province.

The Quebec separatists want independence. In 1992 the federal government, led by Prime Minister Brian Mulroney, proposed a constitutional reform to persuade Quebec to remain part of Canada. The reform, called the Charlottetown Agreement, proposed special rights to Quebec as a "distinct society" within the nation. For many complex reasons, the voters defeated it.

In general, the separatists voted no because they want nothing less than total independence for Quebec. Other Canadians felt that one province should not have special rights that others do not have. Thus the struggle over Quebec's status continues.

The Inuit are native people who have long struggled to preserve their cultural heritage. Today thousands of Inuit live in northern Canada. They have been working to regain land that they believe was always theirs. In 1992 the citizens of the Northwest Territories voted to split that region into two parts. The new part shown on the map on page 599 will become official in 1999. It will be called Nunavut Territory. In Inuit the word *nunavut* means "our land."

Urban Life: Toronto

About 75 percent of all Canadians live in cities and towns, and about 80 percent live within 200 miles of the U.S. border. This southern region is one of the warmer parts of the nation. Toronto, the capital of Ontario, is Canada's largest city. Its location on the St. Lawrence Seaway makes it one of the nation's busiest ports.

In the 1880s the completion of Canada's transcontinental railway system linked the port of Toronto with Canada's timber and mining regions. This link added to the city's industrial growth. Later, its closeness to Detroit, the U.S. car manufacturing center, created an even greater boom in industrial growth.

Toronto is one of the most ethnically diverse cities in the world. More than 80 ethnic groups live there, and approximately 100 languages are spoken. ■

■ *Why can Canada be described as a "cultural quilt"?*

Canada's Achievements

The United Nations has singled out Canada as the world's best place to live based on the education, life expectancy, and income of Canadians. Canadian women live an average of 80 years; men live an average of 73 years.

What other factors make Canada such a great place to live? Some of these include thriving industries, high-quality education, a national health care system, and a wealth of artistic attractions.

Industry

Canada's economy today reflects its urban character. Service industries, including health care, education, and tourism, employ about 72 percent of Canada's workers. Manufacturing, mining, and agriculture follow, with only about 5 percent of the work force employed in agricultural jobs. Canada's major industrial region includes the St. Lawrence River and Great Lakes lowlands.

Canada's economy is strong. It ranks among the top 10 nations in terms of its gross national product (GNP). As you read in Chapter 16, gross national product is the total market value of all goods and services produced yearly by a nation. One reason that Canada's GNP is so high is that the nation has a wealth of natural resources. For example, Canada's natural gas, uranium, crude oil, timber, and coal are purchased by many nations. In fact, the United States buys about 90 percent of Canada's heavy crude oil.

Along with oil and natural gas, Canada has an abundant supply of other energy sources, such as uranium and hydroelectric power. Energy is Canada's second most important export, following cars.

Education and Health

Canada's system of free public schools is similar to that of the United States. Children go to kindergarten and proceed through the system until they graduate from high school.

Across Time & Space

Something that unifies Canadians is their most popular sport—ice hockey. It probably began as a blend of field hockey, a British game, and kolf, a Dutch game played on ice. In 1893 the Canadian governor general, Lord Stanley, donated a silver bowl—the Stanley Cup—for the winners of an annual hockey tournament.

▼ The bustling port city of Toronto takes its name from a Huron word meaning "meeting place." Today it is a center of culture, trade, and industry.

A federal law guarantees all Canadians free health care, funded by federal and provincial taxes. Each province has established its own specific laws regarding the medical services that are available. For example, the province of Quebec extends coverage to include children's dental care.

Founded in 1938, the Royal Winnipeg Ballet is the oldest ballet company in Canada. Other famed cultural attractions include the Canadian Opera Company and the Montreal Symphony Orchestra.

Each province in Canada has the authority to run its public schools. This system allows each region to shape its schools to the specific needs of its multicultural population. Many schools have students from 20 or more different ethnic or cultural groups.

To aid students from different cultures, some Canadian schools have had the Heritage Language Program in use for more than 20 years. Students who wish to learn a language other than English or French can choose from about 60 other languages.

In some provinces teachers in the public schools are allowed to take a year off from teaching every four years. This enables teachers to pursue further training.

Canada also has many excellent public and private trade schools, colleges, and universities. McGill University and the University of Toronto are two examples. The government supports these schools so that the fees students must pay are greatly reduced.

The Arts

Let there be room for magic, room for hope, and room for the imagination.

Paul-Émile Borduas,
French-Canadian painter

Canada has a rich tradition of artistic expression that began thousands of years ago. This unique art includes the towering totem poles of the native peoples of the northwest and the smooth, soapstone sculptures of the Inuit.

Many Canadians have achieved excellence as musicians, writers, and filmmakers. Some Canadian popular musicians who have gained worldwide fame include Anne Murray, Gordon Lightfoot, Neil Young, k. d. lang, and the bands Rush and Triumph. L. M. Montgomery, the author of *Anne of Green Gables* and its sequels, based these famous books on her own childhood on Prince Edward Island. Films produced by the National Film Board of Canada have won many awards. You can read about the art of animation in Canada's films in A Closer Look on page 611. ■

► *Unique Inuit sculptures are prized by many art collectors. This sculpture is of an Inuit woman holding a cutting tool called an* ulu.

■ *What are some of Canada's major achievements in industry, education, health care, and the arts?*

610

Canadian Animation

Many of Canada's animated films are world famous. Artists paint pictures on film cels, but they also use clay and other unusual materials. For many years, they have broken the rules of animation to invent new effects. To make an animated film, pictures, called cels, are repeated with slight changes, one after another. Run at the high speed of 24 frames per second, the changes blend into movement that looks real.

"A-crawlin' in your whiskers, a-crawlin' in your hair . . ." *Blackfly* pits a swarm of pesky flies against Canadian surveyors, and the flies win.

A comical moment from the award winning film *The Big Snit.*

Animator Wendy Tilby creates different textures by painting and scratching film cels.

From the Oscar winning film *The Sand Castle*

Canada's World Vision

Canada's foreign policy has always been one of cooperation and peace. Canada is a member of both the North Atlantic Treaty Organization (NATO) and the United Nations.

Domestic and Foreign Policy

Canada is the only nation in the world to have been involved in every international peacekeeping mission that the United Nations has undertaken. In 1992 Canada joined other nations in sending troops and food supplies to war-torn Somalia.

The Canadian government has sponsored many assistance programs for poor nations. Such programs bring money, food, medicine, agricultural supplies, and knowledge to nations all over the world.

Canada also has a history as a refuge—a place of safety—for people of other nations. Before the U.S. Civil War, Canadians welcomed many African American slaves who reached Canada, where they lived as free men and women. Canada has also welcomed many European and Caribbean immigrants fleeing war or political unrest. During the Vietnam War, Canada's door was open to many young people from the United States. These people came to Canada because they did not support U.S. policies in Vietnam.

Canada and the United States

Canada and the United States share the longest undefended border in the world. This 5,525-mile border stretches from the Atlantic

▼ *Strong domestic anti-pollution policy has reduced acid rain caused by Canadian industries. However, much of Canada's acid rain starts as air pollution blown across the border from U.S. industries.*

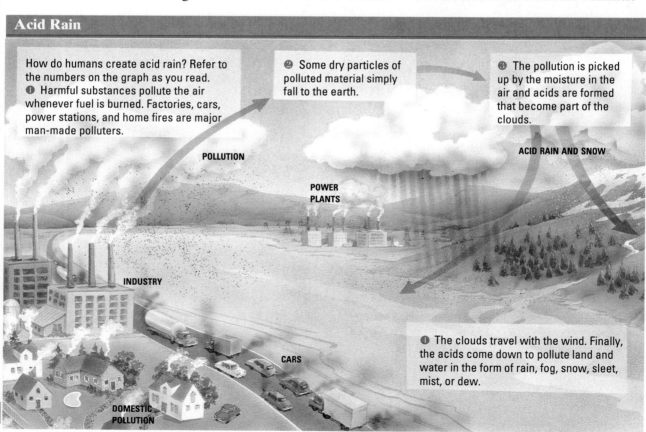

Acid Rain

How do humans create acid rain? Refer to the numbers on the graph as you read. ❶ Harmful substances pollute the air whenever fuel is burned. Factories, cars, power stations, and home fires are major man-made polluters.

❷ Some dry particles of polluted material simply fall to the earth.

❸ The pollution is picked up by the moisture in the air and acids are formed that become part of the clouds.

POLLUTION

POWER PLANTS

ACID RAIN AND SNOW

INDUSTRY

CARS

❹ The clouds travel with the wind. Finally, the acids come down to pollute land and water in the form of rain, fog, snow, sleet, mist, or dew.

DOMESTIC POLLUTION

Ocean and runs through the Great Lakes, which Canada shares with the United States. It then extends west to the Pacific Ocean and along the border of Alaska.

In the 1970s former Canadian prime minister Pierre Trudeau compared Canada's position in relation to the United States as that of "a mouse next to an elephant." Although Canada's world influence has grown, history has taught Canadians to view the United States with some caution. For example, during both the American Revolution and the War of 1812, the United States invaded Canadian soil to attempt to defeat British forces there.

Today, as neighbors and major trading partners, the United States and Canada work together. A Free Trade Agreement in effect since 1989 has enabled Canadian and U.S. exports to cross the border with reduced tariffs, or fees.

The two nations have also cooperated in trying to solve environmental concerns. Pollution of Canada's air and water has come from its own industrial plants and from the U.S. industrial plants across the border. One of the greatest problems is acid rain.

A 20-foot-wide path, called a vista, shows a portion of the boundary between Quebec, on the left, and Maine. This wintry scene is typical of the many miles of undefended border between Canada and the United States.

The diagram on page 612 explains how acid rain is created. Canada and the United States are working to solve the problem through environmental agreements and a commitment to find clean sources of energy.

In spite of neighborly agreements, Canada has no desire to be thought of as an extension of the United States. Although the nation shares many aspects of U.S. culture, Canada wants to keep its own separate identity. Canadians take pride in their independent nation. They have worked hard throughout their history to maintain a peaceful, prosperous "home and native land." ■

■ *What factors of Canada's foreign and domestic policy make it a "good neighbor" to people of other nations?*

R E V I E W

1. **FOCUS** What factors make modern Canada a prosperous, multicultural nation?
2. **POLITICAL SYSTEMS** Explain the change the French-speaking separatists of Quebec want in Canada's political system.
3. **CULTURE** How does life in Toronto provide an example of a multicultural society?
4. **CRITICAL THINKING** The relationship between Canada and the United States has sometimes been described as a "guarded friendship across an unguarded border." Explain what you think that phrase means.
5. **WRITING ACTIVITY** Canada has several programs designed to help its citizens learn and prosper. Two examples are the Heritage Language Program and the national health care policy. Write a letter to an imaginary Canadian penpal. Include questions you would like to have answered about each program.

Canada

Chapter Review

Reviewing Key Terms

bilingual (p. 608)
confederation (p. 603)
dominion (p. 603)

multicultural (p. 607)
permafrost (p. 599)
separatism (p. 608)

A. Answer the following questions regarding selected key terms.
1. What two types of government share the power in a <u>confederation</u>?
2. As a <u>dominion</u>, what was Canada's relationship with Great Britain?
3. What is the goal of the Canadian supporters of <u>separatism</u>? What root word in *separatism* provides a clue to the term's meaning?
4. What are the characteristics of land that has <u>permafrost</u>?

B. The prefix *bi-* means "two." The prefix *multi-* means "many." On your own paper, answer these questions.
1. What does the key term <u>bilingual</u> mean? What clue does the meaning of the prefix give you?
2. What does the key term <u>multicultural</u> mean? What clue does the meaning of the prefix give you?
3. What other words begin with the prefixes *bi-* and *multi-*? List as many words as you can that begin with these prefixes. What do the words mean?

Exploring Concepts

A. Copy the following chart, which lists the political regions of Canada. In the second column, write at least one historical or cultural fact about the region. One entry has been filled in for you.

Region	Historical or Cultural Fact
The Atlantic Provinces	
Ontario	
Québec	Many French-speaking people of Québec want to separate from the rest of Canada.
The Prairie Provinces	
British Columbia	
The Territories	

B. Support each of the following statements with information from the chapter.
1. Canada's Native Americans were helpful to early explorers and settlers.
2. The names of several locations in Canada come from languages spoken by its Native Americans.
3. Canada's motto, "From Sea to Sea," could accurately be changed to "From Sea to Sea to Sea."
4. Unlike many nations who struggled to become independent from their colonial governments, Canada's major steps toward independence were peaceful.
5. Many French-speaking Canadian citizens continue to struggle for independence from the rest of the nation.
6. Canada has worked hard to create laws and programs to benefit all Canadians.
7. Canada is one of the best places to live.
8. Other nations of the world might call Canada "a friendly giant."

Reviewing Skills

1. Study the process diagram on page 606. Then create a process diagram of your own. Use it to explain a simple process to a younger student. Choose something like how to tie a shoe, play a board or video game, make directional signals while riding a bike, or load a camera with film.

2. European explorers searched the rivers and ocean inlets of Canada, hoping to find a route leading west to Asia. Study the map of the world in the Atlas on pages 680–681. Where does that route exist? What types of modern ships might be able to use it? Why might the early explorers have found the route impossible to navigate?

3. Turn to page 602, and reread the account of Alexander Mackenzie's first attempt to find a route to the Pacific Ocean, in 1789. Imagine that you are with him, paddling along the river. Based on your knowledge of the features of the Arctic region, what assumptions would you make about where the river might lead? Support your assumptions with facts. Then summarize the advice you might give Mackenzie.

4. Using the map on page 599, draw an outline map of Canada that includes the provinces and territories. Fill in the major mountain ranges. Do research to find out where most of the people live in Canada today, and complete a population map. Use clusters of dots to show where people are living.

Using Critical Thinking

1. Look at the picture of the maple leaf on page 596. Why do you think the Canadians selected a maple leaf for their national symbol? Based on facts from your reading, what other symbols do you think they might have selected? Explain your answers.

2. Imagine that the Canadian Prime Minister has asked your advice on how to persuade Quebec to remain part of Canada. What ideas would you offer? Explain how your ideas might help solve the conflict.

3. Think about the fact that Canada, the world's second-largest nation, covers over 3.8 million square miles. In what ways does Canada's size, as well as other facts about Canada that you have read in the chapter, make unifying Canada so difficult?

Preparing for Citizenship

1. **COLLECTING INFORMATION** Use the *Readers' Guide to Periodical Literature* to locate current magazine articles about both sides of the separatist issue in Canada. Use this background information to make a list of supporting arguments for each position. Then predict what would result if Quebec separated from Canada.

2. **ARTS ACTIVITY** Make a travel poster to encourage tourists to visit Canada. Combine pictures and written material to emphasize what you consider Canada's most interesting attractions.

3. **COLLABORATIVE LEARNING** In a small group, create an exhibit that might appear at a Canadian multicultural fair. First, work together to select a specific ethnic group of Canadians, from early or current times. For example, you might pick the Inuit, the Iroquois, the Haida, the Algonquin, the British, the French, or the Chinese. Do research to find out about a specific feature of their ethnic culture, such as their foods, religious beliefs, and community values. Then plan and create your group's exhibit, combining pictures with written facts. Share your exhibit with your classmates. After viewing the exhibits, discuss this statement together: "A multicultural society is greater than the sum of its individual parts."

615

Chapter 27
From Many, One Nation

The United States is a land of great diversity—in its geography, its climate, its resources, and above all, its people. Wave after wave of immigrants from the world over have contributed to the growth and the culture of the nation. Today U.S. citizens confront a variety of problems: from discrimination to poverty to pollution. Many people believe that the United States can tackle these problems if citizens work together and help one another.

Starting in colonial times, women held quilting parties where they worked together to sew beautiful quilts like this one. In many families, quilts were passed down from generation to generation.

Millions of buffalo once roamed the Great Plains. Many Native Americans counted on buffalo as a source of food, clothing, and shelter.

| 1375 | 1500 | 1625 |

1400

1565 Spain establishes St. Augustine, Florida, the first permanent European settlement in what is now the United States.

This painted tray from the early 1800s shows Lemuel Haynes, a Revolutionary War hero and a free black preacher.

In pioneer days, wagon trains gathered in St. Louis before making the long journey west. Today the St. Louis Arch marks the "gateway to the west."

Several days of celebration marked the inauguration of Bill Clinton as President of the United States in January 1993. Here Clinton and a crowd of young people walk across the Memorial Bridge in Washington, D. C.

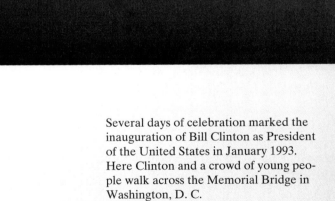

1750

1875

2000

1783 The United States wins its independence from Great Britain.

1964 The Civil Rights Act outlaws racial discrimination in jobs and public places.

Today

617

Land of Diversity

**THINKING
F O C U S**

How have people used the land and the resources of the United States?

Key Term

• conservation

➤ *Native Americans of the Pacific Northwest held many ceremonies to celebrate the resources of their region. The mask shown here was worn by a singer during ceremonies.*

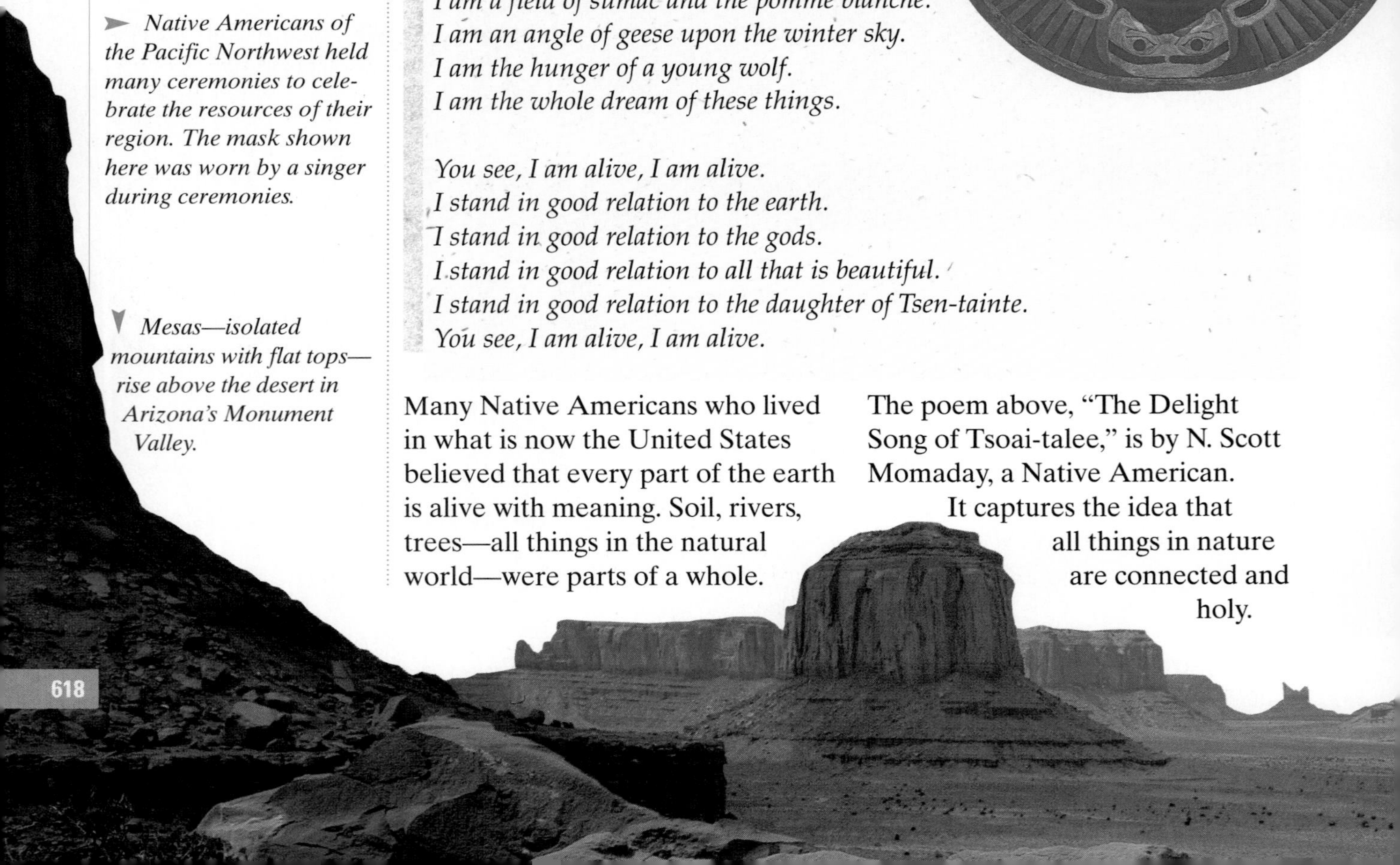

▼ *Mesas—isolated mountains with flat tops—rise above the desert in Arizona's Monument Valley.*

I am a feather in the bright sky.
I am the blue horse that runs in the plain.
I am the fish that rolls, shining, in the water.
I am the shadow that follows a child.
I am the evening light, the lustre of meadows.
I am an eagle playing with the wind.
I am a cluster of bright beads.
I am the farthest star.
I am the cold of the dawn.
I am the roaring of the rain.
I am the glitter on the crust of the snow.
I am the long track of the moon in a lake.
I am a flame of four colors.
I am a deer standing away in the dusk.
I am a field of sumac and the pomme blanche.
I am an angle of geese upon the winter sky.
I am the hunger of a young wolf.
I am the whole dream of these things.

You see, I am alive, I am alive.
I stand in good relation to the earth.
I stand in good relation to the gods.
I stand in good relation to all that is beautiful.
I stand in good relation to the daughter of Tsen-tainte.
You see, I am alive, I am alive.

Many Native Americans who lived in what is now the United States believed that every part of the earth is alive with meaning. Soil, rivers, trees—all things in the natural world—were parts of a whole.

The poem above, "The Delight Song of Tsoai-talee," is by N. Scott Momaday, a Native American. It captures the idea that all things in nature are connected and holy.

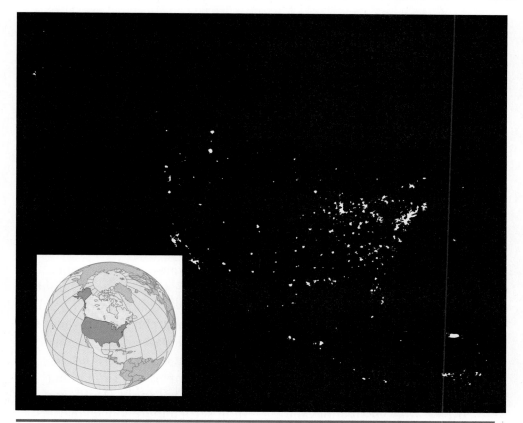

◄ White areas on this satellite map of the United States show population concentration by light use at night. Which side of the country shows the most light, east or west?

A Varied Land

Since the early days of U.S. history, the land has changed forever. Yet it is still a vast and beautiful country.

As you read in Chapter 2, the United States is divided into six regions. Sometimes, however, it is divided in other ways. For example, the northern states are known as the Snowbelt. This name refers to their cold, snowy winters. The band of southern states stretching from the Carolinas to California is often called the Sunbelt.

The map above shows that many people in the United States live along the Gulf coast. Many also live in cities in the Northeast, along the Pacific coast, and along the Great Lakes. In fact, the United States is a nation of cities. Outside the cities, the country is thinly populated. As writer Gertrude Stein put it, "In the United States there is more space where nobody is than where anybody is."

The Coasts of the Country

Use the map on page 573 in the Unit Overview to locate the three coastal regions. They border the Pacific and Atlantic oceans and the Gulf of Mexico.

The Pacific coast is dramatic. Mountains descend to the ocean along a 434-mile road that winds between Los Angeles and San Francisco.

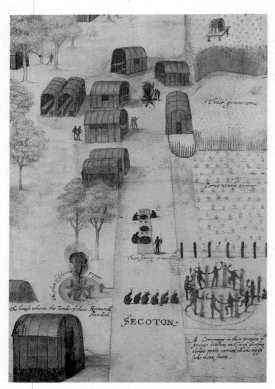

This painting from the 1580s shows a Native American village in the Southeast woodlands. Villagers planted crops such as corn and arranged their houses in orderly rows.

■ *Find evidence to support the following statement: The United States is a vast and diverse land.*

In contrast, the Atlantic coast is mostly flat and dotted with harbors. It also has stretches of beach, rolling hills, and smaller mountains.

The Gulf coast hooks around the Gulf of Mexico. It has much rich soil and many grassy swamps. Many rivers flow into the gulf. The greatest of these is the Mississippi. It has many tributaries, smaller rivers that stretch east and west.

Interior Plains

The Mississippi River links the Gulf coast with the interior of the country. Native Americans once grew corn in the rich soil of the Mississippi valley. Today barges travel from Minneapolis to New Orleans. They carry raw materials and industrial goods.

West of the Mississippi, forests and mountains give way to the flat, treeless Great Plains. Millions of buffalo once grazed on these plains. Native Americans counted on these herds as a source of food, clothing, and shelter. During the 1800s settlers drove the original inhabitants from the plains. These settlers and

newcomers also hunted the buffalo nearly to extinction. Today farms and fields of wheat stretch for miles across the Great Plains.

To the west of the plains are the Rocky Mountains—the "backbone" of North America. They rise to more than 14,000 feet above sea level. The Rocky Mountains are far higher than their eastern cousins, the Appalachians.

From the Arctic to the Tropics

Much of the United States is in the temperate—or mild—climate zone. Some people in the United States, however, must work hard to adapt to their climate. Nowhere in the United States is the climate colder than in parts of Alaska. Winter temperatures can plunge to –30°F. The Yupik, Aleut, and Inuit settled there long ago. These Native Americans had to adapt to a region with no trees or farmland. In south-central Alaska, however, the climate is milder. In the summer, people travel there to fish, sail, and swim.

At the opposite extreme are the tropical islands of Hawaii. Volcanic mountains make up most of the state. It has a warm, wet climate and dense rain forests. One part of Hawaii, in fact, is often called the wettest spot in the world. Its yearly rainfall is 444 inches. ■

Rich Natural Resources

The United States is rich in resources. People have often acted as though these resources were unlimited. In recent years, however, the people of the United States have started to understand that they must use their resources more wisely than they have in the past.

Resources of Land and Sea

Resources of the United States include dense forests, rich soil, fresh water, and varied animal life. The five Great Lakes make up the largest freshwater system in the world. Valuable mineral deposits lie beneath the soil. Alaska's Arctic coast holds the largest oil reserves in North America. Oil and natural gas are also found in Texas, Oklahoma, California, and other states.

The early inhabitants of the Pacific Northwest once used trees for building and carving. Today these forests provide much of the nation's lumber. Forests in the Southeast supply wood pulp to make paper. Some southeastern forests are planted and harvested much like any other crop.

Conserving Resources

Native Americans regarded the land as the giver of life, as holy. They were generally careful not to destroy the resources that fed and clothed them. Europeans, however, saw the land as something to be owned and used. To them the resources of the great new land seemed limitless. Today we know that the resources of this land are limited. We understand the need to use them with care. Yet **conservation**—saving resources—is not always easy.

The Mississippi River is one of the nation's most important transportation and trade routes. Ships and barges on the Mississippi and its tributaries can travel far into the country's interior.

Sometimes, conservation seems to conflict with economic growth. In other cases people must learn new habits of saving rather than consuming or wasting.

For example, 90 percent of the U.S. population own at least one car or truck. Many depend on cars for work and recreation. Yet there is a great price to pay in terms of pollution of the environment.

In addition, people in the United States use huge amounts of coal, oil, and natural gas. After people have used these resources, they are gone for good. Much more can be done to save these fuels for the future. More can also be done to clean up the pollution they produce. ■

◄ *The Tlingit, Native Americans of the Pacific Northwest, carved this wooden ceremonial rattle. Wood continues to be an important resource in the Northwest today.*

■ *Identify three resources of the United States and one place where each is found.*

R E V I E W

1. **FOCUS** How have people used the land and the resources of the United States?
2. **GEOGRAPHY** Look back at the map showing the regions of the United States in Chapter 2 (page 43). Which regions border the Atlantic coast? The Gulf coast? The Pacific coast?
3. **CULTURE** Contrast the climates of Alaska and Hawaii with the temperate climate of many of the other 48 states. How might the climate of Alaska and Hawaii affect the way people live there?
4. **CRITICAL THINKING** Should people living in the United States change the way they use the resources? Tell why or why not.
5. **WRITING ACTIVITY** Make a list of all the resources you use in a single day. Include the reason you use each one. List ways in which you could conserve these resources.

621

L E S S O N   2

People from Many Lands

THINKING FOCUS

Why is the United States called a nation of many peoples?

Key Terms

- quota
- naturalized citizen

▼ *At this Cinco de Mayo celebration in San Antonio, Texas, dancers wear traditional Mexican costumes.*

It is May 5 in a city in the Southwest. For days people have been looking forward to a holiday. It is Cinco de Mayo, the Fifth of May. From all over the city, people hurry to the fiesta.

At school, children have learned about Cinco de Mayo. They know that on May 5, 1862, Mexicans turned back French invaders in the Battle of Puebla. This victory lives on in Cinco de Mayo festivals. They are held in Los Angeles, San Antonio, and other southwestern cities with Mexican American communities.

Today people are coming together to celebrate this victory. As they near the park, they see Mexican flags. They hear the Mexican music. It is played by *mariachis,* Mexican musicians, dressed in black. These musicians wander through the crowd. Near a stage at one end of the park, people gather to watch costumed dancers.

Good smells drift over the crowd. At one food stand, a woman makes tacos. She fills thin pancakes, called tortillas, with beans, lettuce, and tomatoes. Italian pizza and ices as well as hot dogs and ice cream are for sale.

All day people enjoy picnics, parades, street dancing, and games. Not everyone at the fiesta is Mexican, however. African Americans, Asian Americans, and people of many other different ethnic groups join the celebration.

Patterns of Immigration

Any time citizens of the United States get together, the crowd probably will be made up of people whose ancestors came from all over the world. Every ethnic group now living in the United States once came from another land.

Native Americans came first. As you read in Chapter 6, their ancestors crossed a land bridge that linked Asia and Alaska many thousands of years ago.

Settlement by others of what is now the United States began in the early 1500s. This was soon after European explorers arrived and laid claims in the Americas. Spanish missionaries were the first European settlers. They hoped to convert the Native Americans to Catholicism. Spanish missions became centers for settlement in what is now the Southwest, the West, and Florida. In 1565, the Spanish founded St. Augustine in present-day Florida. It became the first permanent European settlement in what is now the United States.

In the early 1600s, French traders and trappers set up forts in the far Northeast and along the Mississippi. At about the same time, the Dutch founded a colony in what became the state of New York. English settlers established their first colonies on the Atlantic coast in the early 1600s. During this period Europeans brought another group to the Americas—Africans. Most Africans came as slaves, taken by force.

Welcoming the World

In time, the English colonies on the Atlantic coast became a new nation. At first, the United States welcomed immigrants. In the 1800s the nation needed people to farm the land and build cities. Immigrants were eager to come to the United States.

Many immigrants had been driven from their countries by war, persecution, disease, and poverty. For them the United States was a "golden land." People came with dreams of freedom and fortune. As one Russian immigrant said, to come to the United States "was the wish, the dream, and the hope of every person."

Between 1820 and 1930, more than 37 million immigrants came to

◀ *Europeans brought their knowledge of farming to the United States. These farmers settled in North Dakota.*

▽ *These Jewish children were one of the many groups to immigrate to the United States in the early 20th century. They had been made orphans by war in Europe.*

623

From Many, One Nation

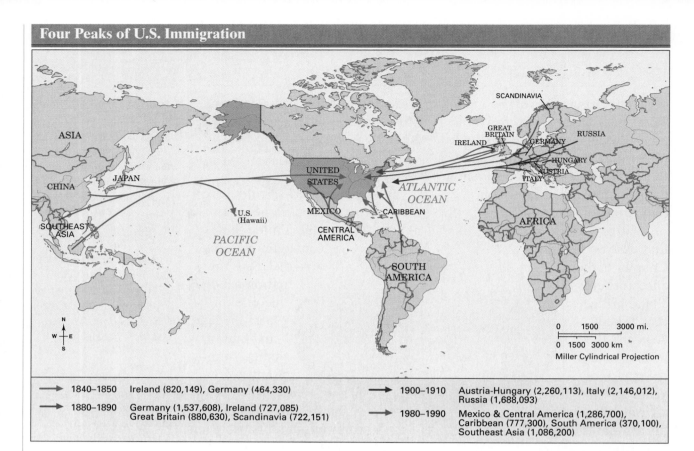

→	1840–1850	Ireland (820,149), Germany (464,330)	
→	1880–1890	Germany (1,537,608), Ireland (727,085) Great Britain (880,630), Scandinavia (722,151)	
→	1900–1910	Austria-Hungary (2,260,113), Italy (2,146,012), Russia (1,688,093)	
→	1980–1990	Mexico & Central America (1,286,700), Caribbean (777,300), South America (370,100), Southeast Asia (1,086,200)	

This map shows some of the peak periods of U.S. immigration. It also shows when immigrants came, where they came from, and where they settled. How did the immigrants' places of origin change from the first part of the 1900s to the last part?

A Chinese immigrant brought this compass from China to help him find his way in his new country.

the United States. Some arrived from Asia and South America. Most, however, came from Europe. In the 1840s and 1850s, for instance, over one and a half million people fled Ireland and came to the United States. The map above and the chart on page 625 show where many other immigrant groups came from and when they arrived.

Closing the Door

Most immigrants faced hardship in their new land. They had to learn a new way of life. Many had to learn a new language. Often the foods were not familiar. Many immigrants arrived with little money. Those who lived in the cities often shared dark, crowded rooms.

To make matters worse, many immigrants had to deal with prejudice. The settled population sometimes feared or hated the newest arrivals. They worried that the newcomers would take

their jobs. They feared the immigrants would change their way of life. Immigrants looking for jobs found signs saying NO IRISH NEED APPLY—or a variation of this idea.

The huge number of immigrants and the fears of settled citizens led many people to call for immigration limits. Chinese applicants were excluded beginning in 1882.

In the 1920s the U.S. Congress passed immigration laws that set quotas. These **quotas** put limits on the number of people allowed into the country.

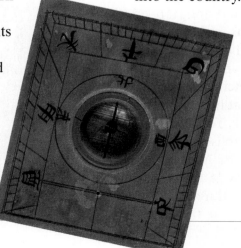

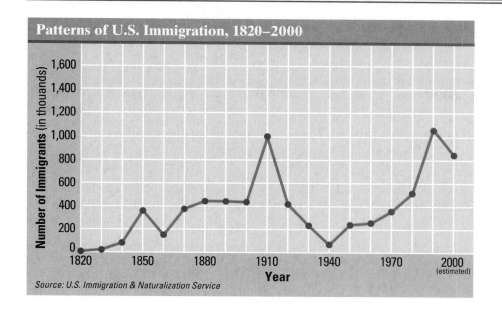

Patterns of U.S. Immigration, 1820–2000

(Line graph: Number of Immigrants (in thousands) on vertical axis from 0 to 1,600; Year on horizontal axis from 1820 to 2000 (estimated))

Source: U.S. Immigration & Naturalization Service

◄ *No one knows exactly how many immigrants will come to the United States by the year 2000. However, scientists make educated guesses, as this chart shows.*

The laws favored northern Europeans. Congress set low quotas for southern and eastern Europeans. The new laws made it difficult for people fleeing war to enter the United States.

Present Immigration Laws

In the 1950s and 1960s, the United States economy began to boom again. There seemed to be enough jobs for everyone. In 1952 Congress removed the ban on Asian immigration. In 1965 Congress changed U.S. immigration policy even more dramatically. New laws greatly expanded quotas in an attempt to treat every country equally. Quotas also favored uniting families who had relatives already living in the United States.

From 1950 to 1980, immigration increased. Many newcomers were fleeing from their governments. These refugees came from Cuba, Central America, South Vietnam, Haiti, Hungary, and the Soviet Union. Immigrants also arrived from Ethiopia, Mozambique, Angola, and the Middle East. Large numbers of Asians arrived from the Philippines, South Korea, China, and India. Other new immigrants came from Mexico and the Caribbean islands.

During these years more people entered the United States than the quotas allowed. In 1986 the government set up new rules to stop illegal immigration. These rules also helped some illegal immigrants in the country become citizens. Understanding Naturalization on page 626 explains how an immigrant becomes a **naturalized citizen.** ■

▼ *This family had fled Armenia at the turn of the century to come to the United States.*

■ *How have immigration laws changed over the years?*

Becoming One Nation

Physicist Albert Einstein, one of the most famous immigrants to the United States, became a U.S. citizen on October 1, 1940. In the photo below he is shown taking the oath of citizenship with his daughter.

For many years historians described the United States as a "melting pot." By this they meant a place where people from many lands lose their separate, national identities. Today some historians believe that "patchwork quilt" better describes the United States. In a patchwork quilt, the separate pieces are each unique. Together they make up a whole. In the "patchwork quilt" that is the United States, people keep their own culture. At the same time, they create a single, unified nation.

Immigrant Contributions

Many ethnic groups have contributed to U.S. growth. In the late 1800s, immigrants helped build the railroads that linked the nation's cities. They also built roads and canals. They dug mines. They set up farms and ranches. In cities

UNDERSTANDING NATURALIZATION

What is a citizen? A citizen is any person who was born or naturalized in a country. Many immigrants to the United States go through a process called naturalization to become citizens. A naturalized citizen has all the rights and responsibilities of a citizen born in this country.

U.S. citizens have the right to vote. Citizens also have many freedoms that are guaranteed by the Constitution of the United States. For example, citizens have the freedom to worship in the religion of their choice, to speak their minds, and to own property.

All citizens have legal responsibilities as well. They must obey the law, pay taxes, and serve on a jury when called. They also have civic responsibilities not required by law. They are supposed to vote and to respect and protect the rights of others.

How Does a Person Become a Citizen?

Any person born in this country is a citizen. Any person whose parent is a citizen is also a citizen. In order for an immigrant to become a naturalized citizen, that person must: (1) be at least 18 years old, (2) be in the country legally, (3) have lived here five years in a row, (4) be able to use English, (5) know about U.S. history and government.

There are several steps in the naturalization process. Immigrants must have their fingerprints taken. They must prove that they meet the naturalization requirements; for example, that they have lived here at least five years. They must take a test to show that they can read, write, and speak English. They must also take a test to show their knowledge of U.S. history and government.

Becoming a naturalized citizen is not simple. Yet thousands of people go through the naturalization process each year. They believe that the rights and benefits of U.S. citizenship are worth the effort.

immigrants ran the machines that made everything from textiles to steel.

Immigrants have enriched life in the United States. They have given much more than muscle power alone. They also have brought their ideas, their traditions, and their dreams.

Music, art, food, writing, and dance in the United States show the influences of many lands. For example, jazz, blues, gospel, and rap are African American contributions to music. Reggae developed in the Caribbean. In any big U.S. city, you can eat foods from all over the world.

A Brighter Future

Many immigrants come to the United States looking for freedom. They want to make their own choices and elect their own leaders. Many find their own dreams through their children. The hope of a brighter future continues to unite many U.S. citizens. Farm worker José Urbina expresses a dream that many can understand.■

Our dream is to be able to give the children the best of everything. We know that, for them to have a better future and purpose in life, they need a good education. . . . We are going to sacrifice for them, so that they can have the profession that they desire.

▲ *Visitors in Washington, D.C., in 1993 view the Emancipation Proclamation, the Civil War document that freed slaves in the United States. On display for the first time since being signed by President Lincoln, it held out hope for a brighter future for African Americans.*

◄ *Ileana Ros-Lehtinen, a Republican from Florida, was born in Havana, Cuba. She is the first Hispanic woman elected to Congress and the first Cuban American to serve. She is shown at a political rally in this photograph.*

■ *What gives many U.S. citizens a common purpose?*

R E V I E W

1. **FOCUS** Why is the United States called a nation of many peoples?

2. **HISTORY** What situations in their birthplaces have led immigrants to come to the United States? Why did the United States seem attractive to them?

3. **GEOGRAPHY** Where did the first European settlers in the Americas come from? Why did they come? Where did they settle?

4. **CRITICAL THINKING** Give two reasons to explain why the United States first began to limit immigration. Do you think that these are good reasons for limiting immigration today? Explain your answer.

5. **ACTIVITY** Imagine that you are a 20-year-old, unmarried man or woman deciding whether to immigrate to the United States. Choose a country of origin. Then fold a sheet of notebook paper in half lengthwise. On one half list the reasons for immigrating, and on the other half list the reasons against.

From Many, One Nation

In Lesson 2 you learned about Chinese immigration to California. The author of this tale has used realistic details about immigrant life as he tells his story of two young lovers living in a California Chinatown.

LITERATURE

Ginger for the Heart

Paul Yee

In 1848 gold was discovered in northern California. This discovery started a world gold rush. People from the East Coast of the United States as well as people from other countries traveled thousands of miles to reach California and try their luck at gold mining. Chinese immigrants poured into California at this time. Many were hired as laborers to help construct the new transcontinental railroad, but others headed for the mountain streams of the Sierra Nevadas, where they panned for gold dust and nuggets that were mixed with the sand in the bottom of the streams. The story below comes from a collection of fictional stories about Chinese immigrants living in the United States. Can you find examples of Chinese traditions in this story?

The buildings of Chinatown are stoutly constructed of brick, and while some are broad and others thin, they rise no higher than four solid storeys. Many contain stained-glass windows decorated with flower and diamond patterns, and others boast balconies with fancy wrought-iron railings.

Only one building stands above the rest. Its turret-like tower is visible even from the harbor, because the cone-shaped roof is made of copper.

In the early days, Chang the merchant tailor owned this building. He used the main floor for his store and rented out the others. But he kept the tower room for his own use, for the sun filled it with light. This was the room where his wife and daughter worked.

His daughter's name was Yenna, and her beauty was beyond compare. She had ivory skin, sparkling eyes, and her hair hung long and silken, shining like polished ebony. All day long she and her mother sat by the tower window and sewed with silver needles and silken threads. They sang songs while they worked, and their voices rose in wondrous harmonies.

ebony a tropical, dark-colored wood often finished to look shiny black

In all Chinatown, the craftsmanship of Yenna and her mother was considered the finest. Search as they might, customers could not discern where holes had once pierced their shirts. Buttonholes never stretched out of shape, and seams were all but invisible.

discern to perceive or detect

One day, a young man came into the store laden with garments for mending. His shoulders were broad and strong, yet his eyes

were soft and caring. Many times he came, and many times he saw Yenna. For hours he would sit and watch her work. They fell deeply in love, though few words were spoken between them.

Spring came and boats bound for the northern gold fields began to sail again. It was time for the young man to go. He had borrowed money to pay his way over to the New World, and now he had to repay his debts. Onto his back he threw his blankets and tools, food and warm jackets. Then he set off with miners from around the world, clutching gold pans and shovels.

Yenna had little to give him in farewell. All she found in the kitchen was a ginger root as large as her hand. As she stroked its brown knobs and bumpy eyes, she whispered to him, "This will warm you in the cold weather. I will wait for you, but, like this piece of ginger, I, too, will age and grow dry." Then she pressed her lips to the ginger, and turned away.

"I will come back," the young man said. "The fire burning for you in my heart can never be extinguished."

extinguished put out

Thereafter, Yenna lit a lamp at every nightfall and set it in the tower window. Rains lashed against the glass, snow piled low along the ledge, and ocean winds rattled the frame. But the flame did not waver, even though the young man never sent letters. Yenna did not weep uselessly, but continued to sew and sing with her mother.

There were few unmarried women in Chinatown, and many men came to seek Yenna's hand in marriage. Rich gold miners and sons of successful merchants bowed before her, but she always looked away. They gave her grand gifts, but still she shook her head, until finally the men grew weary and called her crazy. In

China, parents arranged all marriages, and daughters became the property of their husbands. But Chang the merchant tailor treasured his daughter's happiness and let her be.

One winter, an epidemic ravaged the city. When it was over, Chang had lost his wife and his eyesight. Yenna led him up to the tower where he could feel the sun and drifting clouds move across his face. She began to sew again, and while she sewed, she sang for her father. The lamp continued to burn steadily at the tower window as she worked. With twice the amount of work to do, she labored long after dusk. She fed the flame more oil and sent her needle skimming through the heavy fabrics. Nimbly her fingers braided shiny cords and coiled them into butterfly buttons. And when the wick sputtered into light each evening, Yenna's heart soared momentarily into her love's memories. Nights passed into weeks, months turned into years, and four years quickly flew by.

One day a dusty traveler came into the store and flung a bundle of ragged clothes onto the counter. Yenna shook out the first shirt, and out rolled a ginger root. Taking it into her hand, she saw that pieces had been nibbled off, but the core of the root was still firm and fragrant.

She looked up. There stood the man she had promised to wait for. His eyes appeared older and wiser.

"Your gift saved my life several times," he said. "The fire of the ginger is powerful indeed."

"Why is the ginger root still firm and heavy?" she wondered. "Should it not have dried and withered?"

"I kept it close to my heart and my sweat coated it. In lonely moments, my tears soaked it." His calloused hands reached out for her. "Your face has not changed."

"Nor has my heart," she replied. "I have kept a lamp burning all these years."

"So I have heard," he smiled. "Will you come away with me now? It has taken many years to gather enough gold to buy a farm. I have built you a house on my land."

For the first time since his departure, tears cascaded down Yenna's face. She shook her head. "I cannot leave. My father needs me."

"Please come with me," the young man pleaded. "You will be very happy, I promise."

Yenna swept the wetness from her cheeks. "Stay with me and work this store instead," she implored.

The young man stiffened and stated proudly, "A man does not live in his wife's house." And the eyes that she remembered so well gleamed with determination.

"But this is a new land," she cried. "Must we forever follow the old ways?"

implored pleaded

630

She reached out for him, but he brushed her away. With a curse, he hurled the ginger root into the fireplace. As the flames leapt up, Yenna's eyes blurred. The young man clenched and unclenched his fists in anger. They stood like stone.

At last the man turned to leave, but suddenly he knelt at the fireplace. Yenna saw him reach in with the tongs and pull something out of the flames.

"Look!" he whispered in amazement. "The ginger refuses to be burnt! The flames cannot touch it!"

Yenna looked and saw black burn marks charring the root, but when she took it in her hand, she found it still firm and moist. She held it to her nose, and found the fragrant sharpness still there.

The couple embraced and swore to stay together. They were married at a lavish banquet attended by all of Chinatown. There, the father passed his fingers over his son-in-law's face and nodded in satisfaction.

Shortly after, the merchant Chang died, and the young couple moved away. Yenna sold the business and locked up the tower room. But on nights when boats pull in from far away, they say a flicker of light can still be seen in that high window. And Chinese women are reminded that ginger is one of their best friends.

tongs a grasping tool made of two hinged arms

Further Reading

Dragonwings. Laurence Yep. Moon Shadow is a Chinese immigrant boy who helps his father test their homemade airplane.

Immigrant Girl: Becky of Eldridge Street. Brett Harvey. This book tells of a young Russian girl who grows up in a busy immigrant neighborhood of New York City in 1910.

My Name is San Ho. Jayne Pettit. San Ho is a 12-year-old Vietnamese boy. He travels to the United States to live with his mother and his stepfather, a U.S. Marine, during the Vietnam War.

Summer Endings. Sollace Hotz. This story tells of a young Polish girl who has to come to the United States during the summer of 1945. The family awaits news of the father, who was detained in Poland because he was a political activist.

For the Good of All

**THINKING
F O C U S**

*In what ways have people
in the United States
worked for the good of
all citizens?*

Key Terms

- discrimination
- volunteer

*M*ost of the students looked at me because the way I was dressing was
strange. It was so cold, I wore everything I'd bought. I didn't know
where anything was. I came late to every class. I was confused and I could
not ask people. They told me in sign language, "Go to eat." I went into the
cafeteria. There were hundreds of people. . . . A supervisor knew I was a new
student. He took me to the head of the line to get a hamburger and the other
students got angry. "Why does that boy get to go first?" I told the supervisor,
"I want to wait in the line. Please." He said, "Don't worry about it. Take the food."

This is how Von, an immigrant
from Vietnam, remembers how
difficult his first day in a Detroit
school was. Part of what made it
hard was the reaction of other
students.

Fighting Discrimination

Sometimes, people react to
differences in the same way the
students did to Von. Discrimination
often occurs when people fear
differences between themselves
and others. **Discrimination**
means treating a person
unfairly because of race,
religion, nationality, gender, or
other differences. If a person is
kept from a job, from housing, or
from education for one of these
reasons, this is called discrimination.

In the United States, discrimination is an old problem. As you
have already read in this chapter,
new immigrants
often faced ha-
tred and fear.
Other groups,
such as women
and nonwhites,
also have had
trouble getting
fair treatment in
the United
States.

African
Americans have

➤ *In this photo-
graph, people of many
ages, backgrounds,
and professions are
marching to protest
discrimination. The
buttons above express
their hopes.*

no justice,
NO PEACE

PRACTICE
BROTHERHOOD

fought a long battle against discrimination. The Civil War (1861–1865) ended slavery and gave African Americans citizenship. However, they did not get equal opportunities for jobs, housing, or education along with their freedom.

In 1955 Rosa Parks, an African American from Montgomery, Alabama, refused to give up her bus seat to a white woman. In those days, bus companies in the South often made African Americans sit behind whites. Parks was jailed for defying this rule. To fight this discrimination, the black community boycotted the city buses for more than a year.

Martin Luther King, Jr., joined the struggle. He became a leader of the civil rights movement—or "freedom struggles." The civil rights protests spread. Volunteers from all over the country joined boycotts, marches, and court actions.

The result of the "freedom struggles" was the Civil Rights Act of 1964 and the Voting Rights Act of 1965. The Civil Rights Act made it illegal to keep people from a public place—such as a store or a bathroom—because of their race. It also outlawed racial discrimination in jobs or schools. The Voting

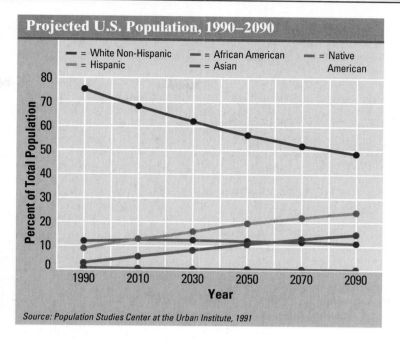

Projected U.S. Population, 1990–2090

= White Non-Hispanic   = African American   = Native American
= Hispanic   = Asian

Percent of Total Population

Year

Source: Population Studies Center at the Urban Institute, 1991

Rights Act allowed more African Americans to register to vote.

The African American "freedom struggles" changed our society. Many schools and colleges that once were closed to African Americans are now desegregated. More African Americans now hold political office. The "freedom struggles" also helped open doors for all minorities and women in the United States.

A Moment in Time on page 634 explains how a young black woman was able to find opportunity in the United States armed services. ■

▲ *The percentages of Asian and Hispanic populations of the United States are growing rapidly while the percentage of the white population is declining. These changes will, in proportion to the whole, affect the nation's ethnic mix in the next century.*

■ *What effect does discrimination have on people's lives?*

The Power of Education

The first step in stopping discrimination is beginning to overcome prejudice. Prejudice is hatred, distrust, or fear of people because of their race, religion, gender, national background, or other differences. Often education helps people to overcome prejudice. They learn to respect and appreciate the differences of others.

The chart on this page shows that the ethnic mix of the United States is changing. Experts predict that by the middle of the 21st century, U.S. citizens of European ancestry will no longer be the majority. Learning to respect others will continue to be important.

The Tradition of Education

The tradition of education goes back to the early days of U.S.

633

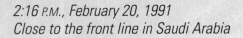

A Gulf War Soldier

2:16 P.M., February 20, 1991
Close to the front line in Saudi Arabia

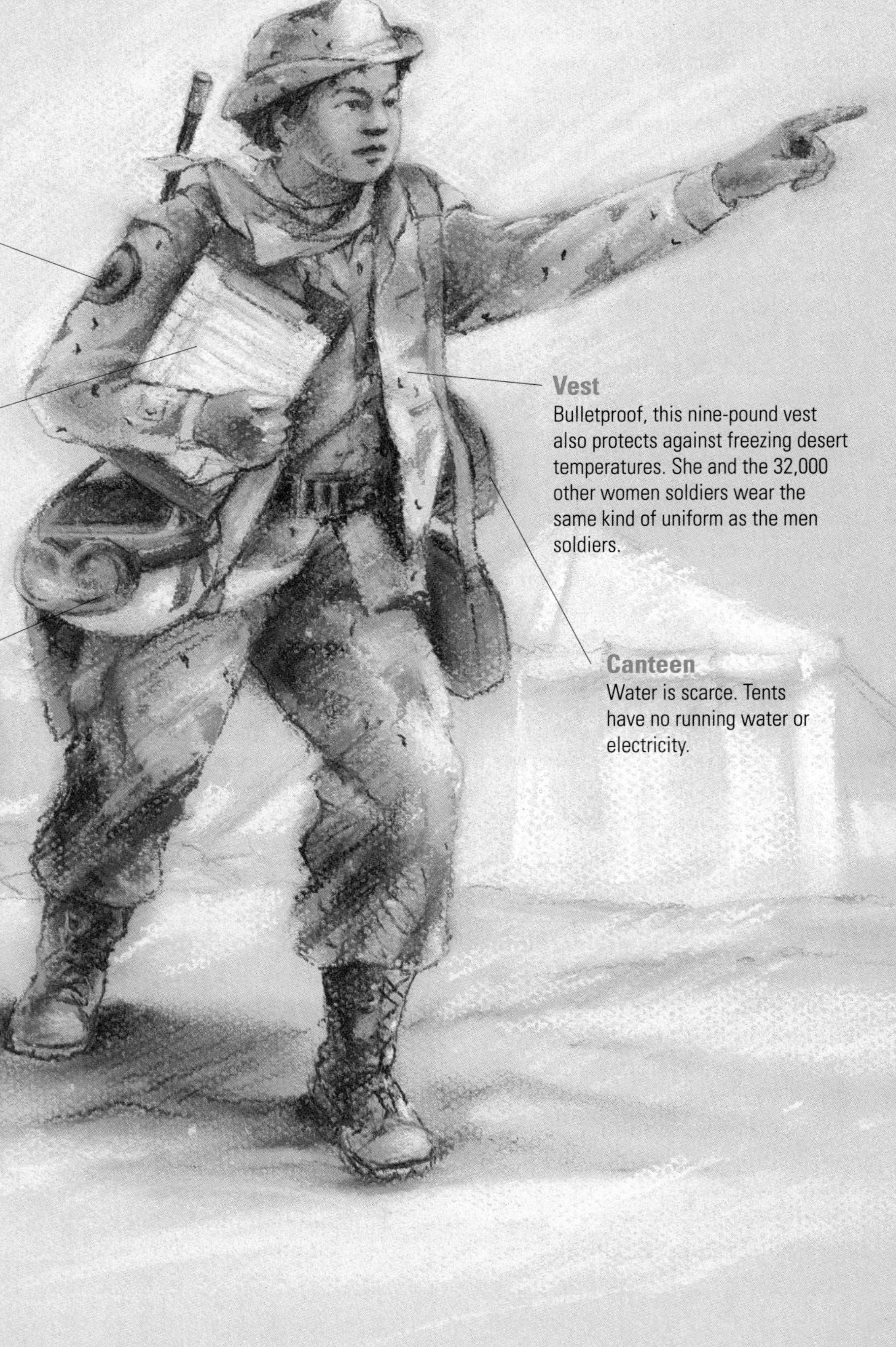

Patch
This shows she is in the
U.S. Army 24th Infantry
Division. She is a captain.
For her service in this war,
she will receive the Bronze
Star, a combat medal.

Orders
These tell her which troops
need supplies. She directs
her supply unit to rush food,
fuel, and ammunition to the
front lines.

Helmet
She told her family that the
"V" on her helmet stands
for "Victory"—her division's
nickname. Her children
were curious about her
protective gear.

Vest
Bulletproof, this nine-pound vest
also protects against freezing desert
temperatures. She and the 32,000
other women soldiers wear the
same kind of uniform as the men
soldiers.

Canteen
Water is scarce. Tents
have no running water or
electricity.

history. New England Puritans wanted their children to know how to read so that they could study the Bible. Other early settlers also worked to educate their children.

After the American Revolution, a major concern in education was to create good citizens. The new nation needed people who would support the government and choose capable leaders. Some people born in the United States believed that education was a way for immigrants to learn about their new culture. Many immigrants also saw education as a way for their children to get ahead.

Yet many children received little education. Often they had to work to help their families survive.

In the mid-1800s, Horace Mann, a Massachusetts educator, led a movement to improve public schools. Mann worked with the state government to ensure that all children would go to school for at least six months of the year.

The Need for Educated Citizens

By the mid-1900s, the United States needed fewer unskilled workers. More and more jobs required special training. Many jobs called for at least a high school education. College became a dream of more and more people. School attendance increased steadily.

Today the need for skilled workers remains a priority. Yet many people are worried that the nation is falling behind other countries in educating and training its citizens. On tests taken by students of many nations, U.S. students no longer score among the highest.

In order for the United States to be competitive in the modern world, it will need to strengthen its schools. Some experts believe that our present educational system will have to change in the future. ■

▲ *A turn-of-the-century class in New York City (above) and an English-language class today (inset).*

■ *List three reasons why education is important.*

Solving Problems

Education is an old tradition in the United States. So is self-reliance. The early settlers had to depend on themselves, their family, and their neighbors for survival. Native Americans have also counted on themselves and their communities for support. Today many people still believe that this nation can tackle its problems if citizens help themselves and one another.

A History of Volunteering

A **volunteer** gives his or her free labor. Volunteer labor means that organizations such as Goodwill, the United Fund, and the Red Cross can give more to the people they serve. Volunteers also help the federal government with certain problems.

When John F. Kennedy became President in 1961, he inspired many

635

From Many, One Nation

Rosalynn Carter, are active in the struggle for civil rights. They work on behalf of women, Native Americans, Hispanic Americans, the homeless, people with AIDS, and other minorities.

Why do so many United States citizens volunteer? Some people have a personal interest in the groups they serve. Other people do volunteer work to prepare for a job. Volunteering in a hospital, for instance, might lead the way to a job in the medical profession.

Many others just feel good about helping others. As one volunteer speaker on AIDS prevention told a teenage audience, "If I can prevent one of you from getting infected, it's worth my time."

Still others see volunteering as a responsibility. For these people, volunteer work is part of being a good citizen.

Whatever their reasons, the volunteers of the United States are following an old and honored tradition. ■

▲ *Former President Jimmy Carter helps build houses for the homeless. His volunteer organization is called Habitat for Humanity.*

U.S. citizens to become volunteers. "Ask not what your country can do for you," he urged. "Ask what you can do for your country."

Many Americans responded to Kennedy's challenge. For example, college graduates from across the United States signed up as Peace Corps volunteers. They helped people in poor countries learn new farming methods. They taught them ways to stay healthy. Other volunteers for VISTA worked in low-income communities in the United States.

Volunteers Today

■ *Identify two problems that volunteers have worked to solve.*

Today volunteers from all walks of life, including former President Jimmy Carter and his wife,

---

R E V I E W

1. **FOCUS** In what ways have people in the United States worked for the good of all of its citizens?
2. **HISTORY** What were the Civil Rights Act of 1964 and the Voting Rights Act of 1965?
3. **HISTORY** In addition to African Americans, what groups were helped by the "freedom struggles" of the 1960s?
4. **CRITICAL THINKING** Why is it important for U.S. schoolchildren to be able to keep up with schoolchildren from other countries?
5. **WRITING ACTIVITY** Identify a problem in your community. Make a list of suggestions explaining how volunteers could help solve the problem.

Identifying Stereotypes

Here's Why

A stereotype is an over-generalized idea about a group of people. For example, "Scandinavians are blond" is a stereotype. So is the statement "All Italians are dark haired." These stereotypes are too simple. Not all Scandinavians are blond. Nor are all Italians dark haired.

Stereotypes are often based on partial truths, like the examples above. As a result, stereotypes can be hard to recognize. You may have some general, partly true ideas about people from a certain country or people of a certain race, religion, age, or gender.

Stereotyping can be harmful. During the 1500s, Europeans made slaves of the peoples of Africa and the Americas. Because those Europeans accepted the stereotype of Africans and Indians as less than human, they did not treat them as fellow humans.

Relating to people as individuals rather than as members of groups will help you overcome stereotypes.

Here's How

This picture shows a family in the United States in the 1950s packing their car for a vacation. Look carefully at the picture to see what it tells you about the stereotypes people had about boys and girls in the 1950s. Notice that the girl holds a doll, and the boy holds a baseball bat. Like her mother, the girl wears a skirt and dressy shoes. The boy wears clothing more suitable for play. Some stereotypes that this picture suggests are that only boys play active games and that girls always wear pretty dresses and play quietly with dolls.

Try It

What stereotypes about males and females do people have today? Look through a magazine for pictures of men and women. Think about what the men and the women are doing in the pictures. Could they change roles?

What stereotypes about men and women do the pictures suggest? Do any of the pictures avoid stereotypes? Write a paragraph about one or two of the most interesting examples. Compare your observations with those of your classmates.

Apply It

The humor in television comedies is sometimes based on stereotypes. Make a list of stereotypes that you notice in a show you watch. Discuss your list with others in your class.

637

From Many, One Nation

Should Puerto Rico Be the 51st State?

*P*uerto Rico is a Latin American nation . . . except for political expression of the fact.

Puerto Rican Senator
Fernando Martin

*O*ne half of the electorate in Puerto Rico would stand to gain economically and personally from a vote for statehood.

Former Governor
Rafael Hernández Colón

Background

Consider these facts:
• Puerto Rico is an island about half the size of New Jersey.
  • Puerto Rico's population is about 3.5 million people.
  • Spanish is the island's official language.
  • About 40 percent of the population speak some English.
  • The island's per capita [per person] income is about $6,000.
    • Its per capita income is higher than that of most other Caribbean islands.
    • Its per capita income is about half that of Mississippi, the poorest state.
• Its unemployment rate is about 14 percent, higher than any state's.

U.S. involvement in Puerto Rico dates back to 1898. Up to that time, Puerto Rico had been a Spanish territory.

In April 1898 the United States went to war with Spain. The war lasted only four months. In that time the United States smashed Spanish fleets near the Philippines and Cuba. In July U.S. troops occupied Puerto Rico with little opposition. After the war Puerto Rico became a U.S. territory.

The following are other important dates in U.S.–Puerto Rican relations:
• **1917** Puerto Ricans were granted U.S. citizenship.
• **1948** Puerto Ricans elected their first governor.
• **1952** The island received U.S. commonwealth status. Thus, Puerto Rico would have its own government and constitution.
• **1967** Puerto Ricans voted to continue commonwealth status.

Luis Muñoz Marín
USA
05
Governor, Puerto Rico

▲ *Luis Muñoz Marín was elected the first governor of Puerto Rico in 1948.*

638

Considering the Alternatives

Puerto Ricans have long been divided over the question of whether Puerto Rico should become the 51st state.

About 41 percent of the Puerto Ricans favor statehood, according to a 1990 poll. They argue that becoming a state would give them representation in the world's most powerful nation. The United States, they say, protects the island from extreme poverty and from dictators. Both have weakened other Caribbean islands. They believe that statehood would also bring Puerto Rico greater benefits and social service programs.

About 36 percent of the islanders, according to this poll, want to continue commonwealth status. They say that Puerto Rico should not give up the benefits of its special association with the United States. However, like those who favor independence, they claim that statehood would weaken Puerto Ricans' culture. What's more, they do not want to pay U.S. taxes. They also fear that statehood would cost them jobs. That's because U.S. companies on the island get special tax benefits that would be lost if the island became a state.

About five percent of the

▲ *Puerto Ricans demonstrate in favor of statehood. What are some of the reasons they favor this change?*

population now want their island to become an independent nation, according to the poll. They say that Puerto Rico is different from the 50 states that make up the United States. They are proud of Puerto Rico's unique Spanish-Caribbean tradition and history. They fear that becoming a state might change their culture.

Puerto Ricans may vote again soon on the question of statehood. How do you think they should vote?

Decision Point

1. If you were a Puerto Rican, which point of view would you support? Why?
2. If you were a member of the U.S. Congress, would you favor Puerto Rican statehood? Why or why not?
3. If you owned a factory in Puerto Rico, would you argue for independence, statehood, or commonwealth status? Give your reasons.
4. What changes might result from adding a new state to the Union? For example, consider the U.S. flag.

Chapter Review

Reviewing Key Terms

conservation (p. 621)
discrimination (p. 632)
naturalized citizen (p. 625)

quota (p. 624)
volunteer (p. 635)

Each statement below uses a key term from this chapter. Tell whether each key term is used correctly. Then explain the reason for your answer.

1. Each <u>volunteer</u> at the Red Cross receives an annual salary from that organization.
2. As a result of applying new <u>conservation</u> methods, natural resources in the United States are being used up at a faster rate than ever before.
3. As soon as an immigrant arrives in the United States, he or she becomes a <u>naturalized citizen</u>.
4. A woman who fails to get a job because of her gender is a victim of <u>discrimination</u>.
5. Because of <u>quotas</u> set in the 1920s, fewer people from southern Europe and eastern Europe were able to immigrate to the United States.

Exploring Concepts

A. Many immigrants to the United States eventually become citizens. Copy and complete the following chart. List the requirements and responsibilities of naturalized citizens. One is done for you.

Becoming a Naturalized Citizen	
Requirements	**Responsibilities of Citizenship**
You must be at least 18 years old.	You must obey the law.

B. Answer each question with information from the chapter.

1. What geographic features dominate the U.S. landscape?
2. To what climate zone does most of the United States belong?
3. What has been the role of the Mississippi River in the United States?
4. How did the Europeans' view of the land differ from that of the Native Americans? What were the consequences of the Europeans' view?
5. Why have the places of origin of immigrants changed over the years? Give an example to support your answer.
6. What hardships did immigrants face in the United States?
7. What contributions have immigrants made to the United States?
8. How did the "freedom struggles" change U.S. society?
9. Tell how the traditions of education and of volunteering in the United States have influenced this nation and its citizens.

Reviewing Skills

1. How can stereotypes be harmful? What can people do to overcome them?
2. What are some stereotypes that relate to age? How do you think these stereotypes came to be?
3. Look through a newspaper or magazine for advertisements. Think about the messages in the ads and what the person or persons are doing. Do they suggest any stereotypes about people from a certain country or of a certain race, age, or sex? Make a list of stereotypes that you notice. Share your list with your classmates. Rewrite an ad to remove stereotypes.

Using Critical Thinking

1. In Lesson 1 you read that "sometimes conservation seems to conflict with economic growth." Do you think conservation limits growth? Tell why or why not. What new jobs might be created by protecting the environment?
2. Prejudice may lead to discrimination. Why do you think this is so? What can be done to stop prejudice?
3. Every ethnic group in the United States once came from another land. Despite this fact, the settled population sometimes reacts to new immigrants with fear and hatred and treats them unfairly. Do you think the condition of the economy in the United States may affect the attitudes of the settled population toward immigrants? Tell why or why not.
4. In Lesson 2 you read that historians often described the United States as a "melting pot." Today, however, some historians believe that "patchwork quilt" better describes the United States. How is it possible for people to keep their own culture and traditions and, at the same time, be part of a single, unified nation?
5. One of the responsibilities of all citizens is to work to improve life in their community. What can you do to improve life in your community?

Preparing for Citizenship

1. **COLLECTING INFORMATION** Imagine you are planning a trip to one of the six regions in the United States. Research the geographic features, the food, customs, climate, resources, recreation areas, and historic places of the region. You may wish to write to the Chamber of Commerce of one or more states in that region for information. Then compile a scrapbook with facts, maps, and photographs. Share the scrapbook with your classmates.
2. **INTERVIEWING** Investigate the national origins of your family or of the family of someone you know. From what country did they come? Why did they come to the United States? How were they received by the settled population? Interview an older family member to find the answers to these questions. Share your findings with the class.
3. **GROUP ACTIVITY** In Lesson 3 you read about Von's first day in school. Interview students in your school who have come from another region or country to learn about their experiences. In small groups, discuss ways you can help newcomers adjust to the school and the community.
4. **COLLABORATIVE LEARNING** Celebrate the contributions of the various ethnic groups in the United States. Plan a Multicultural Festival. Prepare ethnic foods. Research and share stories about immigration to the United States. Tell about customs from another country. Play tapes or records of songs from other countries. Decorate your classroom with flags of different countries. You may wish to invite relatives or another class to the festival.

641

Chapter 28

The United Nations, Israel, and South Korea

In the world today, conflicts threaten many nations. The people of the world need to work together to solve political and environmental problems. After the chaos of World War II, many nations joined together to form the United Nations. This international organization has intervened in many places around the world. The histories of two nations, Israel and South Korea, have been shaped by actions of the United Nations.

Korea University students demonstrate in Seoul in 1987.

This carved *menorah*, a candelabrum or candlestick with many branches, is a symbol of Judaism. It stands in front of the Knesset—Israel's parliament—and depicts scenes from Jewish history.

1948 The State of Israel is created.

| 1930 | 1940 | 1950 | 1960 |

1945 The United Nations is founded.

1950 UN troops fight in the Korean War.

1945

The United Nations has its home in this building in New York City. Here the General Assembly and Security Council meet. These UN stamps illustrate some UN efforts: (far left) promotion of clean oceans, (top) World Bank funding for hydroelectric dams, (right) UN cooperation.

1987 The *intifada* begins.

| 1970 | 1980 | 1990 | 2000 |

1967 Israel conquers land in neighboring countries—the Gaza Strip, the West Bank, and the Golan Heights.

1991 North Korea and South Korea are admitted to the United Nations.

Today

L E S S O N   1

The United Nations

Key Terms

- forum
- veto
- humanitarian

▼ *This UN observer in Bosnia is from France. He carries a sign that was knocked down by bullets.*

W*e, the peoples of the United Nations, determined to save succeeding generations from the scourge of war, which twice in our lifetime has brought untold sorrow to mankind, and to reaffirm faith in fundamental human rights, in the dignity and worth of the human person, in the equal rights of men and women and of nations large and small, and . . . to promote social progress and better standards of life in larger freedom. . . .*

From the Preamble to
the UN Charter

In 1945 the representatives of 51 nations created a new world organization, the United Nations (UN). World War II was the most devastating war in the world's history. Weary of its horrors, people wanted, in the words of U.S. President Harry S. Truman, to win "a victory against war itself."

This chapter will explain how the United Nations works to meet its goals and will give some examples of its achievements. You will then learn how the United Nations helped two countries, Israel and South Korea, to be born.

The United Nations at Work

Membership in the United Nations has more than tripled since its founding in 1945. However, the two main purposes of the organization have remained the same. The first is to keep the peace. The second is to encourage respect for all people and to ease suffering from abuse, ignorance, and disease.

Organization

The two main parts of the United Nations are the General Assembly and the Security Council. The General Assembly is the world's **forum,** or place for talking and exchanging views. Here, all member nations can safely bring up their concerns and discuss them with friend or foe. All nations are equal in that each has one vote.

The Security Council has real power. Unlike the General Assembly, it can use force to keep the peace. It has 15 members. Of these, five are permanent. They are the major powers that won World War II: the United States, the Soviet Union (now Russia), Britain, France, and China. Any one of these nations can **veto,** or block, decisions of the Security Council.

The United Nations has one person who can speak for the whole organization, the secretary-general. A strong secretary-general can have great influence on world public opinion.

Special agencies carry out the **humanitarian** efforts of the United Nations. Humanitarian means having concern for and encouraging human welfare.

Many agencies work together to bring food, shelter, and health care to people in need. In addition, the UN Educational, Scientific, and Cultural Organization (UNESCO) organizes schools, trains and sends out teachers, and provides technical advice in countries that request it. The UN Children's Fund (UNICEF) works to relieve the suffering of children and provide for their future.

Achievements

Some important activities of UN agencies include:

Sarajevo, Bosnia: Security Council
—In 1992 the Security Council approved the use of force to stop all trade with Serbia during its conflict with Bosnia. UN troops from several countries were authorized to board and search vessels entering the Adriatic Sea, to stop all but humanitarian supplies from reaching Serbian forces.

Mogadishu, Somalia: World Food Program
—In 1993 supply jets brought food supplied by the United Nations, after U.S. troops reopened Mogadishu's airport. Civil war had closed supply routes, and thousands had died of starvation. The Security Council voted to send a force to protect food deliveries, leading to the arrival of U.S. and French troops.

Geneva, Switzerland: World Health Organization (WHO)
—The number of children dying every day is in decline. This is in part due to the WHO vaccination programs that are now reaching 80 percent of the world's children.

Paris, France: UNESCO
—UNESCO's program to save places of unique importance in the world includes 358 sites in 83 countries. Among these is the ancient city of Venice in Italy. ■

▼ *(top) Palestinian refugees attend a school run by UNESCO. (bottom) UNICEF doctors and nurses help mothers to care for their children in Afghanistan.*

■ *How is the United Nations organized?*

645

New Roles and Challenges

World events are changing how the United Nations functions today. New kinds of conflicts are spreading, bringing untold suffering. At the same time, the world is more than ever challenged by problems of poverty, hunger, and pollution.

Changing Roles

The end of the Cold War has enabled democratic and former Communist nations to work together on some major issues. Security Council members do not use their veto power as often as in the past, which makes it easier for the United Nations to take a stand.

However, divisions between the rich and poor nations of the world are increasing. Many poorer nations are heavily in debt to the richer nations. This inequality between nations has also caused distrust to grow among members of the United Nations.

New leaders are also beginning to emerge. Germany and Japan are challenging the status of the United States and Russia as the world's most powerful and successful nations. They are claiming a greater role in the United Nations.

The United Nations is also taking on new roles. In Cambodia, for example, it is helping to rebuild a country destroyed by civil war. It is organizing elections, rebuilding roads, constructing bridges, and helping more than 360,000 refugees resettle in their homelands there.

➤ *This statue, called* We Shall Beat Our Swords into Ploughshares, *stands in front of the UN building in New York City.*

New Challenges

The end of the Cold War has increased—not reduced—the UN peacekeeping mission. Look at the map on the next page. In what parts of the world have new UN missions recently started?

The problems of war today are often harder to solve than they were in the past. Ancient ethnic and religious strife—some of it much older than communism—is causing bitter conflicts.

The fight against poverty, hunger, and lack of education is more challenging than ever. Although some diseases like smallpox have been wiped out, new diseases like AIDS are spreading fast.

The growing world population has stretched food supplies to the

WE SHALL BEAT OUR SWORDS INTO PLOWSHARES

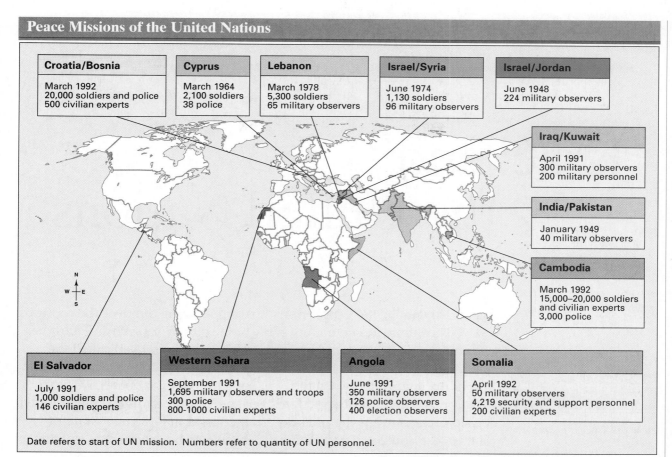

Peace Missions of the United Nations

Croatia/Bosnia
March 1992
20,000 soldiers and police
500 civilian experts

Cyprus
March 1964
2,100 soldiers
38 police

Lebanon
March 1978
5,300 soldiers
65 military observers

Israel/Syria
June 1974
1,130 soldiers
96 military observers

Israel/Jordan
June 1948
224 military observers

Iraq/Kuwait
April 1991
300 military observers
200 military personnel

India/Pakistan
January 1949
40 military observers

Cambodia
March 1992
15,000–20,000 soldiers
and civilian experts
3,000 police

El Salvador
July 1991
1,000 soldiers and police
146 civilian experts

Western Sahara
September 1991
1,695 military observers and troops
300 police
800-1000 civilian experts

Angola
June 1991
350 military observers
126 police observers
400 election observers

Somalia
April 1992
50 military observers
4,219 security and support personnel
200 civilian experts

Date refers to start of UN mission. Numbers refer to quantity of UN personnel.

Source: UN Peace-keeping Operations Information Notes, September 1992

breaking point. More than 500 million people are undernourished.

As poorer nations struggle to improve their economies, richer nations warn of global dangers to the environment. People in poorer countries are cutting down forests to grow more crops. Cattle and sheep, grazing on land that is already poor, are causing erosion. Whole regions are becoming more desertlike every year. The United Nations is trying to offer new solutions for improving food supplies and protecting the environment. It also has to find a way of paying for the rising costs of its many projects.

Although it faces many new challenges, the United Nations remains a forum where nations can talk instead of fight. Through it, worldwide problems and threats of war may be resolved.

Early in its history, the United Nations took a role in shaping the future of Israel and South Korea. As you will learn in the next lessons, the United Nations took action in both countries and may still have a role to play there. ■

▲ *Which is the oldest UN mission still active in 1992?*

■ *What are some new challenges faced by the United Nations?*

R E V I E W

1. **FOCUS** What two main goals have guided the United Nations since its founding?
2. **HISTORY** Why are the United States, Great Britain, France, Russia, and China permanent members of the General Assembly?
3. **POLITICAL SYSTEMS** What effect did the end of the Cold War have on the United Nations?
4. **CRITICAL THINKING** Usually the United Nations does not get involved in a country without the country's permission. How might civil war bring about a change in UN policy?
5. **ACTIVITY** Find a recent newspaper story about UN activities and explain to the class how its action fits in with the UN mission.

The United Nations, Israel, and South Korea

L E S S O N   2

Israel and the United Nations

THINKING
FOCUS

How did Israel become a nation?

Key Terms

- partition
- kibbutz
- intifada

➤ *The six-pointed Star of David, a bas-relief, stands for Judaism. During World War II, the Nazis forced Jews to wear a yellow Star of David, so that everyone would know they were Jews.*

I n November 1947, a special UN commission voted to solve the conflicts between Jews and Arabs in Palestine. It decided to split the country between the two groups. The Jews accepted this decision. The Arabs, who did not want to lose control of any of their land, did not.

On May 14, 1948, the sound of an ancient shofar, or ram's horn trumpet, rang out over the rooftops of the city of Tel Aviv in Palestine. This same sound had called the Jewish people to prayer in the time of King David, about 3,000 years ago. Now the shofar sounded to tell the world that the new State of Israel had been born. For Jews in the new nation, this was a deeply moving moment—their dream of many years had come true.

Israel and Its Borders

The new State of Israel was to be carved out of Palestine, the land west of the Jordan River, as shown on the map on page 649. A UN decision established its original borders.

The Problem of Palestine

As you read in Chapter 3, many Jews left ancient Palestine in the Diaspora. Through the centuries, they were often unwelcome guests in their new countries.

By the late 1800s, some Jews—called Zionists—felt that their people could be safe only in a separate Jewish state. They got together in 1897 and set as their goal "to create for the

Jewish people a home in Palestine secured by public law."

In 1917, in the Balfour Declaration, the British government agreed with the Zionists. However, Palestine was already home to an ancient Arab people. The British also promised that the rights of Palestinian Arabs would not be harmed. Soon, it became clear that these two promises were in conflict.

At the end of World War I, Britain was put in charge of Palestine. As more Jewish settlers arrived in Palestine, local Arabs felt threatened. Violence broke out between Jews and Arabs. The British tried to limit the

The Founding of Israel

1897	First Zionist Congress meets.
1917	Balfour Declaration promises Jewish homeland in Palestine.
1922	British Mandate of Palestine begins.
1933	Nazis come to power in Germany.
1945	World learns of the Holocaust.
1947	United Nations votes in favor of partition of Palestine.
1948	British Mandate ends. Israel declares its independence.

flow of Jewish settlers. After World War II, however, Jewish immigration to Palestine gained support.

The UN Plan

The British turned the Palestine problem over to the United Nations. The United Nations came up with two plans. One called for the **partition,** or division, of Palestine between Jews and Arabs as shown in the first map below. Jerusalem—a holy city for Jews, Christians, and Muslims—was to be international. The other plan called for a united Palestine in which Jews and Arabs would rule themselves.

In 1947, the United Nations voted for the first plan. On May 14, 1948, the Jews proclaimed the State of Israel. The next day, five Arab states invaded Israel. The Jews fought back and extended their borders beyond the UN partition lines to those shown on the second map.

Many Palestinians refused to accept the existence of Israel. They fled and settled in UN refugee camps along Israel's borders.

In 1967, Israel won another war. It gained the lands shown on the third map. Some of these were later returned to Egypt. The others remain Israeli-occupied territories. ■

▲ *(left) Israeli soldiers stay on the lookout along the country's borders. (right) The founding of Israel was the fulfillment of the Zionist dream. (below) How did the 1967 war change the borders of Israel? How have they changed since then?*

■ *How did the United Nations try to solve the Arab-Jewish conflict in Palestine?*

Changing Boundaries of Palestine and Israel

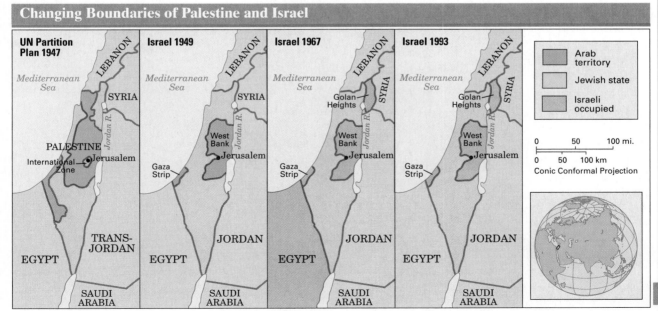

The United Nations, Israel, and South Korea

Everyday Life in Israel

Jewish immigrants have come to Israel from many countries. Since the breakup of the Soviet Union, hundreds of thousands more hope to immigrate.

Israel has created a modern economy along socialist lines. In the **kibbutz,** a type of collective farm, people share the work, daily living, and products of their efforts. Israel has also built factories and modern cities.

At the same time, Israel has to support expensive military forces. This effort uses up the resources needed to solve problems of housing, employment, and water shortages.

Today, UN observers still patrol some of Israel's borders. Palestinian refugees and their children continue to live in UN camps, now in Israeli-occupied territories. ■

▼ *Most Christians and Muslims in Israel are Palestinian Arabs.*

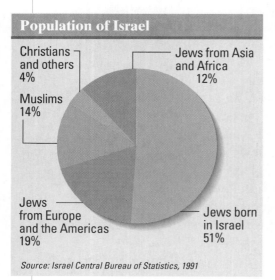

Population of Israel

Christians and others 4%

Muslims 14%

Jews from Asia and Africa 12%

Jews from Europe and the Americas 19%

Jews born in Israel 51%

Source: Israel Central Bureau of Statistics, 1991

▲ *This kibbutz in the Negev in southern Israel grows tomatoes in the desert. Water is piped in from the Sea of Galilee, far to the north.*

▼ *Women serve in the Israeli army.*

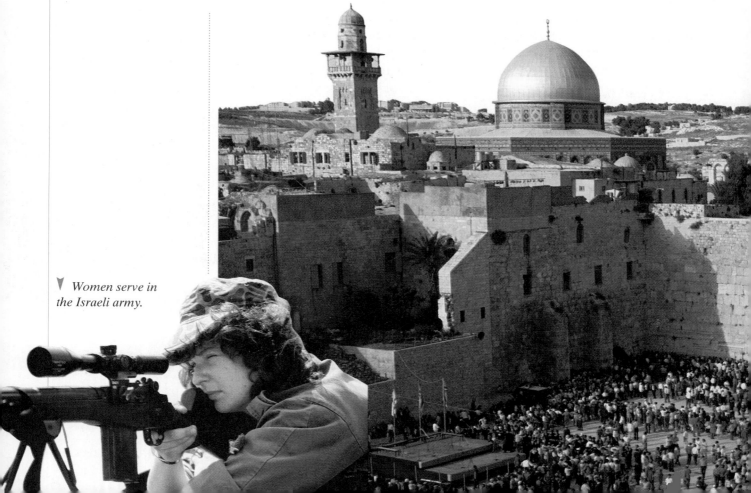

▶ This refugee camp in Gaza has been home to Palestinians for over 40 years.

▼ In Jerusalem, people shop in a street mall.

▲ Orthodox Jews, who strictly follow ancient traditions, wear prayer shawls on their way to pray at the Wailing Wall.

▼ These Jewish children are newly arrived from Ethiopia. It is their third day of school. They are learning to speak Hebrew.

▼ The Wailing Wall in Jerusalem is a remnant of a wall surrounding the Second Temple. Behind it is the Dome of the Rock, a holy site for Islam. In the distance, a church marks a Christian holy site on the Mount of Olives.

■ How do the pictures on these pages show the diversity of people and ways of life in Israel?

651

The Future of Israel

Since December 1987, Palestinian anger in the occupied lands has taken the form of an uprising called **intifada** (*ihn tih FAHD ah*). Palestinians—including women and young boys—have protested against Israel's rule by stone throwing, violent demonstrations, and strikes.

In 1992, Israel, its neighbors, and Palestinians began to discuss terms for peace. Some Israelis favor giving up occupied lands in exchange for peace. Others argue that these lands must not be returned because they are important to Israel's safety. However, the Palestinian population is growing quickly in these territories. If these areas become part of Israel, Arabs might soon outnumber Jews. Palestinians want their own country. What areas would this country include? Perhaps the United Nations will again take a role in solving some of these problems. ■

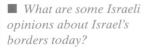
Israeli settlements in the occupied territories (shown on the map) concern Palestinians, who greatly outnumber Jewish settlers there, as the chart below shows. During the intifada, *Palestinian women from the West Bank argue with Israeli soldiers (below).*

■ *What are some Israeli opinions about Israel's borders today?*

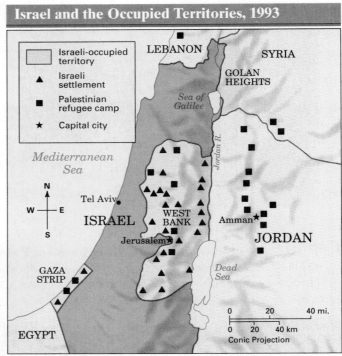

Israel and the Occupied Territories, 1993

Legend:
- Israeli-occupied territory
- ▲ Israeli settlement
- ■ Palestinian refugee camp
- ★ Capital city

LEBANON, SYRIA, GOLAN HEIGHTS, Sea of Galilee, Mediterranean Sea, Jordan R., Tel Aviv, ISRAEL, WEST BANK, Amman, Jerusalem, JORDAN, GAZA STRIP, Dead Sea, EGYPT

0   20   40 mi.
0   20   40 km
Conic Projection

Population

	Jews	Palestinians
Israel	3,946,700	750,000
Occupied Territory	110,000	1,900,000
Total	4,056,700	2,650,000

Source: Israeli Embassy, Information Department

REVIEW

1. **FOCUS** How did Israel become a nation?
2. **HISTORY** What was the aim of the Zionists?
3. **GEOGRAPHY** Why might Israel want to extend its border to the Jordan River?
4. **CRITICAL THINKING** How might the rapid growth of the Palestinian population living in the occupied territories influence Israel's decision to add these territories to the country?
5. **ACTIVITY** Imagine that you are interviewing an Israeli who lived through the founding of Israel in 1948. Write some questions that you have about this person's life since Israel was founded.

L E S S O N   3

South Korea and the United Nations

I t is a tense but quiet place. A strip of land two and a half miles wide divides the Korean peninsula between north and south. Soldiers stand by on either side with machine guns and peer at each other through field glasses.

This no man's land forms the border between North Korea and South Korea. It stretches generally along the 38th parallel, or 38° latitude north. In 1950, UN forces, including troops from many countries, defended this border.

T H I N K I N G
F O C U S

What role did the United Nations play in South Korea's history?

History of Korea

The partition of Korea into North Korea and South Korea first took place in 1945. The years of partition are a tiny slice of time in the history of this ancient land.

Land of the Morning Calm

For more than 1,300 years, Korea was united. Its ancient name, Choson, means "Land of the Morning Calm." The chart on the next page shows different

Key Term

- sanction

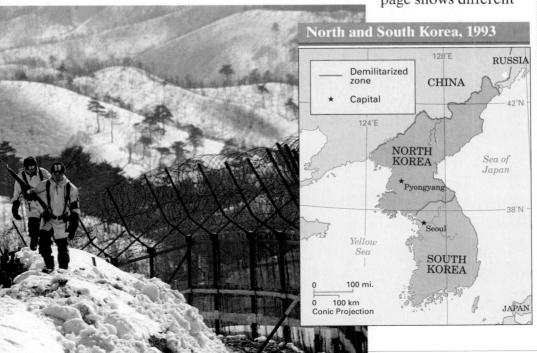

North and South Korea, 1993

- Demilitarized zone
- ★ Capital

128°E

RUSSIA

CHINA

42°N

124°E

NORTH KOREA

Sea of Japan

★ Pyongyang

38°N

★ Seoul

Yellow Sea

SOUTH KOREA

0   100 mi.

0   100 km
Conic Projection

JAPAN

◄ *(left) These cold hillsides behind the barbed wire form the border between North Korea and South Korea. (right) Where is the border between North Korea and South Korea located?*

653

The United Nations, Israel, and South Korea

civilizations that have formed Korea. If you look at the Atlas on page 684, you will see that Korea served as a natural bridge between China and Japan. Korea borrowed from both of these cultures, but it also developed its own language, alphabet, and traditions.

Koreans adopted Buddhism and Confucianism from China. Confucianism still influences daily life and social relationships. Today many Koreans also practice Christianity, which was brought by missionaries in the 1800s. Shamanism, or belief in spirits, still plays a role in the lives of many Koreans.

From the 1600s to 1910, Korea was called the Hermit Kingdom because it closed its borders to outsiders, hoping to prevent new invasions. However, in 1910, Korea was invaded by Japan. It remained a colony of Japan until 1945.

Partition and War

As World War II drew to a close, Koreans hoped to regain their independence. Instead, the Allies divided the country, placing Soviet troops in the north and U.S. troops in the south. (The map on page 653 shows how Korea is divided today.) The superpowers were supposed to cooperate and join the two parts into a single, independent Korea. Instead, the Cold War began, and Korea became a center of conflict.

In 1947 the United Nations decided that free elections should be

▼ *Modern Korea is built on centuries of tradition. Just as an archaeologist uncovers new layers in a dig, you can see the many layers of Korea's history in this chart.*

The History of Korea

1945–Present	**Divided North and South Korea**	
1910–1945	**Japanese Occupation**	
1392–1910	**Choson Dynasty** Hermit Kingdom Manchu and Japanese invasions Korean alphabet Confucianism: state religion	Turtle ships, covered with armor, were invented by Admiral Yi Sun-sin. They helped the Choson dynasty defeat the Japanese navy in 1592.
936–1392	**Koryo Dynasty** Buddhism: state religion Fighting against Mongols First movable type	Celadon pottery was a specialty of the Koryo dynasty.
c. A.D. 668–936	**Unified Silla Dynasty** Golden age Buddhism Strong Chinese influence	Dragons, believed to be powerful creatures, were often used in the Unified Silla kingdom to decorate ancient Korean temples.
c. A.D. 100– c. A.D. 668	**Three Kingdoms: Koguryo, Paekche, and Silla** Korean influence on Japan Buddhism	This observatory, built in 647 in the kingdom of Silla, was used to study the stars. It is the oldest observatory in East Asia.
c. 2333 B.C.– c. A.D. 100	**Old Choson** Shamanism Founding of Korea	This Old Choson rattle was used during shaman rituals in second to third century B.C.

654

Chapter 28

held in all of Korea. In South Korea, elections were held under UN supervision, and the Republic of Korea was created in 1948. In the north, the Soviets set up a Communist government and closed the border to UN observers.

In 1950, North Korean forces, supplied with Soviet arms, poured into South Korea, occupying most of the country. Because of a Soviet boycott, the United Nations was able to use **sanctions** and military force against North Korea. Sanctions are penalties used against a nation breaking international law. After three years of war, the border between North Korea and South Korea was back about where it had been—near the 38th parallel.

Land of Miracles

The war devastated South Korea. Many families were separated. The United Nations formed the Korean Reconstruction Agency in 1950. From 1951 to 1958 the agency helped South Korea as it recovered from the war.

South Koreans worked very hard to start up new industries. The country has done so well in the last 40 years that it has been called the Land of Miracles. Today, South Korea is one of the "four tigers" of Asia, a major producer of heavy machinery, textiles, and electronics. It is also an important trading partner with other countries of the Pacific Rim (see the Atlas, page 684).

Many Koreans have moved from the countryside into the cities. The population of Seoul *(sohl),* the capital, has grown from 500,000 after the Korean War to over 10 million. As you can see in the Minipedia, page 664, it is now the fourth largest city in the world.

Korea's Political Future

In 1948, after UN-supervised elections, South Korea became a republic. Since then it has actually known little political freedom. In the 1980s huge student demonstrations led to some reforms.

In the 1950s and 1960s, many South Koreans emigrated to the United States, seeking greater freedom. Today they are one of the fastest-growing U.S. minorities.

In North Korea, a dictator named Kim Il Sung has ruled since 1948. Under his rule, North Korea has cut itself off from most of the non-Communist world.

The end of the Cold War has eased relations between North Korea and South Korea. In 1991, both were admitted to the United Nations. Representatives from the two countries have started talks to reunite their countries. ■

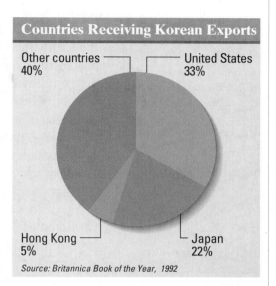

Countries Receiving Korean Exports

Other countries 40%

United States 33%

Hong Kong 5%

Japan 22%

Source: Britannica Book of the Year, 1992

▲ *The United States is South Korea's most important trading partner.*

▼ *Namdae-mun (Great South Gate) is one of the largest gates in Seoul's ancient city wall.*

■ *Why were Koreans hoping for independence at the end of World War II?*

Life in South Korea

Across Time & Space

Korea, like Germany, was divided in two parts after World War II. One part has a free-market economy; the other is Communist. As in Germany, if Korea reunites, its people will have to blend two very different ways of life.

■ *What is important in the life of South Koreans today?*

South Korea has blended modernization with respect for tradition. Confucianism teaches respect for ancestors, the need for order in society, and the importance of education. Families are very important in South Korea, and children are taught to honor their elders. Koreans believe that education is the key to success in life. It is not unusual for parents to make great sacrifices for their children's education. South Korean students study hard, and the country has a very high literacy rate.

Koreans enjoy sports. Apart from traditional self-defense, wrestling, and archery, they have taken up several western sports. Soccer has become a great favorite.

In 1988, South Korea hosted the summer Olympic Games. Its athletes won gold medals in archery, boxing, judo, table tennis, and wrestling. Korea also has a long artistic tradition. This tradition continues to be reflected in its dance, music, and festivals. For example, the National Classic Music Institute serves as a training center for Korean folk music. Folk dances are performed at many ceremonies throughout South Korea. ■

▼ *Education is very important to Korean children and their parents. (below) The Korean martial art of* tae kwon do, *which means "hand and foot fighting," is very popular in many countries.*

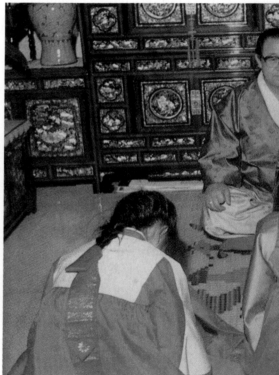

▲ *On New Year's Day, families gather to honor the souls of their ancestors. Children bow deeply to their elders and are given advice and presents.*

▲ *Seoul has become a huge city with sky-scrapers, fast traffic, and parks. To the left is an ancient palace begun in 1392.*

▲ *This street market in Seoul offers a choice of spicy Korean foods.*

▲ *Families work together threshing the harvest.*

▼ *Musicians play the komun-go, a six-stringed zither invented in the seventh century during the Koguryo kingdom.*

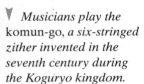

R E V I E W

1. **FOCUS** What role did the United Nations play in South Korea's history?
2. **HISTORY** Following World War II, the Cold War began. How did the Cold War affect Korea?
3. **BELIEF SYSTEMS** What religions and philosophies can be found in Korea?
4. **ECONOMICS** Why has South Korea been called the Land of Miracles?

5. **CRITICAL THINKING** If North Korea and South Korea agree to reunite, how is life likely to change for North Koreans? For South Koreans?
6. **ACTIVITY** Imagine that you are South Korean. Write a letter to the secretary-general of the United Nations explaining how you feel about the partition of your country and what you would like the United Nations to do about it.

The United Nations, Israel, and South Korea

Chapter Review

Reviewing Key Terms

forum (p. 644)
humanitarian (p. 645)
intifada (p. 652)
kibbutz (p. 650)

partition (p. 649)
sanction (p. 655)
veto (p. 644)

Answer the following questions using the key term or terms in parentheses.

1. What are the goals and powers of the United Nations? (forum, humanitarian, veto, sanction)
2. How do Israelis earn a living? (kibbutz)
3. What was the result of Allied decisions about Korea after World War II? (partition)
4. How did Palestinians react to Israeli occupation? (intifada)

Exploring Concepts

Answer each question with information from the chapter.

1. What role did the United Nations play in the creation of Israel?
2. What was unusual about the UN role in Korea in 1950?
3. Why have conflicts between Arabs and Jews continued in Israel?
4. Why did Zionist leaders of the early 1900s believe that the Jewish people needed a nation of their own?
5. What was unusual about South Korea's recovery after the war?
6. What is the relationship between the United Nations and the two Korean governments today?

Using Critical Thinking

1. What qualities do you think the UN secretary-general should have? Make up a list of questions you would ask someone who is being considered for this position. Then write the answers you think he or she should give.
2. Having veto power gives the five permanent members of the Security Council a great deal of influence over UN decisions. Do you think that it is a good idea for these five nations to have this power? Explain why or why not.

Preparing for Citizenship

1. COLLECTING INFORMATION Make a scrapbook of news articles about the ongoing activities of the United Nations and its agencies.
2. COLLABORATIVE LEARNING With your classmates, organize a "model United Nations." Choose five people to represent the permanent members of the Security Council. Choose one person (perhaps your teacher) to act as both secretary-general and moderator.

Other class members should choose the nations they want to represent from a list of current UN members. In an almanac or encyclopedia, each delegate should look up basic information about the country he or she represents. Then choose a committee to research and present three to five issues that your model United Nations will address.

Time/Space
Databank

Minipedia	660
Alphabet	660
Architecture	662
City	664
Highlights in the History of Communication	665
History of the World	669
Countries of the World	674
Atlas	678
World: Political	678
World: Physical	680
Eurasia: Political/Physical	682
Pacific Rim: Political/Physical	684
Africa: Political/Physical	685

North America: Political/Physical	686
South America: Political/Physical	687
World: Religions	688
World: Climate	688
World: Population (Cartogram)	689
World: Land Use, Land and Ocean Resources	689
Glossary of Geographic Terms	690
Gazetteer	692
Biographical Dictionary	696
Glossary	701
Index	708

Alphabet

Alphabet is the series of letters used in writing a language. The name means exactly what the term ABC´s means as a name for the 26 letters of our alphabet. The word comes from *alpha* and *beta,* the first two letters of the Greek alphabet.

Most books, magazines, and newspapers are printed in the 26-letter alphabet called *Roman.* But the Romans did not invent it. They put finishing touches on a system that had been growing for thousands of years.

The earliest writing

In early times, people could communicate with one another only by speaking or by making gestures. They had no way to keep records of important events, unless they memorized the story of a great battle or important happening. They had no way to send messages over long distances unless they passed them from one person to the next by word of mouth, or had one person

memorize the message and then deliver it.

The first stage in writing came when people learned to draw pictures to express their ideas. In *ideography,* each picture conveyed an idea. Ideography enabled even people who did not speak the same language to communicate with each other. Then people learned *logography,* expressing ideas indirectly by using signs to stand for the words of the idea. Instead of drawing pictures of five sheep to show a herd of five animals, a person could draw one sign for the numeral "five" and one for "sheep." Gradually people learned to use a *syllabic* system, in which a sign that stood for one word could be used not only for that word but also for any phonetic combination that sounded like that word. This is what we call *rebus writing.* If we used rebus writing in English, we could draw a sign for the word "bee" followed by a sign for the word "leaf" to stand for the word "belief." Finally, people developed alphabets in which indi-

Development of the English alphabet The English alphabet developed from a number of early writing systems, beginning with the sign writing of Ancient Egypt. The Romans had given most capital letters their modern form by A.D. 114. But the letters *J, U,* and *W* were not added to the alphabet until the Middle Ages.

Some important alphabets The alphabets of five important languages are shown below. Hindi is India's most widely spoken language. People throughout the Middle East and northern Africa use Arabic, which is read from right to left. Gaelic, along with English, is the official language of Ireland.

Greek Α Β Γ Δ Ε Ζ Η Θ Ι Κ Λ Μ Ν Ξ Ο Π Ρ Σ Τ Υ Φ Χ Ψ Ω

Russian АБВГДЕЁЖЗИЙКЛМНОПРСТУФХЦЧШЩЪЫЬЭЮЯ

Hindi अ आ इ ई उ ऊ ऋ ए ऐ ओ औ क ख ग घ ङ च छ ज झ ञ ट ठ ड ढ ण त थ द ध न प फ ब भ म य र ल व श ष स ह

Arabic ا ب ت ث ج ح خ د ذ ر ز س ش ص ض ط ظ ع غ ف ق ك ل م ن ه و ي

Gaelic ᚪ b c ᚈ e ᚠ ᚷ h i l m n o p ᚱ ᚄ ᚈ u

vidual signs stood for particular sounds. Today, most written languages in the world use alphabetic writing systems.

The earliest alphabets

The Egyptians used a system of several hundred signs that stood for full words or for syllables. They could write the word *nefer,* or *good,* with a single sign for the whole word, or with three signs, for the sounds *n, f,* and *r.* These signs specified the consonants in syllables, but not the vowels. Egyptian writing, which developed around 3000 B.C., was formally a picture writing, and structurally a word and syllabic writing.

The Semites, who lived in Syria and Palestine, knew something of the Egyptian writing system. They worked out an alphabetic writing about 1500 B.C. They used signs to show the consonants of syllables, just as the Egyptians did. The Semites seem to have adapted some of the pictures from Egyptian hieroglyphics, but they used these symbols for sounds in their own language. The oldest Semitic alphabet comes from the Sinai Peninsula.

The Phoenicians, who lived along the coast of the Mediterranean Sea, developed a system of 22 signs about 1000 B.C. Their alphabet was structurally related to Semitic and Egyptian, with signs for consonant sounds, not vowel sounds. Early Phoenician writing consists partly of pictographic forms, which they may have borrowed from older pictographic systems, and partly of geometric or diagrammatic signs that they invented. Historians find it difficult to trace the formal relations between Semitic and Phoenician signs, because Phoenician has both pictographic and diagrammatic signs, and because so little is known of the ancient systems used in Syria and Palestine.

The Cypriots, the people of the island of Cyprus, developed an alphabet of their own. Starting with an unknown word-syllable system, they worked out an alphabet of 56 signs, each standing for an initial consonant and a different vowel. The next step was to create separate signs for vowels and consonants.

The Greeks came in contact with Phoenician traders, and learned from them the idea of writing individual sounds of the language. Sometime during the period before 800 B.C., they borrowed Phoenician symbols and modified them to form the Greek alphabet. The Phoeni-

cian alphabet included more consonants than the Greeks needed for their language, so they used the extra signs for vowel sounds. In this way, the Greeks improved on both Phoenician and Cypriot ideas, because they could combine individual letters for both consonants and vowels to spell any word they wanted.

The Greeks took over the Phoenician names for their signs, and in most cases the signs themselves. The first letter of the Phoenician alphabet,✔, and its name, *aleph,* meaning *ox,* became ∆, or *alpha* in Greek. The second letter,⊿ , or *beth,* meaning *house,* became β, or *beta* in Greek. The Greeks later modified the shapes of these letters, adding and dropping some letters, to form the 24-letter Greek alphabet of today.

The Roman alphabet

The Etruscans moved to central Italy from somewhere in the eastern Mediterranean region sometime after 1000 B.C. They carried the Greek alphabet with them. The Romans learned the alphabet from the Etruscans, and gave it much the same form we use today. The early Roman alphabet had about 20 letters, and gradually gained 3 more.

Capital letters were the only forms used for hundreds of years. Many people consider the Roman alphabet to have been perfected by A.D. 114. That year, sculptors carved the inscriptions on a memorial column built to honor the emperor Trajan. The style of lettering they used is considered one of the most beautiful in the world.

Carving letters in stone is not an easy job, and Roman stonecutters rounded or squared, simplified, and polished their letters. They developed the beautiful thick-and-thin strokes we use today. They also added *serifs* (little finishing strokes) at the tops and bottoms of many letters. The practical reason for serifs was that the carvers found it difficult to end wide strokes without ugly blunt lines. And if a chisel slipped while squaring off an end, they could not erase the mistake. But serifs also added a touch of strength and grace to Roman lettering, and are still used today.

Small letters gradually developed from capitals. Scribes who copied books often used *uncials* (rounded letters) that were easier to form than some capitals. True lower-case letters developed later, when scribes saved space in books by using the smaller letters.

Architecture

Architectural terms

Ambulatory is a continuous aisle in a circular building. In a church, the ambulatory serves as a semicircular aisle that encloses the apse.

Apse is a semicircular area. In most churches, the apse is at one end of the building and contains the main altar.

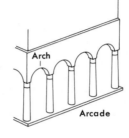

Arcade refers to a series of arches supported by columns or piers. A passageway formed by the arches is also called an arcade.

Arch is a curved structure used to support the weight of the material above it. A stone at the top of an arch, called the *keystone,* holds the other parts in place.

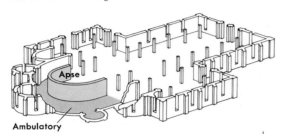

Architrave makes up the lowest part of an entablature. It rests on the capital of a column. For a drawing of an architrave, see Entablature on the opposite page.

Buttress is a support built against an outside wall of a building. A *flying buttress* is an arched support that extends from a column or pier to the wall.

Buttress   Flying Buttress

Cantilever is a horizontal projection, such as a balcony or a beam, which is supported only at one end.

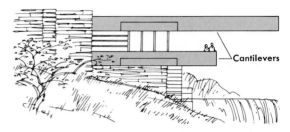

Cantilevers

Capital, in an order, forms the upper part of a column. It separates the shaft from the entablature.

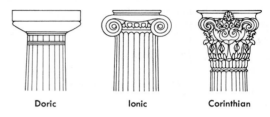

Doric   Ionic   Corinthian

Colonnade means a row of columns, each set an equal distance apart.

Column is a vertical support. In an order, it consists of a shaft and a capital and often rests on a base.

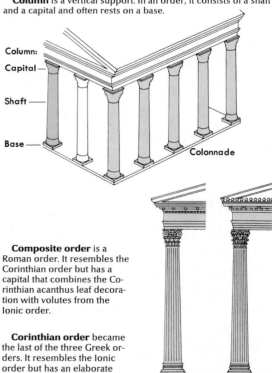

Column:
Capital
Shaft
Base
Colonnade

Composite order is a Roman order. It resembles the Corinthian order but has a capital that combines the Corinthian acanthus leaf decoration with volutes from the Ionic order.

Corinthian order became the last of the three Greek orders. It resembles the Ionic order but has an elaborate capital that is decorated with carvings of leaves of the acanthus plant.

Composite Order   Corinthian Order

Cornice forms the upper part of an entablature and extends beyond the frieze.

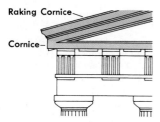

Raking Cornice

Cornice

Doric Order

Doric order was the first and simplest of the three Greek orders. The Doric is the only order that normally has no base.

Entablature refers to the upper horizontal part of an order between a capital and the roof. It consists of three major parts—the architrave, frieze, and cornice.

Entablature:

Cornice

Frieze

Architrave

Facade is the front of a building. Most facades contain an entrance.

Frieze forms the middle part of an entablature and is often decorated with a horizontal band of relief sculpture.

Ionic order was the second of the three Greek orders. It has a capital decorated with carved spiral scrolls called *volutes*.

Module is a measurement, such as the diameter of a column, which architects use to establish the proportions of an entire structure.

Nave is the chief area within a church. It extends from the main entrance to the transept.

Ionic Order

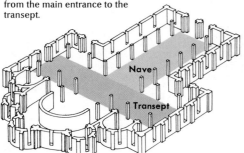

Nave

Transept

Order, in classical architecture, consisted of a column and an entablature. Orders served as the basic elements of Greek and Roman architecture and influenced many later styles.

Pediment is a triangular segment between the horizontal entablature and the sloping roof at the front of a classical-style building.

Pediment

Pendentive is a curved support shaped like an inverted triangle. Pendentives hold up a dome.

Dome

Pendentive

Pier refers to a large pillar used to support a roof.

Post and lintel is a method of construction in which vertical beams (posts) support a horizontal beam (lintel).

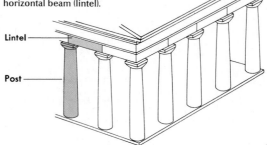

Lintel

Post

Shaft is the main part of a column below the capital. Many shafts have shallow vertical grooves called *fluting*.

Transept forms the arms in a T- or cross-shaped church.

Tuscan order, a Roman order, resembles the Doric order, but the shaft has no fluting.

Vault is an arched brick or stone ceiling or roof. A *barrel vault,* the simplest form of vault, is a single continuous arch. A *groined vault* is formed by joining two barrel vaults at right angles. A *ribbed vault* has diagonal arches that project from the surface.

Tuscan Order

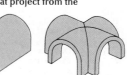

WORLD BOOK illustrations by Robert Keys

Barrel Vault   Groined Vault   Ribbed Vault

City

Comparing the sizes of cities

A city determines its population by counting the people who live within its political boundaries. But cities of the world define their city limits differently, making population comparisons difficult. United States cities fix their limits so that they do not overlap or include other cities and towns. Some foreign cities include other urban and rural areas.

Countries also determine metropolitan areas in various ways. In the United States, metropolitan area boundaries follow county lines. Each metropolitan area includes a county with a large city and perhaps nearby counties. But in most countries, a metropolitan area does not have definite political boundaries.

In these countries, metropolitan areas include the major city and urban and rural areas that are socially or economically identified with the city.

Mexico City has the largest population of any city in the world. Mexico City also has the largest metropolitan area population in the world.

Some governments do not report separate city and metropolitan area populations in their censuses and population estimates. In such cases, the same city proper figure appears in both the cities and the metropolitan areas tables, *below,* to show the existence of a metropolitan area.

50 largest cities in the world

1. Mexico City	10,061,000	27. Ho Chi Minh City	3,419,978
2. Seoul	9,645,932	28. Wuhan	3,340,000
3. Tokyo	8,353,674	29. Calcutta	3,305,006
4. Moscow	8,275,000	30. Madras	3,276,622
5. Bombay	8,227,332	31. Guangzhou	3,220,000
6. New York City	7,071,639	32. Madrid	3,123,713
7. São Paulo	7,033,529	33. Berlin (East and West)	3,062,979
8. Shanghai	6,880,000	34. Chicago	3,005,072
9. London	6,767,500	35. Yokohama	2,992,644
10. Jakarta	6,503,449	36. Sydney	2,989,070
11. Cairo	6,052,836	37. Baghdad	2,969,000
12. Beijing	5,760,000	38. Los Angeles	2,968,579
13. Teheran	5,734,199	39. Lahore	2,952,689
14. Hong Kong	5,705,000	40. Alexandria	2,917,327
15. Istanbul	5,475,982	41. Buenos Aires	2,908,001
16. Tianjin	5,300,000	42. Rome	2,830,569
17. Karachi	5,208,170	43. Chongqing	2,730,000
18. Bangkok	5,153,902	44. Melbourne	2,645,484
19. Rio de Janeiro	5,093,232	45. Pyongyang	2,639,448
20. Delhi	4,884,234	46. Osaka	2,636,260
21. Leningrad	4,295,000	47. Harbin	2,590,000
22. Santiago	4,225,299	48. Hanoi	2,570,905
23. Lima	4,164,597	49. Chengdu	2,540,000
24. Shenyang	4,130,000	50. Bangalore	2,476,355
25. Bogotá	3,982,941		
26. Pusan	3,516,807		

50 largest metropolitan areas in the world

1. Mexico City	15,505,000	26. Bangkok	5,153,902
2. São Paulo	12,588,439	27. Leningrad	4,827,000
3. Shanghai	12,050,000	28. Philadelphia	4,716,818
4. Tokyo	11,618,281	29. Lima	4,608,010
5. Cairo	10,000,000	30. Detroit	4,488,072
6. Buenos Aires	9,927,404	31. Madras	4,289,347
7. Seoul	9,645,932	32. Santiago	4,225,299
8. Beijing	9,470,000	33. Shenyang	4,130,000
9. Calcutta	9,194,018	34. Bogotá	3,982,941
10. Rio de Janeiro	9,018,637	35. Pusan	3,516,807
11. Paris	8,706,963	36. Toronto	3,427,168
12. Moscow	8,537,000	37. Ho Chi Minh City	3,419,978
13. New York City	8,274,961	38. Wuhan	3,340,000
14. Bombay	8,227,332	39. Caracas	3,310,236
15. Tianjin	7,990,000	40. Washington, D.C.	3,250,822
16. Los Angeles-Long Beach	7,447,503	41. Guangzhou	3,220,000
17. London	6,767,500	42. Madrid	3,123,713
18. Jakarta	6,503,449	43. Berlin (East and West)	3,062,979
19. Chicago	6,060,387	44. Athens	3,027,331
20. Manila	5,926,000	45. Yokohama	2,992,644
21. Teheran	5,734,199	46. Sydney	2,989,070
22. Delhi	5,729,283	47. Baghdad	2,969,000
23. Hong Kong	5,705,000	48. Lahore	2,952,689
24. Istanbul	5,475,982	49. Bangalore	2,921,751
25. Karachi	5,208,170	50. Montreal	2,921,357

50 largest cities in the United States

1. New York City	7,071,639	26. St. Louis	452,801
2. Chicago	3,005,072	27. Kansas City, Mo.	448,033
3. Los Angeles	2,968,579	28. El Paso	425,259
4. Philadelphia	1,688,210	29. Atlanta	425,022
5. Houston	1,595,138	30. Pittsburgh	423,959
6. Detroit	1,203,399	31. Oklahoma City	403,484
7. Dallas	904,078	32. Cincinnati	385,457
8. San Diego	875,538	33. Fort Worth	385,164
9. Phoenix	789,704	34. Minneapolis	370,951
10. Baltimore	786,741	35. Portland, Ore.	366,383
11. San Antonio	786,023	36. Honolulu	365,048
12. Indianapolis	700,807	37. Long Beach	361,355
13. San Francisco	678,974	38. Tulsa	360,919
14. Memphis	646,174	39. Buffalo	357,870
15. Washington, D.C.	638,432	40. Toledo	354,635
16. Milwaukee	636,297	41. Miami	346,865
17. San Jose	629,531	42. Austin	345,890
18. Cleveland	573,822	43. Oakland	339,337
19. Columbus, O.	565,032	44. Albuquerque	332,239
20. Boston	562,994	45. Tucson	330,537
21. New Orleans	557,927	46. Newark	329,248
22. Jacksonville, Fla.	540,920	47. Omaha	327,558
23. Seattle	493,846	48. Charlotte	314,447
24. Denver	492,365	49. Louisville	298,694
25. Nashville	455,651	50. Birmingham	284,413

50 largest cities and towns in Canada

1. Montreal	1,015,420	28. Markham	114,597
2. Calgary	636,104	29. Halifax	113,577
3. Toronto	612,289	30. Thunder Bay	112,272
4. Winnipeg	594,551	31. Richmond	108,492
5. Edmonton	573,982	32. St. John's	96,216
6. North York	556,297	33. Nepean	95,490
7. Scarborough	484,676	34. Montréal-Nord	90,303
8. Vancouver	431,147	35. Glouster	89,810
9. Mississauga	374,005	36. Sudbury	88,717
10. Hamilton	306,728	37. Saanich	82,940
11. Etobicoke	302,973	38. Gatineau	81,244
12. Ottawa	300,763	39. Sault Ste. Marie	80,905
13. Laval	284,164	40. Cambridge	79,920
14. London	269,140	41. Delta	79,610
15. Windsor	193,111	42. Guelph	78,235
16. Brampton	188,498	43. Saint John	76,381
17. Surrey	181,447	44. Brantford	76,146
18. Saskatoon	177,641	45. St.-Léonard	75,947
19. Regina	175,062	46. La Salle	75,621
20. Quebec	164,580	47. Sherbrooke	74,438
21. Kitchener	150,604	48. Niagara Falls	72,107
22. Burnaby	145,161	49. Ste.-Foy	69,615
23. York	135,401	50. Coquitlam	69,291
24. Longueuil	125,441		
25. Oshawa	123,651		
26. St. Catherines	123,455		
27. Burlington	116,675		

Sources: 1980 census for the United States cities; 1986 census for Canadian cities; 1976-1990 censuses and estimates for other cities.

Highlights in the history of communication

Prehistoric people used paintings and drawings to tell stories.

About 20,000 B.C.

The Sumerians developed the first known system of writing.

About 3500 B.C.

The Semites developed the first real alphabet.

About 1500-1000 B.C.

59 B.C.

The Romans began a handwritten newssheet that was a forerunner of today's newspapers.

WORLD BOOK illustration by Richard Hook

Deutsches Museum, Munich, West Germany

Deutsches Museum, Munich, West Germany

Smoke signals were one of the earliest forms of long-distance communication. Such signals could send only limited information—a warning, for example.

Cuneiform writing consists of wedge-shaped characters stamped on clay. The clay cylinder above was inscribed during the 500's B.C. in Babylon.

Wax tablets were once a common writing surface. The early Greeks wrote on such tablets with a pointed tool called a *stylus* and laced the tablets together.

T'sai Lun, a Chinese government official, invented paper.

About A.D. 105

Pi Sheng, a Chinese printer, invented movable type.

About 1045

The German metalsmith Johannes Gutenberg reinvented movable type.

Mid-1400's

The English made the first pencils of *graphite,* the substance used today.

Mid-1500's

Printed newssheets called *corantos* appeared.

1600's

Detail of an Italian manuscript (about 1331) by Giovanni de' Nuxiglia; Bibliothèque Nationale, Paris (SCALA/EPA)

Bettmann Archive

During the Middle Ages, artists copied books by hand, letter by letter. They covered their work with gold, silver, and colored decorations called *illumination.*

Printing from movable type was invented in Asia during the 1000's and in Europe during the 1400's. A shop of the 1600's is shown above. At the left, typesetters assemble type to form pages. In the background, an assistant inks a page. At the right, a printer turns a huge screw on the printing press to push paper against the type.

Communication

The French engineer Claude Chappe developed a visual telegraph.

Joseph Nicéphore Niépce, a French physicist, made the first permanent photograph.

| Late 1700's | 1811 | 1826 | 1830's |

Friedrich Koenig, a German printer, invented a steam-powered printing press.

The French painter Louis J. M. Daguerre developed an improved photograph.

American Antiquarian Society, Worcester, Mass.

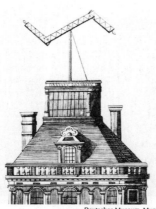

Deutsches Museum, Munich, West Germany

Detail of *Intérieur d'un Cabinet de Curiosités;* Société Française de Photographie, Paris

Postal service was established in many nations during the 1700's. This postrider carried mail between Boston and other cities in the American Colonies.

The Chappe telegraph consisted of a series of towers. An operator in each tower moved a crossbar and two large, jointed arms to send coded messages.

A daguerreotype was an early type of photograph printed on a metal plate. Louis J. M. Daguerre took this picture of a collection of rare objects in 1837.

Thomas A. Edison developed the first practical phonograph.

Ottmar Mergenthaler, a German-born mechanic, patented the Linotype machine.

| 1877 | 1880's | 1884 | 1895 |

The German physicist Heinrich Hertz discovered electromagnetic waves.

The Italian inventor Guglielmo Marconi developed the *wireless telegraph* (radio).

Bettmann Archive

Historical Pictures Service

The Marconi Company

Thomas A. Edison's phonograph recorded sound on a cylinder covered with foil. This picture shows the inventor with an early version of his phonograph.

Linotype machines used a keyboard to set type mechanically. Their introduction sped the production of newspapers and other publications.

Guglielmo Marconi combined the ideas of several scientists to send signals through the air. His invention, the *wireless telegraph,* led to present-day radio.

The American painter Samuel F. B. Morse patented his electric telegraph.

The first successful transatlantic telegraph cable linked Europe and North America.

Alexander Graham Bell patented a type of telephone.

1840   1864   1866   1868   1876

The British physicist James Clerk Maxwell reported his theory of electromagnetism, which led to radio.

Three American inventors patented the first practical typewriter.

Bettmann Archive

Bettmann Archive

Bettmann Archive

Samuel F. B. Morse developed one of the first successful electric telegraphs. He also developed Morse code, a system of sending messages by dots and dashes.

An early typewriter was patented in the 1860's by three American inventors—Carlos Glidden, Christopher Latham Sholes, and Samuel W. Soulé.

Alexander Graham Bell designed one of the first successful telephones and demonstrated it at the 1876 Centennial Exposition in Philadelphia.

Reginald A. Fessenden, a Canadian-born physicist, transmitted voice by radio.

Vladimir K. Zworykin, a Russian-born physicist, demonstrated the first all-electronic TV system.

1906   1907   1929   1936

The American inventor Lee De Forest patented the *triode,* an improved vacuum tube.

The British Broadcasting Corporation made the world's first TV broadcasts.

Bettmann Archive

Bettmann Archive

British Broadcasting Corporation

A motion picture camera of about 1915 was used to film silent movies. Several inventors developed movie cameras in the late 1800's and early 1900's.

Radio became a major source of family entertainment during the 1920's. This photograph shows a singer making a broadcast during the early days of radio.

One of the first TV broadcasts was a demonstration of self-defense techniques. It appeared in 1936 on the British Broadcasting Corporation (BBC).

Extracted from the Communication article in *World Book.* Copyright © 1990 by World Book, Inc.

Communication

┌ Bell Telephone Laboratories
│ developed the transistor.

┌ Television networks began to
│ record programs on videotape.

┌ Xerox Corporation perfected
│ *xerography,* a copying process.

○ 1947   ○ Mid-1950's   ○ 1960

└ Dennis Gabor, a British engineer, invented
  holography (3-D photography).

└ *Echo 1* became the first satellite to receive radio signals from a ground
  station and reflect them back to earth.

Ampex Corporation

American Telephone
& Telegraph Co.

WORLD BOOK photo

Tape recorders that recorded sounds on magnetic tape were developed in the 1930's. This 1948 recorder was the first one manufactured in the United States.

Telstar I, a communications satellite launched in 1962, relayed telephone calls, TV shows, and other communications between the United States and Europe.

Computers revolutionized communication in the 1960's and 1970's. A computer terminal at an airport, *above,* relays information about flights and reservations.

┌ Corning Glass Works produced the first optical
│ fiber suitable for long-range communication.

┌ The first mailgram was trans-
│ mitted by satellite.

○ 1970   ○ 1970's   ○ 1974   ○ Early 1980's

└ Several manufacturers developed
  cassette videotape recorders.

└ Several companies began
  marketing cellular mobile
  telephones.

WORLD BOOK photo

WORLD BOOK photo

© Paul Robert Perry

Fiber-optic communication uses a laser to send signals through glass strands called *optical fibers,* shown above.

A home computer, *above,* helps a girl practice arithmetic problems. Small computers that perform a variety of jobs gained popularity in the late 1970's.

A cellular mobile telephone enables a motorist to make and receive calls. These devices, introduced in the 1980's, greatly improved mobile phone communication.

World, History of the

Major developments in early centers of civilization

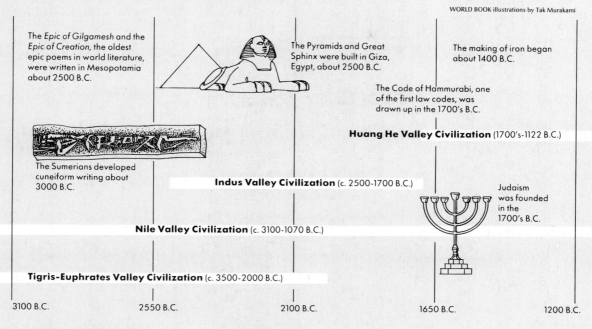

The *Epic of Gilgamesh* and the *Epic of Creation*, the oldest epic poems in world literature, were written in Mesopotamia about 2500 B.C.

The Pyramids and Great Sphinx were built in Giza, Egypt, about 2500 B.C.

The making of iron began about 1400 B.C.

The Code of Hammurabi, one of the first law codes, was drawn up in the 1700's B.C.

Huang He Valley Civilization (1700's-1122 B.C.)

The Sumerians developed cuneiform writing about 3000 B.C.

Indus Valley Civilization (c. 2500-1700 B.C.)

Judaism was founded in the 1700's B.C.

Nile Valley Civilization (c. 3100-1070 B.C.)

Tigris-Euphrates Valley Civilization (c. 3500-2000 B.C.)

| 3100 B.C. | 2550 B.C. | 2100 B.C. | 1650 B.C. | 1200 B.C. |

The earliest civilizations arose in four river valleys in Asia and Africa between about 3500 B.C. and the 1700's B.C. The fertile soil of the valleys supported flourishing farming villages. Civilization began when such villages developed into cities.

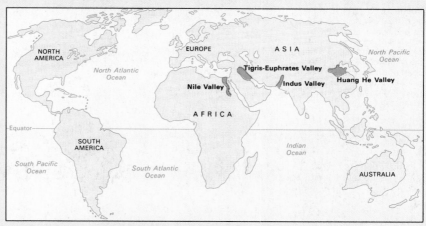

Important dates

c. 9000 B.C. The development of agriculture began with the growing of crops and the domestication of animals in the Middle East.

c. 3500 B.C. A number of small cities, centers of the world's first civilization, appeared in Sumer, the lower part of the Tigris-Euphrates Valley.

c. 3500 B.C. The Sumerians invented the first form of writing. It was later simplified to produce wedge-shaped *cuneiform* writing, which spread throughout the Middle East.

c. 3100 B.C. King Menes of Upper Egypt united Lower and Upper Egypt.

c. 2500 B.C. The Indus Valley civilization began to flourish in the cities of Moen-jo-Daro and Harappa in what is now Pakistan.

c. 2500-1100 B.C. The Minoan civilization on the island of Crete rose and fell.

2300's B.C. Sargon of Akkad conquered the Sumerians and united all Mesopotamia under his rule, creating the world's first empire.

1700's B.C. The Shang dynasty began its rule in the Huang He Valley of China.

c. 1792-1750 B.C. Babylonia flourished under King Hammurabi.

1500's-c. 1100 B.C. The city of Mycenae was the leading political and cultural center on the Greek mainland.

c. 1595 B.C. The Hittites, a warlike people from what is now central Turkey, conquered the Babylonians.

c. 1500 B.C. The Aryans of central Asia began migrating to India.

Major developments from about 1200 B.C. to A.D. 500

WORLD BOOK illustrations by Tak Murakami

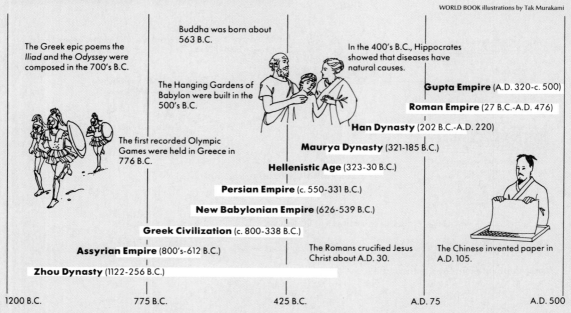

The Greek epic poems the *Iliad* and the *Odyssey* were composed in the 700's B.C.

Buddha was born about 563 B.C.

In the 400's B.C., Hippocrates showed that diseases have natural causes.

The Hanging Gardens of Babylon were built in the 500's B.C.

The first recorded Olympic Games were held in Greece in 776 B.C.

The Romans crucified Jesus Christ about A.D. 30.

The Chinese invented paper in A.D. 105.

Gupta Empire (A.D. 320-c. 500)
Roman Empire (27 B.C.-A.D. 476)
Han Dynasty (202 B.C.-A.D. 220)
Maurya Dynasty (321-185 B.C.)
Hellenistic Age (323-30 B.C.)
Persian Empire (c. 550-331 B.C.)
New Babylonian Empire (626-539 B.C.)
Greek Civilization (c. 800-338 B.C.)
Assyrian Empire (800's-612 B.C.)
Zhou Dynasty (1122-256 B.C.)

1200 B.C.   775 B.C.   425 B.C.   A.D. 75   A.D. 500

Powerful empires emerged as civilization advanced and spread between 1200 B.C. and A.D. 500. The Roman Empire covered much of Europe and the Middle East, and the north coast of Africa. The Han dynasty of China and the Gupta dynasty of India also ruled huge empires.

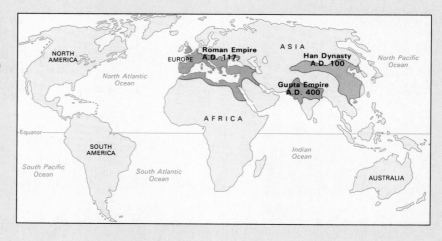

WORLD BOOK map

Important dates

1020 B.C. The Hebrews founded a kingdom in what is now Palestine.

800's B.C. The Etruscans settled in west-central Italy.

750-338 B.C. Athens, Corinth, Sparta, and Thebes were the chief city-states of Greece.

c. 550 B.C. Cyrus the Great established the Persian Empire.

509 B.C. The people of Rome revolted against their Etruscan rulers and established a republic.

338 B.C. Philip II of Macedonia conquered the Greeks.

331 B.C. Alexander the Great defeated the Persians at Arbela, opening the way to his conquest of northern India.

221-206 B.C. The Qin dynasty established China's first strong central government.

202 B.C. The Han dynasty began its 400-year rule of China.

146 B.C. The Romans conquered Greece.

55-54 B.C. Julius Caesar led the Roman invasion of Britain.

27 B.C. Augustus became the first Roman emperor.

c. A.D. 250 The Maya Indians developed an advanced civilization in Central America and Mexico.

313 Constantine issued the Edict of Milan, which granted freedom of worship to Christians of the Roman Empire.

320 India began its golden age under the Gupta dynasty.

395 The Roman Empire split into the East Roman, or Byzantine, Empire and the West Roman Empire.

476 The Germanic chieftain Odoacer overthrew Romulus Augustulus, the last emperor of the West Roman Empire.

World, History of the

Major developments from A.D. 500 to about 1500

WORLD BOOK illustrations by Tak Murakami

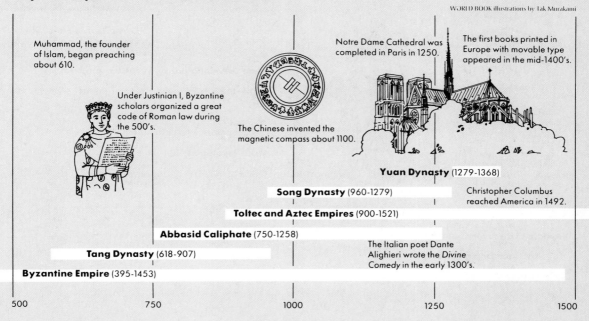

Muhammad, the founder of Islam, began preaching about 610.

Under Justinian I, Byzantine scholars organized a great code of Roman law during the 500's.

The Chinese invented the magnetic compass about 1100.

Notre Dame Cathedral was completed in Paris in 1250.

The first books printed in Europe with movable type appeared in the mid-1400's.

Yuan Dynasty (1279-1368)

Song Dynasty (960-1279)

Christopher Columbus reached America in 1492.

Toltec and Aztec Empires (900-1521)

Abbasid Caliphate (750-1258)

The Italian poet Dante Alighieri wrote the *Divine Comedy* in the early 1300's.

Tang Dynasty (618-907)

Byzantine Empire (395-1453)

| 500 | 750 | 1000 | 1250 | 1500 |

Between 500 and 1500, new civilizations appeared in Africa and the Americas. In the Middle East, the Muslim Arabs rose to power and conquered a huge empire by the mid-700's. In the 1200's, Mongol warriors swept through Asia, creating one of the largest empires in history.

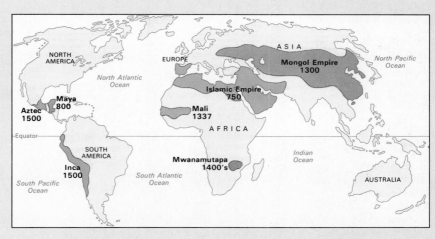

WORLD BOOK map

Important dates

527-565 The Byzantine Empire reached its greatest extent under Emperor Justinian I.

622 Muhammad, founder of Islam, fled from Mecca to Medina. His flight, called the Hegira, marks the beginning of the Islamic calendar.

700's-mid-1000's The Ghana Empire, the first great black empire in western Africa, flourished as a trading state.

732 Charles Martel and the Franks defeated invading Muslims in fighting in west-central France. The victory prevented the Muslims from overrunning Europe.

750 The Abbasids became the caliphs of the Islamic world.

800 Pope Leo III crowned Charlemagne, ruler of the Franks, emperor of the Romans.

c. 988 Vladimir I converted the Russians to Christianity.

1054 Rivalries between the church in Rome and the church in Constantinople resulted in their separation as the Roman Catholic Church and Eastern Orthodox Churches, respectively.

1192 Yoritomo became the first shogun to rule Japan.

1215 English barons forced King John to grant a charter of liberties called Magna Carta.

1279 The Mongols gained control of all China.

1300's The Renaissance began in Italy.

1368 The Ming dynasty began its nearly 300-year rule of China.

1453 The Ottoman Turks captured Constantinople (Istanbul) and overthrew the Byzantine Empire.

Major developments from A.D. 1500 to about 1900

WORLD BOOK illustrations by Tak Murakami

Nicolaus Copernicus proposed in 1543 that the sun is the center of the universe.

Michelangelo completed painting the ceiling of the Sistine Chapel in the Vatican in 1512.

William Shakespeare wrote many of the world's greatest dramas between 1590 and 1616.

Charles Darwin published his theory of evolution in 1859 in *The Origin of Species.*

European Colonial Expansion in Africa and Asia (1870-1914)

Latin-American Wars of Independence (1791-1824)

French Revolution (1789-1799)

Revolutionary War in America (1775-1783)

Industrial Revolution (1700-mid-1800's)

Manchu Rule of China (1644-1912)

Tokugawa Shogunate in Japan (1603-1867)

Mogul Empire (1526-1707)

Voyages of Discovery (1400's-1500's)

Ottoman Empire (1326-1922)

Renaissance (1300-1600)

Ludwig van Beethoven composed many of his greatest symphonies between 1800 and 1815.

Alexander Graham Bell invented the telephone in 1876.

1500   1600   1700   1800   1900

European colonial empires had spread over much of the world by the late 1800's. The largest empires of the period belonged to Great Britain, France, and Germany.

Belgium
France
Germany
Great Britain
Italy
Netherlands
Portugal
Spain

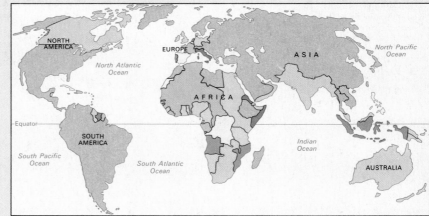

WORLD BOOK map

Important dates

1500's The Reformation led to the birth of Protestantism.

1519-1521 Ferdinand Magellan commanded the first globe-circling voyage, completed in 1522 after his death.

1521 The Spanish conquistador Hernando Cortés defeated the Aztec Indians of Mexico.

1526 Babar, a Muslim prince, invaded India and founded the Mogul Empire.

1588 The Royal Navy of England defeated the Spanish Armada, establishing England as a great naval power.

1644-1912 The Manchus ruled China as the Qing dynasty.

1776 The 13 American Colonies adopted the Declaration of Independence, establishing the United States of America.

1789 The French Revolution began.

1815 Napoleon Bonaparte was defeated in the Battle of Waterloo, ending his attempt to rule Europe.

1853-1854 Commodore Matthew Perry visited Japan and opened two ports to U.S. trade, ending Japan's isolation.

1858 Great Britain took over the rule of India from the East India Company after the Sepoy Rebellion.

1865 Union forces defeated the Confederates in the American Civil War after four years of fighting.

1869 The Suez Canal opened.

1871 Germany became united under the Prussian king, who ruled the new empire as Kaiser Wilhelm I.

1898 The United States took control of Guam, Puerto Rico, and the Philippines following the Spanish-American War.

Major developments from 1900 to 1990

WORLD BOOK illustrations by Tak Murakami

Sigmund Freud developed psychoanalysis about 1900.

The Wright brothers made the first successful airplane flights in 1903.

Albert Einstein published his special theory of relativity in 1905.

World War I (1914-1918)

Alexander Fleming discovered penicillin in 1928.

The first computers were developed in the 1930's and 1940's.

The British Broadcasting Corporation made the world's first TV broadcasts in 1936.

World War II (1939-1945)

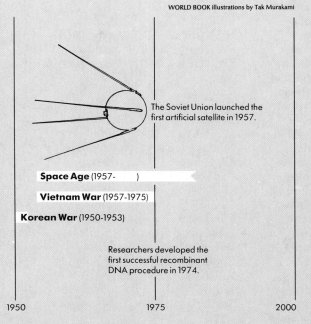

The Soviet Union launched the first artificial satellite in 1957.

Space Age (1957-   )

Vietnam War (1957-1975)

Korean War (1950-1953)

Researchers developed the first successful recombinant DNA procedure in 1974.

1900   1925   1950   1975   2000

The wealth of nations can be compared on the basis of each country's *gross national product* (GNP). The GNP is the value of all goods and services produced by a country in a year. The developing countries of Africa and Asia have the lowest GNP per person.

High GNP per person

Medium GNP per person

Low GNP per person

Very low GNP per person

WORLD BOOK map
Map is based on U.S. government
GNP estimates for 1982.

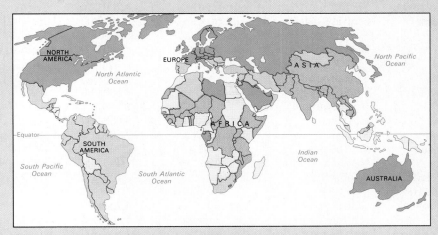

Important dates

1914 The assassination of Archduke Francis Ferdinand of Austria-Hungary started World War I.

1917 The Bolsheviks (Communists) seized power in Russia.

1933 Adolf Hitler became dictator of Germany.

1939 Germany invaded Poland, starting World War II.

1941 The Japanese attacked Pearl Harbor, and the United States entered World War II.

1945 The United Nations was established.

1945 The first atomic bombs used in warfare were dropped by U.S. planes on Hiroshima and Nagasaki.

1945 World War II ended in Europe on May 7 and in the Pacific on September 2.

1949 The Chinese Communists conquered China.

1950 North Korean Communist troops invaded South Korea, starting the Korean War.

1957 The Vietnam War started when South Vietnamese rebels known as the Viet Cong attacked the U.S.-backed South Vietnamese government.

1962 The Soviet Union agreed to U.S. demands that its missiles be removed from Cuba, ending a serious Cold War crisis.

1969 U.S. astronauts made the first manned moon landing.

1975 The Vietnam War ended when South Vietnam surrendered to the Viet Cong and North Vietnam.

1979 Soviet troops invaded Afghanistan to support the leftist Afghan government against rebel tribes.

1989 The Soviet Union completed withdrawal of its troops from Afghanistan.

COUNTRIES OF THE WORLD

Afghanistan   *Djibouti*

Country	Location	Capital	Population*	Area	Area (Metric)
Afghanistan	SW-central Asia	Kabul	16,900,000	250,000 sq mi.	647,500 sq km.
Albania	SE Europe	Tirana	3,300,000	11,100 sq mi.	28,748 sq km.
Algeria	NW Africa	Algiers	26,000,000	919,595 sq mi.	2,381,751 sq km.
Andorra	SW Europe	Andorra la Vella	55,400	175 sq mi.	453 sq km.
Angola	SW Africa	Luanda	8,900,000	481,350 sq mi.	1,246,700 sq km.
Antigua and Barbuda	Caribbean	St. John's	100,000	171 sq mi.	442 sq km.
Argentina	S South America	Buenos Aires	33,100,000	1,072,067 sq mi.	2,776,654 sq km.
Armenia	SW Asia	Yerevan	3,376,000	11,500 sq mi.	29,800 sq km.
Australia	SE of Asia	Canberra	17,800,000	2,966,150 sq mi.	7,682,300 sq km.
Austria	central Europe	Vienna	7,900,000	32,375 sq mi.	83,851 sq km.
Azerbaijan	SW Asia	Baku	7,100,000	33,400 sq mi.	86,600 sq km.
Bahamas	Caribbean	Nassau	254,685	5,380 sq mi.	13,939 sq km.
Bahrain	SW Asia	Manama	500,000	240 sq mi.	620 sq km.
Bangladesh	S Asia	Dhaka	111,400,000	55,598 sq mi.	143,998 sq km.
Barbados	Caribbean	Bridgetown	300,000	166 sq mi.	431 sq km.
Belarus	E Europe	Minsk	10,300,000	80,200 sq mi.	207,600 sq km.
Belgium	W Europe	Brussels	10,000,000	11,781 sq mi.	30,513 sq km.
Belize	Central America	Belmopan	200,000	8,867 sq mi.	22,965 sq km.
Benin	W Africa	Porto-Novo	5,000,000	43,483 sq mi.	112,622 sq km.
Bhutan	central Asia	Thimphu	700,000	18,000 sq mi.	46,620 sq km.
Bolivia	South America	Sucre; La Paz	7,800,000	424,162 sq mi.	1,098,581 sq km.
Bosnia and Herzegovina	SE Europe	Sarajevo	4,200,000	19,741 sq mi.	51,129 sq km.
Botswana	central S Africa	Gaborone	1,400,000	231,800 sq mi.	600,360 sq km.
Brazil	E South America	Brasília	156,275,000	3,286,470 sq mi.	8,511,957 sq km.
Brunei	island of Borneo	Bandar Seri Begawan	300,000	2,226 sq mi.	5,765 sq km.
Bulgaria	SE Europe	Sofia	8,900,000	42,823 sq mi.	110,912 sq km.
Burkina Faso	W Africa	Ouagadougou	9,600,000	105,870 sq mi.	274,200 sq km.
Burma	(see Myanmar)				
Burundi	E Africa	Bujumbura	5,800,000	10,747 sq mi.	27,834 sq km.
Cambodia	SE Asia	Phnom Penh	9,100,000	69,884 sq mi.	181,000 sq km.
Cameroon	W Africa	Yaoundé	12,700,000	183,569 sq mi.	475,442 sq km.
Canada	N North America	Ottawa	27,400,000	3,851,809 sq mi.	9,976,186 sq km.
Cape Verde	W of Africa	Praia	400,000	1,557 sq mi.	4,033 sq km.
Central African Republic	central Africa	Bangui	3,200,000	241,313 sq mi.	625,000 sq km.
Chad	central Africa	N'Djamena	5,200,000	495,752 sq mi.	1,284,000 sq km.
Chile	W South America	Santiago	13,600,000	292,132 sq mi.	756,622 sq km.
China	E Asia	Beijing	1,165,800,000	3,691,521 sq mi.	9,561,000 sq km.
Colombia	NW South America	Bogotá	34,300,000	440,829 sq mi.	1,141,748 sq km.
Comoros	E. of Africa	Moroni	500,000	690 sq mi.	1,787 sq km.
Congo	central Africa	Brazzaville	2,400,000	132,046 sq mi.	342,000 sq km.
Costa Rica	Central America	San José	3,200,000	19,652 sq mi.	50,898 sq km.
Côte D'Ivoire	W Africa	Abidjan; Yamoussoukro	13,000,000	124,502 sq mi.	322,462 sq km.
Croatia	E Europe	Zagreb	4,600,000	21,829 sq mi.	56,537 sq km.
Cuba	Caribbean	Havana	10,800,000	44,218 sq mi.	114,524 sq km.
Cyprus	S. of Europe	Nicosia	710,000	3,572 sq mi.	9,251 sq km.
Czech Republic	central Europe	Prague	10,362,000	30,441 sq mi.	78,864 sq km.
Denmark	N Europe	Copenhagen	5,200,000	16,631 sq mi.	43,075 sq km.
Djibouti	E Africa	Djibouti	400,000	8,490 sq mi.	22,000 sq km.

*Populations are mid-1992 estimates.

Country	Location	Capital	Population*	Area	Area (Metric)
Dominica	Caribbean	Roseau	100,000	290 sq mi.	751 sq km.
Dominican Republic	Caribbean	Santo Domingo	7,500,000	18,704 sq mi.	48,442 sq km.
Ecuador	NW South America	Quito	10,300,000	106,927 sq mi.	276,840 sq km.
Egypt	NE Africa	Cairo	57,758,000	386,900 sq mi.	1,002,000 sq km.
El Salvador	Central America	San Salvador	5,600,000	8,260 sq mi.	21,393 sq km.
Equatorial Guinea	W Africa	Malabo	400,000	10,830 sq mi.	28,051 sq km.
Estonia	NE Europe	Tallinn	1,600,000	18,370 sq mi.	47,549 sq km.
Ethiopia	E Africa	Addis Ababa	54,300,000	472,432 sq mi.	1,223,600 sq km.
Fiji	SW Pacific Ocean	Suva	800,000	7,078 sq mi.	18,333 sq km.
Finland	N Europe	Helsinki	5,000,000	130,119 sq mi.	337,009 sq km.
France	W Europe	Paris	56,900,000	212,918 sq mi.	547,026 sq km.
Gabon	W Africa	Libreville	1,100,000	103,346 sq mi.	267,667 sq km.
Gambia	W Africa	Banjul	900,000	4,093 sq mi.	10,600 sq km.
Georgia	SW Asia	Tbilisi	5,550,000	26,900 sq mi.	69,940 sq km.
Germany	W Europe	Berlin	80,600,000	137,838 sq mi.	357,000 sq km.
Ghana	W Africa	Accra	16,000,000	92,100 sq mi.	238,537 sq km.
Greece	SE Europe	Athens	10,300,000	50,961 sq mi.	131,990 sq km.
Grenada	Caribbean	St. George's	100,000	133 sq mi.	344 sq km.
Guatemala	Central America	Guatemala City	9,700,000	42,042 sq mi.	108,889 sq km.
Guinea	W Africa	Conakry	7,800,000	94,925 sq mi.	245,857 sq km.
Guinea-Bissau	W Africa	Bissau	1,000,000	13,948 sq mi.	36,125 sq km.
Guyana	N South America	Georgetown	800,000	83,000 sq mi.	214,969 sq km.
Haiti	Caribbean	Port-au-Prince	6,400,000	10,714 sq mi.	27,750 sq km.
Honduras	Central America	Tegucigalpa	5,500,000	43,277 sq mi.	112,088 sq km.
Hungary	central Europe	Budapest	10,300,000	35,919 sq mi.	93,030 sq km.
Iceland	N Atlantic Ocean	Reykjavík	300,000	39,709 sq mi.	102,846 sq km.
India	S Asia	New Delhi	882,600,000	1,229,737 sq mi.	3,185,019 sq km.
Indonesia	SE Asia	Jakarta	184,500,000	735,268 sq mi.	1,904,344 sq km.
Iran	SW Asia	Tehran	59,700,000	636,293 sq mi.	1,648,000 sq km.
Iraq	SW Asia	Baghdad	18,200,000	167,920 sq mi.	434,913 sq km.
Ireland	N Atlantic Ocean	Dublin	3,500,000	27,136 sq mi.	70,282 sq km.
Israel	SW Asia	Jerusalem	5,200,000	8,020 sq mi.	20,772 sq km.
Italy	S Europe	Rome	58,000,000	116,500 sq mi.	301,278 sq km.
Jamaica	Caribbean	Kingston	2,500,000	4,411 sq mi.	11,424 sq km.
Japan	E Asia	Tokyo	124,400,000	145,874 sq mi.	377,815 sq km.
Jordan	SW Asia	Amman	3,600,000	34,573 sq mi.	89,544 sq km.
Kazakhstan	W-central Asia	Alma-Ata	16,900,000	1,049,000 sq mi.	2,717,300 sq km.
Kenya	E Africa	Nairobi	26,200,000	224,960 sq mi.	582,646 sq km.
Kiribati	Pacific Ocean	Tarawa	72,298	280 sq mi.	726 sq km.
Kuwait	SW Asia	Kuwait	1,400,000	6,880 sq mi.	17,820 sq km.
Kyrgyzstan	W-central Asia	Bishkek	4,500,000	76,000 sq mi.	198,500 sq km.
Laos	SE Asia	Vientiane	4,400,000	91,429 sq mi.	236,800 sq km.
Latvia	NE Europe	Riga	2,700,000	25,400 sq mi.	65,786 sq km.
Lebanon	SW Asia	Beirut	3,400,000	4,015 sq mi.	10,400 sq km.
Lesotho	S Africa	Maseru	1,900,000	11,720 sq mi.	30,355 sq km.
Liberia	W Africa	Monrovia	2,800,000	43,000 sq mi.	111,370 sq km.
Libya	N Africa	Tripoli	4,500,000	679,536 sq mi.	1,759,998 sq km.
Liechtenstein	W-central Europe	Vaduz	30,000	61 sq mi.	157 sq km.
Lithuania	NE Europe	Vilnius	3,700,000	25,174 sq mi.	64,445 sq km.
Luxembourg	NW Europe	Luxembourg	400,000	999 sq mi.	2,586 sq km.
Macedonia	SE Europe	Skopje	1,900,000	9,928 sq mi.	25,713 sq km.

*Populations are mid-1992 estimates.

Country	Location	Capital	Population*	Area	Area (Metric)
Madagascar	off SE Africa	Antananarivo	11,900,000	226,660 sq mi.	587,050 sq km.
Malawi	E-central Africa	Lilongwe	8,700,000	45,747 sq mi.	118,484 sq km.
Malaysia	SE Asia	Kuala Lumpur	18,700,000	128,328 sq mi.	332,370 sq km.
Maldives	Indian Ocean	Malé	200,000	115 sq mi.	298 sq km.
Mali	W Africa	Bamako	8,500,000	478,819 sq mi.	1,240,142 sq km.
Malta	Mediterranean Sea	Valletta	400,000	122 sq mi.	316 sq km.
Marshall Islands	W-central Pacific Ocean	Majuro	48,000	70 sq mi.	181 sq km.
Mauritania	W Africa	Nouakchott	2,100,000	397,953 sq mi.	1,030,700 sq km.
Mauritius	Indian Ocean	Port Louis	1,100,000	787 sq mi.	2,040 sq km.
Mexico	S North America	Mexico City	87,700,000	761,600 sq mi.	1,972,547 sq km.
Micronesia	W Pacific Ocean	Kolonia	100,000	271 sq mi.	703 sq km.
Moldova	E Europe	Kishinev	4,400,000	13,000 sq mi.	33,700 sq km.
Monaco	S Europe	Monaco	29,700	.73 sq mi.	1.9 sq km.
Mongolia	central Asia	Ulan Bator	2,300,000	604,250 sq mi.	1,565,000 sq km.
Morocco	NW Africa	Rabat	26,200,000	172,413 sq mi.	446,550 sq km.
Mozambique	SE Africa	Maputo	16,600,000	303,073 sq mi.	799,380 sq km.
Myanmar	SE Asia	Yangon	42,500,000	261,220 sq mi.	676,560 sq km.
Namibia	SW Africa	Windhoek	1,500,000	318,261 sq mi.	824,296 sq km.
Nauru	W-central Pacific Ocean	Yaren	9,500	8.2 sq mi.	21 sq km.
Nepal	central Asia	Kathmandu	19,900,000	54,463 sq mi.	141,059 sq km.
Netherlands	NW Europe	Amsterdam; The Hague	15,300,000	16,041 sq mi.	41,548 sq km.
New Zealand	Pacific Ocean	Wellington	3,400,000	103,884 sq mi.	269,062 sq km.
Nicaragua	Central America	Managua	4,100,000	50,180 sq mi.	130,000 sq km.
Niger	W Africa	Niamey	8,300,000	489,206 sq mi.	1,267,044 sq km.
Nigeria	W Africa	Abuja	88,500,000	356,700 sq mi.	923,853 sq km.
North Korea	E Asia	Pyongyang	22,200,000	46,768 sq mi.	121,129 sq km.
Norway	N Europe	Oslo	4,300,000	125,049 sq mi.	323,877 sq km.
Oman	SW Asia	Muscat	2,070,000	82,030 sq mi.	212,458 sq km.
Pakistan	S Asia	Islamabad	121,700,000	310,400 sq mi.	803,936 sq km.
Panama	Central America	Panama City	2,400,000	29,761 sq mi.	77,082 sq km.
Papua New Guinea	SW Pacific Ocean	Port Moresby	3,900,000	178,704 sq mi.	462,840 sq km.
Paraguay	South America	Asunción	4,500,000	157,047 sq mi.	406,752 sq km.
Peru	W South America	Lima	22,500,000	496,222 sq mi.	1,285,216 sq km.
Philippines	E Asia	Manila	63,700,000	115,830 sq mi.	300,000 sq km.
Poland	E Europe	Warsaw	38,400,000	120,727 sq mi.	312,683 sq km.
Portugal	S Europe	Lisbon	10,500,000	35,550 sq mi.	92,075 sq. km.
Qatar	SW Asia	Doha	500,000	4,000 sq mi.	11,437 sq km.
Romania	E-central Europe	Bucharest	22,760,000	91,700 sq mi.	237,500 sq km.
Russia	E Europe; N Asia	Moscow	148,542,700	6,592,800 sq mi.	17,075,400 sq km.
Rwanda	E Africa	Kigali	7,700,000	10,169 sq mi.	26,338 sq km.
St. Kitts and Nevis	Caribbean	Basseterre	40,000	100 sq mi.	260 sq km.
St. Lucia	Caribbean	Castries	200,000	238 sq mi.	616 sq km.
St. Vincent and the Grenadines	Caribbean	Kingstown	100,000	150 sq mi.	389 sq km.
San Marino	N Italy	San Marino	20,000	23.6 sq mi.	62 sq km.
São Tomé and Príncipe	off W Africa	São Tomé	100,000	370 sq mi.	958 sq km.

*Populations are mid-1992 estimates.

Country	Location	Capital	Population*	Area	Area (Metric)
Saudi Arabia	SW Asia	Riyadh	16,100,000	865,000 sq mi.	2,250,070 sq km.
Senegal	W Africa	Dakar	7,900,000	75,954 sq mi.	196,722 sq km.
Seychelles	off E Africa	Victoria	100,000	175 sq mi.	453 sq km.
Sierra Leone	W Africa	Freetown	4,400,000	27,700 sq mi.	71,740 sq km.
Singapore	SE Asia	Singapore	2,800,000	246.7 sq mi.	639 sq km.
Slovakia	E Europe	Bratislava	5,278,700	18,928 sq mi.	49,035 sq km.
Slovenia	E Europe	Ljubljana	1,962,600	7,819 sq mi.	20,251 sq km.
Solomon Islands	SW Pacific Ocean	Honiara	400,000	11,500 sq mi.	29,785 sq km.
Somalia	E Africa	Mogadishu	8,300,000	246,199 sq mi.	637,655 sq km.
South Africa	S Africa	Pretoria	41,700,000	471,440 sq mi.	1,221,030 sq km.
South Korea	E Asia	Seoul	44,300,000	38,031 sq mi.	98,500 sq km.
Spain	W Europe	Madrid	39,301,000	194,884 sq mi.	504,750 sq km.
Sri Lanka	off SE India	Colombo	17,600,000	25,332 sq mi.	65,610 sq km.
Sudan	E Africa	Khartoum	26,500,000	967,491 sq mi.	2,505,802 sq km.
Suriname	N South America	Paramaribo	400,000	63,251 sq mi.	163,820 sq km.
Swaziland	SE Africa	Mbabane	800,000	6,704 sq mi.	17,363 sq km.
Sweden	N Europe	Stockholm	8,700,000	173,800 sq mi.	449,964 sq km.
Switzerland	W Europe	Bern	6,900,000	15,941 sq mi.	41,288 sq km.
Syria	W Asia	Damascus	13,700,000	71,498 sq mi.	185,180 sq km.
Taiwan	off SE China	Taipei	20,800,000	13,895 sq mi.	35,988 sq km.
Tajikistan	W Asia	Dushanbe	5,500,000	55,300 sq mi.	143,100 sq km.
Tanzania	E Africa	Dar es Salaam	27,400,000	364,879 sq mi.	945,037 sq km.
Thailand	SE Asia	Bangkok	56,300,000	198,455 sq mi.	514,000 sq km.
Togo	W Africa	Lomé	3,800,000	21,925 sq mi.	56,785 sq km.
Tonga	SW Pacific Ocean	Nuku'alofa	96,800	290 sq mi.	751 sq km.
Trinidad and Tobago	Caribbean	Port-of-Spain	1,300,000	1,980 sq mi.	5,128 sq km.
Tunisia	N Africa	Tunis	8,400,000	63,379 sq mi.	164,152 sq km.
Turkey	S Europe/SW Asia	Ankara	59,200,000	300,947 sq mi.	779,452 sq km.
Turkmenistan	W Asia	Ashkhabad	3,900,000	188,500 sq mi.	488,100 sq km.
Tuvalu	W Pacific Ocean	Funafuti	9,300	10 sq mi.	26 sq km.
Uganda	E Africa	Kampala	17,500,000	91,459 sq mi.	236,880 sq km.
Ukraine	E Europe	Kiev	52,100,000	233,000 sq mi.	603,700 sq km.
United Arab Emirates	SW Asia	Abu Dhabi	2,500,000	32,000 sq mi.	82,880 sq km.
United Kingdom	off W Europe	London	57,533,000	94,247 sq mi.	244,100 sq km.
United States	North America	Washington, D.C.	255,600,000	3,536,341 sq mi.	9,159,123 sq km.
Uruguay	E South America	Montevideo	3,100,000	68,040 sq mi.	176,224 sq km.
Uzbekistan	W Asia	Tashkent	21,300,000	172,700 sq mi.	447,400 sq km.
Vanuatu	SW Pacific Ocean	Port Vila	200,000	5,700 sq mi.	14,763 sq km.
Vatican City	central Italy	—	778	.17 sq mi.	.44 sq km.
Venezuela	N South America	Caracas	18,900,000	352,143 sq mi.	912,050 sq km.
Vietnam	SE Asia	Hanoi	69,200,000	127,246 sq mi.	329,566 sq km.
Western Samoa	S Pacific	Apia	200,000	1,093 sq mi.	2,831 sq km.
Yemen	SW Asia	Sanaa	10,400,000	203,850 sq mi.	527,970 sq km.
Yugoslavia**	SE Europe	Belgrade	10,000,000	26,940 sq mi.	69,775 sq km.
Zaire	central Africa	Kinshasa	37,900,000	905,365 sq mi.	2,344,885 sq km.
Zambia	S Africa	Lusaka	8,400,000	290,586 sq mi.	752,618 sq km.
Zimbabwe	S Africa	Harare	10,300,000	150,698 sq mi.	390,308 sq km.

*Populations are mid-1992 estimates.
**Present-day Yugoslavia comprises the republics of Serbia and Montenegro.

WORLD: *Political*

ABBREVIATIONS

BOS. AND HERZ.
    Bosnia and Herzegovina
CEN. AFR. REP.
    Central African Republic
DEN. Denmark
FR. France
GR. Greece
IT. Italy
N. North, Northern
NETH. Netherlands
N.Z. New Zealand
PORT. Portugal
S. South
SP. Spain
U.A.E. United Arab
    Emirates
U.K. United Kingdom
U.S. United States
W. Western

—— National boundary

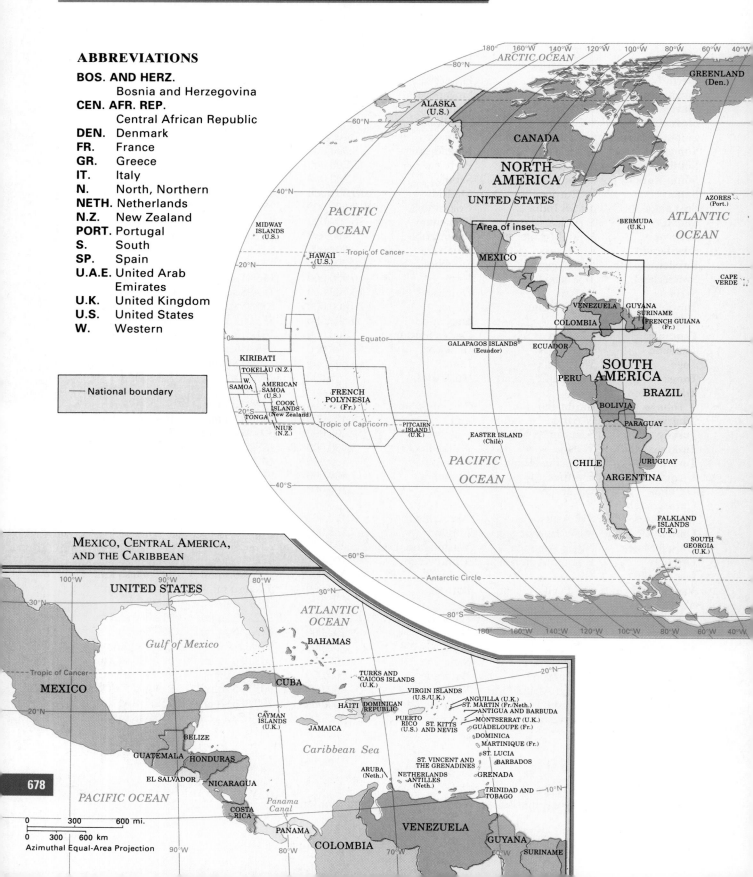

MEXICO, CENTRAL AMERICA, AND THE CARIBBEAN

0   300   600 mi.

0   300   600 km

Azimuthal Equal-Area Projection

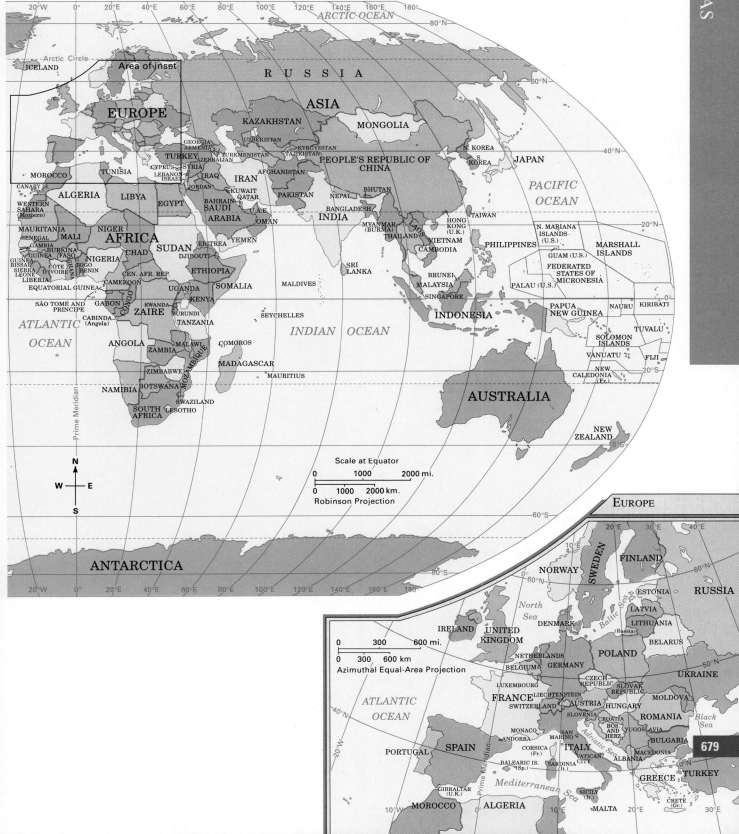

Scale at Equator

0   1000   2000 mi.

0   1000   2000 km.

Robinson Projection

EUROPE

0   300   600 mi.

0   300   600 km

Azimuthal Equal-Area Projection

679

WORLD: *Physical*

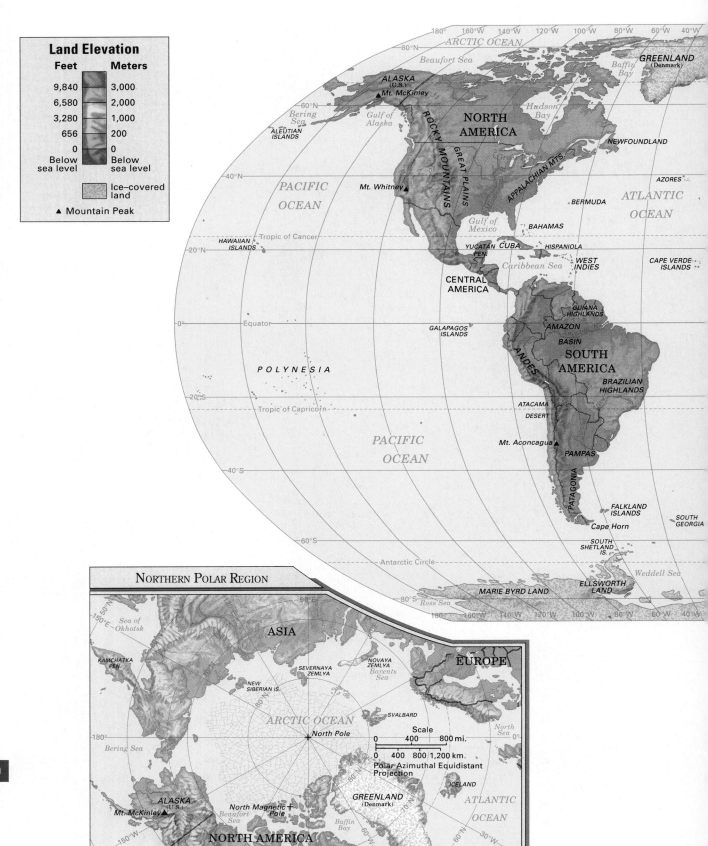

Land Elevation

Feet	Meters
9,840	3,000
6,580	2,000
3,280	1,000
656	200
0	0
Below sea level	Below sea level

Ice–covered land

▲ Mountain Peak

ARCTIC OCEAN
Beaufort Sea
GREENLAND (Denmark)
Baffin Bay
ALASKA (U.S.)
▲ Mt. McKinley
Hudson Bay
NORTH AMERICA
NEWFOUNDLAND
Bering Sea
Gulf of Alaska
ROCKY MOUNTAINS
GREAT PLAINS
APPALACHIAN MTS.
AZORES
ALEUTIAN ISLANDS
PACIFIC OCEAN
Mt. Whitney ▲
BERMUDA
ATLANTIC OCEAN
Gulf of Mexico
BAHAMAS
HAWAIIAN ISLANDS
Tropic of Cancer
YUCATAN PEN.
CUBA
HISPANIOLA
WEST INDIES
CAPE VERDE ISLANDS
CENTRAL AMERICA
Caribbean Sea
Equator
GALAPAGOS ISLANDS
GUIANA HIGHLANDS
AMAZON BASIN
POLYNESIA
ANDES
SOUTH AMERICA
BRAZILIAN HIGHLANDS
Tropic of Capricorn
ATACAMA DESERT
PACIFIC OCEAN
Mt. Aconcagua ▲
PAMPAS
PATAGONIA
FALKLAND ISLANDS
SOUTH GEORGIA
Cape Horn
SOUTH SHETLAND IS.
Antarctic Circle
Weddell Sea
MARIE BYRD LAND
ELLSWORTH LAND
Ross Sea

NORTHERN POLAR REGION

Sea of Okhotsk
ASIA
KAMCHATKA PEN.
NEW SIBERIAN IS.
SEVERNAYA ZEMLYA
NOVAYA ZEMLYA
Barents Sea
EUROPE
ARCTIC OCEAN
SVALBARD
North Sea
North Pole
Scale
0   400   800 mi.
0   400   800 1,200 km.
Polar Azimuthal Equidistant Projection
Bering Sea
ALASKA (U.S.)
▲ Mt. McKinley
North Magnetic Pole
Beaufort Sea
GREENLAND (Denmark)
ICELAND
ATLANTIC OCEAN
Baffin Bay
NORTH AMERICA

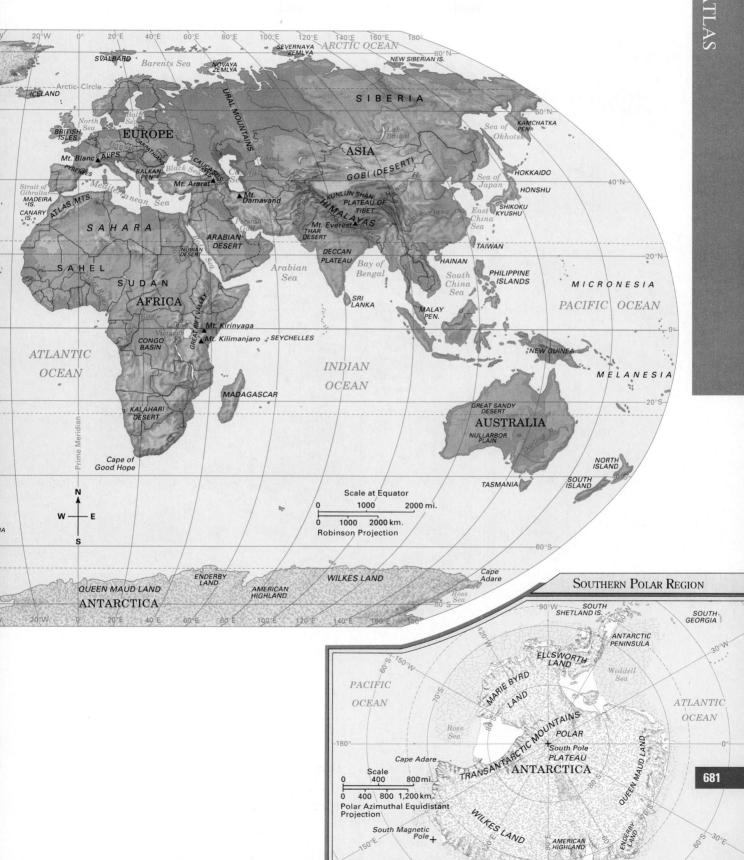

20°W 0° 20°E 40°E 60°E 80°E 100°E 120°E 140°E 160°E 180°

SEVERNAYA
ZEMLYA
ARCTIC OCEAN
80°N

SVALBARD
Barents Sea
NEW SIBERIAN IS.

NOVAYA
ZEMLYA

ICELAND
Arctic Circle

URAL MOUNTAINS
SIBERIA
60°N

KAMCHATKA
PEN.

North
Sea
BRITISH
ISLES
EUROPE
Baltic
Sea

Lake
Baikal
Sea of
Okhotsk

HOKKAIDO

Mt. Blanc
ALPS
PYRENEES
CARPATHIANS
CAUCASUS
MTS.
Black Sea
Caspian
Sea
ASIA
GOBI (DESERT)
He
Sea of
Japan
HONSHU
40°N

BALKAN
PEN.
Mt. Ararat
Mt.
Damavand
KUNLUN SHAN
PLATEAU OF
TIBET
Huang
SHIKOKU
KYUSHU

Strait of
Gibraltar
MADEIRA
IS.
Mediterranean Sea
ATLAS MTS.
Persian
Gulf
HIMALAYAS
Mt. Everest
THAR
DESERT
Chang Jiang
East
China
Sea

CANARY
IS.
SAHARA
ARABIAN
DESERT
DECCAN
PLATEAU
TAIWAN
20°N

SAHEL
NUBIAN
DESERT
Arabian
Sea
Bay of
Bengal
HAINAN

SUDAN
South
China
Sea
PHILIPPINE
ISLANDS
MICRONESIA

AFRICA
SRI
LANKA
MALAY
PEN.
PACIFIC OCEAN

ATLANTIC
OCEAN
Lake
Victoria
Mt. Kirinyaga
Mt. Kilimanjaro
SEYCHELLES
INDIAN
OCEAN
NEW GUINEA

CONGO
BASIN
GREAT RIFT VALLEY
MELANESIA
20°S

MADAGASCAR
GREAT SANDY
DESERT

KALAHARI
DESERT
AUSTRALIA

Prime Meridian
NULLARBOR
PLAIN
Darling

Cape of
Good Hope
NORTH
ISLAND

N
W   E
S
Scale at Equator
0   1000   2000 mi.
0 1000 2000 km.
Robinson Projection
TASMANIA
SOUTH
ISLAND
60°S

IA

QUEEN MAUD LAND
ENDERBY
LAND
AMERICAN
HIGHLAND
WILKES LAND
Cape
Adare
Ross
Sea
80°S

ANTARCTICA
20°W 0° 20°E 40°E 60°E 80°E 100°E 120°E 140°E 160°E 180°

SOUTHERN POLAR REGION

90°W
SOUTH
SHETLAND IS.
SOUTH
GEORGIA

120°W
60°W
ANTARCTIC
PENINSULA
30°W

PACIFIC
OCEAN
150°W
70°S
ELLSWORTH
LAND
MARIE BYRD
LAND
Weddell
Sea
ATLANTIC
OCEAN

180°
Ross
Sea
TRANSANTARCTIC MOUNTAINS
South Pole
POLAR
PLATEAU
80°S
0°

Cape Adare
ANTARCTICA
QUEEN MAUD LAND

Scale
0   400   800 mi.
0 400 800 1,200 km.
Polar Azimuthal Equidistant
Projection
WILKES LAND
AMERICAN
HIGHLAND
ENDERBY
LAND
30°S

South Magnetic
Pole
150°E
120°E
90°E
60°E

681

EURASIA: *Political/Physical*

NORTH AMERICA

SVALBARD (Norway)

FRANZ JOSEF LAND

Barents Sea

NOVAYA ZEMLYA

Norwegian Sea

Murmansk

Arctic Circle

Reykjavik ICELAND

White Sea

R U S S I A

Trondheim

NORWAY SWEDEN FINLAND

Gulf of Bothnia

Helsinki

Oslo Stockholm Tallinn

Lake Ladoga

St. Petersburg

Volga River

Moscow

Ob River

Novosibirsk

ATLANTIC OCEAN

North Sea

Edinburgh

Copenhagen DENMARK

Riga LATVIA

ESTONIA

Baltic Sea

Volga River

Samara

Dublin IRELAND UNITED KINGDOM

Amsterdam NETH.

Gdansk

LITHUANIA

Vilnius

Minsk BELARUS

The Hague

London BELG. GERMANY

Berlin

POLAND

Warsaw

Kiev UKRAINE

Kharkov

URAL MOUNTAINS

Irtysh River

Brussels LUX. Bonn Prague CZECH REP.

Elbe R.

Vistula

Don River

Volgograd

KIRGHIZ STEPPE

Lake Balkhash

Paris *Rhine River* *Loire R.*

Bern SWITZ. LIECH Vienna AUST. SLOVAK REP.

Bratislava HUNG.

Budapest

CARPATHIANS

MOLDOVA

Kishinev

Sea of Azov

Aral Sea

KAZAKHSTAN

Sea of Biscay

FRANCE ALPS

Venice

Zagreb CRO. SLO. BOS.

Danube R.

ROMANIA

Bucharest

Black Sea

GEORGIA

CAUCASUS MTS.

Tbilisi

Caspian Sea

UZBEKISTAN

Alma-Ata

Bishkek KYRGYZSTAN

MONACO ANDORRA CORSICA (Fr.)

SAN MARINO

APENNINES

Adriatic Sea

Sarajevo YUGO. Belgrade

BULGARIA Sofia

Tirana MACE.

ALB.

ARMENIA Yerevan

AZERBAIJAN

Baku

TURKMENISTAN

Ashkhabad

Tashkent

Dushanbe

PAMIRS

TAJIKISTAN

KUNLUN

Barcelona

PORTUGAL Madrid

Lisbon SPAIN

Rome ITALY

SARDINIA (Italy)

Tyrrhenian Sea

BALEARIC ISLANDS (Sp.)

SICILY (Italy)

MALTA

Ionian Sea

GREECE Athens

Aegean Sea

ASIA MINOR

Istanbul

Ankara TURKEY

KURDISTAN

Tigris R.

Euphrates R.

ELBURZ MTS.

Tehran

ZAGROS MOUNTAINS

PLATEAU OF IRAN

HINDU KUSH

Kabul AFGHANISTAN

Islamabad

HIMALAYAS

PYRENEES

Nicosia CYPRUS

SYRIA

Beirut LEBANON Damascus

Jerusalem ISRAEL Amman JORDAN

Baghdad

IRAQ

IRAN

Kuwait KUWAIT

New Delhi

PAKISTAN

THAR DESERT

Kathmandu NEPAL

Ganges R.

Mediterranean Sea

Tropic of Cancer

BAHRAIN QATAR

Riyadh

Abu Dhabi U.A.E. Muscat OMAN

Karachi

INDIA

Red Sea

SAUDI ARABIA

Mecca

RUB AL KHALI (DESERT)

OMAN

Arabian Sea

Bombay

DECCAN PLATEAU

WESTERN GHATS

EASTERN GHATS

Sanaa YEMEN

Aden *Gulf of Aden* SOCOTRA (Yemen)

Madras

AFRICA

LACCADIVE ISLANDS (India)

SRI LANKA

Colombo

Male MALDIVES

Equator

INDIAN OCEAN

Prime Meridian

Legend

⊛ National capital

• Major city

– National boundary

N / W E / S

| 0 | 400 | 800 mi. |
| 0 | 400 | 800 km. |

Robinson Projection

ARCTIC OCEAN

75°N

NORTH
AMERICA

SIBERIA

60°N

Bering Sea

Lena River

River

STANOVOI RANGE

Sea of
Okhotsk

Irkutsk

Lake
Baikal

SAKHALIN

180°

DA HINGGAN LING

Amur River

KURIL ISLANDS

45°N

Ulan Bator

ALTAI MTS.

MONGOLIA

Harbin

GOBI (DESERT)

Vladivostok

Sapporo

Beijing

N. KOREA
Pyongyang

Sea of
Japan

Seoul
S. KOREA

JAPAN

Tokyo

Huang He

Yellow
Sea

Osaka

PEOPLE'S REPUBLIC
OF CHINA

Jiang

Shanghai

PACIFIC

30°N

AN

PLATEAU
OF
TIBET

Chang

East
China
Sea

OCEAN

Brahmaputra R.

Thimphu
BHUTAN

Xi Jiang

Taipei
TAIWAN

BANGLADESH
Dhaka

MACAO
(Port.)

Guangzhou

HONG
KONG
(U.K.)

Philippine

Irrawaddy R.

Calcutta

MYANMAR
(BURMA)

LAOS

Hanoi

Gulf
of
Tonkin

HAINAN

Sea

15°N

Mekong

Vientiane

Yangon
(Rangoon)

THAILAND

Da Nang

Bay of
Bengal

Bangkok

CAMBODIA

VIETNAM

Manila

PHILIPPINES

ANDAMAN
ISLANDS
(India)

Phnom
Penh

Ho Chi Minh City
(Saigon)

NICOBAR
ISLANDS
(India)

South China
Sea

Bandar Seri
Begawan
BRUNEI

MALAYSIA

Kuala Lumpur

MALAYSIA

Singapore
SINGAPORE

BORNEO

SUMATRA

CELEBES

0°

INDONESIA

NEW GUINEA

Java Sea

Jakarta
JAVA

Arafura Sea

Timor
Sea

15°S

683

AUSTRALIA

90°E   105°E   120°E   135°E   150°E   165°E   180°   165°W   150°W   135°W   120°W

PACIFIC RIM: *Political/Physical*

ARCTIC OCEAN

RUSSIA

ASIA

MONGOLIA

Arctic Circle

ALASKA (U.S.)
• Anchorage

CANADA

NORTH AMERICA

Vancouver
• Seattle

Ottawa

Bering Sea

KAMCHATKA

SAKHALIN

Beijing
PEOPLE'S REPUBLIC OF CHINA

NORTH KOREA
• Vladivostok
Pyongyang
Seoul
SOUTH KOREA

KURIL IS. (Russia)

JAPAN
Tokyo

PACIFIC OCEAN

San Francisco

UNITED STATES

Washington

Los Angeles

Shanghai

East China Sea

RYUKYU IS.(Japan)

VOLCANO IS. (Japan)

WAKE ISLAND (U.S.)

MIDWAY ISLANDS (U.S.)

Tropic of Cancer

MEXICO

BAHAMAS

Hanoi
HONG KONG (U.K.)
Taipei
TAIWAN

Philippine Sea

NORTHERN MARIANA ISLANDS (U.S.)

MARSHALL ISLANDS

Honolulu

HAWAII (U.S.)

Mexico City

CUBA

HAITI

LAOS
VIETNAM
THAILAND
CAMBODIA

Manila
PHILIPPINES

GUAM (U.S.)

MICRONESIA

Kolonia

Majuro

GUATEMALA
EL SALVADOR

BELIZE
HONDURAS
NICARAGUA

South China Sea

PALAU (U.S.)

FEDERATED STATES OF MICRONESIA

Tarawa

Equator

COSTA RICA
PANAMA

Bogotá

Kuala Lumpur
MALAYSIA
BRUNEI

Yaren
NAURU

GALAPAGOS IS. (Ecuador)

COLOMBIA

ECUADOR
Quito
Guayaquil

SINGAPORE

INDONESIA

NEW GUINEA

PAPUA NEW GUINEA

Jakarta

Arafura Sea
Timor Sea

Port Moresby

Gulf of Carpentaria

SOLOMON ISLANDS
Honiara

TUVALU
Funafuti

TOKELAU (N.Z.)

WESTERN SAMOA

POLYNESIA

KIRIBATI

AMERICAN SAMOA (U.S.)

FRENCH POLYNESIA (Fr.)

PERU
Lima

SOUTH AMERICA

INDIAN OCEAN

GREAT SANDY DESERT

MACDONNELL RANGE

GREAT DIVIDING RANGE

DARLING RANGE

AUSTRALIA

Great Barrier Reef

Coral Sea

VANUATU

Port-Vila

WALLIS AND FUTUNA IS. (Fr.)
Apia
TONGA
Suva
FIJI
Nuku'alofa

NIUE (N.Z.)

COOK ISLANDS (N.Z.)

Tropic of Capricorn

PITCAIRN I. (U.K.)

EASTER I. (Chile)

CHILE

Valparaíso
Santiago

NEW CALEDONIA (Fr.)

Great Australian Bight

Sydney
Canberra

TASMANIA

NORFOLK I. (Aust.)

NEW ZEALAND

Auckland

Wellington

KERMADEC ISLANDS (N.Z.)

Tasman Sea

CHATHAM IS. (N.Z.)

PACIFIC OCEAN

Scale at Equator

0   1000   2000 mi.

0   1000   2000 km

Miller Cylindrical Projection

60°S

Antarctic Circle

684

⊛ National capital

• Major city

— National boundary

ANTARCTICA

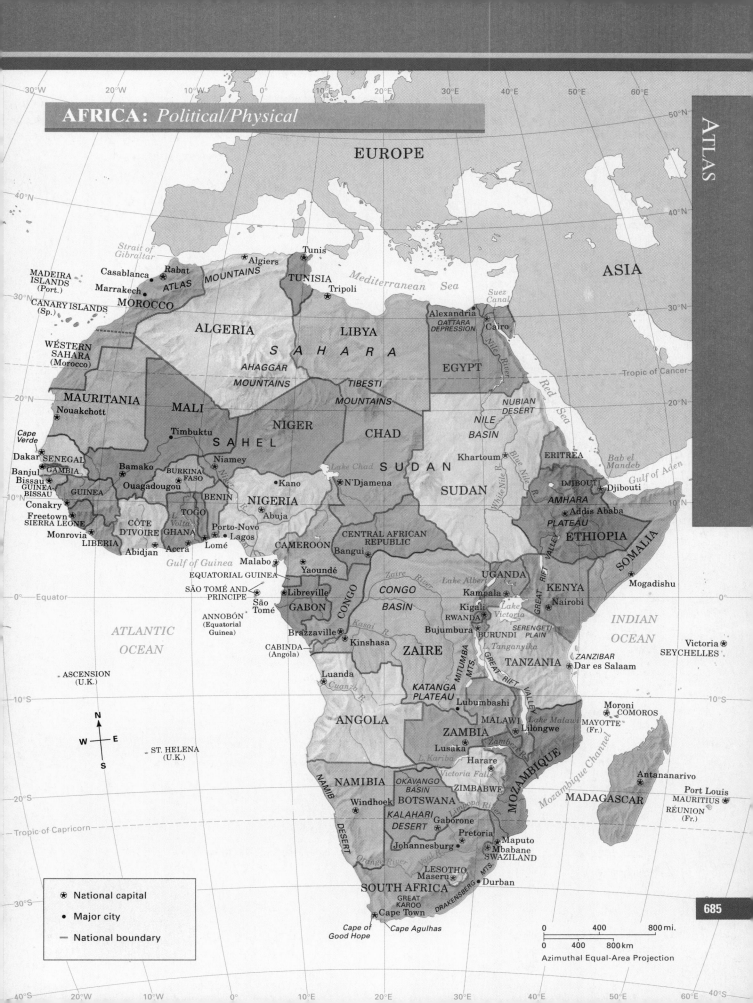

AFRICA: *Political/Physical*

EUROPE

ASIA

Strait of Gibraltar

MADEIRA ISLANDS (Port.)

Casablanca
Rabat ⊛
ATLAS MOUNTAINS
Marrakech
MOROCCO

Algiers ⊛
Tunis ⊛
TUNISIA
Tripoli ⊛

Mediterranean Sea

Suez Canal

Alexandria
QATTARA DEPRESSION
Cairo ⊛

CANARY ISLANDS (Sp.)

WESTERN SAHARA (Morocco)

ALGERIA

LIBYA

EGYPT

S A H A R A

Tropic of Cancer

AHAGGAR MOUNTAINS

TIBESTI MOUNTAINS

Red Sea

NUBIAN DESERT

MAURITANIA
Nouakchott ⊛

MALI

NIGER

CHAD

NILE BASIN

SAHEL

Timbuktu

Khartoum ⊛

ERITREA

Bab el Mandeb

Gulf of Aden

Cape Verde

Dakar ⊛ SENEGAL
Banjul ⊛ GAMBIA
Bissau ⊛ GUINEA-BISSAU
Conakry ⊛ GUINEA
Freetown ⊛ SIERRA LEONE
Monrovia ⊛ LIBERIA

Bamako ⊛
BURKINA FASO
Ouagadougou ⊛
BENIN
CÔTE D'IVOIRE
GHANA
Abidjan
Accra ⊛

Niamey ⊛

Kano

L. Volta
TOGO
Porto-Novo ⊛
Lomé ⊛ Lagos
Abuja ⊛

NIGERIA

N'Djamena ⊛

SUDAN

SUDAN

DJIBOUTI ⊛
Djibouti

AMHARA
Addis Ababa ⊛
PLATEAU

ETHIOPIA

SOMALIA

CAMEROON

CENTRAL AFRICAN REPUBLIC

Bangui ⊛

Gulf of Guinea
Malabo ⊛
EQUATORIAL GUINEA
Yaoundé ⊛
SÃO TOMÉ AND PRINCIPE
São Tomé
ANNOBÓN (Equatorial Guinea)

Libreville ⊛

Zaire River

CONGO BASIN

Lake Albert

UGANDA
Kampala ⊛
Lake Victoria
RWANDA
Kigali ⊛
BURUNDI
Bujumbura ⊛
SERENGETI PLAIN

KENYA
Nairobi ⊛

Mogadishu

Equator

GABON

CONGO

Kasai R.

Brazzaville ⊛
Kinshasa ⊛
CABINDA (Angola)

ZAIRE

GREAT RIFT VALLEY

L. Tanganyika

TANZANIA
ZANZIBAR
Dar es Salaam ⊛

INDIAN OCEAN

ATLANTIC OCEAN

ASCENSION (U.K.)

Luanda ⊛
Cuanza R.

KATANGA PLATEAU

MITUMBA MTS.

Victoria ⊛
SEYCHELLES

ANGOLA

Lubumbashi

MALAWI
Lilongwe ⊛
Lake Malawi

Moroni ⊛
COMOROS
MAYOTTE (Fr.)

ST. HELENA (U.K.)

N
W   E
S

NAMIB DESERT

OKAVANGO BASIN

ZAMBIA
Lusaka ⊛

Zambezi R.

Harare ⊛
L. Kariba
Victoria Falls

MOZAMBIQUE

Mozambique Channel

Antananarivo ⊛

MADAGASCAR

Port Louis ⊛
MAURITIUS
RÉUNION (Fr.)

NAMIBIA
Windhoek ⊛

BOTSWANA

ZIMBABWE

Tropic of Capricorn

KALAHARI DESERT
Gaborone ⊛
Limpopo River

Pretoria ⊛
Johannesburg
Maputo ⊛
Mbabane ⊛
SWAZILAND

Orange River
Vaal R.
LESOTHO
Maseru ⊛
DRAKENSBERG MTS.
Durban

SOUTH AFRICA

GREAT KAROO
Cape Town ⊛

Cape of Good Hope
Cape Agulhas

⊛ National capital

• Major city

— National boundary

685

0   400   800 mi.
0   400   800 km
Azimuthal Equal-Area Projection

NORTH AMERICA: *Political/Physical*

ASIA

ARCTIC OCEAN

EUROPE

Bering Strait

Beaufort Sea

BROOKS RANGE

Bering Sea

ALASKA RANGE
Fairbanks
Anchorage
KODIAK ISLAND
Gulf of Alaska

Yukon River

QUEEN ELIZABETH ISLANDS

BANKS ISLAND

ELLESMERE ISLAND

GREENLAND (Denmark)

Baffin Bay

VICTORIA ISLAND

Mackenzie River

Great Bear Lake

BAFFIN ISLAND

ALEXANDER ARCHIPELAGO

QUEEN CHARLOTTE ISLANDS

COAST MOUNTAINS

Great Slave Lake

LAURENTIAN SHIELD

UNGAVA PENINSULA

Labrador Sea

VANCOUVER ISLAND

Vancouver
Puget Sound
Seattle

Edmonton

Calgary

Lake Winnipeg

CANADA

Hudson Bay

LABRADOR

NEWFOUNDLAND

PRINCE EDWARD ISLAND

CAPE BRETON ISLAND

Portland

ROCKY MOUNTAINS

Columbia River

Winnipeg

Quebec

St. Lawrence River

Bay of Fundy

San Francisco

COAST RANGES

SIERRA NEVADA

Great Salt Lake

Salt Lake City

BLACK HILLS

Missouri River

Minneapolis

Milwaukee

Chicago

Lake Superior

L. Michigan

Lake Huron

Toronto

Detroit
Cleveland

Montreal
Ottawa

L. Ontario

Lake Erie

Boston
Cape Cod

New York

ATLANTIC OCEAN

Los Angeles
San Diego

MOJAVE DESERT

Denver

Kansas City

Omaha

Indianapolis

St. Louis

Ohio River

Louisville

APPALACHIAN MTS.

Philadelphia
Baltimore
Washington

Colorado River

GRAND CANYON

UNITED STATES

Wichita

Nashville

Charlotte

Cape Hatteras

BERMUDA (U.K.)

Phoenix

Red River

Fort Worth

Atlanta
Birmingham

PACIFIC OCEAN

Rio Grande

Austin

San Antonio

Houston

New Orleans

Jacksonville

Cape Canaveral

Tropic of Cancer

Ciudad Juárez
Chihuahua

SIERRA MADRE OCCIDENTAL

Gulf of California

BAJA CALIFORNIA

Miami

Nassau
BAHAMAS

Cabo San Lucas

Monterrey

SIERRA MADRE ORIENTAL

Havana

CUBA

VIRGIN ISLANDS (U.S., U.K.)

San Juan
ANGUILLA (U.K.)
ANTIGUA AND BARBUDA

Gulf of Mexico

Santiago de Cuba

PUERTO RICO (U.S.)

ST. KITTS AND NEVIS

GUADELOUPE (Fr.)

MEXICO

PLATEAU OF MEXICO

Guadalajara

Mexico City

Puebla
Veracruz

YUCATÁN PENINSULA

Port-au-Prince
HAITI

DOMINICAN REPUBLIC

Kingston

JAMAICA

Santo Domingo

DOMINICA Roseau

MARTINIQUE (Fr.)

Castries ST. LUCIA

ST. VINCENT AND THE GRENADINES

Kingstown

BARBADOS
Bridgetown

CAYMAN ISLANDS (U.K.)

Acapulco

ISTHMUS OF TEHUANTEPEC

Belmopan
BELIZE

St. George's
GRENADA

Port-of-Spain
TRINIDAD AND TOBAGO

GUATEMALA

Guatemala City

HONDURAS

Tegucigalpa

NICARAGUA

MOSQUITO COAST

NETHERLANDS ANTILLES (Neth.)

ARUBA (Neth.)

Caribbean Sea

San Salvador
EL SALVADOR

Managua

Lago de Nicaragua

N
W E
S

San José
COSTA RICA

ISTHMUS OF PANAMA

Panama City

PANAMA

SOUTH AMERICA

Equator

⊛ National capital

• Major city

— National boundary

0   400   800 mi.

0   400   800 km

Azimuthal Equal-Area Projection

SOUTH AMERICA: *Political/Physical*

CENTRAL
AMERICA

Caribbean Sea

*ATLANTIC
OCEAN*

Barranquilla
Cartagena
• Maracaibo
⊛ Caracas

*Gulf
of
Panama*

LLANOS

VENEZUELA

Orinoco River

Georgetown
Paramaribo

GUYANA

Angel Falls

GUIANA HIGHLANDS

SURINAME

FRENCH
GUIANA
(Fr.)

• Cayenne

• Medellín

⊛ Bogotá

COLOMBIA

OCCIDENTAL MTS
Magdalena R.
Cauca R.

MALPELO∘
(Colombia)

Rio   *Negro*

River

Equator

⊛ Quito
ECUADOR

AMAZON

• Belém

GALÁPAGOS
ISLANDS
(Ecuador)

Guayaquil

*Gulf of
Guayaquil*

• Iquitos

Solimões   *River*

• Manaus

Amazon

BASIN

Tapajós River

Xingu River

BRAZIL

• Fortaleza

Madeira

River

PERU

• Trujillo

Tocantins River

São Francisco River

• Recife

PACIFIC

A
N
D
E
S

Lima ⊛
• Cuzco

Lake Titicaca

PLATEAU OF
MATO GROSSO

BRAZILIAN

Salvador •

OCEAN

Arequipa •

• La Paz

BOLIVIA

ALTIPLANO

⊛ Sucre

⊛ Brasília

HIGHLANDS

Paraguay River

• Belo Horizonte

Antofagasta •

ATACAMA DESERT

GRAN CHACO

PARAGUAY

Paraná River

São Paulo •

• Rio de Janeiro

Tropic of Capricorn

SAN FÉLIX
ISLAND
(Chile)

SAN AMBROSIO
ISLAND
(Chile)

⊛ Asunción

• Santos

Salado River

Paraná

River

• Pôrto Alegre

JUAN FERNÁNDEZ
ISLANDS
(Chile)

CHILE

A
N
D
E
S

• Córdoba

Rosario •

URUGUAY

Valparaíso •
Santiago •

Buenos Aires ⊛

⊛ Montevideo

ARGENTINA

Rio de la Plata

ATLANTIC

Concepción •

PAMPAS

Colorado R.

• Bahía Blanca

OCEAN

Valdivia •

Gulf of San Matías

N
W   E
S

P
A
T
A
G
O
N
I
A

• Comodoro Rivadavia
Gulf of San Jorge

⊛ National capital

• Major city

— National boundary

| 0 | 400 | 800 mi. |
| 0 | 400 | 800 km |

Azimuthal Equal-Area Projection

*Strait of
Magellan*

FALKLAND
ISLANDS
(U.K.)

687

TIERRA
DEL FUEGO

Cape Horn

SOUTH GEORGIA
(U.K.)

Drake Passage

WORLD: *Religions*

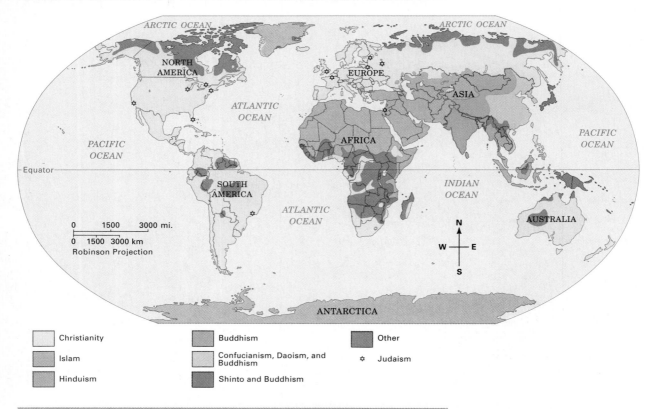

Christianity

Islam

Hinduism

Buddhism

Confucianism, Daoism, and Buddhism

Shinto and Buddhism

Other

✡ Judaism

WORLD: *Climate*

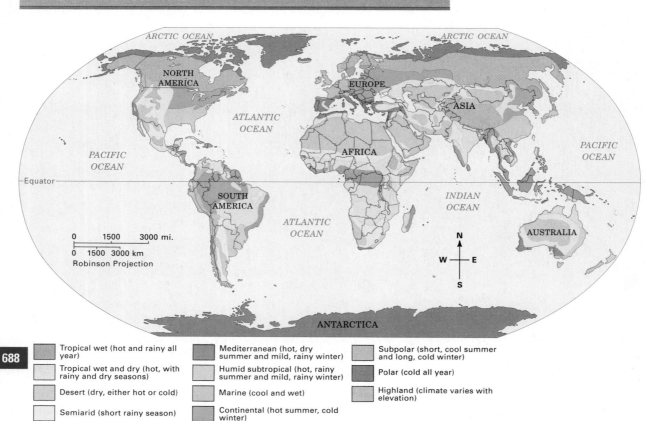

Tropical wet (hot and rainy all year)

Tropical wet and dry (hot, with rainy and dry seasons)

Desert (dry, either hot or cold)

Semiarid (short rainy season)

Mediterranean (hot, dry summer and mild, rainy winter)

Humid subtropical (hot, rainy summer and rainy winter)

Marine (cool and wet)

Continental (hot summer, cold winter)

Subpolar (short, cool summer and long, cold winter)

Polar (cold all year)

Highland (climate varies with elevation)

WORLD: *Population*

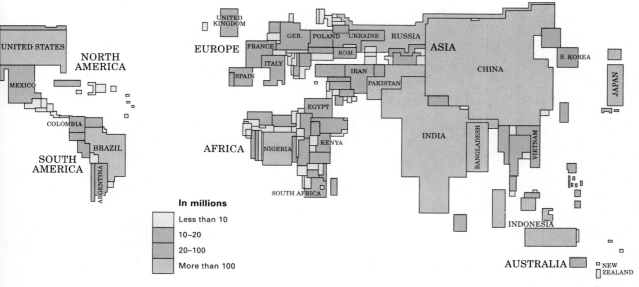

UNITED STATES

NORTH AMERICA

MEXICO

COLOMBIA

BRAZIL

SOUTH AMERICA

ARGENTINA

UNITED KINGDOM

EUROPE

FRANCE

ITALY

SPAIN

GER. POLAND UKRAINE RUSSIA

ROM.

IRAN

PAKISTAN

EGYPT

AFRICA

NIGERIA

KENYA

SOUTH AFRICA

ASIA

CHINA

S. KOREA

JAPAN

INDIA

BANGLADESH

VIETNAM

INDONESIA

AUSTRALIA

NEW ZEALAND

In millions

Less than 10

10–20

20–100

More than 100

Each country's size in the cartogram represents the size of its population compared with those of other countries in the world. Based on information in *The World Factbook, 1991.*

WORLD: *Land Use, Land and Ocean Resources*

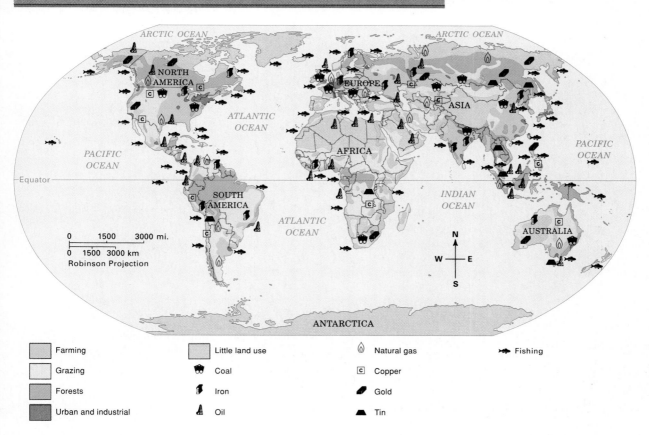

ARCTIC OCEAN

ARCTIC OCEAN

NORTH AMERICA

ATLANTIC OCEAN

EUROPE

ASIA

PACIFIC OCEAN

AFRICA

PACIFIC OCEAN

Equator

SOUTH AMERICA

ATLANTIC OCEAN

INDIAN OCEAN

AUSTRALIA

0   1500   3000 mi.

0   1500   3000 km

Robinson Projection

N
W   E
S

ANTARCTICA

Farming		Little land use	◊ Natural gas	Fishing
Grazing		Coal	C Copper	
Forests		Iron	Gold	
Urban and industrial		Oil	Tin	

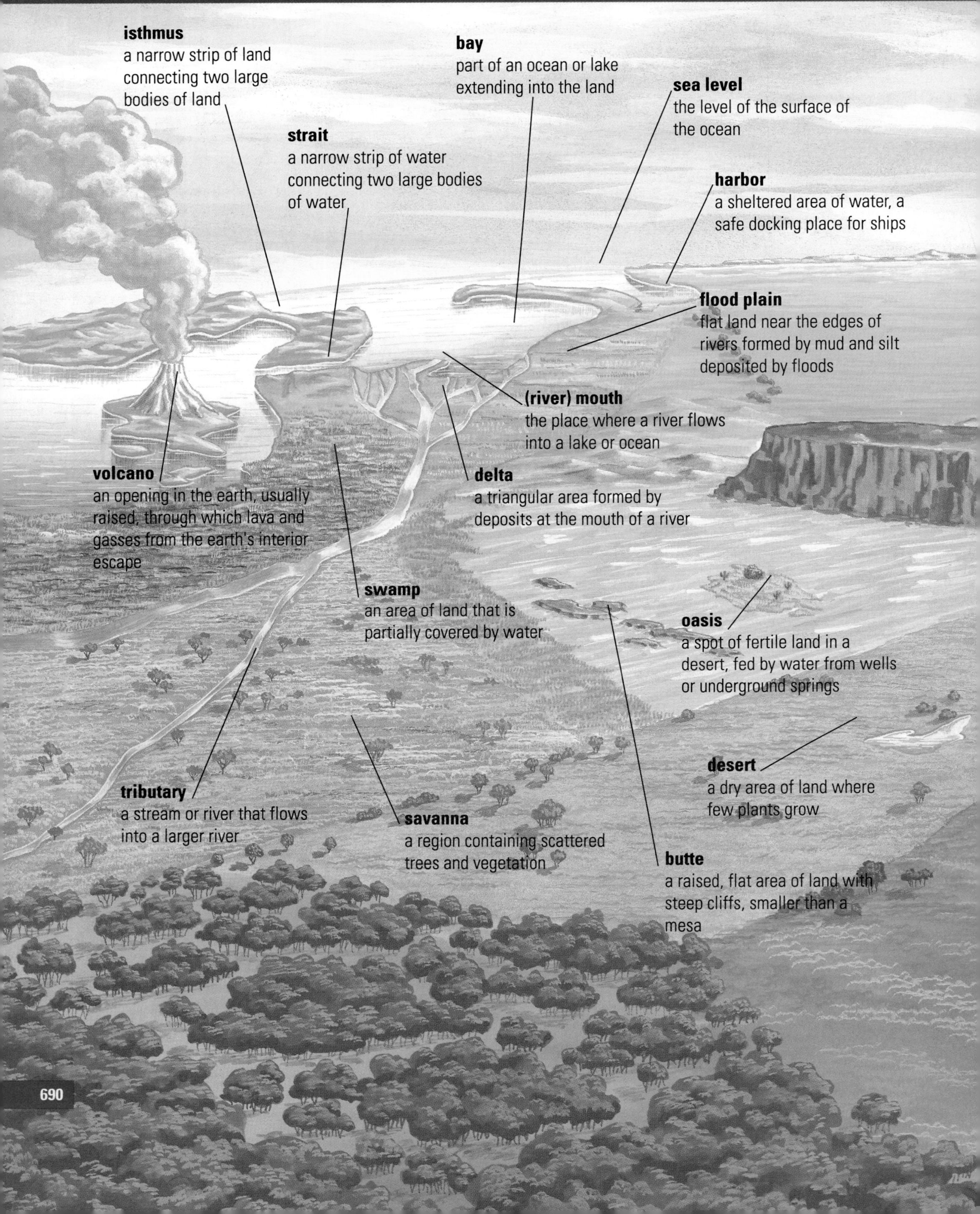

GLOSSARY OF GEOGRAPHIC TERMS

isthmus
a narrow strip of land connecting two large bodies of land

bay
part of an ocean or lake extending into the land

sea level
the level of the surface of the ocean

strait
a narrow strip of water connecting two large bodies of water

harbor
a sheltered area of water, a safe docking place for ships

flood plain
flat land near the edges of rivers formed by mud and silt deposited by floods

(river) mouth
the place where a river flows into a lake or ocean

volcano
an opening in the earth, usually raised, through which lava and gasses from the earth's interior escape

delta
a triangular area formed by deposits at the mouth of a river

swamp
an area of land that is partially covered by water

oasis
a spot of fertile land in a desert, fed by water from wells or underground springs

desert
a dry area of land where few plants grow

tributary
a stream or river that flows into a larger river

savanna
a region containing scattered trees and vegetation

butte
a raised, flat area of land with steep cliffs, smaller than a mesa

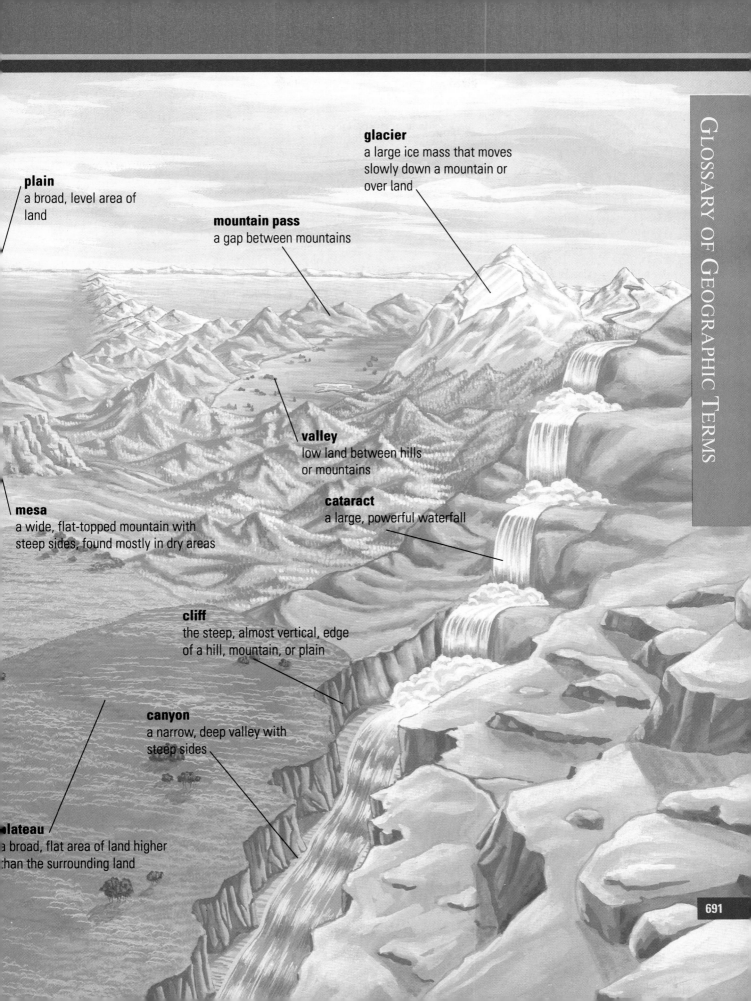

glacier
a large ice mass that moves
slowly down a mountain or
over land

plain
a broad, level area of
land

mountain pass
a gap between mountains

valley
low land between hills
or mountains

mesa
a wide, flat-topped mountain with
steep sides, found mostly in dry areas

cataract
a large, powerful waterfall

cliff
the steep, almost vertical, edge
of a hill, mountain, or plain

canyon
a narrow, deep valley with
steep sides

plateau
a broad, flat area of land higher
than the surrounding land

691

GAZETTEER

This Gazetteer will help you locate many of the places discussed in this book. Latitude and longitude given for large areas of land and water refer to the centermost point of the area; latitude and longitude of rivers refer to the river mouth. The page number tells you where to find each place on a map.

PLACE	LAT.	LONG.	PAGE
A			
Accra (capital of Ghana)	6°N	0°	**282**
Aegean Sea (part of the Mediterranean Sea)	39°N	25°E	**155**
Alexandria (city in Egypt founded by Alexander the Great)	31°N	30°E	**178**
altiplano (high plateau, as in the Andes region)	19°S	68°W	**687**
Amazon R. (in South America; largest in the world)	1°S	52°W	**557**
Andes (mountain system in South America)	13°S	75°W	**687**
Angel Falls (in S.E. Venezuela; world's highest waterfall)	5°N	62°W	**687**
Arabian Sea (in Asia; meets the Indian Ocean)	16°N	65°E	**190**
Aral Sea (inland sea between Kazakhstan and Uzbekistan)	45°N	60°E	**494**
Argos (ancient Greek city-state)	38°N	23°E	**155**
Ashanti (region in central Ghana)	7°N	2°W	**282**
Assur (ancient city of Assyria; in modern Iraq)	35°N	43°E	**71**
Athens (ancient city-state; capital of modern Greece)	38°N	24°E	**155**
Attica (ancient region in central Greece)	38°N	24°E	**155**
B			
Babylon (ancient city-kingdom and capital of Babylonia)	33°N	44°E	**67**
Baghdad (capital of modern Iraq)	33°N	44°E	**215**
Baikal, Lake (in S. Siberia)	53°N	109°E	**494**
Baja California (peninsula in N.W. Mexico; between the Pacific Ocean and the Gulf of California)	27°N	114°W	**585**
Baltic Sea (in N. Europe)	55°N	17°E	**494**
Beijing (capital of China)	40°N	116°E	**348**
Benares (city in north-central India; now known as Varanasi)	25°N	83°E	**324**
Bengal, Bay of (part of the Indian Ocean)	18°N	87°E	**324**
Bering Strait (waterway separating Asia and North America)	65°N	169°W	**686**
Berlin (capital of Germany)	53°N	13°E	**473**

PLACE	LAT.	LONG.	PAGE
Black Sea (between Europe and Asia)	43°N	35°E	**178**
Bombay (city in W. India where the British first traded)	19°N	73°E	**324**
Brasília (capital of Brazil)	16°S	48°W	**551**
Buenos Aires (capital of Argentina)	34°S	59°W	**687**
C			
Cairo (capital of Egypt)	30°N	31°E	**240**
Calcutta (chief commercial port in India)	23°N	88°E	**324**
Cape Town (capital of South Africa)	34°S	18°E	**294**
Caribbean Sea (area of the western Atlantic Ocean bounded by Central and S. America and West Indies)	15°N	73°W	**509**
Caspian Sea (largest salt lake and inland sea in the world; between Europe and Asia)	42°N	51°E	**169**
Chang Jiang (river in China; also known as the Yangtze R.)	32°N	121°E	**115**
Constantinople (modern Istanbul; capital of the Byzantine and Ottoman empires)	41°N	29°E	**413**
Corinth (ancient Greek commercial city)	38°N	23°E	**155**
Crete (island of Greece; in the Mediterranean Sea)	35°N	25°E	**155**
Crimea (in Ukraine; peninsula extending into the Black Sea)	45°N	34°E	**419**
Cuzco (in Peru; capital of the Inca Empire)	14°S	72°W	**139**
D			
Danube R. (second longest river in Europe)	45°N	30°E	**169**
Dasht-e-Kavir (salt desert in north-central Iran)	35°N	54°E	**205**
Dasht-e-Lut (desert in east-central Iran)	32°N	59°E	**205**
Delhi (in India; capital of the Mughal Empire)	29°N	77°E	**324**
E			
Elburz Mts. (mountain range in N. Iran)	37°N	51°E	**205**
Elmina (seaport in Ghana)	2°W	5°N	**269**

PLACE	LAT.	LONG.	PAGE
Ephesus (ancient city in modern Turkey)	38°N	27°E	**155**
Euphrates R. (in S.W. Asia; along with the Tigris R., the site of several ancient civilizations)	31°N	47°E	**67**
Everest, Mt. (part of the Himalaya range; highest mountain in the world)	28°N	87°E	**115**

F

Fuji, Mt. (volcano in Japan, inactive since 1707)	35°N	139°E	**361**

G

Ganges R. (in India; Hindu holy river)	23°N	91°E	**331**
Gao (in Mali; capital of the Songhai Empire)	16°N	0°	**256**
Good Hope, Cape of (on the S.W. coast of Africa)	34°S	19°E	**298**
Great Rift Valley (land depression stretching from Jordan to S.E. Africa)	0°	36°E	**224**
Guadalajara (city in S.W. Mexico)	21°N	103°W	**585**
Guangzhou (city in China)	23°N	113°E	**348**
Guiana Highlands (plateau and mountain region in northern South America)	3°N	60°W	**687**
Guinea, Gulf of (part of the Atlantic Ocean off the coast of western Africa)	2°N	1°E	**269**

H

Hanoi (capital of Vietnam)	21°N	106°E	**387**
Himalayas (mountain system in Asia)	28°N	84°E	**115**
Hindu Kush (mountain range in central Asia)	36°N	70°E	**324**
Hiroshima (city in S.W. Japan)	34°N	132°E	**361**
Hormuz, Strait of (connects the Persian Gulf to the Gulf of Oman)	27°N	57°E	**205**
Horn, Cape (southernmost tip of South America)	56°S	67°W	**503**
Huang He (river in China; also known as the Yellow R.)	38°N	117°E	**115**
Hudson Bay (inland sea in Canada)	60°N	86°W	**599**

PLACE	LAT.	LONG.	PAGE

I

Indus R. (in Pakistan; longest of the Himalayan rivers)	24°N	68°E	**331**
Isfahan (city in Iran)	33°N	52°E	**209**
Ithaca (Greek island)	38°N	21°E	**155**

J

Jakarta (capital of Indonesia)	6°S	107°E	**387**
Jericho (ancient city in present-day Occupied Territory)	32°N	35°E	**67**
Johannesburg (city in South Africa)	26°S	28°E	**294**
Jordan R. (forms the boundary between Israel and Jordan, and Israel and Syria)	32°N	36°E	**652**

K

Khyber Pass (narrow mountain pass on the border between W. Afghanistan and N. Pakistan)	34°N	71°E	**324**
Kiev (capital of Ukraine)	50°N	31°E	**494**
Kumasi (capital of the Ashanti Region in Ghana)	7°N	2°W	**269**
Kunlun Shan (mountain range in China)	36°N	88°E	**115**
Kyoto (city in Japan)	35°N	136°E	**361**

L

Lima (capital of Peru)	12°S	77°W	**687**
London (capital of the United Kingdom)	52°N	0°	**682**

M

Machu Picchu (in Peru; ruined Inca citadel)	13°S	73°W	**139**
Mackenzie Mts. (mountain range in N.W. Canada)	64°N	129°W	**599**
Mackenzie R. (in N.W. Canada)	69°N	134°W	**599**
Manila (capital of the Philippines)	15°N	121°E	**387**
Mecca (in Saudi Arabia; holiest city of Islam)	21°N	40°E	**190**
Medina (in Saudi Arabia; holy city of Islam)	24°N	40°E	**190**
Mediterranean Sea (between Europe and Africa)	35°N	20°E	**178**

PLACE	LAT.	LONG.	PAGE
Memphis (ancient city in Lower Egypt; capital of most rulers of the Old Kingdom)	30°N	31°E	86
Meroë (ancient city on east bank of the Nile; capital of Nubia)	17°N	34°E	86
Mesopotamia (region in S.W. Asia; site of Babylonia and Assyria)	34°N	44°E	67
Mexico City (capital of Mexico)	19°N	99°W	585
Montréal (in Canada; French settlement)	46°N	74°W	599
Moscow (capital of Russia)	56°N	38°E	494

N

PLACE	LAT.	LONG.	PAGE
Napata (ancient capital of Nubia in Egypt)	19°N	32°E	86
Nile R. (in Africa; longest river in the world)	30°N	31°E	83
North Sea (part of the Atlantic Ocean, between Great Britain and the European continent)	56°N	3°E	494
Nubia (ancient empire in N.E. Africa)	21°N	33°E	83

O

PLACE	LAT.	LONG.	PAGE
Olympus, Mt. (highest mountain in Greece; on the Macedonia-Thessaly border)	40°N	22°E	155
Orinoco R. (river in Venezuela)	9°N	61°W	687

P

PLACE	LAT.	LONG.	PAGE
Pampas (plains in S. South America)	37°S	65°W	687
Panama Canal (in Panama; opened in 1914)	9°N	81°W	543
Paraná R. (in S.E. South America)	34°S	59°W	557
Paris (capital of France)	49°N	2°E	682
Peloponnesus (peninsula of Greece)	38°N	22°E	155
Persepolis (in Iran; ancient capital of Persia)	30°N	53°E	205
Persian Gulf (part of the Arabian Sea; between Iran and the Arabian Peninsula)	27°N	51°E	215
Pinatubo, Mt. (volcano in the Philippines; erupted in June 1991)	15°N	120°E	401
Pretoria (administrative capital of South Africa)	26°S	28°E	294

PLACE	LAT.	LONG.	PAGE
Pyongyang (capital of North Korea)	39°N	126°E	653

Q

PLACE	LAT.	LONG.	PAGE
Québec (in Canada; French settlement)	47°N	71°W	599
Quito (capital of Ecuador)	0°	79°W	687

R

PLACE	LAT.	LONG.	PAGE
Red Sea (between the Arabian Peninsula and N.E. Africa)	20°N	38°E	234
Rhone R. (in Switzerland and France)	43°N	5°E	169
Rio de Janeiro (seaport in Brazil)	23°S	43°W	557
Rio Grande (river that forms the boundary between Texas and Mexico)	26°N	97°W	585
Rome (capital of Italy; center of ancient Roman Empire)	42°N	13°E	169

S

PLACE	LAT.	LONG.	PAGE
Sahara (largest desert on the earth; stretches across northern Africa)	24°N	2°W	224
San José (capital of Costa Rica)	10°N	84°W	543
São Paulo (city in Brazil)	24°S	47°W	557
Seoul (capital of South Korea)	38°N	127°E	653
Siberia (vast region in Russia; covers the northern third of Asia)	57°N	97°E	683
Sicily (island of Italy in the Mediterranean Sea)	38°N	14°E	178
Sierra Madre del Sur (part of the Sierra Madre range on the coast of southern Mexico)	17°N	100°W	585
Sierra Madre Occidental (part of the Sierra Madre range in Mexico; runs almost parallel to the Gulf of California and the Pacific Ocean)	21°N	105°W	585
Sierra Madre Oriental (part of the Sierra Madre range in Mexico; runs almost parallel to the Gulf of Mexico)	21°N	99°W	585
Sinai Peninsula (easternmost part of Egypt; between the Gulf of Suez and the Gulf of Aqaba)	30°N	34°E	240
Sparta (ancient city-state of Greece)	37°N	22°E	155

PLACE	LAT.	LONG.	PAGE
St. Petersburg (in Russia; Peter the Great's capital)	60°N	30°E	**494**
Susa (ancient city in Persia)	32°N	49°E	**209**

T

PLACE	LAT.	LONG.	PAGE
Tehran (capital of Iran)	36°N	52°E	**205**
Tema (city in Ghana)	6°N	0°	**282**
Tenochtitlan (modern Mexico City; capital of the Aztec Empire)	19°N	99°W	**130**
Tian Shan (mountain range in Asia)	42°N	80°E	**115**
Tibet, Plateau of (region of China; highest plateau in the world)	33°N	92°E	**115**
Tigris R. (in S.W. Asia; along with the Euphrates R., site of several ancient civilizations)	31°N	47°E	**67**
Timbuktu (in modern Mali; city in Songhai Empire)	17°N	3°W	**256**
Titicaca, Lake (in Bolivia and Peru; center of early South American civilizations)	16°S	69°W	**139**
Tokyo (Edo; center of the Tokugawa shogunate; capital of Japan)	36°N	140°E	**361**
Toronto (city in Ontario, Canada)	44°N	79°W	**599**

U

PLACE	LAT.	LONG.	PAGE
Ur (city in ancient Sumer)	31°N	46°E	**67**

PLACE	LAT.	LONG.	PAGE
Ural Mts. (mountain range in Russia; form the border between Europe and Asia)	56°N	58°E	**453**
Uxmal (in Mexico; capital of the later Mayan Empire)	20°N	90°W	**130**

V

PLACE	LAT.	LONG.	PAGE
Vancouver (city in British Columbia, Canada)	49°N	123°W	**599**
Veracruz (city in Mexico)	19°N	96°W	**585**
Vladivostok (seaport in Russia)	43°N	132°E	**494**
Volga R. (in Russia; longest river in Europe)	46°N	49°E	**494**
Volta R. (in Ghana)	5°N	1°E	**269**
Volta, Lake (reservoir in Ghana)	7°N	1°W	**282**

X

PLACE	LAT.	LONG.	PAGE
Xi'an (early capital of China; on Wei He)	34°N	109°E	**341**

Y

PLACE	LAT.	LONG.	PAGE
Yucatán Peninsula (mainly in S.E. Mexico)	20°N	89°W	**130**
Yukon R. (in North America; flows from Canada across Alaska)	62°N	165°W	**599**

Z

PLACE	LAT.	LONG.	PAGE
Zagros Mts. (mountain range in western Iran)	34°N	47°E	**205**

BIOGRAPHICAL DICTIONARY

This dictionary lists many of the important people introduced in this book. The page number refers to the main discussion of that person in the book. For more complete references see the Index.

Pronunciation Key

This chart presents the system of phonetic respellings used to indicate pronunciation in the Biographical Dictionary and in the chapters of this book.

Spellings	Symbol	Spellings	Symbol	Spellings	Symbol
pat	a	kick, cat, pique	k	thin, this	th
pay	ay	lid, needle	l	cut	uh
care	air	mum	m	urge, term, firm, word, heard	ur
father	ah	no, sudden	n		
bib	b	thing	ng	valve	v
church	ch	pot, horrid	ah	with	w
deed, milled	d	toe	oh	yes	y
pet	eh	caught, paw, for	aw	zebra, xylem	z
bee	ee	noise	oy	vision, pleasure, garage	zh
life, phase, rough	f	took	u		
gag	g	boot	oo	about, item, edible, gallop, circus	uh
hat	h	out	ow		
which	hw	pop	p	butter	ur
pit	ih	roar	r		
pie, by	eye, y	sauce	s	Capital letters indicate stressed syllables.	
pier	ihr	ship, dish	sh		
judge	j	tight, stopped	t		

A

Abbas I 1571–1629, shah of Persia (1587–1629) who strengthened the Safavid dynasty and encouraged great artistic and cultural achievements (p. 210).

Abdul Aziz *(AHB dul, ah ZEEZ)* c. 1880–1953, also known as ibn-Saud, founder of the Kingdom of Saudi Arabia and its first king, (1932–1953) (p. 194).

Abraham c. 2000 B.C., according to the Bible, the ancestor of the Israelites (p. 73).

Akbar *(AK bahr)* 1542–1605, Mughal emperor of India (1556–1605) who transformed the region into a major cultural center (p. 323).

Alexander II 1818–1881, czar of Russia (1855–1881) who emancipated the serfs (1861) (p. 455).

Alexander the Great 356–323 B.C., king of Macedonia, (336–323 B.C.) who conquered the Persians and established an empire stretching from Egypt to India. His conquests spread Greek culture (p. 159).

Aquino, Benigno 1932–1983, opposition leader in the Philippines during a period of martial law under President Marcos; assassinated by the military upon his return to the Philippines from the United States (p. 393).

Aquino, Corazón (Cory) 1933–, president of the Philippines (1986–1992) after succeeding her husband, Benigno, as the leader of the opposition to Marcos (p. 393).

Arias Sánchez, Oscar *(AH ryahs SAHN chez)* 1941–, president of Costa Rica (1986–1990) and Nobel Peace Prize winner (1987) (p. 545).

Aristotle *(AIR ihs taht uhl)* 384–332 B.C., Greek philosopher and scientist, student of Plato, and teacher of Alexander the Great (p. 160).

Aryabhata *(ah ree ah BAHT uh)* 476–c. 550, Indian mathematician who worked mainly in the fields of astronomy and trigonometry (p. 318).

Ashoka *(ah SHOH kah)* died c. 238 B.C., last major emperor of the Mauryan dynasty in India; responsible for spreading Buddhism in India and beyond (p. 113).

Ashurbanipal *(ah shur BAH nuh pahl)* seventh century B.C., last great Assyrian king; known for assembling a major library in the ancient Middle East (p. 72).

Augustus 63 B.C.–A.D. 14, first Roman emperor (27 B.C.–A.D. 14) who defeated Antony and Cleopatra and ruled the Greco-Roman world (p. 169).

Aurangzeb *(AWR ehng zehb)* 1618–1707, last great ruler of the Mughal Empire in India (p. 323).

B

Begin, Menachem 1913–1992, prime minister of Israel (1977–1983) who negotiated with President Sadat of Egypt in an attempt to settle the Arab-Israeli conflict (p. 237).

Bolívar, Simon *(boh LEE vahr)* 1783–1830, Venezuelan leader who led the independence movement in South America (p. 532).

Bonaparte, Napoleon 1769–1821, French general, emperor of France (1804–1814) who controlled Continental Europe (p. 552).

Botha, Louis *(BOH tuh)* 1862–1919, first prime minister of the Union of South Africa (p. 301).

Botha, Pieter Willem 1916–, prime minister of South Africa (1978–1989) who refused to abolish the policy of apartheid (p. 305).

Bowdich, Thomas Edward 1791–1824, British traveler who negotiated peace with the Ashanti kingdom, leading to an increase in British influence in Africa (p. 274).

Bruegel, Pieter (the Elder) *(BROY guhl)* c. 1525–1569, Flemish Renaissance painter known for landscapes and scenes of peasant life (p. 428).

Brunelleschi, Filippo *(broo nuh LEHS kee)* 1377–1446, Italian Renaissance architect; best known for the dome of the Florence cathedral (p. 426).

Buthelezi, Mangosuthu *(boo tuh LEH zee)* 1928–, Zulu chief and head of the Inkatha Freedom Party in South Africa (p. 305).

C

Caboto, Giovanni (John Cabot) c. 1450–c. 1498, Italian-born navigator who led the first English expedition to North America (p. 601).

Cabral, Pedro Álvares 1467/1468–1520, Portuguese explorer who claimed Brazil for Portugal in 1500 (p. 551).

Caesar, Julius 100–44 B.C., Roman general who ruled Rome as a dictator from 49 B.C. until his assassination (p. 169).

Calvin, John 1509–1564, French-born Swiss Protestant reformer, whose ideas heavily influenced the development of Protestantism in Europe (p. 432).

Cárdenas, Lázaro 1895–1970, president of Mexico (1934–1940) who worked to carry out the goals of the Mexican Revolution (p. 582).

Cartier, Jacques *(ZHAHK kahr tee AY)* 1491–1557, French navigator who explored the St. Lawrence River and claimed the region for France (p. 601).

Castro, Fidel 1926/1927–, Communist leader of Cuba since 1959, after leading a revolution to overthrow the Batista regime (p. 520).

Catherine the Great 1729–1796, empress of Russia (1762–1796); greatly increased the size of the empire and brought Russia closer to Europe politically and culturally (p. 455).

Champlain, Samuel de c. 1567–1635, French explorer who founded the Canadian city of Québec in 1608 (p. 601).

Charlemagne *(SHAR luh mayn)* c. 742–814, king of the Franks who conquered and united most of western Europe (p. 412).

Chiang Kai-shek *(chang ky shehk)* 1887–1975, Chinese general; head of the Nationalist government in China (1928–1949); later headed the Chinese Nationalist government in exile in Taiwan (p. 344).

Churchill, Winston 1874–1965, British prime minister (1940–1945 and 1951–1955) who led Great Britain through World War II (p. 470).

Cleopatra VII 69–30 B.C., queen of Egypt; Cleopatra's and Mark Antony's forces were defeated by Octavian's Roman forces (p. 229).

Collor de Mello, Fernando *(COH lawr dee MEHL lu)* 1949–, president of Brazil (1990–December 1992) (p. 553).

Columbus, Christopher 1451–1506, Italian explorer who reached the Americas in 1492 and claimed the area for Spain while attempting to find a westward sea route to Asia (pp. 440, 513).

Confucius (K'ung Ch'iu) *(kung chee oo)* c. 551–479 B.C., Chinese teacher and philosopher whose ideas influenced all the Asian civilizations (p. 118).

Constantine I c. 280–337, first Roman emperor to support Christianity; protected Christians in the empire and made Constantinople its new capital (pp. 178, 412).

Copernicus, Nicolaus *(koh PUR nuh kuhs)* 1473–1543, Polish astronomer who developed the theory that Earth and the other planets revolve around the sun (p. 429).

Cortés, Hernán 1485–1547, Spaniard who conquered the Aztec Empire and claimed Mexico for Spain (p. 578).

D

da Silva, Benedita 1942–, first African Brazilian woman elected to the Brazilian congress (1987) (p. 563).

Darius I *(duh RY uhs)* 550–486 B.C., king of Persia (522–486 B.C.) who enlarged the empire, standardized gold and silver coins, and built Persepolis (p. 209).

Darwin, Charles 1809–1882, British naturalist famous for his theory of evolution, as set forth in his work, *Origin of Species* (p. 448).

David second king of Israel who ruled from c. 1000 B.C. until his death (c. 962 B.C.); made Jerusalem the capital of Israel and founded a lasting dynasty (p. 75).

de Klerk, Frederik Willem 1936–, president of South Africa since 1989 who released Nelson Mandela from prison and began repealing apartheid laws (p. 305).

Deng Xiaoping *(duhng shyow pihng)* 1904–, strongest leader of the Chinese Communist party late 1970s–1990 (p. 348).

d'Este, Isabella *(DEHS tay)* 1474–1539, Renaissance patron of the arts who helped her husband's family rule the Italian city-state of Mantua (p. 427).

Dias, Bartolomeu *(DEE uhs)* c. 1450–1500, Portuguese explorer who led the first European expedition to sail around the Cape of Good Hope (1488) (p. 297).

Díaz, Porfirio 1830–1915, president of Mexico (1877–1880 and 1884–1911) who created a strong central government (p. 581).

Djoser *(DZOH suhr)* second king of the Third Dynasty of Egypt (c. 2650–c. 2575 B.C.) who ordered the construction of the Step Pyramid (p. 93).

Drake, Sir Francis c.1540–1596, first English navigator to circumnavigate the globe; vice admiral of the fleet that defeated the Spanish Armada (p. 513).

E

Einstein, Albert 1879–1955, German-born U.S. physicist who developed the theory of relativity (p. 626).

F

Farouk 1920–1965, king of Egypt from 1936 until his overthrow by Nasser in 1952 (p. 236).

Ferdinand 1452–1516, king of Aragon who, with his wife, Isabella of Castile, united and ruled Spain (p. 438).

Foch, Ferdinand *(fosh)* 1851–1929, French marshal and commander-in-chief on the western front during World War I; helped lead the Allied forces to victory (p. 463).

Francis Ferdinand 1863–1914, archduke of Austria whose assassination triggered World War I (p. 462).

G

Gama, Vasco da c. 1460–1524, Portuguese navigator who led the first European expedition to India, helping make Portugal a world power (p. 551).

Gandhi, Mohandas K. 1869–1948, Indian leader of the independence movement against the British; known for his use of nonviolent civil disobedience (pp. 299, 326, 450).

Gorbachev, Mikhail *(GAWR buh chawf)* 1931–, general secretary of the Communist party of the USSR (1985–1991) and president of the USSR (1990–1991) who began reforms that helped bring about the end of the Cold War and the breakup of the USSR (p. 474).

Gutenberg, Johannes *(GOOT n burg)* c. 1400–c. 1468, German printer who invented a printing press that used moveable type (p. 428).

H

Hammurabi ruler of Babylonia 1792–1750 B.C., recorded a system of laws known as the Code of Hammurabi (p. 69).

Hatshepsut *(haht SHEHP soot)* ruler of ancient Egypt (c. 1472–1458 B.C.) who took the title of pharaoh for herself (p. 85).

Havel, Václav 1936–, Czech playwright, poet, and protest leader; became Czechoslovakia's president in 1989 after the collapse of communism; president of the newly formed Czech Republic (1993) (p. 478).

Haynes, Lemuel 1753–1833, African American minister and Revolutionary War soldier (p. 617).

Henry (the Navigator) 1394–1460, Portuguese prince who sponsored voyages to Africa and advanced shipbuilding, cartography, and commerce (p. 550).

Henry VIII 1491–1547, king of England (1509–1547). His refusal to obey the Pope led to the establishment of the Church of England (p. 432).

Hidalgo y Costilla, Miguel 1753–1811, Mexican priest who led an uprising against Spanish domination; known as the father of Mexican independence (p. 580).

Hippocrates *(hih PAHK ruh teez)* c. 460–c. 377 B.C., ancient Greek physician who is considered the founder of medicine (p. 160).

Hitler, Adolf 1889–1945, leader of the Nazi party in Germany from 1921; dictator of Germany's Third Reich (1933–1945); ordered the killing of millions of Jews and others during World War II (p. 468).

Ho Chi Minh *(hoh chee minh)* 1890–1969, founder of the Indochina Communist party; president of North Vietnam (1945–1969) (p. 397).

Homer ninth or eighth century B.C., Greek poet considered the creator of the two great epic poems, the *Iliad* and the *Odyssey* (p. 154).

Hugo, Victor 1802–1885, French author of *The Hunchback of Notre Dame, Les Misérables,* and many other works (p. 480).

I

Ibn Battuta 1304–1368/1369, Arab traveler and author who journeyed throughout the Muslim countries and to the Far East (p. 250).

Ibn Khaldun *(IHB uhn kal DOON)* 1332–1406, Arab historian who wrote the first significant history of Muslim North Africa (p. 232).

Imhotep *(ihm HOH tehp)* 27th century B.C., architect, physician, and chancellor under Djoser, later worshiped in Egypt and Greece as the God of medicine (p. 93).

Isabella 1451–1504, queen of Castile who, with her husband, Ferdinand of Aragon, united and ruled Spain; sponsored the voyages of Christopher Columbus (p. 438).

Ivan III (the Great) 1440–1505, prince of Moscow (1462–1505) who fought off the dominance of the Tatars and laid the foundation for a unified Russian state (p. 454).

Ivan IV (the Terrible) 1530–1584, first czar of Russia (1547–1584); fought unsuccessful wars with Sweden; carried out a reign of terror against the aristocracy (p. 454).

J

Jacob (or Israel) according to the Bible, grandson of Abraham. His 12 sons became the ancestors of the 12 tribes of Israel (p. 74).

Jesuit a member of the Society of Jesus (S.J.), the Roman Catholic order founded in 1530 by Ignatius of Loyola for teaching and missionary work (p. 433).

Jesus c. 6 B.C.–A.D. 30, great religious leader called the Christ by his followers; believed by most Christians to be the son of God (p. 175).

João VI 1767–1826, king of Portugal (1816–1826). During the time of his rule Brazil was declared independent (1822) (pp. 552–553).

Juárez, Benito 1806–1872, president of Mexico (1861–1872); fought against foreign domination by Napoleon III of France and Maximilian of Austria (p. 581).

K

Khomeini, (Ayatollah) Ruholla *(AY uh tohl lah koh MAY nee)* 1900–1989, Shiite religious leader, although in exile, directed the Iranian revolution that overthrew the shah in 1979; head of state of Iran (1979–1989) (p. 214).

Khufu *(KOO foo)* second king of Egypt's Fourth Dynasty (2500s B.C.), who built the Great Pyramid at Giza (p. 88).

King, Martin Luther, Jr. 1929–1968, U.S. minister, leader of the U.S. civil rights movement from the mid-1950s until his assassination (pp. 432, 633).

Krishna eighth incarnation of the Hindu God Vishnu (p. 109).

L

Las Casas, Bartolomé de 1474–1566, Spanish missionary in the Americas who called for the abolition of Indian slavery (p. 443).

Lenin 1870–1924, founder of the Bolsheviks (Russian Communist party); a leader of the Russian Revolution (1917); first head of the Soviet Union (p. 465).

Leo Africanus 1485–c. 1554, Arabian traveler who wrote about Africa and Islam (p. 251).

Leonardo da Vinci 1452–1519, Italian Renaissance artist, inventor, and scientist whose paintings include *Mona Lisa* and *The Last Supper* (p. 427).

Luther, Martin 1483–1546, German priest whose ideas inspired the Protestant Reformation; translated the Bible from Latin to German (p. 430).

M

MacArthur, Douglas 1880–1964, U.S. general who commanded the Allied troops in Asia in World War II; headed the U.S. occupation forces in Japan (p. 392).

Mackenzie, Alexander c. 1755–1820, Scottish-born explorer of Canada for whom the Mackenzie River in Canada is named (p. 602).

Magellan, Ferdinand c. 1480–1521, Portuguese navigator and explorer whose European expedition was the first to complete the trip around the globe (p. 390).

Mahmud *(mah MOOD)* 971–1030, sultan (ruler) of the kingdom of Ghazna; one of the early Muslim leaders who invaded India (p. 322).

Mandela, Nelson 1918–, South African activist and head of the African National Congress (p. 292).

Mann, Horace 1796–1859, U.S. educator whose work led to reforms in public education, including a longer school year and teacher training programs (p. 635).

Mansa Musa died c. 1332/1337, emperor of Mali (1307–1332) who made an extravagant pilgrimage to Mecca (p. 248).

Mao Zedong *(mow dzuh dahng)* 1893–1976, Chinese leader who helped found the Chinese Communist party; established the People's Republic of China (1949) (p. 345).

Marconi, Guglielmo 1874 –1937, Italian physicist who invented the wireless (p. 12).

Marcos, Ferdinand 1917–1989, Philippine head of state (1966–1986) who was overthrown by a popular rebellion (p. 392).

Margaret I of Denmark 1353–1412, queen who united the Scandinavian countries of Denmark, Norway, and Sweden (p. 415).

Marie de France flourished late 12th century; earliest known French woman poet whose famous work was *Ysopet,* a collection of fables (p. 415).

Marx, Karl 1818–1883, German philosopher whose political theories started the movement called Marxism and whose famous book with Friedrich Engels is the *Communist Manifesto* (p. 450).

Medici (family) *(MEHD uh chee)* wealthy Italian family that ruled Florence during the Renaissance, making important contributions to the arts, politics, and religion (p. 425).

Menchú, Rigoberta 1959–, Guatemalan Nobel Peace Prize winner (1992) (p. 542).

Mendes, Chico *(SHEE ku MEHN dehz)* 1944?–1988, Brazilian environmental activist who promoted sustainable development (p. 562).

Mengzi c. 371–289 B.C., Chinese philosopher and follower of Confucius (p. 340).

Michelangelo *(my kuhl AN juh loh)* 1475–1564, Italian Renaissance sculptor, painter, and architect whose works include paintings in the Sistine Chapel and the sculpture *David* (p. 426).

Montezuma c. 1466–1520, Aztec emperor defeated by Cortés in 1520 (p. 578).

Moses c. 14th–13th century B.C., according to the Bible, Hebrew prophet and law giver who led the Israelites out of slavery in Egypt (p. 74).

Mubarak, Hosni 1928–, president of Egypt since 1981 (p. 237).

Muhammad c. 570–632, religious prophet and founder of Islam (p. 186).

Muhammad Ali *(ah LEE)* 1769–1849, founder of the Egyptian dynasty that ruled from the early 1800s to the mid-1900s (p. 234).

N

Nasser, Gamal Abdel *(NAS uhr)* 1918–1970, Egyptian revolutionary and president (1956–1970) who instituted broad reforms and ordered the building of the Aswan Dam (p. 236).

Nebuchadnezzar II c. 630–562 B.C., king of Babylonia who captured Jerusalem and had the Israelites brought to Babylon (p. 76).

Nehru, Jawaharlal *(juh wah hur LAHL NAY roo)* 1889–1964, activist for independence in India; first prime minister of independent India (1947–1964) (p. 327).

Nicholas II 1868–1918, last Russian czar who was killed by the Bolsheviks (Communists) during the Russian Revolution (p. 464).

Nkrumah, Kwame *(KWAH may uhng KROO muh)* 1909–1972, leader of the Ghanaian independence movement against British rule, president of Ghana (1960–1966) (p. 280).

Noriega, Manuel 1940–, military dictator of Panama (1983–1989) (p. 543).

O

Odysseus *(oh DIHS ee uhs)* Perhaps mythical Greek hero and central character in Homer's epic poem the *Odyssey.* (p. 154).

P

Pachacuti *(pah chah KOO tee)* Inca emperor 1438–1471, who greatly expanded the Inca Empire in South America (p. 142).

Pahlavi, Mohammed Reza Shah 1919–1980, shah of Iran (1941–1979) overthrown by Islamic fundamentalists (p. 214).

Pahlavi, Reza Shah 1878–1944, Iranian general who became the shah of Iran and started reform of the country (p. 213).

Parks, Rosa 1913–, African American civil rights activist whose refusal in 1955 to give up her seat to a white bus rider stirred the U.S. civil rights movement (p. 633).

Paul c. A.D. 5–c. A.D. 67, Jewish convert to Christianity who became one of its most important apostles (p. 175).

Pedro I 1798–1834, Portuguese prince who declared Brazil's independence from Portugal (1822); served as its first emperor (1822–1831) (p. 553).

Pedro II 1825–1891, second and last emperor of Brazil (1831–1889); during his reign slavery was abolished (p. 553).

Pericles *(PEHR ih kleez)* c. 495–429 B.C., political and cultural leader of Athens during its Golden Age (p. 158).

Perón, Eva Duarte de *(puh ROHN)* 1919–1952, Argentinean social reformer and supporter of women's rights (p. 540).

Perón, Juan Domingo *(puh ROHN)* 1895–1974, president of Argentina (1946–1955 and 1973–1974) (p. 540).

Perry, Matthew C. 1794–1858, U.S. naval officer who led the expedition to force Japan to open its doors to foreign trade (1853–1854) (p. 370).

Peter the Great 1672–1725, czar of Russia (1682–1725) who extended Russian territory, introduced Western technology, greatly reformed the government and military forces, and built St. Petersburg (p. 454).

Philip II 1527–1598, king of Spain (1556–1598) who sent the Spanish Armada on an unsuccessful invasion of England (1588) (p. 443).

Philip II 382–336 B.C., king of Macedonia who conquered Greek city-states; father of Alexander the Great (p. 159).

Pizan, Christine de *(pee ZAHN)* c. 1365–1430, French poet known for her love poems and writings about women (p. 427).

Plaatje, Solomon *(PLAHT juh)* 1877–1932, black South African interpreter and journalist whose diary provides an important account of the South African War (p. 301).

Plato c. 427–c. 348 B.C., ancient Greek philosopher; a student of Socrates who recorded his teacher's ideas (p. 160).

R

Raffles, Sir (Thomas) Stamford 1781–1826, administrator of British holdings in East India and founder of Singapore (1819) (p. 395).

Ramesses II *(RAM ih seez)* king of Egypt (1279–1213 B.C.), known for his major building projects and the many statues of himself in Egypt and Nubia (p. 85).

Ramos, Fidel 1928–, army chief of staff in the Philippines who led the protest against Marcos; elected president in 1992 (p. 393).

Roosevelt, Franklin D. 1882–1945, U.S. president (1933–1945) who brought the country through the Great Depression (1929–1941) with the economic reform program called the New Deal; led the country during World War II (p. 472).

S

Sadat, Anwar *(suh DAHT)* 1918–1981, Egyptian military leader and president of Egypt (1970–1981) who worked for peace with Israel (p. 236).

Saladin 1138–1193, Muslim sultan of Egypt who captured Jerusalem and defended it during the Third Crusade (p. 233).

San Martín, José de *(san mahr TEEN)* 1778–1850, Argentinian general and leader of the independence movement against Spanish rule in Argentina, Chile, and Peru (p. 532).

Shaka c. 1787–1828, Zulu chief and founder of the Zulu kingdom in southern Africa (p. 299).

Shakespeare, William 1564–1616, English playwright and poet, often considered the greatest dramatist in history whose plays include *Romeo and Juliet* and *Hamlet* (p. 428).

Shakti Hindu deity who is worshiped as the mother Goddess of Hinduism (p. 109).

Shi huangdi *(see hwahng dee)* c. 259–210 B.C., first emperor of the Qin dynasty who built the Great Wall and unified most of China (p. 121).

Shōtoku 574–622, Japanese ruler (593–622) who made major changes in culture and education (p. 363).

Siddhartha Gautama *(sihd DAHR tah GAW tah mah)* c. 563–c. 483 B.C., the Buddha or "Enlightened One" whose teachings formed the basis of Buddhism (p. 110).

Socrates *(SOK ruh teez)* c. 470–399 B.C., ancient Greek philosopher; teacher of Plato (p. 160).

Solomon flourished mid-10th century B.C., generally considered the greatest king of Israel; built the famous temple in Jerusalem (p. 75).

Sonni 'Ali *(SOH nee AHL ee)* died 1492, leader of the Songhai Empire that conquered the ancient Mali Empire (p. 251).

Stalin, Josef 1879–1953, Soviet head of state (1922–1953) who ruled as a dictator and made the USSR a world power (p. 467).

Sun Yat-sen 1866–1925, leader of the revolution against the Manchu dynasty; first leader of the new Republic of China (p. 344).

Sundiata *(sun dee AHT ah)* died 1255, West African monarch who founded the empire of Mali (p. 249).

T

Thompson, David 1770–1857, English explorer who mapped much of western Canada (p. 602).

Tokugawa Ieyasu *(ih yeh YAH soo)* 1543–1616, founder of the last shogunate (military government) in Japan, which lasted from 1603 until 1867 (p. 368).

Tolstoy, Leo 1828–1910, Russian writer whose novels include *War and Peace* and *Anna Karenina* (p. 455).

Toussaint L'Ouverture *(too SAN loo vehr TUR)* 1743–1803, leader of the Haitian independence movement who helped emancipate enslaved Africans (p. 515).

Trudeau, Pierre 1919–, prime minister of Canada (1969–1979 and 1980–1984), during whose administration Canada was granted full independence from Great Britain (p. 613).

Truman, Harry S. 1884–1972, U.S. president (1945–1953) who ordered the dropping of two atomic bombs on Japan, which ended World War II; led the United States during the Korean War (p. 473).

Tutankhamon *(toot ahng KAH muhn)* Egyptian king (1333–1323 B.C.) whose tomb was discovered intact in 1922 (p. 85).

Tutu, Osei late 17th century, launched the Ashanti Empire by uniting the Akan tribes in what is now Ghana (p. 273).

V

Vesalius, Andreas *(vih SAY lee uhs)* 1514–1564, Flemish Renaissance biologist who wrote one of the first textbooks on anatomy (p. 429).

Vespucci, Amerigo *(vehs POO chee)* 1454–1512, Italian explorer of South America; gave his name to the American continents (p. 536).

Vladimir I c. 956–1015, Russian prince who is credited with bringing Orthodox Christianity to Russia; later made a saint (p. 453).

W

Walesa, Lech *(wah LEHN sah)* 1943–, Polish labor leader, chairman of the trade union Solidarity and president of Poland since 1990 (p. 491).

Y

Yaa Asantewa c. 1840/1860–1921, leader of the Asante in West Africa who stirred her people to resist British attempts to take power (p. 276).

Yeltsin, Boris 1931–, first secretary of Moscow City Party Committee who became Russia's first freely elected president (p. 474).

Z

Zapata, Emiliano 1879–1919, Mexican revolutionary who fought for land reform (p. 581).

Pronunciation Key

This chart presents the pronunciation key used in this Glossary. For a key to the phonetic respellings used to indicate pronunciation in the text of the chapters, see page 696.

Spellings	Symbol	Spellings	Symbol	Spellings	Symbol
pat	ă	kick, cat, pique	k	thin	th
pay	ā	lid, needle	l	this	*th*
care	âr	mum	m	cut	ŭ
father	ä	no, sudden	n	urge, term, firm,	ûr
bib	b	thing	ng	word, heard	
church	ch	pot, horrid	ŏ	valve	v
deed, milled	d	toe	ō	with	w
pet	ĕ	caught, paw, for	ô	yes	y
bee	ē	noise	oi	zebra, xylem	z
life, phase, rough	f	took	o͝o	vision, pleasure,	zh
gag	g	boot	o͞o	garage	
hat	h	out	ou	about, item, edible,	ə
which	hw	pop	p	gallop, circus	
pit	ĭ	roar	r	butter	ər
pie, by	ī	sauce	s		
pier	îr	ship, dish	sh	Primary stress ´	
judge	j	tight, stopped	t	Secondary stress ´	

A

acid rain (ăs´ĭd rān) rain that has very high amounts of acids; caused by pollution.

adapt (ə-dăpt´) to adjust to meet new situations (p. 33).

Afrikaner (ăf´ rĭ-kä´nər) an Afrikaans-speaking South African descended from the early Dutch, German, and French settlers (p. 297).

afterlife (ăf´tər-līf) according to some beliefs, the life that follows death (p. 89).

agriculture (ăg´rĭ-kŭl´ chər) the practice of cultivating the soil to produce crops and to raise livestock; farming (p. 59).

alliance (ə-lī´əns) agreement made between nations for a common cause (p. 461).

anthropologist (ăn´ thrə-pŏl´ə-jĭst) a scientist who studies the origins, behavior, and development of human beings (anthropology) (p. 23).

apartheid (ə-pärt´hīt´) an official policy of racial separation and white supremacy practiced in the Republic of South Africa, now being reversed (p. 293).

apostle (ə-pŏs´əl) one of Jesus' twelve original followers and other missionaries of the early Christian Church (p. 175).

aqueduct (ăk´wĭ-dŭkt´) a large pipe built to carry water from a distant source; also, the structure that carries the pipe (p. 173).

archaeologist (är´kē-ŏl´ə-jĭst) a scientist who recovers and studies the tools, graves, buildings, pottery, and other remains of past human life and culture (p. 58).

archipelago (är´kə-pĕl´ə-gō) a large number of islands in a group (p. 387).

arid (ăr´ĭd) having little rainfall, or none at all (p. 205).

B

ban (băn) to forbid by law or policy.

bankrupt (băngk´rŭpt´) declared by law as being without the means to pay off debts.

barter (bär´tər) a system of trading in which people exchange goods or services directly, without using money (p. 134).

basin (bā´sĭn) an area drained by a river and its tributaries (p. 529).

belief (bĭ-lēf´) an idea that a person holds to be true (p. 8).

bilingual (bī-lĭng´gwəl) able to speak two languages fluently; written in two languages (p. 608).

boom-and-bust (bo͞om ənd bŭst) a rapid expansion in economic activity, followed by a rapid decline (p. 559).

border (bôr´dər) an area or line that separates two regions or nations (p. 586).

boycott (boi´kŏt´) an organized form of protest by a group that refuses to use, deal in, or buy certain products or services from specific businesses or nations (p. 295).

Buddhism (bo͞o´dĭz´əm) a religion founded in India by Siddhartha Guatama; Buddhism stresses freedom from worldly desires and nonviolence (p. 110).

C

caliph (kā´lĭf) religious head of a Muslim state (p. 189).

capital (kăp´ĭ-təl) money used to start, or invest in, businesses; also, a city where the head of a state or federal government is located (p. 561).

caravan (kăr´ə-văn) a group of merchants or pilgrims journeying together, usually through desert regions (p. 277).

cash crop (kăsh krŏp) a crop that is grown primarily to sell rather than to keep (p. 277).

caste (kăst) one of the four social classes in Hindu society in India (p. 106).

cataract (kăt´ə-răkt´) a steep rapid in a river (p. 83).

caudillo (kô-dēl´yō) a military dictator (p. 537).

censor (sĕn´sər) to control what people read, write, hear, or see; to prohibit free expression of ideas (p. 197).

circumnavigate (sûr´kəm-năv´ĭ-gāt´) to travel completely around; for example, to sail around the earth (p. 390).

citizen (sĭt´ĭ-zən) a person who owes loyalty to a town, city, state, or nation and in return is protected by its government (p. 156).

citizenship (sĭt´ĭ-zən-shĭp´) the possession of rights, duties, and privileges of every citizen of a city, state, or country.

city-state (sĭt´ē-stāt´) an independent state including a city and the surrounding area (p. 155).

civil disobedience (sĭv´əl dĭs´ə-bē´dē-əns) the refusal to obey certain laws because they are thought to be unjust and in order to effect change in government policy or laws (p. 326).

civilization (sĭv´ə-lĭ-zā´shən) a complex society with, among other features, a highly developed government and culture (p. 67).

civil war (sĭv´əl wôr) a war fought between groups or regions within a country.

class (klăs) a group of people who share similar economic and social conditions (p. 67).

classics (klăs´ĭks) the collection of literature of the ancient Greek and Roman cultures (p. 426).

clergy (klûr´jē) the group of people ordained to serve as religious leaders; for example, priests, ministers, and rabbis (p. 411).

climate (klī´mĭt) the average weather conditions of a particular region, including temperature, wind, and precipitation.

cold war or **Cold War** (kōld wôr) an intense rivalry between countries, stopping short of military engagement, especially as existed between Soviet-bloc and Western-bloc countries after World War II (p. 473).

collective (kə-lĕk´tĭv) a large farm or business where people work together to produce a product, usually under government supervision.

colonialism (kə-lō´nē-ə-lĭz´əm) a policy by which a nation obtains and controls foreign lands as colonies, usually for economic gain (p. 440).

Columbian exchange (kə-lŭm´bē-ən ĭks-chānj´) the exchange of people, goods, culture, and ideas that occurred among Europe, Asia, Africa, and the Americas after the arrival of Columbus in America (p. 442).

command economy (kə-mănd´ ĭ-kŏn´ə-mē) a system of government ownership and control of farms and factories in which the government decides what to produce and sets all prices (p. 490).

common market (kŏm´ən mär´kĭt) an economic union formed to increase trade and cooperation among its member countries (p. 484).

commonwealth (kŏm´ən-wĕlth´) union of countries that share common goals (p. 496).

communism (kôm´yə nĭz´əm) a social system without social classes or private ownership in which the state controls the production and distribution of goods (p. 344).

community (kə-myōō´nĭ-tē) a group of people living in the same area and usually having common ties of language or culture.

confederation (kən-fĕd´ə-rā´shən) a unified political state in which power is shared between national and local governments (p. 603).

Confucianism (kən-fyōō´shən-ĭz-əm) the ethical teachings of Confucius, emphasizing social harmony, devotion to family, and personal virtue (p. 118).

conquistador (kŏn-kwĭs´tə-dôr´) a leader in the Spanish conquest of Mexico, Central America, and Peru during the 16th century (p. 578).

conservation (kŏn´sûr-vā´shən) the careful use and protection of natural resources, such as forests and rivers (p. 621).

continental climate (kôn´tə-nĕn´təl klī´mĭt) a climate marked by warm, short summers and long, cold winters (p. 482).

contribution (kŏn´trĭ-byōō´shən) the act of giving something for a special purpose.

converso (kŏn-vĕr´sō) a person of the Jewish faith who converted to Christianity during the reign of Ferdinand and Isabella (p. 439).

convert (kən-vûrt´) to change from one religion to another (p. 552).

Coptic Church (kŏp´tĭk chûrch) a Christian church of Egyptian origin.

coup (kōō) a sudden takeover of the government (p. 540).

Creole (krē´ōl´) in Latin America, people whose ancestors came from Europe; a person of European descent born in Spanish America; in the United States, people descended from French settlers.

crusade (krōō-sād´) one of the military expeditions carried out by European Christians during the Middle Ages in an attempt to recapture the Holy Land from the Muslims (p. 416).

cultural diffusion (kŭl´chər-əl dĭ-fyo͞o´zhən) the spreading of elements of one culture (arts, customs, beliefs, ideas, institutions) to another culture (p. 15).

culture (kŭl´chər) the institutions, beliefs, values, art, technology, and other achievements of a group of people, passed on from one generation to the next (p. 5).

currency (kûr´ən-sē) any items used as a medium of exchange during a given time (p. 134).

custom (kŭs´təm) a way of doing things that has become accepted by a people (p. 6).

customs check (kŭs´təmz chĕk) a border inspection (p. 485).

czar (zär) any of the male emperors who ruled Russia before the revolution of 1917 (p. 454).

D

deforestation (dē-fôr´ĭ-stā´shən) the removal, usually by fire or clear-cutting, of forest trees and other plants (p. 35).

delta (dĕl´tə) a triangular area of fertile land at the mouth of a river (p. 83).

demilitarized zone (dē-mĭl´ĭ-tə-rīzd´ zōn) an area where no military personnel or equipment are allowed.

democracy (dĭ-mŏk´rə-sē) a form of government in which the citizens are entitled to influence the making of laws and policies, either directly or through elected representatives (p. 158).

depression (dĭ-prĕsh´ən) a period marked by severe economic decline. It is usually a time of enormous unemployment and hardship.

desalination (dē-sǎl´ə-nā´shən) the process of taking away salts and other chemicals, especially from ocean water or soil (p. 198).

diagnosis (dī´əg-nō´sĭs) an identification of an illness and its cause (p. 189).

dictator (dĭk´tā´tər) a ruler who holds absolute power, usually by force (p. 467).

discrimination (dĭ-skrĭm´ə-nā´shən) the unfair treatment of a person because of the person's race, nationality, gender, age, disabilities, or other factors (p. 632).

dissident (dĭs´ĭ-dənt) a person who does not agree with an accepted opinion or belief; a protester (p. 350).

distribution (dĭs´trə-byo͞o´shən) the act of allotting or apportioning specific goods or resources; the geographic occurrence of a given feature (p. 142).

diversity (dĭ-vûr´sĭ-tē) the variety or differences characterizing a group of people, things, or places (p. 129).

divine right (dĭ-vīn´ rīt) the belief that monarchs receive their right to rule directly from God.

dominion (də-mĭn´yən) a self-governing nation within the British Commonwealth (p. 603).

drought (drout) a long period in which there is little or no rainfall (p. 256).

dynasty (dī´nə-stē) a series of rulers from the same family (p. 84).

E

ejido (ĕ-hē´dō) Mexican rural lands recognized by the government as belonging to Native Americans and commonly used for agricultural purposes.

elevation (ĕl´ə-vā´shən) the height of a given point above sea level, usually expressed in feet or meters (p. 138).

emancipation (ĭ-mǎn´sə-pā´shən) the act of freeing people from bondage or slavery (p. 515).

embargo (ĕm-bär´gō) a ban by a government on trade with a foreign nation (p. 398).

emigrant (ĕm´ĭ-grənt) a person who leaves a native land to make a new home in another place (p. 41).

endangered (ĕn-dān´jərd) threatened with extinction (p. 35).

entrepreneur (ŏn´trə-prə-nûr) one who organizes and operates a business (p. 493).

environment (ĕn-vī´rən-mənt) all the living and nonliving things surrounding a person or organism (p. 12).

epic (ĕp´ĭk) a long poem or literary work that tells the story of a heroic character (p. 319).

ethnic group (ĕth´nĭk gro͞op) a group of people who can be characterized by their similar culture, religion, race, ancestry, or language (p. 21).

exile (ĕg´zīl) to banish; also, the state of being banished from one's native land (p. 215).

export (ĭk-spôrt´) to send the goods of a country abroad for sale or trade; a good sent out of the country (p. 277).

extinct (ĭk-stĭngkt´) no longer living or existing (p. 35).

F

famine (fǎm´ĭn) an extreme shortage of food, leading to hunger and starvation (p. 341).

favela (fə-vĕl´ə) a poor community in Brazilian cities (p. 562).

fellahin (fĕl´ə-hēn´) farmers or peasants in an Arab country, such as Egypt (p. 228).

felucca (fə-lo͞o´kə) a narrow sailing vessel used on the Nile or in the Mediterranean (p. 240).

feudalism (fyo͞od´əl-ĭz´əm) a political and economic system in which lords granted land to vassals in exchange for protection and other services (p. 367).

fiesta (fē-ĕs´tə) a religious or patriotic festival, generally held in Spanish-speaking countries to celebrate an important person or event (p. 588).

foreign policy (fôr´ĭn pŏl´ĭ-sē) set of guidelines that a government adopts in order to define its interactions with other nations.

forum (fôr´əm) a public meeting place for discussion (p. 644).

free enterprise (frē ĕn´tər-prīz´) the freedom of private businesses to operate for profit, with little government control (p. 347).

fundamentalism (fŭn´də-mĕn´təl-ĭz´əm) a movement based on the strict following of certain beliefs, such as those put forth in the Bible or Qur'an.

G

galleon (găl´ē-ən) a large, three-masted wooden trading ship or warship, with a square rig and two or more decks; used by Spain from the 15th to the 17th century (p. 391).

genocide (jĕn´ə-sīd´) the planned killing of an entire racial, national, political, or ethnic group (p. 470).

geography (jē-ŏg´rə-fē) the study of the earth and the relationship between human beings and the earth, including the study of natural features, population, and resources (p. 29).

glacier (glā´shər) a huge mass of ice that flows slowly over land (p. 128).

global (glō´bəl) worldwide in scope or influence.

Gospel (gŏs´pəl) one of the first four books of the New Testament, in which the life and teachings of Jesus are recorded (p. 176).

gross national product (grōs năsh´ə-nəl prŏd´əkt) the total value of all goods and services that a nation produces in a given time period (p. 374).

guerrilla (gə-rĭl´ə) a member of a small group of fighters who organize against the government (p. 540).

guild (gĭld) an association of artisans who do the same type of work, or of merchants who engage in the same type of business.

H

hacienda (hä´sē-ĕn´də) a large ranch or estate in Spanish-speaking countries (p. 579).

hierarchy (hī´ə-rär´kē) a body of authority figures, such as the clergy, organized by rank.

hieroglyphics (hī´ər-ə-glĭf´ĭks) a type of writing in which pictorial symbols stand for meanings or sounds (p. 87).

Hinduism (hĭn´dōō-ĭz´əm) the major religion in India, based on a belief in a supreme being of many forms (p. 108).

Holocaust (hŏl´ə-kôst´) the genocide of Jews and others by the Nazis during World War II (p. 471).

homogeneous (hō´mə-jē´nē-əs) having the same ethnic or racial composition (p. 378).

hostage (hŏs´tĭj) a person who is held by one party so that certain terms will be met by an opposing party (p. 216).

humanist (hyōō´mə-nĭst) someone who studies the classics; someone concerned with the welfare of humankind (p. 426).

humanitarian (hyōō-măn´ĭ-târ´ē-ən) concerned with the welfare and needs of people (p. 645).

hunter-gatherer (hŭn´tər-ga*th*´ər-ər) a person who gets food by hunting wild animals and gathering wild plants (p. 59).

I

ideology (ī´dē-ŏl´ə-jē) a system of ideas and beliefs (p. 348).

immigration (ĭm´ĭ-grā´shən) the act of entering and permanently resettling in a country to which one is not native (p. 39).

imperialism (ĭm-pîr´ē-ə-lĭz´əm) the policy of increasing a nation's authority by acquiring or controlling other nations (p. 325).

import (ĭm-pôrt´) to bring goods into one country from another through trade; a good brought into a country (p. 277).

indentured servant (ĭn-dĕn´chərd sûr´vənt) a person under contract to serve another for a specified amount of time (p. 513).

independence (ĭn´dĭ-pĕn´dəns) the state of being free or self-governing.

indulgence (ĭn-dŭl´jəns) in the Roman Catholic church, the medieval practice of pardoning sin in exchange for a gift of money (p. 430).

Industrial Revolution (ĭn-dŭs´trē-əl rĕv´ə-lōō´shən) the far-reaching changes brought about by technological advances in the way goods were produced; it began in England around 1760 and spread to other countries (p. 446).

inflation (ĭn-flā´shən) a continuing rise in prices due to an increase in available money (p. 561).

infrastructure (ĭn´frə-strŭk´chər) the basic public services and facilities, such as roads, canals, and bridges, needed by a community or society (p. 230).

Inquisition (ĭn´kwĭ-zĭsh´ən) during the Middle Ages, the tribunal, or church court, set up by the Roman Catholic church to find and punish people considered heretics (p. 433).

institution (ĭn´stĭ-tōō´shən) an organization, especially one that is dedicated to public service (p. 7).

interaction (ĭn´tər-ăk´shən) the act of two or more parties affecting each other.

intervene (ĭn´tər-vēn´) to enter into in order to change a course of events.

intifada (ĭn-tĭ-fä´də) the Arab uprising started in 1987 against the Israeli occupation of the Gaza Strip, the West Bank, and parts of Jerusalem (p. 652).

iron curtain (ī´ərn kûr´tən) the military, political, and ideological barrier that separated the Soviet bloc from Western Europe and the United States after World War II (p. 472).

irrigation (ĭr´ĭ-gā´shən) the practice of supplying dry lands with water by means of canals, ditches, pipes, and streams (p. 67).

isolation (ī´sə-lā´shən) the state of being separated from others (p. 362).

isthmus (ĭs´məs) a thin strip of land connecting two larger pieces of land (p. 235).

J

jingoism (jĭng′gō-ĭz′əm) a warlike feeling of extreme nationalism (p. 460).

K

kabuki (kə-bōō′kē) the traditional Japanese drama that evolved from No theater, with songs and dances performed in costume (p. 650).

kibbutz (kĭ-bōōts′) a collective farm in Israel (p. 650).

kinship (kĭn′shĭp′) relationship by blood, marriage, or adoption (p. 271).

knight (nīt) a mounted, armed soldier in medieval Europe who served a monarch or feudal lord (p. 416).

L

labor-intensive (lā′bər-ĭn-těn′sĭv) requiring a greater amount of human power than resources (p. 522).

landform (lănd′fôrm′) a feature on the surface of the earth, such as a hill, plain, or valley (p. 29).

landlocked (lănd′lŏkt′) enclosed by land (p. 256).

latitude (lăt′ĭ-tōōd′) how far north or south of the equator a place is (p. 29).

legion (lē′jən) a unit of the ancient Roman army, consisting of 3,000 to 6,000 foot soldiers, along with some cavalry; a large number (p. 170).

liberation (lĭb′ə-rā′shən) the act of being set free from confinement or control.

life expectancy (līf ĭk-spěk′tən-sē) the number of years a person is expected to live (p. 261).

Line of Demarcation (līn əv dē′mär-kā′shən) an imaginary line that split the non-Christian world (p. 550).

lineage (lĭn′ē-ĭj) the descendants of a common ancestor (p. 271).

literacy rate (lĭt′ər-ə-sē rāt) the percentage of a given population that can read and write (p. 283).

longitude (lŏnj′ĭ-tōōd′) how far east or west of the prime meridian a place is (p. 29).

M

Mandate of Heaven (măn′dāt′ əv hěv′ən) the doctrine that an emperor has received the right to rule from heaven (p. 116).

manor (măn′ər) the estate of a feudal lord in medieval Europe (p. 415).

marine climate (mə-rēn′ klī′mĭt) a fairly mild climate; its main air mass forms over oceans (p. 482).

market economy (mär′kĭt ĭ-kŏn′ə-mē) the private ownership of land, farms, and factories; free enterprise (p. 490).

martial law (mär′shəl lô) temporary military rule during an emergency (p. 392).

matrilineal (măt′rə-lĭn′ē-əl) relating to tracing ancestry through the maternal line (p. 270).

media (mē′dē-ə) the means used to communicate in society, such as newspapers, magazines, radio, and television (p. 21).

Mediterranean climate (měd′ĭ-tə-rā′nē-ən klī′mĭt) the climate of the Mediterranean region, characterized by mild winters and sunny, hot summers (p. 482).

mestizo (měs-tē′zō) a person of mixed racial ancestry (p. 391).

middleman (mĭd′l-măn′) a trader who buys goods from one party and sells to another; a go-between (p. 250).

migrant worker (mī′grənt wûr′kər) a worker who moves from place to place, as crops ripen (p. 543).

migration (mī-grā′shən) the movement of people from one country, place, or region to another (p. 39).

modernize (mŏd′ər-nīz′) to update, or make modern, in order to meet current needs (p. 214).

monarchy (mŏn′ər-kē) government by a monarch (a ruler such as a king, queen, or emperor).

monastery (mŏn′ə-stěr′ē) a community of persons living under religious vows, especially monks (p. 411).

monocrop (mŏn′ō-krŏp) the only major crop in a region (p. 522).

monotheism (mŏn′ə-thē-ĭz′əm) the belief that there is only one God (p. 73).

mosque (mŏsk) a house of worship for Muslims (p. 186).

Mughal (mōō′gəl) the Muslim dynasty that ruled India from 1526 to 1857 (p. 323).

multicultural (mŭl′tē-kŭl′chər-əl) including many cultures (p. 607).

mummy (mŭm′ē) a body embalmed after death in the manner practiced by the ancient Egyptians (p. 89).

N

nationalism (năsh′ə-nə-lĭz′əm) devotion to a nation and its interests and culture; desire for national independence (p. 280).

nationalize (năsh′ə-nə-līz′) to transfer control of an industry from private ownership to government ownership (p. 537).

naturalization (năch′ər-ə-lĭ-zā′shən) the act of giving full citizenship to a person of foreign birth.

naturalized citizen (năch′ər-ə-līzd sĭt′ĭ-zən) an immigrant who has met naturalization requirements to become a citizen of the new country (p. 625).

navigable (năv′ĭ-gə-bəl) being wide and deep enough to allow passage of a vessel.

Nazi (nät′sē) a member of the National Socialist German Workers' Party, which ruled Germany under Adolf Hitler from 1933 to 1945.

negotiate (nĭ-gō′shē-āt′) to discuss with another party in order to come to an agreement (p. 544).

nuclear (nōō′klē-ər) using energy that is derived from the nuclei of atoms.

O

oasis (ō-ā′sĭs) a fertile area around a spring or water hole in the desert (p. 185).

P

pampas (păm´pəz) the grassy, treeless plains of Argentina and some other parts of South America (p. 528).

papyrus (pə-pī´rəs) a long, thin reed; a type of paper made from this plant by ancient people, especially Egyptians (p. 94).

parliament (pär´lə-mənt) a body of representatives that makes laws for a country.

partition (pär-tĭsh´ən) division or separation of something into parts (p. 649).

patriarch (pā´trē-ärk´) the male leader of a family.

patrilineal (păt´rə-lĭn´ē-əl) relating to tracing ancestry through the paternal line (p. 270).

patron (pā´trən) one who supports the arts, an institution, or a cause (p. 425).

peninsula (pə-nĭn´syə-lə) a piece of land mostly surrounded by water and attached to a larger land mass (p. 155).

peon (pē´ŏn´) a landless peasant laboring in Spanish America (p. 579).

permafrost (pûr´mə-frôst´) the permanently frozen subsoil of the Arctic (p. 599).

pharaoh (fâr´ō) a ruler of ancient Egypt (p. 85).

philosophy (fĭ-lŏs´ə-fē) the study and love of wisdom; the search for knowledge (p. 160).

pilgrimage (pĭl´grə-mĭj) a journey to a place that is sacred, like Mecca or Jerusalem (p. 184).

plague (plāg) a highly contagious, widespread disease, which is often fatal (p. 418).

plateau (plă-tō´) an elevated area of relatively flat land (p. 205).

pluralism (plŏŏr´ə-lĭz´əm) the state of having many different ethnic and cultural groups existing together in a society.

pollute (pə-lōōt´) to make dirty; to contaminate (p. 35).

prehistoric (prē´hĭ-stôr´ĭk) of the time before the development of writing (p. 59).

prejudice (prĕj´ə-dĭs) hatred or suspicion of persons of a particular race, ethnic group, or religion (p. 23).

propaganda (prŏp´ə-găn´də) information designed to win people over to a certain doctrine (p. 467).

prophet (prŏf´ĭt) a religious leader who is believed to proclaim the wishes of a God (p. 76).

Protestant (prŏt´ĭ-stənt) a member of one of the Christian churches that broke away from the Roman Catholic church starting in the 16th century (p. 431).

province (prŏv´ĭns) a territory governed as a unit within a country or empire (p. 170).

pyramid (pĭr´ə-mĭd) a large monument such as those found in ancient Egypt and Mexico, with a rectangular base and four triangular sides, built as a tomb or temple.

Q

quota (kwō´tə) an allotment; the maximum number of people allowed to enter a country, group, or institution (p. 625).

R

rabbi (răb´ī) a teacher and spiritual leader of Jews (p. 77).

racism (rā´sĭz´əm) discrimination based on race (p. 23).

rain forest (rān fôr´ĭst) a dense forest, usually tropical, that is green throughout the year and has an annual rainfall of at least 100 inches (p. 130).

raw materials (rô mə-tîr´ē-əls) the natural products used for industry and manufacturing (p. 448).

Reconquista (rē´kŏng-kē´stə) the Spanish re-conquest of the Iberian peninsula from the Muslims in a series of wars in the 1400s (p. 439).

Reformation (rĕf´ər-mā´shən) a political and religious movement in 16th-century Europe to reform the Roman Catholic church; the result was the establishment of Protestant churches (p. 431).

region (rē´jən) an area with shared features that set it apart from surrounding areas (p. 42).

reincarnation (rē´ĭn-kär-nā´shən) the rebirth of a soul into another body after death, according to some religious traditions (p. 109).

Renaissance (rĕn´ĭ-säns´) the period of intellectual and artistic rebirth in Europe that began in Italy in the late 1300s (p. 424).

republic (rĭ-pŭb´lĭk) a nation without a monarch, in which political power may lie with the citizens (p. 169).

resistance (rĭ-zĭs´təns) the act of opposing, especially an enemy or an attack.

reunification (rē-yōō´nə-fĭ-kā´shən) the process of making whole again something that has been separated.

revolution (rĕv´ə-lōō´shən) political rebellion that results in overthrow of a government and formation of a new government (p. 465).

rhythm (rĭ*th*´əm) a movement that occurs repeatedly and in a regular sequence.

rural (rŏŏr´əl) pertaining to the country (p. 41).

S

Sahel (sə-häl´) the hot, dry region in Africa that lies between the Sahara and the savanna vegetation zone (p. 256).

samurai (săm´ə-rī´) the Japanese warriors who owed their allegiance to the nobility in feudal times (p. 367).

sanction (săngk´shən) a penalty against nations for breaking international law (p. 655).

satrap (sā´trăp) a provincial governor in ancient Persia (p. 208).

savanna (sə-văn´ə) the flat, largely treeless grasslands found in warm or tropical regions (p. 257).

scribe (skrīb) a writer, secretary, or copyist, especially in ancient times (p. 88).

segregation (sĕg´rĭ-gā´shən) the act of separating or isolating one group of people from another group, based on race or social class (p. 293).

separatism (sĕp´ər-ə-tĭz-əm) being in favor of separating from a group, a nation, or an established church (p. 608).

serf (sûrf) a peasant; a member of the lowest feudal class, bound to the land and controlled by a lord (p. 415).

shah (shä) the title of a hereditary monarch of Iran, used before the 1979 revolution (p. 208).

Shinto (shĭn´tō) the earliest Japanese religion, which emphasizes worship of nature and spirits (p. 362).

shogun (shō´gən) a military ruler of Japan from 1192 to 1867 (p. 366).

silt (sĭlt) a material of very fine particles (p. 243).

social interaction (sō´shəl ĭn´tər-ăk´shən) the way that people relate to each other at all levels in a community (p. 14).

social justice (sō´shəl jŭs´tĭs) fairness for all people in a society (p. 305).

specialization of labor (spĕsh´ə-lĭ-zā´shən ŭv lā´bər) having specific people performing specific jobs; a feature of civilization (p. 67).

standard of living (stăn´dərd əv lĭv´ĭng) the economic level at which an individual, family, or nation lives (p. 376).

steppe (stĕp) a vast, grassy plain (p. 452).

subcontinent (sŭb´kŏn´tə-nənt) a large landmass, such as India, that is to some extent separate but still part of a continent (p. 329).

sultan (sŭl´tən) a ruler of the former Ottoman Empire or of a Muslim country (p. 234).

superpower (soo´pər-pou´ər) a country that is a military, political, and economic giant (p. 472).

surplus (sûr´pləs) an excess amount or quantity (p. 67).

synagogue (sĭn´ə-gŏg´) a house of worship for people of the Jewish faith.

T

taiga (tī´gə) the northern region of Europe and Asia that is covered with forest. The ground is frozen during winter and swampy in summer.

Talmud (tăl´mood) the collection of ancient books containing the laws and customs that developed in the Jewish tradition (p. 77).

tariff (tăr´ĭf) a government tax on imports or exports (p. 485).

technology (tĕk-nŏl´ə-jē) the application of scientific knowledge, particularly in industry (p. 16).

tithe (tī*th*) one-tenth of a person's income, which is paid to a church each year (p. 411).

Torah (tôr´ə) the first five books of the Hebrew scriptures (p. 74).

toxic (tŏk´sĭk) poisonous.

trade agreement (trād ə-grē´mənt) an agreement on the rules about exchanging goods and services between different countries (p. 593).

trade imbalance (trād ĭm-băl´əns) when a country exports more than it imports from another country (p. 379).

trade union (trād yoon´yən) an organization of workers formed to look after their interests (p. 447).

tradition (trə-dĭsh´ən) elements of a culture that are handed down from generation to generation.

trek (trĕk) a long and difficult journey (p. 298).

triangle trade (trī´ ăng´gəl trād) a three-way trade system, originated by the Dutch. The original triangle included the exchange of European goods for slaves, and the exchange of slaves for sugar and other Caribbean goods (p. 514).

tributary (trĭb´yə-tĕr´ē) a river or stream that flows into a larger river or stream (p. 103).

tribute (trĭb´yoot) a gift or payment made for protection, or to show respect, submission, or admiration (p. 137).

tropical (trŏp´ĭ-kəl) hot and humid; characteristic of the tropics (p. 510).

tundra (tŭn´drə) the treeless area of the Arctic region, with only low-growing plants.

typhoon (tī-foon´) a severe tropical cyclone that develops in the western Pacific and Indian oceans (p. 387).

U

unemployment (ŭn´ĕm-ploi´mənt) being without a job.

untouchable (ŭn-tŭch´ə-bəl) a member of the class that is excluded from Hindu rituals and is considered unclean (p. 106).

urban (ûr´bən) pertaining to cities (p. 43).

V

value (văl´yoo) an amount considered fair in an exchange; a principle, standard, or quality considered worthwhile or desirable (p. 9).

vassal (văs´əl) a person who was granted land by a feudal monarch, in exchange for military service or tribute (p. 415).

vertical zone (vûr´tĭ-kəl zōn) a climate and vegetation at different altitude levels (p. 529).

veto (vē´tō) refusal to approve a bill or a decision that otherwise would be enforced (p. 644).

volunteer (vŏl´ən-tîr´) a person who provides labor or services without expectation of financial reward (p. 635).

W

westernize (wĕs´tər-nīz´) to adapt to the culture and technology of the West (p. 370).

work unit (wûrk yoo´nĭt) in Communist China, a team of state workers who are provided with housing, education, health care (p. 353).

Italic numbers refer to pages on which illustrations appear.

A

Abbas I, shah of Persia, 210, 212
Abbasid family, 210
Abdul Aziz, king of Saudi Arabia, 183, 194–195, 196, 199
Abraham, 56–57, 73–74, 151
Abu Simbel, 241
Abu-Bakr, caliph, 189
Acacia trees, 253
Accra, Ghana, 267, *270,* 282, 283
Acid rain, 406, *612*
Acropolis, *152,* 484
Adaptation, 32–33
Aegean Sea, 155
Afghanistan, United Nations presence in, *645*
Africa
    in Columbian exchange, 442
    crafts in, 278–279
    festivals in, *21*
    geography of, 222, *223*
    history of, 225
    maps of, G6–G7, G9, *685*
    population of, *225*
    rainfall in, 49
    storytelling in, 284–286
    topography of, 224, *224*
African Americans
    in Brazil, *548, 556, 563, 564*
    in Canada, 612
    in the Caribbean, *507,* 511, *515,* 515, *519*
    in Central America, 505, 530, 531
    discrimination against, 633
    forebears of, 514
    migration of, 40, 41
    in South America, *526,* 536, 539
    in the U.S., *20, 21,* 40, *40, 523, 523,* 622, 627, 632–633, *634*
African National Congress (ANC), 292
Afrikaans language, 302
Afrikaners, 297–302
Afterlife, 89
Agriculture, 59
    origins of, 129
Agyeman-Rawlings, Nana Konadu, 267
Akbar, Mughal emperor, 323
Akhenaton, pharaoh of Egypt, 85
Akosombo Dam, 267

Al-Azhar University, 234, 242
Al-Fustat, 233
Al-Idrisi, 182
Alaska, *151,* 437, *453,* 572
    climate of, 620
    earthquakes in, 574
    oil in, 621
Albania, 461
Alberta, *598,* 599
Alberti, Leon, 426
Aleijadinho, *552*
Aleut people, 620
Alexander II, czar of Russia, 455
Alexander III, czar of Russia, 465
Alexander the Great, 152, 159, 160, 209–210, 226, 229
    conquests of, *G12*
Alexander VI, pope, 550
Alexandra, empress of Russia, 466
Alexandria, Egypt, G15, 226, 229
Alexis, prince of Russia, 466
Alfonso, king of Portugal, 438
Algeria, immigration into, 261
Algonquin people, 600
Ali, caliph, 190
Alliance, defined, 461
Alpenhorn, 406
Alphabets, 660–661
    Hebrew, *73*
Alps, *45,* 480, *480*
Altiplano, 139
Amazon Basin, 529, 557
Amazon rain forest, 504
    as resource, 566–567
    wildlife in, 504, *504*
Amazon River, 528, 529, 557, 558
Amber, *279*
American Indians. *See* Native Americans.
American Revolution, 532, 613, 617, 635
Amish, 45
Amsterdam, the Netherlands, 470
Anastasia, princess of Russia, 466
ANC (African National Congress), 292
Anchorage, Alaska, 47
Andes (mountains), G13, 32, *32,* 54, *502, 527,* 528–529
    civilizations in, 138–142
    zones of, *528*

Angel Falls, 528
Angola, emigration to U.S. from, 625
Antarctica, 528
Anthropologist, *22*
    defined, 23
Antigua, British rule over, 445
Antilles, Greater and Lesser, 509–510
Antoninus Pius, emperor of Rome, *146–147*
Apache people, 14, *14*
Apartheid, 293–295, 302
    combating of, 295, 305
    defined, 293
    world view of, 295, 307
Apostles, 175
Appalachian Mountains, 620
Aqueducts, *171,* 173
Aquino, Benigno, 393
Aquino, Corazón, *385,* 393
Ar-Razi, 189
Arabia
    rule over Egypt, 228, 232–234
    trade with China, 384
    trade with India, 319, 384
    trade with Southeast Asia, 384, 389
    See also Saudi Arabia.
Arabian peninsula, 185
Arabian Sea, 185
Arabic language, 187
Arafat, Plain of, 184, 194
Aral Sea, *494*
Arawak people, *506,* 512
Archaeology, 58
Archipelago, 387
Architectural terms, 662–663
Argentina
    agriculture in, 539
    climate of, *529*
    demography of, 531, *531,* 539
    education in, 540
    gauchos in, *538, 539*
    government of, 539–540
    independence of, 532
    industry in, 539
    land regions of, *G13*
    population density of, *G13*
    women in, 540
Arias Sánchez, Oscar, 545, *545*
Arid, defined, 205
Aristotle, 152, 160
Arizona, *618–619*
    Apache ceremony in, 14, *14*

Armenia, *494*
    emigration to U.S. from, *625*
    membership in CIS, 496
    Turkish persecution of, 471
Armistice, 463
Arthur, king of England, 415
Artifacts, interpreting, 583
Aryabhata, 318
Aryans, 105–106
Asante people, 266, 268–270
    kinship system of, 270–271
    modern, 282–283
Ashanti Empire, 266, 267, 273–274, 276
Ashoka, king of India, 113
Ashura, 207, 213
Ashurbanipal, 72
Asia
    economy of, 314
    geography of, 312–314, *313*
    physical map of, *683*
    Southeast. *See* Southeast Asia.
    transportation in, *312*
Assiniboine people, 600
Assumptions, recognizing, 554
Assyria, 57, 70, 71–72, *71,* 92
Astronomy
    Arabic, 191
    Egyptian, 229
    Korean, *654*
Aswan, Egypt, *86,* 239, 240
Aswan High Dam, *227,* 239, *239,* 241, 243
Athens, Greece, *152,* 156, 158, 484
Atlantic City, New Jersey, *26*
Atlas, 679–689
Atlas mountains, *224*
Attica, Greece, 156
Augustus Caesar, 169, 175
Aurangzeb, Mughal emperor, 323
Auschwitz concentration camp, 471
Australia, 58, 315
    aboriginal customs, 6
    geography of, G2
    settlement of, 623
    Sydney, 33, *33*
    wildlife of, *437*
Austria, 461
    German invasion of, 469

Austro-Hungarian Empire, 461
  end of, 463
  World War I alliances of, 461, 462
Axis powers, 371, 469
Azerbaijan, *494*
  membership in CIS, 496
  people of, 206
Azeri language, 206
Aztecs, 136–137, 145, 576
  culture of, *127,* 135–137, 583
  economy of, 134
  fall of, 578, 579
  modern borrowings from, 591
  origin of, 132
  religion of, 135–136
  riches of, 513
  society of, 137

B

Babbage, Charles, 447
Babylonia, G12, 69, 71
Baghdad, *66*
Bahamas, *507, 509,* 513
Bahasa Indonesia language, 396
Balfour Declaration, 648, 649
Bali, agriculture in, *310–311, 388*
Balkans, 461
  modern conflict in, 492
Baltic states, 496
Bamako, Mali, 254, 259, 261, *262*
Bambara people, 258, 259
Bananas, 543
Banda Aceh, Indonesia, *396*
Banerji, R. D., 102
Bangladesh
  formation of, 327, 331
  Muslims in, 190
Bani River, 256
Bantu languages, G14, 296
Bantu people, migration of, G14
Barbados, 509
  British rule over, 445
  currency of, *522*
Barbuda, 510
Barter, 134
Baseball, 518
Bashō, 364
Basin, defined, 529
Bataan, 392
Bay, defined, 690
Bedouins, 185
Begin, Menachem, 237
Beijing, China, *338,* 346, 349–350

Belarus
  membership in CIS, 496
  nuclear weapons in, 497
Belém, Brazil, 559
Belgium, *478*
  Common Market and, 484
  Spanish rule over, 441
  in World War II, 470, 472
Beliefs, 8–9
Belize, 542
  demography of, 530, *530,* 531
Belo Horizonte, Brazil, 557
Beringia, 128, 129, *129*
Berlin, Germany, division of, 472, 473
Berlin blockade, 473
Berlin Wall, *459,* 471, *472*
Bermuda, British rule over, 445
Betancourt, Romulo, 537
Bible, 175–176, 412
  art based on, 426, 432
  book of Psalms in, 75–76
  Gospels in, 175–176
  and Gutenberg's press, 428
  preservation of, 411
  and prophets, 75–76
  translated into German, 431
Bilingual, defined, 608
Biographical dictionary, 696–700
Bishops, 179
Black Death, 418
Blacks. *See* African Americans.
Blake, William, 457
Boer War, 301
Boers. *See* Afrikaners.
Bolívar, Simon, 527, 532, *532*
Bolivia, 32, *32*
  demography of, 531, *531*
Bombay, India, 324
  population density of, *315*
Bonaparte, Napoleon, 552
Bonsai, 363
Boom-and-bust, defined, 559
Bora, Katherine von, *431*
Border
  defined, 586
  types and functions of, 586
Borduas, Paul-Émile, 610
Borobudur, *384*
Bosnia-Herzegovina, conflict in, 479, 490, 492, *644,* 645

Botha, Louis, 301
Botha, P. W., 305
Botswana, 293
Boukman, 515
Bowdich, Edward, 274
Boycott, defined, 295
Bozo people, 258
Brasília, Brazil, 559, 562
Brazil, *34*
  abolition of slavery in, 553, 569
  culture of, 564–565
  democracy movement in, 553
  demography of, 531, *531*
  economy of, 559–561
  ethnic population in, 556
  festivals in, 565, *565*
  geography of, 555–557, *557, 559*
  history of, 548–549
  independence of, 549, 552
  industry in, 559–560
  life in, 563–564
  modern, 562–563
  plantations in, *548*
  Portuguese settlement of, 550–552
  rain forests of, 529, 566–567
  religion in, 564–565, *564*
Bristol, England, *437*
Britain
  Norse settlements in, 414
  Roman rule of, 153, 170
  See also British Empire; Great Britain.
British Columbia, 599
  ethnic communities in, 607
British East India Company, 317, 324–325, 395
British Empire, *26, 445, 449*
  decline and fall of, 450
  expansion of, 448
  rise of, 443
  setbacks to, 446
Brooklyn, New York, Caribbean influence on, 523, *523*
Bruegel, Pieter, *428,* 429, 435
Brunei, population of, 387
Brunel, Isambard K., *446*
Brunelleschi, Filippo, 426, *426*
Buddhism, 110–112
  in China, 101
  in Korea, 654
Buenos Aires, Argentina, G13, 539, *539*

Buildings, purposes of, *9*
Bulgaria, 461
Burma
  religion in, 112
  See also Myanmar.
Bush, George, 497
Buthelezi, Mangosuthu, 305
Butte, defined, 690
Byron, Augusta Ada, Lady Lovelace, 447
Byzantine Empire, 178, 231, 412
  architecture of, *408*
  influence on Egypt, 228

C

Caboto, Giovanni (Cabot, John), 596, 601
Cabral, Pedro Álvares, 548, 551, 564
Caesar Julius, 153, 169
Cai Lung, 120
Cairo, Egypt, 191, *227,* 232, 233, 236, *236,* 242–243, 249
Calcutta, India, 324
California, *16,* 619
  migrant workers in, 39
  Chinese immigrants in, 628–631
  earthquakes in, 574
  gold rush in, 628
  migrant workers in, 39
  oil in, 621
Caliph, defined, 189
Calvin, John, 432
Calvinists, 432
Cambodia, 386, 471, 647
  Communist rule over, 398
  population of, 387
  United Nations presence in, 646
Caminha, Pero Vaz de, 551
Canaan, 56, 57, 75
Canada, 12, *13,* 31 , 572
  achievements of, 609
  African Americans in, 612
  arts in, 610, 611
  border with U.S., 612–613, *613*
  British rule over, 446
  climates and topography of, 599
  cultures of, 596–597, 607–608, 615
  economy of, 609
  education in, 609–610
  festivals in, *575*
  French and British settlement of, 601–602

geography of, *599*
government of, 604–605
health care in, 610
immigration to, 604
industry in, 609
international relations of, 612–613
legal system of, 605
Native Americans in, *597, 600*
natural resources of, 599
North American trade of, 593
provinces of, 598–599
quality of life in, 609
separatism in, 615
trade with U.S., 613
transportation in, 606
westward expansion of, 602–604
in World War I, 604
in World War II, 605
World War II alliances of, 469
Canadian Rockies, *598*
Canadian Shield, 599
Canal Zone, 543
Canals, *505*
Candomblé, 564–565
Canyon, defined, 691
Cape Breton, *597*
Cape Colony, 301
Cape of Good Hope, 297
Cape Town, South Africa, *291*
Capital, defined, 561
Caracas, Venezuela, *537*
Caravan, defined, 185
Cárdenas, Lázaro, 582
Carib people, 512
Caribana, 608
Caribbean islands
agriculture in, 510 , 519
city life in, 519
climate of, 504, 510, 523
cultures of, 502, 511
economy of, 522
emigration to U.S. from, 625
geography of, 502, 509–510
history of, 511
languages of, 511
music of, 521, 627
Native Americans in, 512
plantations on, 513, 514
Spanish rule over, 441
sports in, 518
wildlife in, 510
Caribbean Sea, 508, 509
marine life in, *509*
Carnival, 504, *504,* 511, *511, 521, 523,* 565, *565*

Carter, Jimmy, 237, 238, 636, *636*
Carter, Rosalynn, 636
Carthage, 169
Cartier, Jacques, 601
Cartograms, 372–373
Cartoons, 475
Cash crop, defined, 277
Caspian Sea, *494*
Caste system, 106, 320, 335
Castiglione, Baldassare, 427
Castro, Fidel, 520
Catacombs, *177*
Cataract, defined, 83, 691
Cathedral, defined, 411
Catherine the Great, empress of Russia, 455
Catholic Church
medieval, 410–412
Orthodox split from, 408, 412–413, *413*
post-Reformation, 433
in Reformation, 432–433
Caudillo, defined, 537
Cause and effect, 107
Cayman Islands, 516
Cebu, Philippines, *390*
Celadon pottery, *654*
Cennini, Cennino, 424, 435
Censor, defined, 197
Census, described, 590
Central America
African Americans in, 505
agriculture of, 543
cities of, 533
climate of, 504, 529
cultures of, 502
economy of, 543
exports of, 543, *543*
geography of, 502, 528
independence movements in, 532
migrant workers in, 543
peace plan for, 545
peoples of, 530–531, *530,* 531–532
social injustice in, 542
unrest in, 542, 543–544
Champlain, Samuel de, 596, 601
Chang Jiang (river), *53,* 54, 115
Chapultepec Park, G2
Charlemagne, king of France, 408, 412–413, 492
Charles I, king of Spain, 390
Charles V, Holy Roman Emperor, 431
Charles V, king of Spain, 584

Charlottetown Agreement, 608
Chavín civilization, 126, 139
Chernobyl nuclear disaster, 471
Cherrapunji, India, 312
Chesapeake and Delaware Canal, *505*
Chiang Kai-shek, 344
Chiapas, Mexico, *588*
Chicago, Illinois, 40, 46–47
Chichén Itzá, *126,* 131
Chile, 139
demography of, *531*
independence of, 532
Chili peppers, *531*
China, 38, *52,* 101, 192, 356
achievements of, 120–121
agriculture in, 352
ancient, 114
ancient, history of, 100–101, 116
civil service in, 101, 120
cultural heritage of, 117–120
daily life in, 351–353
democracy movement in, 349–350
economic and social reform in, 348
emigration to U.S. from, 624, 625
festivals in, 7, *7*
future of, 354
geography of, 115, *115, 348*
history of, 338–339
international trade of, 342–343
Manchu rule over, 342–343
modern, 347–349
Mongol rule over, 341
Nationalist, 344
population of, 312, *348*
relations with West, 343–344
religion in, 101, 112
trade with Arabs, 384
trade with India, 319
trade with Philippines, 391
trade with Southeast Asia, 389
transportation in, *339*
urban life in, 353
war with Japan, *344,* 345, 371
Chinese Americans, 21
Chinese language, 117
dialects of, 355
Chinese New Year, 7

Choson kingdom, 653, *654*
Christianity, 73
Coptic, 231
crusades of, 416
east-west division of, 408, 412–413, *413*
growth of, 177–179, *178*
Islam on, 188
Jerusalem and, 649, *651*
Jesus in, 175–177
medieval, 410–412
origins of, 148, 151, 153
Chronological order, 107
Chu Yüan-chang, 342
Churchill, Winston, *472*
Ciboney people, 512
Cinco de Mayo, 581, 622, *622*
Circumnavigate, defined, 390
Circus Maximus, 170
CIS (Commonwealth of Independent States)
economic situation in, *475*
environmental problems in, 497
ethnic conflict in, *494*
formation of, 496
future of, 496–497
nuclear weapons in, 497
Citizen, defined, 156
Citizenship, 156–158
rights and responsibilities of, 626
Roman, 170, 171
U.S., by naturalization, 625, 626
City-state, defined, 155
Civil disobedience, 326
Civil Rights Act of 1964, 617, 633
Civil War (U.S.), 633
Civilization, 67
ancient, *53,* 54–55
See also names of individual civilizations.
Class structure
Aryan, 106
defined, 67
Mesopotamian, 68
Classics, defined, 426
Clemente, Roberto, 518
Cleopatra VII, queen of Egypt, 226, 229
Clergy, defined, 411
Cliff, defined, 691
Clinton, Bill, 617
Clovis, New Mexico, 128
Clovis point, *128*
Cocoa, 281, *281*
Code of Hammurabi, 69, 71, 209

Codex Mendoza, *136,* 137
Coffee, 543, *543,* 544, 559
Cold War, 471, 472–473
    end of, 646
    Korea in, 655
Coleridge, Samuel Taylor,
    457
Colombia, 139
    demography of, *531*
    rain forests of, 529
Colonialism, 440
Color de Mello, Fernando,
    553
Colorado, *570–571*
Colosseum, 153, 170
Columbian exchange,
    442–443
Columbus, Christopher
    discovery of Venezuela
        by, 536
    racial attitudes of, 525
    voyages of, 440–441, 502,
        506, 509, 512, 513, 526
Command economy, 490
Commerce. *See* Trade.
Common Market, *485,* 497
    building, 484–485
    defined, 484
Commonwealth, defined,
    496
Commonwealth of Inde-
    pendent States. *See*
    CIS; Russia; Soviet
    Union.
Communication
    advances in, 17
    history of, 665–668
Communism
    defined, 344
    functioning of, 345
    in Russia, 465
Comparison and contrast,
    107
Compass rose, defined, G2
Concentration camps, 471
Concorde (airplane), *479*
Confederation, defined, 603
Conflicts, resolving, 483
Confucianism, 118, 120
    in Korea, 654, 656
Confucius, 118, 120
Congo Basin, G9
Conquistadors, 578
Conservation, 621
Constantine, emperor of
    Rome, 153, 178, 179
Constantinople, 178, 412,
    413
    international trade of,
        409, 453
    See also Istanbul, Turkey.
Constitution, Roman
    antecedents of, 171

Constructive criticism, 517
Continental climate,
    defined, 482
Conversion, religious, 552
Converso, defined, 439
Cook, James, 437, *445,* 600
Copán, 131
Copernicus, Nicolaus, 429
Coptic Christianity, 231
Coptic language, 231
Córdoba, Spain, 192
Cortés, Hernán, 578
Costa Rica, 542
    democracy in, 544–545
    demography of, *530*
    future of, 545
    tranquility of, 544, *545*
Cotton, 235
Countries of the world, 43,
    675–677
Coup, defined, 540
Courlander, Harold, 262
Cree people, 600
Creole language, 511
Creoles, 533
Cricket, 518
Criticism, constructive, 517
Croatia
    modern, 492
    unrest in, 479
Crusade
    defined, 416
    knights of, *417*
Cuba, 391, 506, 509, 638
    abolition of slavery in, 515
    demographics of, 520
    economy of, 520
    emigration to U.S. from,
        625
    future of, 520–521
    sports in, 518
Cultural diffusion, 15
Cultural Revolution, 346,
    347
Culture
    in civilization, 67
    defined, 5
    diversity of, 4, 21, 23
    elements of, 6–9
    factors affecting, 12–17,
        138–139
    regional, 45
    spread of, 15
    in U.S., 20–21
Cuneiform, 70
Cunha, Euclides da, 555,
    565
Cunninghame Graham,
    R. B., 528
Currency, 134
Customs, 6
Customs check, defined,
    485

Cuzco, Peru, 140, *527*
Cyrus, shah of Persia, 202,
    209
Czar, defined, 454
Czech Republic, 490, 491
Czechoslovakia
    breakup of, 479, 490, 491
    German invasion of, 469
    per capita income in, *485*
    Velvet Revolution of,
        478

D

Dagomba people, 274
Dai Jin, 342
Damascus, Syria, 192
Damavand, Mount, 205
Darius I, king of Persia,
    209
Dark Ages. *See* Middle
    Ages.
Darwin, Charles, 448, 450
David, king of Israel, 75
Deforestation, *34, 35, 561*
Degrees, 29
De Klerk, F. W., 305
Delhi, India, *334*
Delphi, Greece, 148
Delta, defined, 83, 690
Democracy
    birth of, 156–157
    defined, 157
    forms of, 157
Deng Xiaoping, 348, 349,
    350
Denmark, 414, 415
    Common Market and, 485
    German invasion of, 470
    per capita income in, *485*
    Reformation in, 433
    rejection of Maastricht
        Treaty, 487
Desalination, *198*
    defined, 198
Desert, 224
    defined, 690
Desert Storm, Operation,
    197
Detroit, Michigan, 40, 608
Dhaka, Bangladesh, popu-
    lation density of, *315*
Di-xin, Chinese emperor,
    340
Día de los Muertos, 588,
    592
Diagnosis, 189
Dialects, 355
Dias, Bartolomeu, 297
Diaspora, 648
Díaz, Porfirio, 581, *581*
Dictator, defined, 467
Dionysus Exiguus, 75
Diossé, Koumi, 254

Diré, Mali, 247
Direct democracy, 157
Discrimination
    defined, 632
    in South Africa, 301–302
    in U.S., 632–633
Disease, introduction to
    the Americas, 442,
    513, 532
Dissident, defined, 350
Distribution, defined, 142
Diversity, defined, 129
Djenné, Mali, 249, *251*
Djoser, pharaoh of Egypt,
    93
Dolores, Mexico, 580
Dominican Republic, 509,
    510
    currency of, *522*
    language of, 511
    sports in, 518
Dominion, defined, 603
Dorris, Michael, 512
Drake, Francis, 513
Drought
    defined, 256
    effects of, 260–261
Dublin, Ireland, 484
Dubois, Eugene, 396
Dutch East India Com-
    pany, 297
Dutch language, 406
Dynasty
    defined, 84
    in China, 116

E

Earth Summit, 549, 563
Earthquakes, 204, 361
Easter Island, 18–19, *18*
Eastern Europe
    conflicts in, 492
    democracy in, 490
    progress in, 491
EC. *See* Common Market.
Economic systems, 8
Economics, defined, 23
Economy
    boom-and-bust, 559
    command, 490
    market, 490
Ecuador, 139
    demography of, 531, *531*
Edelweiss, 406
Edo (Tokyo), Japan, 370
Education
    Argentine, 540
    Canadian, 609–610
    importance of, 635
    Japanese, 375–376,
        380–381
    Japanese vs. U.S.,
        380–381

Peruvian, 533
South Korean, *656*
U.S., 633, 635
UN and, 645
Egypt, *54, 55,* 245, 249
agriculture in, 235
ancient, 82–85
ancient, achievements of, 93–94
ancient, death rituals in, 99
ancient, history of, 80–81
ancient, religion in, 89
ancient, society in, 87–88
Arab rule over, 232–234
art of, 96–97
British rule over, 235–236
Byzantine rule over, 226–227
foreign influences in, 228–229
history of, 226–227
international trade of, 234, 235–236
modern, 236–237, *240*
Muslims in, 190, 226
Ottoman rule over, 234–235
religion in, 231, 233, 237
Roman rule over, 229, 230
Suez Canal, *505*
wars with Israel, 236–237, 649
Eiffel, A. G., 29
Einstein, Albert, *626*
El Dorado, 505
El Salvador, G15, 542
crafts in, *530*
demography of, 530
government of, 544
peace plan for, 545
unrest in, 542, 544, 545
Elevation, G9
defined, 138
maps of, 399
Elizabeth I, queen of England, 513
Elizabeth II, queen of England, *407, 605*
Elmina, Ghana, 266, 274
Emancipation, 515, 553, 569
Embargo, defined, 398
Emigrant, defined, 41
Empire, defined, 136
Empty Quarter (Arabia), 185, 194
Endangered species, 35, *35*
England, 414
defeat of Spanish Armada, 437, 443, 444

Reformation in, 432, 433
religious conflict in, 433
See also British Empire; Great Britain.
English Channel, tunnel under, *407*
Enlightenment, 447
Enrile, Juan Ponce, 393
Entrepreneur, defined, 493
Environment, 12–13
changing, 33–34
culture and, 138–139
Epic, defined, 319
Epidaurus, *161*
Equator, G4
Eratosthenes, 160
Este, Isabella d', 427
Estonia, independence of, 496
Ethiopia, 225
emigration to Israel from, *651*
emigration to U.S. from, 625
famine in, 243
marriage customs of, 6
Muslims in, 190
Ethnic group, defined, 21
Euphrates River, 54, *54,* 66, 67
Europe, *481*
eastern. *See* Eastern Europe.
economic unity of, 496–497
ethnic diversity of, *462*
geography of, *404,* 406–407
great plain of, 481
physical map of, *682*
regions of, 480–481
western. *See* Western Europe.
European Economic Community. *See* Common Market.
Evidence, identifying, 263
Ewe people, 272
Exchange, currency, 486
Exile, 215
Export, defined, 277
Extinct, defined, 35

F
Fabergé, Carl, 466
Facts, 18–19
Fahd, king of Saudi Arabia, 195
Faisal, king of Saudi Arabia, 195, 199
Falkland Islands, *26*
Family, as institution, 8
Famine, defined, 341

Fante people, 274
Farming. *See* Agriculture.
Farouk, king of Egypt, 236
Farsi language, 206, 210
Fatima, 190
Favela, defined, 562
Faxian, 321
Fellahin, defined, 228
Felucca, defined, 242
Ferdinand, king of Spain, 436, 438, 439, 440, 506
Fertile Crescent, *56–57,* 67, *67*
Festa Del Gallo, 7
Festivals, 6–7
Feudalism, 367, 414–418
structure of, 415
Fez, Morocco, 192
Fiesta, defined, 588
Flood plain, defined, 690
Florence, Italy, 427
as trade center, 418, 425
Florida, 509, 616, 623
Cuban emigration to, 523
Spanish rule over, 441
Flow charts, 61
Foch, Ferdinand, 463
Folsom, New Mexico, 128
Forbidden City, *338*
Forum, defined, 644
Fossils, *26*
France, *29, 29–31, 30,* 155
Caribbean possessions of, 511, 513, 514
Catholicism in, 433
colonial expansion of, 460
competition with Britain, 445–446
currency of, 486
economic isolationism in, *487*
influence over Canada, 602, 608
medieval empire of, 412–413
nationalism of, 460
Norse settlements in, 414
per capita income in, *485*
resistance to Nazis in, 470
rule over Egypt, 228
rule over Mali, 247, *251,* 253–254
rule over Mexico, 581
rule over Vietnam, 397
Seven Years' War with Britain, 597
trade with China, 342
trade with Southeast Asia, 389
World War I alliances of, 461, 462

in World War II, 470, 472
World War II alliances of, 469
Francis Ferdinand, archduke of Austria, 462
Franco, Francisco, 469
Frank, Anne, 470
Frankincense, 185
Frederick the Wise, prince of Saxony, 431
Free enterprise, defined, 347
French and Indian War, 445–446, 601–602
French language, 406
Fuji, Mount, 314
Fulani people, 258

G
Galilee, Sea of, *650*
Galleons, 391
Gama, Vasco da, 225, 324
Gandhi, Indira, 327, *327*
Gandhi, Mohandas, 299, 326–327, *326,* 337
Ganges River, *329*
Gao, Mali, 249, 250
Gauchos, *538, 539*
Gaza, *651*
Gazetteer, 692–695
Geneva, Switzerland, 645
Genghis Khan, 341
Genoa, Italy, as trade center, 418, 425
Genocide, 470, 471, 492
Geographic terms, 690–691
Geography, G15
Arabic, 191
defined, 21, 29
five themes of, 28
See also Maps.
George V, king of England, 299
Georgics (Virgil), 168
Germany
aggression of, 469
alliance with Japan, 371
colonial expansion of, 460
Common Market and, 484
division of, 472, *473*
economy of, 373
emigration to U.S. from, 625
Gulf War and, 197
industrialization of, *461*
inflation in, 468
manners in, 6
Nazi, 468–470
neo-Nazism in, 487
oil resources of, 373
per capita income in, *485*

Reformation in, 430–431, 433
reunification of, 459, 491, 655
World War I alliances of, 461, 462
World War I peace talks, 463, 465
in World War II, 470–472
World War II alliances of, 469
Ghana, 225, 289
colonization of, 267, 276–277
crafts in, *266, 271, 275*
demographics of, 283
festivals in, 268, 273
geography of, 269
history of, 266
independence of, 280–281
international trade of, 274–275
modern, 282–283
natural resources of, 277, 281, 282
proverbs of, 272
religion in, 271, 276
Gil, Gilberto, 565
Gilgamesh, 62–65
Giza, Egypt, 242
pyramids at, 88–89, *88, 227*
Glacier, defined, 128, 574, 691
Globe, using, G4
Glossary, 701–708
of geographic terms, 690–691
GNP (gross national product), 374
Gokason, 365
Gold Coast, 276, 277, 280
Golden Stool, 273, 276
Good, Paul, G7
Goodwill, 635
Gorbachev, Mikhail, 474, *474,* 480, 493, 494
Gospels, 175–176
Government
as institution, 8
Roman influences on, 171
types of, 525
Granada, Spanish conquest of, 440
Grand Canal (China), *338*
Graphs, comparing, 451
Great Britain, 12
Caribbean possessions of, 511, 513, 514, 515, 516

colonial expansion of, 460
colonization of Ghana, 267, 276–277
Common Market and, 485
competition with France, 445–446
culture of, 450
currency of, 486
economy of, 373
empire of. *See* British Empire.
festivals in, 7
fuel consumption of, 457
government of, 407
international influence of, 448, 450
mountains of, 480
oil resources of, 373
per capita income in, *485*
reform efforts in, 447
rule over Canada, 601, 602, 603–605
rule over Egypt, 228, 236
rule over India, 317, 324–325
rule over Palestine, 648, 649
rule over South Africa, 298, 301
Seven Years' War with France, 597
sports in, 518
trade with China, 342
trade with Southeast Asia, 389
transportation in, 16
World War I alliances of, 461, 462
in World War II, 450, 470, 472
World War II alliances of, 469
Great Lakes, *574,* 599, 600, 609, 620
Great Leap Forward, 346
Great Migration, 40
Great Plains, 33, *616,* 620
Canadian, 600
Great Rift Valley, G9, 224, *224*
Great Trek, 290, 298–299, *298*
Great Wall, 121, 342
benefits and costs of, 122–123
Greater Antilles, 509, 510
natural resources of, 510
Greece, 461, *481*
climate of, 482
Common Market and, 485
culture of, 148

geography of, 155
per capita income in, *485*
resources of, 155
Greek Empire, *149*
achievements of, 159–161
conquest of Persia, 209–210
culture of, 161
engineering in, 174
Golden Age of, 156–158
influence on Egypt, 228
mythology of, 164–166
philosophy in, 160
religion in, 159–160
science in, 160
size of, 155
Greek language, 406, 412
Greenland, G6
Grenada, 521
Grid, map, G2, G3
Gross national product (GNP), 374
Guadeloupe, 506
government of, 511
Guangzhou, China, *344*
Guarani language, 532
Guatemala, G15, *44,* 134, 542
arts in, *527*
demography of, *530,* 531
dictatorship in, 542
festivals of, *530*
peace plan for, 545
unrest in, 544
Guerrillas, defined, 540
Guiana Highlands, 529
Guild, defined, 425
Gulf of Mexico, 620
Gulf Stream, 482
Gulf War, 197, 199, *634*
Gum arabic, 253
Gupta dynasty, 316, 320
achievements of, 318–319
decline of, 321
Gutenberg, Johannes, 428
Guyana, demography of, *531*

H

Habitat for Humanity, *636*
Hacienda, defined, 579
Haida people, 600
Haiti, 509, 515
economy of, 522
emigration to U.S. from, 625
independence of, 507, 516, 532
language of, 511
Halloween, 21
Hammurabi, 69, 71
Hanoi, Vietnam, 398
Harappa, 104

Harbor, defined, 690
Hatshepsut, queen of Egypt, 85
Havel, Václav, 478
Hawaii, climate of, 620
volcanoes in, 26
Haynes, Lemuel, *617*
Hebrew language, *73*
Heian period, 363
Hemisphere, 529
of globe, G4
Henry IV, king of Castile, 438
Henry the Navigator, prince of Spain, 550
Heritage Language Program, 610
Hermit, defined, 654
Herodotus, 94
Hidalgo y Castillo, Miguel, 580
Hieroglyphics, 87, 95
Hijra, 186
Himalayas, 115, 312, 314, 331
Hindi language, 332, 333
Hindu Kush (mountains), 105, 331
Hindu New Year, *108*
Hinduism, 108–110
culture of, 100
customs of, 316, 320–321
funeral customs of, 6
suppression by Muslims, 322
Hippocrates, 160
Hiroshima, Japan, 371
Hispaniola, 442, 509, 513
History, defined, 21, 23
History of the Indies (de las Casas), 443
Hitler, Adolf, 468, *468,* 469, 470, 472
Ho Chi Minh, 397
Ho Chi Minh City, Vietnam, 398, *398*
population density of, *315*
Ho-ti, emperor of China, 120
Hockey, 609
Hodgson, Frederick, 276
Hokkaido, 360
Holland. *See* Netherlands.
Holocaust, 470–471, 649
Holy Land, 416
Homer, 93, 154
Homo sapiens, 59–60
Homogeneous, defined, 378
Honduras, G15, 542, 544
British rule over, 445
demography of, *530*
peace plan for, 545

Hong Kong
  economy of, *315*
  future of, 354
  population density of, 315
Honolulu, Hawaii, G10
Honshu, 360
Hostage, defined, 216
House of Commons, 407
House of Lords, 447
Housing, 31
Houston, Texas, 31
Huang He (river), 54, *54,*
  115
Hudson Bay, 599
Hugo, Victor, 480
Humanism, defined, 426
Humanitarian, defined, 645
Hung-wu, Chinese em-
  peror, 342
Hungary, 461
  emigration to U.S. from,
  625
Huns, white, 321
Hunter-gatherers, 58, 129
Husayn, 207, 214
Hypotheses, making, 419

I
Ibn Battuta, 191, 250, 251
Ibn Juzayy, 251
Ibn Khaldun, 232
Ideology, defined, 348
Idioms, 25
Iffat, queen of Saudi Arabia, 195
Imhotep, 93
Immigration, 39, 623–624
  current laws on, 625
  patterns of, *625*
  quotas on, 624–625
  value of, 626–627
Imperialism, defined, 325
Import, defined, 277
Inca Empire, 142, 145
  accomplishments of, 143
  culture of, 140
  heritage of, *502*
  people of, 140, 143
  riches of, 513
  roads of, 141
  ruins of, *527*
Indentured servants, 513,
  516, *516*
India, 38, 192
  ancient, 100
  ancient, arts in, 319
  ancient, civilization of,
  102–103
  ancient, crafts in, 319
  ancient, governments in,
  321
  ancient, religion in, 105,
  316

ancient, science and
  medicine in, 318–319
ancient, social system in,
  106
ancient, trade in,
  103–104, 319
British rule over, 317,
  324–325, 445
conflict with Pakistan,
  332
cultures of, 332
democracy in, 335
emigration to U.S. from,
  625
festivals in, *108*
funeral customs of, 6
geography of, 329,
  331–332
history of, 316–317
independence movement
  in, 325–327
international trade of,
  319, 324
languages and peoples
  of, 332–333
Mughal rule over,
  323–324, *324*
Muslims in, 190, *191*
overthrow of British rule,
  337
population of, 312, 335
providing labor to Saudi
  Arabia, 198
rainfall in, 312
religion in, 112, 333
revolts against Britain,
  446
self-government for, 327
social progress in,
  333–335
trade with Arabs, 384
trade with Southeast
  Asia, 389
See also Hinduism.
Indo-European languages,
  206
Indo-Europeans, 105
Indonesia, 396–397, *399*
  agriculture in, *310–311,
  388*
  arts in, *384*
  economy of, *315*
  climate of, *G8*
  Muslims in, 190
  population of, 387
  trade with India, 319
Indulgences, defined, 430
Indus River, G12, 54, *54,*
  103, 389
  civilizations along, 100
Industrial Revolution, 437,
  446–447
Inflation, 560, 587

defined, 561
Information, recording, 303
Infrastructure, defined, 230
Inquisition
  defined, 433
  Spanish, 439
Inset, defined, G2
Institutions, 7–8
International Date Line,
  610
Inti Raymi, *142*
Intifada, 652
Inuit people, 597, 600, *600,*
  607, 608, 620
  art of, *610*
Ipuky, 96
Iran, 219
  agriculture in, 205
  commerce in, *203*
  earthquakes in, 204
  festivals in, 207, 213
  geography of, 205
  government of, 214, 215,
  216
  history of, 202–203
  languages of, 206
  modernization of,
  213–214
  Muslims in, 190
  natural resources of, 196
  oil in, *215*
  peoples of, 206
  plateau of, 205
  relations with U.S.,
  214–216
  religions of, 206
  war with Iraq, 197, 216
  See also Persian Empire.
Iraq
  Gulf War and, 197
  natural resources of, 196
  war with Iran, 197, 216
Ireland, 38
  Common Market and,
  485
  emigration to U.S. from,
  624
  Norse settlements in, 414
  per capita income in, *485*
  potato famine in, 624
Irish Americans, 41, 624
Iron curtain, 472
Iroquois people, 600
Irrigation, 34, 67, 206
Isabel, princess of Brazil,
  553, 569
Isabella, queen of Spain,
  438, 439, 440, 506
Isfahan, 210, 212
Islam, *479*
  growth of, 189–191, *190*
  origins of, 148, 151,
  186–187

sects of, 190, 207, 210
Shi'a, 190, 203, 206, 207,
  210, 232
in Southeast Asia, 384
Sunni, 190
teachings of, 187–188
See also Muslims.
Ismail, 235, 237
Isolation, defined, 362
Israel, 416
  ancient, 56–57, 75
  borders of, 648
  demography of, *650*
  everyday life in, 650, *651*
  founding of, 642
  future of, 652
  immigration to, 650, *651*
  independence of, 649
  population of, *652*
  religion in, *650, 651*
  territories occupied by,
  643, *652*
  UN and, 648–649, 650
  wars with Egypt,
  236–237, 649
  women in, *650*
Istanbul, Turkey, 178, 412
  See also Constantinople.
Isthmus, defined, 235, 690
Italy, 155
  Catholicism in, 433
  climate of, 482
  culture of, 148
  currency of, 486
  festivals in, 7
  per capita income in, *485*
  Renaissance, 425
  World War I alliances of,
  461
  in World War II, 472
  World War II alliances
  of, 469
  See also Roman Empire.
Ivan the Great, czar of
  Russia, 454
Ivan the Terrible, czar of
  Russia, 454

J
Jacob, 74
Jakarta, Indonesia, 396
  population density of, *315*
Jamaica, 509
  government of, 511
  language of, 511
  natural resources of, 510
  sports in, 518
Japan
  arts in, *358–359*
  Chinese influence in, 363
  colonization of Korea,
  363, *654*
  conflict with Russia, 495

economy of, *315,* 373, 374–376
education in, 375–376, 380–381
environment of, 378
family life in, 376–377
future of, 378–379
geography of, G1, 360–362, *361*
Gulf War and, 197
history of, 358–359, 366–371
international relations of, 379
language in, 363
leisure in, 377–378
literacy rate of, 375
minorities in, 378
natural resources of, 361–362
occupation of Philippines, 392
oil resources of, 373
poetry of, 364–365
religion in, 112, 362, 363
shogunates of, 366–368, 370
standard of living in, 376
tea ceremony in, *369*
war with China, *344,* 345, 371
war with Russia, 371
in World War II, 371, 472
World War II alliances of, 469
Java, 396, *384*
Java man, 396
Jerusalem, 75, *75,* 649
Turkish rule over, 416
Jesuits, 433, 552
Jesus
life of, 175–177
See also Christianity.
Jingoism, 460
João, prince of Portugal, 552, 553
Johannesburg, South Africa, 299, *305*
John, apostle, 175
Jomon people, 362–363
Jordan, Gulf War and, 197
Joseph, Lynn, 508
Juárez, Benito, 581
Judah, 75
Judaism
Christianity and, 175
in Egypt, 229, 230
holy days of, 7, 74, 77
inquisitions against, 433
Islam on, 188
Israel and, 648
Jerusalem and, 416, 649, *651*

marriage customs of, 6
Nazi persecution of, 468, 469, 470, 648
origins of, 73–77, 148, 151
Spanish persecution of, 439
symbols of, *642*
in U.S., 77, *623*
Judgments, making, 18–19
Julius II, pope, 426
Justice, social, 306

K

Kabuki theater, 315
Kaiapó people, 563
Kalahari Desert, *224*
Kampuchea, genocide in, 471
Kapital, Das (Marx), 450
Kayes, Mali, 254
Kazakhstan
membership in CIS, 496
nuclear weapons in, 497
Ka'bah, *183,* 184, 185, *186,* 187
Keita, Modibo, 254
Kennedy, John F., 635–636
Kente cloth, 271, 274, 275
Kenya, *222*
Kenya, Mount, *224*
Kerinci, Mount, 399
Kerma kingdom, 81, *86,* 90
Khadijah, 186
Khafre, pharaoh of Egypt, 88
Khartoum, Sudan, 83
Khmer people, persecution of, 471
Khoikhoi people, 296
Khoisan people, 290, 296, 297
Khomeini, ayatollah of Iran, 214–216
Khufu, pharaoh of Egypt, 88, 89–90
Khyber Pass, 322
Kibbutz, defined, 650
Kiev, Ukraine, 471
Kievan Russia, Viking rule over, 453
Kilimanjaro, Mount, G9, *224*
Kim Il Sung, 655
King, Martin Luther, Jr., 350, 633
Kinship, 270–271
defined, 271
Kipling, Rudyard, 448, 449
Knesset, *642*
Knight, *417*
defined, 416
Koguryo kingdom, *654*
Konaré, Alpha Oumar, 247, 262

Koran. *See* Qu'ran.
Korea
arts in, *3,* 654
in Cold War, 655
geography of, G1, 654
history of, 653–654, *654*
Japanese control over, 363, *654*
partition of, 653, 654–655
religion in, 112, 654
science in, *654*
UN and, 653, 655
See also North Korea; South Korea.
Korean Reconstruction Agency, 655
Korean War, *642*
Koryo kingdom, *654*
Kraft, Adam, *409*
Kremlin, *493*
Kristallnacht, 469
Krupp family, *461*
Kublai Khan, 338, 341
Kumasi, Ghana, 273, 274, 276, 277, 283
Kuna people, 500
Kurile Islands, 495
Kush, 86, 90, 92, 94
Kuwait
Gulf War and, 197
natural resources of, 196
Kwanzaa, *21*
Kyrgyzstan, membership in CIS, 496
Kyoto, Japan, 363, 366
Kyushu, 360

L

La Paz, Bolivia, 32, *32*
Labor
indentured, 513, 516, *516*
migrant, 39, 543
specialization of, 67
trade unions, 447
Labor-intensive, defined, 522
Lancaster, Pennsylvania, 45
Landform, defined, 29
Landlocked, defined, 256
Lang, k. d., 610
Language
alphabets, 660–661
development of, 39
Indo-European, 206
Laos, 386
Communist rule over, 398
population of, 387
Las Casas, Bartolomé de, 442–443
Last Supper, 176–177, *179*

Latin America, 45, *52*
See also Central America; South America.
Latin language, 173, 413
Latitude
defined, G2, 29
lines of, G4
using, G5
Latvia, independence of, 496
Lawrence, Jacob, 40
Le Clerq, François, 513
League of Nations, 604
League of the Five Nations, 600
Leakey, Louis, 222
Leakey, Mary, 222
Lebanon, unrest in, 197
Lee, Manuel, 518
Legend, map, G2, G3, G9
Legion, defined, 170
Lenin, Vladimir, 465, 467
Leo Africanus, 251, 253
Leo III, pope, 408, 412
Leo X, pope, 431
Leonardo da Vinci, 427, *429*
Lessac, Frané, *508*
Lesser Antilles, 509, 510
Liberia, 225
Libya, Gulf War and, 197
Life expectancy, defined, 261
Lightfoot, Gordon, 610
Lima, Peru, 533
Line of demarcation, 550
Lineage, defined, 271
Lintong, China, 119
Literacy rate, defined, 283
Literature, 10–11, 62–65, 164–166, 284–286, 364–365, 420–423, 534–537, 628–631
Lithuania, independence of, 496
Location, 30
Locator inset, G2, G3
Lock, functioning of, *606*
London, England, Caribbean influence on, 523
Longitude
defined, G2, 29
lines of, G4
using, G5
Lord, feudal, 415
Lorenzetti, Ambrogio, *425*
Los Angeles, California, G10, *16, 572,* 622
Lothal, 104
Louisburg, Canada, 602
Louisiana, 43
Louvre museum, 407, *407*

Luke, apostle, 175, 176
Luther, Martin, 409,
    430–431, 432
Lutherans, 431
Luxembourg
    Common Market and,
        484
    German invasion of, 470
Luxor, Egypt, 242
Luzon, Philippines, 390

M
Maastricht Treaty, 487,
    496–497
MacArthur, Douglas, 371,
    392
Macedonia, 461
Machu Picchu, *126,* 140
Mackenzie, Alexander,
    602–603, *602*
MacNeish, Richard, 128
Madras, India, 324
Magellan, Ferdinand, 385,
    389, 390
Mahabharata, 319
Mahmud of Ghazna, 316,
    322
Main idea, identifying, 143
Maine, border with Que-
    bec, *613*
Malaya, natural resources
    of, 550
Malaysia, 386
Malaysia, population of,
    387
Mali, 21, 225
    agriculture in, 255, 257
    crafts in, 252, 265
    culture of, 262
    demographics of, 261
    empire of, 246–250
    French rule over, 247,
        251, 253–254
    future of, 262
    history of, 246–247
    international trade of,
        250
    Islam in, 248–249, 250,
        251, 258
    life expectancy in, 265
    natural resources of, 260
    peoples of, 258
Malinke people, 249, 258
Manchus, rule over China,
    339, 342–343
Mandate of Heaven, 116,
    340
Mandela, Nelson, 291, 292,
    294, 295, 305, 309
Manetho, 84
Manila, Philippines, 391, 394
Manitoba, 599
Mann, Horace, 635

Manners, 6
Manor, defined, 415
Mansa Musa, king of Mali,
    246, 248–249, 250
Mantua, Italy, 427
Manuel, king of Portugal,
    551
Mao Zedong, 339, 345–346,
    348
Map and Globe Hand-
    book, G1–G15
Maps
    comparing, G13
    cultural, G14
    defined, G1
    elevation, 399
    geographic references
        on, G15
    historical, G11
    physical, G9
    reading, G2–G3
    symbols on, 372–373
    thematic, 46–47
    types of, G9–G12
    using, 29–30
    world, 679–689
Maquiladoras, 587, *587*
Maracaibo, Lake, 537, *537*
Marathon, Battle of, 158
Marconi, Guglielmo, 12, 25
Marcos, Ferdinand, 385,
    392–393
Marcos, Imelda, 393
Margaret I, queen of Den-
    mark, 415
Marie de France, 415
Marine climate, defined, 482
Maritime provinces, 598,
    599, 604
Maritz, Gert, *290*
Mark, apostle, 175
Market, defined, 415
Market economy, 490
Marseilles, France, 155
Martial law, defined,
    392–393
Martinique
    government of, 511
    language of, 511
Marx, Karl, 450
Marx, Roberto Burle, 565
Massachusetts, 523, 596
Matrilineal, defined, 270
Matthew, apostle, 175, 176
Mauritania, *279*
Mauryas, 113
May Day, *7*
Mayans, *52, 55, 126,*
    130–131
    achievements of, 131
McGill University, 610
Mecca, 151, *183,* 184, 185,
    186, 187, 233, 248

Media
    defined, 21
    effect on democracy,
        157
Medici family, 425, 427
Medicine
    Arabic, 189, 191
    Indian, 319
Medina, 186, 188
Mediterranean Sea, *149*
    climate of, 150, 482
    trade around, 150
Meiji Restoration, 370–371
Mekong River, 398
Memphis, Egypt, *86*
Menchú, Rigoberta, 527,
    542
Mendes, Chico, 562–563,
    563
Mengzi, 340
Mercator, Gerardus, G6
Meroë, *86, 94,* 95
Mesa, defined, 618, 691
Mesoamerica, *130*
    early cultures in, 129–131
Mesopotamia, *55,* 66–72
Mestizos, 391, 530
Mexica. *See* Aztecs.
Mexico, 572
    agriculture in, 585
    border with U.S., 586
    climates of, 585
    colonization of, 578–579
    crafts in, 3
    cultures of, 591
    emigration to U.S. from,
        625
    family life in, 589
    festivals in, *575,* 588, *588,*
        591, 592
    folk traditions in, 591
    French rule of, 581
    geography of, 584–585
    government of, 593
    history of, 576–577
    independence of,
        580–581
    industry in, 582, 586–587
    international relations of,
        593
    land reform in, 582
    modernization of, 582
    native cultures in, 513
    natural resources of, 585
    relations with U.S., 582,
        586, 593
    religion in, 579, 589
    revolutions in, 577,
        581–582
    rural life in, 588–589
    Spanish rule over, 441
    unrest in, *581*
    urban life in, 589–590

    war with U.S., 580
    women's role in, 589
Mexico City, G2, *576, 577,*
    590
    earthquakes in, 574
Meyer, Elana, 304
Mfecane, 299
Miami, Florida, G10
Michelangelo, 426, 427
Middle Ages, 410
    Christianity in, 410–413
    crusades in, 416, 417
    daily life in, *408,* 415
    end of, 418
    feudalism in, 415
Middle East, emigration to
    U.S. from, 625
Middleman, defined, 250
Midwest, of U.S., 43
Migrant workers, 543
Migration, 39, 41
Milan, Italy, as trade
    center, 418, 425
Minamoto family, 366
Mindanao, Philippines, 394
Minerals, *26*
Ming dynasty, 338, 342
Minneapolis, Minnesota,
    620
Missionaries, 177, 276
Mississippi, 638
Mississippi River, 620, *621,*
    623
Moche civilization, 139
Montezuma, Aztec em-
    peror, 578
Modernization, defined, 214
Mogadishu, Somalia, 645
Mohammed Reza Pahlavi,
    shah of Iran, 214, 215,
    216
Mohenjo-Daro, *12,*
    102–103, *103,* 125
Moldova, membership in
    CIS, 496
Moluccas, 387
Momaday, N. Scott, 618
Monastery, defined, 411
Mongols
    invasion of Russia,
        453–454
    rule over China, 338, 341
Monocrop, defined, 522
Monotheism, 73
Monsoons, 314, 329, 330,
    387
Mont Blanc, France, *1*
Montenegro, modern, 492
Montgomery, Alabama,
    boycotts in, 633
Montgomery, L. M., 598,
    610
Montreal, Quebec, 572, 610

Morocco, Muslims in, 190
Moscow, Russia, *405,* 474, *478*
  rise of, 454
Moses, 74
Mosques, 186
Mosul, Iraq, 192
Mount of Mercy, 184
Mountain pass, defined, 691
Mouth (river), defined, 690
Mozambique, 293
  emigration to U.S. from, 625
Mubarak, Hosni, 237
Mughal Empire, 323–324, *324*
Muhammad, 151, 182, 184, 188, 190
  life of, 186–187
Muhammad Ali, 226, 234, 235
Mulroney, Brian, 608
Multicultural, defined, 607
Multiculturalism Act (Canada), 608
Mummy, defined, 89–90
Murray, Anne, 610
Muslims, 73
  achievements of, 191–192
  in Balkans, 492
  crusades against, 416
  inquisitions against, 433
  Jerusalem and, 416, 649, *651*
  and Spanish culture, 439
  See also Islam.
Myanmar, 386
  population of, 387

N

Nagasaki, Japan, 371
Nagorno-Karabakh, *494*
Nairobi, Kenya, *222*
Nalanda, India, 318
Namibia, 293
Napata, *86,* 92
Nascimento, Abdias do, 565
Nascimento, Milton, 565
Nasser, Gamal Abdel, 227, 236, 239
Natal, 301, 302
National Film Board of Canada, 610
Nationalism, 460
  defined, 280
  in modern Europe, 487
Nationalization, defined, 537
Native Americans
  in Alaska, 620, 620
  arrival in North America, 623

art of, 527
  Canadian, *597,* 600, *600,* 607, 608
  Caribbean, *506,* 512
  in Central and South America, 532
  Columbus on, 525
  in French and Indian War, 601–602
  North American, 14, *14*
  in Pacific Northwest, *621*
  philosophy of, 618
  pre-Columbian cultures of, 502
  trade by, 619
  villages of, *620*
NATO (North Atlantic Treaty Organization), 612
Natural resources, 34
Naturalized citizen
  becoming, 626
  defined, 625
Nazi party, 468–470, 649
Nebamun, 96
Negev Desert, *650*
Negotiate, defined, 544
Nehru, Jawaharlal, 317, 327
Netherlands, 34
  colonization of Africa by, *277,* 290, 297–298
  Caribbean possessions of, 511, 513
  Common Market and, 484
  currency of, 486
  German invasion of, 470
  Reformation in, 432, 433
  resistance to Nazis in, 470
  rule over Indonesia, 396
  settlement of New York, 623
  Spanish rule over, 441
  and triangle trade, 514, *514*
  trade with Southeast Asia, 389
Netherlands Antilles, 509, *519*
New Brunswick, 598
  confederation of, 603
  in dominion of Canada, 603
New Jersey, *27*
New Mexico, archaeological excavations in, 128
New Orleans, Louisiana, 620
New Testament, 175–176
New York, 572
New York, New York, *38*

Caribbean influence on, 523, *523*
  population density of, *315*
  settlement of, 623
  United Nations in, *643*
Newfoundland, 12, 598, 599, 601
  confederation of, 603
  ethnic communities in, 607
Nicaragua, 542, 544
  demography of, *530,* 531
  elections in, 544
  peace plan for, 545
  unrest in, 542, 544, 545
Nicholas, bishop of Myra, 416
Nicholas II, czar of Russia, 464, 465, 466
Niger, immigration into, 261
Niger River, 255, 256, 263
Nigeria, Muslims in, 190
Nile River, 54, *54,* 80, *227,* 245
  civilizations on, 82–93
  geography of, 83
  lower, 240, 242
  upper, 242–243
Nîmes, France, G11
Ninety-Five Theses (Luther), 430
Nineveh, 71
Nkrumah, Kwame, 280, *280,* 281
Nobunaga, Oda, 367–368
Noh theater, 315
Noriega, Manuel, 543
Norsemen, 414
North America
  ethnic communities in, *572*
  European rule of, 572
  exploration of, 596
  geography of, *573,* 574–575
  map of, *686*
  natural resources of, 575
North American Free Trade Agreement, 593
North Atlantic Treaty Organization (NATO), 612
North Dakota, *624*
North Korea, 643
  government of, 655
  military aggression of, 655
  relations with South Korea, 655
North, Marianne, 448, 450
Northeast, of U.S., 43

Northern Hemisphere, G4
  tilt of, G8
Northwest Territory, 599, 608
Norway, 414, 415
  German invasion of, 470
  mountains of, 480
Note taking, 303
Nova Scotia, *597,* 598
  confederation of, 603
  in dominion of Canada, 603
Novgorod, Viking rule over, 453
Now Rouz, 207, 208
Nubia, 85–86, *85,* 90, 92
  achievements of, 94–95
  modern, 95, 240
  nobility of, *91*
  relations with Egypt, 81
Nuclear weapons, 371, 473
  control of, 497
Nunavut Territory, *597,* 608
Nuremberg, Germany, 468
Nzima people, 280

O

Oasis, defined, 185, 690
Octavian. *See* Augustus Caesar.
Odwira festival, 268, 273, 282
Odysseus, 154
Odyssey (Homer), 154
Oil
  importance of, 196–198, 199
  Saudi Arabian, 196–198
  U.S. reserves of, 621
  Venezuelan, 536–537
  world resources of, 373
Ojibwa people, 600
Oklahoma, oil in, 621
Old Testament, 175, *176*
Olinda, Brazil, 556
Olmec, *126,* 130
Olympia, Greece, 148
Olympic Games, 148
Ontario, 599, 602, 608
  confederation of, 603
  in dominion of Canada, 603
Ontario, Lake, 599
OPEC (Organization of Petroleum Exporting Countries), 196, 199, 537
Operation Desert Storm, 197
Opinions, 18–19
Opium War, 344
Oral report, presenting, 541

Orange Free State, 298, 299
Organization of Petroleum
　　Exporting Countries
　　(OPEC), 196, 199, 537
Organization, patterns of,
　　107
Orientus, 410
Orinoco River, 529
Orthodox Church, 408,
　　412–413, *413, 436*
Ottoman Empire, *234,* 461
　　rule over Egypt, 234–235
　　war with Russia, 454
Ouro Prêto, Brazil, 552

P

Pacific Northwest, 621
Pacific Rim, 315, 655
　　map of, *684*
Paekche kingdom, *654*
Pahlavi family, 213–214
Pakistan, *12,* 13
　　conflict with India, 332
　　formation of, 327,
　　　331–332
　　Muslims in, 190
　　providing labor to Saudi
　　　Arabia, 198
Palestine
　　British rule over, 648,
　　　649
　　partition of, 649, *649*
　　refugees from, *645, 650,
　　　651, 652*
Pamir mountains, *50–51*
Pampas, G13, 528
Pan American games, 545
Panama, 528, 542
　　climate of, *529*
　　crafts in, *500–501*
　　demography of, *530*
　　dictatorship in, 542
　　Spanish rule over, 441
Panama Canal, 505, *505,*
　　543
Panatal, Brazil, 559
Panchatantra, 319
Papyrus, 94, *94*
Parachico people, *588*
Paraguay
　　ancient languages of, 532
　　demography of, *531*
Parallel timelines, 199
Paris, France, *29,* 29–31, *30,*
　　484, 645
Parks, Rosa, 633
Parthenon, *152,* 158, 484
Partition, defined, 649
Pass, mountain, 691
Passover, 74, 77
Patagonia, G13
Patrilineal, 270
Patrilocal, defined, 270

Patron, defined, 425
Patterns, identifying, 107
Paul, apostle, 175, 176, 177
Pax Romana, 169
Paz, Octavio, 588
Peace Corps, 636
Pearl Harbor, Hawaii, 371,
　　392, 472
Pearl Mosque, 192
Pedro I, king of Brazil,
　　552–553
Pedro II, king of Brazil,
　　553
Peksowa, Ewelina, *3*
Pelé (Edson Arantes do
　　Nascimento), 563
Peloponnesian War
　　(Thucydides), 158
Peloponnesus, *155,* 156
Peninsula, defined, 155
Pennsylvania, 45
Peon, defined, 579
Pepin, king of France, 420
Pericles, 158
Permafrost, defined, 599
Perón, Eva Duarte de, 540,
　　541
Perón, Juan, 540
Perry, Matthew C., 370
Persepolis, 208, *208*
Persian Empire, *149,* 158,
　　209
　　achievements of, 210–212
　　crafts in, *202,* 219
　　history of, 209–210, 212
　　religion in, 202, 203
　　trade in, 208, 209
　　war with Russia, 454
　　See also Iran.
Persian Gulf War, 197, 199,
　　634
Peru, 54, 55, *502,* 528
　　ancient languages of,
　　　532
　　commerce in, *533*
　　cultures of, 138–142
　　demography of, 531, *531*
　　education in, 533
　　festivals in, *142*
　　independence of, 532
　　native cultures in, 513
　　Spanish rule over, 441
　　wedding customs of, *531*
Peter the Great, czar of
　　Russia, *453,* 454–455
Peters, Arno, G6
Petrograd, 464, 470
Pharaoh, defined, 85
Philip II, king of Spain,
　　390, 443
Philip, king of Macedon,
　　159
Philippines, 638

　　colonial rule over,
　　　390–392
　　economy of, *315*
　　emigration to U.S. from,
　　　625
　　festivals in, *385*
　　independence of, 392–393
　　Japanese occupation of,
　　　392
　　literacy rate of, 394
　　modern, 394
　　population of, 387
　　providing labor to Saudi
　　　Arabia, 198
　　religion in, 390–391, 393
　　Spanish Rule over, 385,
　　　390–391
　　volcanoes in, 388
Philosophy, 160
Physical environment,
　　12–13
Physical features, 31
Pilgrimage, defined, 184
Pilipino language, 394
Pinatubo, Mount, 388
Pizan, Christine de, 427
Plague, 409, *419*
　　defined, 418
Plain, defined, 691
Plantations, 514, 553, 559
　　labor force for, 513, 514,
　　　516, 552
Plateau, defined, 205, 691
Plato, 160
Pol Pot, 471
Poland
　　arts in, *3*
　　democracy in, 491
　　German invasion of, 469
　　per capita income in, *485*
　　resistance to Nazis in,
　　　470
　　science in, 429
　　trade unions in, 478
　　in World War I, *458*
Political cartoons, 475
Pollution, 35
　　industrial, 447
Population, of large cities,
　　664
Porter, John, 566
Portugal
　　climate of, 482
　　colonization of Ghana,
　　　266, 274
　　colonization of South
　　　America, 526, 532,
　　　548, 550–552
　　Common Market and, 485
　　rivalry with Spain, 550
Portuguese language, 45
Porus, Indian prince, G12
Potato famine, 38, 41

Powell, Colin, 523
Prague, Czechoslovakia,
　　491
Predictions, making, 217
Prehistoric, defined, 50
Prejudice, 624
　　combating, 633
　　defined, 23
Prime meridian, G4
Prince Edward Island, 598
　　confederation of, 603
　　in dominion of Canada,
　　　603
Printing, movable-type,
　　428, 432
Process diagram, reading,
　　606
Profile, G9
Projection
　　defined, G2
　　examples of, G6–G7
Pronunciation key, 701
Propaganda, defined, 467
Prophets, 76–77
Protestant
　　and Anglican church, 432
　　and biblical art, *432*
　　Calvinists as, 432
　　defined, 431
　　and Inquisition, 433
　　and John Calvin, 432
　　Lutherans as, 431
　　and Martin Luther, 409,
　　　430–431
　　and spread of Reforma-
　　　tion, 432, *433*
Proverbs, 272
Province, defined, 170
Psalms, 75
Ptolemy dynasty, 229, 233
Pu Yi, Chinese emperor,
　　344
Puebla, Battle of, 581, 622
Puerto Rico, 509
　　demographics of, 520
　　economy of, 520
　　festivals in, *507*
　　government of, 507, 638
　　Spanish rule over, 638
　　sports in, 518
　　statehood and indepen-
　　　dence movements in,
　　　520, 639
　　U.S. rule over, 638
　　urban life in, 519, *522*
Punic Wars, 169
Pyramids, 88–89, *88, 92,* 242

Q

Qing dynasty, 342–343
Qu'ran, 73, *182,* 187, 188,
　　192, 195, 201
Quadrant, *603*

Quebec, 599, 601, 602
  border with Maine, *613*
  confederation of, 603
  in dominion of Canada,
    603
  ethnic communities in,
    607
  health care in, 610
  legal system of, 605
  separatist movement in,
    607, 608
Quechua language, 532
Quechua people, 528
  crafts of, 532
Quotas, immigration,
  624–625
Qustul, *86*

R

Rabbi, defined, 77
Racism, defined, 23
Raffles, Stamford, 395
Rain forests, 130, 529,
  566–567
Rajputs, 324
Ramayana, 319
Ramesses II, pharaoh, 85,
  241
Ramos, Fidel, 393, 394
Raphael, *402–403, 424*
Rashid family, 194
Rasputin, *466*
Rattray, R. S., 268
Raw materials, defined,
  448
Rawlings, Jerry, 267, 282
Readers' Guide, 328
Recife, Brazil, 556
Reconquista, 439
Red Cross, 635
Red Guard, 346
Red River (Vietnam), 398
Red Sea, 185
Red Square, *478,* 493
Reformation, 409
  beginning of, 430–431
  spread of, 432–433, *433*
Regions
  defined, 42
  of U.S., 42–43
  of world, 44–45
Reincarnation, 109, 111
Religion
  ancient Egyptian, 89
  ancient Indian, 105, 316
  Aryan, 105–106
  Aztec, 135–136
  Brazilian, 564–565, *564*
  Burmese, 112
  Chinese, 101, 112
  conversion, 552
  Egyptian, 231, 233, 237
  Ghanaian, 271, 276

Greek, 159–160
  as institution, 8
  Indian, 112, 333
  Iranian, 206
  Israeli, *650, 651*
  Japanese, 112, 362, 363
  Korean, 112, 654
  Mexican, 579, 589
  Persian, 202, 203
  Philippine, 390–391, 393
  Russian, 436
  South American, 505
  world distribution of,
    688
  See also names of indi-
    vidual religions.
Remus, 168
Renaissance
  arts in, *409,* 426–427
  city life in, 425
  defined, 424
  Italian, 425
  northern, 428–429
  science in, 429
Reports, oral, 541
Representative democracy,
  157
Republic, defined, 169
Resistance, 470
Revolution, 465
Reza Shah Pahlavi, 203,
  213–214
Rig-Veda, 105
Ring of Fire, 574
Rio Bravo del Norte (Rio
  Grande), 586
Rio de Janeiro, Brazil, 549,
  549, 552, 557
Riyadh, Saudi Arabia, *183,*
  194
Robinson, Arthur, G7
Rocky Mountains, 43, 47
  Canadian, 620
Roman Empire, *149, 153*
  achievements of, 171, 173
  agriculture in, *230*
  culture of, 148
  decline of, 171
  engineering in, *172, 174*
  expansion of, G11
  extent of, *153, 169*
  fall of, 410
  influence on Egypt, 228
  laws of, 171, 173
  military organization of,
    174
  origins of, 168
  rise of, 168–169
  rule over Egypt, 229, 230
  trade with India, 319
Romance languages, 173
Romanian language, 406
Romanov family, 454

Romantic movement, 447,
  457
Rome, 413, 426
  Treaty of, 484–485
  See also Roman Empire.
Romulus, 168
Roosevelt, Franklin D., *472*
Rosen, Barry, 216
Rosetta stone, 87
Rosh Hashanah, 7, 74
Ross, John, *603*
Royal Canadian Mounted
  Police, 604
Rubber, *315*
  as natural resource, 559,
    559
Rudbar, 204
Rumania, 461
Rural, defined, 41
Russia, 155, 192
  colonial expansion of,
    460
  conflict with Japan, 495
  early history of, 453–454
  economic conditions in,
    499
  emigration to U.S. from,
    623, 625
  empire of, *453,* 454–455
  expansionism of, 454–455
  geography of, 452
  modernization of,
    454–455
  Mongol invasion of,
    453–454
  Norse settlements in, 414
  rail travel in, 436
  religion in, 436
  religious conflict in, 433
  rise of, 454–455
  war with Japan, 371
  World War I alliances of,
    461, 462
  World War I peace talks,
    463, 465
  See also CIS; Soviet
    Union.
Russian language, 406
Russian Republic, 474
Russian Revolution of
  1905, 470
Russian Revolution of
  1917, *459, 464–465*

S

Saba, Netherlands Antilles,
  519
Sadat, Anwar, 236–237, 238
Sadat, Jehan, 237, 238
Safavid Empire, 210, 212
Sahara (desert), 82, *224, 274*
Sahel, 13, 31, 39, 41, *224,*
  256–257, 260, 261, 263

St. Augustine, Florida, 616,
  623
Saint Domingue, 515, 516
St. John, Newfoundland,
  572
St. Lawrence River, 599,
  600, 601, 609
St. Lawrence Seaway, 606,
  608
St. Louis, Missouri, *617*
St. Lucia, 523
St. Peter's cathedral, 426,
  430
St. Petersburg.
  See Petrograd.
Sako, Ousmane, 262
Salamis, Battle of, 158
Salinas de Gortari, Carlos,
  593
Salvador, Brazil, 552
Samba, 565
Samurai, 359, 367
San Antonio, Texas, 622
San Francisco, California,
  572
San Juan Mountains
  (Colorado), *570–571*
San Juan, Puerto Rico, 519,
  522
San Martín, José de, 527,
  532
San people, 296
Sanctions, defined, 655
Sankoré Mosque, *246*
Sanpū, 364
Sanskrit language, 105, 319
Santayana, George, 402
Santiago (St. James), *576*
Santo Domingo, Domini-
  can Republic, 506, 513
Santos, Brazil, 552
São Francisco River, 556
São Paulo, Brazil, 552, 555,
  556, 557, 560
São Vicente, Brazil, 552
Saqqara, 93
Sarajevo, Bosnia, 462, 645
  destruction of, 490
  Olympics in, 478
Sardis, Persia, 209
Sarmiento, Domingo, 540
Saskatchewan, *598,* 599
  ethnic communities in,
    607
Sassanian Empire, 209–210
Satrap, defined, 209
Saud family, 194
Saudi Arabia, *13,* 151, *183,*
  184
  agriculture in, *198*
  customs of, 193
  history of, 194–196
  resources of, 196–198

rainfall of, *150*
Savafids, 203
SAVAK, 214, 215
Savanna, *257*
  defined, 257, 690
Scale, defined, G2
Scandinavia
  unification of, 415
  Vikings in, 414
Science
  Arabic, 191
  Egyptian, 229
  Indian, 318–319
  Renaissance, 429
Scotland, Reformation in, 432
Scribe, defined, 88
Sea level, defined, 690
Seasons, G8
Segregation, defined, 293
Seljuk Turks, rule over Jerusalem, 416
Senegal River, 253, 256
Seoul, South Korea, *642, 655*, 656
Separatism, defined, 608
Serbia, 461
  modern, 492
  unrest in, 479
  World War I alliances of, 461, 462
Serf, defined, 415
Seven Years' War, 446, 597
Shah, defined, 208
Shaka, Zulu king, 299
Shakespeare, William, 428–429
Shamanism, 654, *654*
Shang dynasty, 100, 340
Sharpeville, South Africa, 295
Shi huang-di, emperor of China, 119, 121, 122–123
Shiite Muslims, 190
  in Egypt, 232
  in Iran, 203, 206, 207, 210
Shikoku, 360
Shinto, 362
Shogun, defined, 366
Shogun government, 359, 366–370
Shtōku, prince of Japan, 363
Siberia, *453*
  environmental crisis in, 495
Siddhartha Gautama, 110–111
Sierra Madre, 39
Sikhs, 324, *332*
Silk Road, *50*, 121, 341
Silla kingdom, *654*

Silt, defined, 243
Silva, Benedita da, 563
Sima Xiangru, 114
Singapore, G5, 395–396
  economy of, *315*
  population of, 387
Sisal fiber, *225*
Sistine Chapel, 426, *427*
Slavery, 623
  abolition of, 515, 553, 569
  in Brazil, 552, 553
  in Ghana, 274–275
  in Latin America, 533
  triangle trade, 514, *514*
Slavs, 452
Slovak Republic, 490, 491
Slovakia, *8*
Slovenia, 492
  unrest in, 479
Social interaction, 14–15
Social justice, 306
Social sciences, defined, 21, 23
Socrates, 160
Solomon, king of Israel, 75
Somalia, *220–221*
  relief efforts in, 612, 645
Songhai Empire, 246, 250–251, 253
Songhai people, 258
Sonni 'Ali, 246, 250, 251
Sources, evaluating, 238
South Africa, 225, 292, 326
  apartheid in, 293–295
  demography of, *294*
  government of, 293
  history of, 290–291, 296–299, 301–302
  mining in, 299, 300
  modern, 304–306
  world relations of, 307
South African War, 301
South America, 528
  cities of, 533
  climates of, 504, *504*, 529
  cultures of, 502, 505
  emigration to U.S. from, 625
  geography of, 502, *503*
  independence movements in, 532
  languages of, 505
  map of, *687*
  peoples of, 530–531, *531*, 531–532
  religion in, 505
  Spanish rule over, 441
  topography of, 528–529
South Korea, 643
  border with North Korea, 653, *653*
  daily life in, 656, *656, 657*
  economy of, *315*

education in, *656*
  emigration to U.S. from, 625, 655
  family life in, 656, *656*
  holidays in, *656*
  industrialization of, 655
  international trade of, *656*
  protests in, *642,* 655
  sports in, 656, *656*
Southeast Asia
  climate and resources of, 387
  cultures of, 389
  international trade in, 384, 389
  physical geography of, 386–387
Southeast, of U.S., 43
Southern Hemisphere, G4
  tilt of, G8
Soviet Union
  breakup of, *478,* 493–495
  collapse of, 474
  emigration to Israel from, 650
  emigration to U.S. from, 625
  ethnic problems in, 492
  foreign aid to Cuba, 520
  formation of, 465
  modernization of, 467
  transformation into CIS, 496
  World War II alliances of, 469
  See also CIS; Russia.
Soweto, South Africa, *291,* 292, 295
Space exploration, *41*
Spain, 155, 190
  agriculture in, *482*
  Catholicism in, 433
  civil war in, 469
  climate of, 482
  colonization of South America, 442–443, 513, 532
  Common Market and, 485
  currency of, 486
  empire of, 440–443, *441*
  Inquisition in, 439
  per capita income in, *485*
  religious conflict in, 433
  rivalry with Portugal, 550
  rule over Central America, 542
  rule over Mexico, 578–579
  rule over Philippines, 385, 390–391
  rule over South America, 420–423, 526

settlement of North America, 442–443, 506, 519
  unification of, 438, 439
Spanish Armada, 437, 443, 444, 484
Spanish language, 45, 406
Spanish-American War, 385, 391
Sparta, Greece, 156, 158
Spatial order, 107
Specialization of labor, defined, 67
Sphinx, *80–81*
Spice Islands, 387
Sri Lanka, providing labor to Saudi Arabia, 198
Stalin, Josef, *459,* 467, 468, *472,* 473
Stalingrad, 472
Standard of living, defined, 376
Stanley Cup, 609
States, 43
Statute of Westminster, 604–605
Steel drums, 521
Stein, Gertrude, 619
Stephens, John Lloyd, 131
Steppe, defined, 452
Stereotypes, identifying, 637
Stockholm, *3*
Strait, defined, 690
Strategic Arms Reduction Treaty (START II), 497
Subcontinent, defined, 329
Sudan, 83, 95
  famine in, 243
Suez Canal, 235–236, *505*
Sugar, as natural resource, 522, 556, 559
Sultan, defined, 234
Sumatra, 399, *399*
Sumer, 68
  birth of writing in, 56
  culture of, 69
Sun Yat-sen, 344
Sunbelt, 619
Sundiata, king of Mali, 249, 250
Sung dynasty, 101
Sunni Muslims, 190
Superpower, defined, 472
Suriname, demography of, *531*
Surplus, defined, 67
Susa, Persia, 209
Sustainable development, defined, 563
Swamp, defined, 690
Swaziland, 293

Sweden, 414, 415
  mountains of, 480
  Reformation in, 433
  war with Russia, 454–455
Swedish Americans, 21
Switzerland, *480*
  per capita income in, *485*
  Reformation in, 432
Sydney, Australia, 33, *33*
Syria, agriculture in, *56*

T
Tagalog language, 394
Taharka, emperor of
  Nubia, *81*
Taira family, 366
Taj Mahal, 323
Tajikistan, membership in
  CIS, 496
  religion in, *479*
Takoma, Washington, *9*
Talbot, William Henry
  Fox, 447
Talmud, 77
Tangier, Morocco, 191
Tanzania, *224*
  human origins in, 222
Tarahumara Indians, 39, 41
Tariffs, defined, 485
Technology
  and culture, 16–17
  space exploration, *41*
Tehran, Iran, *205*, 215, 216
Tel Aviv, Israel, 648
Television, 17, 21
  effect on democracy, 157
Tema, Ghana, *282*
Ten Commandments, 74
Tenochtitlan, *127,* 132, 133,
  133, 135, 576
  destruction of, 578
Teotihuacán, 127, 132, 134
Tetzel, Johannes, 430, 431
Texas, 31
  independence of, 580,
  580
  oil in, 621
Texcoco, Lake, 132, 133
Thailand, 386
  population of, 387
Thanksgiving, 21, *575*
Thebes, *86*
Thompson, David, 602
Thucydides, 158
Tiananmen Square, 346,
  349–350, *350*
Tibet, religion in, 112
Tigris River, 54, *54, 66,* 67
Tilby, Wendy, *611*
Timbuktu, 246, *246,*
  250–251, 253
Time zones, G10
Timelines, parallel, 199

Tiradentes, 552
Tithe, defined, 411
Titicaca, Lake, *138,* 502
Tlatelolco, 132, 134
Tlingit people, *621*
Tokugawa Ieyasu, 368
Tokugawa shogunate, 359,
  368–370
Tokyo, Japan, 370, 374, 376
Tolstoy, Leo, *455*
Toluca, Mexico, *584*
Torah, *57,* 74, *74*
Toronto, Ontario, 608, *608,*
  609
Toronto, University of, 610
Tourism, 522, 587
Toussaint L'Ouverture,
  515, *515, 516*
Toxic waste, 35
Trade agreement, defined,
  593
Trade imbalance, defined,
  379
Trade
  Arab, 319, 384, 389
  Byzantine, 171
  British, 342, 389
  Canadian, 613
  Chinese, 319, 342–343,
  384, 389, 391
  Dutch, 389
  Egyptian, 93, 234, 235–236
  French, 342, 389
  Ghanaian, 274–275
  in India, 103–104, *104,*
  319, 324, 384, 389
  Indonesian, 319
  in Italy, 418, 425
  Japanese, 374–376
  in Mali, 250
  Mediterranean, 150
  Native American, 619
  in Persian Empire, 208,
  209
  Roman, 319
  South Korean, *656*
  Southeast Asian, 384, 389
  triangle, 514, *514*
  U.S., 342, 593, 613
  world, 451
Trade unions, 447
Tradition, defined, 268
Trans-Siberian Railway,
  436
Transportation, 16–17, 31,
  38–39
Transvaal, 299
Treblinka concentration
  camp, 471
Trek, defined, 298
Triangle trade, 514, *514*
Tributary, defined, 103, 690
Tribute, defined, 137–138

Trinidad and Tobago, 506,
  508, 509, 521, 523
  festivals in, *504, 511*
  natural resources of, 510
  sports in, *518*
Trinity, 179
Trojan War, 154
Tropical, defined, 509
Trudeau, Pierre, 613
Truman, Harry S., 473, 644
Tsumshian people, 600
Tuareg people, 261
Tulu, Derartu, 304
Tundra, 387
Tupi people, *548,* 551
Turkey, 155, 178, 461
  Muslims in, 190
  persecution of Armeni-
  ans, 471
  rule over Egypt, 228
  See also Ottoman
  Empire.
Turkmenistan, member-
  ship in CIS, 496
Tusaik Palace, 195
Tutankhamon, pharaoh of
  Egypt, 85
Tutu, Osei, 225, 267, 273
Typhoons, 387

U
Ukraine
  membership in CIS, 496
  nuclear weapons in, 497
Umar, caliph, 232
Umayyad family, 190
Ummayyads, 210
UNESCO (UN Educa-
  tional, Scientific, and
  Cultural Organiza-
  tion), 645
UNICEF (United Nations
  Children's Fund), 645
United Fund, 635
United Nations, *643*
  achievements of, 645
  formation of, 459, 471,
  642
  Gulf War and, 197
  importance of, 646–647
  Israel and, 649, 650
  Korea and, 655–656
  peacekeeping role of,
  492, 642, 646, *647*
  structure of, 644–645
United Silla kingdom, *654*
United States, 572
  border with Canada,
  612–613, *613*
  border with Mexico, 586
  Caribbean possessions
  of, 511, 516
  Civil War of, 633

climates of, 620
crafts in, 616
cultures of, 626–627
demographic changes in,
  633
diversity of, 616
economy of, 373
education in, 380–381,
  633, 635
energy consumption of,
  621
festivals in, 7, *7, 21,* 622,
  622
formation of, 446
geography of, 46–47, *46,*
  47
Gulf War and, 197
immigration to, 623–627
independence of, 532,
  617
literacy rate of, 375
manners in, 6
marriage customs of, 6
natural resources of,
  620–621
North American trade
  of, 593
occupation of Japan, 359
oil dependency of, 196,
  199
oil resources of, 373
overthrow of British rule,
  337
per capita income in, 485
purchase of Alaska, 437,
  453
regions of, 42–43, *43,*
  619–620
relations with Central
  America, 543
relations with Iran,
  214–216
relations with Japan, 379
relations with Mexico,
  582, 586, 593
relations with Saudi Ara-
  bia, 196
relations with South
  Korea, *656*
relations with Vietnam,
  385, 397, 398
religion in, 623
rule over Philippines,
  391–392
satellite map of, *619*
trade with Canada, 613
trade with China, 342
transportation in, 16–17,
  31, 38–39, 621
war with Mexico, 580
World War I alliances of,
  46
in World War II, 472

World War II alliances of, 469
Untouchable, defined, 106
Ur, 68, 103
Urban, defined, 43
Uruguay, demography of, *531*
USSR. *See* Soviet Union.
Uzbekistan, membership in CIS, 496

V
Valley, defined, 691
Values, defined, 8
Vancouver, British Columbia, 600
Vassal, defined, 415
Vedas, 105
Velvet Revolution, 478
Venezuela
   agriculture in, 536
   cultures of, 526, 536
   natural resources of, 536–537
   demography of, *531*
   native peoples of, *536*
   natural resources of, 196
Venice, Italy, 536
   restoration of, 645
   as trade center, 418, 425
Versailles, Treaty of, 463
Vertical zones, 529
Vesalius, Andreas, 429
Vespucci, Amerigo, 536
Veto, defined, 644
Victoria, queen of England, 325, 448, 470
Vietnam, 386, 397–398
   Communist rule over, 397–398
   emigration to U.S. from, 625
   population of, 387
Vietnam War, 385, 397, 612
Vikings, 414
   rule over Russia, 453

Virgil, 168
Virgin Islands, 516
VISTA, 636
Vladimir I, Kievan prince, 436, 453
Volcanoes, G15, *26,* 361, 387, 388
   defined, 690
Volga River, 454
Volta River, 267, 269
Volunteer, defined, 635
Voting Rights Act of 1965, 633

W
Wailing Wall, *651*
Walcott, Derek, 523
Walesa, Lech, 478, 491
Warfare
   Greek, 158, 159
   modern, 462–463, 472–473
   Roman, 174
   nuclear, 371, 473
War of 1812, 613
Warsaw, Poland, 469, *470,* *458, 490,* 491
Washington, D.C., 617
West, Benjamin, *601*
West Indies Federation, 521
West Indies. *See* Caribbean Islands.
Western Europe
   climates of, 482
   economic union in, 484–485
   future of, 487
   productivity of, 481, 482
Westernization, defined, 371
Winnipeg, Manitoba, *610*
Wittenberg, Germany, 430
Wolfe, James, *601*
Women
   in Argentina, 540

in Babylonia, 69
in China, 351
in Ghana, 267, 270
in Inca culture, 140
in India, 335
in Iran, 214, 215, 216
in Israel, *650*
in Japan, 363, 376
in Mexico, 589
in Muslim culture, 187, 193
in Renaissance, 427
in Rome, 170
in Saudi Arabia, 196
in U.S., 632
   stereotypes of, 637
Wordsworth, William, 457
Work unit, 353
World Bank, *643*
World
   climates of, *688*
   countries of, 675–677
   hemispheres of, 44
   history timetables of, 669–673
   largest cities of, 664
   physical map of, *680–681*
   population distribution of, *689*
   regions of, 44–45, *44*
   religions of, *688*
   resource distribution of, *689*
World Food Program, 645
World Health Organization (WHO), 645
World War I, 462–463
   alliances of, 462
   antecedents of, 460
   costs of, 458
World War II
   aftermath of, 472–473
   costs of, 459, 472
Writing
   alphabetic, *73,* 660–661
   birth of, 56
   cuneiform, 70

hieroglyphics, 87, 95
Wu, Chinese emperor, 340

X
Xhosa language, 292
Xhosa people, 298
Xochimilco, 134

Y
Yaa Asantewa, queen mother of Ghana, 276, *277*
Yalta peace conference, *472*
Yamato people, 358, 363
Yamin, Mohammad, 386
Yangdi, emperor of China, 123
Yangtse. *See* Chang Jiang.
Yathrib, 186
Yeltsin, Boris, 474, *475,* 496, *496,* 497
Yemen, 194, 234
   Gulf War and, 197
Yi Sun-sin, *654*
Yom Kippur, 74
Yoritomo, shogun, 366
Young, Neil, 610
Yoyoi people, 363
Yuan dynasty, 341
Yugoslavia, breakup of, 479, 490, 492
Yukon Territory, 599
Yupik people, 620

Z
Zagros mountains, 205
Zapata, Emiliano, 581
Zapotec people, 582
Zheng He, 343
Zhou dynasty, 340
Zimbabwe, 293
Zionists, 648
Zoroaster, 206–207
Zoroastrianism, 206–207, 210
Zulu kingdom, 299
Zuni people, 572

Text (continued from page iv)

ii From "Auguries of Innocence" by William Blake from the Pickering Manuscript, about 1803. **10** "I Love the World," "The Pier," "A Wish," "Winter" from *Miracles: Poems by Children of the English-speaking World,* collected by Richard Lewis. Copyright © 1966 by Richard Lewis. Reprinted by permission of Richard Lewis. **11** "Sailing Homeward" by Chang Fang-Sheng from *Translations from the Chinese,* by Arthur Waley, New York: Alfred E. Knopf, Inc., 1941. **38** Quote by Elihu Burritt as it appears in *Eyewitness to History,* edited by John Carey, Cambridge, Massachusetts: Harvard University Press, 1987. **64** "The Luring of Enkidu" from *Gilgamesh* by Bernarda Bryson. Copyright © 1966 by Bernarda Bryson. Reprinted by permission of Bernarda Bryson Shahn. **73** Genesis 12: 1–2 from *The Holy Bible,* New Revised Standard Version, Oxford University Press, © 1989. **89** From Spell 125 from *The Book of the Dead* translated by Raymond O. Faulkner, edited by Carol Andrews, New York: Macmillan Publishing Company, 1985. **113** From *The Edicts of Asoka* translated by N. A. Nikam and Richard McKeon, Chicago: University of Chicago Press, 1959. **114** From "The Shang-lin Park" translated by Burton Watson, in *Anthology of Chinese Literature,* compiled and edited by Cyril Birch. Copyright © 1965 by Grove Press. Reprinted by permission of the publisher. **132** From a Náhuatl lyric poem in *Pre-Columbian Literatures of Mexico* by Miguel León-Portilla, translated from the Spanish by Grace Lobanov and the author. Copyright © 1969 by the University of Oklahoma Press. Reprinted by permission of University of Oklahoma Press. **154** Quote from *The Odyssey of Homer* translated by Richmond Lattimore, New York: Harper and Row, 1965. **158** Quote by Pericles from "Pericles' Funeral Speech" as it appears in "Athens at War," from *The History of the Peloponnesian War of Thucydides* retold by Rex Warner, New York: E. P. Dutton & Company, 1970. **164** "Demeter and Persephone" from *D'Aulaires' Book of Greek Myths* by Ingri and Edgar Parin D'Aulaire. Copyright © 1962 by Ingri and Edgar Parin D'Aulaire. Used by permission of Doubleday, a division of Bantam Doubleday Dell Publishing Group, Inc. **175** Acts 16:30–1 from *The Holy Bible,* New Revised Standard Version, Oxford University Press, © 1989. **176** Matthew 22:37–40 from *The Holy Bible,* New Revised Standard Version, Oxford University Press, © 1989. **188** From *The Holy Koran: An Introduction with Selections* by A. J. Arberry, New York: Macmillan, 1953. **189** Quote by ar-Razi from *A History of Medicine* by Arturo Castiglioni, translated from the Italian and edited by E.B. Krumbhaar, New York: Jason Aronson, 1975. **212** Poem by an unknown Sufi poet as it appears in *Fall of the Peacock Throne* by William H. Forbis, New York: Harper & Row Publishers, 1980. **216** Quote by Barry Rosen as it appears in *444 Days: The Hostages Remember* by Tim Wells, Orlando: Harcourt Brace Jovanovich, 1985. **232** Quote by ibn Khaldun as it appears in *Egypt* by Mary Cross, Orlando: Harcourt Brace Jovanovich, 1991. **235** Quote by Nasser as it appears in "Letter from Alexandria" by Amos Elon, *The New Yorker,* July 18, 1988. **236** From a 1935 letter by Gamal Abdel Nasser to a friend in *Nasser* by Anthony Nutting, London: Constable and Company, 1972. **236** Quote by King Farouk as it appears in "Letter from Alexandria" by Amos Elon in *The New Yorker,* July 18, 1988. **237** From a letter by Jihan Sadat as it appears in *Sadat and His Statecraft* by Felipe Fernández-Armesto, London: The Kensal Press, 1982. **245** From *Those I Have Known* by Anwar el-Sadat, New York: Continuum, 1984. **249** Quote by al-Omari from *History of African Civilization* by E. J. Murphy, New York: Delta, 1972. **250** Quote by Ibn Battuta as it appears in *Ancient Ghana and Mali* by Nehemia Levtzion, New York: Africana Publishing Company, 1980. **253** Quote by Leo Africanus as it appears in "Bound and Free in 1508" by Mahmud Kati in *The African Past* by Basil Davidson, Boston: Atlantic Monthly Press, 1964. **262** From *The Heart of the Ngoni* by Harold Courlander with Ousamane Sakeo. Copyright © 1982 by Harold Courlander. Reprinted by permission of Harold Courlander. **268** From *Religion and Art in Ashanti* by R. S. Rattray, Oxford, England: Clarendon Press, 1927. **280** From *I Speak of Freedom* by Kwame Nkrumah, London: Panaf Books, 1973. **280** Quote by Kwame Nkrumah from *The Africans* by David Lamb, New York: Random House, 1982. **284** "The Cow-Tail Switch" from *The Cow-Tail Switch and Other West African Stories* retold by Harold Courlander and George Herzog. Copyright © 1947 by Harold Courlander, renewed 1975 by Harold Courlander. Reprinted by permission of Henry Holt, Inc. **294** From an excerpt of an April 20, 1964, speech by Nelson Mandela as it appears in *The Land and People of South Africa* by Jonathan Paton, New York: J. B. Lippincott, 1990. **307** Quote by Jane Mogase as it appears in The Open School Children's Art Calendar, 1992. Reprinted by permission of the publisher. **322** From *The Book of Kings* by Firdawsi, quoted in *A History of the World* by Stanley Chodorow, New York: Harcourt Brace Jovanovich, 1986. **327** From an excerpt of an August 14, 1947, speech by Nehru in *Nehru: A Political Biography* by Michael Brecher, Abridged Edition, Boston: Beacon Press, 1962. **347** From "Joining Forces" in *Chinese Lives: An Oral History of Contemporary China* by Zhang Xinxin and Sang Ye, translated by W. J. F. Jenner and Delia Davin, London: Macmillan London, 1987. Previously published in China as *Beijingren,* Shanghai: Shanghai Cultural Publishing House, 1986. **350** From a 36-line poem displayed in a shop window in Tiananmen Square as it appears in *The Iron House* by Michael S. Duke, Layton, Utah: Gibbs-Smith Publisher, 1990. **351** Quotes from Meng Maying and Xiao Wenxin as they appear in *Portraits of Ordinary Chinese* edited by Liu Bing-Wen and Xiong Lei, Peking: Foreign Language Press, 1990. **352** Adapted from "Population, Plenty and Poverty" by Paul R. Ehrlich and Anne H. Ehrlich from *National Geographic,* December 1988. **364** From *An Introduction to Haiku* by Harold G. Henderson. Copyright © 1958 by Harold G. Henderson. Reprinted by permission of Doubleday, a division of Bantam Doubleday Dell, Inc. **364** "The kite with a full stomach . . ." "When I think it's mine . . ." and "Wondering . . ." text and accompanying art from *Senryu Poems of the People,* calligraphy and illustrations by J. C. Brown. Copyright © 1991 by Charles E. Tuttle, Co., Inc. Reprinted by permission of Charles E. Tuttle, Co., Inc. **366** From *The Tale of the Heike,* anonymous, translated by Helen Craig McCullough, Stanford: Stanford University Press, 1988. **368** Quote from Ieyasu Tokugawa as it appears in *The Japanese* by Peter Tasker, New York: E. P. Dutton, 1987. Originally published in Great Britain as *Inside Japan,* London: Sidgwick & Jackson, Ltd. **386** Excerpt from poem by Mohammed Yamin and translated by Burton Raffel as it appears in *The Development of Modern Indonesian Poetry* edited by Burton Raffel. Translation copyright © 1967. Reprinted by permission of Burton Raffel. **394** Quote by Pope Pius XII as it appears in *Corazon Aquino: The Story of a Revolution* by Lucy Komisar, New York: George Braziller, 1987. **402** From *The Life of Reason* by George Santayana, New York: Scribners, 1905. **414** Translation of a Latin prayer which appears in *The Vikings in History* by F. Donald Logan, Second Edition, London: HarperCollins Academic, 1991. **415** From a song of the Second Crusade as it appears in *English in the Making of the Middle Ages* by R. W. Southern, New Haven: Yale University Press, 1953, and cited to *Les Chansons de Croisade* Paris: J. Bédier and P. Aubrey, 1909. **418** From a March 14, 1525, letter by Michael Behaim to his cousin in *Three Behaim Boys* by Steven Ozment, New Haven: Yale University Press, 1990. **420** Chapter 6 from *Valentine and Orson* by Nancy Ekholm Burkert. Copyright © 1989 by Nancy Ekholm Burkert. Reprinted by permission of Farrar, Straus, and Giroux, Inc. **424** From *The Craftsman's Handbook* by Cennino d'Andrea Cennini, translated by Daniel V. Thompson, Jr., New Haven: Yale University Press, 1933. **426** Quote by Leon Battista Alberti as it appears in *The Day the Universe Changed* by James Burke, Boston: Little, Brown and Company, 1985. **426** Quote by a contemporary of Michaelangelo as it appears in "The Sistine Restoration" by David Jeffrey in *National Geographic,* Vol. 176, No. 6, December 1989. **427** Quote by The Magnifico from *The Book of the Courtier* by Count Baldesar Castiglione, translated by Leonard Eckstein Opdycke, New York: Horace Liveright, 1901. **430** Quote by Martin Luther from "The Ninety-Five Theses" in *Here I Stand: A Life of Martin Luther* by Roland H. Bainton, Nashville: Abingdon Press, 1950. **431** Quote by Martin Luther as it appears in *Here I Stand: A Life of Martin Luther* by Roland H. Bainton, Nashville: Abingdon Press, 1950. **442** Quote by Christopher Columbus as it appears in "Edible Treasures" by Shari Lyn Zuber in *Cobblestone,* January 1992. **443** Quote by Bartolomé de las Casas as it appears in *A People's History of the United States* by Howard Zinn, New York: Harper Colophon, 1980. **444** Quote by Bentivollo as it appears in *The Spanish Armadas* by Winston Graham, Garden City: Doubleday and Company, 1972. **447** Quote by William Wordsworth from *Evening Voluntaries* by William Wordworth. **448** From *The White Man's Burden* (The United States and the Philippines Islands) by Rudyard Kipling, 1899. **460** From a song by Gilbert Hastings McDermott as it appears in *Age of Progress* by S. C. Burchell, Amsterdam, Holland: Time-Life Books, 1966. **463** Quote by Ferdinand Foch as it appears in *World War II: A 50th Anniversary History* by the writers and photographers of The Associated Press, New York: Henry Holt, 1989. **470** Quote from the "Report of the Jewish Resistance Movement" as it appears in *The Holocaust: The Nazi Destruction of Europe's Jews* by Gerhard Schoenberner, translated from the German by Susan Sweet, Edmunton: Hurtig Publishers, 1985. **470** From *Anne Frank: The Diary of a Young Girl,* New York: Doubleday & Company, 1967. **474** Quote from "Good-bye Soviet Union" by Bill Walter in *Junior Scholastic,* October 19, 1991. **480** Quote by Victor Hugo as it appears in *Euroquake* by Daniel Burstein, New York: Simon & Schuster, 1991. **488** Quote by Kim Jensen as it appears in "Making the Pieces Fit" by David Lawday in *U.S. News and World Report,* June 1, 1992. **488** From a letter by Aristides H. Liakopoulos as it appears in in *The European,* July 16–19, 1992. **493** From "It's a Kiosk! It's a Mall! No, It's Slavyansky Ryad!" by Celestine Bohlen in *The New York Times,* December 23, 1992. **495** Quote by Nikolai Karanko from "Glasnost's Children" by Lauren Tarshis and Judith Goldberg in *Scholastic Update,* Vol. 124, No. 7, December 6, 1991. **508** From *A Wave in Her Pocket: Stories from Trinidad* by Lynn Joseph, New York: Clarion Books, 1991. **512** From *Morning Girl* by Michael Dorris, New York: Hyperion Books for Children, 1992. **515** Quote from a letter which appeared in *Written in Blood: The Story of the Haitian People, 1492–1971,* by Robert Debs Heinl, Jr., and Nancy Gordon Heinl, Boston: Houghton Mifflin, 1978. **528** From "La Pampa" in *The South American Sketches of R. B. Cunninghame Graham,* selected and edited by John Walker, Norman: University of Oklahoma Press, 1978. **534** From *The Captive* by Scott O'Dell. Copyright © 1979 by Scott O'Dell. Reprinted by permission of Houghton Mifflin Company. **536** Quote by Amerigo Vespucci as it appeared in "Letter from Seville" from *Amerigo Vespucci: Pilot Major* by Frederick J. Pohl, New York: Octagon Books, 1944. **551** From a May 1, 1500, letter of Pero Vaz de Caminha to King Manuel, written at Porto Seguro (Brazil) as it appeared in *Portugal Brazil: The Age of Atlantic Discoveries* by Bertrand Editora, Franco Maria Ricci, and the Brazilian Cultural Foundation, New York: Brazilian Cultural Foundation, 1990. **555** From *Rebellion in the Backlands* by Euclides da Cunha, translated by Samuel Putnam, Chicago: University of Chicago Press, 1944. **588** From *The Labyrinth of Solitude* by Octavio Paz, translated by Lysander Kemp, New York: Grove Press, 1961. **598** From *Anne of Green Gables* by L. M. Montgomery, Boston: L. C. Page & Company, 1908. **600** Quote by James Cook as it appears in *Canada* by the Editors of Time-Life Books, Amsterdam, Holland: Time-Life Books, 1987. **602** Quote by David Thompson as it appeared in *The Canadians* by George Woodcock, Cambridge: Harvard University Press, 1979. **618** "The Delight Song of Tsai-talee" in *The Gourd Dancer* by N. Scott Momaday. Copyright © 1976 by N. Scott Momaday. Reprinted by permission of N. Scott Momaday. **627** Quote by José Luis as it appears in "Mojados" from *New Americans: An Oral History* by Al Santoli, New York: Viking Penguin, 1988. **628** "Ginger for the Heart" from *Tales from Gold Mountain* by Paul Yee. Copyright © 1989 by Paul Yee. Reprinted by permission of Macmillan and Douglas & McIntyre, Ltd. **632** From *New Kids on the Block: Oral Histories of Immigrant Teens* by Janet Bode, New York: Franklin Watts, 1989. **636** Quote from a volunteer speaker as it appears in the *AIDS Action Committee of Massachusetts Update,* Vol. 7, No. 3, Summer 1992.

Illustrations

Ligature 9, 17, 36, 41, 60, 61, 76, 78, 85, 95, 98, 107, 111, 112, 117, 120–121, 187, 190, 199, 298–299, 308, 336, 356, 357, 387, 400, 441, 445, 451, 453, 456, 457, 470, 471, 476, 483, 499, 521, 524, 530, 531, 594, 639, 640, 649, 652, 654, 674–675, 676, 677. **Precision Graphics** 6, 54, 134, 150, 198, 214, 215, 227, 237, 261, 281, 294, 314, 315, 316, 333, 334, 348, 374, 413, 415, 485, 505, 528, 552, 581, 587, 625, 633, 650, 656. **Brian Battles** 112. **John T. Burgoyne** 298. **Young Sook Cho** 22, 634. **Ebet Dudley** 55, 226, 241, 574, 612. **Amy Fagin** 73. **Simon Galkin** 561. **Tyrone Geter** 252. **Andrea Golden** 489, 602, 603. **Hank Iken** 135, 171, 606. **Charley Liu** 118. **Al Lorenz** 102, 184, 260, 271. **Chuck MacKey** 88 (adapted from an illustration by Mark Lehner), 407, 442. **Judy Reed** 84. **Mike Rodericks** 369, 538. **Kirsten Tarnowski** 30. **Richard Waldrep** 91, 172.

Maps

R. R. Donnelley & Sons Company Cartographic Services 149(t), 223, 313, 372, 373, 375, 404, 503, 573, 678–689. **Mapping Specialists** G1–G14, 43, 44, 46, 47, 49, 53, 59, 67, 71, 83, 86, 104, 115, 129, 130, 139, 149(b), 150, 155, 169, 178, 184, 190, 205, 209, 215, 224, 230, 234, 240, 250, 251, 256, 269, 282, 294, 297, 298, 314, 318, 324, 331, 333, 341, 348, 355, 361, 387, 391, 399, 401, 406, 413, 416, 419, 433, 441, 445, 453, 462, 473, 481, 485, 494, 504, 509, 514, 516, 529, 543, 551, 557, 574, 580, 585, 590, 599, 602, 624, 647, 649, 652, 653.

Photographs

AR—Art Resource, New York; **BM**—British Museum, London; **P.A.I.**—Polish Information Agency; **PR**—Photo Researchers; **RHPL**—Robert Harding Picture Library; **SP**—Schlowsky Photography; **TM, SAP**—Tony Morrison, South American Pictures

Front Cover Globe courtesy of Replogle Globes, Inc.; photo by Peter Bosy. **Back Cover** The British Library, London, Bridgeman. **G8** Tony Stone Images (l). **G12** Scala, AR (bl). **G1** T. Van Sant, Geosphere Project, SPL, PR (l,r). **G11** © Michael Holford. **ii** Sovfoto (b); BM, Bridgeman (t). **iii** Museum Expedition courtesy of Museum of Fine Arts, Boston (r); © Jerry Howard, Positive Images (l). **vi** © Lee Boltin (c); By courtesy of the Board of Trustees of the Victoria & Albert Museum (b). **vii** Nelson Gallery-Atkins Museum (Nelson Fund), Kansas City (t); © Popperfoto (c); © Wolfgang Kaehler (b). **viii** © D. Donne Bryant (c); © Craig Duncan, D. Donne Bryant (b). **ix** SP. **x** © Loren McIntyre, Woodfin Camp & Assoc. **0–1** Hubert Le Campion, ANA, Viesti Assoc. **2** © O'Connor School Portraits & Assoc. (b). **3** J. Langevin, Sygma (tr); Stanislaw Momot, P.A.I. (bl); TM, SAP (tl); © Martha Cooper, Viesti Assoc. (br). **4** © 1993 Steven Greenberg (l); © Linc Cornell, Light Sources Stock (r). **5** © 1993 Steven Greenberg. **6** SP (cr); © Laura Dwight, Peter Arnold Inc. (tl). **7** SP (both).**8** © Dean Conger, © National Geographic Society (l); © Eastcott, Momatiuk, The Image Works (r). **9** Eric Simmons, Stock Boston. **12** © Dilip Mehta, Woodfin Camp & Assoc. **13** James Balog, Black Star (t); © Robert Azzi, Woodfin Camp & Assoc.(b). **14** © Stephen Trimble (b). **14–15** Addison Geary, Stock Boston. **16** © Al Zwiazek, Tony Stone Images (t); © Chad Ehlers, Tony Stone Images (br); Culver Pictures (bl). **18** Werner Forman Archive. **20** Jerry Howard, Positive Images. **21** Maddy Miller (t); Julie Bidwell, Stock Boston (b). **23** SP (r); © Gerd Ludwig, Woodfin Camp & Assoc. (t). **26** SP (b); Steven Raymer, © National Geographic Society (l); © Lee Allen Thomas (c). **26–27** © Joe Viesti, Viesti Assoc. **27** SP (b); NASA (r). **28–29** SP. **29** © Mark Antman, The Image Works. **30** © Arthus-Bertrand, Explorer. **31** SP. **32** © TM, SAP. **33** Hiroyuki Matsumoto, Black Star. **34** © Michael Nichols, Magnum. **35** Courtesy of David Clendenen, Hooper Mountain National Wildlife Refuge California Condor Recovery Program. **36** SP. **37** SP. **38** Museum of The City of New York, 33.169, Gift of Mrs. Robert M. Littlejohn. **38–39** UPI/Bettmann. **40** The Phillips Collection, Washington, D.C. (c); © The Library of Congress (tr); SP (br, l). **41** NASA. **42** Rhoda Sidney, Stock Boston. **44** © Robert Frerck, Odyssey Productions. **45** © Hubert Le Campion, Viesti Assoc. **50–51** © R. & S. Michaud, Woodfin Camp & Assoc. **52** © Henri Cartier-Bresson, Magnum (b); Werner Forman Archive, National Museum of Anthropology, Mexico City (t). **54** Georg Gerster, Comstock (l); © U.S. Geological Survey (r). **55** John Ross, RHPL (l); TM, SAP (c); Georg Gerster, Comstock (r). **56** Ralph J. Brunke. **56–57** Michael Jennes, RHPL. **57** Jewish Museum, AR (b); © Michael Holford, BM (t). **58** BM (br); Ralph J. Brunke (bl). **59** Scala, AR. **60** © Michael Holford, BM. **66** Georg Gerster, Comstock. **68** BM, Bridgeman (t); Georg Gerster, Comstock (b). **69** Erich Lessing, AR (b); Scala, AR (t). **70** SP (b); BM (r); Kelsey Museum of Ancient and Medieval Archaeology, University of Michigan, Ann Arbor (t). **72** BM. **74** By permission of the British Library, ADDMS 10456-Folio. **75** © Photographic Archive of the the Jewish Theological Seminary of America, New York. **77** SP (t); Richard T. Nowitz (b). **80** AR. **80–81** John Ross, RHPL (c); Harvard University-MFA Expedition, courtesy of Museum of Fine Arts, Boston (t). **81** Museum Expedition, courtesy of Museum of Fine Arts, Boston (r,b). **82** Photothèque du Musée de l'Homme, Paris (t); © Susan Lapides, Woodfin Camp & Assoc. (c). **84** © Michael Holford, BM. **85** Erich Lessing, Scala, AR. **86** Museum Expedition, courtesy of Museum of Fine Arts, Boston. **87** © Michael Holford, BM. **89** © Michael Holford, BM (tr); The Metropolitan Museum of Art (bl); The Metropolitan Museum of Art, Rogers Fund, 1915 (bc). **90** Peter Clayton (b); Museum Expedition, courtesy of Museum of Fine Arts, Boston (t). **92** © Francis Geus (r); BM (l). **93** Ashmolean Museum, Oxford. **94** BM. **95** © Timothy Kendall, Museum of Fine Arts, Boston. **96** The Metropolitan Museum of Art. **97** The Metropolitan Museum of Art. **100** Ralph J. Brunke (b); J.H.C. Wilson, RHPL (l). **100–101** Laurie Platt Winfrey, Inc. (t). **101** Laurie Platt Winfrey, Inc. (r); © Ralph J. Brunke (b). **102** P. Koch, PR (b). **103** SP (bl); © Christine Pemberton, Hutchison Library (r). **104** AR (r); © Josephine Powell (l). **105** © R. & S. Michaud, Woodfin Camp & Assoc. **106** K. Rodgers, Hutchison Library. **108** SUPERSTOCK. **109** © Michael Holford, Musée Guimet. **110** © Michael Holford, BM. **111** AR. **113** Asoka School of Oriental and African Studies. **114** © George Bosio, Gamma-Liaison (c); © Manfred Gotschalk, Tom Stack & Associates (b). **116** © Michael Holford, BM. **117** In the Collection of the C. V. Starr East Asian Library, Columbia University. **118** BM. **119** SP (bl); Tony Waltham,

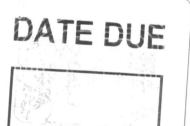